AWS®
Certified Security Study Guide

Specialty (SCS-C02) Exam

Second Edition

AWS® Certified Security Study Guide

Specialty (SCS-C02) Exam

Second Edition

Mauricio Muñoz, Darío Goldfarb,
Alexandre Matos da Silva Pires de Moraes, Omner Barajas,
Andrés González Santos, Rogerio Kasa

Copyright © 2025 by John Wiley & Sons, Inc. All rights reserved, including rights for text and data mining and training of artificial intelligence technologies or similar technologies.

Published by John Wiley & Sons, Inc., Hoboken, New Jersey.
Published simultaneously in Canada.

No part of this publication may be reproduced, stored in a retrieval system, or transmitted in any form or by any means, electronic, mechanical, photocopying, recording, scanning, or otherwise, except as permitted under Section 107 or 108 of the 1976 United States Copyright Act, without either the prior written permission of the Publisher, or authorization through payment of the appropriate per-copy fee to the Copyright Clearance Center, Inc., 222 Rosewood Drive, Danvers, MA 01923, (978) 750-8400, fax (978) 750-4470, or on the web at www.copyright.com. Requests to the Publisher for permission should be addressed to the Permissions Department, John Wiley & Sons, Inc., 111 River Street, Hoboken, NJ 07030, (201) 748-6011, fax (201) 748-6008, or online at http://www.wiley.com/go/permission.

The manufacturer's authorized representative according to the EU General Product Safety Regulation is Wiley-VCH GmbH, Boschstr. 12, 69469 Weinheim, Germany, e-mail: Product_Safety@wiley.com.

Trademarks: Wiley and the Wiley logo are trademarks or registered trademarks of John Wiley & Sons, Inc. and/or its affiliates in the United States and other countries and may not be used without written permission. All other trademarks are the property of their respective owners. John Wiley & Sons, Inc. is not associated with any product or vendor mentioned in this book.

Limit of Liability/Disclaimer of Warranty: While the publisher and author have used their best efforts in preparing this book, they make no representations or warranties with respect to the accuracy or completeness of the contents of this book and specifically disclaim any implied warranties of merchantability or fitness for a particular purpose. No warranty may be created or extended by sales representatives or written sales materials. The advice and strategies contained herein may not be suitable for your situation. You should consult with a professional where appropriate. Neither the publisher nor author shall be liable for any loss of profit or any other commercial damages, including but not limited to special, incidental, consequential, or other damages. Further, readers should be aware that websites listed in this work may have changed or disappeared between when this work was written and when it is read. Neither the publisher nor authors shall be liable for any loss of profit or any other commercial damages, including but not limited to special, incidental, consequential, or other damages.

For general information on our other products and services, please contact our Customer Care Department within the United States at (800) 762-2974, outside the United States at (317) 572-3993. For product technical support, you can find answers to frequently asked questions or reach us via live chat at https://sybexsupport.wiley.com.

If you believe you've found a mistake in this book, please bring it to our attention by emailing our reader support team at wileysupport@wiley.com with the subject line "Possible Book Errata Submission."

Wiley also publishes its books in a variety of electronic formats. Some content that appears in print may not be available in electronic formats. For more information about Wiley products, visit our web site at www.wiley.com.

Library of Congress Control Number: 2025911987

ISBN: 9781394253463 (paperback)
ISBN: 9781394253470 (epub)
ISBN: 9781394253487 (ePDF)

Cover Design: Wiley
Cover Image: © Jeremy Woodhouse/Getty Images

SKY10119766_062625

Acknowledgments

First and foremost, we offer our most profound thanks to our spouses, children, and families, whose support and understanding during our many long hours of writing and reviews gave us the time and strength to create this book. This book would not have been possible without our wonderful families.

We would also like to show our appreciation for Amazon Web Services (AWS) for providing cloud-computing platforms, APIs, and the Specialty Exam to the world at large. We are excited to be an active part of this transformative growth and development of secure cloud computing in the world today.

We'd also like to thank associate publisher Jim Minatel and acquisitions editor Ken Brown for entrusting us with the role of creating this study guide for Wiley. We also appreciate the insights of technical editor Rogerio Kasa, whose attention to detail elevated this book to the next level. Thanks also goes to managing editor Pete Gaughan, project manager Robyn Alvarez, production specialist Bala Shanmugasundaram, copy editor Kezia Endsley, and the entire team at Wiley for their guidance and assistance in making this book. We'd also like to thank all of our colleagues and experts who consulted with us while we were writing this book—too many to name here, but we are grateful for your suggestions and contributions.

And perhaps more than anyone else, we would like to thank our readers. We are grateful for the trust that you have placed in us to help you study for the exam. We wrote this book to support you in your journey.

—The Authors

About the Authors

Mauricio Muñoz is a Principal Technologist at Amazon Web Services (AWS), where he guides global customers in their journey to implement mission-critical applications into the AWS Cloud. With over 25 years of experience in information security and a CISSP certification since 2005, Mauricio has continuously expanded his expertise across various domains, including networking, application integration, analytics, and cloud computing. A passionate advocate for learning and knowledge sharing, Mauricio has served as an authorized instructor for CISSP and CEH certification training, as well as other technical certifications, including recent AWS architectural training. He is a sought-after speaker at both cloud computing and industry events, bringing valuable insights to diverse audiences. His international career spans Latin America and the United States, enriching his global perspective in technology consulting. Academically, Mauricio holds an electronics engineering degree from Pontificia Universidad Javeriana (PUJ—Colombia) and an executive MBA from Insper (Brazil), combining technical prowess with strategic business acumen.

Darío Goldfarb is a security solutions architect at Amazon Web Services in Latin America with more than 18 years of experience in cybersecurity, helping organizations from different industries improve their cyber-resiliency. Dario enjoys sharing security knowledge through speaking at public events, presenting webinars, teaching classes for universities, and writing blogs and articles for the press. He has a significant number of certifications, including CISSP, the Open Group Master IT Architect, and the AWS Security Specialty certification, and he holds a degree in systems engineering from UTN (Argentina) and a diploma in cybersecurity management from UCEMA (Argentina).

Alexandre Matos da Silva Pires de Moraes, CCIE No. 6063, worked as a systems engineer for Cisco Brazil from 1998 to 2014, in projects involving not only security and VPN technologies but also routing protocol and campus design, IP multicast routing, and MPLS networks design. He is the author of *Cisco Firewalls* (Cisco Press, 2011) and has delivered many technical sessions related to security in market events, such as Cisco Networkers and Cisco Live (Brazil, United States, United Kingdom). In 2014, Alexandre started a new journey as a director for Teltec Solutions, a Brazilian systems integrator that is highly specialized in the fields of network design, security architectures, and cloud computing. Alexandre holds the CISSP and three CCIE certifications (routing/switching, security, and service provider). He graduated with a degree in electronic engineering from the Instituto Tecnológico de Aeronáutica (ITA—Brazil) and holds a master's degree in mathematics (group theory) from Universidade de Brasília (UnB—Brazil). Alexandre also contributes, as a mathematics teacher, to preparing candidates for the national exams of military universities in Brazil, such as ITA and IME (Instituto Militar de Engenharia).

Andrés González Santos is a senior security specialist solution architect at Amazon Web Services in Latin America with more than 20 years of experience in cybersecurity. Andrés has served in various security positions, including consultant, IT architect, and security auditor, helping organizations across diverse industries strengthen their security posture. His experience spans multiple countries, including Colombia, Ecuador, and Peru, where he has implemented strategic technological solutions for both national and international enterprises. Andrés holds a master's degree in systems engineering and a master's degree in information security. He also holds a significant number of certifications, including CISSP, CISA, CISM, CRISC, ABCP and AWS Certified Security—Specialty, AWS Networking Specialty, and AWS Certified Solutions Architect.

Omner Barajas is a security specialist solution architect at Amazon Web Services in Latin America with more than 15 years of experience in cybersecurity. During those years, Omner has taken multiple roles as security consultant, IT architect, and security auditor while helping organizations from different industries to improve their security posture. Omner has a master's degree in information security and holds a significant number of certifications, including CISSP, CISA, CISM, AWS Certified Security—Specialty, AWS Certified Solutions Architect—Professional, and PCI Internal Security Assessor (ISA).

Rogerio Kasa is a Security Solutions Architect at Amazon Web Services (AWS), where he helps organizations strengthen their cloud security posture through strategic advisory and technical leadership. Since joining AWS in 2019, he has established himself as a trusted advisor in cloud security, leading the internal extended Security Community in Brazil, implementing risk-based security controls, governance frameworks, and compliance requirements. A certified professional holding CISSP/ISC2, CISM/ISACA, CCSK/CSA, and multiple AWS certifications, Rogerio combines deep technical expertise with strategic insight to help organizations navigate their cloud security challenges. His work spans security automation, incident response, network security, IAM, detection/response, data protection, and the implementation of comprehensive security controls across multi-account environments.

Contents at a Glance

Introduction		*xxi*
Assessment Test		*xxvii*
Chapter 1	Security Fundamentals	1
Chapter 2	Cloud Security Principles and Frameworks	45
Chapter 3	Management and Security Governance	67
Chapter 4	Identity and Access Management	87
Chapter 5	Security Logging and Monitoring	131
Chapter 6	Infrastructure Protection	191
Chapter 7	Data Protection	293
Chapter 8	Threat Detection and Incident Response	385
Appendix A	Answers to Review Questions	431
Appendix B	Creating Your Security Journey in AWS	441
Appendix C	AWS Security Services Portfolio	449
Appendix D	DevSecOps in AWS	467
Index		*501*

Contents

Introduction		*xxi*
Assessment Test		*xxvii*
Chapter 1	**Security Fundamentals**	**1**
	Understanding Security	2
	Basic Security Concepts	6
	Vulnerability, Threat, and Security Risk	6
	Security Countermeasures and Enforcement	7
	Confidentiality, Integrity, and Availability	7
	Accountability and Nonrepudiation	7
	Authentication, Authorization, and Accounting	8
	Visibility and Context	8
	Foundational Networking Concepts	9
	The OSI Reference Model	9
	The TCP/IP Protocol Stack	11
	From IPv4 to IPv6	14
	IPv6 Address Format and Addressing Architecture	16
	Main Classes of Attacks	18
	Reconnaissance	18
	Password Attacks	18
	Eavesdropping Attacks	19
	IP Spoofing Attacks	19
	Man-in-the-Middle Attacks	19
	Denial-of-Service Attacks	19
	Malware Attacks	20
	Phishing Attacks	21
	Risk Management	21
	Firewalls	22
	Web Proxies	23
	Web Application Firewalls	23
	API Discovery and Protection	23
	Intrusion Detection and Intrusion Prevention	25
	Protecting Email Services	26
	Virtual Private Networks	27
	Protecting DNS and Using Insights from DNS	27
	Tools for Vulnerability Analysis and Management	28
	Correlation of Security Information and Events	29

xii Contents

	Network Detection and Response Systems	30
	TLS/SSL Offload and Visibility	31
	Handling Security Incidents	32
	Structured Malware Protection	33
	Well-Known Security Frameworks and Models	33
	Sample Practical Models for Guiding Security Design and Operations	34
	The Security Wheel	34
	The Attack Continuum Model	35
	The Zero-Trust Model	38
	Summary	39
	Exam Essentials	39
	Review Questions	42
Chapter 2	**Cloud Security Principles and Frameworks**	**45**
	Introduction	46
	Cloud Security Principles Overview	46
	The Shared Responsibility Model	47
	Different Powers, Different Responsibilities	49
	AWS Compliance Programs	52
	AWS Artifact Portal	56
	AWS Well-Architected Framework	58
	Well-Architected Lenses	59
	Using the AWS Well-Architected Tool	60
	The AWS Marketplace	61
	Summary	62
	Exam Essentials	63
	Review Questions	64
Chapter 3	**Management and Security Governance**	**67**
	Introduction	68
	Multi-Account Management Using AWS Organizations	68
	Management Policies	70
	Authorization Policies	70
	Delegated Administration	71
	AWS Control Tower	73
	Secure and Consistent Infrastructure Deployment in AWS	75
	Infrastructure as Code Using AWS CloudFormation	75
	Tagging Strategies	77
	Sharing Resources across AWS Accounts	77
	Deploying Portfolios of Approved Services	78
	Evaluating Compliance	78
	Data Classification Using Amazon Macie	78

Contents xiii

	Evaluate Configuration Using AWS Config	79
	AWS Audit Manager to Collect Compliance Evidence	80
	Architecture Review and Cost Analysis	80
	AWS Trusted Advisor	81
	AWS Cost Explorer	81
	Summary	82
	Exam Essentials	83
	Review Questions	85
Chapter 4	**Identity and Access Management**	**87**
	Introduction	88
	IAM Overview	88
	How AWS IAM Works	89
	Principals	89
	AWS Security Token Service	96
	IAM Roles Anywhere	99
	Access Management with Policies and Permissions	100
	Access Management in Amazon S3	106
	Policy Conflicts	109
	Secure Data Transport in Amazon S3	109
	Cross-Region Replication in Amazon S3	112
	Amazon S3 Pre-Signed URLs	113
	Identity Federation	114
	Identity Use Cases	115
	Amazon Cognito	115
	AWS IAM Identity Center	118
	Microsoft AD Federation with AWS	118
	Protecting Credentials with AWS Secrets Manager	120
	Secrets Permission Management	120
	Automatic Secrets Rotation	120
	Choosing Between AWS Secrets Manager and AWS Systems	
	Manager Parameter Store	121
	IAM Security Best Practices	121
	Multifactor Authentication	121
	Apply Least-Privilege Principle	122
	Regularly Review Access to Your Environment	122
	Use Conditions in IAM Policies to Further Restrict Access	122
	Use IAM Roles to Provide Temporary Credentials	122
	Use Federation for Your Workforce Accounts	122
	Security Best Practices for Your Root User	123
	Common Access Control Troubleshooting Scenarios	124
	Identity Federation Problems	124

xiv Contents

	Summary	125
	Exam Essentials	126
	Review Questions	128

Chapter 5   **Security Logging and Monitoring**   **131**

Introduction	132
Stage 1: Resources State	134
AWS Config	135
AWS Systems Manager	142
Stage 2: Events Collection	143
AWS CloudTrail	143
Amazon CloudWatch Logs	157
Amazon CloudWatch	162
AWS Health	166
Stage 3: Events Analysis	167
AWS Config Rules	167
Amazon Inspector	170
Amazon Security Lake	172
Amazon GuardDuty	174
AWS Security Hub	174
AWS Systems Manager: State Manager, Patch Manager, and Compliance	175
AWS Trusted Advisor	177
Stage 4: Action	178
Summary	184
Exam Essentials	185
Review Questions	187

Chapter 6   **Infrastructure Protection**   **191**

Introduction	192
AWS Networking Constructs	192
Network Address Translation	209
Security Groups	215
Network Access Control Lists	219
Amazon VPC Transit Gateways	225
Elastic Load Balancing	231
VPC Endpoints	241
VPC Flow Logs	246
AWS Web Application Firewall	249
AWS Shield	257
AWS Network Firewall	259
Amazon Inspector	263
AWS Systems Manager Patch Manager	267

Contents xv

	EC2 Image Builder	273
	Network and Connectivity Troubleshooting Scenarios	276
	VPC Network Reachability	276
	Network Access Analyzer	277
	VPC Security and Filtering	281
	Route Tables	282
	Network Gateways	282
	VPC Peering	284
	VPC Flow Logs	286
	Summary	286
	Exam Essentials	287
	Review Questions	290
Chapter 7	**Data Protection**	**293**
	Introduction	294
	Symmetric Encryption	296
	Asymmetric Encryption	296
	Hash Algorithms	298
	AWS Key Management Service	300
	Managed and Data Key	303
	Customer-Managed Key and Key Hierarchy	305
	KeyID, Alias, and ARN	305
	Permissions	307
	Managing Keys in AWS KMS	312
	Creating a Key Using the Console	313
	Deleting Keys in AWS KMS	315
	Rotating Keys in KMS	316
	Understanding the Cloud Hardware Security Module	328
	Using CloudHSM with AWS KMS	333
	SSL Offload Using CloudHSM	334
	AWS Certificate Manager	335
	AWS Secret Protection Mechanisms	338
	AWS Secrets Manager	338
	AWS Systems Manager Parameter Store	341
	Protecting Your S3 Buckets	344
	Default Access Control Protection	344
	S3 Block Public Access (BPA)	344
	S3 Access Points	346
	S3 Object Lock and S3 Glacier Vault Lock	347
	Bucket and Object Encryption	350
	Amazon Macie	365
	Protecting Data on the Move in AWS	370
	Data Protection Troubleshooting Scenarios	374

xvi Contents

	Summary	376
	Exam Essentials	377
	Review Questions	381

Chapter 8	**Threat Detection and Incident Response**	**385**
	Introduction	386
	Threat Detection	386
	Identifying Risks vs. Detecting Active Threats	387
	Automated vs. Custom Threat Detection	387
	Threat Detection Services	388
	Amazon GuardDuty	388
	AWS Security Hub	393
	AWS Trusted Advisor	397
	Amazon Detective	398
	Other Threat Detection Capabilities in AWS Services	400
	Incident Response	401
	Incident Response Life Cycle	401
	People, Technology, and Processes	403
	AWS Customer Incident Response Team	404
	Creating Your Incident Response Plan	404
	Step 1: Prepare	405
	Step 2: Implement	405
	Step 3: Monitor and Test	407
	Step 4: Update	407
	Reacting to Specific Security Incidents	408
	Abuse Notifications	408
	Insider Threat and Former Employee Access	409
	Amazon EC2 Instance Compromised by Malware	410
	Leaked Credentials	411
	Application Attacks	412
	Automating Incident Response	413
	Why Leverage Security Automations	413
	When to Automate	414
	Structure of a Security Automation	415
	How to Automate	417
	Summary	426
	Exam Essentials	426
	Review Questions	428

| | Contents | xvii |

| Appendix A | **Answers to Review Questions** | **431** |

Chapter 1: Security Fundamentals 432
Chapter 2: Cloud Security Principles and Frameworks 433
Chapter 3: Management and Security Governance 434
Chapter 4: Identity and Access Management 435
Chapter 5: Security Logging and Monitoring 436
Chapter 6: Infrastructure Protection 437
Chapter 7: Data Protection 438
Chapter 8: Threat Detection and Incident Response 439

| Appendix B | **Creating Your Security Journey in AWS** | **441** |

Introduction 442
How to Prioritize Your Security Initiatives 442
It's a Journey 443
Security Maturity Model 444

| Appendix C | **AWS Security Services Portfolio** | **449** |

Amazon Cognito 450
Amazon Detective 451
Amazon GuardDuty 451
Amazon Inspector 452
Amazon Macie 453
Amazon Security Lake 453
Amazon Verified Permissions 454
AWS Artifact 455
AWS Audit Manager 455
AWS Certificate Manager 456
AWS CloudHSM 456
AWS Directory Service 457
AWS Firewall Manager 458
AWS Identity and Access Management 459
AWS IAM Identity Center 459
AWS Key Management Service 460
AWS Network Firewall 460
AWS Organizations 461
AWS Payment Cryptography 462
AWS Private Certificate Authority 462
AWS Resource Access Manager 463
AWS Secrets Manager 464
AWS Security Hub 464
AWS Shield 465
AWS Web Application Firewall 466

xviii   Contents

Appendix D   DevSecOps in AWS   **467**

Introduction   468
  Cultural Philosophies   468
  Practices   469
  Tools   471
Dev + Sec + Ops   472
AWS Developer Tools   473
  AWS CodeCommit   473
  AWS CodeBuild   474
  AWS CodeDeploy   475
  AWS X-Ray   475
  Amazon CloudWatch   476
  AWS CodePipeline   476
Creating a CI/CD Using AWS Tools   477
  Creating a Repository   477
  Creating an AWS CodePipeline Pipeline   480
Evaluating Security in Agile Development   492
Creating the Correct Guardrails Using SAST and DAST   495
Security as Code: Creating Guardrails and Implementing
    Security by Design   496
  The Top 10 Proactive Controls   496
  The 10 Most Critical Web Application Security Risks   498

Index   *501*

Table of Exercises

Exercise 2.1	Generating a PCI DSS Report in the AWS Artifact Portal	57
Exercise 2.2	Checking the ISO 27001 and ISO 27017 Reports	58
Exercise 2.3	Using the Well-Architected Tool	61
Exercise 3.1	Viewing Compliance of Your AWS Resources	80
Exercise 3.2	Enabling Organization View in Trusted Advisor	81
Exercise 4.1	Change the Root Account Password	90
Exercise 4.2	Enable Virtual Multifactor Authentication for the Root Account	92
Exercise 4.3	Create an IAM User with Administrator Access Permissions	93
Exercise 4.4	Create an IAM Group with Amazon S3 Read-Only Access Role	107
Exercise 4.5	Create an Amazon S3 Bucket	108
Exercise 4.6	Add a User to the AmazonS3Viewers Group	108
Exercise 4.7	Force TLS Encryption for an Amazon S3 Bucket	110
Exercise 5.1	Set Up AWS Config	141
Exercise 5.2	Set Up a Trail in CloudTrail	155
Exercise 5.3	AWS CloudTrail Integration with Amazon CloudWatch Logs	160
Exercise 5.4	Create a Metric and an Alarm in Amazon CloudWatch	165
Exercise 5.5	AWS Config Rules	170
Exercise 5.6	AWS CloudTrail Integration with Amazon EventBridge	182
Exercise 6.1	Create a VPC and Subnets	208
Exercise 6.2	Create an Internet Gateway	208
Exercise 6.3	Create NAT Gateways	214
Exercise 6.4	Create Security Groups	219
Exercise 6.5	Create an NACL	225
Exercise 6.6	Create a Transit Gateway Attachment for VPC	231
Exercise 6.7	Elastic Load Balancing	240
Exercise 6.8	Work with VPC Endpoints	246
Exercise 6.9	Check VPC Flow Logs	249
Exercise 6.10	Create and Test an AWS Web Application Firewall	256
Exercise 7.1	Create a KMS Key	313
Exercise 7.2	Create an S3 Bucket and Use a KMS Key to Protect It	319
Exercise 7.3	Protecting RDS with KMS	321
Exercise 7.4	Protecting EBS with KMS	326

xx Table of Exercises

Exercise 7.5	Protect Your S3 Buckets with Block Public Access Settings and Service Control Policy.	357
Exercise 7.6	Replicate Encrypted S3 Objects Across Regions	360
Exercise 7.7	Protect Your S3 Buckets with a Resource Policy and VPC Endpoints.	362
Exercise 8.1	Enable Amazon GuardDuty in Your Account.	392
Exercise 8.2	Enable AWS Security Hub in Your Account.	397
Exercise 8.3	Enable Amazon Detective in Your Account	400
Exercise 8.4	Rotate AWS IAM Credentials	411
Exercise 8.5	Isolate Instances Using a TOR Anonymization Network	424

Introduction

As the pioneer and world leader of cloud computing, Amazon Web Services (AWS) has positioned security as its highest priority. Throughout its history, the cloud provider has constantly added security-specific services to its offerings as well as security features to its ever-growing portfolio. Consequently, the AWS Certified Security—Specialty certification offers a great way for IT professionals to achieve industry recognition as cloud security experts and learn how to secure AWS environments, both in concept and practice.

According to the AWS Certified Security Specialty Exam Guide, the corresponding certification attests your ability to demonstrate the following:

- An understanding of specialized data classifications and AWS data protection mechanisms
- An understanding of data-encryption methods and AWS mechanisms to implement them
- An understanding of secure Internet protocols and AWS mechanisms to implement them
- A working knowledge of AWS security services and features of services to provide a secure production environment
- Competency from two or more years of production deployment experience in using AWS security services and features
- The ability to make trade-off decisions regarding cost, security, and deployment complexity to meet a set of application requirements
- An understanding of security operations and risks

Through multiple choice and multiple response questions, you will be tested on your ability to design, operate, and troubleshoot secure AWS architectures composed of compute, storage, networking, and monitoring services. It is expected that you know how to deal with different business objectives (such as cost optimization, agility, and regulations) to determine the best solution for a described scenario.

The AWS Certified Security—Specialty exam is intended for individuals who perform a security role for three to five years with at least two years of hands-on experience securing AWS workloads.

What Does This Book Cover?

To help you prepare for the AWS Certified Security Specialty (SCS-C02) certification exam, *AWS Certified Security Study Guide Specialty (SCS-C02) Exam, Second Edition* explores the following topics:

Chapter 1: Security Fundamentals   This chapter introduces you to basic security definitions and foundational networking concepts. It also explores major types of attacks, along with the AAA architecture, security frameworks, practical models, and other solutions. In addition, it discusses the TCP/IP protocol stack.

Chapter 2: Cloud Security Principles and Frameworks This chapter discusses critical AWS Cloud security concepts such as its shared responsibility model, AWS hypervisors, AWS security certifications, the AWS Well-Architected Framework, and the AWS Marketplace. It also addresses both security *of* the cloud and security *in* the cloud. These concepts are foundational for working with AWS.

Chapter 3: Management and Security Governance This chapter discusses strategies to govern your workloads effectively using multiple AWS accounts and AWS Organizations to centrally manage security services with delegated administration and applying guardrails such as SCPs (Service Control Policies) as a technical solution to enforce policies across your organization. It also addresses how AWS Control Tower helps to consistently deploy architectures based on best practices and security guardrails to protect your workloads.

Chapter 4: Identity and Access Management This chapter explores AWS Identity and Access Management (IAM), which establishes the foundation for all resource interactions within AWS accounts. It covers authentication methods through various interfaces (AWS Console, CLI, and SDKs) and explains how to implement authorization through policies and permissions. The chapter also addresses critical security features, including multifactor authentication, identity federation, and AWS Secrets Manager, while emphasizing best practices for securing AWS environments. Key concepts include role-based access, cross-account permissions, and the principle of least privilege.

Chapter 5: Security Logging and Monitoring This chapter discusses how to gather information about the status of your resources and the events they produce through a four-stage framework: resources state, events collection, events analysis, and action. Key services include AWS Config, CloudTrail, CloudWatch, Inspector, Security Lake, Systems Manager, Trusted Advisor, and EventBridge, which work together to provide comprehensive visibility and automated responses to security events in AWS environments.

Chapter 6: Infrastructure Protection This chapter explores AWS networking concepts such as Amazon VPC, subnets, route tables, and other features that are related to network address translation (NAT gateways and NAT instances) and traffic filtering (security groups and network access control lists). It also addresses AWS Elastic Load Balancing and how security services such as AWS Web Application Firewall can provide secure access to your cloud-based applications. Finally, it discusses the AWS Shield and AWS's unique approach to mitigate distributed denial-of-service attacks.

Chapter 7: Data Protection This chapter discusses protecting data using a variety of security services and best practices, including AWS Key Management Service (KMS), the cloud hardware security module (CloudHSM), and AWS Certificate Manager. It also covers creating a customer master key (CMK) in AWS KMS, protecting Amazon S3 buckets, and how Amazon Macie can deploy machine learning to identify personal identifiable information (PII).

Chapter 8: Threat Detection and Incident Response This chapter covers AWS threat detection services (including GuardDuty, Security Hub, Trusted Advisor, and Detective) and incident response procedures, emphasizing both manual and automated approaches to handling security incidents. It covers the incident response life cycle, common security scenarios, and best practices for creating and implementing response plans while leveraging AWS services and automation capabilities to detect and remediate security issues effectively.

Appendix A: Answers to Review Questions This appendix provides the answers to the review questions that appear at the end of each chapter throughout the book.

Appendix B: Creating Your Security Journey in AWS This appendix discusses how to create your strategy to improve your security posture, consistently prioritizing the most important initiatives that can provide you security benefits, such as mitigating critical risks as soon as possible, thus optimizing your team's results.

Appendix C: AWS Security Services Portfolio This appendix provides an overview of the 24 AWS cloud services dedicated to security, identity, and compliance.

Appendix D: DevSecOps in AWS This appendix introduces DevSecOps, the AWS family of services that implement DevOps practices, and how security controls can be implemented in an automated pipeline.

How to Contact the Publisher

If you believe you've found a mistake in this book, please bring it to our attention. At John Wiley & Sons, we understand how important it is to provide our customers with accurate content, but even with our best efforts, an error may occur.

In order to submit your possible errata, please email it to our Customer Service Team at wileysupport@wiley.com with the subject line "Possible Book Errata Submission."

Interactive Online Learning Environment and Test Bank

Studying the material in the *AWS Certified Security Study Guide: Specialty (SCS-C02) Exam* is an important part of preparing for the AWS Certified Security Specialty (SCS-C02) certification exam, but we provide additional tools to help you prepare. The online test bank will help you understand the types of questions that will appear on the certification exam. The online test bank runs on multiple devices.

Sample Tests: The sample tests in the test bank include all the questions at the end of each chapter as well as the questions from the assessment test. In addition, there are two practice exams with 50 questions each. You can use these tests to evaluate your understanding and identify areas that may require additional study.

Flashcards: The flashcards in the test bank will push the limits of what you should know for the certification exam. There are 100 questions provided in digital format. Each flashcard has one question and one correct answer.

Glossary: The online glossary is a searchable list of key terms introduced in this exam guide that you should know for the AWS Certified Security Specialty (SCS-C02) certification exam.

Go to www.wiley.com/go/sybextestprep to register and gain access to this interactive online learning environment and test bank with study tools. To start using these tools to study for the AWS Certified Security Specialty (SCS-C02) exam, go to www.wiley.com/go/sybextestprep to register your book and receive your unique PIN. Once you have the PIN, return to www.wiley.com/go/sybextestprep, find your book, and click register or login and follow the link to register a new account or add this book to an existing account.

AWS Certified Security Study Guide—Specialty (SCS-C02) Exam Objectives

This table shows the extent, by percentage, of each domain represented on the actual examination.

Domain	Percent of Examination
Domain 1: Threat Detection and Incident Response	14%
Domain 2: Security Logging and Monitoring	18%
Domain 3: Infrastructure Security	20%
Domain 4: Identity and Access Management	16%
Domain 5: Data Protection	18%
Domain 6: Management and Security Governance	14%
Total	100%

Exam objectives are subject to change at any time without prior notice and at AWS's sole discretion. Visit the AWS Certified Security–Specialty website (aws.amazon.com/certification/certified-security-specialty) for the most current listing of exam objectives.

Objective Map

Objective	Chapters
Domain 1: Threat Detection and Incident Response	
1.1: Design and implement an incident response plan.	2,8
1.2: Detect security threats and anomalies by using AWS services.	1,5,8
1.3: Respond to compromised resources and workloads.	8
Domain 2: Security Logging and Monitoring	
2.1: Design and implement monitoring and alerting to address security events.	1,5
2.2: Troubleshoot security monitoring and alerting.	5
2.3: Design and implement a logging solution.	5
2.4: Troubleshoot logging solutions.	5
2.5: Design a log analysis solution.	5
Domain 3: Infrastructure Security	
3.1: Design and implement security controls for edge services.	1,6
3.2: Design and implement network security controls.	1,6
3.3: Design and implement security controls for compute workloads.	6
3.4: Troubleshoot network security.	2,6
Domain 4: Identity and Access Management	
4.1: Design, implement, and troubleshoot authentication for AWS resources.	1,4
4.2: Design, implement, and troubleshoot authorization for AWS resources.	4
Domain 5: Data Protection	
5.1: Design and implement controls that provide confidentiality and integrity for data in transit.	7
5.2: Design and implement controls that provide confidentiality and integrity for data at rest.	7

Objective	Chapters
5.3: Design and implement controls to manage the life cycle of data at rest.	1,7
5.4: Design and implement controls to protect credentials, secrets, and cryptographic key materials.	7
Domain 6: Management and Security Governance	
6.1: Develop a strategy to centrally deploy and manage AWS accounts.	3
6.2: Implement a secure and consistent deployment strategy for cloud resources.	3
6.3: Evaluate the compliance of AWS resources.	3,5
6.4: Identify security gaps through architectural reviews and cost analysis.	3

Assessment Test

1. Which one of the following components should not influence an organization's security policy?

   A. Business objectives

   B. Regulatory requirements

   C. Risk

   D. Cost–benefit analysis

   E. Current firewall limitations

2. Consider the following statements about the AAA architecture:

   I. Authentication deals with the question "Who is the user?"

   II. Authorization addresses the question "What is the user allowed to do?"

   III. Accountability answers the question "What did the user do?"

   Which of the following is correct?

   A. Only I is correct.

   B. Only II is correct.

   C. I, II, and III are correct.

   D. I and II are correct.

   E. II and III are correct.

3. What is the difference between denial-of-service (DoS) and distributed denial-of-service (DDoS) attacks?

   A. DDoS attacks have many targets, whereas DoS attacks have only one each.

   B. DDoS attacks target multiple networks, whereas DoS attacks target a single network.

   C. DDoS attacks have many sources, whereas DoS attacks have only one each.

   D. DDoS attacks target multiple layers of the OSI model and DoS attacks only one.

   E. DDoS attacks are synonymous with DoS attacks.

4. Which of the following options is incorrect?

   A. A firewall is a security system aimed at isolating specific areas of the network and delimiting domains of trust.

   B. Generally speaking, the web application firewall (WAF) is a specialized security element that acts as a full-reverse proxy, protecting applications that are accessed through HTTP.

   C. Whereas intrusion prevention system (IPS) devices handle only copies of the packets and are mainly concerned with monitoring and alerting tasks, intrusion detection system (IDS) solutions are deployed inline in the traffic flow and have the inherent design goal of avoiding actual damage to systems.

xxviii   Assessment Test

    D. Security information and event management (SIEM) solutions are designed to collect security-related logs as well as flow information generated by systems (at the host or the application level), networking devices, and dedicated defense elements such as firewalls, IPSs, IDSs, and antivirus software.

5. In the standard shared responsibility model, AWS is responsible for which of the following options?

    A. Regions, availability zones, and data encryption

    B. Hardware, firewall configuration, and hypervisor software

    C. Hypervisor software, regions, and availability zones

    D. Network traffic protection and identity and access management

6. Which AWS service allows you to generate compliance reports that enable you to evaluate the AWS security controls and posture?

    A. AWS Artifact

    B. AWS Trusted Advisor

    C. AWS Well-Architected Tool

    D. Amazon Inspector

7. Which of the following contains a definition that is not a pillar from the AWS Well-Architected Framework?

    A. Security and operational excellence

    B. Reliability and performance efficiency

    C. Cost optimization and availability

    D. Security and performance efficiency

8. Which of the following services provides a set of APIs that controls access to your resources on the AWS Cloud?

    A. AWS AAA

    B. AWS IAM

    C. AWS Authenticator

    D. AWS AD

9. Regarding AWS IAM principals, which option is *not* correct?

    A. A principal is an IAM entity that has permission to interact with resources in the AWS Cloud.

    B. They can only be permanent.

    C. They can represent a human user, a resource, or an application.

    D. They have three types: root users, IAM users, and roles.

10. Which of the following is *not* a recommendation for protecting your root user credentials?

   A. Use a strong password to help protect account-level access to the management console.

   B. Enable MFA on your AWS root user account.

   C. Do not create an access key for programmatic access to your root user account.

   D. If you must maintain an access key to your root user account, you should never rotate it using the AWS Console.

11. In AWS Config, which option is *not* correct?

   A. The main goal of AWS Config is to record configuration and the changes of the resources.

   B. AWS Config Rules can decide if a change is good or bad and if it needs to execute an action.

   C. AWS Config cannot integrate with external resources like on-premises servers and applications.

   D. AWS Config can provide configuration history files, configuration snapshots, and configuration streams.

12. AWS CloudTrail is the service in charge of keeping records of API calls to the AWS Cloud. Which option is *not* a type of AWS CloudTrail event?

   A. Management

   B. Insights

   C. Data

   D. Control

13. In Amazon VPCs, which of the following is *not* correct?

   A. You can deploy only private IP addresses from RFC 1918 within VPCs.

   B. VPC is the acronym of Virtual Private Cloud.

   C. VPCs do not extend beyond an AWS region.

   D. You can configure your VPC to not share hardware with other AWS accounts.

14. In NAT gateways, which option is *not* correct?

   A. NAT gateways are always positioned in public subnets.

   B. Route table configuration is usually required to direct traffic to these devices.

   C. NAT gateways are highly available by default.

   D. Amazon CloudWatch automatically monitors traffic flowing through NAT gateways.

15. In security groups, which option is *not* correct?

   A. Security groups only have allow (permit) rules.

   B. The default security group allows all outbound communications.

   C. The default security group allows all outbound communications to any destination.

   D. You cannot have more than one security group associated with an instance's ENI.

xxx Assessment Test

16. In network ACLs, which option is *not* correct?

    A. They can be considered an additional layer of traffic filtering to security groups.

    B. Network ACLs have allow and deny rules.

    C. The default network ACL has only one inbound rule, denying all traffic from all protocols and all port ranges, from any source.

    D. A subnet can be associated with only one network ACL at a time.

17. In AWS KMS, which option is *not* correct?

    A. KMS can integrate with Amazon S3 and Amazon EBS.

    B. KMS can be used to generate SSH access keys for Amazon EC2 instances.

    C. KMS is considered multitenant, not a dedicated hardware security module.

    D. KMS can be used to provide data-at-rest encryption for RDS, Aurora, DynamoDB, and Redshift databases.

18. Which option is *not* correct with regard to AWS KMS customer managed keys?

    A. A CMK is a 256-bit AES for symmetric keys.

    B. A CMK has a key ID, an alias, and an ARN (Amazon Resource Name).

    C. A CMK has two policies roles: key administrators and key users.

    D. A CMK can also use IAM users, IAM groups, and IAM roles.

19. Which of the following actions is *not* recommended when an Amazon EC2 instance is compromised by malware?

    A. Take a snapshot of the EBS volume at the time of the incident.

    B. Change its security group accordingly and reattach any IAM role attached to the instance.

    C. Tag the instance as compromised together with an AWS IAM policy that explicitly restricts all operations related to the instance, the incident response, and forensics teams.

    D. When the incident forensics team wants to analyze the instance, they should deploy it into a totally isolated environment—ideally a private subnet.

20. Which of the following actions is recommended when temporary credentials from an Amazon EC2 instance are inadvertently made public?

    A. You should assume that the access key was compromised and revoke it immediately.

    B. You should try to locate where the key was exposed and inform AWS.

    C. You should not reevaluate the IAM roles attached to the instance.

    D. You should avoid rotating your key.

21. Which of the following options may *not* be considered a security automation trigger?

    A. Unsafe configurations from AWS Config or Amazon Inspector

    B. AWS Security Hub findings

    C. Systems Manager Automation documents

    D. Event from Amazon CloudWatch Events

22. Which of the following options may *not* be considered a security automation response task?

A. An AWS Lambda function can use AWS APIs to change security groups or network ACLs.

B. A Systems Manager Automation document execution run.

C. Systems Manager Run Command can be used to execute commands to multiple hosts.

D. Apply a thorough forensic analysis in an isolated instance.

23. Which of the following may not be considered a troubleshooting tool for security in AWS Cloud environments?

A. AWS CloudTrail

B. Amazon CloudWatch Logs

C. AWS Key Management Service

D. Amazon EventBridge

24. Right after you correctly deploy VPC peering between two VPCs (A and B), inter-VPC traffic is still not happening. What is the most probable cause?

A. The peering must be configured as transitive.

B. The route tables are not configured.

C. You need a shared VPC.

D. You need to configure a routing protocol.

25. A good mental exercise for your future cloud security design can start with the analysis of how AWS native security services and features (as well as third-party security solutions) can replace your traditional security controls. Which of the options is not a valid mapping between traditional security controls and potential AWS security controls?

A. Network segregation (such as firewall rules and router access control lists) and security groups and network ACLs, Web Application Firewall (WAF)

B. Data encryption at rest and Amazon S3 server-side encryption, Amazon EBS encryption, Amazon RDS encryption, and other AWS KMS-enabled encryption features

C. Monitor intrusion and implementing security controls at the operating system level versus Amazon GuardDuty

D. Role-based access control (RBAC) versus AWS IAM, Active Directory integration through IAM groups, temporary security credentials, AWS Organizations

Answers to Assessment Test

1. **E.** Specific control implementations and limitations should not drive a security policy. In fact, the security policy should influence such decisions, and not vice versa.

2. **D.** Accountability is not part of the AAA architecture; accounting is.

3. **C.** When a DoS attack is performed in a coordinated fashion, with a simultaneous use of multiple source hosts, the term *distributed denial-of-service* (DDoS) is used to describe it.

4. **C.** It's the other way around.

5. **C.** AWS is responsible for its regions, availability zones, and hypervisor software. In the standard shared responsibility model, AWS is not responsible for user-configured features such as data encryption, firewall configuration, network traffic protection, and identity and access management.

6. **A.** AWS Artifact is the free service that allows you to access compliance-related reports.

7. **C.** Availability is not a pillar from the AWS Well-Architected Framework.

8. **B.** AWS Identity and Access Management (IAM) gives you the ability to define authentication and authorization methods for using the resources in your account.

9. **B.** IAM principals can be permanent or temporary.

10. **D.** If you must maintain an access key to your root user account, which is a bad practice, you should regularly rotate it using the AWS Console.

11. **C.** AWS Config can also integrate with external resources like on-premises servers and applications, third-party monitoring applications, or version control systems.

12. **D.** CloudTrail events can be classified as management, insights, and data.

13. **A.** You can also assign public IP addresses in VPCs.

14. **C.** You need to design your VPC architecture to include NAT gateway redundancy.

15. **D.** You can add up to five security groups per network interface.

16. **C.** The default network ACL also has a Rule 100, which allows all traffic from all protocols and all port ranges, from any source.

17. **B.** Key pairs (public and private keys) are generated directly from the EC2 service.

18. **D.** IAM groups cannot be used as principals in KMS policies.

19. **B.** To isolate a compromised instance, you need to change its security group accordingly and detach (not reattach) any IAM role attached to the instance. You also remove it from Auto Scaling groups so that the service creates a new instance from the template and service interruption is reduced.

20. **A.** As a best practice, if any access key is leaked to a shared repository (like GitHub)—even if only for a couple of seconds—you should assume that the access key was compromised and revoke it immediately.

21. **C.** Systems Manager Automation documents are actually a security automation response task.

22. **D.** A forensic analysis is a detailed investigation for detecting and documenting an incident. It usually requires human action and analysis.

23. **C.** AWS KMS is a managed service that facilitates the creation and control of the encryption keys used to encrypt your data, but it doesn't help you troubleshoot in other services.

24. **B.** VPC peering requires route table configuration to direct traffic between a pair of VPCs.

25. **C.** Monitor intrusion and security controls at the operating system level can be mapped to third-party solutions, including endpoint detection and response (EDR), antivirus (AV), host intrusion prevention system (HIPS), anomaly detection, user and entity behavior analytics (UEBA), and patching.

Chapter 1

Security Fundamentals

THE AWS CERTIFIED SECURITY SPECIALTY EXAM OBJECTIVES THAT LEVERAGE CONCEPTS EXPLAINED IN THIS CHAPTER INCLUDE THE FOLLOWING:

✔ **Domain 1: Incident Response**

- 1.2. Verify that the Incident Response plan includes relevant AWS services

✔ **Domain 2: Logging and Monitoring**

- 2.1. Design and implement security monitoring and alerting

✔ **Domain 3: Infrastructure Security**

- 3.1. Design edge security on AWS
- 3.2. Design and implement a secure network infrastructure

✔ **Domain 4: Identity and Access Management**

- 4.1. Design and implement a scalable authorization and authentication system to access AWS resources

✔ **Domain 5: Data Protection**

- 5.3. Design and implement a data encryption solution for data at rest and data in transit

An understanding of the concepts explained in this chapter is critical in your journey to pass the AWS Certified Security Specialty exam. We introduce the following topics:

- Basic security definitions
- Foundational networking concepts
- Main classes of attacks
- Risk management
- Well-known security frameworks and models

In this chapter, you learn about basic security concepts and some foundational terminology that comes from the information technology (IT) infrastructure knowledge domain. Even if your sole objective is to conquer the AWS Certified Security Specialty certification, this chapter is relevant for any professional, particularly for the officially accredited ones, to demonstrate a good level of general education on the security subject matter (be it related to cloud-based or to traditional on-premises environments).

If you are already an experienced information security expert, you can still use this chapter for concept review purposes.

Understanding Security

The world of data communications has evolved considerably over the years, irrevocably impacting learning methods, business models, human interaction possibilities, and even the dynamics of most day-to-day activities. The networks of today are powerful, enabling individuals and companies to quickly transport data, voice, and video in an integrated fashion, thus providing access from multiple types of devices to all kinds of applications, which may reside anywhere in the world.

Virtually limitless use cases are brought to existence by the omnipresent network of networks. Conversely, this almighty global entity, which came to be known as *the Internet*, turned out to be a platform that embeds dangerous characteristics such as user anonymity, the ability to simultaneously control multiple remote computing devices, and the possibility to automate execution of tasks. Unfortunately, from a technical perspective, this all-encompassing network may be used for both good and evil.

Being aware of the adverse results that may be derived from widespread connectivity, it is natural to look for ways to ensure that only legitimate or noble uses of networked systems are allowed. Effective resources that compensate for the absence of natural boundaries on the Internet must be implemented. There should be structured means of defining what the acceptable activities are, from either a productivity or a protection standpoint. Conditional access to networked resources should be put in place, instead of simply providing unrestricted access and naively relying on inherent humankind's goodwill. Dealing with this variety of challenges is what the security practice lends itself to.

When the subject is connectivity, the trending topic of artificial intelligence (AI) can no longer be overlooked. It is here to stay and revolutionize the world but, as is common for such a broad concept, it can be employed in diametrically opposed directions. On the one hand, AI makes it simpler and faster for hackers to perform cyberattacks, mainly because of its data-gathering and -processing capabilities, user behavior learning, and potential for attack automation. On the other hand, the AI capabilities of analyzing vast amounts of data, establishing what is standard behavior, and detecting deviations from this reference are very useful on the defense side. Commercial solutions that embed AI are quickly proliferating and showing their potential to help security operations teams handle vulnerabilities and incidents, either from a detection or response perspective.

But where do you start your journey to learn security? The first step in solving a problem is recognizing that there is one. The second most effective step is ensuring that you understand what needs to be solved; in other words, what is the problem? If you are presented with questions for which there may be multiple answers (or multiple choices, as in your certification exam), a good starting point is to eliminate all those options that do not apply. In an attempt to summarize what the practice of security could signify, it is probably easier to begin by defining what it is not:

- **Security is neither a product nor a service.** First of all, there is no single product that can act as a "magic black box" that can automatically solve every problem. Moreover, the available capabilities of a given product are helpful only when they are properly enabled for actual use.

- **Security is not a technology.** Technologies, including those that provide visibility and the ability to block traffic as well as respond to attack situations, may be grouped to form an important defensive system. However, the threat landscape is an ever-changing object, meaning that several techniques and tools that have been largely employed on well-known attack scenarios may prove ineffective when facing the newest challenges.

- **Security is not static.** It is not something that you do once and quickly forget. Processes must exist for dealing with planning, implementation, testing, and updating tasks. All of these items must involve people and discipline.

- **Security is not a check box.** You should know what you are protecting against and, once you determine that, look for resources that can demonstrate true security effectiveness.

- **Security is not made only by nominal security elements.** In spite of the existence of dedicated security hardware and software products, security is not limited to them. For example, there are countless contributions that can be brought to the overall security process by well-configured network infrastructure devices such as routers and switches.

- **Security is not a beautiful graphical user interface (GUI).** You should always understand what is going on behind the scenes—what is in the brain of the system and not relying blindly, for instance, on reports that state "you are protected."

Now that you've learned what security is not about, it is time to start getting acquainted with what it can be. One general principle that has proved valuable in many fields is to move from global concepts to specifics, and not in the opposite direction. In that sense, if the assigned duty is to protect the relevant digital assets of a particular organization, it is highly advisable that you understand the organization's vision, mission, objectives, and possible competitors. All of these items are considered in a high-level document known as the *organizational security policy*, which establishes the foundation for all initiatives and tasks pertaining to security.

Among the typical pieces of information that are used to guide policy creation, some deserve special mention:

- **Business objectives:** The main references for policy definition, these are related to the classic questions—*Why we are here?* and *What are we trying to achieve?*—that are answered in mission statements or company strategies for a period.

- **Regulatory requirements:** These are specific to the industry sector to which the organization belongs and must be always considered. These requirements normally indicate what type of data is valuable in that particular industry.

- **Risk:** The acceptable level of risk, from the point of view of senior leadership, should be included in the policy. There can be various categories of risks, such as direct financial loss, improper disclosure of intellectual property, strategic information theft, or damage to the public image of the organization.

- **Cost/benefit analysis:** This analysis should always be considered for the mitigation of the identified risks. The cost/benefit ratio of implementing a certain control must always be taken into account, and this calculation involves not only investment in products but also the cost of specialized personnel to make it possible.

A security policy is related to an organization's business strategy and, as such, is usually written using broader terms. To have practical applicability, the general rules and principles it states need to be carefully described in a set of companion documents, which are tactical in nature. The most common of these elements are as follows:

- **Standards:** These specify mandatory rules, regulations, or activities.

- **Guidelines:** These encompass sets of recommendations, reference actions, and operational guides to be considered under circumstances in which standards are not applicable.

- **Baselines:** These documents are meant to define the minimum level of security that is required for a given system type.

- **Procedures:** These include step-by-step instructions for performing specific tasks. They define how policies, standards, and guidelines are implemented within the operating environment.

FIGURE 1.1 Positioning the security policy.

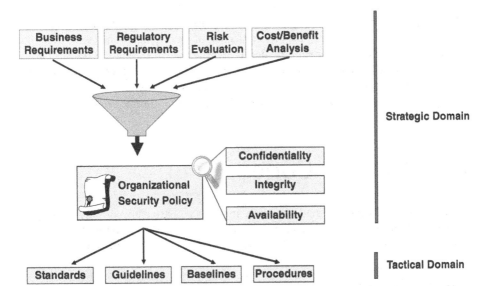

Figure 1.1 depicts the relationship of the security policy with its companion documents and main sources of information. It also displays some important attributes that must be present in the policy.

You should be aware of several important principles, especially if you are in charge of defending critical digital assets. First, you should be aware that *attacks happen*. It does not matter whether or not you detect them. It is not even relevant whether those attacks have already been successful (even if they haven't, they might be someday—it's just a matter of time). In dealing with security, it is crucial to have an attack-and-defense culture in place so that you are always reflecting on potential exposures and can learn how to mitigate the associated risk.

You should also notice that every networked element is a potential attack target. This is the case with servers (e.g., web, application, and database servers), client devices of any kind, intermediary elements such as Application Programming Interfaces and even infrastructure devices, such as routers, switches, and wireless access points.

Hope is not a strategy. You should make sure your security strategy directly states the access policies and clarifies what types of traffic are permitted and under what conditions. There should be precisely documented network topologies that provide easy understanding of allowed connections, from sources to destinations. You should deploy elements acting as established policy enforcement points, instead of assuming that users and devices will behave properly.

Much like onions, security is built in layers. By considering the hypothesis that a certain defense may be circumvented, you should build additional protection layers along the path that leads to your valuable resources.

At this point of the discussion, some questions may arise, such as how can you link the macro statements from the overarching security policy to those down-to-earth requirements of configuring a certain access control rule? Or what does a particular traffic flow permission have to do with a given business objective of an organization?

To respond to such inquiries, begin by identifying the critical business systems of your organization. What communication protocols are involved in connecting to those systems? What are the inherent risks of having these protocols running on your network? Are there reported vulnerabilities that could be exploited? What are the suitable security measures for risk mitigation?

Basic Security Concepts

Imagine that you have been assigned a mission and that you are truly committed to accomplishing it. Before you begin executing the specific tasks that compose the major objective of your journey, you must understand, at a minimum, the following:

- What rules are involved?

- What are the restrictions?

- What is available in your toolkit?

- What kind of help can you count on?

- What are the parameters that indicate that you have succeeded?

Likewise, if your particular mission has something to do with protecting a given computing environment, you must have solid knowledge not only of the available security building blocks but also of the typical terminology that relates to risk, exposure, threats, and the absence of proper safeguards. The purpose of this section is to provide a reference, within the realm of IT security, that you can revisit while reading the rest of this book.

Vulnerability, Threat, and Security Risk

The concepts of vulnerabilities, threats, and security risks are distinct and yet interrelated:

- A *vulnerability* is a weakness in a computer system that can be exploited to perform unauthorized actions.

- A *threat* is defined by any entity (such as a person or a tool) that can exploit a vulnerability, intentionally or by accident. Such an entity is also known as a *threat actor* or *threat agent*.

- A *security risk* relates to the probability of a certain vulnerability being exploited by a threat actor. A risk also depends on the value of the digital asset under analysis. For instance, if the same software bug (an example of vulnerability) is present on a lab virtual machine and a production application server, a higher security risk should be associated with the latter.

Basic Security Concepts

Security Countermeasures and Enforcement

Within a computing environment, the mechanisms aimed at risk mitigation are called *security countermeasures* (or *security controls*). They can come in multiple formats, including the following:

- Software patching (to eliminate a previously detected vulnerability)
- Implementation of security capabilities that are specifically designed as defensive resources to reduce or eliminate risk, thus avoiding vulnerability exploitation (some examples of such capabilities are explored in the "Risk Management" section later in this chapter)
- Verification of user identity before granting access to critical data

The mere process of defining security policies and their component rules is not enough for effective security. You must have a means to ensure that those rules are implemented and obeyed—or, in other words, there must be an enforcement.

Confidentiality, Integrity, and Availability

The following are foundational attributes that you should consider not only for policy definition but also for evaluation of security effectiveness:

- **Confidentiality:** This principle is concerned with preventing unauthorized disclosure of sensitive information and ensuring a suitable level of privacy at all stages of data processing. Encryption is a typical example of a technology designed with confidentiality in mind.
- **Integrity:** This principle deals with the prevention of unauthorized modification of data and with ensuring information accuracy. Hash message authentication codes, such as HMAC-SHA (largely employed by the Internet Protocol Security [IPsec] framework), are mathematical functions conceived to protect the integrity of the data transmitted in Internet Protocol (IP) packets.
- **Availability:** This principle focuses on ensuring reliability and an acceptable level of performance for legitimate users of computing resources. Provisions must be made against eventual failures in the operating environment, which includes the existence of well-designed recovery plans at both physical and logical levels.

In many publications, the confidentiality, integrity, and availability security principles are also referred to as the *CIA triad*.

Accountability and Nonrepudiation

Accountability is an attribute related to a certain individual or organization being held responsible for its actions. The idea is to ensure that all operations performed by systems or processes can be identified and precisely associated with their author.

Nonrepudiation is the property of ensuring that no one can deny that they have performed an action in an effort to avoid being held accountable. In the IT security world, repudiation examples include someone denying that a certain system transaction has been carried out or users denying the authenticity of their own signatures.

Authentication, Authorization, and Accounting

Authentication, authorization, and accounting are three security functions that are usually combined to deliver access control services. This interaction inspired the creation of the AAA architecture, in which the meaning of each "A" is more easily grasped when associated with the question it was designed to answer:

- **Authentication:** Deals with the question *Who is the user?* The process to find this answer essentially involves extracting user-related information (such as a username and its corresponding password) from an access request to a system and comparing it to a database of previously defined valid users. Certain environments may treat unregistered users as guests or generic users, thus granting a basic level of access.

- **Authorization:** Addresses the question *What is the user allowed to do?* This user should have been authenticated before authorization occurs in order to differentiate the access privileges, or authorization attributes. The authorization failures that appear on an AAA service report can help characterize improper access attempts.

- **Accounting:** Answers the question *What did the user do?* Through this process, an accounting client—for instance, a networking device—collects user activity information and sends it to an accounting server (or service in the case of the AWS Cloud). This function not only provides information about legitimate use but also spots unexpected user behavior (in terms of traffic volume, abnormal access hours, or failed access attempts, for instance).

Visibility and Context

It is certainly much easier to protect your computing systems from the threats that are visible. Fortunately, in today's computing environments, visibility is not restricted to what you are able to directly see. Tools and techniques have been specifically developed to provide information about many parameters of packet flows, including the hidden ones.

Another important concept for the current security practice is *context*. Providing context relates to the ability to gather additional information around the main one use so that ambiguity is removed before making policy decisions. Here are some examples:

- The same user may be granted different levels of access to corporate resources, depending on the device being used. On a domain-registered personal computer, the user will be provided with full access, whereas on a personal device, the same user will have only basic access to applications.

- Access to certain strategic systems may be deemed normal only for a specific time of day or day of the week. Any deviation from what is considered standard may indicate misuse and should trigger further investigation.

- A certain traffic pattern may be deemed an attack according to the source IP address that it comes from.

Foundational Networking Concepts

Chances are that you may be the security architect in charge of protecting companies that view the AWS Cloud as an interesting disaster recovery option for its critical workloads. You may also be responsible for providing security for companies that are adapting applications so that they can be migrated to the AWS Cloud. Or you may be the security consultant for a cloud-native organization. In any of these scenarios, it is important to keep in mind that, although hosted in a virtual private network, your cloud-based systems could still be reachable through the Internet using standard data communication protocols. Consequently, it is not possible to perform cloud security well without a good knowledge of network security, which, in turn, is not achievable unless you are familiar with the basics of networking.

This section visits two network communication models: the Open Systems Interconnection (OSI) model and the TCP/IP protocol stack, which is what came to be the most prevalent and successful standard for network-based communications. This approach proves insightful and allows you to quickly locate the layer over which an attack is taking place, thus making it easier to determine what types of protection mechanisms may the most appropriate.

The OSI Reference Model

The OSI model was developed by the International Organization for Standardization (ISO) in 1984. This example of a divide-and-conquer approach for explaining network-based communications was aimed at reducing the overall perception of complexity and, undoubtedly, has contributed to generations of professionals and students working in this field. OSI divides the communication system into seven abstract layers, each of which is in charge of a well-defined job, while working in a collaborative way, in order to achieve data transmission between two given systems.

Some of the OSI benefits are listed here:

- It allows the standardization of interfaces among devices, making interoperability possible between diverse systems, even those created by distinct vendors.

- It enables modularity, from engineering and development standpoints, making it possible to design features that belong to a particular layer, without worrying, at least momentarily, about what happens on another layer.

10 Chapter 1 ▪ Security Fundamentals

- It makes it possible to build specialized devices that may act on a specific layer or, eventually, on just some of them.

- It allows more direct isolation of problems, which is useful not only for troubleshooting efforts but also for security planning.

Now that you know the motivation behind the creation of this famous conceptual model, whose hierarchy is illustrated in Figure 1.2, we briefly describe the main functions associated with each of the seven numbered layers:

1. **Physical layer:** The lowest layer is responsible for the physical connection between the devices and is concerned with transmitting raw bits over a communication channel. The main design issues include dealing with mechanical, electrical, optical, and timing interfaces as well as with ensuring that when one side sends a 1 bit, it is accurately received by the other side as a 1 bit, and not as a 0 bit.

2. **Data Link layer:** This layer is in charge of node-to-node delivery of the message in the form of larger and sequential units of data called *frames*. For proper identification of end hosts, it defines a physical addressing scheme, which has only local significance, such as the 48-bit MAC address used by the Ethernet network interface cards (NICs). Some of the issues this layer deals with are error-free delivery, flow control (thus avoiding a fast transmitter from overwhelming a slow receiver), and controlled access to shared media (including those that allow broadcast transmission, such as Ethernet).

3. **Network layer:** The main task of this layer concerns routing a unit of data (the so-called Layer 3 packet) from one given source to a destination that resides on a different network, potentially connected by means of a different Data Link layer technology. This layer introduces the concept of the *logical address*, of which the IP address is the most important example. This addressing paradigm, which treats an individual host as part of a larger logical entity (known as a Layer 3 *subnet*), is what makes global delivery of

FIGURE 1.2 The OSI model.

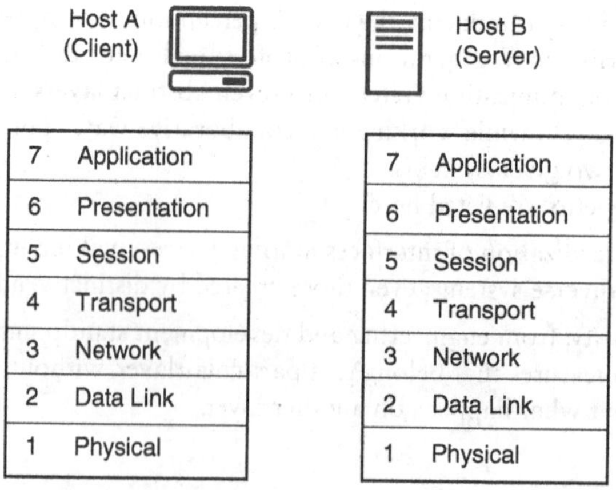

Host A (Client)		Host B (Server)	
7	Application	7	Application
6	Presentation	6	Presentation
5	Session	5	Session
4	Transport	4	Transport
3	Network	3	Network
2	Data Link	2	Data Link
1	Physical	1	Physical

packets accurate, scalable, and flexible, independently of the Layer 2 media (and the correspondent Layer 2 address of the destination node).

4. **Transport layer:** This layer is aimed at providing reliable message delivery, from the source to the destination host, irrespective of the types and number of physical or logical (Layer 3) networks traversed along the path. The Transport layer can also confirm (or acknowledge) successful data transmission and trigger retransmission when errors are detected. Layer 4 introduces the concepts of source and destination ports, thus allowing multiple service processes to run (and be identified) within the same computing node. The most common transport protocols are Transmission Control Protocol (TCP) and User Datagram Protocol (UDP), both of which belong to the TCP/IP stack, which is discussed later, in the "The TCP/IP Protocol Stack" section.

5. **Session layer:** A session consists of the coordinated exchange of requests and responses between application processes running on endpoint machines. The main functions associated with this layer are session handling (establishment, maintenance, and termination), controlling the dialogue between the two communicating parties (half-duplex and full-duplex transmission), and inserting synchronization control points into the data flow (which makes it possible for a large transfer to be restarted from the point where it was interrupted, rather than retransmitting everything).

6. **Presentation layer:** This layer is sometimes called the *Translation layer* because it deals with the syntax and semantics of the data being transmitted. This makes it possible for devices that employ different data representations to communicate. The data structures being exchanged can be defined in an abstract way, along with a standard encoding to be used over the transmission media.

7. **Application layer:** This is the top layer of the OSI reference model and the closest to the end user. Many examples of application protocols are very well known for the typical end user; the most common being the Hypertext Transfer Protocol (HTTP), the File Transfer Protocol (FTP), and the auxiliary Domain Name System (DNS), which acts as the mapping agent between site names and IP addresses before the actual application connection takes place.

The TCP/IP Protocol Stack

Sponsored by the U.S. Department of Defense, the academic network known as the Advanced Research Projects Agency Network (ARPANET) is considered the ancestor of today's Internet. It already employed packet switching (instead of circuit switching) and was the first network to implement the TCP/IP protocol suite.

Even though it is always instructive, during the learning process, to contrast a certain protocol stack with the OSI model, you should not forget that other suites of protocols were in use before OSI was established. This was the case of the TCP/IP stack, which survived the test of time and, despite any eventual criticism, became the de facto standard for internetworking. Due to the practical importance of protocols such as IP, TCP, and UDP, we provide a dedicated analysis that, although brief, may be useful to you later. Figure 1.3 compares TCP/IP and the OSI layers.

FIGURE 1.3 Comparison between the OSI model and the TCP/IP stack.

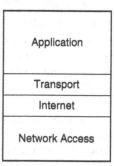

The Internet Protocol (IP) is almost a synonym of the OSI network layer, and packet routing is its most relevant task. IP routing deals with the choice of a path over which the IP packets (or datagrams), destined to a particular host, will be sent. Even though some techniques employ additional attributes (the source IP address, for example), the classic definition of routing considers the destination IP address as the only criterion for path selection. The IP routing function can be divided into four basic activities:

1. **Gathering routing information:** This can be achieved by manual definition of static routes or by using dynamic routing protocols, such as Open Shortest Path First (OSPF), Routing Information Protocol (RIP), or Border Gateway Protocol (BGP).

2. **Building the routing table:** Before installing a path in this table, a router sequentially performs two comparisons: (1) If more than one equal-length network prefix is available to a destination, the router will prefer the one with the lowest administrative distance (a measure of the trustworthiness among static routes, dynamic routes originated from routing protocols, or a mixture of both), and (2) for two equal-length prefixes that have the same value for the administrative distance parameter, a router will choose the one with the lowest cost under the perspective of the particular routing protocol.

3. **Searching for the longest prefix match:** When a packet arrives at the incoming interface, its destination IP address is extracted and compared to the available entries in the routing table. The comparison that results in the longest bitwise match for the network mask is selected. If a match is not found, the last possibility of finding one is to use a default route (in case one is available).

4. **Forwarding the packet on the outgoing interface:** When a match happens in Step 3, it will point to an entry in the routing table that has a corresponding outgoing interface. This last step includes building the appropriate Layer 2 header for this interface.

The TCP/IP model defines two end-to-end transport layer protocols: TCP and UDP. The choice will depend on the requirements of the application protocol being used. TCP is connection-oriented, reliable, and includes flow control, while UDP is a much simpler option that provides best-effort delivery of individual packets. UDP is connectionless and unreliable but nevertheless is well suited for real-time traffic (such as

FIGURE 1.4 The IPv4 header.

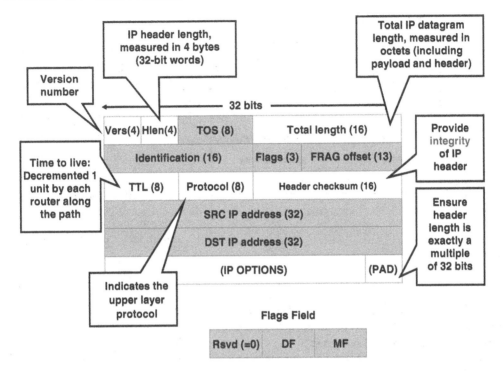

voice and video) and other applications that use a client-server communication model with simple request-reply queries.

The types of fields included in the header of a communication protocol can tell a lot about its operational capabilities and flexibility. The way a packet with such a header is processed by end hosts or routers along the path can also reveal insightful information about potential protocol vulnerabilities that, if exploited, may lead to security issues. You should therefore have a good understanding of the IP, TCP, and UDP headers. We also recommend that you pay attention to header elements whenever a new protocol is introduced.

Figure 1.4 shows the IPv4 header and Figure 1.5 shows the UDP and TCP headers, with a special reference to the TCP flags field. These flags, in conjunction with the Sequence and Acknowledgement numbers, are key resources for materializing the so-called *TCP State Machine* and rendering TCP a truly stateful L4 protocol.

Besides its regular unicast transmission, an IP (version 4) network allows two other modes of operation: broadcast and multicast.

In a broadcast, a datagram is transmitted to all hosts in a network (or subnet) and, in general, does not require a response. Two classic protocols that employ broadcasting are the *Address Resolution Protocol* (ARP), used to map L3 and L2 addresses within a LAN, and *Dynamic Host Configuration Protocol* (DHCP), the protocol of choice for automatic IP address assignment for endpoint computers.

FIGURE 1.5 UDP and TCP headers.

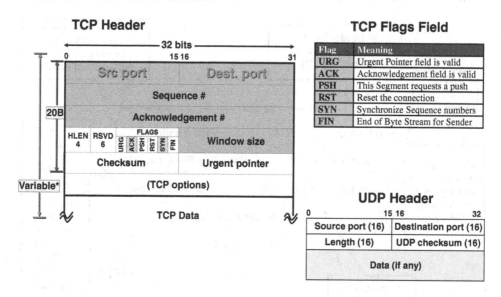

Multicast is concerned with sending data from a source unicast address to a given set of receivers represented by a group address. Typical tasks in the context of IP multicasting are group creation, signaling the interest of hosts in participating in a certain group, and routing multicast packets from the source toward those routers that have connected receivers for that group. The two main protocols pertaining to IP multicast are *Internet Group Membership Protocol* (IGMP), which is in charge of the host-to-router communication, and *Protocol Independent Multicast* (PIM), the routing protocol of choice for implementing real-life multicast networks.

From IPv4 to IPv6

Even among the most visionary connectivity enthusiasts, it is unlikely that someone could have foreseen, in the early 1980s, that a network originally conceived to interconnect universities would grow the way the Internet did. It gained so much importance, both for individuals and business activities, that it is almost impossible to imagine our current life without it.

But this tremendous increase in size, global reach, and use cases did not come without challenges. On the one hand, transport capabilities had to be adapted in a way that would allow the Internet to be a truly multiservice platform. On the other hand, as the Internet grew, so did the need to provide more and more IP addresses, potentially including several access devices per person, physical server hosting applications on virtual machines or containers, and all sorts of remotely controlled elements within the context of the Internet of Things (IoT) and operating technologies (OT).

The successor of the Internet Protocol version 4 (IPv4) is IPv6, which was initially designed in 1995 and standardized by the Internet Engineering Task Force (IETF) in 1998. Although not new at all, IPv6 has not been able yet to break through the inertia and completely replace IPv4. One of the main contributors to the long life of IPv4 is the Network Address Translation (NAT) technique, particularly in its many-to-one operation mode known as Port Address Translation (PAT). This resource allows multiple internal IP addresses to be mapped to a single external ("public") address, thus helping to work around v4 address depletion.

The major changes introduced by IPv6 are described here:

- **Much larger addressing capability:** IPv6 addresses are 128 bits long, which corresponds to 2^{96} times the size of the whole IPv4 addressing space. This huge number is beyond a human's ability to express quantities in words. Even with this almost unmeasurable amount, the Internet Assigned Numbers Authority (IANA) has created a very conservative and organized model for distributing v6 addresses to the regional registries (such as the ARIN and the RIPE NCC). The allocation is hierarchical (with IANA at the top level), thus providing visibility of addressing needs and simplifying address aggregation.

- **End-to-end connectivity made possible:** Given the virtually unbound addressing space, NAT should no longer be a concern. Technically speaking, two native IPv6-based elements can simply use their public v6 network addresses for direct communication.

- **Base header format simplification:** To reduce the processing effort in the most common situations of packet routing and forwarding, some IPv4 fields were removed from the IPv6 specification. For instance, IP options are conveyed as purpose-specific extension headers and not as a part of the base header anymore. Figure 1.6 illustrates the IPv6 base header and some examples of extension headers.

FIGURE 1.6 The IPv6 header and sample extension headers.

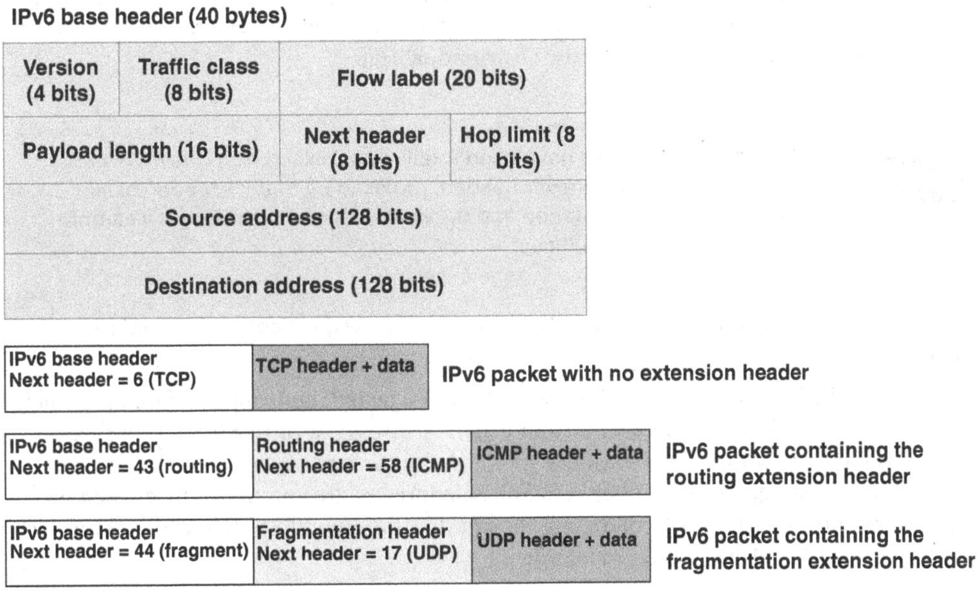

IPv6 base header (40 bytes)

Version (4 bits)	Traffic class (8 bits)	Flow label (20 bits)	
Payload length (16 bits)		Next header (8 bits)	Hop limit (8 bits)
Source address (128 bits)			
Destination address (128 bits)			

IPv6 base header Next header = 6 (TCP)	TCP header + data	IPv6 packet with no extension header

IPv6 base header Next header = 43 (routing)	Routing header Next header = 58 (ICMP)	ICMP header + data	IPv6 packet containing the routing extension header

IPv6 base header Next header = 44 (fragment)	Fragmentation header Next header = 17 (UDP)	UDP header + data	IPv6 packet containing the fragmentation extension header

IPv6 Address Format and Addressing Architecture

The 128 bits of an IPv6 address are organized as eight fields of 16 bits (four hexadecimal digits per field), separated by colons. The basic rules for representing IPv6 addresses are as follows:

- The hexadecimal digits are not case-sensitive.
- Leading zeros within a field may be omitted. For example, 2001:0db8:000C:00AB:0045:0303:000D:0E0E may be written as 2001:db8:C:AB:45:303:D:E0E, with no loss of information.
- Successive fields containing only zeros can be represented as a double colon (::). To avoid ambiguity, the double colon is allowed only once in the address. Some examples:
  - 2001:db8::A is equivalent to 2001:db8:0000:0000:0000:0000:0000:000A.
  - The loopback address is written as ::1 or ::1/128 (the first 127 bits are zero).
  - The unspecified address is composed of 128 zeros and represented as :: or ::/128.

IPv6 uses prefix lengths instead of subnet masks to represent the network portion of an address. The notation 2001:db8::25/64 means that 64 bits are used to specify the subnet within this address. In this example, the host address is 25 and belongs to the subnet 2001:db8:0:0::/64 (or, simply, 2001:db8::/64). There are three types of IPv6 addresses:

- **Unicast:** Identifies a single interface.
- **Anycast:** Identifies a set of interfaces that typically belong to distinct nodes. A packet sent to an anycast address will be delivered to the closest host, according to the routing protocol measure of distance.
- **Multicast group address:** Identifies a set of interfaces that typically belong to different nodes. A packet sent to a multicast address is delivered to all interfaces identified by that group address, following a Multicast Distribution Tree.

> Broadcast addresses have been totally suppressed from the IPv6 framework and, whenever needed, replaced by multicast addresses. Layer 2 address resolution and duplicate address detection are sample tasks that employ multicast.

These are the two main subtypes of IPv6 unicast addresses, which are outlined in Figure 1.7.

- **Link-local addresses:** Designed for use within a single link and employed on tasks such as automatic address configuration and neighbor discovery, or in situations where no routers are present. Routers must not forward any packets containing link-local source or destination addresses to other links. These addresses are automatically created on IPv6-enabled interfaces by combining the link-local prefix, FE80::/10, with a sequence of 54 zeros and a 64-bit interface identifier.

- Global unicast addresses (RFC 3587): Employed for generic IPv6 addressing and conceived with the possibility of aggregation in mind.

 In order to identify interfaces on a link, IPv6 unicast addresses employ *interface identifiers*. They must be unique within a given subnet but may be reused on multiple interfaces on a single node, in case they are part of different subnets. All unicast addresses, with the exception of those that start with binary 000, require interface IDs to be built in Modified EUI-64 format.

An extended unique identifier (EUI), as per RFC2373, allows a host to assign itself a unique 64-bit IPv6 interface identifier (EUI-64). This feature is a key benefit over IPv4, as it eliminates the need for manual configuration or DHCP. The IPv6 EUI-64 format address is obtained through the 48-bit MAC address. The MAC address is first separated into two 24-bit parts, with one being an organizationally unique identifier (OUI) and the other being NIC specific. The 16-bit 0xFFFE is then inserted between these two 24-bit parts for the 64-bit EUI address. IEEE has chosen FFFE as a reserved value that can only appear in EUI-64 generated from an EUI-48 MAC address. Figure 1.8 shows the connection between the MAC address and the interface identifier.

FIGURE 1.7 Main types of IPv6 unicast addresses.

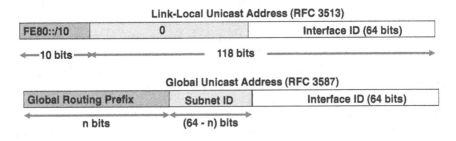

FIGURE 1.8 Deriving the interface identifier from the MAC address.

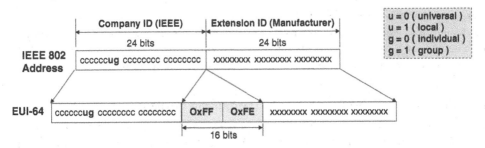

Main Classes of Attacks

Even though cyberattacks have always been around, when you compare current threats with those of the Internet's humble beginnings, the difference is essentially related to the intent of the individuals (or groups) carrying out the exploitation attempts. If notoriety was the main motivation early on, the possibility of quick personal profit is typically the motive of today's threats. Stealing intellectual property, having access to digital products without paying for them, illegally transferring money from someone else's bank account, and even using the Internet as a weapon for warfare between nations (or specific political groups within a country) are just a few examples of what can be done.

Another relevant challenge faced by the security professionals of today is that new exploit tools are made available daily, whereas the technical knowledge required to operate them is constantly decreasing. Most of them come with examples of use, scripts for attack automation, and sometimes even a GUI, which can make the cyberattack an even simpler task.

This section provides an overall view of the main classes of threats. Before starting the actual discussion, though, a word of warning: The descriptions that follow are not complete, mainly because this is a dynamic subject matter. Furthermore, it is common to find some types of attacks falling within more than one class.

Reconnaissance

Reconnaissance is normally defined as an attack preparation phase rather than an attack class on its own. The underlying goal is to obtain as much information as possible about potential targets without actually attacking their main application. Internet Control Message Protocol (ICMP) ping sweeps, port scanning (both on UDP and TCP), and observing a host's behavior under particular conditions (such as exposure to fragmented IP packets) are mechanisms that belong to the class of reconnaissance attacks.

Frequently considered harmless (and, as such, overlooked), this practice may be an indicator that attacks are about to happen.

The new challenge here is the availability of AI-based tools, which allow attackers to map the network very quickly and jump to the most dangerous phases.

Password Attacks

It is very natural for inside users to have more access rights to the systems of an interconnected organization. Being aware of this characteristic, many attackers leverage techniques that allow them to be authenticated as regular privileged users in such environments. Two possible ways of accomplishing such a goal are by:

- Creating a new privileged account
- Compromising an existing account and elevating its privileges

Brute-force attacks are those in which all possible combinations of letters, numbers, and symbols are sequentially tried by a program. A *dictionary* attack assumes that users tend to select a common word (typically small) or phrase to build their passwords. If the attacker gets access to an encrypted file that contains all the passwords, it will be possible to apply the same encryption to a dictionary of frequently used passwords and compare the results.

Eavesdropping Attacks

Network eavesdropping, also called *sniffing*, is an attack targeted at the confidentiality attribute of data. One typical goal here is to obtain valid credentials. In *passive eavesdropping*, the attacker listens to the message exchange that takes place over the network. This is achievable in many ways: by installing a wiretap, by connecting to shared media, such as an Ethernet hub, or by configuring switch port mirroring (using the attacker's machine as the destination). In *active eavesdropping*, the attacker tries to produce the mirroring effect by acting as a relay. Some examples are the exploitation of weaknesses in auxiliary local area network (LAN) protocols such as Dynamic Host Configuration Protocol (DHCP) or Address Resolution Protocol (ARP).

IP Spoofing Attacks

IP spoofing is the act of copying or falsifying a trusted source IP address. It is frequently used as an accessory resource for performing several types of attacks. Typical motivations behind IP spoofing are as follows:

- Impersonating a trusted user (or host) and taking advantage of the privileges associated with this trust relationship.
- Diverting attention away from the actual attack originator in an attempt to remain undetected.
- Casting suspicion on a legitimate host.

Man-in-the-Middle Attacks

Man-in-the-middle (MitM) is a broad class of attacks that involve a hacker maliciously inserting a third system into a two-party network conversation or transaction. To achieve this, the attacker establishes independent connections with the target machines and relays the exchanged messages, thus tricking both target machines into believing they are directly communicating.

Denial-of-Service Attacks

Since the early days of computer networking, attackers have employed many different techniques to take advantage of system vulnerabilities. Whereas many of the attack categories are focused on compromising the confidentiality or integrity attributes, there are also attempts to affect the availability of services. This last form of doing harm to networked organizations is the practice of *denial of service* (DoS), which induces exhaustion

20 Chapter 1 ▪ Security Fundamentals

of processing or network resources (on either connectivity devices or computing hosts), thus keeping legitimate users from accessing the intended applications. DoS attacks can occur in many layers of the OSI reference model, as illustrated in the following examples:

- **Layer 7 DoS:** Application layer DoS attacks target Layer 7 in the OSI model. The attacks attempt to overwhelm the server resources with a flood of traffic (typically HTTP requests). As an example, an HTTP DoS attack will focus on disrupting specific functionality of an online service by leveraging a vulnerability or some business logic inconsistency in the application. Another attack might induce a web application to perform a resource-intensive task, such as a database search, with the goal of increasing the consumption of server resources each time the search is performed.

- **Layer 4 DoS:** The TCP SYN flood is a classic attack that exploits the three-way handshake that TCP uses for connection setup. Normally, a TCP three-way handshake consists of a client sending a SYN message to the server, which acknowledges it by sending a SYN-ACK back to the client, causing the client to establish the connection via an ACK message. In this DoS attack, the client never sends the ACK message, creating a substantial number of half-open connections on the server that may exhaust its computing resources.

- **Layer 3 DoS:** Earlier examples of Layer 3 DoS attacks were the Ping of Death (where a large ICMP Echo message is maliciously sent to a host to cause buffer overflow when it attempts to reassemble the malformed packet), the Smurf attack (where an attacker broadcasts an ICMP Echo message using a target host IP as its source, thus causing all other hosts to flood this host with ICMP Echo Reply messages), and the teardrop attack (where an attacker sends fragmented IP packets to a target host, which may cause it to crash when trying to reassemble them).

- **Layer 2 DoS:** The Spanning Tree Protocol (STP) was created to remove looped connections in an Ethernet LAN. Switches deploying the same STP version exchange communication during a time interval to decide which links must be blocked to avoid such loops. An attacker may send false messages to initiate STP recalculations that can lead to a LAN environment becoming unavailable.

When a DoS attack is performed in a coordinated fashion, with simultaneous use of multiple source hosts, the term *distributed denial-of-service* (DDoS) is used to describe it.

Malware Attacks

Broadly speaking, *malware* is a software program designed to perform unauthorized actions on computer systems, sometimes reaching the limit of causing irreversible damage to them. Malware enters the network through vulnerabilities and can perform multiple types of malicious actions, including blocking access to network elements; installing additional hostile software on the initial target; propagating to neighboring hosts; creating communication channels with remote control machines in order to perpetuate illegal access; and, eventually, rendering systems unusable. Reflecting their main purpose or the way they act, malware is known under various names:

- **Virus:** A specific type of malware that depends on some kind of human action to start its job. A virus replicates itself by inserting its code into other programs and files, or even into a computer's boot sector. Viruses may be distributed through peripheral devices (such as flash drives), email attachments, or infected websites.

- **Worm:** This malware type does not require a program to trigger its execution, as it self-replicates and propagates. Once installed in a targeted system, it can create multiple copies of itself and spread through the network, infecting any devices that do not have suitable protection in place.

- **Trojan horse:** This is a destructive program that deceives the user by posing as a genuine application. It is very common for Trojans to create backdoors, thus providing attackers with continuous access to the infected system and allowing, for instance, the theft of information.

- **Adware:** This malware class is focused on presenting unwanted advertising to users and is typically bundled with free software or browser toolbars.

- **Launcher:** This accessory malware is used to download other malicious software. It is normally used for the initial compromise of a target.

- **Keylogger:** This malware is designed to stealthily record everything that is typed on a computer keyboard and transmit the data to a remote agent.

- **Ransomware:** This type of malware encrypts all user files on the target machine. After the initial compromise, the victim receives a message offering to restore access in return for the payment of a ransom.

Phishing Attacks

Phishing is the practice of sending fraudulent emails that appear to have come from trusted sources, with the objective of obtaining personal information or inducing the victim to perform some action, such as clicking on a hyperlink that will install malware.

Spear phishing is a more advanced technique in which the attackers include information that looks personal and is meaningful to the victims. With this investment in time and special preparation, the received message is more likely to be considered genuine.

Risk Management

Now that you have an understanding of common attack categories and how they operate, it is time to start working on the defense-related activities. Such practices involve, but are not limited to, the following:

- Understanding what each of the security technologies in your protection toolbox can bring to the game

22   Chapter 1 ▪ Security Fundamentals

- Knowing your key security personnel and determining the level of security education of your organization
- Designing the security processes to be implemented
- Spreading the security culture inside your team and organization

This section provides a quick review of the main security solutions and services available in the market. You can use this section as a reference that you can revisit while you read the remaining chapters of this study guide.

Firewalls

In the context of networking, a *firewall* is a security system aimed at isolating specific areas of the network and delimiting domains of trust. The firewall acts as a sort of conditional gateway, specifying the traffic types allowed to go from one domain to another by means of access control policies. It is important to keep in mind that a firewall is capable of controlling only the traffic that passes through it. Therefore, you must have a clear knowledge of the location of clients (connection initiators) and servers in the network before defining your policy.

Firewalls are the classic example of a specialized (and dedicated) security device and are pivotal elements in any defense system. Their evolution, through decades of service, has a lot to do with the OSI layers in which they act. Here's a brief review of the various generations of firewalls:

- **Packet filters:** Packet filters focus their access control efforts on static parameters related to the network and transport layers. They are stateless in essence, acting only over individual packets instead of connections.
- **Circuit-level proxies (or generic proxies):** These proxies establish sessions, as defined in Layer 5 of the OSI model, to the intended destinations, on behalf of requesting source hosts. The classic implementation of this category is the SOCKS5 software.
- **Application-level proxies (or dedicated proxies):** These proxies understand and interpret the commands within the application protocol they are providing services for. Given their application awareness, they can provide extra functionality such as caching, detailed logging, and user authentication. The trade-offs are the need to develop specific client software for each protected application and their CPU-intensive nature.
- **Stateful firewalls:** These firewalls incorporate the concept of connections and state to the original packet filters. Their access control rules act on groups of packets that belong to the same connection (or *flow*), rather than on individual packets. A stateful firewall not only analyzes source/destination IP and L4 port combinations but also verifies the consistency of the TCP Flags field with the Sequence and Acknowledgement numbers. This class of firewalls has been widely deployed, not only because their capabilities are much more advanced than those of packet filters but also because they provide much higher performance than dedicated proxies.
- **Next-generation firewalls (NGFWs):** NGFWs have been developed using stateful inspection as a starting point. They include the critical capability of identifying

applications, regardless of the TCP or UDP service port they use for transport. This is quite relevant because, with the advent of Web 2.0, many applications try to disguise themselves inside HTTP flows (which are always allowed through stateful firewalls), thus avoiding the use of their originally assigned service ports. This modern class of firewalls also includes easy ways of creating user-based rules and integration with auxiliary tools that dynamically analyze the content inside the IP packets, thus helping overall malware detection and prevention efforts. They are also capable of categorizing and filtering uniform resource locators (URLs) and decrypting Transport Layer Security (TLS) channels to inspect the content in the communication data payload. Many NGFWs also deploy intrusion-mitigation techniques, which is explained in the "Intrusion Detection and Intrusion Prevention" section later in this chapter.

Web Proxies

A *web proxy* (also known as a web gateway) is an important example of an application-level firewall, typically used to control the access of internal corporate users to outside web servers (outbound access control). Among many other features, this class of device is capable of blocking malware, enforcing acceptable-use policies, categorizing and filtering URLs, and controlling content based on the reputation of the sites hosting it. The main objective of web proxies is to keep external content requested by internal clients from harming the organization. Nevertheless, given the evolution of NGFWs, this well-known security element is falling into obsolescence.

Web Application Firewalls

The web application firewall (WAF) is a specialized security element that acts as a full-reverse proxy, protecting applications that are accessed through the HTTP protocol. Whereas web proxies protect the client side, WAF devices protect the server side of the connection from application layer attacks. A typical WAF analyzes each HTTP command, thus ensuring that only those actions specified in the security policy can be performed. A reference for WAF action is mitigation for the vulnerabilities identified by the Open Web Application Security Project (OWASP). Among the most common vulnerabilities are code injection and cross-site scripting. Figure 1.9 contrasts the insertion of web proxies and WAF devices in the network topology.

You should not confuse the Application Visibility and Control (AVC) capabilities of NGFWs, which are focused on controlling outbound user access, with the services provided by WAFs. Instead of replacing one with another, they can actually work in conjunction.

API Discovery and Protection

Application Programming Interfaces (APIs) act as intermediaries that enable connectivity and data transfer between different software components, which may reside on the same machine or interact by means of a network. APIs typically establish a set of rules that govern

Chapter 1 ▪ Security Fundamentals

FIGURE 1.9   Contrasting WAF and a web proxy.

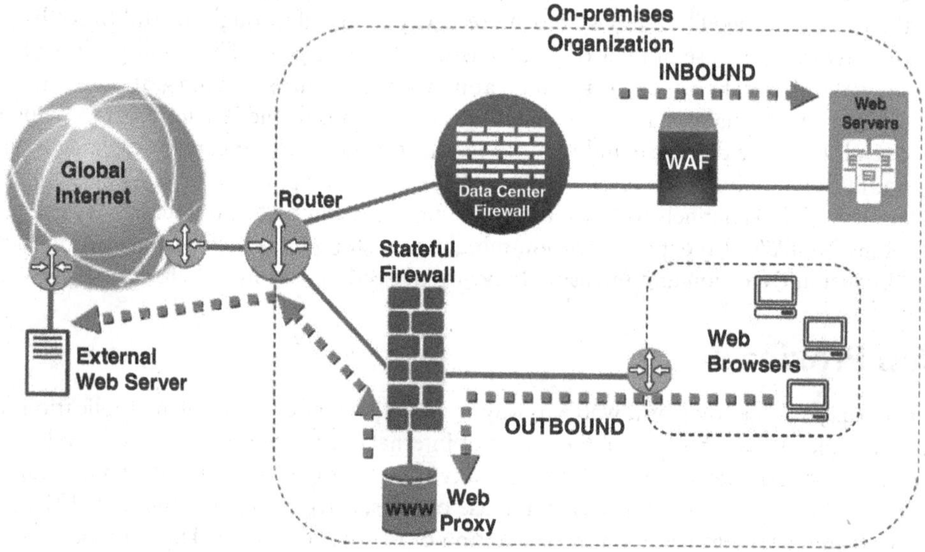

how services from a system are exposed to applications, defining attributes such as data format, operations, input, and output.

APIs are key elements of modern applications and have become particularly common for cloud migrations and software integrations. They allow for the automation of tasks and for ensuring data portability, reducing the compatibility issues when migrating data between different cloud environments. They also accelerate software development, by allowing integration of capabilities and data from other applications, thus avoiding the need to build everything from scratch.

These benefits, however, do not come without risks. The more quickly they proliferate, the greater the attack surface of the service infrastructure.

As usual, security solutions have been developed to deal with these new challenges, which include shadow APIs, vulnerability exploits, credential abuse, and DoS attacks.

It is typical for API protection tools to start their work by scanning the web application environment and building a sort of tree that contains the discovered API endpoints, as shown in Figure 1.10. The associated methods, attributes, and authentication characteristics (if any) are also mapped.

Some protection features that deserve special mention are the following:

- Rate limiting requests toward a given API endpoint
- Enforcing compliance with the published schema for a given version of the API
- Use of WAF signatures designed for API protection
- Blocking unauthenticated access attempts to the API

FIGURE 1.10 Sample API endpoint tree.

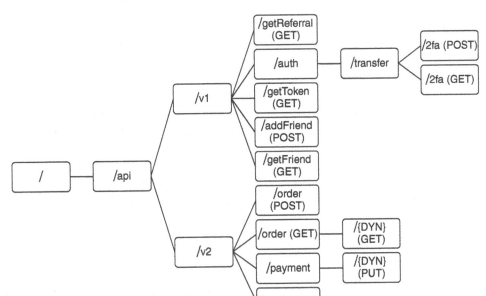

 It is very common for vendors to bundle WAF and API protection functionality into a single commercial product. This has led to the creation of the new term—*Web Application and API Protection* (WAAP).

Intrusion Detection and Intrusion Prevention

Intrusion-detection and intrusion-prevention technologies provide in-depth inspection capabilities so that the occurrence of malicious traffic can be discovered inside network packets, at either their header or data portion. While intrusion-detection system (IDS) devices handle only copies of the packets and are mainly concerned with monitoring and alerting tasks, intrusion-prevention system (IPS) solutions are deployed inline in the traffic flow and have the inherent design goal of avoiding actual damage to systems.

IDSs and IPSs can look for well-known attack patterns within packet streams and take an action according to the configured policy. Some typical actions are packet drop, connection block, denying further access to the address that sourced the attack, and sending an alert when an attack indication (i.e., a signature) is spotted.

IPSs act as a normal companion to stateful firewalls, mainly for data center protection (inbound traffic). They provide detailed analysis for the connections permitted by firewalls, thus complementing their work. An IPS concentrates most of its analysis at the Network,

FIGURE 1.11 Sample inbound topology.

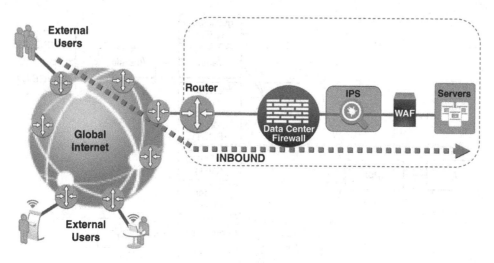

Transport, and Application layers, possibly maintaining state (*stateful pattern matching*) and executing traffic anomaly detection.

There are many possible formats for practical IPS deployment:

- As a dedicated appliance
- As a dedicated hardware (or software) module inside a stateful firewall
- As a resource that is enabled on a per-firewall rule basis on NGFWs

Figure 1.11 displays a typical coordination of protection devices that are well suited for controlling inbound access.

Protecting Email Services

Simple Mail Transfer Protocol (SMTP) uses TCP transport and employs a client-server model for sending and receiving email.

Due to the nature of its message exchange, SMTP protection typically relies on an email proxy (or gateway) to control the interaction of external clients with the company's email server. This gateway may be considered an application-level firewall and is ideally deployed behind a network firewall.

A frequent mistake concerning email security is to think it is just about anti-spam, a feature that many times comes bundled with the mail service itself. There is more to it. For instance, email security should include analysis of the sender's reputation, inspection of SMTP commands, content type filtering, and Data Loss Prevention (DLP), just to name a few.

The modern protection mechanisms complement the traditional defense capabilities by focusing on the identification of phishing attempts. Considering that the techniques to impersonate a legitimate sender are always more sophisticated, AI inspection engines have been developed to help in the detection of recent phishing attacks.

Virtual Private Networks

The term *virtual private network* (VPN) is used to refer to technologies that reproduce the characteristics of a private corporate network, even when traffic is being transported over a shared network infrastructure. VPNs were created to provide a secure extension of corporate networks, without requiring a dedicated infrastructure based on expensive WAN circuits.

But security has a broad meaning and may represent very different resources when considered from the standpoint of a particular VPN technology. To further your understanding, we summarize the main categories.

The IPsec framework provides answers for questions such as confidentiality, integrity, and authentication of VPN participants and management of cryptographic keys. All of these tasks are accomplished by using standardized protocols and algorithms, a fact that contributed to render IPsec ubiquitous. IPsec supports both client-to-site (or *remote access VPN*) and site-to-site (or *LAN-to-LAN*) deployment models. IPsec operates at the Network layer (Layer 3) and, as such, can protect native IP protocols (ICMP, for instance) or any application carried over TCP or UDP.

SSL VPN is another remote access VPN technology that does not require a dedicated client. When it was created, SSL VPN was even considered a synonym of clientless access (because web browsers are considered a sort of universal client that is available on any networked machine). This possibility of providing secure remote access, even for those stations that were not managed by corporate IT, sounded appealing to administrators. Not long after the inception of SSL, customers started to request a *client-based* SSL-VPN option that could eventually replace IPsec as the standard remote-access VPN solution. One benefit is the fact that SSL is used everywhere (mainly for HTTP protection) and, as a result, is permitted through firewalls and routers along the path. A classic topology for VPN termination (either IPsec or SSL-based) is shown in Figure 1.12.

A third common use of the term VPN relates to the Multiprotocol Label Switching (MPLS) space, where the service known as *MPLS VPN* was designed to achieve logical network segmentation and optimized routing (in an any-to-any or full-mesh topology). Although segmentation means providing native traffic isolation among tenants that are transported through the MPLS backbone, there is no provision for the security mechanisms that IPsec deals with (integrity, confidentiality, and authentication). IPsec can be used to add security services for the virtual circuits that characterize MPLS VPN. Although MPLS VPN is primarily used by telecommunication providers to isolate tenant traffic in a shared backbone, we included it here to show you how flexible the term *VPN* is.

Protecting DNS and Using Insights from DNS

The Domain Name System (DNS) is a hierarchical and decentralized directory that maps the assigned hostnames of resources connected to the Internet, or other IP networks, to their corresponding IP addresses. The motivation is to simplify access to applications by

FIGURE 1.12 Classic topology for VPN termination.

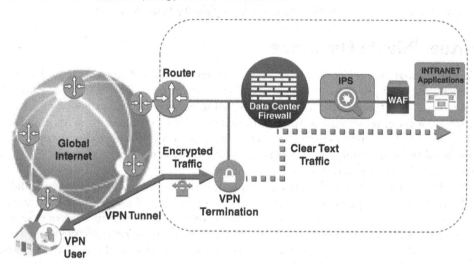

using (ideally) easy-to-remember names, thus avoiding the need for the end user to know the machine-readable IP addresses. This name-to-IP association process, which precedes the actual application request, lies at the heart of the Internet's operation. This official distributed database is constructed in a collaborative way, and the exchange of information pertaining to this process relies on the DNS protocol.

Given the foundational role played by DNS on the Internet architecture, research on two mutually complementary fields has increased:

- Understanding how the protocol operates and its inherent vulnerabilities. The objective is to protect not only message exchange (client-to-server and server-to-server) but also the integrity of the directory data.

- Leveraging the information on such a large and dynamic database to keep users from connecting to well-known malicious domains, in an attempt to minimize the likelihood that a legitimate user brings harmful content inside the organization.

Tools for Vulnerability Analysis and Management

As defined in the earlier section "Basic Security Concepts," a vulnerability is a weakness that can be exploited. It may be seen as a sort of door that should not be opened. In the context of IT, the vulnerability assessment process involves identifying and classifying vulnerabilities in the digital entities that compose the computing environment under analysis (such as end-user machines, operating systems, applications, container images, and key networking devices). After this information-gathering phase, the findings should be presented in a structured fashion so that the corrective actions can be prioritized according to the risk level.

Although the grouping of topics may vary among vendors, the typical tasks included in the process may be summarized as follows:

- **Inventory compiling:** It is very difficult to protect a resource you are not aware of. Building a hardware and software inventory of the environment is a basic step toward the goal of minimizing the attack surface. The assets that are mission-critical must be identified and grouped according to their business value.

- **Identification of vulnerabilities:** Running scanning tools throughout the inventory will help you create a list of current vulnerabilities (mainly software bugs and misconfigurations) and where they reside. The Common Vulnerabilities and Exposures (CVE) system provides a reference method for publicly known, information-security vulnerabilities and exposures.

- **Definition of priorities:** Not all vulnerabilities have the same level of criticality and, as such, must not be deemed equally urgent. Considering the business relevance of each potential target will guide the IT staff on prioritizing efforts. If your tool of choice can automate the categorization of vulnerabilities and assign some sort of risk rating, instead of just presenting a long list of affected entities, it will bring more value.

- **Remediation:** By using the risk-oriented list of the previous step, you can build a roadmap of actions to be taken so that you reduce the exposure level. If the chosen tool automatically identifies the corrections that must be made, it will be even more useful.

- **Effectiveness measurement:** Knowing that you took the right path, and having some perception of progress, positively affects the morale of the team. "How much did we reduce the exposure level?" and "How does our company compare with our competitors in the same market segment?" are two simple evaluations that should follow remediation. This can be done manually or, ideally, by selecting a tool that automates it.

Security is not just about technology. It is a continuous process. It involves people. Regardless of the particular tool you eventually choose and the way it structures and presents the vulnerability data, going through these typical steps must be a part of your security team's routine, with a suitable recurrence.

Correlation of Security Information and Events

Security information and event management (SIEM) solutions are designed to collect security-related logs as well as flow information generated by systems (at the host or application level), networking devices, and dedicated defense elements such as firewalls, IPSs, IDSs, proxies, and endpoint protection software. They work by aggregating, normalizing, and categorizing the received information and then applying intelligence algorithms that allow them to correlate events that refer to particular sessions. Here are some reasons you might employ SIEM solutions:

- To lower the volume of data that must be dealt with by removing ambiguous session information and avoiding the generation of events for legitimate resource use

30 Chapter 1 ▪ Security Fundamentals

- To provide real-time insights on security alerts, clearly separating what is meaningful, in an attempt to minimize the occurrence of false positives
- To prioritize response actions so that the most critical issues are investigated first (according to the associated risk level)

Modern SIEM solutions include artificial intelligence (AI) and user behavior analytics (UBA) so that they can quickly spot deviations from the normal activity profile for a particular user, which may indicate intentional misuse or, eventually, derive from system compromise. In a sense, SIEM solutions tend to complement the vulnerability management practice. Whereas the latter deals with the somehow static measures of closing the doors that do not need to remain open, the former is more dynamic in nature, providing real-time visibility of what is flowing through the doors.

One critical thing you can do to make your SIEM project successful is devote time to event filtering so that you can limit the amount of data that will be collected. This approach not only improves performance but also impacts cost, because most products (and services) are charged based on storage amount or events per second (EPS). Another factor in your SIEM selection is to understand how ready it is for the correlation tasks regarding the systems within your particular environment. To determine that, ask the following questions:

- Are there native integration agents so that my systems start sending logs to the SIEM?
- Do I need to send every log to the system and then select the security events? Is it possible for the systems of interest to send only security-related information?
- How "plug-and-play" is the solution? What is the average customization time for putting it to work?
- How does the system scale?
- Does the SIEM integrate with incident response tools?

SIEM is a classic example of a solution that has tremendous potential for alleviating the operational burden of security monitoring. But, to really benefit from it, you need to invest in training, thus making sure that the team gets acquainted with the capabilities of the tool. It is also advisable to ensure that a detailed documentation of the environment is available and to determine what types of logs and flow data are generated by each of the monitored sources. This process is not only about acquiring a product or service.

Network Detection and Response Systems

Network Traffic Analysis (NTA) is a process based on real-time traffic monitoring and inspection, which can be of great value if the objective is to gain visibility of network activity. NTA starts with some method for directing copies of the packets that flow through the network to a given analysis tool. The information gathered by means of NTA may be used for several purposes, including troubleshooting and, of course, security.

Network Detection and Response (NDR) systems leverage NTA functionality in order to detect and investigate anomalous behaviors, threats, and risky activity throughout the layers of the OSI model.

By continuously monitoring and inspecting network activity with intelligent packet analysis engines, it becomes possible to establish communication patterns and define what is "the normal behavior" of users and devices connected to the network.

The main components of an NDR solution are as follows:

- **Machine learning algorithms:** To learn from network traffic and detect abnormal behaviors.
- **Behavioral analytics:** To perform pattern recognition for identifying deviations from network activities that are considered "normal."
- **Threat intelligence:** To enhance the embedded detection and analysis capabilities so that more precise actions can be taken based on risk level.
- **Response automation:** To trigger automated responses or alerts to reduce the time required for threat mitigation.

NDR systems are sometimes considered an evolution of IPS. They go much deeper on packet inspection and include response functionality, which makes this type of product a key element for the toolbox of security operations.

TLS/SSL Offload and Visibility

The Secure Sockets Layer (SSL) protocol was developed to provide services such as data integrity, confidentiality, and peer authentication for application protocols that are carried over TCP. The motivation behind the construction of such a generic layer of security was to avoid the need for embedding security for every application. SSL was updated up to version 3.0, which was deprecated in 2015 and replaced by the standards-based Transport Layer Security (TLS) protocol.

Some studies show that TLS/SSL usage is growing continuously. What should be deemed an evolution of the overall security practice brings the collateral effect of lack of visibility, thus allowing malicious traffic to hide inside the encrypted channels. To address this new challenge, many security solutions—such as NGFWs, WAFs, and IPSs—started supporting decryption of the TLS streams before going through the analysis activities they were designed for.

By deploying TLS-offload operations, these solutions can provide the following benefits:

- Web servers can be offloaded from any encryption duties (or leverage less-intensive encryption algorithms), which allow them to serve more concurrent clients with a better response time.
- The security solutions can now process and analyze Layer 7 information that was originally encrypted (and, therefore, reaching application services without any protection).
- The security solutions can centralize public certificates and allow the use of private certificates (which are less expensive and easier to maintain) on the web servers.

TLS Orchestration

Because TLS decryption can be relatively CPU-intensive, it can negatively impact the performance of specialized on-premises appliances that deploy TLS offload (such as NGFWs, WAFs, and IPSs) and introduce latency in their filtering operations. To deal with such a scenario, a solution known as *TLS orchestration* was devised. The idea is to provide a centralized TLS decryption service whose operations include the following:

1. TLS traffic arriving on a centralized device calls the TLS orchestrator, where such traffic is decrypted.
2. The cleartext traffic is dynamically steered to the inspection elements, according to their individual capabilities.
3. After going through the chain of inspection services, the legitimate traffic is sent back to the TLS orchestrator.
4. Traffic is re-encrypted by the orchestrator and delivered to the original destination.

Figure 1.13 displays a typical topology for inbound TLS orchestration.

FIGURE 1.13 Sample topology for inbound TLS orchestration.

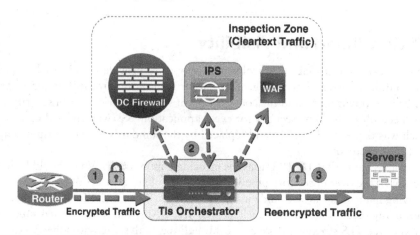

Handling Security Incidents

In the context of information security, an *incident* is defined as a violation (or a threat of violation) of security policies, acceptable-use policies, or standard security practices. Among the consequences of an incident are a negative impact on an organization's reputation, a loss of intellectual property, or unauthorized access to data.

To deal with these sorts of events, you should establish an *incident handling program*. For instance, you should define the meaning of "incident" within your organization. Another important step is to assign an incident response team, with clearly defined responsibilities, among which creating an incident response plan deserves special mention.

As in other domains, incident response may also leverage certain tools in order to make the daily tasks of security analysts a bit easier. For example, a new class of products, grouped under the term *security orchestration, automation, and response* (SOAR), has been developed. SIEM solutions are a natural source of information to SOAR systems, which focus on coordinating and automating response actions among multiple protection elements using the concept of playbooks. The ability to create response templates for incidents that happen often may free a significant amount of time for analysts, thus allowing them to focus on what is different or new.

Structured Malware Protection

As discussed, there are various categories of computer programs that can be grouped under the name *malware*. There is no absolute strategy for providing protection against malware attacks. Therefore, the next section introduces an approach to structured malware protection as a practical usage example of a security model.

Well-Known Security Frameworks and Models

The concept of security risk is based on the likelihood of a certain vulnerability being exploited and its respective potential impact, which depends on the value of the digital asset under analysis.

The underlying goal of reducing risk inspired the creation of security frameworks, which are published materials that typically include standards, guidelines, sample policies, recommended security safeguards and tools, risk management approaches, relevant technologies, and recognized best practices for protection of certain computing environments.

At a tactical level, the contents inside the framework will translate into security controls, which must map to the specific threats a company may be exposed to. A basic design principle that will help in selecting the appropriate controls is to add more layers of defense according to the criticality of the asset being protected.

Many frameworks were developed with a particular goal in mind, such as providing guidance for a given industry segment (according, for instance, to the type of data that is more relevant to that sector, the most valuable systems, and the associated communication protocols). On the other hand, there are examples of frameworks that are meant for general purpose. Among the various examples that are in use, some deserve special mention:

- **Payment Card Industry Data Security Standard (PCI DSS):** Created with the goal of increasing the level of protection for issuers of credit cards by requiring that merchants meet minimum levels of security when they process, store, and transmit card holder data.

- **Health Insurance Portability and Accountability Act (HIPAA):** A set of security standards for protecting certain health information that is transferred or held in electronic form.
- **National Institute for Standards and Technology Cybersecurity Framework (NIST CSF):** A publication that results from a collaborative work among industry, academia, and the U.S. government. The framework recognizes that the cybersecurity activities inside an organization should be guided by its business drivers. It also establishes that the overall risk management process should include the risks related to the cybersecurity domain. The CSF assembles standards, guidelines, and practices that have proved effective and may be used by entities belonging to any market segment.
- **General Data Protection Regulation (GDPR):** A set of rules created by the European Union (EU) that requires businesses to protect the personal data and privacy of EU citizens. GDPR not only applies to transactions that occur within the EU members but also governs the transfer of personal data outside the EU. This regulation states that foreign entities willing to conduct business with EU companies also need to demonstrate their compliance with GDPR. This fact motivated the creation of GDPR-like standards outside Europe.

Instead of focusing on security standards that apply to the type of organization you are in charge of protecting, you should become familiar with those principles that can be employed in a broader sense.

Sample Practical Models for Guiding Security Design and Operations

Security controls are implemented to reduce the level of risk to which an organization is exposed. Generically speaking, they are divided into three main categories:

- **Physical controls:** Designed to protect facility, personnel, and material resources. Some examples are locks, fencing, monitoring cameras, and security agents. This type of control is inherently present in the data centers belonging to large cloud service providers such as AWS.
- **Logical controls:** Many examples of this category of controls are provided in the section "Risk Management" earlier in this chapter.
- **Administrative controls:** Some examples of this class are the risk management process, security documentation, and training (not only specific to operations but also to promote overall security awareness within the organization).

The Security Wheel

Figure 1.14 portrays the security wheel, a closed-loop model for security operations that is centered on the foundational concept of security policy, discussed earlier in the "Understanding Security" section. This model recognizes that the security practice has a continuous and cyclical nature and is structured in five basic stages:

FIGURE 1.14 The security wheel.

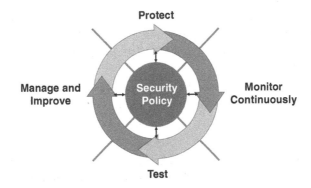

1. **Develop a security policy:** Start with a high-level policy that clearly establishes and documents the strategic goals that relate to the business drivers or mission of the organization. The policy should refer to the appropriate standards, guidelines, procedures, and baselines that will guide the actual implementation.
2. **Implement security measures:** Having defined the assets that need to be protected and the appropriate protection level (according to business relevance), you next deploy the security controls that will contribute to risk mitigation. Many layers of defense, such as those described in the "Risk Management" section, may be coordinated to provide better security.
3. **Monitor continuously:** At this stage, resources such as logging, intrusion detection, and SIEM are employed to spot violations of the access policies.
4. **Test:** Even though you may have invested a lot in protection and monitoring capabilities, you should not take them for granted. Systems evolve rapidly and new ways to exploit their weaknesses will be readily available. Vulnerability analysis and management apply well to this stage.
5. **Manage and improve:** Using the feedback that comes from Stages 3 and 4, improvements can be applied to Stage 2 in the form of new or updated controls. Depending on the specific findings, you may need to review the security policy (for instance, in case it was too permissive or too simple in its original definitions and that reference led to exposure and high risk to the organization's assets).

The Attack Continuum Model

Security is a moving target. No matter the investment of time, effort, and financial resources to protect the organization, new challenges will be faced every day due to the continuous attack attempts happening around the world. Despite the security structure you might have in place, falling victim to a cyberattack is just a matter of time. Of course, the more solid the

36   Chapter 1 ▪ Security Fundamentals

construction of your layered defense system, the lower the probability of the effects of the attack being spread throughout the company.

Building on the principle that attacks happen, the attack continuum model associates the security controls with the phase to which they relate most: before, during, or after the attack. Figure 1.15 represents the attack continuum model and suggests some security solutions that may fit each of the model phases.

- **Before:** The tools and methods used here refer mainly to attack prevention tasks. The motivation is to have the controls that allow you to minimize the attack surface.

- **During:** Detection and monitoring tools, which provide visibility and awareness of what is going on during live daily operations, are the key types of resources for this stage.

- **After:** It is increasingly common that modern attack tools are programmed to have an initial dormant phase, with the underlying goal of remaining undetected for a certain period. A good defense implementation needs retrospective security capabilities so that these intentionally delayed threats can be detected (and stopped) before any damage. The protection mechanisms for this phase should identify the point of entry, understand its reach, contain the propagation, and remediate any eventual damage or disruption.

Of course, once a threat is found in the after-the-attack stage, the implicit feedback loop of this model must be used so that the prevention resources of the before-the-attack stage are updated to avoid reinfection.

As a practical illustration, a range of protection mechanisms that can be effective in fighting against malware are positioned within the attack continuum model, as displayed in Figure 1.16.

FIGURE 1.15 The attack continuum model.

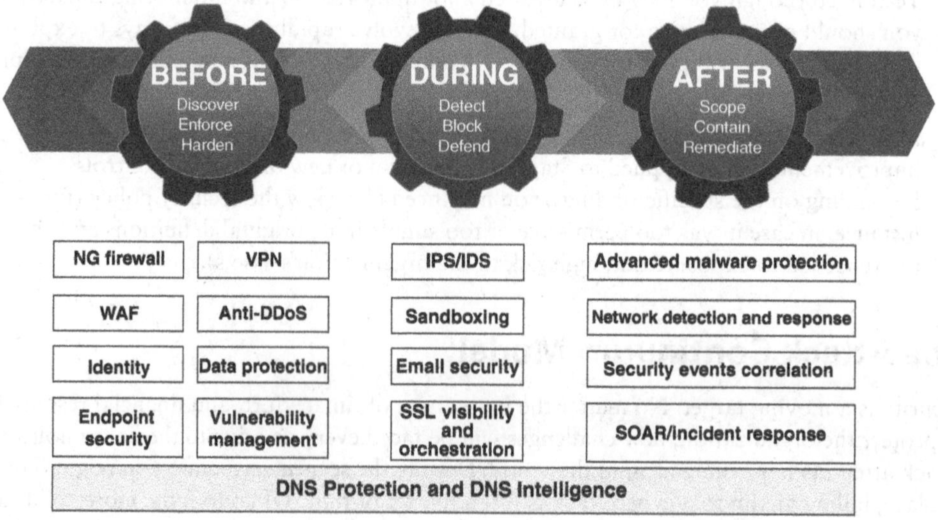

FIGURE 1.16 The attack continuum model applied to malware protection.

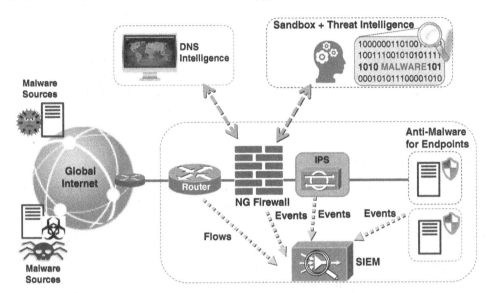

- **Before the attack:** An effective antimalware measure is to avoid the connection of internal users to well-known malicious domains and to IP addresses that have been used to host domains with bad reputations. To achieve that, tools that provide insights into the current DNS infrastructure and help identify domain generation algorithms are very useful. NGFWs and modern IPSs that can block traffic, after evaluating the content being transported, can also contribute to this effort. For instance, they can block files that are deemed harmful, based on hash information that comes from cyberintelligence sources, thus avoiding their entry into the organization. TLS orchestration systems can play the important auxiliary role of providing visibility for all the inspection devices.
- **During the attack:** While the allowed packets are flowing through the network, monitoring tools should be in place. For instance, IPSs (or IDSs) should be searching for attack patterns. Moreover, files that come through email or web vectors (and whose reputation are not known) can be dynamically evaluated by interaction with sandbox solutions, which execute untrusted applications in a separate environment without risking production systems.
- **After the attack:** Even after all the efforts carried out in the previous phases, some attacks may still be successful. Consider this an invitation to invest even more in an organized work method. A good start here relates to answering questions such as the following: Was the attack a result of misconfiguration of one of my protection elements? Was it a result of an unpatched vulnerability? Was the attack totally

unknown? In the two first cases, it is a matter of hard and structured work to apply the appropriate corrections. In the last case, a good option is to have endpoint protection software running on the endpoints, which should be considered the last line of defense. By looking for abnormal behavior, this kind of element can block malicious activities taking place on end hosts, without need of specific previous knowledge. An access attempt to an external command and control source, from a dormant threat on the inside, can also be an indicator of a new threat (DNS insight tools are useful for that purpose). SIEM solutions can also identify that certain actions, when combined, represent an attack.

The Zero-Trust Model

Once upon a time, in an ideal land, there existed clearly defined perimeters for corporate networks. Branch offices connected through leased lines or IPsec VPNs to the company headquarters, and there was a central point of access to the Internet. The classic firewalls were able to delimit the borders of the organization and establish the access control conditions for traffic to flow between two domains of trust. The simplest logical division was to consider the inside networks as the trusted domain and all those IP addresses falling outside the organization as untrusted.

Nonetheless, times have changed significantly, and computer communication has not only become ubiquitous but also much more complex. The options of access technologies have been multiplied, and each user now likely owns several devices. Branch offices connect directly to the Internet, thus greatly expanding the frontiers that need supervision and protection. Most companies are moving at least a portion of their workloads to cloud computing environments and, as a result, need to coordinate the security efforts so that they have compatible levels of defense, independently of the data being located on-premises or on the cloud. The extranet connections that, on the one hand, simplify business transactions among partners, on the other hand may create shared vulnerabilities, especially if one of the companies is less experienced with security. These are only a few examples of the common challenges faced, on a daily basis, by network administrators.

To adapt to this context, a relatively recent framework, *zero trust*, has established itself as a reference for security design. The model is based on the principle of least privilege, which states that organizations should grant the minimal amount of permissions that are strictly necessary for each user or application to work. Therefore, they should not implicitly trust any entity, at any time, no matter if it resides outside or inside the organization domains.

The great philosophy change brought about by zero trust is concerned with avoiding a blind trust of inside hosts and networks. The typical assumption that internal systems are reliable is flawed, because if a single inside host is compromised, lateral movement and associated threat spread will become easy tasks. From a network traffic standpoint, this new security paradigm advocates heavy use of network segmentation, encryption technologies, and identity-based access controls, both at the user and the device levels.

The zero-trust approach is an interesting architecture for cloud environments, which are usually multitenant by design and, as such, do not allow you to implicitly trust a shared network. Some relevant controls guided by this model are as follows:

- Using advanced authentication and authorization resources, before granting access, is key for avoiding undesired use of your computing resources or, even worse, unauthorized access to data under your control.

- Promoting granular segmentation of the network, up to the point where you are able to define access control rules down to a single instance level (when necessary), is another key measure associated with the new "shared land" reality. This fine-grained rule-building practice is frequently called *microsegmentation*.

- The use of encryption technologies everywhere is key to bringing the confidentiality and integrity attributes to the scene, thus helping you ensure that data privacy has not been compromised and that data remains unaltered.

Summary

This chapter reviewed general concepts and terminology that are crucial both for demonstrating a good level of education on the security subject matter and for a better understanding of the upcoming chapters.

After exploring basic networking and security definitions, we introduced the main classes of attacks as well as the typical elements that can be used to protect against them. Taking into consideration the critical principle that security is not a product, we reviewed some well-known security frameworks. These particular security models have been selected among the countless options available, not only for being very practical in nature but also because they are complementary.

We discussed the security wheel, designed to remind you of the importance of building a security policy and having processes in place to deal with daily security challenges. We next examined the attack continuum model, which shows you how to position the available security controls according to their capability of adding value to dealing with a particular attack stage. Finally, we introduced the zero-trust security model, which is based on the principle of least privilege, thus providing the recommended mindset for creating controls on the shared computing environments that are so characteristic of cloud computing.

Exam Essentials

Understand basic security definitions. Review the definitions of vulnerability, threat, and security risk. The attributes of the Confidentiality, Integrity, and Availability (CIA) triad, the Authentication, Authorization, Accounting (AAA) architecture, and the concepts of accountability and nonrepudiation should also be revisited.

Understand the OSI model and the TCP/IP stack. The *OSI model* divides data communication into seven layers: physical, data link, network, transport, session, presentation, and application. The *TCP/IP stack* is the de facto standard for computer networks of all sizes. IP, TCP, and UDP are the main protocols to become familiar with.

Understand common classes of attacks. You should get acquainted with the main classes of attacks, and the related terminology presented, such as reconnaissance, IP spoofing, brute force, man-in-the-middle, denial-of-service (DoS), and phishing.

Be able to define malware. *Malware* is a software program designed to perform unauthorized actions on computer systems, sometimes causing irreversible damage to them. According to the way malware acts, it may be classified as virus, worm, Trojan horse, adware, launcher, keylogger, or ransomware.

Understand firewalls and their related technologies. A *firewall* is used for isolating specific areas of a network and delimiting domains of trust. The main categories of firewalls are application-level proxies, stateful firewalls, and next-generation firewalls. A *web proxy* is an application-level firewall used to control the access of internal corporate users to outside web servers. A *web application firewall* (WAF) is a specialized security element that protects applications that are accessed through HTTP.

Know the difference between IDS and IPS technologies. Intrusion detection and prevention technologies provide in-depth inspection capabilities so that the occurrence of malicious traffic can be determined inside network packets at either their header or data portions.

Be able to define VPNs. *Virtual private networks (VPNs)* refer to technologies that reproduce the characteristics of a private corporate network, even when traffic is being transported over a shared network infrastructure.

Be familiar with SIEM, SOAR, and NDR solutions. SIEM solutions collect and correlate security-related information, generated by end systems, networking devices, and dedicated defense elements (e.g., firewalls, IPSs, and IDSs). SOAR products use response templates to deal with incidents that happen often, thus allowing analysts to focus on what is different or new. NDR systems perform deep analysis of network traffic and spot deviations from normal user behavior. NDR is somewhat considered an evolution of IPS with the embedded capabilities of incident response.

Know the main security frameworks. The Payment Card Industry Data Security Standard (PCI DSS) was created to increase the level of protection for issuers of credit cards, by requiring that merchants meet minimum levels of security when handling card holder data. The Health Insurance Portability and Accountability Act (HIPAA) is a set of security standards for protecting certain health information that is transferred or held in electronic form. The National Institute for Standards and Technology Cybersecurity Framework (NIST CSF) is a framework that assembles security standards, guidelines, and practices that have proved effective and may be used by entities belonging to any market segment. The General Data Protection Regulation (GDPR) is a set of rules created by the European Union (EU), requiring businesses to protect the personal data and privacy of EU citizens.

Know the main security models. The *security wheel* is a closed-loop practical model that has a continuous and cyclical nature and is structured in five basic stages: develop a security policy, implement security measures, monitor continuously, test, and manage and improve. The *attack continuum model* is based on the principle that attacks happen, and it associates the security controls with each phase they relate to the most: before, during, or after the attack. Finally, the *zero-trust* security model is based on the *principle of least privilege*, which states that organizations should grant permissions that are strictly necessary for each user or application to work. Therefore, they should not implicitly trust any entity, at any time, no matter if it resides outside or inside the organization's domains.

42   Chapter 1 ▪ Security Fundamentals

Review Questions

1. Read the following statements and choose the correct option:

a. A vulnerability is a weakness within a computer system that can be exploited to perform unauthorized actions.

b. A security risk is defined as any entity (such as a person or a tool) that can exploit a vulnerability intentionally or by accident.

c. A threat relates to the probability of a certain vulnerability being exploited by a threat actor, which will depend on the value of the digital asset under analysis.

    A. Options a, b, and c are correct.

    B. Only option a is correct.

    C. Only option b is correct.

    D. Only option c is correct.

2. Read the following statements and choose the correct option:

a. Confidentiality can be addressed through data encryption.

b. Integrity can be addressed via hashing algorithms.

c. Availability can be addressed with recovery plans.

    A. Options a, b, and c are correct.

    B. Only option a is correct.

    C. Only option b is correct.

    D. Only option c is correct.

3. What term defines "the property of ensuring that someone cannot deny an action that has already been performed so that they can avoid attempts of not being accountable"?

    A. Accountability

    B. Nonrepudiation

    C. Responsibility

    D. Verification

    E. Authentication

4. Which option correctly defines the AAA architecture?

    A. Accountability, authorization, availability

    B. Authentication, authorization, anonymity

    C. Authentication, authorization, accountability

    D. Authentication, authorization, accounting

    E. Authorization, anonymity, accountability

5. Which option represents the seven OSI model layers in the correct order?

   A. Physical, Data Link, Network, Transport, Session, Presentation, and Application

   B. Physical, Data Link, Network, Transport, Session, Application, and Presentation

   C. Physical, Data Link, Routing, Transport, Session, Presentation, and Application

   D. Bit, Frame, Packet, Connection, Session, Coding, and User Interface

   E. Physical, Media Access Control, Network, Transport, Session, Presentation, and Application

6. Which of the following options is *not* correct?

   A. UDP is part of the TCP/IP stack.

   B. IP can be related to the Network layer of the OSI model.

   C. ICMP, OSPF, and BGP are dynamic routing protocols.

   D. TCP is a connection-oriented and reliable transport protocol.

   E. UDP is a connectionless and unreliable transport protocol.

7. Which well-known class of cyberattacks is focused on affecting the availability of an application, connectivity device, or computing hosts?

   A. Man-in-the-middle

   B. Phishing

   C. Malware

   D. Reconnaissance

   E. Denial of service

8. Which of the following options is *not* correct?

   A. A firewall is a security system aimed at isolating specific areas of the network and delimiting domains of trust.

   B. A typical WAF analyzes each HTTP command, thus ensuring that only those actions specified on the security policy can be performed.

   C. All VPNs were created to provide a secure extension of corporate networks, without the need of using a dedicated infrastructure but ensuring data confidentiality.

   D. IPsec deals with integrity, confidentiality, and authentication.

   E. SIEM stands for security information and event management.

9. Which security framework was created with the goal of increasing the level of protection for issuers of credit cards?

   A. HIPAA

   B. GDPR

   C. PCI DSS

   D. NIST CSF

   E. CS STAR

44 Chapter 1 ▪ Security Fundamentals

10. Which concept guides the zero-trust security model?

    A. Develop, implement, monitor continuously, test, and improve

    B. Before, during, and after an attack

    C. Principle of least privilege

    D. In transit and at rest

    E. Automation

Chapter 2

Cloud Security Principles and Frameworks

THE AWS CERTIFIED SECURITY SPECIALTY EXAM OBJECTIVES THAT LEVERAGE CONCEPTS EXPLAINED IN THIS CHAPTER INCLUDE THE FOLLOWING:

✔ **Domain 1: Threat Detection and Incident Response**
- 1.1. Design and implement an incident response plan

✔ **Domain 3: Infrastructure Security**
- 3.4. Design and implement security controls for compute workloads

Introduction

In this chapter, you learn critical cloud security concepts that will help you create the foundation to go deeper into all the topics covered in the next chapters.

These concepts are critical in your journey to pass the AWS Certified Security Specialty exam. We introduce the following topics:

- Cloud security principles
- The Shared Responsibility Model
- AWS compliance programs
- AWS Well-Architected Framework
- AWS Marketplace

Cloud Security Principles Overview

As a general rule, the concepts and controls studied in Chapter 1, "Security Fundamentals," apply to both on-premises and cloud-based environments. Nonetheless, before moving your workloads to the cloud, you must understand what controls will remain under your responsibility and what tasks will be taken care of by the cloud service provider (CSP) of your choice. The sum of these efforts is usually referred to as the *Shared Responsibility Model*.

One noticeable challenge regarding cloud security is the inherent perception of loss of control. This initial suspicion may be a result of the lack of visibility into the provider's environment or by not understanding security tools and rules used in the cloud, as compared to those resources your company is familiar with. Although it may sound obvious, you should not move to a provider that you do not trust. And moving from doubt to trust does not mean simply verifying that the CSP has a famous security certification or accreditation displayed on its website. It is *essential* to understanding the security practices and controls available on the provider's infrastructure and, even more important, how to enable and enforce those controls.

Generally speaking, physical controls are more readily available and consistent in the cloud. That happens because, in order to be attractive and reliable to their potential customers, CSPs must invest in highly available data centers and enforce restrictive rules for physical access to facilities. Doing so might prove to be impracticable for most companies, which will, most frequently, have third parties in charge of those activities. Moreover, some IT security teams from more traditional organizations may frown at the need to take care of these physical aspects or even consider them as secondary concerns for someone who is in charge of *infrastructure specifics*.

As the pioneer and clear leader of the cloud service provider market, Amazon Web Services (AWS) has focused its development efforts on embedding security controls in each of its cloud services (such as Amazon EC2, Amazon S3, and Amazon VPC). In addition, AWS created innovative security services such as AWS Identity and Access Management (IAM), AWS Security Hub, Amazon GuardDuty, AWS Shield, AWS Web Application Firewall (WAF), AWS Key Management Service (KMS), Amazon Macie, AWS Artifact, Amazon Detective, and AWS Secrets Manager, among others. Moreover, AWS offers hundreds of industry-leading products from third-party security-focused partners to leverage existing controls and skills that are already in place in your organization.

Therefore, before you decide to move your first workload to the AWS Cloud, it is crucial that you familiarize yourself with the AWS security and compliance services, tools, best practices, and responsibilities, as well as have a good understanding of your own duties during your organization's cloud adoption journey. With this background, you will be able to maintain and steadily improve your security posture using the AWS Cloud, creating a better security program and implementing your security controls based on industry best practices, frameworks, and regulations with which your organization must be compliant.

The Shared Responsibility Model

AWS provides a global IT secure infrastructure, with compute, storage, networking, database, and higher-level services, like artificial intelligence (AI), machine learning (ML), analytics, and Internet of Things (IoT). To access the company's more than 200 available services (at the time of this writing), you can use the AWS Management Console, shown in Figure 2.1.

If you have ever watched an AWS presentation, you have probably observed that security is stated as AWS's "top priority," because of the company's mission to release cloud services with security by design controls and divulge best practices on how to use them. Embedding security controls in the cloud services and establishing best practices for them will ensure that your cloud environments are more secure and compliant with security evaluations and certifications based on the AWS Information Security Management System (ISMS). This includes a set of AWS information security policies and processes, as well as industry-specific security and compliance frameworks.

FIGURE 2.1 Services available from the AWS Management Console.

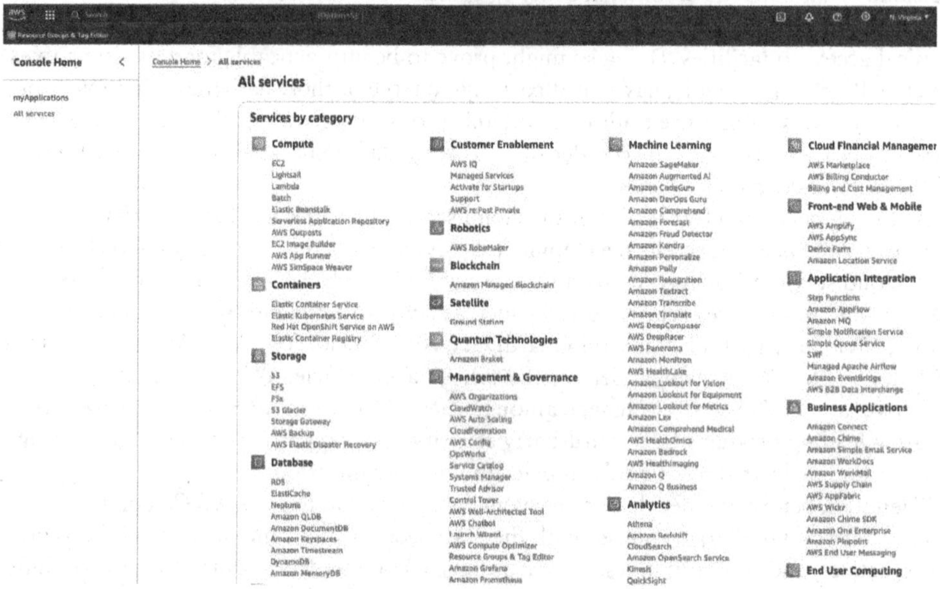

The Shared Responsibility Model defines the boundaries and responsibilities belonging to AWS and those belonging to the customer regarding security and compliance. Generally speaking, AWS is in charge of security and compliance *of the cloud*, and customers are in charge of security and compliance *in the cloud*. That means that AWS controls the security and compliance aspects of its infrastructure, which includes hardware and software, as you can see in Figure 2.2.

AWS is in charge of physical security and compliance of all data center facilities, in all regions, availability zones, and edge locations. AWS is also responsible for hardware security in all of its facilities around the globe, as well as for compute, storage, database, and networking security. For instance, AWS executes patch management in all routers, switches, and network equipment that are part of the AWS network infrastructure. In the same way, customers own the security management in all storage, network, and computing resources that they request and provision in the AWS Cloud.

As you can see in Figure 2.2, AWS is responsible for implementing the security of the software layer that runs on top of the hardware components. One example of this layer is a *hypervisor*, which is the underlying platform that virtualizes CPU, memory, storage, and networking infrastructure. Through such software, AWS leverages a rich set of management capabilities and controls how these hardware systems will serve each AWS customer. Consequently, when you create your Amazon EC2 instance, AWS is in charge of implementing the security patches, hardening guidelines, and best practices in the

FIGURE 2.2 Standard Shared Responsibility Model.

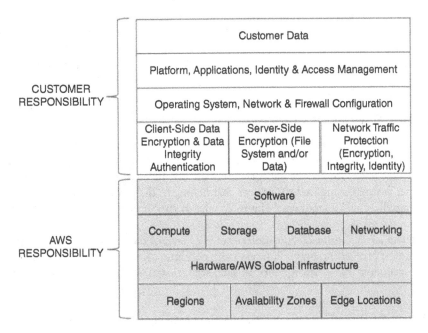

hypervisor layer. You are in charge of updating the instance's operating system (OS) patches, implementing system configuration best practices, and creating security policies that align with your organization's security policy.

Also in Figure 2.2, you can see that you (as an AWS customer) are always in charge of data encryption, OS security (in the case of Amazon EC2 instances), network firewall rules and configurations, IAM throughout your AWS Cloud environment (including your Amazon VPCs and AWS accounts), and your own application security that is running in the AWS Cloud.

Different Powers, Different Responsibilities

As a cloud security professional, you should remember that AWS offers a variety of cloud services, such as Amazon EC2 instances, Amazon RDS databases, and AWS Lambda functions. The Shared Responsibility Model has features that depend on the type of service you are deploying.

To understand such peculiarities, the next sections discuss three main categories of AWS compute services and explain how each of them produces a slightly different responsibility division between AWS and the customer.

Infrastructure Category

The infrastructure category includes AWS Cloud services such as Amazon EC2, Amazon Elastic Block Store (Amazon EBS), AWS Auto Scaling, and Amazon Virtual Private Cloud (Amazon VPC). Therefore, if you are deploying such services, you are in charge of the deployed operating system, security controls, identity and access management, data encryption, firewall rules, and network configuration, as shown in Figure 2.2.

Container Services Category

The container services category includes AWS services that commonly run on Amazon EC2 instances (or other compute instances available in the AWS Cloud) where you, as a customer, do not manage their OS or their platform components. In such services, AWS manages more elements when compared to services that belong to the infrastructure category, providing application "containers." Figure 2.3 shows the Shared Responsibility Model for container services.

As you can see in Figure 2.3, customers are in charge of data protection and encryption, network traffic protection, firewall access rules definitions, and IAM administration of their AWS accounts and environments. In such scenarios, AWS takes care of the container

FIGURE 2.3 Shared Responsibility Model for container services.

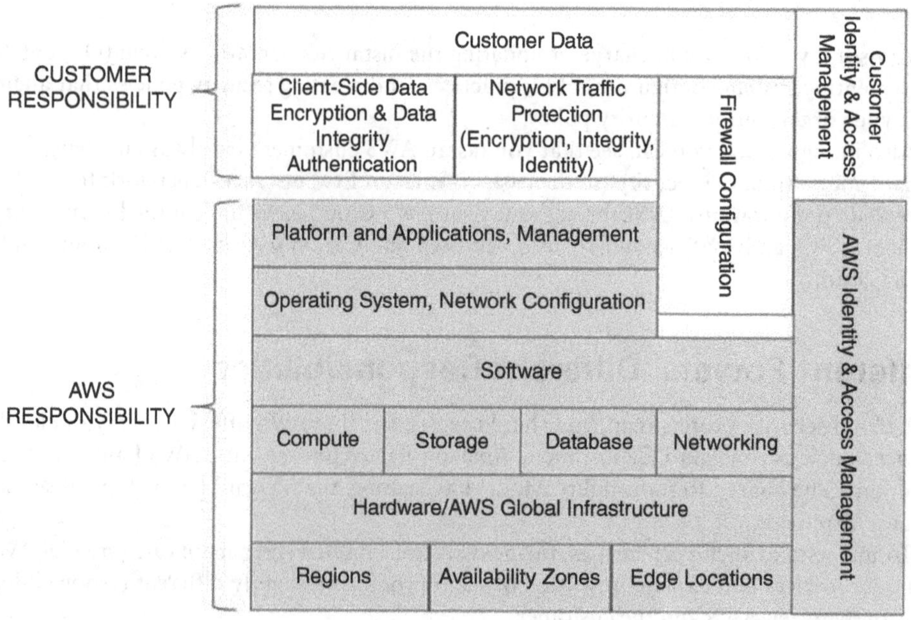

platform and management (including patching), OS security controls, as well as all other lower-layer-based controls.

The AWS shared responsibility for container services applies to AWS services such as Amazon RDS, Amazon EKS, and Amazon ECS, because AWS manages the underlying infrastructure, the OS, and their application platform. Because they are *managed* services, their AWS-controlled application platform also offers more sophisticated features such as orchestration, data backup, and recovery tools. Nonetheless, it is up to you to define and configure your disaster recovery and business continuity policy.

Abstracted Services Category

The abstracted services category encompasses higher-level services such as Amazon Simple Storage Service (S3), Amazon DynamoDB, Amazon Simple Queue Service (SQS), and Amazon Simple Email Service (Amazon SES). As a customer, in these cases you are interacting with only AWS endpoints and APIs, whereas AWS manages all of their components, including applications and the operating system. As a customer, you are using a multitenant platform that is configured to securely isolate your data.

In Figure 2.4, you can see that, as a customer, you are still in charge of data protection using encryption as well as IAM policies to control access to services that belong to the abstracted services category.

AWS provides a set of documentations with security best practices for each of its cloud services. These documentations are intended to help you implement your controls in your cloud environments on the AWS Cloud platform (see Figure 2.5). You can find this web page at https://docs.aws.amazon.com/security.

FIGURE 2.4 Shared Responsibility Model for abstracted services.

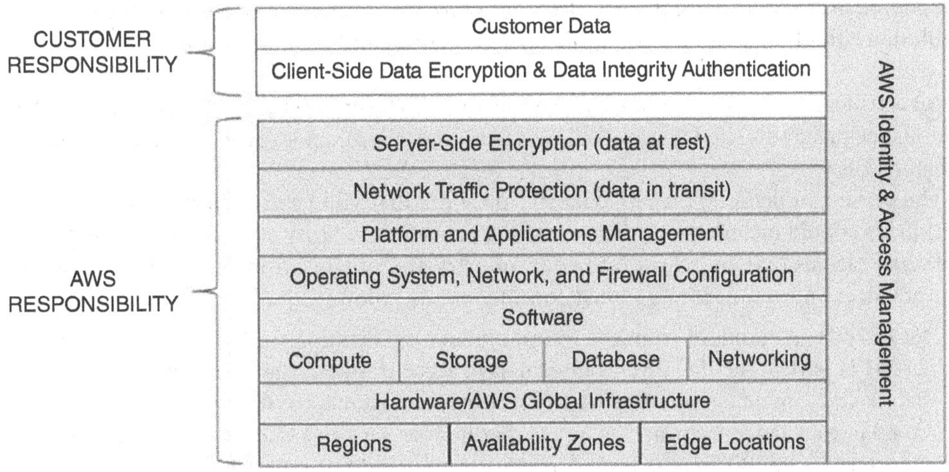

FIGURE 2.5 AWS security documentation.

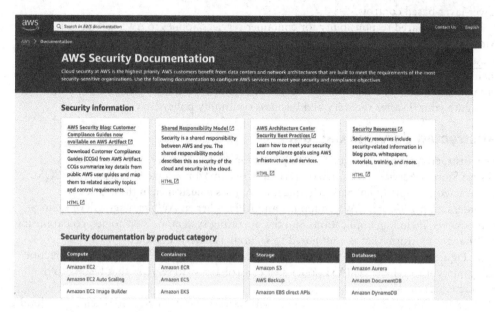

AWS Compliance Programs

When you are running your workloads in the AWS Cloud, you inherit all the security controls and compliance best practices that AWS has developed for its most security-demanding customers. Also, due to its global presence, AWS must comply with various regulations and best practices for security, compliance, and data protection around the world.

All certifications and compliance programs that AWS supports can be found in the AWS compliance programs site (https://aws.amazon.com/compliance/programs), as you can see in Figure 2.6.

The process of defining the cloud service provider that will be used to run your workloads should include an evaluation of the provider's security controls, best practices, and certifications that are relevant to your industry and organization. Some of the security best practices and standards you must consider are as follows:

- **ISO 27001:** A standard from the International Organization for Standardization, ISO 27001 is part of the ISO 27000 information security standards family. It is used to define and implement an information security management system (ISMS), which helps companies manage information assets that include sensitive data. This standard also leverages ISO 27002 as the basis for security controls best practices.

FIGURE 2.6 AWS compliance programs site.

- **ISO 27017:** Another standard that is part of the ISO 27000 family, ISO 27017 is focused on the information security practices for cloud computing. It defines the best practices and security controls that a cloud service provider must implement, supplementing the guidance explained in ISO 27002.
- **ISO 27018:** This standard establishes guidelines to protect *personally identifiable information* (PII) for public cloud computing environments.
- **PCI DSS:** The Payment Card Industry Data Security Standard is an information security standard for organizations that process and store credit card information.
- **CSA STAR:** The Cloud Security Alliance (CSA) is a not-for-profit organization with a mission to promote the use of best practices for providing security assurance within cloud computing environments. The CSA Security, Trust, Assurance, and Risk (STAR) Level 3 standard helps cloud service providers, customers, auditors, and consultants verify that available cloud security controls meet the adequate level of assurance required to protect data.
- **SOC 1, SOC 2, and SOC 3:** The System and Organization Controls (SOC) reports are independent third-party examination reports that demonstrate how AWS achieves compliance and controls objectives, helping your auditors understand the AWS security control models.

Chapter 2 ▪ Cloud Security Principles and Frameworks

In case you decide to focus your attention on the PCI DSS standard, AWS has published a very interesting compliance of version 4.0 (the latest one at the time of writing this chapter) that you can refer to when implementing security controls based on the Shared Responsibility Model. You can find the report at `https://d1.awsstatic.com/whitepapers/compliance/pci-dss-compliance-on-aws-v4-102023.pdf`, and a glimpse of its table of contents is shown in Figure 2.7. This guide can also help you understand the technical controls that you must implement as a part of your responsibility.

In Figure 2.8 (and at `https://aws.amazon.com/compliance/csa`), you can see that AWS is in compliance with the CSA STAR while also providing the CSA STAR consensus assessment, which explains how AWS is implementing the controls the standard requires (see Figure 2.9). The latter can be found here: `https://d1.awsstatic.com/whitepapers/compliance/CSA_Consensus_Assessments_Initiative_Questionnaire.pdf`.

FIGURE 2.7 AWS PCI DSS compliance guide.

Contents

Introduction	1
Changes from PCI DSS v3.2.1 to v4.0	2
PCI DSS compliance status of AWS services	2
AWS Shared Responsibility Model	3
Scope and cardholder data environment	4
Customer PCI DSS scope	4
Scope determination and validation	5
Segmentation	6
Diagrams and inventories	7
Data flow diagrams	7
Network diagrams	9
System component and data storage inventories	10
Guide for PCI DSS Compliance on AWS	11
AWS Well-Architected Framework	11
Customized Approach	12
Targeted risk analysis	12
PCI DSS Requirements	13
Requirement 1	13
Requirement 2	15
Requirement 3	17
Requirement 4	19

FIGURE 2.8 AWS CSA compliance site.

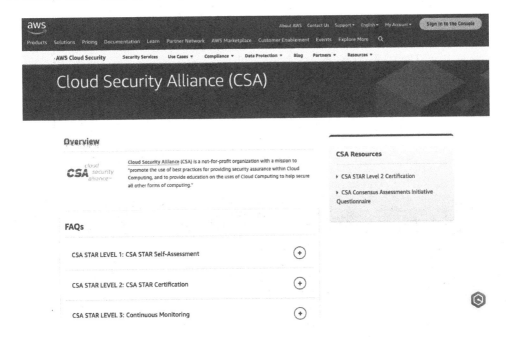

The AWS SOC 1 Type 2 Report evaluates the effectiveness of AWS controls that might affect internal controls over financial reporting (ICFR), and the auditing process is aligned to the SSAE 18 and ISAE 3402 standards. The AWS SOC 2 Privacy Type I Report assesses the AWS controls that meet the American Institute of Certified Public Accountants (AICPA) criteria for privacy. The AWS SOC 2 Security, Availability, & Confidentiality Report assesses the AWS controls that meet the American Institute of Certified Public Accountants (AICPA) criteria for security, availability, and confidentiality. Finally, the AWS SOC 3 Security, Availability, & Confidentiality Report summarizes the AWS SOC 2 report.

Using the ISO 27000 certifications, SOC reports, and other necessary regulations and accreditation models, you can evaluate how the security controls are implemented in the AWS data centers and services, and thus determine whether the level of compliance will achieve the protection you desire for your business.

Even if PCI DSS is not a requirement for your business, the security controls discussed in the standard can be used as a basis for you to define the controls needed for your environment, especially when you are dealing with sensitive data.

FIGURE 2.9 CSA consensus assessment initiative questionnaire.

Introduction

The Cloud Security Alliance (CSA) is a "not-for-profit organization with a mission to promote the use of best practices for providing security assurance within Cloud Computing, and to provide education on the uses of Cloud Computing to help secure all other forms of computing." For more information, see https://cloudsecurityalliance.org/about/.
A wide range of industry security practitioners, corporations, and associations participate in this organization to achieve its mission.

CSA Consensus Assessments Initiative Questionnaire

Questi on ID	Question	CSP CAIQ Answer	SSRM Control Ownership	CSP Implementation Description (Optional/Recommended)	CSC Responsibilities (Optional/Recommended)	CCM Control ID	CCM Control Specification	CCM Control Title	CCM Domain Title
A&A-01.1	Are audit and assurance policies, procedures, and standards established, documented, approved, communicated, applied, evaluated, and maintained?	Yes	CSP-owned	AWS has established formal policies and procedures to provide employees a common baseline for information security standards and guidance. The AWS Information Security Management System policy establishes guidelines for protecting the confidentiality, integrity, and availability of customers' systems and content. Maintaining customer trust and confidence is of the utmost importance to AWS. AWS works to comply with applicable federal, state, and local laws, statutes, ordinances, and regulations concerning security, privacy and data protection of AWS services in order to minimize the risk of accidental or unauthorized access or disclosure of customer content.		A&A-01	Establish, document, approve, communicate, apply, evaluate and maintain audit and assurance policies and procedures and standards. Review and update the policies and procedures at least annually.	Audit and Assurance Policy and Procedures	Audit & Assurance

AWS Artifact Portal

Once you define the controls, certifications, and regulations necessary to meet your business protection requirements, you will need to perform periodic assessments and audits of those controls in AWS. Using a model based on total transparency and self-service principles, AWS created a service portal called AWS Artifact. You can access the Artifact portal using the AWS Management Console or the API directly, and there are no costs to using it.

In AWS Artifact, you can get the compliance reports that allow you to evaluate the AWS security controls and ISVs who sell their products on AWS Marketplace. In Figure 2.10, you can see how the AWS Artifact portal appears in the AWS Management Console.

Exercise 2.1 shows how to use the AWS Artifact portal to generate a PCI DSS report.

FIGURE 2.10 AWS Artifact portal.

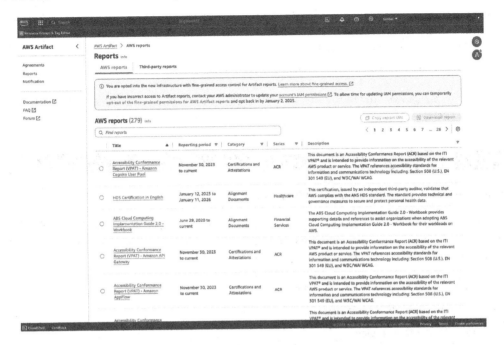

EXERCISE 2.1

Generating a PCI DSS Report in the AWS Artifact Portal

In this exercise, you will use the AWS Artifact portal available on the AWS Management Console to generate a PCI DSS report and evaluate what your (and AWS's) responsibilities for each requirement are. For assistance in completing this exercise, refer to the AWS Artifact documentation at `https://docs.aws.amazon.com/artifact`.

1. Open the AWS Management Console.
2. Search for the Artifact service.
3. Open the Artifact service. Click the View Reports button.
4. Search for the report PCI DSS Attestation of Compliance (AOC) and Responsibility Summary – Current. Select the radio button and click Download Report.
5. If needed, accept the terms and conditions; the download will begin.
6. Open the generated PDF using Adobe Acrobat Reader. (Be sure to use Adobe Acrobat or Adobe Reader to reliably view the files within the download.)

58 Chapter 2 ▪ Cloud Security Principles and Frameworks

7. In the PDF, follow the instructions to open the artifact.

8. You can explore the PCI Responsibility Summary PDF report as well as the Microsoft Excel file with all the necessary security controls, explaining in detail all requirements and the AWS and customer responsibilities.

Exercise 2.2 shows how to use the AWS Artifact portal to check the ISO 27001 and ISO 27017 reports.

EXERCISE 2.2

Checking the ISO 27001 and ISO 27017 Reports

In this exercise, you will check the ISO 27001 and ISO 27017 reports using the AWS Artifact portal in your AWS Management Console. For assistance in completing this exercise, refer to the AWS Artifact documentation at `https://docs.aws.amazon.com/artifact`.

1. Open the AWS Management Console.

2. Search for the Artifact service.

3. Open the Artifact service.

4. Search for the reports ISO 27001:2022 Certification, ISO 27001:2022 Statement of Applicability (SoA), SO 27017:2015 Certification, and ISO 27017:2015 Statement of Applicability (SoA). Select the radio button and click Download Report.

5. If needed, accept the terms and conditions; the download will begin.

6. Open the generated PDF using Adobe Acrobat Reader. (Be sure to use Adobe Acrobat or Adobe Reader to reliably view the files in the download.)

AWS Well-Architected Framework

The *AWS Well-Architected Framework* was developed to help you, as a customer, build secure, high-performing, resilient, and efficient infrastructure for your applications. The framework defines best practices in six pillars: security, operational excellence, reliability, performance efficiency, cost optimization, and sustainability.

The *AWS Well-Architected security pillar* shows how you can implement a strong security posture in the cloud, defining and implementing security best practices to protect your data and systems, control access, and respond automatically to security events, while also generating business value for your organization.

The security pillar has seven security design principles:

- **Implement a strong identity foundation:** Use the least privilege and enforce separation of duties, using the proper IAM roles and permissions, defining the appropriate authorization for each resource that will interact with the AWS Cloud, limiting and centralizing privileged accesses, and eliminating long-term credentials when possible.

- **Maintain traceability:** Enable audit logs by centralizing log collection, ingestion, protection, and enrichment, and by creating alerts that should be monitored by one or several teams that will respond to each kind of alert, based on required playbooks and runbooks.

- **Apply security at all layers:** Defense-in-depth is a must. You cannot use just one layer of protection; it is a must to implement network security, OS security, load balancer security, application security, and so on. You must implement security best practices in all AWS Cloud services and components that will be part of your application.

- **Automate security best practices:** Automation is a key function in cloud security. The best way to deploy an agile and secure environment is to leverage automation, implement security as code, and transform your paper security policies into real and coded security controls. As you create infrastructure as code and insert embedded security controls to achieve automated security, you can scale your cloud environments while maintaining the same level of protection.

- **Protect data in transit and at rest:** You must understand your data in order to protect sensitive information in both data exchange and storage, using encryption, tokenization, and masking resources to achieve it. You should also create and enforce access control policies to limit access to sensitive data wherever it is stored.

- **Keep people away from data:** You must create mechanisms and tools to reduce or eliminate manual and human access to production data, thus reducing attack surface and operation risks related to human mistakes when handling sensitive data.

- **Prepare for security events:** You must define an incident response management practice, running incident simulations, creating tools, using automation, and developing playbooks to improve the security incident capabilities.

Well-Architected Lenses

The lenses are designed to extend the guidance offered by the Well-Architected Framework, but focus on specific industry and technology domains such as financial services, games industry, SAP, IoT, serverless, and machine learning. As an example, some of the lenses available at the time of writing this chapter include these:

- **Migration lens:** Best practices for how to migrate to the AWS Cloud.

- **Data analytics lens:** Customer-proven best practices for designing analytics workloads.

- **Serverless applications lens:** Best practices for architecting your serverless applications on AWS.

- **Hybrid networking lens:** Processes for designing, deploying, and architecting hybrid networking on AWS Cloud.
- **Financial services industry lens:** A guide focused on financial services industry workloads.

 It is recommended to use applicable lenses along with Well-Architected Framework and its six pillars to fully evaluate your workload in the cloud.

Using the AWS Well-Architected Tool

This tool is offered as a service from the AWS Management Console, and it is designed to help builders and architects evaluate the state of their workloads against architectural best practices offered by the Well-Architected Framework. After reviewing your applications, you should be able to identify areas of improvement, get recommendations, improve your security controls, and track progress over time.

Using the Well-Architected Tool, it is possible to share workloads, custom lens, or profiles, or review templates to other AWS accounts even with all or specific users, but they can only be shared within the same region.

Figure 2.11 shows the tool, which has no associated cost and is available to every AWS user.

Exercise 2.3 shows you how to use the Well-Architected Tool to simulate an evaluation.

FIGURE 2.11 AWS Well-Architected Tool.

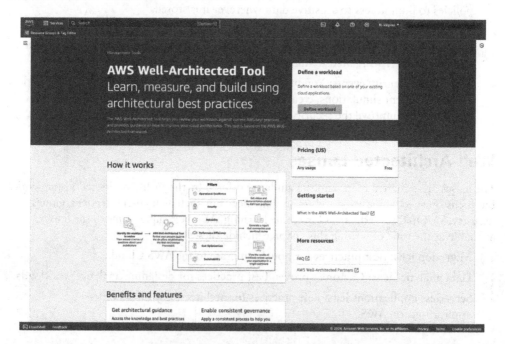

The AWS Marketplace 61

EXERCISE 2.3

Using the Well-Architected Tool

In this exercise, you will simulate a Well-Architected evaluation using the AWS Well-Architected Tool inside the AWS Management Console. For assistance in completing this exercise, refer to the AWS Well-Architected Tool documentation at https://docs.aws.amazon.com/wellarchitected.

1. Open the AWS Management Console.

2. Search for the Well-Architected Tool in the console.

3. Open the Well-Architected Tool Service.

4. Click Define Workload (the orange button) and select the Define Workload option.

5. Specify workload properties by completing all the fields.

6. When you have finished completing the form, click the Next button and select or create a profile if needed. Click the Next button again.

7. Apply a lens from the catalog or choose a custom one if available. Click Define Workload.

8. You can start executing the assessment by clicking Start Reviewing.

9. For each Well-Architected pillar, you need to answer specific questions. Documentation is available to help you understand the context and how to evaluate and implement the recommended best practices. Comprehending the Well-Architected Framework security pillar will help you go deeper and understand the security concepts and tools. These concepts and tools will help you not only pass the AWS Certified Security Specialty exam but also build secure workloads in the future.

The AWS Marketplace

The AWS Marketplace is a digital catalog that offers thousands of software solutions from third-party software manufacturers that make it easy to find, test, buy, and deploy software that runs on AWS. Naturally, it has many security solutions that you can use to improve your security controls when using the AWS Cloud. You can acquire many different solutions and use the pay-as-you-go model that is normally expected from cloud computing environments.

Through the AWS Marketplace, you can purchase the solutions directly from technology partners and quickly provision such specialized workloads within your AWS account, with just a few clicks.

As an illustration, Figure 2.12 depicts the first look at the Security category in the AWS Marketplace.

The solutions available from the marketplace are organized into various categories and are available from several strategic partners, enabling you to replicate and migrate

FIGURE 2.12 AWS Marketplace security solutions.

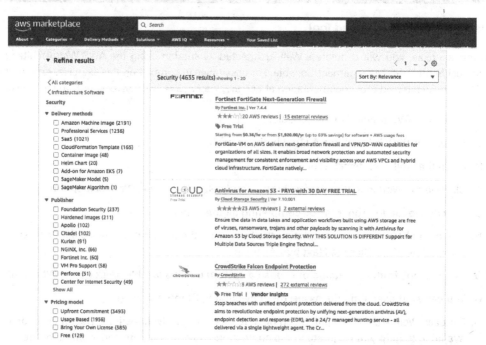

security solutions from your on-premises environment to the AWS Cloud with little effort. Furthermore, many solutions allow you to use your previously available licenses on a process that is also known as the bring-your-own-license (BYOL) model.

Summary

In this chapter, you learned how important it is to understand the Shared Responsibility Model and its guidance when adopting different types of services in the AWS Cloud.

Based on the model, AWS is responsible for the security *of* the cloud, while you (the customer) are always responsible for security *in* the cloud. This means you are responsible for securing your workloads running in your AWS environments while leveraging the security services and features AWS offers, including data protection and encryption, application security, network security configuration, and access control to your AWS environment.

Depending on the type of service you are using, you may have more or fewer security responsibilities. For example, if you are using managed services such as AWS Lambda, Amazon RDS databases, and Amazon S3, you have to deal with fewer security controls than you would if you were only using Amazon EC2 instances. Still, you will always be responsible for controlling access to your data and for protecting your applications.

AWS adopts security best practices to comply with various rules and regulations from different countries around the globe, and all certifications and reports are available on the AWS Artifact portal inside the AWS Management Console. Amazon offers this portal as a free service to allow you to access information about AWS compliance, assurance reports, and security best practices using AWS and third-party reports.

You can also use the AWS Well-Architected Tool in the AWS Management Console to evaluate the security and compliance of your workloads. Both resources are based on seven design principles that can be applied to assess your workloads running in the AWS Cloud or even on-premises.

Finally, you can use the AWS Marketplace to implement security solutions in your cloud environment in just a few clicks, which helps you deploy solutions and improve your security posture using AWS security partners.

Exam Essentials

Understand the Standard Shared Responsibility Model. Clearly understand the difference between security "of the cloud" and security "in the cloud."

Know the Shared Responsibility Model details. If you are using abstracted or container services, you (and AWS) will have slightly different security responsibilities. Understand these differences in detail.

Be familiar with the most important security certifications. It is essential for you to understand the objectives and context of the following certifications and reports: ISO 27001, ISO 27002, PCI DSS, SOC (1,2,3), and CSA STAR.

Know how to use the Well-Architected Framework. Understand that the AWS Well-Architected Framework has six pillars, one of which is security. In the security pillar, there are seven security design principles:

1. Implement a strong identity foundation.

2. Maintain traceability.

3. Apply security at all layers.

4. Automate security best practices.

5. Protect data in transit and at rest.

6. Keep people away from data.

7. Prepare for security events.

Be familiar with the AWS Marketplace. You can find many security solutions in the AWS Marketplace that you can use to improve your security posture. You can use strategic AWS security partners. You can use your own licenses in a bring-your-own-license model. The pay-as-you-go model is another option available to you.

Review Questions

1. In an Amazon EC2 instance deployment, who is in charge of the data center facilities security, based on the Shared Responsibility Model?

   A. AWS

   B. The customer

   C. The responsibility is shared

   D. Depends on the region

2. In a database implementation of Amazon RDS running MySQL, who is in charge of the operating system security patching, based on the Shared Responsibility Model?

   A. The customer

   B. The responsibility is shared

   C. AWS

   D. Depends on the region

3. From where can you download ISO 27001, ISO 27017, ISO 27018, and other certification files in PDF format?

   A. AWS Security portal

   B. AWS Artifact service

   C. AWS GuardDuty

   D. AWS public website

4. What is the SOC-1 Type 2 report?

   A. It evaluates the effectiveness of AWS controls that might affect internal controls over financial reporting (ICFR).

   B. It is a summary of the AWS SOC 2 report.

   C. It evaluates the AWS controls that meet the American Institute of Certified Public Accountants (AICPA) criteria for security, availability, and confidentiality.

   D. It is a comprehensive evaluation of a service organization's controls designed to ensure the protection and security of data.

5. What is the SOC 2 Security, Availability, and Confidentiality report?

   A. It evaluates the effectiveness of AWS controls that might affect internal controls over financial reporting (ICFR).

   B. It is a summary of the AWS SOC 2 report.

   C. It evaluates the AWS controls that meet the American Institute of Certified Public Accountants (AICPA) criteria for security, availability, and confidentiality.

   D. It is a comprehensive evaluation of a service organization's controls designed to ensure the protection and security of data.

6. Which option best defines the AWS Well-Architected Framework?

A. It is a framework developed by AWS that describes best practices to help customers build secure, high-performing, resilient, and efficient cloud-based applications and systems.

B. It is a paid service developed by AWS that defines best practices to help customers to build their environments, improving security, operational excellence, reliability, performance efficiency, and cost optimization.

C. It is a no-cost framework developed by AWS that defines best practices, helping customers implement their environments, improving security, operational excellence, reliability, performance efficiency, and cost optimization.

D. It is a tool in the AWS Management Console that helps customers automatically implement architecture best practices.

7. What are the design principles defined in the AWS Well-Architected security pillar?

A. Identity and access management, detective controls, and infrastructure protection

B. Data protection, and identity and access management

C. Implement a strong identity foundation, maintain traceability, apply security at all layers, automate security best practices, keep people away from data, and prepare for security events

D. Implement a strong identity foundation, maintain traceability, apply security at all layers, automate security best practices, protect data in transit and at rest, keep people away from data, and prepare for security events

8. Who is in charge of the AWS hypervisor security when you, as a customer, are deploying Amazon EC2 instances in the AWS Cloud?

A. AWS is always in charge of the hypervisor security.

B. The customer is in charge of the hypervisor security.

C. It depends on the type of instance.

D. This is a Shared Responsibility Model, so the customer and AWS have the responsibility of the hypervisor security.

9. You are looking for an endpoint protection solution, and you want to use the same solution that you are using on-premises today to improve your workload protection running on your Amazon EC2 instances. Where can you find endpoint protection solutions to protect your servers running in the AWS Cloud?

A. AWS Management Console

B. AWS website

C. AWS Security Services

D. AWS Marketplace

66 Chapter 2 ▪ Cloud Security Principles and Frameworks

10. What is the pillar of the Well-Architected Framework that emphasizes the protection of data, systems, and assets?

A. Reliability

B. Financial lens

C. Sustainability

D. Security

Chapter 3

Management and Security Governance

THE AWS CERTIFIED SECURITY SPECIALTY EXAM OBJECTIVES THAT LEVERAGE CONCEPTS EXPLAINED IN THIS CHAPTER INCLUDE THE FOLLOWING:

✓ **Domain 6: Management and Security Governance**

- 6.1. Develop a strategy to centrally deploy and manage AWS accounts
- 6.2. Implement a secure and consistent deployment strategy for cloud resources
- 6.3. Evaluate the compliance of AWS resources
- 6.4. Identify security gaps through architectural reviews and cost analysis

Introduction

In this chapter, you learn strategies to manage multiple AWS accounts using AWS Organizations. We also cover AWS Control Tower as a service to consistently deploy a landing zone architecture based on best practices and security controls to protect your workloads. In addition, you learn how to use service control policies (SCPs) as a technical solution to enforce central control over the maximum available permissions across your organization and to centrally manage security services using delegated administrator accounts.

You also learn how to use a service such as AWS CloudFormation to deploy cloud resources consistently and securely, enforcing security best practices within your Infrastructure as Code (IaC) strategy. Also, you can use AWS Service Catalog to create a portfolio of approved services to be deployed in your organization.

From a management and security governance perspective, it is important to evaluate compliance of your cloud resources, starting with correct data classification and identification of sensitive information. You learn that a service such as Amazon Macie can help you achieve that objective. You also discover how using AWS Config can help you assess and evaluate configurations of your AWS resources.

Finally, in this chapter, you learn how to identify security gaps by detecting anomalies based on resource utilization and trends using services such as AWS Trusted Advisor and AWS Cost Explorer or the AWS Well-Architected Framework.

Multi-Account Management Using AWS Organizations

You can use the AWS Organizations service to manage all your AWS accounts in one place. This service provides a centralized view of billing and the ability to share resources across accounts. Furthermore, you can automate account provisioning by using the account factory feature and quickly add those accounts to their respective groups.

Using AWS Organizations, you can group your AWS accounts into organizational units (OU) and attach SCPs to control the maximum available permissions within that account.

OUs allow you to group accounts and other organizational units in a hierarchical structure. Such a composition gives you the ability to mimic your own organizational structure and break down the OUs into teams, environments, business units, and regulatory requirements, while using SCPs to limit the service usage.

Figure 3.1 illustrates a sample account hierarchy using AWS Organizations.

In Figure 3.1, there are three OUs (Development, UAT, and Production). Attached to each OU is an SCP that controls the maximum available permissions to AWS services. Note also that there is a separate account, "Security Account," that is not under any OU but has a corresponding SCP attached to it.

Organizations offer two types of policies—management and authorization—which we review in the following sections.

FIGURE 3.1 AWS Organizations account hierarchy.

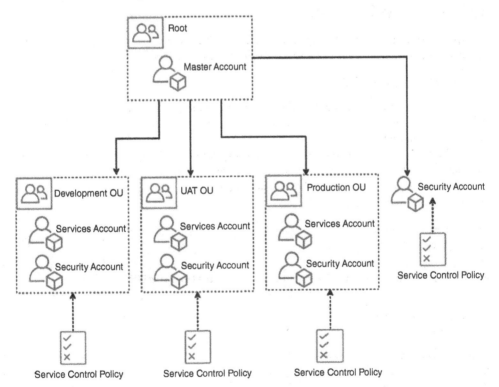

Management Policies

Management policies are used to centrally configure and manage AWS services and their behavior. There are three types of policies:

- **Artificial intelligence (AI) services:** Some AI services might store and use customer content for development and improvement of other AWS services. Using this type of policy, you can opt out of having your content stored and enforce the selected setting for all your members' accounts in your organization.

- **Backup policies:** This type of policy allows you to create backup plans for the accounts in your organization.

- **Tag policies:** With this type of policy, you can centrally manage the rules to use tags across resources in your organization.

Management policies have a different syntax that includes an inheritance operator, which enables users to add fine granularity, specifying elements that can be modified when inherited by organizational units or accounts, resulting in an effective policy that applies to each account.

Authorization Policies

This type of policy helps you manage the security on the accounts in your organization. It specifically focuses on the service control policies (SCP) described here.

Service Control Policies

You can use SCPs to centrally control the maximum available permissions across multiple AWS accounts within your AWS Organization deployment. SCPs are similar to IAM policies and have the same syntax.

In truth, an SCP is similar to an *IAM permissions boundary*, which restricts the actions that identities within that account can actually perform.

Example 3.1 shows a sample SCP that denies access to any Amazon DynamoDB (AWS's NoSQL database service) actions.

Real World Scenario

Example 3.1: Sample SCP Denying Access to DynamoDB

```
{
 "Version": "2012-10-17",
 "Statement": [
 {
 "Sid": "DenyDynamoDBAccess",
 "Effect": "Deny",
 "Action": "dynamodb:*",
 "Resource": "*"
 }
 ]
}
```

Note that SCPs act as permissions boundaries and do not grant any permission by themselves. Consequently, you still need to use identity-based and resource-based policies within your account to allow access to AWS resources. The SCPs limit the maximum available permission granted by these policies, and the user cannot perform any actions that the applied SCPs do not allow.

Also remember to validate which services and actions are allowed in the SCP attached to the account when you are dealing with debugging permission issues. The SCP boundaries always take precedence over the permissions defined through identity and resource-based policies. Last, it's important to note that in member accounts of an AWS Organization, the root user is also affected by SCP boundaries.

Service control policies are not available if you only enable consolidated billing in your organization.

Service control policies do not affect identities in the management account. That type of policy only takes effect in the members' accounts in your organization.

Delegated Administration

It is a good practice to use the organization management account for activities that must be executed by that account only. From that perspective, the term *delegated administrator* is used when one or more member accounts are used as administrator of a specific service that allows you to reduce the usage of the management account. When you register an account as a delegated administrator, you grant access to perform policy actions that are, by default, available only to the management account for that service.

There is an extensive list of services that support delegated administrators, but we mention some of the security services more relevant to the Security Specialty certification.

AWS Account Management

Using this service, you can delegate the administration of alternate contact information for all accounts in your organization. It is a best practice to keep your security contacts up to date in order to receive important notifications related to your accounts, such as security events impacting your resources.

AWS Audit Manager

Delegating the administration of this service allows you to continuously audit your accounts across your organization. It automates evidence collection to assess risk and compliance with regulations and industry standards.

AWS CloudTrail

An identity in the delegated administrator account can create an organization trail that logs all events in all accounts in your organization. We strongly recommend setting a centralized management log of all activities in your organization.

AWS Config

Using AWS Config, you can assess, audit, and evaluate configuration of your AWS resources. Once this service has been delegated, you can get an aggregate view of your resources' configuration and compliance data for your entire organization.

Amazon Detective

Amazon Detective integrates with AWS Organization, enabling you to analyze, investigate, and quickly identify the root cause of security findings or suspicious activities to conduct faster and more efficient security investigation in your organization. Delegating administration for this service allows you to separate this task from a management account, restricting access and enforcing the principle of minimum privilege.

AWS Firewall Manager

Besides separating the administration of the service from your management account, AWS Firewall Manager allows you to centrally configure and manage AWS WAF, AWS Shield Advanced, Amazon VPC security groups and network ACLs, AWS Network Firewall, and Amazon Route 53 Resolver DNS Firewall across the accounts in your organization.

Amazon GuardDuty

Once you delegate administration of Amazon GuardDuty for one of your member's accounts, you can view findings to identify suspicious and potentially malicious activity for all accounts in your organization. In addition, you can manage the service that allows you to add members in your organization automatically, enabling the service and its additional protection plans in your delegated account.

IAM Access Analyzer

Using IAM Access Analyzer, you can delegate an administrator account that allows you to create organization-wide analyzers to identify resources shared with external principals and unused access findings in one account for further analysis and investigation. The service analyzes the policies attached to your resources to detect unintended or overly permissive access, helping to secure your environment and meet compliance requirements.

Amazon Inspector

Amazon Inspector allows you to automatically scan your EC2, Lambda, and ECR resources for security vulnerabilities. Once you delegate the administration to a member account, you can enable or disable the scan of specific accounts in your organization. In addition, you can aggregate findings for the entire organization and manage suppression rules.

Amazon Macie

With the delegation of Amazon Macie, you can have a consolidated view all of your sensitive objects in your S3 buckets, discovering and classifying your sensitive data. From the delegated administrator account, you can configure the service to automatically detect resources in new accounts and get alerts for policy misconfiguration across S3 buckets in your organization.

AWS Security Hub

Using AWS Security Hub from a delegated administration account, you can have a single interface to view the security posture of the entire organization. In addition, you can configure the service to automatically enable it for all the members' accounts in your organization, aggregating findings including from third-party products and custom security tools.

AWS IAM Identity Center

IAM Identity Center lets you centrally configure and manage user access to AWS accounts and applications. It is a security best practice to delegate the administration of IAM Identity Center to centrally manage access to the accounts in your organization outside of your management account. Delegation allows you to manage the users and set policies to control access to your organization without the need to configure identity providers in each member account.

AWS Trusted Advisor

AWS Trusted Advisor is a service that helps you optimize your AWS environment by providing guidance and recommendations to improve security, performance, cost optimization, and reliability. Once it has been delegated, you can run Trusted Advisor checks for all the member accounts in your organization.

AWS Control Tower

AWS Control Tower offers a way to build and govern a multi-account environment following best practices and security recommendations by setting up a landing zone using multiple AWS services such as AWS Organization, AWS Identity Center, and AWS Service Catalog.

Control Tower uses controls to enable best practices, extending capabilities of AWS Organizations. For example, you can use security controls to guarantee that API activity is being captured by CloudTrail and that it is protected against tampering.

Account Factory is another good feature of Control Tower that allows you to provision new accounts and infrastructure, facilitating account deployment and governance by enforcing standardized configuration and security controls in your environment.

We review some of the most important features that Control Tower offers to manage multi-account organizations.

Control Tower creates several resources when launching a new landing zone. In order to keep your landing zone from entering an unmanaged state, it's important that you not modify or delete those resources.

Landing Zone

A landing zone is a concept that applies to a well-architected muti-account environment based on security and compliance best practices. It is a reference architecture that holds all accounts in your organization, and it is structured using organizational units, roles, users, and other resources. The common structure of a landing zone includes the following:

- **Root:** Parent that contains all other OUs.
- **Security OU:** This organizational unit contains two accounts created by Control Tower—Log Archive and Audit. It is possible to customize those names when launching your landing zone or when bringing existing accounts under Control Tower management.
- **Sandbox OU:** This is an optional organizational unit commonly used for experimentation purposes.
- **Identity Directory:** This cloud-native directory in AIM Identity Center holds preconfigured groups and permissions. However, you can also manage your own identity provider if you do not want to use the default configuration.
- **Users:** These are the identities that your users can assume to log in to your accounts. We highly recommend you federate with your authoritative directory service.

Controls

A control is a security guardrail that supports the governance of your AWS accounts. There are three types of controls:

- **Preventive:** As its name implies, it prevents an action from occurring, for example, removing CloudTrail from the Log Archive account.
- **Detective:** This control detects specific events when they occur and logs the action for further analysis in a Config Compliance Rule. For example, when a new S3 bucket is created with a public read/write access setting.
- **Proactive:** These rules have the capacity to check compliance before the actual resource is provisioned in your accounts using Infrastructure as Code (IaC) with CloudFormation hooks, preventing the creation if resources are not compliant.

Three categories of guidance apply for controls: mandatory, strongly recommended, and elective. You can decide to enforce strongly recommended and elective controls from Control Tower, but mandatory controls cannot be changed.

Account Factory

Control Tower offers Account Factory as a built-in account template that can be used to standardize the provisioning of a new account with approved account settings. It is possible to update, manage, and even close accounts that you create using Account Factory. In addition, it is possible to use this feature to change the organizational unit for an account in your environment.

This Account Factory feature is also known as a "vending machine," as it creates and enrolls new AWS accounts and automates the process of configuring controls and policies for those accounts that are joining your organization.

We strongly discourage running any type of production workload in your Control Tower management account.

Secure and Consistent Infrastructure Deployment in AWS

It is possible to treat deployment of infrastructure in the same way that developers treat code development: using principles of DevOps. That means code is expected to be developed in a defined format and syntax and stored in a source control system that logs historic changes to create applications in a consistent, reliable, and repeatable way.

AWS provides mechanisms and services to create, deploy, orchestrate, and maintain infrastructure, also using DevOps principles, just like developers write code in a programmatic, descriptive, and declarative way.

The following sections review some core services and features that will help you secure and consistently deploy infrastructure in AWS.

Infrastructure as Code Using AWS CloudFormation

AWS CloudFormation is a service that allows you to create templates to design, provision, and manage AWS resources in a predictable and reliable way by taking care of configurations and dependencies.

It is possible to replicate your infrastructure in different accounts or even different regions, reusing your templates to create resources in a repeatable manner. Since those templates are text (YAML or JSON), you can easily track changes using a version control system, opening the possibility to roll back changes or just use a previous version if needed.

Stacks

CloudFormation offers a simple way to manage Infrastructure as a Code, using templates to create a stack as a collection of resources that are provisioned in an orderly manner as a single unit. The service makes underlying API calls to the same services declared in your template; therefore, it needs proper permissions to successfully complete those actions.

Since all resources in a stack are treated as a group, they all need to be created or deleted for the stack to work properly. If a resource cannot be created, the CloudFormation service rolls back and deletes all resources created previously. If a resource cannot be deleted, all other resources are retained until the stack can be successfully deleted.

When you need to make changes to a stack, you can apply changes instead of deleting or creating a completely new stack. To do so, you submit the new template, and CloudFormation compares the current state of your stack and updates only the changed resources.

StackSets

AWS CloudFormation StackSets is a feature that extends capabilities of stacks by enabling you to manage stacks in multiple accounts and regions. You can manage your StackSets from a central administrator account and use your templates as a source for provisioning stacks with resources on target accounts and regions in your organization.

Figure 3.2 shows a logical representation of how a StackSet is used to deploy stacks in multiple accounts and different regions.

FIGURE 3.2 Logical representation of a StackSet model.

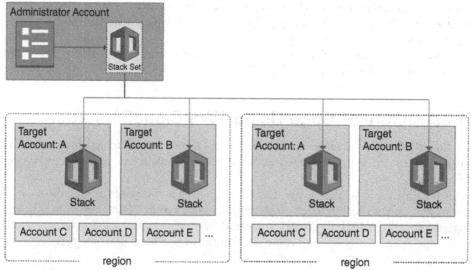

Tagging Strategies

A good way to organize your AWS resources is by using tags. Tags are key-value pairs that act as metadata that can be added when you create or update your resources, such as Amazon EC2 instances or Amazon S3 buckets.

Tags are useful to manage, identify, search, and filter resources. They are commonly used to add categories by purpose, owner, organizational unit, billing department, or even environment. Tag names and tag values are case sensitive.

Real World Scenario

Example 3.2: Sample Tags

CostCenter=222233334444
In this example the key is CostCenter. The tag value is 222233334444.

Another common use case is to get billing reports with costs broken down by tag. In Example 3.2, you can see a business tag with a traditional cost allocation dimension by cost center. Some services support the createdBy tag, which is generated by AWS and is used for cost allocation purposes when resources are uncategorized.

It is important to highlight that IAM policies support tag-based conditions, letting you enforce permissions based on tags or tags values. However, keep in mind that support for tag-based and resource-level permissions is specific per service. Be sure to restrict who can modify tags of your resources when using them to control access through IAM policies to avoid bypassing your access controls.

Best Practices for Tagging

Some best practices to use for your tagging strategy are as follows:

1. Use a standardized, case-sensitive format.
2. Do not include sensitive data in tags.
3. Use automated tools such as Tag Editor to help manage resource tags.
4. Enforce tagging standards using AWS Organization through service control policies.

Sharing Resources across AWS Accounts

In a multi-account environment, it is possible to create a resource and share it with other accounts or organizational units using AWS Resource Manager (AWS RAM). This feature gives you the possibility of avoiding duplication of resources in every account, reducing operational overhead and simplifying security management, since all access in RAM resources is managed by a single set of policies and permissions.

A good example of using AWS RAM is for sharing a private certificate authority (CA) resource, allowing AWS Certificate Manager users in other accounts to issue certificates signed by your centralized CA.

Deploying Portfolios of Approved Services

AWS Service Catalog is a service that allows you to centrally manage a portfolio of resources to govern your Infrastructure as Code (IaC) templates, which can be developed in CloudFormation or Terraform standards.

Using Service Catalog, you can offer a curated catalog of resources for your customers to quickly provision approved architectures without needing direct access to underlying services. These services can include container images, servers, databases, and more.

End users can be your development team, data analysts, or any other cloud consumer. Users can browse a list of products they have access to, select what they need, and launch it on their own, while administrators can restrict where the product can be deployed, the type of instances to be used, and many other configuration options, resulting in a standardized provisioned product.

Administrators of catalogs can use resource tags during deployment and then grant access to the final product using AWS IAM users, groups, policies, and conditions.

Add a product to any number of portfolios without creating additional copy. Updating the product to a new version will propagate the update to every portfolio that references it.

Evaluating Compliance

One important aspect of evaluating compliance in your environment is to understand what needs to be protected and apply a correct classification to the data so you can, in turn, apply adequate security controls to protect it.

In this section, we review three important services that can help you effectively evaluate compliance in your AWS workloads.

Data Classification Using Amazon Macie

Using a service such as Amazon Macie, you can automatically discover sensitive data in your Amazon S3 buckets. The service gives you the possibility of doing that in two different ways. The first is by evaluating your inventory on a daily basis and using sampling techniques to identify representative objects from your buckets. The second way is enabling discovery jobs that provide a deeper, more targeted analysis where you can select the scope and criteria to be used. In addition, you can configure on-demand only once or on a recurring basis to maintain continuous monitoring of your data.

Data Identifiers

Amazon Macie has two types of data identifiers that you can use to discover sensitive data in your buckets:

- **AWS-managed:** These are built-in identifiers designed to detect specific types of sensitive data. For example, AWS access keys, credit card numbers or identification numbers from multiple regions and countries, personally identifiable information (PII), and financial information.
- **Custom identifiers:** You can create custom criteria for detecting sensitive data. Identifiers are built using regular expressions (regex), defining a text pattern to match character sequence and a proximity rule. These can be used to define specific use cases that are not covered by AWS-managed identifiers.

There is an additional element that you can use to refine the results. The *allow lists* function gives you the ability to specify checks and patterns to be ignored during discovery of sensitive data, for example, credit card numbers when using a test environment. Amazon Macie will not report an occurrence of matching if an element is declared in your list and found in managed or custom identifiers.

Amazon Macie can help you meet compliance with your data security requirements by producing reports of sensitive data found during analysis. A finding is sensitive data found in an S3 object, and a data discovery result is the actual record of the analysis performed.

 At the time of writing this chapter, Amazon Macie only supports discovering sensitive data in Amazon S3 buckets. However, keep in mind that you can still move data, such as snapshots of databases in parquet format or any other format supported by the service, temporarily to buckets for analysis.

Evaluate Configuration Using AWS Config

AWS Config is a service that can help you audit resources to ensure compliance with policies and best practices by accessing historical configuration and changes. A good example is the possibility of accessing historical configuration of security groups assigned to an EC2 instance, including port rules that were open at a specific time.

You can use Config Rules or Conformance Packs to configure AWS Config. The first allows you to evaluate compliance for the type of resource you select, to record activity and send the results to an Amazon S3 bucket, or to set up a topic to get notifications using Amazon SNS. The second is a collection of rules that can be deployed and monitored as a single entity.

80 Chapter 3 ▪ Management and Security Governance

The service also gives you the opportunity to use aggregators to get a centralized view of your resource inventory and compliance. An aggregator collects configuration and compliance data from multiple accounts and regions in a single place.

In Exercise 3.1, you use the AWS Console to view compliance of your resources using AWS Config.

EXERCISE 3.1

Viewing Compliance of Your AWS Resources

In this exercise, you will view compliance of resources using AWS Console.

1. Log in to your AWS account and open the AWS Config service. Select Resources from the left-side menu.

2. On the Resource Inventory page, you can filter by category, type, and compliance status. Choose Include Deleted Resources. The table will show the results. Note that resource identifier can be an ID or a resource name.

3. Choose a resource from the Resource Identifier column.

4. Click the Resource Timeline button.

5. If needed, filter further by configuration, compliance, or CloudTrail events.

AWS Audit Manager to Collect Compliance Evidence

Audit Manager can help you audit usage of other AWS services and simplify how to manage compliance with regulations and standards. The service can automate the collection of data to assess whether your security controls are operating effectively. In addition, Audit Manager can help you manage stakeholders involved in reviews and generate audit reports based on pre-built or custom frameworks.

Once you create an assessment from a selected framework, Audit Manager will start automatically to collect data from your AWS accounts and services defined as the scope for your audit.

Some of the pre-built standard frameworks that you can use to assist you in collecting relevant evidence are PCI DSS, AWS Well-Architected, ISO/IEC 27001, and SOC2.

Architecture Review and Cost Analysis

It is important to have a process for continuous improvement, especially to review your architectures to identify issues that might need to be fixed. We recommend implementing a lightweight process to be designed in a consistent and repetitive manner instead of a manually heavy procedure to be run against your workloads.

We review some services and tools that can help you automate the process of revision and continuously evaluate your architecture against well-known frameworks and best practices.

AWS Trusted Advisor

AWS Trusted Advisor is a service that continuously evaluates your environment to make recommendations across the categories of cost optimization, performance, resilience, operational excellence, security, and service limits, along with deviation from best practices.

Depending on the support plan you have in your account, you can access different levels of recommendations. Basic and Developer Support plans give you access to all validations in the Service Limit category and six checks in the Security category. For Business and Enterprise Support, you can access all checks in all categories, including CloudWatch and Security Hub events, to monitor status.

Trusted Advisor integrates with AWS Organization, which allows you to aggregate and check results for all accounts in your organization. Exercise 3.2 shows you how to enable organization view in the service.

EXERCISE 3.2

Enabling Organization View in Trusted Advisor

In this exercise, you will enable organization view in Trusted Advisor.

1. Log in to your organization management account and open the Trusted Advisor service.
2. In the Navigation pane, under Preferences, choose the Your Organization option.
3. Under Enable Trusted Access with AWS Organization, turn on Enabled.

The level of support determines which Trusted Advisor checks are available for each account even when organization view has been enabled.

AWS Cost Explorer

AWS Cost Explorer is a service that can help you analyze the usage of AWS services and the costs associated with them. Using this service, you can access data from the last 13 months while forecasting how much you are likely to spend for the next 12 months. It is possible to enable this service by opening it from the AWS Cost Management console.

Within an AWS Organization, you should be able to launch Cost Explorer from a member account if the management account has it enabled. However, management account can deny access for member accounts.

Cost Anomaly Detection

Cost Anomaly Detection is another feature from the Cost Management service. It uses machine learning to detect anomalous spending patterns in your AWS services. It can also be configured to provide monitoring alongside a daily summary subscription, which will let you know, for example, if spending exceeds one hundred dollars and 40 percent of your expected spending per service.

Summary

In this chapter, you learned how using AWS Organization can help you establish a strategy for managing all your accounts in a single place, by consolidating billing, managing access control, and sharing resources. In addition, you can use organizational units (OUs) to group accounts by business department, environment, and so on, and you can attach service control policies (SCPs) to apply controls and limit service usage across your organization. Using management policies in your organization, you can control the behavior of services in your organization, such as tag policies, which can help you standardize the tags attached to resources in your organization's accounts.

Remember that it is a good practice to delegate administration of services in your organization to avoid using the management account. When you delegate administration to a member account, you grant administrative permissions for that service, including read-only activity for your organization. Some of the security services that support administration delegation are Amazon GuardDuty, Amazon Inspector, IAM Access Analyzer, AWS Security Hub, Amazon Detective, and AWS IAM Identity Center.

Control Tower is a tool that will help you build a multi-account environment while keeping best practices and security recommendations by setting up a landing zone that includes guardrails to support the governance of your organization.

AWS provides services that can help you create, deploy, and orchestrate infrastructure in a programmatic way. For example, AWS CloudFormation allows you to create templates to provision resources while taking care of configurations and dependencies. Conversely, a good way to keep your AWS resources organized is using tags, which can be used to apply IAM policies in a more granular way while using tags as a condition.

After building a consistent landing zone with best practices and security controls, it is important to demonstrate compliance with either internal policies or international standards. Using services such as Amazon Macie, you can discover sensitive data in your S3 buckets that will allow you to correctly apply controls to protect data according to its classification. In addition, you can use AWS Config to frequent audit resources to ensure compliance and access historical configurations and changes. Audit Manager is a tool that can help you collect compliance evidence and delegate responsibilities while creating reports to validate compliance against international frameworks such as PCI DSS or SOC2.

Exam Essentials

Multi-account strategies. AWS Organization is the core service to create a multi-account strategy by creating an organization that allows you to consolidate billing and policies and share resources across members. You can use organizational units (OUs) to better group resources and apply policies to control and limit services usage along with security controls. Support your governance with the use of tags, which will help you improve your permissions policies with better granularity.

Control Tower offers a way to build and govern a multi-account environment following best practices and security recommendations by setting up a landing zone that includes controls to enforce best practices, extending capabilities of AWS Organizations.

Delegated administration. When possible, avoid the use of an administrative management account. As a good practice, delegate administration of your security services to member accounts, granting the permission to manage such services. Some of the security services that support administration delegation are Amazon GuardDuty, Amazon Inspector, IAM Access Analyzer, AWS Security Hub, Amazon Detective, and AWS IAM Identity Center.

Best practices for tagging. Some of the best practices and recommendations for tagging your resources are as follows:

- Use a standardized, case-sensitive format.
- Do not include sensitive data in tags.
- Use automated tools to help manage resource tags.
- It is possible to enforce tagging standards using SCPs.

Data classification. Using Amazon Macie, you can automatically discover sensitive data in your S3 buckets. The service gives you the option to perform data discovery in two different ways. The first is by evaluating your inventory and using sampling techniques to identify representative objects from your buckets. The second is by enabling discovery jobs that provide a deeper and more targeted analysis where you can select the scope and criteria to be used.

Assess, audit, and evaluate configurations. AWS Config is a service that can help you audit resources to ensure compliance with policies and best practices by accessing historical configuration and changes. Using Config Rules, you can evaluate compliance for the type of resource you want and record and report compliance results. You can also use the included conformance packs, which are a collection of rules that can be deployed and monitored as a single entity.

84 Chapter 3 ▪ Management and Security Governance

AWS cost and usage for anomaly detection. Cost Explorer is a tool that can help you analyze usage of AWS services and the costs associated with them. Using this service, you can access data from the last 13 months while forecasting how much you are likely to spend for the next 12 months. Cost Anomaly Detection is another feature from the Cost Management service. It uses machine learning to detect anomalous spending patterns in your AWS services, and it is configured to provide monitoring along with a daily summary alert subscription, which will let you know, for example, of spending exceeding one hundred dollars and 40 percent of your expected spending per service.

Review Questions

1. What is a feature offered by AWS Organization service?
   A. Consolidated vendors report
   B. Centralized network logs
   C. Catalog of services to be deployed over a multi-account environment
   D. Central access management using IAM Identity Center

2. Is it possible to use service control policies (SCPs) to restrict actions for identities in the organization management account?
   A. Yes
   B. No
   C. This relationship does not make sense
   D. More information is needed

3. Which of the following is an AWS service that integrates with organizations and support to become delegated administrator?
   A. Amazon Macie
   B. Amazon Bedrock
   C. Amazon VPC
   D. Control Tower

4. What is not a type of control that supports the governance of your environment using Control Tower?
   A. Preventive
   B. Detective
   C. Corrective
   D. Proactive

5. What could be the most efficient way to create a group of resources across multiple accounts and regions in a single operation?
   A. A CloudFormation template
   B. A CloudFormation stack
   C. A CloudFormation StackSet
   D. A CloudFront distribution

Chapter 3 · Management and Security Governance

6. You need to issue an X.509 certificate from multiple accounts using Certificate Manager as your private certificate authority (CA). In order to avoid the creation of one private CA per account where you need to issue certificates, what service allows you to share resources across your organization?

   A. AWS Resource Access Manager

   B. AWS Tag Editor

   C. Amazon Share Services

   D. AWS Certificate Manager

7. What is one type of data identifier available in Amazon Macie to discover sensitive data in your S3 buckets?

   A. PII

   B. PCI DSS

   C. HIPAA

   D. Managed data identifier

8. What is one valid channel that AWS Config can use to deliver configuration items?

   A. Event Bridge notifications

   B. Amazon S3 buckets

   C. Amazon ACLs

   D. Amazon SES

9. How many security checks are available in Trusted Advisor for customers with a Basic or Developer Support plan?

   A. All security checks are available.

   B. None; with basic support, Trusted Advisor is not supported.

   C. All checks in Service Limits and some checks in the Security category.

   D. All checks, but in read-only mode.

10. What is a valid pre-built standard framework available in the AWS Audit Manager library?

    A. DORA 2024

    B. SSAE-18 SOC 3

    C. PCI DSS v2.2

    D. PCI DSS v4.0

Chapter 4

Identity and Access Management

THE AWS CERTIFIED SECURITY SPECIALTY EXAM OBJECTIVES THAT LEVERAGE CONCEPTS EXPLAINED IN THIS CHAPTER INCLUDE THE FOLLOWING:

✓ **Domain 4: Identity and Access Management**

- 4.1. Design, implement, and troubleshoot authentication for AWS resources
- 4.2. Design, implement, and troubleshoot authorization for AWS resources

Introduction

In this chapter, you learn what AWS Identity and Access Management (IAM) is and how it sets the foundation for all interactions among the resources in your AWS account. We also cover the various access methods for the AWS IAM services:

- AWS Management Console
- AWS Command Line Tools
- AWS Software Development Kits (SDKs)
- IAM Query API

We also cover the various principals that can interact with AWS and how they are authenticated. We then discuss how to write policies that define permitted access to services, actions, and resources, and explain how to associate these policies with authenticated principals.

Finally, we explore additional AWS IAM features that can help you secure your AWS Cloud environment, including multifactor authentication (MFA), rotating keys, federation, AWS IAM roles, and other security best practices.

IAM Overview

AWS Identity and Access Management provides the necessary infrastructure through a set of APIs that control access to your resources on the AWS Cloud. AWS IAM gives you the ability to define authentication and authorization methods for using the resources in your account.

When you create your account, you receive a single identity that gives you full access to the resources in the account. The login information is in the form of an email address. This identity is called the *root account* or *root user*, and due to its high level of permissions, AWS recommends restricting the access to these credentials to a few people and using it sparingly. For additional security, AWS recommends that you enable MFA on your root account and do not create root access keys to make programmatic requests to AWS. You cannot reduce the permissions associated with your AWS root account, unless service control policies (SCPs) are used in member accounts from the management account in an AWS Organization.

AWS IAM empowers you to define strict access rules for individuals and other systems for interacting with resources in a specific account. For example, you can specify that a user can call a specific API from a specific IP address only during a certain period of the day. AWS IAM makes access to AWS resources possible for applications that are running on-premises or in the AWS Cloud. Such granularity allows systems administrators to comply with security and regulations that are relevant for their organizations.

AWS IAM is designed to protect the resources in your AWS account, and it should not be used as an identity provider (IdP) for your applications. If you are planning to migrate your on-premises application to the AWS Cloud and it has its own IdP, you should continue to use it as your authoritative directory. For example, if your application uses Microsoft Active Directory (AD) as its IdP, you can extend it into AWS by using the AWS Directory Service, an Active Directory–compatible directory service that is capable of integrating with your on-premises AD. On the other hand, if you plan to implement a new web or mobile application, you may consider Amazon Cognito for identity management in your applications.

How AWS IAM Works

The AWS IAM service provides the necessary infrastructure for you to implement authentication and authorization in your AWS account. To better understand the AWS IAM architecture, this section explores the main elements that compose it.

Principals

A *principal* is an AWS IAM entity that has permission to interact with resources in the AWS Cloud. Whether it is permanent or temporary, this principal can represent a human user, a resource, or an application. There are three types of principals: root users, IAM users, and IAM roles (or temporary security credentials). Principals include federated users and assumed roles.

Root Users

When you create your first account on AWS, you begin with a single identity that has complete access to all AWS resources in the account; this identity is called the *root user identity*. You can

Chapter 4 • Identity and Access Management

log in to the AWS Console using the email address and password that you provided when you created your account.

The root user credentials give you unrestricted access to all the AWS services in your account. This access covers (but is not limited to) viewing billing information, changing your root account password, and performing the complete termination of your account and deletion of its resources.

For daily operations in your AWS account, it is not necessary to use the root user. Moreover, AWS highly recommends that you not share the root user credentials with anyone, simply because doing so gives them unrestricted access to your account. There is no way to restrict the access given to the root user in the account. However, if the account is a member of an AWS Organization, it is possible to use SCPs to restrict root user account permissions.

Once you have set up your AWS account, the most important thing that you should do is protect your root user credentials by following these recommendations:

- Use a strong password to help protect account-level access to the management console.

- Enable virtual or hardware MFA with time-based one-time passwords on your AWS root user account.

- Remember that you should avoid creating an access key for programmatic access to your root user account unless such a procedure is mandatory. You can create another IAM user with the required permissions to perform the necessary actions on your account. It is possible to give administrative permissions to an IAM user.

- In case you must maintain an access key to your root user account, you should regularly rotate it using the AWS Console. You need to log in using your account's email address and password to rotate (or even delete) your access key credentials for your root account.

- Remember, never share your root user password or access keys. Anyone with access to the root user account can terminate and destroy all resources in your AWS account.

Resetting Root Users

You must be signed in as the root user to change the root user password or anything else related to the user. To execute such a procedure, take the steps shown in Exercise 4.1.

EXERCISE 4.1

Change the Root Account Password

In this exercise, you will reset the root account password.

1. Use your email address and password to log in to the AWS Console as the root user.

2. Click on the name of your account in the upper-right corner.

How AWS IAM Works 91

3. Choose Account option from the menu.

4. In the Account page, next to the Account Settings pane, click Edit.

5. Once you click, you will be redirected to the Login page to confirm your root credentials. From the options presented, choose Root User and enter the email registered for your root account.

6. Click Next, and on the following screen, enter your root password and click the Sign In button.

7. If you have MFA enabled on your root account, enter the MFA code at the prompt.

8. After you confirm your root credentials, you'll see the Update Account Settings page. Click the Edit button next to the Password field.

9. Use a strong password for your account, with a minimum of 8 and a maximum of 128 characters. It should contain a combination of the following character types: uppercase, lowercase, numbers, and special characters. Don't use simple passwords, such as *january, password, p4ssw0rd*, or your date of birth, which can be easily cracked through dictionary attacks.

You can change user account names, passwords, and email settings on the Update Account Settings page, which is shown in Figure 4.1.

If you need to reset the root account credentials, remember to delete the previous two-factor authentication information, as well as any access and secret keys that might exist for the root account. It's important to remember to reenable MFA on the account and avoid creating root access keys.

In Exercise 4.2, you can take your root account security management further by setting up MFA.

FIGURE 4.1 Update Account Settings page.

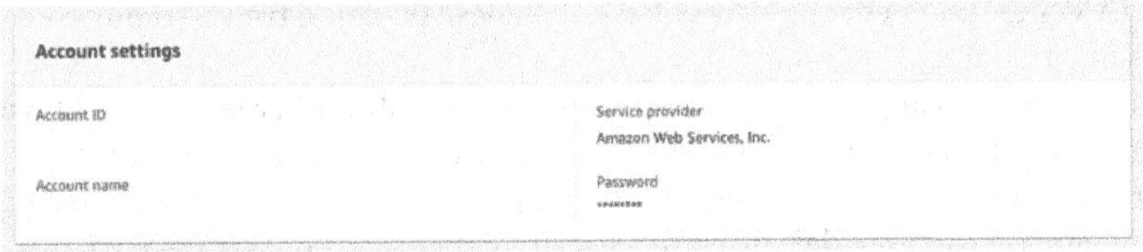

92   Chapter 4 ▪ Identity and Access Management

EXERCISE 4.2

Enable Virtual Multifactor Authentication for the Root Account

In this exercise, you will enable virtual MFA for the root account.

1. Log in to your AWS account using your root account credentials.

2. Click the name of your account and then select Security Credentials.

3. On the My Security Credentials screen, close to the Multifactor Authentication (MFA) pane, click on Assign MFA Device.

4. On the Select MFA Device screen, type a name in the Device Name field and select the Authenticator App option. Then click Next.

5. Ensure that you have an authenticator app on your mobile phone or computer. A list of compatible applications can be found on the setup device screen.

6. On the next screen, click Show QR Code and scan it using your authenticator app.

7. Enter the two consecutive codes in the MFA Code 1 and MFA Code 2 fields.

8. Click Add MFA. Now, every time you log in with your root credentials, you must provide an MFA code as part of the login process.

IAM Users

IAM users are people or applications in your organization. They live within the AWS accounts where they were created but may have cross-account permissions if configured to do so. Each IAM user has its own username and password that give them access to the AWS Console. Additionally, it is possible to create an access key to provide users with programmatic access to AWS resources.

IAM users is an entity that gives administrators the granularity required to control how users should interact with AWS resources. Note that an IAM user is not necessarily a person. It can be an application (such as SalesApp) that runs on AWS or on your corporate network and needs to interact with resources in your account. If your application is running on AWS, you should use IAM roles to provide temporary credentials for the application to access AWS resources. However, if your application is running on your corporate network, you can create an IAM user and generate access keys, so SalesApp can have the required credentials to access your resources.

In order to avoid using your root user account, you should create an IAM user or assume an IAM role and then assign administrator permissions for your account so that you can add more users when needed. Figure 4.2 shows such a scenario. In the figure, you can see the user details page as well as the list of policy permissions attached to the user.

FIGURE 4.2 IAM users and account permissions.

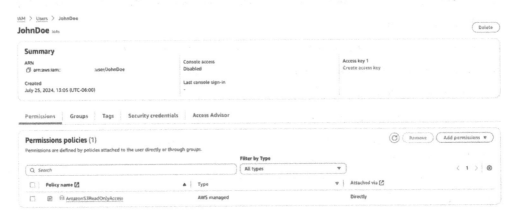

 Always remember to enforce the principle of least privilege when creating your users—that is, users should have only the minimum level of permissions they need to perform their assigned tasks. You should define fine-grained policies associated with your IAM users. Policies will be covered later in this chapter in "Access Management with Policies and Permissions."

You can create IAM users and set whatever permissions are necessary. Exercise 4.3 shows you how to create an IAM user with administrator access.

EXERCISE 4.3

Create an IAM User with Administrator Access Permissions

In this exercise, you will learn how to create a new IAM user with administrator permissions.

1. Log in to your AWS account and open the IAM service. Select Users from the left-side menu.
2. From the Users pane, click Create User.
3. In the User Name field, type **MyAdminUser**. Click on the combo box to provide access to the AWS Management Console.
4. For User type, select "I want to create an IAM user."
5. Choose whether you want to use an autogenerated password or provide your own in the Console Password section.
6. Keep selected the option to create a new password at the next sign-in.

94 Chapter 4 ▪ Identity and Access Management

EXERCISE 4.3 *(continued)*

7. Click the Next button.

8. On the Set Permissions page, select the Attach Policies Directly option.

9. Choose Administrator Access from the policy list.

10. Click the Next button.

11. On the Review page, click the Create User button.

12. On the next screen, you can send the credential details by email or download a CSV file with the credential information.

IAM Groups

An *IAM group* is a good way to allow administrators to manage users with similar permissions requirements. Administrators can create groups that are related to job functions or teams, such as administrators, developers, QA, FinOps, and operations. They can then assign fine-grained permissions to these groups.

When you add IAM users to a group, they inherit the group's permissions. With such a simple practice, it becomes easier to manage bulk changes in your environment and move IAM users around as they change or gain new responsibilities in the company.

One important thing for you to note: An IAM group is not an identity because it cannot be referred to as a principal when you're setting up permission policies. It is just a logical organization that allows you to attach policies to multiple users all at once.

Try to avoid assigning permissions directly to IAM users since these permissions are hard to track when your organization scales and users move to different organizational positions.

Figure 4.3 describes the relationship between users and groups with their related permissions.

IAM Roles

Similar to IAM users, *IAM roles* can have a permission policy that determines what the IAM role can and cannot do in AWS. IAM roles are not exclusively associated with an IAM user or group; they can also be assumed by other entities, such as applications or services.

Additionally, IAM roles do not have long-term credentials or access keys directly assigned to them during creation. When a role is assumed, it is granted temporary credentials by a service called *AWS Security Token Service (STS)*. Such temporary credentials are valid throughout the role session usage. The default lifetime of temporary security tokens issued by STS is for a maximum of 12 hours and can be configured from 15 minutes to 36 hours. These security credentials can be requested for a root user but restricted to a duration of 1 hour due to security reasons.

Roles can be used to delegate access to resources that services, applications, or users do not normally have. For example, you can allow an application to assume a role that provides

FIGURE 4.3 Groups and IAM users.

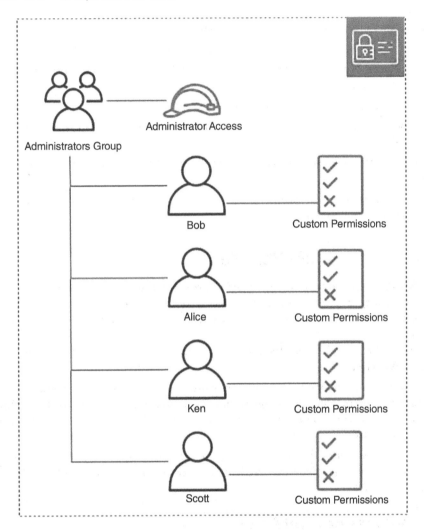

access to a resource in a different AWS account even if its original permissions did not allow such access. Another example is if your user only has access to a development account and you grant them the ability to publish content in the production account by assuming an IAM role. Yet another example is if you grant an external application access to AWS resources, but instead of using fixed credentials inside the application (which are easy to extract and hard to rotate once deployed), you can leverage an IAM role for this purpose.

Furthermore, if you want to give access to users who already have identities on your corporate authoritative directory or from another IdP, it is possible to change these credentials to IAM role credentials that provide them with temporary access to AWS resources.

IAM roles can be used in the following scenarios:

- Grant permissions to an IAM user in the same AWS account as the role.
- Grant permissions to an IAM user in a different AWS account than the role, which is also called *cross-account access*.
- Provide access for non-AWS workloads using temporary credentials.
- Provide access to your accounts by a third party by creating roles to assume with correct permissions.
- Grant permissions to AWS services by controlling what a service can access using service roles.
- In user federation scenarios, it's possible to use IAM roles to grant permissions to external users authenticated through a trusted IdP.

AWS Security Token Service

The AWS Security Token Service is designed to provide trusted users and services with temporary security credentials that control access to AWS resources. This service provides the foundation for other features such as cross-account access, service roles, and identity federation.

The main differences between long-term access keys and temporary security credentials issued by AWS STS are as follows:

- When you issue a temporary security credential, you can specify the expiration interval of that credential, which can range from a few minutes to several hours. Once expired, these credentials are no longer recognized by AWS, and any API requests made with them are denied.
- Temporary credentials are dynamic and generated every time a user requests them. A user can renew the temporary credentials before their expiration if they have permission to do so.

Roles for Cross-Account Access

Roles for cross-account access grant users of one AWS account access to resources in a different account. Such a procedure enables a different set of scenarios such as API, CLI, calls or AWS Console access.

One common use case can be two AWS accounts, such as Dev and Prod, where users from the Dev account need specific access on the Prod account. The regular permissions for a developer in the Dev account do not allow them to directly access the resources in the Prod account. However, it is possible to define a trust policy that allows a developer in the Dev account to assume a role in the Prod account. Once the trust policy is attached to the Prod role, a Dev account with the permission to assume the production role (with a `sts:AssumeRole` directive) can access the Prod account with the permissions defined by the role assumed.

In Example 4.1, the trust relationship policy definition attached to the role ProdAccess in the Prod account allows an IAM user or role in the Dev account to perform the `AssumeRole` action. Note that the policy is specifying the Dev AWS account identifier in its definition.

Real World Scenario

Example 4.1: ProdAccess Role Trust Relationship Policy Definition in the Prod Account

```
{
  "Version": "2012-10-17",
  "Statement": {
  "Effect": "Allow",
  "Principal": { "AWS": "arn:aws:iam::dev-aws-account-id:root" },
  "Action": "sts:AssumeRole",
  }
}
```

In Example 4.2, it is the policy definition attached to the user or role in the Dev account that allows them to perform the `AssumeRole` action on the ProdAccess role in the Prod account.

Real World Scenario

Example 4.2: Assume Role Permission Policy

```
{
  "Version": "2012-10-17",
  "Statement": [{
  "Effect": "Allow",
  "Action": ["sts:AssumeRole"],
  "Resource": "arn:aws:iam::prod-account-id:role/ProdAccess"
  }]
}
```

In Example 4.3, the policy definition attached to the `ProdAccess` role provides Amazon S3 bucket operations in the `production-bucket`.

Real World Scenario

Example 4.3: `ProdAccess` **Permission Policy**

```
{
 {
 "Effect": "Allow",
 "Action": [
 "s3:ListBucket",
 "s3:GetBucketLocation"
 ],
 "Resource": "arn:aws:s3:::production-bucket"
 },
 {
 "Effect": "Allow",
 "Action": [
 "s3:GetObject",
 "s3:PutObject",
 "s3:DeleteObject"
 ],
 "Resource": "arn:aws:s3:::production-bucket/*"
 }
 ]
}
```

Another common use case is when you want to grant access for a third party to your AWS resources, for example, when an external company is hired to provide monitoring and needs access to read logs from your account. Using the same model, it is possible to use IAM roles to grant access without sharing security credentials. Instead, the third party can access by assuming the role you created in your account.

In Example 4.4, the trust policy definition attached to the role provides access to a third party by specifying the AWS account number as the `Principal`. In addition, a `Condition` is included in the trust policy to validate an `ExternalId` to be used as a context key.

Real World Scenario

Example 4.4: Third-Party Trust Policy

```
"Principal": {"AWS": "Third party AWS account ID"},
"Condition": {"StringEquals": {"sts:ExternalId": "Unique ID shared by
Third Party"}}
```

AWS Service Role

The *AWS Service Role* is an IAM role that can be attached to multiple Amazon EC2 instances, which allows your applications to securely make API requests from your instances without the need to manage the security credentials that the applications use.

To further understand what this feature actually does, imagine a scenario where an application running on an Amazon EC2 instance needs to post a message to Amazon Simple Queue Service (SQS). In this scenario, you do not need to set up an IAM user with the required policies to post a message to Amazon SQS and then share the user's access keys with the developer to manage directly inside the application configuration file. Instead, you can create a role for an EC2 instance and attach a policy to the role (with the required permission to access Amazon SQS), allowing the application to assume the role and perform the actions with temporary credentials.

The same permissions apply with other AWS services, when roles are used to control what a service can access and they have a specialized purpose for a service, also known as *service-linked roles*.

When running your applications on Amazon EC2 instances, always use AWS service roles for an EC2 instance to give your applications access to AWS resources.

IAM Roles Anywhere

The *AWS Identity and Access Management Roles Anywhere* service can be used to obtain temporary security credentials for servers or applications that are running outside of AWS but are using IAM policies and IAM roles to access AWS resources.

To use this service, your workloads need to use X.509 certificates issued by your private certificate authority to establish trust between your public-key infrastructure and IAM Roles Anywhere. Then, create a signature with the certificate and call the service to get temporary security credentials.

A common use case is the possibility to enable roles for non-AWS workloads, when you have applications or services running in your data center or other infrastructure running outside of AWS but need to interact with your AWS resources. To avoid the creation, maintenance, and distribution of long-term access keys, you can use IAM Roles Anywhere. Once you have established the trust between IAM Roles Anywhere and your CA, you can create IAM roles to be assumed by your applications to get temporary credentials, taking advantage of the same policies and trust declared in the IAM service.

Access Management with Policies and Permissions

Access to AWS resources is managed through *policy documents*, which are attached to IAM identities or AWS resources. A policy is a JavaScript Object Notation (JSON) file that defines all the permissions that an identity or a resource has. When an identity or a resource makes an API request to a service, the AWS Cloud evaluates its permissions and allows the request to go through or denies it, based on a policy definition.

Here are the key points you should learn to understand how the AWS Cloud evaluates policies during API requests:

- All requests are denied by default because they follow the principle of least privilege (implicit deny).

- If your policy has an explicit allow directive, it will override the default.

- Permissions boundaries, service control policies, and session policies can override the permissions defined in policy documents.

- If you place an explicit deny on your policy, it will override any allow directive present in the document.

JSON Policy Documents

The AWS Certified Security Specialty exam requires you to understand the JSON syntax and the policy document structure. When designing simple policies, you can use the visual editor available in the AWS Console, which covers most of the everyday scenarios. In situations where you need to write more complex policies, you should leverage the JSON editor that is also available in the AWS Console.

The JSON policy document consists of the following elements:

- **Version:** This is the version of the policy language. The latest version is 2012-10-17.

- **Id (Optional):** This is an optional identifier, which is used differently depending on the service. It is allowed in resource-based policies only.

- **Statement:** This contains the remaining elements of the policy.

- **Sid (Optional):** This is an identifier used to differentiate statements. As a best practice, for complex or more customized policies, use this field as a small description of that statement.

- **Effect:** Use this element to specify whether the policy *allows* or *denies* something.

- **Principal:** Use this element only when defining resource-based policies, where you define which principal is affected by that specific statement. In identity-based policies, the principal is implicit.

- **NotPrincipal:** This element is used to deny access to all principals except the principal specified.

- **Action:** This is the list of methods that the policy allows or denies.

- **NotAction:** This element is used to explicitly match everything except the specified list of actions.

- **Resource:** This defines the resources that the policy statement applies. You specify a resource using an Amazon Resource Name (ARN).
- **NotResource:** This element matches every resource except those specified.
- **Condition (Optional):** This element allows you to implement custom logic to test values of specific keys in the context of the request. For example, you can use it to test whether the user making the request has MFA enabled (aws:MultiFactorAuthPresent).

Example 4.5 shows a JSON policy that allows read access to Amazon S3.

Real World Scenario

Example 4.5: S3 Read-Only JSON Policy

```
{
 "Version": "2012-10-17",
 "Statement": [
 {
 "Effect": "Allow",
 "Action": [
 "s3:Get*",
 "s3:List*"
 ],
 "Resource": "*"
 }
 ]
}
```

As you can see in Example 4.5, the JSON policy allows read access using Get and List operations on Amazon S3. Additionally, this policy is not restricted to a specific resource because it is using the * directive on the Resource element.

If you are not comfortable editing JSON documents to create your policies, you can use the visual editor from the AWS Console. You can see a summary of the permissions, which helps you troubleshoot and fix common errors encountered when creating IAM policies.

AWS provides a set of policy types that are available to use in different scenarios. The remainder of this section covers the most common ones.

Identity-Based Policies

Identity-based policies are JSON permissions policies that you can attach to an identity such as IAM users, IAM groups, or IAM roles. These policies define the actions that the principal can perform, and for which resources and in which conditions it might do so. AWS categorizes these policies into two types:

- **Managed policies:** Stand-alone policies that you can attach to multiple users, groups, and roles. There are two types of managed policies:
  - **AWS-managed policies:** These are policies provided and managed by AWS. They are essentially curated policies that allow you to quickly start setting up permissions to IAM identities and cover the most common use cases. For example, you can find policies by job function such as Administrator, Billing, and Database Administrator. These policies may change based on AWS's discretion. For example, when a change is made to the policy, it might impact the identities using the existing policy.
  - **Customer-managed policies:** These are policies that you create and manage in your AWS account. Once you have better understanding of your users and applications, you can start defining fine-grained permissions policies that are reusable within your AWS account.
- **Inline policies:** This type of policy is directly embedded in the entity. For example, when you create an IAM user and attach an inline policy to it, that policy will live within that entity and cannot be shared. If you delete the entity, the policy is also deleted. This type of policy gives the administrators a one-to-one relationship between the IAM entity (user, group, or role) and its permission policy.

> Managed policies provide you with features that make the day-to-day administration activities easier. These policies have the following advantages:
>
> - Reusability
> - Central change management
> - Versioning and rollback
> - Delegation of permission management

Resource-Based Policies

A resource-based policy allows you to directly attach permissions to AWS resources, such as an Amazon SQS queue or an Amazon S3 bucket. It also allows you to specify who has access to that resource even if it does not have an explicit identity-based policy that says so. Figure 4.4 shows an example of a resource-based policy for Amazon S3.

In Figure 4.4, user John does not have explicit permissions to perform the GetObject operation on the Amazon S3 bucket. However, the policy attached to the Amazon S3 bucket allows full access to the users within the AWS account, which allows the request to complete successfully.

FIGURE 4.4 Resource-based policy example.

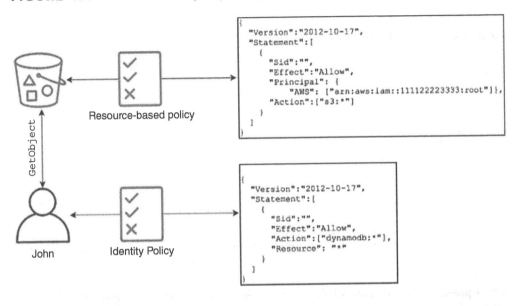

 Cross-account resource access is used in scenarios where you need to access resources in different accounts. For example, say SalesApp needs to send a message (SendMessage) to an Amazon SQS queue in the Message Broker AWS account. You should explicitly allow the role attached to SalesApp to make requests to the Amazon SQS queue on the Message Broker account. Additionally, you must add a resource-based policy to the Amazon SQS queue that allows SalesApp to perform the actions required, in this case SendMessage.

Permissions Boundaries

Permissions boundaries allow you to define the maximum permissions a user or application can be granted by IAM identity-based policies. You can use a customer-managed or an AWS-managed policy to set the permissions boundaries for an IAM user or role.

The boundaries assigned to the user or role do not give them permissions, but rather define the limits of the permissions attached to them, as shown in Examples 4.6 and 4.7.

104 Chapter 4 ▪ Identity and Access Management

> ### 🌐 Real World Scenario
>
> #### Example 4.6: Administrator User Policy
>
> ```
> {
>   "Version": "2012-10-17",
>   "Statement": [
>   {
>   "Effect": "Allow",
>   "Action":"*",
>   "Resource": "*"
>   }
>   ]
> }
> ```

> ### 🌐 Real World Scenario
>
> #### Example 4.7: Permissions Boundary to Restrict Access to Amazon S3 Operations
>
> ```
> {
>   "Version": "2012-10-17",
>   "Statement": [
>   {
>   "SID": "AllowAmazonS3AccessOnly",
>   "Effect": "Allow",
>   "Action":["s3:*"],
>   "Resource": "*"
>
>   } }
>   }
>   ]
> }
> ```

In Example 4.6, a permission policy allows administrative permission for a user or role. However, the permissions boundary assigned to the user restricts access only to Amazon S3 operations for any given bucket. Although the user has a permission policy that gives administrator access, if they try to access any other resources or services besides Amazon S3, it fails due to the permissions boundary assigned to them.

Figure 4.5 shows how the effective permissions work when you are using permissions boundaries. You can see that IAM determines the effective permissions for one specific IAM user or role and they must be allowed on both its policies and permissions boundaries.

FIGURE 4.5 Effective permissions example.

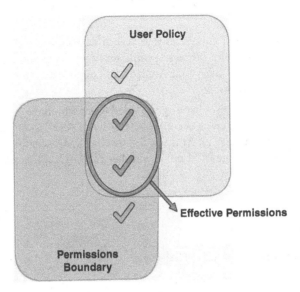

Service Control Policies

When you enable an AWS Organization service to centrally manage AWS accounts, you can use service control policies to specify the maximum permissions for one account or organizational unit. The SCPs provide a set of limits for entities in accounts within an organization, which include the root user.

Similar to the discussion about permissions boundaries, SCPs alone are not sufficient for allowing or denying access in the accounts in your organization. However, SCPs define a guardrail for what actions the principals can perform.

Access Control Lists

Access control lists (ACLs) are used to control which principals in other accounts can access specific resources. ACLs cannot be used to control access for principals in the same account. ACLs are similar to resource-based policies, but they do not use the JSON document format and are supported by few services, such as Amazon S3, AWS WAF, and Amazon VPC.

Session Policies

This type of policy can be used to limit the permissions of a session during the assume role. It is important to note that these policies do not grant permissions but only limit created sessions.

Access Management in Amazon S3

On top of the AWS IAM permission policies that you can attach to users and roles to manage AWS resources, Amazon S3 offers a specific set of resource-based policies that allows even finer-grained control over your Amazon S3 environment. Such resource-based policies are divided into two types:

- **Access control lists:** An ACL is a list of grants and users who have permission for them. It is possible to define cross-account read or write permissions using ACLs. Unlike IAM policies, ACLs use an Amazon S3–specific XML schema. AWS generally recommends that you leverage IAM policies rather than ACLs. Example 4.8 shows an Amazon S3 ACL.

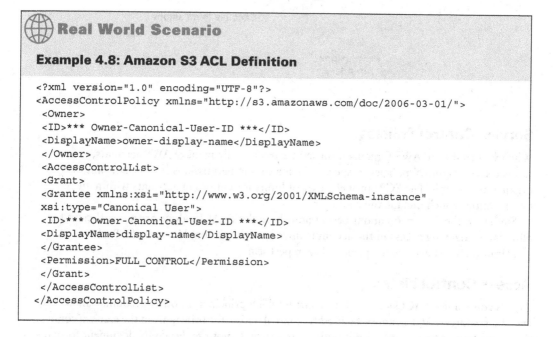

- **Bucket policy:** A bucket policy provides you with a simple way to define cross-account access to your S3 buckets without setting up IAM roles. It also gives you centralized management of your bucket permissions. Just like IAM, these policies are defined using a JSON format. You should be diligent with bucket policies to avoid making your files publicly accessible by accident. These policies can be managed per user-level, which means that you can create a bucket policy that sets specific permissions per user within a bucket. Example 4.9 shows one bucket policy that allows full read permissions to anonymous users. Bucket policies are applied at the bucket level and do not extend to object-level granularity.

Real World Scenario

Example 4.9: Amazon S3 Bucket Policy

```
{
 "Version":"2012-10-17",
 "Statement": [
 {
 "Effect":"Allow",
 "Principal": "*",
 "Action":["s3:GetObject"],
 "Resource":["arn:aws:s3:::my-bucket/*"]
 }
 ]
}
```

Be very cautious when granting anonymous access to your Amazon S3 bucket. If you do, anyone on the Internet can access the contents of your bucket. Never grant anonymous access to your buckets unless you're required to do so—for example, when you're working with static website hosting.

In Example 4.9, when specifying resources on your bucket policy statement, pay attention to the specified resource ARN of your bucket. It should contain the /* notation at the end; otherwise, you'll get an error stating that the action does not apply to any resources.

There are many ways you can manage access management from the AWS Management Console and the IAM Console. You can create IAM groups and set their level of access to Amazon S3, as shown in Exercise 4.4.

EXERCISE 4.4

Create an IAM Group with Amazon S3 Read-Only Access Role

In this exercise, you will create an IAM group and attach a role allowing read-only access to Amazon S3.

1. Log in to the AWS Management Console using the MyAdminUser credentials.
2. Go to the IAM console and select User Groups from the left-side menu.

108   Chapter 4 ▪ Identity and Access Management

EXERCISE 4.4 (continued)

3. Click Create Group.

4. For the User Group name, enter **AmazonS3Viewers**.

5. On the Attach Permissions Policies pane, search for the `AmazonS3ReadOnlyAccess` policy and then click to select it.

6. Click Create Group button.

You can also create Amazon S3 buckets, as shown in Exercise 4.5.

EXERCISE 4.5

Create an Amazon S3 Bucket

In this exercise, you will create an Amazon S3 bucket and block all public access to it.

1. Using the `MyAdminUser` credentials, log in to the AWS Management Console and go to the Amazon S3 Console.

2. Click Create Bucket.

3. Choose a region and enter a name for your bucket. Remember that Amazon S3 buckets must be unique.

4. Leave the "Block All Public Access" option selected.

5. Click the Create Bucket button.

Exercise 4.6 shows you how to add a user to your S3 group.

EXERCISE 4.6

Add a User to the AmazonS3Viewers Group

In this exercise, you will add a user to the AmazonS3Viewers group.

1. Open the IAM Console.

2. Select User Groups from the left-side menu.

3. Click on the **AmazonS3Viewers** group from the list.

4. For the Users tab, click on the Add Users button.

5. Select the user you want to add from the list.

6. Click on the Add Users button.

Policy Conflicts

When Amazon S3 needs to authorize a request to a bucket or object, it evaluates all access policies, such as user policies and resource-based policies (bucket policy, bucket ACL, and object ACL) associated with the respective target of the request.

You should always remember that when dealing with policy conflicts on Amazon S3, the AWS Cloud follows the principle of least privilege, where everything is denied by default, unless instructed otherwise by an allow. You should also observe that any explicit deny overrides any other allow policy statement.

In your preparation for the exam, remember the following steps when evaluating the policy conflicts:

1. Every bucket and object is private by default (principle of least privilege).
2. Access policies, user policies, and resource-based policies (bucket policy, bucket, and object ACLs) are all evaluated.
3. If an explicit deny is found, evaluation stops and the request is denied.
4. If an explicit allow is found, evaluation stops and the request is allowed.
5. In any other case, the request is denied (implicit deny).

Secure Data Transport in Amazon S3

Amazon S3 supports HTTP and HTTPS requests by default. However, if you want to guarantee that all data is encrypted in transit, you must create a specific bucket policy that denies any requests that meet the condition `"aws:SecureTransport": "false"`. Example 4.10 shows such a condition in action in an Amazon S3 bucket policy.

Real World Scenario

Example 4.10: Enforce HTTPS (TLS) Bucket Policy

```
{
  "Version": "2012-10-17",
  "Statement": [
    {
```

110 Chapter 4 ▪ Identity and Access Management

```
"Sid": "AllowRequests",
"Effect": "Allow",
"Principal": "*",
"Action": "s3:*",
"Resource": "arn:aws:s3:::your-s3-bucket/*"
},
{
"Sid": "ForceSSLRequests",
"Effect": "Deny",
"Principal": "*",
"Action": "s3:*",
"Resource": "arn:aws:s3:::your-s3-bucket/*",
"Condition": {
"Bool": {
"aws:SecureTransport": "false"
}
}
}
]
}
```

In Example 4.10, the policy starts by allowing all requests to the bucket. The previous statement uses a condition to deny all the requests that match the `"aws:SecureTransport": "false"` condition.

Another thing you can do is force SSL encryption for an Amazon S3 bucket, as Exercise 4.7 shows.

EXERCISE 4.7

ForceTLS Encryption for an Amazon S3 Bucket

In this exercise, you will learn how users can access your bucket files using SSL encryption through bucket policies.

1. Log in to the AWS Management Console using the **MyAdminUser** credentials.

2. Open the Amazon S3 Console and select the bucket that you created in Exercise 4.5.

3. Select the Permissions tab.

4. Click the Edit button in the Block Public Access (bucket settings) pane.

5. Deselect the Block All Public Access check box, and then click Save Changes. Type **confirm** to apply the changes, then click on the Confirm button.

6. Click Edit in the Bucket Policy pane.

7. In the Bucket Policy Editor, add the following bucket policy:

```
{
    "Version": "2012-10-17",
    "Statement": [
      {
        "Sid": "AllowRequests",
        "Action": "s3:*",
        "Effect": "Allow",
        "Resource": "arn:aws:s3:::your-s3-bucket/*",
        "Principal": "*"
      },
      {
        "Sid": "ForceSSLRequests",
        "Action": "s3:*",
        "Effect": "Deny",
        "Resource": "arn:aws:s3:::your-s3-bucket/*",
        "Condition": {
          "Bool": {
            "aws:SecureTransport": "false"
          }
        },
        "Principal": "*"
      }
    ]
}
```

8. Replace *your-s3-bucket* with the name of your bucket.

9. Click Save Changes.

10. Create a file named `hello.txt`, enter the text `AWS Security Specialty Exam`, and then click Save.

11. Upload the `hello.txt` file to your bucket.

12. Click the `hello.txt` file in the bucket.

13. In the Overview panel, search for the Object URL field and copy and paste this address into your web browser. The message "AWS Security Specialty Exam" should appear.

14. Change the protocol from HTTPS to HTTP in the Object URL. It should present an Access Denied message, confirming that the policy is working.

Cross-Region Replication in Amazon S3

Cross-region replication (CRR) replicates objects from one region to another in an asynchronous fashion. Such replication can happen between buckets owned by the same AWS account or by different accounts. Consequently, CRR allows cloud environment administrators to meet compliance requirements that demand aggregating logs into a single bucket in a different AWS account and region, miles away from the original stored data.

Additionally, you can use CRR to change object ownership at the destination bucket, restricting access to the replicated objects. Moreover, you can change the class of objects at your destination to achieve more cost-effective storage designs.

Replication only happens in a one-to-one relation, or simply, from one source to one destination. Once the object is replicated, it is not possible to replicate it again. Furthermore, when you enable CRR, you do not need to write custom policies to enforce SSL encryption during the replication, because this is done by default.

The following items detail what is replicated when CRR is enabled:

- New objects created after the replication is activated. Old objects will not be replicated unless they are changed after the replication was activated.

- Unencrypted objects.

- Encrypted objects by SSE-S3-managed keys or customer-managed keys (CMKs) stored in Amazon KMS (SSE-KMS). The latter should be explicitly enabled to work.

- Object metadata, ACL updates, any existing tags, and lock retention information.

- If you perform a `delete` operation to mark an object as deleted, this marker will be replicated.

Conversely, the following items represent what is not replicated by the CRR:

- Objects created before the CRR was enabled.

- Any objects created with SSE-C, or customer-provided encryption keys.

- Objects deleted through a `delete` operation with a version ID specified. This prevents malicious deletion of your data.

For cross-region replication to work, you should pay attention to these key requirements:

- Versioning should be enabled in both buckets (source and destination).

- Make sure that the replication role specified gives all the necessary permissions to replicate and access the objects on the source bucket.

- If the destination bucket is owned by a different AWS account, the account owner of the destination must grant the required permission to store the replicated objects. It is also possible to change object ownership during replication to the destination bucket.

- If the owner of the source bucket does not have permissions on the stored objects, the read and read_acp permissions should be granted; otherwise, replication of these objects will fail.

- The bucket owner must have permissions to access objects (ACLs) to perform the replication.

Amazon S3 Pre-Signed URLs

As mentioned in the "Policy Conflicts" section, all objects in your Amazon S3 bucket are private by default, unless you set up policies to make them accessible. However, there are situations in which you need to share objects with other users, services, or even the whole Internet through a finer-grained approach.

For such scenarios, you can leverage *pre-signed URLs*, which allow users and applications to access private objects for a limited period of time. It is important that you observe that anyone who has access to a pre-signed URL will have access to the object.

To create pre-signed URLs, you must provide security credentials, the bucket name, the expiration time interval, and the object key that you want to share. Keep in mind that the credentials being used to generate the pre-signed URL must have the right permissions to access the Amazon S3 object. The permissions defined by the pre-signed URL are scoped at the object level and do not allow any other operations at the bucket level.

You can use the Amazon S3 console, AWS API, the AWS CLI, or one of the AWS SDKs available to generate a pre-signed URL. Example 4.11 uses the AWS CLI to generate a pre-signed URL from an Amazon EC2 instance with an IAM role attached that has the `AmazonS3FullAccess` policy attached to it.

Real World Scenario

Example 4.11: Generating a Pre-Signed URL Using AWS CLI

```
> aws s3 presign s3://security-bucket-example-0009/hello.txt

# Command Output

> https://security-bucket-example-009/hello.txt?AWSAccessKeyId=AKIAEXAMPLEAC
CESSKEY&Signature=EXHCcBe%EXAMPLEKnz3r8OOAgEXAMPLE&Expires=1555531131
```

Example 4.11 uses the `presign` command, assuming there is a `hello.txt` file in the `security-bucket-example-0009` bucket. The command output is the pre-signed URL that can be shared with other users and applications.

The `presign` command has a parameter called `--expires-in` that allows you to set the expiration time of a pre-signed URL. Although it has a default value of 3600 seconds, you can increase it to up to 7 days. If want to use the Amazon S3 console to generate the pre-signed URL, the maximum expiration time is 12 hours only.

Identity Federation

Identity federation provides you with the ability to perform access management of your AWS account at one single place. In simpler terms, it allows you to exchange valid credentials from external IdPs, such as Microsoft Active Directory, through open standards, such as Security Assertion Markup Language (SAML) 2.0 and OpenID Connect (OIDC), for temporary AWS credentials provided by the Amazon STS.

To grasp the main aspects of deploying identity federation in the AWS Cloud, study these key terms:

- **Identity:** A user in your corporate or web identity store, such as Microsoft Active Directory or Facebook.
- **Identity store:** Central location where identities are stored. It represents services such as Microsoft Active Directory, Amazon, Facebook, and Google.
- **Identity broker:** A client application that performs the authentication of the users against the IdPs, then obtains AWS temporary security credentials, and finally provides the users with access to the AWS resources.

Figure 4.6 explains the identity federation process with Microsoft Active Directory to allow you to log in to the AWS Console.

The identity federation process shown in Figure 4.6 follows these steps:

1. The user logs in to an identity broker using their corporate credentials.
2. The IdP authenticates the user against the LDAP-based identity store.

FIGURE 4.6 Identity federation workflow.

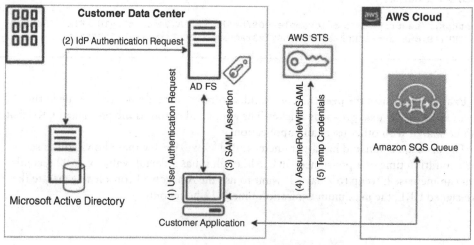

3. The IdP generates a SAML assertion with all the required user information and submits the assertion to the identity broker.

4. The identity broker calls the `AssumeRoleWithSAML` STS API, passing the SAML assertion and the role ARN to assume.

5. The API response, if successful, includes AWS temporary security credentials with its associated permissions.

6. With the temporary credentials, the client application can perform operations on AWS resources.

Identity Use Cases

There are typically two use cases for identity management and access control capabilities—customer and workforce identities. Each has its own peculiarities, such as different use cases, unique traffic patterns, and of course, different requirements for the end-user experience.

Customer Identity

Customer identities are capabilities that allow users to interact and access applications, websites, and services through a variety of channels, including computers, phones, TVs, and other devices. Usually, solutions dedicated to this use case can be critical because they focus on customers accessing applications, which can lead directly into revenue for an organization.

It is expected that a customer identity solution offer APIs with modern authentication support and scale with the numbers of users supported, usually up to 1,000 transactions per minute.

Workforce Identity

On the other side, *workforce identity* usually refers to the mechanism to control which employees have access to what resources from an organization, such as applications, data, and a set of tools that allow those users to do their job.

Amazon Cognito

In scenarios where your mobile or web applications need access to AWS resources, you can take advantage of web identity federation. Web identity federation allows you to federate access through large-scale web-based identity providers such as Amazon, Google, Facebook, or any other platform that supports OIDC and SAML IdPs.

When a user successfully authenticates in one of the IdPs, the user can exchange an authentication code, such as JSON Web Token (JWT), with temporary AWS security credentials.

To reduce complexity in scenarios where you want to implement custom authentication workflows within your web or mobile applications, AWS created Amazon Cognito, which abstracts all heavy lifting related to application authentication. Amazon Cognito offers the following built-in features:

- Sign-up, sign-in, and "forgot my password" flows
- Web user interface customization and custom authentication domain
- Custom authentication flow with CAPTCHA or MFA
- Supports OAuth 2.0, SAML 2.0, and OpenID Connect
- Fully managed user directory for your application
- Guest user support
- Access control using role-based access control (RBAC)
- User data synchronization between devices

Amazon Cognito User Pools

A *user pool* is a secure directory within Amazon Cognito that allows you to manage the users of your web or mobile applications in one place.

Users in a user pool can sign in with their registered credentials or by using a social identity from web providers such as Amazon, Google, or Facebook. Additionally, they can use SAML 2.0 or OpenID Connect with enabled identity providers.

Upon successful authentication, Amazon Cognito returns a set of JWTs that the application developer can use to secure and authorize access to application APIs. Figure 4.7 describes the sign-in flow using the Amazon Cognito user pool.

In Figure 4.7, a user from the Amazon Cognito user pool performs a successful authentication and receives JWTs in exchange that they can use in the application.

Amazon Cognito Identity Pools

Amazon Cognito identity pools allow you to create unique identifiers for guest users who access your application and authenticate these users with identity providers. You can then

FIGURE 4.7 User pool authentication flow.

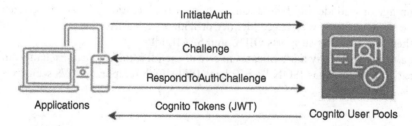

FIGURE 4.8 Cognito identity pools authentication flow.

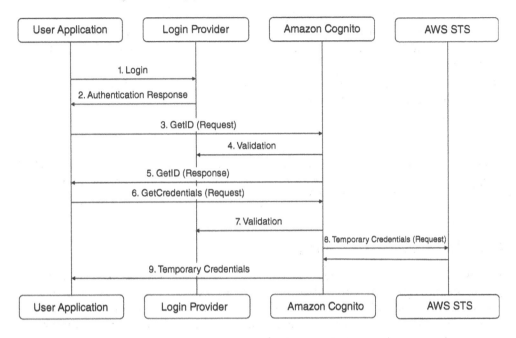

exchange these identities with temporary, limited-privilege AWS temporary credentials to access other AWS services.

Identity pools specify two types of identities—authenticated and unauthenticated—with both of them always associated with an IAM role. *Authenticated identities* represent the users who are verified by a web identity provider (Amazon Cognito user pools, Facebook, Amazon, or Google) or a custom backend authentication process. *Unauthenticated identities* represent guest users.

Figure 4.8 shows the authentication flow for Amazon Cognito identity pools using an external provider. It illustrates the following steps:

1. The user application logs in by using one of the supported web identity providers (Login Provider).
2. Upon successful authentication, the Login Provider returns a session key for the user.
3. With the session key for the user, the application issues a call to the Amazon Cognito GetId API to retrieve a unique identifier for the user.
4. Amazon Cognito validates the provided session key against the Login Provider.
5. If the session key provided is valid, the GetId API returns a unique identifier for the user.
6. The user application then sends a request to the Amazon Cognito GetCredentialsForIdentity API, passing the unique identifier returned by the GetId API, the session key from the Login Provider, and the role ARN.

7. Amazon Cognito validates the provided session key against the Login Provider and the unique identifier.

8. Upon successful validation, Amazon Cognito issues a call to the AWS STS service to retrieve temporary credentials for the user based on the role permissions specified in Step 6.

9. Amazon Cognito returns the temporary credentials to the user application, which in turn uses them to access AWS resources.

> In order to help your organization scale, you can take advantage of the AWS IAM Identity Center service, which allows you to manage single sign-on access to multiple AWS accounts in a central place.

AWS IAM Identity Center

AWS IAM Identity Center, previously known as AWS SSO, is a single sign-on managed service that provides a centralized place for your workforce to access AWS accounts and other cloud applications. The service can manage access for all AWS accounts under your AWS Organizations or for a single account, creating an account instance ideal for testing.

AWS IAM Identity Center supports identity federation using SAML 2.0 and third-party applications such as Azure Active Directory (MS Entra), Office 365, Concur, and Salesforce, or integration with AWS Managed Microsoft AD.

Additionally, IAM Identity Center provides support for the System for Cross-Domain Identity Management (SCIM) v2.0 protocol. Using SCIM, your identities are kept in sync with your IdP, providing automatic provisioning, updates, and deprovisioning of users with your IdP.

AWS IAM Identity Center is recommended to manage workforce identities, enabling improvements over accessing AWS resources using regular IAM users, for example:

- A centralized set of identities for your workforce and single sign-on for your applications
- One place to access accounts across your entire AWS Organization
- Connect your existing Identity Provider
- Multifactor authentication enforcement for your users

Microsoft AD Federation with AWS

AWS enables you to implement identity federation or integration to sign in to AWS Console using Microsoft Active Directory credentials. With this, you can use an existing corporate AD to perform all user administration and thus avoid manually creating user credentials in

Identity Federation   119

FIGURE 4.9 Authentication workflow using federation between an AWS account and Microsoft AD FS.

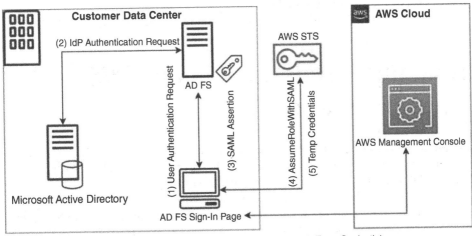

AWS. It reduces the administration overhead and enables users to use a single sign-on in the AWS Console.

When implementing AD federation, you should be aware of Microsoft Active Directory Federation Services (AD FS), a Microsoft solution that provides single sign-on access and acts as the identity broker between AWS and the Microsoft Active Directory. It resides inside your on-premises infrastructure. This setup manually exchanges SAML metadata between the two parties. The metadata contains issuer name, creation date, expiration date, and keys that AWS can use to validate the authentication information (assertions) issued by AD FS.

Although the AWS Certified Security Specialty exam does not require you to configure a Microsoft AD federation with AWS, you should have a clear understanding of how the process works. Figure 4.9 is a visual representation of the authentication workflow using identity federation with AD and your AWS account.

In Figure 4.9, you can observe the user authentication process in an identity federation with Microsoft AD following these steps:

1. A user from your corporate network logs in to AD FS, providing their Active Directory credentials.
2. Active Directory validates the user credentials.
3. Upon a successful login, AD FS returns a SAML 2.0 assertion containing all the necessary user information.
4. The user is redirected to the AWS sign-in page, which extracts the SAML 2.0 assertion.

5. The AWS sign-in page then exchanges the SAML assertion with AWS temporary credentials using the `AssumeRoleWithSAML` API.

6. With the credentials obtained in the previous step, the user is then redirected to the AWS Management Console, authenticated with their assume role temporary credentials.

Protecting Credentials with AWS Secrets Manager

AWS Secrets Manager is a managed service that allows developers, IT, and security administrators to store, rotate, manage, and retrieve database credentials (RDS and non-RDS), API keys, and other secrets throughout their life cycle.

Using AWS Secrets Manager, you can remove hard-coded credentials, passwords, and any other type of sensitive information in your code with an API call to the AWS Secrets Manager to retrieve and store secrets programmatically. AWS Secrets Manager provides integration with AWS CloudFormation through resource types that enable you to create secrets as part of an AWS CloudFormation template.

AWS Secrets Manager uses Amazon Key Management Service (KMS) to encrypt your secrets at rest. Every secret stored can have a corresponding AWS KMS CMK associated with it. In short, users can use the default AWS Managed Keys for the account or provide their own CMK.

Secrets Permission Management

You can manage the permissions associated with the secrets stored in AWS Secrets Manager by using identity-based and resource-based policies. You should always assess your environment to evaluate which type of policies to use. Keep in mind that you should choose the type that reduces your administration overhead and evolves as your organization scales.

With identity-based policies, you can grant access to many secrets for that identity, which is useful when you are setting up an IAM role for an application that requires access to more than one secret.

On the other hand, using resource-based policies enables you to grant multiple principals access to a secret. Additionally, you can define cross-account permissions for your secrets, especially in scenarios where you have a centralized security account containing all secrets that your applications require.

Automatic Secrets Rotation

AWS Secrets Manager enables you to rotate your credentials automatically for selected AWS services and databases. The rotation process takes advantage of AWS Lambda functions to orchestrate the secret rotation process.

Some services support managed rotation, where configuration and rotation are managed for you, so you don't have to use the lambda function to update the secret and credentials in the database. Services that offer managed rotations include the following:

- Amazon RDS for master user credentials
- Amazon Aurora for master user credentials
- Amazon Redshift for admin passwords

Moreover, you can implement your custom AWS Lambda rotation function for third-party services and other databases.

When you turn on automatic rotation for your supported database, AWS Secrets Manager will immediately rotate the secret once you save the configuration. Keep in mind that before enabling rotation, you need to update all of your application code to retrieve credentials from AWS Secrets Manager. Otherwise, your application will not be able to recover the secret.

Choosing Between AWS Secrets Manager and AWS Systems Manager Parameter Store

In the scenarios in which you need to store database credentials for AWS or third-party databases, manage credential rotation, and provide cross-account access, you should choose AWS Secrets Manager because it has these functionalities already built in.

On the other hand, AWS Systems Manager Parameter Store offers a central place to store environment configuration for your applications, user-defined parameters, and any other type of encrypted or plain-text information with no additional charge.

IAM Security Best Practices

The following security best practices are a set of recommendations to be used as guidelines only and do not represent a complete solution for your environment. However, they are going to be helpful to apply security principles that work for your real-world use cases.

Multifactor Authentication

It is strongly recommended to use multifactor authentication for those IAM users in your account as an additional security control to protect access to your resources. MFA uses an authentication challenge in addition to a password to complete the sign-in process.

Apply Least-Privilege Principle

Using the least-privilege principle involves granting only the permissions a user or role requires to perform their duties. This can be achieved by defining the actions that can be taken under well-known conditions for specific resources in your accounts. Using IAM policies, it is possible to assign only the required permissions for a role and reduce those permissions later, if needed, during periodic reviews.

Regularly Review Access to Your Environment

It is a best practice to perform periodic reviews to remove users, roles, groups, permissions, policies, and access keys that are no longer needed in your AWS accounts. That action will help you reduce the risk of having an account compromised or allowing the workforce, customers, or applications that no longer need access to your resources to maintain access. In addition, periodic reviews can reduce the operational work needed to monitor the activities of those accounts.

Use Conditions in IAM Policies to Further Restrict Access

As described in previous sections, you can use conditions within your IAM policies to further restrict access to your resources by validating when and how a policy statement is in effect. Use this best practice to further enforce the least-privilege principle when assigning IAM policies to your identity-based or resource-based policies.

Use IAM Roles to Provide Temporary Credentials

Especially for applications that require access to your AWS resources, when possible, use IAM roles to assign specific permissions, by relying on temporary security credentials with assume role sessions. You can assign IAM policies to that role in order to assign permissions needed for your workloads. If you have machine identities outside of your AWS environment, do not forget that it is possible to use AWS IAM Roles Anywhere, as described previously.

Use Federation for Your Workforce Accounts

It is a best practice to use temporary credentials when accessing AWS resources or accounts. It is recommended to use an identity provider to provide federated access by assuming roles and receive temporary credentials that allow requests to the AWS Cloud. For workforce identities, you can use AWS IAM Identity Center to centrally manage user identities or connect to an external identity provider that you use in your organization.

Security Best Practices for Your Root User

Protecting your root user account is important, since that account has all privileges to control your AWS resources. The following sections review some best practices to protect the root account.

Use a Strong Password

Not only for root but all your user accounts, it is recommended to use a strong password. AWS requires your password to meet the following conditions:

- Minimum of 8 and maximum of 128 characters
- Minimum of three of the following: uppercase, lowercase, numbers, and symbols (!@#¢∞¬][]{}|+-_=)
- Must not be identical to the account name or email address

Secure Your Root User Credentials

Protect your root user ID and password to prevent unauthorized use. Do not share your credentials, access keys, or private certificates with anyone except those with a valid business reason. It is recommended to use an external vault to save your credentials without dependencies on AWS services in the same account because if you forget your password, you won't be able to access AWS Secrets Manager.

Do Not Create Access Keys for Your Root User

There are few tasks and activities that need to be executed by the root user account. For that reason, you should avoid the use of access keys for the root user, and instead sign in to the AWS Management Console to complete root user tasks.

Monitor Access and Usage of Your Root Account

It is important to know when a root user account is used and which tasks were executed with the highest level of privileges, since those tasks are performed infrequently. Increased activity in the root account could indicate that the account has been compromised. It is recommended to use your usual tracking mechanism to monitor and alert when a root user signs in to an AWS account or executes API calls.

Common Access Control Troubleshooting Scenarios

As you learned in this chapter, AWS Identity and Access Management allows you to manage access to AWS services and resources securely. IAM helps you create and control AWS users and groups and use permissions to grant or deny access to AWS resources.

You can also create users and groups in IAM, and then assign individual security credentials to them (access keys, passwords, and MFA) to provide users with access to AWS services and resources. You can also manage permissions to control which operations a user can perform.

You can create roles in IAM and manage permissions to control which operations can be performed by the identity or the AWS service that assumes the role. It is also possible to define which identity is allowed to assume this role. As an AWS administrator, you can use service-linked functions to delegate permissions to AWS services that create and manage AWS resources on your behalf.

It is possible to enable identity federation to allow your current authoritative directory in your company to access the AWS Management Console, call the AWS APIs, and access resources, without the need to create an IAM user for each identity.

By default, access permissions on AWS are denied, meaning that you must be explicit about which permissions users and groups must have. When you are working with multiple policies, actions will only be allowed if no policies have explicit deny policies and at least one allow policy provides explicit access. That is, an explicit deny overrides allowed permission.

Finally, if you are using resource-based access policies (such as Amazon S3 bucket policies), do not forget to verify how these policies are configured and make sure they do not conflict with your IAM policies.

Identity Federation Problems

In AWS, there are three APIs that can be used with federated entities in the STS: `AssumeRole`, `AssumeRoleWithWebIdentity`, and `AssumeRoleWithSAML`.

The `STS:AssumeRole` API is used when you need to assume a specific role after authenticating with your AWS account or by an AWS Service.

The `STS:AssumeRoleWithWebIdentity` API is used in cases of federation with OIDC providers such as Amazon Cognito, Login with Amazon, Facebook, and Google. For example, after authenticating with an external provider, you must call the `STS:AssumeRoleWithWebIdentity` API, sending the web identity-generated token to assume a role on the platform.

Finally, the `STS:AssumeRoleWithSAML` API is used to assume a role when authenticated by a SAML-compliant service or provider, such as Microsoft Azure AD or AWS partners like Okta and OneLogin.

One thing to keep in mind when dealing with a role's identity-based policies is how they interact with session policies. A *session policy* is an inline policy that you can create on the fly and pass in the session during role assumption to further scope down the permissions of the role session. Therefore, be mindful that the effective permissions of the session are the intersection of the role's identity-based policies and the session policy.

Whenever you have problems with the authorization process, make sure you are using the correct API.

It is common to use cross-account IAM roles to access a resource that is in another AWS account. In this case, it is important to verify that the source account that will make the request is assigned the permission for the STS `AssumeRole`. Also, the IAM trust policy on the target account must authorize the source account to perform the assume role action, and there might also be a resource policy in the destination account that could prevent access.

Summary

An essential part of the success of your cloud journey is how you leverage the ability to experiment with new ideas and create solutions to quickly respond to business demands. At the same time, as the administrator of a new cloud environment, you want to maintain or improve your organization's existing security controls.

AWS Identity and Access Management (IAM) lets you build a scalable and easy-to-manage solution. With JSON-based policies, you can define fine-grained permissions for the resources in your AWS accounts. Furthermore, using IAM roles, you can control access between resources that are located in different AWS accounts.

When designing your identity and access strategy, you can take advantage of the AWS IAM Identity Center to provide a single place for your users to access all of your company's AWS accounts.

If you are building mobile or web applications that need to scale to hundreds of millions of users, you can use Amazon Cognito to integrate users with third-party identity providers such as Google, Facebook, and Amazon. And in case you need to continue to use your corporate identity provider for such applications, you can use SAML 2.0 federation methods available on AWS. Additionally, you can take advantage of AWS Secrets Manager to store, rotate, manage, and retrieve database credentials and other secrets.

Finally, Amazon S3 provides security features that allow you to use resource-based and identity-based policies to define who can access the data in your buckets and how it can be accessed. You can also use these policies in association with access control lists to create fine-grained per-object permissions. You can also replicate data across regions and accounts using cross-region replication to meet compliance requirements that might dictate that you store data in different AWS regions.

126 Chapter 4 • Identity and Access Management

Exam Essentials

Understand the criticality of the root account user. The root account user provides complete and unrestricted access to all the services and resources in your account. It is crucial that you use a strong password, enable MFA for your root account user, and keep the usage of this account to a bare minimum. It is best not to create a root user access key, unless you *must* have one. If an administrator leaves the company, make sure that you create a new password, re-create the MFA, and delete or disable any access keys. Additionally, review IAM users periodically to guarantee that they are valid and still needed, otherwise remove them.

Understand how IAM works. AWS Identity and Access Management provides the constructs and necessary infrastructure for you to manage authentication and authorization for your AWS account and all the resources in it. Principals can represent a person or an application that uses an IAM user or an IAM role to send requests to the AWS Cloud. When you create a user or role, by default, it does not have permission to perform any actions on your account. You define the required permissions by using IAM policies, which are JSON documents that specify the resources and actions that the specified principal can perform.

Understand Amazon S3. A bucket policy is a type of resource-based policy directly attached to your Amazon S3 bucket. When using bucket policies, you have a central location to manage how principals access your bucket. Moreover, you use bucket policies to define cross-account access to your bucket. These policies can be fine-grained to the user level. For example, user John can only make PUT objects while Mike can perform READ and PUT actions.

Amazon S3 ACLs are a legacy mechanism for managing permissions for your Amazon S3 bucket and objects. Different from JSON policies, ACLs use XML syntax to define permissions. You can use Amazon S3 ACLs to define permissions to individual objects, whereas Amazon S3 bucket policies only apply to the bucket level. For the exam, remember that Amazon S3 ACLs can only grant permissions to other AWS accounts, and you cannot use them to define permissions to users in your account. Finally, you cannot explicitly define DENY permissions using Amazon S3 ACLs.

AWS follows the principle of least privilege, which denotes that any permission evaluation defaults to a DENY unless an explicit ALLOW exists. When authorizing a request, Amazon S3 evaluates whether the principal performing the request action has all the permissions to perform that action. It gathers all access policies, identity policies, and resource-based policies to validate if the request can complete successfully. If any of the policies evaluated have an explicit DENY for the specified action in the request, the evaluation process stops, and the requisition is not allowed.

Cross-region replication allows you to copy objects across Amazon S3 buckets between regions and AWS accounts. The replication process retains object metadata, deletion markers (the deletes for versions are not retained), and storage classes. You can specify different storage classes for your objects during replication. All the replication has SSL/TLS enabled by default.

Understand identity federation using Microsoft Active Directory. AWS allows you to implement identity federation using identity providers (IdPs) that support SAML 2.0 standards, providing access for your corporate users to the AWS Console or the AWS CLI. To enable identity federation with Microsoft Active Directory, you are required to create a SAML provider in AWS to establish a connection with Microsoft Active Directory Federation Services. In addition, you need to create IAM roles that map to Microsoft Active Directory groups. This way, when a user logs in, the AWS Security Token Services creates temporary security credentials based on the permissions defined in the assigned role. Finally, with the provided temporary credentials, the federated user can access resources and services in your AWS account.

128 Chapter 4 • Identity and Access Management

Review Questions

1. When you first create your AWS account, what is a good practice to protect your root account and provide secure access to your AWS resources?

    A. Create access keys and secret keys for the root account.

    B. Avoid the use of contact information with the intention to protect confidential information.

    C. Create an easy-to-remember password for the root account.

    D. Enable multifactor authentication for the root account.

2. When you're creating resource-based policies, can you use IAM groups as principals?

    A. Yes.

    B. No.

    C. This relationship does not make sense.

    D. More information is needed.

3. When writing a resource-based policy, what are the minimum required elements for it to be valid?

    A. Version, Statement, Effect, Resource, and Action

    B. Version, Statement, Effect, Principal, SID, and Action

    C. Version, Statement, Effect, Principal, and Action

    D. Version, Statement, Effect, Resource, and Condition

4. What IAM feature can you use to control the maximum permission an identity-based policy can grant to an IAM entity?

    A. Service control policy (SCP)

    B. Session policies

    C. Permissions boundary

    D. All the above

5. How do you enforce SSL when you have enabled cross-region replication for your Amazon S3 bucket?

    A. In the configuration wizard, you must select Use SSL when you enable cross-region replication.

    B. Create a bucket policy that denies requests with a condition where `aws:SecureTransport` is `false`.

    C. SSL is enabled by default when using cross-region replication.

    D. Enable `SecureTransport` in the Amazon S3 console.

6. You created an S3 bucket and assigned it a resource-based policy that allows users from other AWS accounts to upload objects to this bucket. What is the only way to manage the permissions for the uploaded objects?

A. Create a bucket policy specifying the path where the objects were uploaded.

B. Create an IAM role that gives full access permissions to users and groups that have this role attached.

C. The owner of the objects must use ACLs to manage the permissions.

D. None of the above.

7. What is a valid amount of time that temporary credentials issued by AWS Security Token Services (STS) can be requested?

A. Temporary credentials do not expire.

B. From 15 minutes up to a maximum of 12 hours.

C. From 1 to 15 minutes.

D. It is not possible to control the valid amount of time when requesting a temporary credential.

8. Developers in your company are building a new platform where users will be able to log in using their social identity providers and upload photos to an Amazon S3 bucket. Which actions should you take to enable the users to authenticate to the web application and upload photos to Amazon S3? (Choose two.)

A. Configure the SAML identity provider in Amazon Cognito to map attributes to the Amazon Cognito user pool attributes.

B. Configure Amazon Cognito for identity federation using the required social identity providers.

C. Create an Amazon Cognito group and assign an IAM role with permissions to upload files to the Amazon S3 bucket.

D. Create an IAM identity provider, with the Provider Type set to OpenID Connect.

9. One of your administrators created an Amazon S3 pre-signed URL and shared it with an external customer to upload system logs. However, the user's access is denied when they try to upload the logs. What are the possible reasons that the user cannot upload the logs? (Choose two.)

A. Users uploading the files are not providing the correct access and secret keys.

B. The administrator who generated the pre-signed URL does not have access to the S3 bucket where the logs need to be uploaded.

C. There is a bucket policy not allowing users to access the bucket using pre-signed URLs.

D. The pre-signed URL has expired.

130 Chapter 4 ▪ Identity and Access Management

10. Which of the following are best practices for AWS IAM to help secure your AWS resources? (Choose two.)

  A. Require MFA.

  B. Assign only permissions required for a role using the least-privilege principle.

  C. Review and remove users that are no longer in use in a daily basis.

  D. Use default password policies in IAM for users accessing your account.

Chapter 5

Security Logging and Monitoring

THE AWS CERTIFIED SECURITY SPECIALTY EXAM OBJECTIVES THAT LEVERAGE CONCEPTS EXPLAINED IN THIS CHAPTER INCLUDE THE FOLLOWING:

✔ **Domain 1: Threat Detection and Incident Response**
  - 1.2. Detect security threats and anomalies by using AWS services

✔ **Domain 2: Security Logging and Monitoring**
  - 2.1. Design and implement monitoring and alerting to address security events
  - 2.2. Troubleshoot security monitoring and alerting
  - 2.3. Design and implement a logging solution
  - 2.4. Troubleshoot logging solutions
  - 2.5. Design a log analysis solution

✔ **Domain 6: Management and Security Governance**
  - 6.3. Evaluate the compliance of AWS resources

Introduction

An important part of the security cycle is being able to understand what is actually happening in an environment. Think about this: if a tree falls in the middle of the forest and nobody hears it, does it make a sound?

Well, as a security professional, it is important for you to notice when trees go down, even if there seems to be no sound or other consequences. Such observation can be an indicator of something not working as expected or a warning of a future, undesired consequence. That is why security experts put effort into having sensors in the right place to learn what is happening. At some point, even if you cannot see inside a system, you should at least infer what is happening within it through its generated events. This practice is known as *observability*.

Think of resources in your AWS account as observable objects. These resources and the information they manage (extract, process, store, transmit, analyze, generate, or archive) are the assets you want to protect. These resources follow a life cycle and are also executing actions as part of their job inside a system. And the resources are not isolated: they interact with internal and external components and respond to those interactions. Therefore, these resources are dynamic.

In this chapter, you learn how to gather information about the status of your resources and, most importantly, the events related to them. These events represent how the resources are being affected and how they are interacting with other resources, either internal or external to your organization.

Detecting, logging, monitoring, and presenting events in the form of observable records is not the end of the process. In the AWS Cloud, you have great capabilities, such as those for big data analysis and automation, that add value to this detection process. Big data analytical capabilities provide tools to extract findings out of the huge amount of raw detected data and deliver as processed events in the form of observable records. Automation allows you to evolve from being a mere viewer to a security enforcer. Although the remediation controls are not in the scope of this chapter, you do learn the basics about automated remediation capabilities of the detective controls. Blend these capabilities with the enlarged visibility the AWS Cloud provides and you will understand one of the main reasons multiple professionals acknowledge that they are more secure in the cloud.

Introduction

To explain the various detective controls, this chapter follows the framework presented in the form of a flow shown in Figure 5.1.

As you can see in Figure 5.1, the framework is split into four main stages: resources state, events collection, events analysis, and action.

The flow starts with a collection of resources and the act of keeping track of its configuration and status over time. These resources are the "objects" that are under observation. They can be AWS resources (such as Amazon EC2 instances or REST APIs published on Amazon API Gateway), external resources (such as software-as-a-service [SaaS] or custom applications), or AWS Cloud services themselves (for example, a service reporting the API calls it receives or a network component reporting the traffic it is processing).

In essence, these services do not focus on detecting changes but on establishing a series of static pictures. Just like in a movie, if you have enough snapshots over a period of time, you can observe movement by watching the sequence of these pictures. This resource collection is the first stage, the resources state.

Because these resources commonly serve business processes, they change over time, either due to the intrinsic automation of cloud computing environments or in order to accommodate changes to generate better business outcomes. All of it represents movement or, simply, modifications in the environment.

An event is the representation of such a change or an action on the environment. Just like a tree falling in the middle of a forest, an event can happen at any time, and you need the right tools to record it as an observable record. The second stage, events collection, deals with registering the events occurring in the environment. The creation of these records can

FIGURE 5.1 Detective controls flow framework.

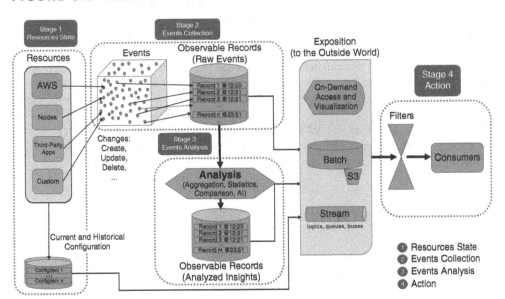

be passive or active. A record is passively created when external sources are responsible for sending event notifications to the detective control. By contrast, a record is actively created if the detective service intentionally looks for information. There are AWS Cloud services that use both methods.

Detective services can generate a large amount of information, and the security professional faces the challenge of extracting value from that information. It is at this point that you enter the third stage, events analysis, where the raw records are processed to produce value-added information. This analysis can be done in different ways. For instance, it can compare the event with a best practice or a baseline and inform you when differences exist between the desired and the current situation.

A service can also use statistics to determine whether the event is normal, or even leverage machine learning techniques to identify suspicious operations. At this stage, the service can also have a passive or active posture. In comparison, a passive posture characterizes an analysis based on the received observable records, while an active posture intentionally gathers additional information from the environment. The final result of the third stage is also a repository of observable records, but in this case, they are a direct result of an analytical process.

AWS services can provide a user-friendly view of these observable records (both before and after the event analysis stage). Tools are available to manage those records, supporting a workflow to give the proper follow-up to security events.

Both the unfiltered observable records and the analyzed records repositories provide mechanisms for consuming them, in addition to visualizing or requesting the records via API calls. These mechanisms can be classified as batches or streams in light of how they grant access to the information. Processing as a batch means producing a historical view of the records that you can work on. Services can also provide access to observable records as a stream, which allows you to receive the event as soon as it is reported.

In the fourth stage, the action stage, you connect the detection controls with reactive actions, through the magic of automation in the cloud. In Chapter 8, "Threat Detection and Incident Response," you learn about automatic reactions, but this chapter introduces you to how some detective services can generate a response to observable events. In the action stage, Amazon EventBridge is arguably one of the most powerful tools in the AWS Cloud. The role of EventBridge is to connect the source of events with consumers who can respond to those events.

This chapter introduces several AWS Cloud services supporting different detective activities. Although most of them carry out tasks for multiple stages in the detective controls flow framework, you analyze each one in light of its primary goal within the framework.

Stage 1: Resources State

The first stage in the detective framework focuses on knowing the state of the monitored resources. AWS provides tools that assess the current situation of resources at different levels and keep historical track of their state. Of course, having that kind of information enables AWS services to work into other stages via trigger actions and calls to other services.

AWS Config

AWS resources inside your account have their own configuration at each point in time. AWS Config is the service that allows you to keep track of the configuration of these AWS resources.

In Chapter 2, "Cloud Security Principles and Frameworks," you learned about the AWS Shared Responsibility Model. The observability of events is heavily based on that model. AWS Config provides you with information about monitored resources, visible to AWS because it falls in their part of the shared responsibility model. For example, according to the shared responsibility model, AWS Config obtains information like Instance ID, IAM role, IP addresses, and security groups from Amazon EC2 instances, but it does not have access to the processes that are running inside the instance (as they belong to the customer portion of the shared responsibility model).

AWS Config allows you to monitor several types of resources inside your account, including compute, serverless, databases, storage, and security, among many others. It starts monitoring by turning on a configuration recorder. This component's mission is to keep track of configuration items (a document containing the configuration information of a resource) for the monitored resources, updating them each time a resource is created, updated, or deleted. The service provides one configuration recorder per account per region. You can define the resources you want to monitor per configuration recorder, as a choice between all supported resource types (current and future), define exceptions, or define a subset of them. AWS Config documentation provides an updated list of supported resource types. This collection of resources is called the recording group. Once you have the configuration recorder created, you can stop and start it via API calls or through the AWS Management Console. After the configuration recorder is successfully started, it is in "recording on" mode, and it tracks changes of the monitored resources by recording a new configuration item when a change in the configuration is detected, either in the monitored resource itself or in any of its related monitored resources (called *relationships*, which you learn about later in this section). The CLI command `describe-configuration-recorder-status` returns the status of the configuration recorder.

The configuration recorder captures information by calling the APIs of the monitored resources. It takes a few minutes for the configuration recorder to update the changes after they occurred.

In essence, the configuration recorder saves each monitored resource's configuration and updates the information according to the detected changes. The information gathered from each monitored resource is stored in a construct called the *configuration item*. You can think of a configuration item as a JSON object that contains the configuration of a resource from the AWS point of view. In fact, this JSON file contains the following information: metadata, attributes (including tags, resource ID, resource type, creation time, Amazon Resource Name, and availability zone), relationships, and current configuration. The current configuration section corresponds to the information that is retrieved by calling the describe or list APIs of the resource.

Relationships are descriptions of connections among different resources. For example, an Amazon EC2 instance has a relationship with a network interface. From the network interface's standpoint, the relationship has the name "is attached to" (the instance); from the instance's point of view, the relationship has the name "contains" (the network interface). Such information is described as part of the JSON object. The available relationships are described in detail in the AWS Config documentation, if you are looking for more information.

You can define the retention period for the configuration items, from 30 days to 2,557 days (7 years, the default configuration).

AWS Config provides you with a repository of configurations for each monitored resource. You can look for a specific resource (or group of resources) and ask for their current configuration item. You can do it through the AWS Config Console, under the Resources menu, or you can use the BatchGetResourceConfig API.

You can also use a SQL-like syntax to query information from the current configuration state of a monitored resource. This feature, called *advanced queries*, allows you to look for resource information directly inside the configuration items, without directly calling APIs to the resource. The queries can be executed directly within the AWS Management Console or by calling the SelectResourceConfig API.

Moreover, AWS Config can provide a holistic picture of the current configuration: a configuration snapshot. In practice, a configuration snapshot is a JSON file that contains the current configuration for all the monitored resources. This file is delivered into an Amazon S3 bucket you own. You can manually create such a snapshot by calling the DeliverConfigSnapshot API at any time, or by scheduling a periodic delivery to occur every 1, 3, 6, 12, or 24 hours.

At this point, you have seen AWS Config recording static configurations; however, these resources are not static in nature. As they change their configuration over time, AWS Config (with its configuration recorder on) keeps track of those changes. Not only that, but AWS Config also correlates the changes in a resource with the events that produced it (for example, the API call that produced a change in the resource's configuration). AWS Config takes a "photo" of the new configuration each time a detected change happens and stores that new configuration in conjunction with information about what caused the change. This sequence of "pictures" for a specific resource is known as a *resource timeline*.

Consequently, AWS Config keeps the observable records of events along with configuration items. The service acts in a passive way when resources inform AWS Config that a change occurred, but it also acts in an active way because at that point, AWS Config calls the APIs to get information about the new status of the resource.

In the AWS Config Console, you can access the current configuration of a monitored resource by accessing the Resource view (as shown in Figure 5.2).

From there, click the Resource Timeline button, and the AWS Config Console will present you with a time-ordered list of recorded events that affected the resource, composed of

Stage 1: Resources State

configuration, compliance, and CloudTrail events (as shown in Figure 5.3). If you want to obtain a list of configuration items (current and past) for a monitored resource, you should call the `GetResourceConfigHistory` API.

FIGURE 5.2 AWS Config Console: Resource view.

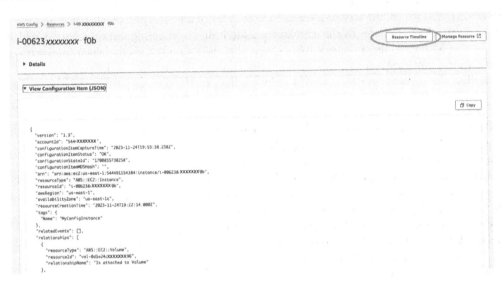

FIGURE 5.3 AWS Config Console: Resource Timeline view.

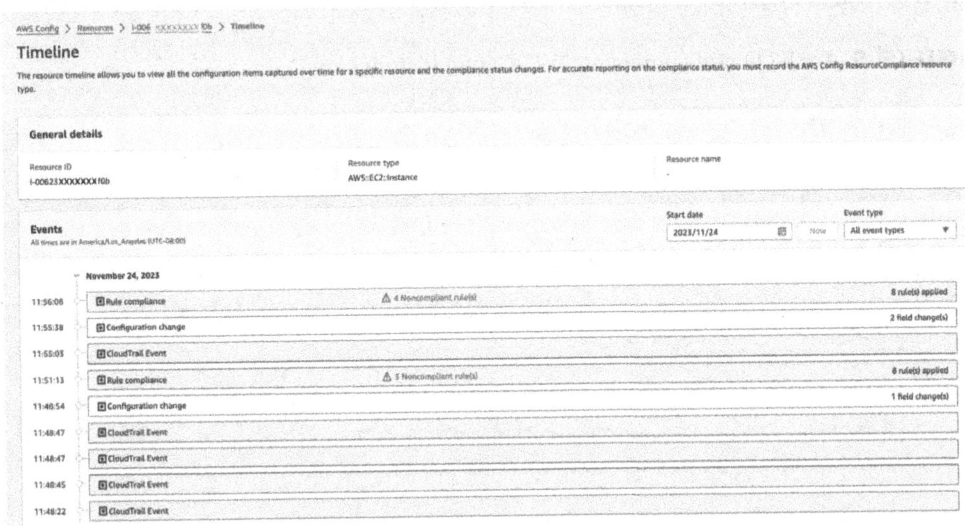

138 Chapter 5 ▪ Security Logging and Monitoring

By default, the AWS Config Console provides a list of events in reverse chronological order. So, the Start Date field refers to the most recent date for which the history is requested.

As you can see, AWS Config records very useful information. To expose such information to the external world, the service leverages the concept of a delivery channel. Think about the delivery channel simply as the mandatory setup inside your configuration recorder, which defines an S3 bucket and an optional SNS topic that AWS Config uses to deliver information (such as the configuration snapshots) and notifications. You can create a delivery channel by calling the `PutDeliveryChannel` API or by configuring the settings page in the AWS Config Console.

Depending on how the information is organized and delivered through the delivery channel, you can have different views. Besides configuration snapshots and configuration timelines, AWS Config also provides a configuration history: a collection of recorded configuration items that changed over a specified time period. AWS Config automatically delivers configuration history files every 6 hours to the S3 bucket configured in the delivery channel. Such a collection contains all configuration items of the monitored resources that changed since the last delivery (if there were several changes during that period, each one of the configuration items would be part of the configuration history files). Each configuration history file corresponds to a different resource type.

To better illustrate this, Figure 5.4 shows an example of AWS Config history files delivered to an S3 bucket.

The information collected by AWS Config can also be provided in a stream, which means being notified as soon as a change is detected. This method is called a configuration stream, and it uses the topic defined in the delivery channel. The same topic is used to deliver several notifications (like the creation of a historical record or a snapshot), so AWS

FIGURE 5.4 S3 bucket containing AWS Config History files.

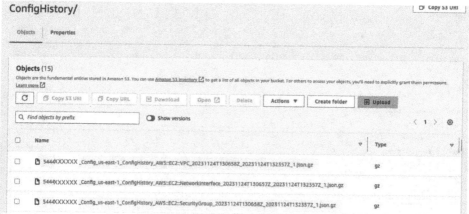

Stage 1: Resources State   **139**

TABLE 5.1   Comparison of Different "Views" for Configuration Items

Configuration View	Contains	Frequency	Delivery Channel
Configuration History files	Files with all configuration items (grouped by resource type) of resources that changed since last delivery	6 hours (fixed)	Amazon S3 bucket (`ConfigHistory` prefix)
Configuration Snapshot	One file with all the current configuration items	Manual or configurable to 1, 3, 6, 12, 24 hours	Amazon S3 bucket (`ConfigSnapshot` prefix)
Configuration Stream	Configuration items as messages in a topic, delivered as soon as they were detected by Config	Continuous (within minutes)	Amazon SNS topic `messageType:` `Configuration` `ItemChangeNotification`

Config uses the `messageType` key inside the message body to signal which information the notification contains. For the configuration stream, the value for the `messageType` key is `ConfigurationItemChangeNotification`.

Table 5.1 compares the different views that AWS Config provides.

With what you have learned, you can already insert the AWS Config capabilities in the detective framework proposed in this chapter's introduction. Figure 5.5 shows the AWS Config concepts we have presented so far and how they are related to the framework.

The main goal of AWS Config is to record configuration and changes of the resources and not analyze them. In other words, AWS Config does not judge if a change is good or bad, or if it needs to execute an action. Such a role will be accomplished by a component called *AWS Config Rules*, which is discussed in the "Stage 3: Events Analysis" section.

When considering multiple AWS accounts and regions, AWS Config provides the concept of an aggregator. An *aggregator* is a Config resource type that allows you to access information about resources and compliance outside your current region and account. To set up an aggregator, first you choose one account and region to host it. Then, you configure the accounts and regions your aggregator will have access to (referred as source accounts and source regions). AWS Config integrates with the concept of AWS Organizations, so you can easily make all the accounts inside one organization report to an aggregator. An aggregator can read configuration and compliance data recorded by AWS Config, but it cannot modify a resource's configuration.

AWS Config can also integrate with external resources like on-premises servers and applications, third-party monitoring applications, or version control systems. You can

FIGURE 5.5 AWS Config and the detective framework.

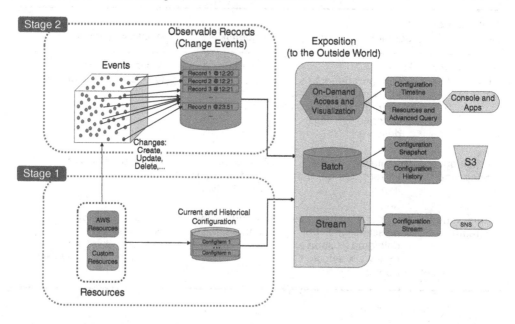

publish configuration items for these resources to AWS Config, so you can manage the resource inventory. You can also have the resources registered with AWS CloudFormation. In this case, if you apply changes to the resources using AWS CloudFormation templates, they will be recorded by AWS Config.

The AWS Config recorder component can be disabled at any time, which will cause it to stop checking for new changes of the monitored resources, and so any other analysis will be disabled from that point on. However, the recorder will keep available previous records until the end of the configured retention period.

To complete the exercises in this chapter, use the AWS Management Console. Start by logging in and choosing a region of your preference. One highly recommended option is to tag the resources created during these exercises with a `Cost Center` key and a `security-chapter5` value.

In Exercise 5.1, you practice how to set up AWS Config to start monitoring resources in your AWS account.

Stage 1: Resources State   **141**

EXERCISE 5.1

Set Up AWS Config

1. Access the AWS Config Console.

2. If this is the first time you've configured AWS Config in the chosen region, use the Get Started wizard. Otherwise, open the Settings menu, click in the Edit button, and make sure the Enable Recording check box is selected.

3. Under the General Settings section, choose "Record All Current and Future Resource Types Supported in this Region" as your recording strategy. Select "Create AWS Config Service-Linked Role" (or "Use an Existing AWS Config Service-Linked Role" if you're not using the wizard) as the IAM role for AWS Config. Leave the "Include Globally Recorded Resource Types" check box unselected.

4. Under the Delivery Method section, select Create a Bucket. Use the S3 bucket name of your preference, and type `security-chapter5` as its prefix. This will be the S3 bucket where AWS Config will deliver its files.

5. Still within the Delivery Method section, mark the "Stream Configuration Changes and Notifications to an Amazon SNS Topic" check box. Select Create a Topic and name the topic `config-topic-security-chapter5`.

6. If you are using the Get Started wizard, click Next to finish the first part of the configuration. Otherwise, click Save and skip to Step 9.

7. Click Next in the AWS Managed Rules page (at this point, you won't configure any AWS Config rules).

8. Review the final page and click Confirm.

9. Subscribe an email account to the Amazon SNS topic you created in Step 5.

10. Execute changes in your account: launch a new EC2 instance. Once the new instance is running, modify the configuration of the security group attached to it.

11. Wait 15 minutes.

12. In the AWS Config Console, open the Resources menu. Select AWS EC2 Instance and AWS EC2 Security Group under the Resource Type field. The recently launched instance and the modified security group appear in the list.

13. In the resource list, click on the security group ID. Browse through the configuration item and resource timeline details. Do the same with the resource representing the recently launched EC2 instance.

14. Check the email account you configured in Step 9. You should have received notifications related to your newly launched EC2 instance, and the modified security group.

142　Chapter 5 ▪ Security Logging and Monitoring

EXERCISE 5.1 *(continued)*

15. (Optional) Using AWS CloudShell, execute the `deliver-config-snapshot` command to have a snapshot delivered (use the `describe-delivery-channels` command to gather information about Config delivery channels). Check the S3 bucket you created in Step 4. Look for snapshot files with `ConfigSnapshot` in the prefix.

16. (Optional) Wait for 6 hours and check the S3 bucket for history files with `ConfigHistory` in their prefix.

AWS Systems Manager

AWS Systems Manager is a comprehensive service that assembles many capabilities. As a whole, the service simplifies the administration of large fleets of instances (Amazon EC2, on-premises servers, or other cloud providers), especially for operational activities. In the past, this service was known as AWS EC2 Simple Systems Manager. Today, you can refer to it simply as SSM (an acronym you will find in this book, as well as in the AWS official documentation).

Because of its myriad features, when approaching the AWS Systems Manager service, it is easier to analyze through the lens of its capabilities instead of the whole service. AWS Systems Manager's capabilities are grouped under these four categories:

- **Operations management:** Provides the current state of your environment and how its components are performing. It covers features such as Explorer, OpsCenter, CloudWatch Dashboard, and Incident Manager.

- **Application management:** Administers applications distributed among several components, environments, and AWS accounts.

- **Change management:** Allows you to specify a sequence of actions to be executed on your managed instances, and how to control its execution.

- **Node management:** Manages instances and nodes at scale.

Some SSM capabilities allow you to interact with monitored resources (instances) at deeper levels (like gathering information directly from the operating system or applications, executing commands inside the operating system, or establishing a terminal administration channel into the instances). This deeper interaction is possible due to a software component called the *SSM agent*. The agent acts as the representative of the service inside the instance.

One of the SSM's capabilities, called *inventory*, leverages the SSM agent to extract metadata (such as software and applications deployed within the instance), enabling the state tracking of these resources. Once the information is collected, SSM can export it to an S3 bucket you own (by configuring a component called *resource data sync*). In SSM Inventory, you define the type of data you want to collect and how frequently; once an initial sync is completed, the resource data sync will keep the information in your Amazon S3 bucket updated accordingly.

To access such information, you can query the Inventory capability in SSM (via console or API calls) or the information in S3 (through Amazon Athena, or Amazon QuickSight). You can also use an embedded functionality in the SSM Inventory console called *detailed view*, which provides a way to directly query inventory information in your S3 bucket (exported by a resource data sync). This functionality in fact uses Amazon Athena and AWS Glue.

Next, the application manager capability (under the Application Management category) provides you with a better view of AWS resources in your account by grouping them under the concept of an *application* (a logical group of resources that you want to operate as a single unit). You can create a custom application by defining resource groups, or by a set of tags that your components share. You can also create a custom enterprise workload (like SAP HANA). Finally, you can define applications by importing group of resources from AWS CloudFormation, Amazon EKS, Amazon ECS, AWS Service Catalog AppRegistry, and AWS Launch Wizard. Once your application is defined in Application Manager, it will consolidate data provided by other services like AWS Config, AWS Billing, and Amazon CloudWatch, as well as providing other SSM capabilities.

The Operations Management category is mostly applicable to stage 1 of the detective framework. The Explorer, Ops Center, and CloudWatch dashboards capabilities grouped under this category do not create or analyze new information. Their focus is to provide a central point of view for several operational metrics (like CloudWatch dashboards), and a list of created operational tickets (ops items). As such, this capability is a visualization tool that aggregates different information into a single pane.

Stage 2: Events Collection

Events are at the core of the detection task. These events represent the activities that are happening, affecting the resources and producing changes. In a dynamic environment, these changes are constantly occurring. A detective system will capture those changes and convert them into observable records.

At the second stage of the framework presented in the chapter's introduction, the focus is not on deciding if the event is good or bad, but on capturing as many interesting events as possible and representing them as records in a repository. Therefore, the collection of events into observable records is at the core of a detective control in this stage.

AWS CloudTrail

All the requests to AWS Cloud services happen through authenticated and authorized API calls. AWS CloudTrail is the service in charge of keeping records of these calls. The service also records non-API events related to service actions and to sign-in attempts for the AWS Console, AWS Discussion Forums, and AWS Support Center.

144 Chapter 5 ▪ Security Logging and Monitoring

Actions taken by an IAM principal (such as a user, a role, or an AWS service) are recorded as events in AWS CloudTrail. The basic unit of activity recording in AWS CloudTrail is called an *event*, which is represented by the record that contains the logged activity. There are three types of events:

- **Management:** Operations performed on AWS resources, or control plane operations, and non-API events, like sign-in operations.

- **Data:** Logs of API operations performed on or within a resource, also known as data plane operations (for example, `PutObject` or `GetObject` operations on an Amazon S3 object or an `Invoke` operation on an AWS Lambda function).

- **Insights:** "Meta-events," generated by CloudTrail when it detects unusual management API activity.

The fields of a recorded event (as shown in Example 5.1) include the activity description and metadata. They provide information about *what* was done (for example, `eventName`, `eventSource`, `requestParameters`, `responseElements`, or `resources`), *who* did it (information about the principal and how it was authenticated; for example, `userIdentity`, which itself includes other attributes like `type`, `principalID`, `arn`, and `accountID`), *when* (`eventTime`), and *where* (for example, `awsRegion`, `sourceIPAddress`, `userAgent`, or `recipientAccountId`). In addition, there is context information about the event itself, like `eventVersion`, `eventType`, `eventCategory`, and `tlsDetails` attributes. Depending on the event, the `eventCategory` field takes one of the three values: Management, Data, or Insight.

🌐 **Real World Scenario**

Example 5.1: CloudTrail's Management Event

```
{
    "eventVersion": "1.08",
    "userIdentity": {
        "type": "AssumedRole",
        "principalId": "AROAUUEDLRTHJNMAUHIJK:i-2131480aa11ee2233",
        "arn": "arn:aws:sts::123456789012:assumed-role/<role>",
        "accountId": "123456789012",
        "accessKeyId": "ASIARICARTVPIMD4MMACE",
        "sessionContext": {
            "sessionIssuer": {
                "type": "Role",
                "principalId": "AROAUUEDLRTHJNMAUHIJK",
                "arn": "arn:aws:iam::123456789012:role/<role>",
                "accountId": "123456789012",
                "userName": "<user name> "
            },
```

```
            "webIdFederationData": {},
            "attributes": {
                "creationDate": "2024-01-01T18:14:24Z",
                "mfaAuthenticated": "true"
            },
            "ec2RoleDelivery": "2.0"
        }
    },
    "eventTime": "2024-01-01T19:06:28Z",
    "eventSource": "ssm.amazonaws.com",
    "eventName": "UpdateInstanceInformation",
    "awsRegion": "us-east-1",
    "sourceIPAddress": "123.222.111.33",
    "userAgent": "aws-sdk-go/1.44.260 (go1.20.10; linux; amd64)
amazon-ssm-agent/",
    "requestParameters": {
        "instanceId": "i-2131480aa11ee2233",
        "agentVersion": "3.2.1798.0",
        "agentStatus": "Active",
        "platformType": "Linux",
        "platformName": "Amazon Linux",
        "platformVersion": "2",
        "iPAddress": "10.0.0.10",
        "computerName": "ip-10-0-0-10.ec2.internal",
        "agentName": "amazon-ssm-agent",
        "availabilityZone": "us-east-1b",
        "availabilityZoneId": "use1-az2",
        "sSMConnectionChannel": "ssmmessages"
    },
    "responseElements": null,
    "requestID": "8044381c-70ae-430b-af05-7a9d0290a525",
    "eventID": "656e695e-0532-48a5-9ed5-8ab94a3f4e76",
    "readOnly": false,
    "eventType": "AwsApiCall",
    "managementEvent": true,
    "recipientAccountId": "123456789012",
    "eventCategory": "Management",
    "tlsDetails": {
        "tlsVersion": "TLSv1.2",
        "cipherSuite": "ECDHE-RSA-AES128-GCM-SHA256",
        "clientProvidedHostHeader": "ssm.us-east-1.amazonaws.com"
    }
}
```

While management, data, and insights events share most of the attributes in the JSON structure, insights events contain an additional attribute, called insightDetails. Example 5.2 shows an insights event.

Real World Scenario

Example 5.2: CloudTrail's Insights Event

```
{
    "eventVersion": "1.09",
    "eventTime": "2024-01-01T20:46:00Z",
    "awsRegion": "us-east-1",
    "eventID": "9d876c5b-ae01-432b-88ce-1a876a11fb9b",
    "eventType": "AwsCloudTrailInsight",
    "recipientAccountId": "123456789012",
    "sharedEventID": "fe6368fd-2286-4297-b127-157fd96d45ca",
    "insightDetails": {
        "state": "Start",
        "eventSource": "cloudshell.amazonaws.com",
        "eventName": "SendHeartBeat",
        "insightType": "ApiCallRateInsight",
        "insightContext": {
            "statistics": {
                "baseline": {
                    "average": 0.0001765848
                },
                "insight": {
                    "average": 0.6
                },
                "insightDuration": 5,
                "baselineDuration": 11326
            },
            "attributions": [
                {
                    "attribute": "userIdentityArn",
                    "insight": [
                        {
                            "value": "arn:aws:sts:: 123456789012:<role>",
                            "average": 0.6
                        }
                    ],
                    "baseline": [
                        {
                            "value": "arn:aws:sts::544491154384:<role>",
                            "average": 0.0001765848
                        }
                    ]
                },
                {
                    "attribute": "userAgent",
                    "insight": [
                        {
                            "value": "<agent description>",
                            "average": 0.6
```

```
                }
            ],
            "baseline": [
                {
                    "value": "<agent description>",
                    "average": 0.0001765848
                }
            ]
        },
        {
            "attribute": "errorCode",
            "insight": [
                {
                    "value": "null",
                    "average": 0.6
                }
            ],
            "baseline": [
                {
                    "value": "null",
                    "average": 0.0001765848
                }
            ]
        }
    ]
    },
    "eventCategory": "Insight"
}
```

AWS CloudTrail is enabled at the creation of an AWS account. Management events recorded within the past 90 days are available in the Event History menu of AWS CloudTrail. This feature (available through the AWS Management Console or via the `LookupEvents` API) allows you to view, search, and download management events related to the account during that timeline.

AWS CloudTrail event history only shows management events, and not all management events are supported to appear in event history.

Insights events are events generated when CloudTrail detects an abnormal volume of API call rates (anomalous call rate in write APIs) and API error rates (anomalous error rate in both read and write APIs). CloudTrail Insights use mathematical models and continuous monitoring of management events.

Insights events are available through the AWS Management Console and through the `LookupEvents` API.

In the Insights console, you can access a list of insights events recorded for the last 90 days, see details of reported unusual activity, and view a timeseries graph.

You have learned that you can access Management events and insights events for the last 90 days. However, effectively managing an account requires a persistent layer that allows you to record events for longer than 90 days. In addition, to store records for future use (e.g., as evidence for audits), a persistent layer can also provide the foundations to analyze, visualize, and respond to events. CloudTrail provides two options for that persistent layer: trails and AWS CloudTrail Lake.

A *trail* allows you to store AWS CloudTrail events in an Amazon S3 bucket that you own, in the form of log files. This way, you can control the life cycle policy and the retention and protection policies of the persisted data. You can create multiple trails. For each trail, you choose the type of events to record (management, data, or insights). Every trail must record management or data events (and it can record both), and a trail recording insights events must record management events.

When creating a trail to receive data events, you use selectors to establish which data to collect in the trail. Basic selectors are available for Amazon S3 and AWS Lambda data events. For all other supported services, you use advanced selectors, where you can filter events you want to collect by Amazon Resource Name, read/write operations, or event name.

Each log file is compressed (in `gzip` format) and contains one or more JSON-formatted records, where each record represents an event. AWS CloudTrail delivers log files several times an hour (about every 5 minutes). Typically, the log files for management and data events appear in your S3 bucket within 15 minutes after the activity was executed in the account. Insights events typically appear within 30 minutes after detecting the unusual activity. AWS CloudTrail stores management and data events in different log files (objects) from insights events.

A trail has several configuration options. However, the minimum information required to create a new trail is its name and the Amazon S3 bucket name to store log files. By default, a trail records all management events and no insight or data events. The trail is always encrypted (using S3 server-side encryption), but other default options differ depending on whether you use the console or the API.

AWS CloudTrail shows insights events in the Management console (or in the `LookupEvents` API) only if there is a trail configured to record those insights events.

Once the records are stored in Amazon S3, you can use services, like Amazon Athena and Amazon QuickSight, to visualize and analyze them. Amazon Athena requires the creation of a table to define the structure of the data and its location within S3. Simply enough, AWS CloudTrail provides a way to create that table directly from its console, by clicking the Create Athena Table button on the Event History page.

NOTE Using the AWS CloudTrail's console for creating the trail's table is not mandatory; you can also manually create the table in Athena.

To protect the stored records, AWS CloudTrail provides encryption and integrity validation mechanisms. Because the records are stored in an Amazon S3 bucket, they are protected at least with the base level of encryption (using Amazon S3 managed keys). However, you can choose to use your own AWS Key Management Service (KMS) keys, specifying one key per trail. If you choose this option, the key policy must allow CloudTrail to use it to encrypt the files and allow chosen principals in the AWS account to decrypt them.

NOTE You learn about AWS KMS in Chapter 7, "Data Protection."

AWS CloudTrail also embeds a trail integrity validation mechanism. This mechanism uses asymmetric cryptographic techniques (digital signatures) applied to the files delivered in S3 buckets. Using these techniques, AWS CloudTrail protects the records and allows you to determine if a delivered log file was modified, deleted, or unchanged. On an hourly basis, AWS CloudTrail delivers a digest file as an object in the trail S3 bucket, digitally signed using a service-managed private key (the digital signature is attached to the object in its metadata, specifically in the `x-amz-meta-signature` key, as is shown in Figure 5.6). The digest file contains a list (in JSON format) of log files and corresponding SHA-256 hashes, delivered within the past hour.

NOTE Each digest file includes information about the previous digest file hash and signature, which establishes a sequential chain of digest files. Example 5.3 shows the header of a CloudTrail digest file.

FIGURE 5.6 AWS CloudTrail digest file object metadata.

Metadata (4)

Metadata is optional information provided as a name-value (key-value) pair. Learn more

Type	Key	Value
System defined	Content-Encoding	gzip
System defined	Content-Type	application/json
User defined	x-amz-meta-signature-algorithm	SHA256withRSA
User defined	x-amz-meta-signature	716ccd0bc6aebe932d641744107171c5c1098a66407313b7dcd014e3bf8f33a5ceaf25ef58f3f4cd495db2C

Real World Scenario

Example 5.3: AWS CloudTrail Digest File Header

```
{
  "awsAccountId": "123456789012",
  "digestStartTime": "2024-01-01T23:19:16Z",
  "digestEndTime": "2024-01-02T00:19:16Z",
  "digestS3Bucket": "cloudtrail",
  "digestS3Object": "<path to current digest S3 object>.json.gz",
  "digestPublicKeyFingerprint": "1234567890b5dc9467b26b16602a50ce",
  "digestSignatureAlgorithm": "SHA256withRSA",
  "newestEventTime": "2024-01-02T00:18:58Z",
  "oldestEventTime": "2024-01-01T23:08:48Z",
  "previousDigestS3Bucket": "cloudtrail",
  "previousDigestS3Object": "<path to digest S3 object from last hour>.json.gz",
  "previousDigestHashValue": "<hash value>",
  "previousDigestHashAlgorithm": "SHA-256",
  "previousDigestSignature": "<digest signature>",
  "logFiles": [
    <structured list including s3Bucket, s3Object, hashValue, hashAlgorithm, newestEventTime, and oldestEventtime for each log file delivered in the past hour>
    ...
  ]
}
```

AWS CloudTrail provides a simple way of validating the integrity of the log files, using the `validate-logs` AWS CLI command.

Trails also provide the option to export CloudTrail events as a stream of events (consistently with the detection framework proposed at the beginning of this chapter). AWS CloudTrail integrates with Amazon CloudWatch Logs, Amazon SNS, and Amazon EventBridge to deliver these streams. The first two integrations (Amazon CloudWatch Logs and Amazon SNS) are configured inside the trail, but it is in Amazon EventBridge configuration where you can set up the third integration.

 You learn more about Amazon CloudWatch Logs later in "Amazon CloudWatch Logs" and about Amazon EventBridge in "Stage 4: Action." At this point, it is important to note that this integration allows you to capture events in Amazon EventBridge for every service supported by AWS CloudTrail.

Configuring an Amazon SNS topic for a trail allows you to receive notifications whenever a log file is delivered to the trail's S3 bucket. If you subscribe to an Amazon SNS notification, you can choose a topic residing in your own account or in another account. In any case, the topic access policy must allow AWS CloudTrail to post messages to it.

The second mechanism AWS CloudTrail provides for persistent storage of events is the CloudTrail Lake. CloudTrail Lake consolidates events records in structures called *event data stores*. You have the option to create event data stores for CloudTrail events, CloudTrail insights events, AWS Config configuration items, and external events. The data schema is different for each one of those four types of events. Therefore, each event data store is able to contain only one event type. Data ingested into an event data store is stored in Apache ORC format, which makes it more efficient to store and run queries. You can use SQL expressions to query data in your event data stores (you can even use SQL JOIN expressions to query multiple event data stores). You can also define the retention period to a maximum of 10 years.

An event data store for CloudTrail events stores management and data events. You can use advanced selectors (the same concept you learned for trails) to define the data events you want to record.

An event data store for CloudTrail insights events is unique, in that it is considered a destination event data store. It requires an existing event data store for CloudTrail events recording management events to act as its source event data store. A CloudTrail events data store can be the source of one and only one CloudTrail Insights event data store.

AWS Config configuration items event data store allows you to collect configuration items generated by AWS Config recorders. The recorders will provide information of configuration items when they detect a change, or when taking a Config snapshot. Once you have data in your configuration items event data store, you can issue queries to correlate data with other data stores (in contrast to AWS Config queries, which only allow you to query AWS Config data).

The external events data store can hold data coming from sources outside of AWS. In this case, in addition to creating the data store, you also designate a channel (or integration). A channel is a resource that exposes an endpoint (webhook), used by external applications to ingest events into CloudTrail Lake. The integration can be of type *direct* (the external application directly calls the channel endpoint using the PutAuditEvents API and includes an externalID) or *solution* (the third party runs an application within your AWS account, which in turn calls the PutAuditEvents API). The channel resource can be protected by a resource policy.

Finally, CloudTrail Lake supports a special type of event data store to hold records generated by the AWS Audit Manager evidence finder. Audit Manager automatically creates the event data store when you enable the evidence finder functionality. You learned about AWS Audit Manager in Chapter 3, "Management and Security Governance." Evidence finder allows you to filter and group data available as part of Audit Manager assessments. Once Audit Manager creates the data store, you can manage it using CloudTrail Lake. You can even query your data using the interface of either service.

Once your data store is created, CloudTrail Lake allows you to run Presto SQL Select queries on it. The service provides different ways of running the queries. One option is accessing the CloudTrail Lake Dashboard in the AWS Management Console. The Dashboard will present you with a set of graphs, each one representing the result of one predefined SQL query. For you to run your own queries, CloudTrail Lake offers you the Query menu (also under the console). Using the Query functionality, you will be able to run any valid Presto SQL Select query on your event data store. You can choose to run one of the sample queries or create your own. The results will be available through the AWS Management Console. You can run queries programmatically and store the results in an S3 bucket you own by calling the startQuery API. Finally, if you enable federation for an event data store, CloudTrail Lake shares metadata with AWS Glue, creates a data catalog, and configures a role, so you can query your data store from Amazon Athena. Because CloudTrail registers the IAM role and data catalog with AWS Lake Formation, you can use Lake Formation to apply fine-grained access control to your event data stores.

CloudTrail Lake event data stores are always encrypted. By default, CloudTrail Lake encrypts them using an AWS-managed KMS key, but you can also encrypt with a KMS key you manage. However, once you select a customer managed KMS key, you cannot change it.

Table 5.2 provides a summary of the main CloudTrail event types.

AWS CloudTrail is a regional scoped service: events reported at the event history level are related to your account and region. However, you can consolidate events from different regions and accounts.

When creating a new trail, you define its scope by choosing the regions the trail covers (options are Current Region or All Regions). When a trail is configured to apply to All Regions (the recommended configuration and mandatory when using the management console), it will create a multiregion trail. That trail will have the current region as its home region, and it will automatically configure trails for every AWS region enabled in that account. Events will be recorded in each region. However, AWS CloudTrail will deliver the log files from all the enabled regions to the centralized Amazon S3 bucket, defined in the multiregion trail. Within the Amazon S3 bucket structure, the log files will be delivered under a prefix that identifies the region they come from. If configured, the Amazon SNS topic will receive a notification for each one of those written log files.

> If a trail applies for all regions, when a new AWS region is added and enabled in the account, AWS CloudTrail will automatically create the trail for that region.

If a trail is not chosen to apply to all regions, it will exist only in the current region. The trail will receive event logs only from the region where it was created.

A trail can also have an organization's scope. You can create a trail in an organization's management account that will log events from all the accounts under it. This scope is independent of the regional scope. All of the organization's member accounts will be able

TABLE 5.2 AWS CloudTrail: Event Types

Event Type	Type of Activity	AWS CloudTrail Console (90 Days)	API (90 Days)	Trail	Event Data Store
Management	API activity (control plane), service events, sign-in events	Event history	`LookupEvents`	Available (Filter to log read, write, or both)	CloudTrail events (Filter to log read, write, or both)
Data	API activity (data plane)	Not available	Not available	Available (Filter using Basic or Advanced selectors)	CloudTrail events (Filter using Advanced selectors)
Insight	"Meta-events": unusual activity associated with API calls and errors	Insights	`LookupEvents` (using the `EventCategory` parameter)	Available, as long as the trail also records management events (Select Insights for API call rate, error rate, or both)	CloudTrail insights events; requires a CloudTrail event as its source event data store (Select Insights for API call rate, error rate, or both)

to see the trail, but they won't have privileges to modify it. By default, they won't have privileges to access the trail's S3 bucket either.

Another possible centralization mechanism is to have trails produced by different accounts storing log files in a centralized Amazon S3 bucket (if you don't use the organizational scope, you will need to configure the right access privileges for different accounts to put objects in the bucket).

Although you cannot disable event history, you can disable the log collection at the trail level. When you disable a trail, you are not going to record events during the period in which the trail is disabled (or deliver trails into the Amazon S3, Amazon SNS, or Amazon CloudWatch logs). You can also disable the collection of only insights or data events at the trail level.

CloudTrail events data stores and configuration items data stores can also be scoped for a single region or all regions, and as a single account or as organizational. When scoped for a single region, the data store will record events from the region where it is created. The same applies for a single-account data store. If it's configured as all regions, CloudTrail will consolidate events originating from all regions into that single data store. The data store will only exist in the region where it was created (it cannot be accessed from other regions). From the management account of AWS Organizations, you can create an organizational CloudTrail data store. In that case, the data store will record events from other accounts in your organization. The member accounts will not have access to the data store.

CloudTrail insights data stores cannot be multiregion or multi-account. These data stores are attached to a source event data store and will produce insights events based on the events recorded therein.

CloudTrail evidence finder data stores are always created as single-region, single-account. The final type of data stores, external event data stores, also cannot be multi-account or multiregion. They store all records ingested in the attached channel. You are responsible for applying the proper resource policy to allow principals from other accounts to ingest records in the corresponding channel.

Now that you have learned about CloudTrail and its capabilities, review Table 5.3, which compares the two mechanisms that CloudTrail offers for persistent storage of events: trails and event data stores.

TABLE 5.3 AWS CloudTrail: Trails and Event Data Stores

	Trail	Event Data Store
Storage format	Compressed JSON files	Apache ORC
Storage location	User-defined Amazon S3 bucket	Event data store
Retention	Defined by S3 bucket life cycle (customer defined) Can be modified at any time	Retention is defined at event data store creation time and not modifiable. Two options: One year, with option to extend at the end of each year, until a maximum of 10 years (cost effective when ingesting less than 25TB per month) Seven years fixed (cost effective when ingesting more than 25TB per month)
Event types supported	Management Data Insights	Management Data Insights Configuration items Audit Manager evidence finder External (integrations)

Stage 2: Events Collection   **155**

	Trail	Event Data Store
Data structure for records	Management and data events recorded in the same JSON file Insights events recorded in the same S3 bucket but in a different JSON file (different keys)	Management and data events are stored in a CloudTrail Events event data store The other event types are stored in their own event data stores
Selectors for data event types	Basic and Advanced selectors	Advanced selectors
Encryption	Always encrypted; can choose between SSE-S3 (KMS key managed by Amazon S3) and SSE-KMS (using a customer managed KMS key)	Always encrypted; can choose between CloudTrail-managed KMS key and customer-managed KMS key
Query options	CloudWatch Logs (if enabled in the trail) Amazon Athena (CloudTrail console simplifies the process of creating the Athena table)	CloudTrail Dashboard (predefined queries) CloudTrail Query Amazon Athena (if event data store is Federation-enabled)
Single vs. multi-account	Single account or whole organization	Single account or whole organization
Single vs. multiregion	Current region or all regions	Current region or all regions
Delegated administrator	CloudTrail allows you to assign an organization's member account as a delegated administrator to manage trails and event data stores. The owner of the created resources is still the organization's management account.	

In Exercise 5.2, you will practice how to create a trail in your AWS account.

EXERCISE 5.2

Set Up a Trail in CloudTrail

1. Access the AWS CloudTrail console.

2. Create a new trail with the name `security-chapter5`.

3. Apply the trail to all regions and record all management and insights events.

4. Monitor S3 activity related to all S3 buckets in your account (data events).

EXERCISE 5.2 *(continued)*

5. Create a new bucket to store the trail, using a unique name and the prefix `security-chapter5`.

6. Encrypt your log files using a new KMS key called `security-chapter5`.

7. Choose the SNS topic `security-chapter5` to send notifications.

8. Generate API activity in your account (access other services, create or modify AWS resources).

9. Wait 15 minutes and check the files in your CloudTrail S3 bucket.

10. Validate that you received SNS notifications related to the delivered files into S3.

11. (Optional) Wait 30 minutes and check for events in insights (inside your S3 bucket).

12. Wait 1 hour and validate the integrity of the digest and log files. Use the `validate-logs` CLI command.

13. (Optional) Follow the procedure indicated in this link to manually validate the integrity of the log files: https://docs.aws.amazon.com/awscloudtrail/latest/userguide/cloudtrail-log-file-custom-validation.html.

After you create the trail, it may take a few minutes for the first events to appear in the S3 bucket. If you don't see records in the bucket, check that the trail has been successfully created and is active on the console.

If the trail is active, check that the bucket name you provided matches the name of the bucket you intended to use. Check that the bucket policy allows CloudTrail to write events, as shown in Example 5.4.

 Real World Scenario

Example 5.4: S3 Bucket Policy That Allows CloudTrail to Write Events

```
{
    "Version": "2012-10-17",
    "Statement": [
        {
            "Sid": "AWSCloudTrailAclCheck20150319",
            "Effect": "Allow",
            "Principal": {
                "Service": "cloudtrail.amazonaws.com"
            },
            "Action": "s3:GetBucketAcl",
            "Resource": "arn:aws:s3:::<YOUR BUCKET NAME>"
        },
```

```
        {
            "Sid": "AWSCloudTrailWrite20150319",
            "Effect": "Allow",
            "Principal": {
                "Service": "cloudtrail.amazonaws.com"
            },
            "Action": "s3:PutObject",
            "Resource": "arn:aws:s3:::<YOUR BUCKET NAME>/AWSLogs/
<YOURACCOUNT ID>/*",
            "Condition": {
                "StringEquals": {
                    "s3:x-amz-acl": "bucket-owner-full-control"
                }
            }
        }
    ]
}
```

If you are having trouble accessing CloudTrail, make sure your user has at least read access to the service by using the `AWSCloudTrailReadOnlyAccess` policy.

Amazon CloudWatch Logs

Applications, services, resources, and almost every technological component produce observable records of activity. Those records can take the form of logs, metrics, or traces. Amazon CloudWatch Logs is a scalable, highly available, and managed service that allows you to manage the logs produced by systems throughout their life cycle.

In the AWS Management Console, Amazon CloudWatch Logs appear under the CloudWatch umbrella. However, they use a different set of APIs. Later in the chapter, you learn about Amazon CloudWatch, the AWS-managed metrics monitoring service.

The basic unit of Amazon CloudWatch Logs is the *log event*. These events are generated by sources like AWS services or by other external sources. They are sent to the service using the `PutLogEvents` API. Following the AWS Shared Responsibility model, AWS services can seamlessly ingest information for log events. AWS provides the unified Amazon CloudWatch agent that you install in your EC2 instances or other computing instances you own to collect those events that occur inside the instances and are not visible to AWS. The agent can extract logs from applications running in compute instances and ingest them into Amazon CloudWatch Logs. It is supported across different operating systems and allows you to gather both predefined operating system logs and custom metrics (via `collectd` and `StatsD` collectors). A configuration file inside the agent allows you to define the agent behavior about which metrics, logs, and traces to collect, and attributes such as metric's namespace (`CWAgent` is the default namespace) or appended dimensions.

 The unified Amazon CloudWatch agent can collect logs, metrics, and traces. It will ingest the collected data into different AWS services (CloudWatch Logs, CloudWatch, and X-Ray, correspondingly).

If you are unable to view logs generated by an Amazon CloudWatch agent installed in an EC2 instance, verify that the agent is correctly installed, look for errors in the log files of the agent (ensure you validate issues with the configuration file reported in the `configuration-validaton.log` file), confirm the agent is running (using the `amazon-cloudwatch-agent-ctl` command directly in the instance where the agent is running, or via Systems Manager), and validate the privileges for the agent to ingest data into the AWS services. See Example 5.5 for a sample policy that allows data ingestion into Amazon CloudWatch Logs.

> **Real World Scenario**
>
> **Example 5.5: CloudWatch Agent Policy Example**
>
> ```
> {
>     "Version": "2012-10-17",
>     "Statement": [
>         {
>             "Effect": "Allow",
>             "Action": [
>                 "logs:CreateLogGroup",
>                 "logs:CreateLogStream",
>                 "logs:PutLogEvents",
>                 "logs:DescribeLogStreams"
>             ],
>             "Resource": [
>                 "arn:aws:logs:*:*:*"
>             ]
>         }
>     ]
> }
> ```

For more details on agent settings, refer to `https://docs.aws.amazon.com/AmazonCloudWatch/latest/monitoring/Install-CloudWatch-Agent.html`.

Each log event is a record representing an event reported to the service and contains two main parts: timestamp (date and time the event occurred, as reported by the source in the PutLogEvents call) and raw message (specific data the source is reporting). Log events are stored in the service, but to make it easier to manage them, incoming records are grouped in a structure called a *log stream* (usually, you want log events inside a log stream to come from a single source and use the same message format).

To increase manageability of the information stored in log streams, they are hierarchically grouped inside another structure: the log group. Configuration parameters are defined at the log group level, so all log streams inside it share the same set of configuration parameters. You can see a graphical representation of this structure in Figure 5.7.

When you create a log group (and only at that moment), you can specify one of two classes: Standard or Infrequent Access. The Infrequent Access class comes with a subset of the available functionality, at a lower ingestion cost than the Standard class. When using the Infrequent Access class, you cannot directly get, filter, or search for events in log streams. Instead, you need to use CloudWatch Logs Insights to view those log events. Other features that are available only to the Standard class log groups are data protection (audit and mask sensitive fields in logs), anomaly detection (report deviations from a baseline), metric filters, subscription filters, and contributor insights. See the CloudWatch Logs documentation for a full list of supported features in each class.

As an example of an AWS service reporting log events to Amazon CloudWatch Logs, an AWS CloudTrail trail can deliver events to a log group. This log group (created in the same AWS region as the home region of the AWS CloudTrail trail) receives the events the trail is configured to monitor (management, insights, or data events). You can see this integration by completing Exercise 5.3.

FIGURE 5.7 Representation of CloudWatch Log hierarchical grouping.

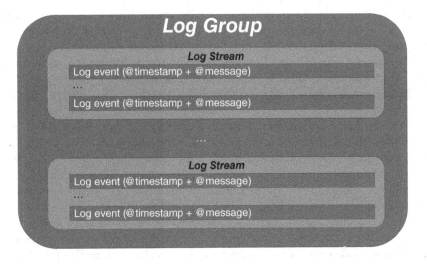

> **EXERCISE 5.3**
>
> **AWS CloudTrail Integration with Amazon CloudWatch Logs**
>
> 1. Access the AWS CloudTrail Console and edit the trail you created in Exercise 5.2.
> 2. Configure the trail to send the events to a new Amazon CloudWatch Logs log group called `CloudTrail/security-chapter5`.
> 3. Generate activity in your AWS account.
> 4. Access the Amazon CloudWatch Logs Console, look for the log group you created, and check that you received events.

Log events within a log group are always encrypted at rest. By default, CloudWatch Logs encrypts the data using a key managed by the service. You can choose to encrypt using an AWS KMS Customer Master Key (CMK). You learn more about AWS KMS keys in Chapter 7, "Data Protection." Amazon CloudWatch Logs will decrypt the data on your behalf when accessing them. If you associate a new KMS key to a log group, the events from that moment on will be encrypted based on the new key. If you disassociate a KMS key from the log group, the new events after that moment will be encrypted using the default mechanism.

As a best practice, use a different KMS key for each log group. Also, use a condition in the KMS key policy to restrict the usage of each key to only the account and log group it is intended to encrypt.

Retention is another aspect you can configure at the log group level. You control how long CloudWatch Logs keeps the log events. By default, there is no retention limit (configured as Never, meaning that the log events will never be deleted). You can configure the retention period in days, using specific values that range from 1 to 3,653 days.

Once the log events are part of a log stream, you can retrieve those log events through the management console or API calls (if using the Standard log class). Also, you will usually analyze the ingested information. It is at this point that Amazon CloudWatch Logs Insights comes in handy.

Amazon CloudWatch Logs Insights provides a query syntax to apply to one or more log groups. As with any query language, everything starts with how the data is structured. Logs Insights automatically discovers the data fields of AWS service logs and any JSON-based logs in Standard class log groups. When it cannot detect the specific type of a log, the purpose-built query language provides the `parse` command to define ephemeral fields and to use them in the specific query. Logs Insights generates the following system fields when a log event arrives to CloudWatch Logs: `@message` (the raw log event), `@timestamp` (timestamp reported by the source), `@ingestionTime` (timestamp when CloudWatch Logs received the event), `@logStream` (the name of the log stream), and `@log` (the unique ID of the log group).

You may also be interested in extracting and summarizing information from the log events. With that goal in mind, Amazon CloudWatch Logs provides a mechanism called a *metric filter* (defined at the log group level, available for the Standard class). A metric filter extracts information from an event log and converts it into a number to be plotted in a timeseries representation (in Amazon CloudWatch).

To establish a metric filter, you first define a filter. This filter defines how Amazon CloudWatch Logs selects the interesting log events. It is expressed in the form of a filter pattern that looks for attributes in a JSON object. The filter shown in Example 5.6 applies to a log group receiving events from CloudTrail. It looks for events generated by any subject that assumed a role in the AWS account.

Example 5.6: Filter Pattern in Amazon CloudWatch Logs

`{ ($.eventVersion="1.08") && ($.userIdentity.type="AssumedRole") }`

After selecting the interesting events, the next definition is to create the metric. The objective of a metric is to establish what number will be reported to Amazon CloudWatch (to store and plot). The metric is aggregated and reported on a per-minute basis. You can choose to report a fixed floating-point number per matched event, or a number in any numeric field of the event. For example, if you decide to report a count of "1" per each matched event, the number reported is the count of log events matched by the filter per-minute.

To finish the definition of a metric filter, you will define both the name of the metric and its namespace. A metric namespace is a label that allows you to group metrics. Think of it as a folder in a hierarchical structure that contains different metrics: even if there are two metrics that share the same name, they will be considered different metrics if they belong to different namespaces. You will also establish a default value: the number to be reported for each log event that does not match the filter.

Specifically, by creating metric filters on top of log groups receiving events from AWS CloudTrail, you can monitor and alert according to the number of occurrences of any event reported in a trail.

At the log group level, you can set up how to send log events data outside Amazon CloudWatch Logs. For the Standard log class, you can export the log events to an Amazon S3 bucket you own and manage. Choose the data to export by defining the start and end times, an optional prefix of the log stream, the destination S3 bucket, and an optional bucket prefix. Information in a log group can take up to 12 hours to be available for exporting.

This method will provide you with the batch historic view. Once in Amazon S3, you can use services like Amazon Athena and Amazon QuickSight to create additional analysis and visualization of the data.

FIGURE 5.8 Schematic representation of log data for cross-account consumption.

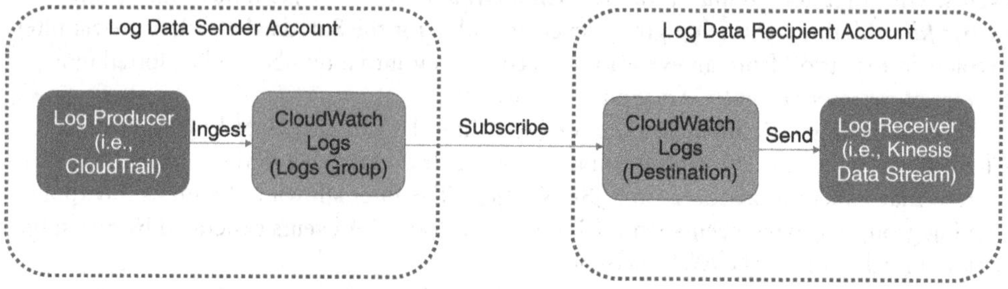

[Diagram: Log Data Sender Account containing Log Producer (i.e., CloudTrail) → Ingest → CloudWatch Logs (Logs Group); Subscribe → Log Data Recipient Account containing CloudWatch Logs (Destination) → Send → Log Receiver (i.e., Kinesis Data Stream)]

To expose the records in a stream-like fashion, Amazon CloudWatch Logs provide another mechanism, available for Standard class log groups: subscriptions. In a subscription, Amazon CloudWatch Logs produce a near real-time stream of events and deliver them to a consumer. The consumer can be Amazon Kinesis Data Streams, Amazon Kinesis Data Firehose, Amazon OpenSearch Service, or an AWS Lambda function (which allows further customization). When defining a subscription, you will also have the option to define a filter in the same way as described in the previous section. The filter allows you to choose which events are sent to the consumer.

Eventually, you will want to configure subscriptions to feed log events to another account's resources (an Amazon Kinesis Firehose or data stream in another account). This special cross-account subscription is called a *destination*. On the receiving account, you will need to create a CloudWatch Logs destination resource (using the `PutDestination` API) and link it to the Amazon Kinesis resource that will receive the events. The destination resource acts as the receiving end of a conduit between the accounts. Figure 5.8 shows the different concepts.

> The Amazon CloudWatch Logs destination resource itself is protected by a resource-level access policy.

Using the destinations construct, you can centralize events in a single AWS account. Another common way of centralizing logs managed by CloudWatch Logs is by having them exported into an S3 bucket. Exporting logs to S3 is an asynchronous operation, available for Standard class log groups.

Amazon CloudWatch

Think of Amazon CloudWatch as a metric repository service. In a nutshell, its function is to record information in a time sequence by storing a number (metric) for each period of time. Note that it can receive more than one number during each period of time, so Amazon CloudWatch can also make calculations (such as average, maximum, and minimum) to establish the metric to report in the period of time. Amazon CloudWatch receives data from either AWS services or custom data sources (custom metrics from your own applications). You can also entrust the unified Amazon CloudWatch agent to collect internal information from a system, such as memory utilization. Amazon CloudWatch allows you to collect data from other external data sources, like Amazon OpenSearch service, Prometheus and Amazon Managed Service for Prometheus, Amazon RDS, Amazon S3, and Microsoft Azure Monitor.

At the time of ingesting data into Amazon CloudWatch, the ingesting source defines a namespace, a metric name, and (optionally) metric dimensions to group the information. For each metric, you will define one of two possible resolutions: Standard or High. Standard resolution stores data with 1-minute granularity, whereas High resolution metrics have a 1-second granularity. By default, AWS Services publish metrics in Standard resolution. High-resolution metrics are available for custom metrics.

Amazon CloudWatch retains the metrics for up to 15 months, aggregating data of higher resolution as that data becomes older. Once the metrics are stored in a repository of observable records (as named in the detection framework in Figure 5.1), organized by namespace, dimensions, and metric names, Amazon CloudWatch can plot them in a timeline graph (*graphed metrics*).

The definitions of *accumulation period* and *statistic* influence the way Amazon CloudWatch plots the graphed metrics. *Accumulation period* refers to a time range. You can choose accumulation periods from 1 second to 30 days. The *statistic* is the math expression applied to the data points in the selected accumulation period. For example, you can choose to report the average of the metric in that period, but you can also select the minimum, the maximum, the sum, or even the number of samples recorded for that period. At the minute level, Amazon CloudWatch also stores aggregated information of the minimum, maximum, sum, and number of samples.

Because the metrics represent organized data points in a timeline, you can use SQL expressions to query and generate additional timeseries. You do that using CloudWatch Metrics Insights, which allows you to run queries across different metrics. You can create your queries from scratch or use one of the provided sample queries.

Amazon CloudWatch dashboards allow you to visualize in a single page a set of graphed metrics you define, so you can easily access them at a central location. Using CloudWatch Explorer functionality, you can use a user-friendly interface to generate graphed metrics from a collection of metrics that you can add to a dashboard.

Amazon CloudWatch provides you with infrastructure monitoring insights functionalities (not to be confused with CloudWatch Metrics Insights). Container Insights and Lambda Insights allow you to collect, aggregate, and consolidate metrics from your applications running on container platforms (ECS, EKS, or Kubernetes on EC2), or serverless applications built on top of AWS Lambda. Contributor Insights functionality allows you to understand how individual components (contributors) are affecting (contributing to) the final metrics results. Using Contributors Insights, you can better understand how a metric is being affected by individual contributors, its number of unique contributors, its Top-N contributors, and the maximum contributor value. Amazon CloudWatch Application Insights functionality uses machine learning technology (powered by Amazon SageMaker) to suggest a configuration that collects and displays metrics and logs from an application you define using SSM Application Manager or a Resource Manager group. Application Insights monitors the collected metrics and logs to identify anomalies.

Using metric streams, you can consume Amazon CloudWatch metrics in a stream-like way. With metrics streams, you set up a set of your metrics as a source to be streamed to an Amazon S3 bucket, an Amazon Kinesis Firehose, or a metric stream's AWS partner (like Datadog, Dynatrace, New Relic, Sumo Logic, or Splunk).

Amazon CloudWatch alarms let you configure automatic actions to execute (invoke a Lambda function, create an entry in Systems Manager, or execute Auto Scaling or EC2 actions) and to send notifications (via an Amazon SNS topic) when your metrics achieve specific conditions.

To specify the conditions you want to evaluate, you select one metric, or you can produce a combined metric using math expressions operating on individual metrics.

Next, you assign a threshold. If your metric breaches the threshold (a number of consecutive times or even using an M out of N expression), it will go to an ALARM state. If it does not breach the threshold, the state is OK. A third option is to go to INSUFFICIENT DATA state, when Amazon CloudWatch has not received data points to calculate the timeseries. To avoid the last state, you alternatively define if your alarm treats missing data points as good or bad, or should ignore them. You configure your alarm to take the automatic action whenever it is in one of those three states.

Basic thresholds are defined as static values. However, a static threshold may not be always suitable (for example, when the behavior of the metric depends on seasonality). In such cases, Amazon CloudWatch offers the option for an alarm to use a dynamic band as a threshold. Amazon CloudWatch's anomaly detection functionality determines that dynamic band. Based on machine learning models and statistics, anomaly detection establishes the dynamic range considered normal at different points in time.

Other than simple alarms, you also can create composite alarms. Instead of getting its status from a metric (or set of metrics), a composite alarm's status is defined by the status of other alarms. Using composite alarms allows you to reduce alarm noise and provide a more comprehensive context when receiving notifications.

Amazon CloudWatch Observability Access Manager (OAM) gives you the capability of monitoring several accounts in the same region from a single monitoring account. You can configure this cross-account observability through the CloudWatch console or by using the Amazon CloudWatch OAM APIs (including via CLI). The source accounts share observability data (CloudWatch Logs, CloudWatch metrics, CloudWatch Application Insights, and AWS X-Ray traces) with a centralized monitoring account. For the sharing to work, both source and monitoring accounts should separately agree to share the data. The monitoring account establishes a resource called a *sink*. The source account establishes a resource called an *observability link*. The telemetry types (logs, metrics, traces, application insights) that each account wants to share are defined in the corresponding resources. Once both parties (source and monitoring accounts) successfully complete the configuration, the observability link is established and the monitoring account has access to the shared

FIGURE 5.9 Visualization of source account telemetry (logs) in a monitoring account.

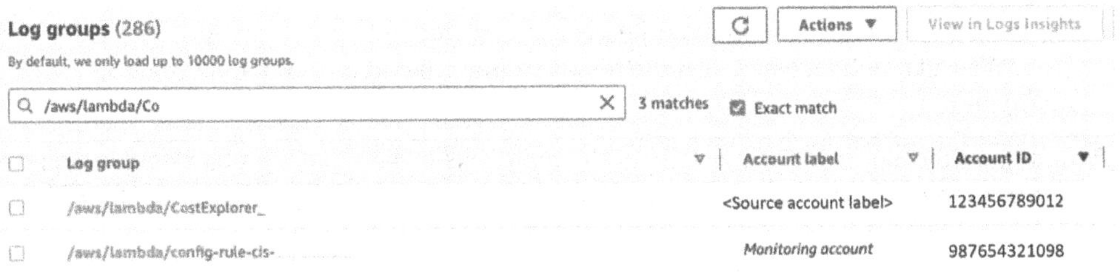

Log group	Account label	Account ID
/aws/lambda/CostExplorer_	<Source account label>	123456789012
/aws/lambda/config-rule-cis-	Monitoring account	987654321098

telemetry types (using the same CloudWatch interfaces). You can see in Figure 5.9 how a log group from a source account is visualized in the monitoring account.

A different way to access CloudWatch data from different accounts is using CloudWatch dashboard for cross-region, cross-account access. This way, you can have access to metrics, alarms, and dashboards, but not to other telemetry types like logs, traces, or application insights from other accounts and regions.

Amazon CloudWatch cross-account observability (using Observability Access Manager) is the preferred way to share telemetry data among AWS accounts.

It is time to consolidate in practice the concepts you have learned so far. In Exercise 5.4, you will use the Amazon CloudWatch Logs log group created in Exercise 5.3 as the source to create a metric and an alarm in Amazon CloudWatch. The alarm will send a notification when an S3 bucket is created or deleted.

EXERCISE 5.4

Create a Metric and an Alarm in Amazon CloudWatch

1. In the Amazon CloudWatch Logs Console, access the log group you created in Exercise 5.3.

2. Create a metric filter for that log group with the following expression:

   { ($.eventSource = "s3.amazonaws.com") && (($.eventName = "CreateBucket") || ($.eventName = "DeleteBucket")) }

3. Name the filter and the namespace security-chapter5.

4. Name the metric bucket-create-delete.

5. Use a metric value of 1 and a default value of 0.

166   Chapter 5 ▪ Security Logging and Monitoring

EXERCISE 5.4 *(continued)*

6. Create the alarm. Once the filter and metric are created, go back to the Amazon CloudWatch Logs Console. Select the filter you just created and click the Create Alarm button.

7. Configure the alarm so that, whenever the metric achieves a value greater than or equal to 1, it sends a notification to the Amazon SNS topic `security-chapter5`. Name the alarm `security-chapter5`.

8. Wait a few minutes and check in the CloudWatch metrics console that the namespace/metric pair `security-chapter5/bucket-create-delete` was created.

9. Go to the S3 management console and create a new test S3 bucket.

10. Check that the metric `bucket-create-delete` reports a number 1 and that the alarm triggered.

11. (Optional) Create an alarm to detect when a root user logs in.

12. (Optional) Follow the examples here: `https://docs.aws.amazon.com/awscloudtrail/latest/userguide/cloudwatch-alarms-for-cloudtrail.html`.

At this point, you can appreciate the close relationship between logs and metrics. As you experienced in Exercise 5.4, logs are a common and effective source for metrics. Because of that close relationship, Amazon CloudWatch introduced a log format called *embedded metric format.* The format specifies a JSON structure where you provide both log information and metric information. Logs submitted to Amazon CloudWatch Logs using the embedded metric format are parsed automatically to create metrics in Amazon CloudWatch, with no coding required. You can build your application to produce logs in the embedded metric format, either following the specification or using one of the software client libraries provided by AWS.

AWS Health

AWS Health is the AWS service that provides information about the underlying infrastructure (under the AWS portion of the shared responsibility model) that could affect your AWS account. AWS Health reports both public information about regional availability of AWS services and specific events affecting your accounts.

Such information is uncovered in a dashboard called AWS Health Dashboard in the AWS Management Console. There, you will find information about recent issues, notifications, and scheduled changes (both upcoming and from the past 7 days). AWS Health also provides a console, with a list of the events reported within the past 90 days.

The AWS Health Dashboard visualizes events for all AWS regions within the current AWS account. You can create filters to view only your regions of interest. From the master account of AWS Organizations, you can also set up an AWS Health organizational view. This view shows consolidated information about events on all your AWS Organizations' accounts and aggregates health events. It is also possible to set up a delegated administrator account to have the AWS Health organizational view of your AWS Organizations.

Events reported by AWS Health are available to be processed by Amazon EventBridge. You learn more about Amazon EventBridge in the following sections.

If you are subscribed to business or higher support plans, you are entitled to call the AWS Health API (the API that supports AWS Health). Doing so gives you access to AWS Health functionalities in a programmatic way. For example, you can work with information about specific events and aggregations, such as the description of event types and summary counts, in an automated way.

Although you cannot disable the AWS Health service on your account, you can enable and disable the organizational view.

Stage 3: Events Analysis

According to the detective framework presented in this chapter's introduction, after collecting the events, you should focus on analyzing them—or, in other words, use the observable records as raw material and execute an analytical process to produce a list of "processed" events (or findings). These processed events are also records that give you value-added information.

In the following sections, you learn about AWS Config Rules (continuing your exploration of the AWS Config service), Amazon Inspector, Amazon Security Lake, AWS Systems Manager (specifically State Manager, Patch Manager, and Compliance capabilities), and AWS Trusted Advisor. While Amazon GuardDuty and AWS Security Hub provide event analysis and monitoring functionality, they are covered in Chapter 8, "Threat Detection and Incident Response."

AWS Config Rules

AWS Config tracks configuration items of your monitored resources (and how they change over time), providing you with a configuration timeline for each of these resources.

AWS Config is notified when a change in a resource happens. This notification allows the service to establish what is the resource's compliance status after the change, by comparing it with a template that defines what the desired configuration is. You can even compare the configuration of a resource you have not yet deployed against the template to understand in advance if the resource will be compliant once deployed.

An AWS Config rule defines the template, which resources it will evaluate, when the evaluation will occur, and what remediation action to take (if any).

There are three types of AWS Config rules:

- **Custom rules:** Rules that you define from scratch, specifying the configuration you want to test in the evaluated resource. You create custom rules by associating an AWS Lambda function you own or using the Guard policy language. In the case of Lambda functions, AWS Config passes the information about the monitored resource to your function at triggering time. You develop the function in a way that returns the resource's compliance status.
- **Managed rules:** Predefined and customizable rules provided by AWS Config, so you can choose one to configure instead of creating it yourself.
- **Service-linked rules:** A special type of managed rule that only AWS services can create and deploy (you cannot edit them). They represent good practices defined as standards by AWS service development teams.

When is a rule triggered? An AWS Config rule can be configured to trigger in three ways (not mutually exclusive): on a periodic basis (you can choose to execute every 1, 3, 6, 12, or 24 hours), when a configuration change is detected (creating a sort of continuous audit on your monitored resources), or on demand (either by an API call or via the AWS Management Console). You can restrict the resources the rule will act upon, defining resource types and resource identifiers in the rule configuration.

When creating a rule, you define its evaluation mode as detective, proactive, or both. A rule in detective mode is executed against resources that are already deployed, and it is meant to provide information about the compliance status (defined by the rule). If you run a rule in proactive mode, you pass information about the resource configuration along with the request to evaluate the rule. As a result, you will receive information about the compliance status of the resource if it would be deployed.

> If the result of a detective evaluation is a noncompliant status, the rule can apply a remediation action, which you learn more about in Chapter 8, "Threat Detection and Incident Response."
>
> A rule in proactive evaluation mode will not remediate or prevent a noncompliant resource from being deployed.

Rule parameters (key-value pairs) further extend the flexibility of the execution of AWS Config rules since they can receive external inputs as part of the rule configuration. For custom rules, you define the configuration, parameters, and the AWS Lambda function AWS Config will actually summon. In contrast, managed rules predefine (and do not allow you to modify) the configuration related to the trigger type and the parameter's key attributes.

AWS Config keeps a record of the rules' execution. For each rule, the service maintains a list of the monitored resources and their reported status (compliant or noncompliant).

FIGURE 5.10 AWS Config Console: Resource timeline.

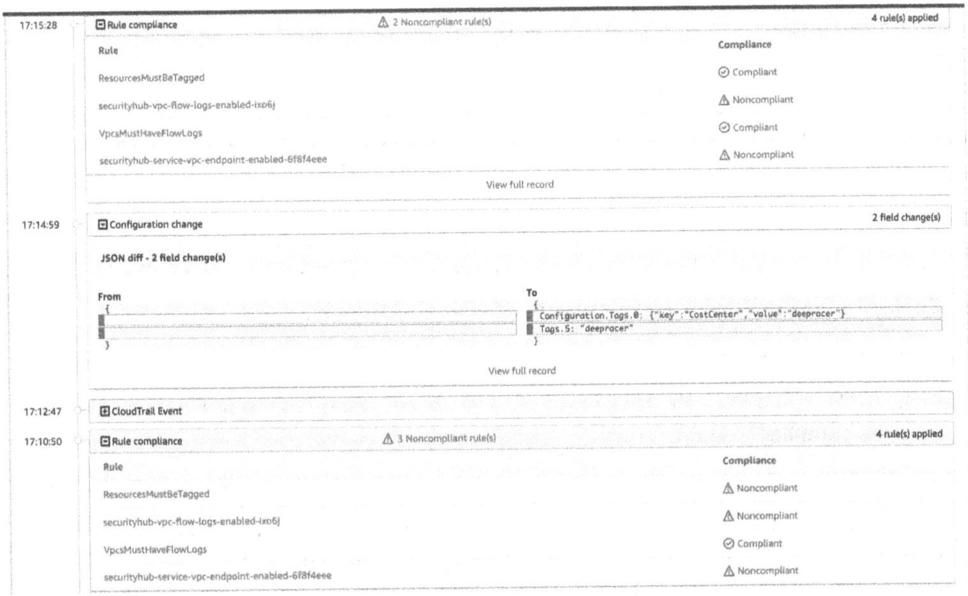

In consequence, you can have a rule-centric view (with a summary of resources and its status on a per-rule basis). You also have access to a resource-centric view, which shows information about the resource and all rules applied to it (with its corresponding compliance status).

AWS Config displays a resource timeline showing the configuration changes on a resource over time. Using the same timeline, the service presents the rule compliance changes for each monitored resource. The resource timeline is a graphical timeseries view that shows the configuration changes and compliance status of a resource over time, as shown in Figure 5.10. This visualization allows you to easily understand when a configuration change affected a resource's compliance state.

Within the notifications the AWS Config delivery channel sends to the defined Amazon SNS topic, you'll see notifications of when a rule is applied to a resource and when the compliance status of a resource changes.

An AWS Config aggregator offers a consolidated view of rules in the same way it consolidates information about different resources across accounts, as explained in "Stage 1: Resources State."

In Exercise 5.5, you will practice with AWS Config rules by configuring a rule to validate the existence of a specific tag in your resources.

EXERCISE 5.5

AWS Config Rules

1. Open the AWS Config Console.
2. Open the Rules menu. Choose to add an AWS managed rule. Use the `required-tags` template.
3. Name the rule `security-chapter5`.
4. Set the rule to trigger when detecting a change in the EC2 instance created in Exercise 5.1.
5. Configure the rule to look for a tag with the key `CostCenter`.
6. Wait until the new rule is evaluated.
7. In the AWS Config Console, look for the EC2 instance created in the previous exercise and check its compliance status.
8. In the EC2 console, modify the EC2 instance by creating a tag key called `CostCenter`, with any non-empty value.
9. Reevaluate the `security-chapter5` AWS Config rule. Check the EC2 instance compliance status regarding this rule.
10. In the AWS Config Console, open the resource timeline for the EC2 resource. See that the timeline shows the progress of the configuration and how it complied with the rule.

Amazon Inspector

We started the chapter talking about how logging and monitoring services capture data and provide observability about the systems. Sometimes data is generated at the monitored component and sent to the service. In some cases, the service assesses the monitored resources, actively looking for the data. Amazon Inspector is a vulnerability management service that actively runs assessments on the monitored systems, obtaining information about software vulnerabilities, and networking access.

Amazon Inspector provides a previous version of the service, called Amazon Inspector Classic. Across this book, we only consider Amazon Inspector (and not Amazon Inspector Classic), as Amazon Inspector provides increased coverage and additional features.

Amazon Inspector scopes to monitor compute systems: EC2 instances, container images belonging to your private Amazon ECR registries, and AWS Lambda functions (software packages and function code).

Stage 3: Events Analysis **171**

When assessing resources, Amazon Inspector can run package vulnerability scans (analyzing operating systems, application programming languages, and dependencies' vulnerabilities), code vulnerability scans (analyzing your custom application code, available for AWS Lambda functions), and network reachability scans (analyzing open networking paths, available for EC2 instances).

Table 5.4 shows how Amazon Inspector works for each compute resource it analyzes.

TABLE 5.4 Amazon Inspector: Available Types of Inspection

	Compute Instances	Container	Lambda
Monitored Resources	EC2	Images in a private Amazon ECR registry	AWS Lambda functions
Findings Scope	Package vulnerability Network reachability	Package vulnerability	Package vulnerability Code vulnerability
Scanning Types	N/A	Basic (provided by ECR) Enhanced (provided by Inspector)	Standard (package vulnerability) Code scanning (package and code vulnerability)
Agent	Package vulnerability scan modes: Agent-based. AWS Systems Manager agent Hybrid (or agentless). Use SSM agent when available; EBS snapshots as second option No agent required for network reachability scan	Not required	Not required
Scan Behavior	Package vulnerability, agent based: Continuously (at launch, when new software is installed, and when a new relevant CVE is added) Package vulnerability, agentless: Continuously, every 24 hours Network reachability: Continuously, every 24 hours	Continuously, (at push time, and when a relevant CVE is added*) with end date defined by the automated rescan duration parameter	Continuously (when a lambda function is first deployed, when it is updated, and when a new relevant CVE is added)

*You can enable scan only when an image is pushed to the repository.

172 Chapter 5 • Security Logging and Monitoring

Amazon Inspector produces information about what was found when running the assessments, in the form of findings. A finding contains detailed information about the detected vulnerability, including a title and description, affected resource, severity rating and scoring, and remediation options. Amazon Inspector console provides a visual interface to list and filter findings. You can also query the service by calling the ListFindings API. For a consolidated view of statistics about findings, the service provides the Amazon Inspector dashboard. Within the dashboard, you get a quick overview of the coverage, risk-based remediations, and critical findings (aggregated and per monitored resource category). In addition to external scores, Amazon Inspector provides an Inspector score that takes into consideration the external scores and the context of the affected resource (for example, Inspector score will be revised for a network exploited vulnerability, if the affected resource is not openly accessible on the Internet). Amazon Inspector findings follow a life cycle, starting with active (initial state when a finding is reported), then moving to suppressed (hidden findings, matching user-created suppression rules), and finally ending with closed (when a previously identified vulnerability is remediated). Closed findings are deleted after an AWS-defined period.

For consumption of Amazon Inspector findings outside the service, you have several options. Amazon Inspector publishes each finding as an event to Amazon EventBridge, so you can consume those events in a stream-like way by subscribing to an event bus (you learn more about Amazon EventBridge in the next sections). You can also use AWS Security Hub to view findings generated from Amazon Inspector. AWS Security Hub provides mechanisms to manage findings generated by different security tools (you learn more about AWS Security Hub in Chapter 8, "Threat Detection and Incident Response"). Finally, to consume Amazon Inspector findings in a batch-like way, you can export findings in CSV or JSON formats to an Amazon S3 bucket you own.

In addition to the off-the-shelf integration with compute resources that Amazon Inspector offers, you can also integrate Amazon Inspector scans in your CI/CD pipelines. In that situation, you use the Amazon Inspector Software Bill of Materials (SBOM) generator feature. The SBOM generator is a binary tool that scans containers and images and produces a file with the list of detected installed packages and versions. Then, you can call the Amazon Inspector scan API with the SBOM file as input. Amazon Inspector will return a package vulnerability report. Integrating the SBOM generator and scan API into your CI/CD pipelines (Amazon Inspector also provides plugins for easy integration with selected CI/CD solutions) allows you to detect and remediate vulnerabilities before deploying your software.

Amazon Security Lake

Managing data records at scale can be a burden. A data lake is a storage solution that establishes the definitions to manage large volumes of data. It covers definitions like the central repository for raw and processed data, and the required governance to manage it (e.g., data schema, access control, storage structure, ingestion, consumption, and life cycle, among other tasks). Amazon Security Lake provides a managed data lake for security records. Records are stored in a common schema called Open Cybersecurity Schema Framework (OCSF). OCSF defines schemas for a series of event classes. Event classes can be system activities (like file system, kernel, and memory), identity and access management activities, network activities, discovery activities, application activities, or security findings (vulnerability findings, compliance findings, detection findings, or incident findings).[1] Producers (sources) ingest their security records into Amazon Security Lake following an OCSF schema. Similarly, subscribers access and query security records stored in Amazon Security Lake using the OCSF structure.

Amazon Security Lake relies on other AWS Services. The security records are stored in parquet format inside customer-owned Amazon S3 buckets (inheriting capabilities like encryption, access control, and life cycle management). AWS Glue provides the data catalog capabilities, while AWS Lake Formation contributes governance functions like establishing granular access controls. Once you create your Amazon Security Lake, you will see the corresponding objects in each one of those services.

At the core of the Amazon Security Lake are the concepts of sources and subscribers. A *source* is the representation of a producer of records. A source can be native (i.e., an AWS service: Route53 resolver query logs, Security Hub findings, VPC Flow Logs, CloudTrail management events, or CloudTrail data events from S3 or Lambda), or custom. In either case, Amazon Security Lake creates a separate table for the source that contains records from a single OCSF event class. When defining a custom source, Amazon Security Lake configures the IAM permissions, sets up the storage structure in Amazon S3, and creates the corresponding entries in AWS Glue and AWS Lake Formation. The producer is then in charge of ingesting the records into the Security Lake according to the configured structures. Amazon Security Lake provides integration with several third-party producers and can integrate with multiple other corporate applications via AWS AppFabric. Custom sources can also ingest the records into Amazon S3 directly or via Amazon Kinesis Firehose.

Native sources automatically convert the records to the required schema and format. Custom sources need to provide the records already transformed to the OCSF schema, and in parquet format. Using Kinesis Firehose makes it easier to execute those preprocessing tasks.

Subscribers represent the consumers of the information stored in the Security Lake. When defining a subscriber, you can granularly establish which sources the subscriber will have access to. The subscriber will then have access only to the data ingested by the authorized sources and located in the local region where the subscriber is being created.

---

[1] For an updated list of OCSF event classes, check the OCSF documentation at https://schema.ocsf.io/.

> When you configure Amazon Security Lake, you decide in which regions it will be enabled. The service will create the data lake structure in each one of the regions. You can then define one or more regions (contributing regions) to make a copy of their records into a centralized (rollup) region. You give a subscriber access to records from several regions by creating it in the rollup region. A region can contribute to several rollup regions; however, a rollup region cannot be a contributing region.

Amazon Security Lake gives two options to restrict the access of subscribers to the data lake records: data access and query access. Data access allows the subscriber to consume the data directly from the Amazon S3 bucket where it resides. The subscriber is notified when a new object is uploaded to the data lake, either via a message in an Amazon SQS queue (pull mechanism), or by synchronously receiving a message in a configured HTTPS endpoint, via Amazon EventBridge (push mechanism). When selecting query access, the subscriber accesses the records by querying the data lake tables as defined in Lake Formation (that in turn, exist in the AWS Glue Data Catalog). The subscribers query the Amazon Security Lake using any of the query services offered by AWS Glue, like Amazon Athena, Amazon Redshift (spectrum), Spark SQL, or third-party solutions (such as Splunk).

Amazon Security Lake is tightly integrated with AWS Organizations. When you enable Amazon Security Lake for AWS Organizations, you must designate a delegated administrator account (it cannot be the AWS Organizations management account), and the service can be enabled for all accounts in the organization (in all the selected regions). You can only make changes in the configurations of Amazon Security Lake from the delegated administrator account.

Amazon GuardDuty

Amazon GuardDuty analyzes selected logs to produce observable records of suspicious activities, which are known as *findings*. You learn more about Amazon GuardDuty and its relationship with automated incident response in Chapter 8, "Threat Detection and Incident Response."

AWS Security Hub

AWS Security Hub is a service that consolidates security findings related to your AWS resources and presents them in a single pane view. AWS Security Hub receives information from other AWS security services (such as Amazon GuardDuty, Amazon Inspector, Amazon Macie, AWS Firewall Manager, and IAM Access Analyzer), as well as integrated third-party security products or from your own custom security applications.

> Input and output data in AWS Security Hub conforms to a standardized format called AWS Security Finding Format (ASFF).

You learn more about AWS Security Hub in Chapter 8, "Threat Detection and Incident Response."

AWS Systems Manager: State Manager, Patch Manager, and Compliance

These three capabilities of AWS Systems Manager (State Manager, Patch Manager, and Compliance) are categorized under the group node management of the service.

State Manager and Patch Manager capabilities work by specifying the desired state of a managed resource (by documenting a set of desired parameters) and constantly act to keep the fleet adhering to that state. Compliance capability shows you the current adherence status both for State Manager and Patch Manager.

State Manager relies on the concept of associations. An association is a construct that defines a desired state of an instance in the form of an AWS SSM document. The documents specify actions to evaluate and update an instance to a desired state. An association also defines which instances are covered by this desired state and a schedule to periodically execute the checks. For example, you can use a predefined AWS SSM document to confirm whether an antivirus program is installed and updated. If it is not installed, the document defines the actions for installing it. If it is already installed, the document defines the actions for updating it. If the two conditions are fulfilled, the system is marked as compliant.

SSM documents are JSON- or YAML-formatted files that describe the actions to be executed and their workflow. They receive parameters at execution time. SSM documents can be of different types. The ones more relevant for this discussion are *command* and *automation*. Command documents are used with the State Manager capability. Automation documents are executed by the Automation capability of SSM. You can create an association that uses an Automation document in State Manager, but it will be triggered by the Automation capability.

State Manager can also use a document of type *policy*. It uses that document to gather inventory information.

Whereas State Manager keeps track of the desired status of an instance by periodically executing associations, Patch Manager orchestrates actions to keep nodes in the desired state, specifically regarding OS and application patches. It also consolidates patching compliance information in a common location. Patch Manager relies on the concept of patch baselines. A patch baseline is a Patch Manager construct that contains a set of rules to auto-approve patches for a specific operating system. Therefore, a patch baseline represents a list of patches that a node with a specific operating system is approved to have installed at that time. There are AWS-managed patch baselines for each available operating system, but you can also create your own. Patch baselines consider the operating system, application (for the Windows OS), product names, classification (such as security, enhancement, bugfix, featurepack, and drivers), its severity (low to critical), and time since the patch release. Patch Manager can run scan, and scan and install operations. In either case, Patch Manager always compares the current node status with its corresponding patch baseline to produce compliance reports (scan) or to install missing patches (scan and install).

Using patch policies allows you to run scan and install operations across a whole AWS Organization, including all regions. A patch policy defines the scope (target nodes, accounts, and regions), the type of operation (scan, or scan and install), the patch baselines, and the schedule to run. Once you define a patch policy, Patch Manager will take care of all the tasks to execute the operations as per the patch policy definition.

Because patch policies allow you to configure all patching operations in the same place, with a comprehensive coverage (multi-account and multiregion), it is the preferred method for running Patch Manager operations.

> AWS Systems Manager offers a Host Management configuration that can update agents, collect inventory data, and scan instances for missing patches (based on the patch baselines). While this option also covers multi-account, multiregion environments, it only permits scanning operations (it does not install missing patches).

Patch Manager can also run patching operations by running a select list of AWS System Manager command documents. You can see the documentation (https://docs.aws.amazon.com/systems-manager/latest/userguide/patch-manager-ssm-documents.html) for a list of SSM documents used to run patching operations. While each document has its own particularities, they all are used to execute either scan, or scan and install patching operations. You can use State Manager to run an association based on one of those patching documents, or you can schedule an AWS Systems Manager maintenance window to run one of those patching documents.

Directly from the Patch Manager console, you can execute a patch now operation that immediately executes a patching operation on the selected resources. Under the hood, the Patch Manager patch now operation creates an AWS-PatchNowAssociation association that runs once, based on one of the aforementioned patching documents.

The AWS-RunPatchBaseline, AWS-RunPatchBaselineAssociation, and AWS-RunPatchBaselineWithHooks documents run patching operations according to a patch baseline. To identify the patch baseline to apply to a node, Patch Manager implements the concept of *patch groups*. A patch group is a list of nodes that you can associate with a patch baseline. When running one of the baseline patching documents in a node, the node's SSM agent will try to match the patch group where the node belongs to its corresponding patch baseline. If the node does not belong to any patch group, or if the patch group has not associated a patch baseline, Patch Manager informs the SSM agent to use the default patch baseline for the node's operating system. You configure a patch group by assigning a tag with the key PatchGroup or Patch Group to the node.

Patch Manager operations running on patch policies do not rely on patch groups (because the patch policy defines the patch baselines to use).

When Patch Manager runs patching operations, the nodes executing the actions can report the patch compliance status back to the service. In the Patch Manager console, the Patch Manager dashboard provides an overview of the compliance status across all managed nodes, as well as a list of the most recent patching operations related to patching policy executions.

The Patch Manager compliance reporting console provides the most recent patching compliance information for the managed nodes. You can consume the information in batches by generating on-demand or scheduled reports in CSV format to be exported to an Amazon S3 bucket you own.

Each time Patch Manager runs a patching operation, it reports the compliance status, overwriting the previous compliance information. If you are using different patch baselines for the same node (for example, running patch policies and running a maintenance window with conflicting patch baselines for the same node), the compliance status can change, providing inexact results. AWS recommends using only one method to run patching operations, to avoid those inconsistencies.

The SSM Compliance capability offers an overview of the status of the monitored nodes according to the patch and status compliance definitions (given by the Patch Manager and State Manager capabilities). With Patch Manager and State Manager, you define your desired state and constantly compare it with the current state of your monitored resources. The Compliance dashboard provides you with an easy way to access that information in a single panel. You can consume this information either directly through the Compliance console or through API calls.

To consume observable records from AWS SSM Compliance in a batch-like mode, use the SSM Resource Data Sync feature (part of the Inventory capability of AWS SSM). When setting up a resource data sync, you define an Amazon S3 bucket (from one of your accounts), where the Inventory capability will deliver inventory information (in the form of JSON files). These files contain information about your managed instances. The resource data sync will update the information when new compliance data is gathered.

Use Amazon EventBridge to consume compliance events in a stream-like fashion. To do that, configure an EventBridge rule to detect Configuration Compliance State Changes event types, from AWS Systems Manager. You learn about Amazon EventBridge in the following sections.

AWS Trusted Advisor

Any discussion about gathering security insights on your AWS account would be incomplete without mentioning AWS Trusted Advisor. This service provides a list of checks that compare your current account status against a set of good practices grouped under the categories security, cost optimization, fault tolerance, performance, service limits, and operational excellence. Basic and Developer support plans have access via a console to the whole service limits category and to a subset of the security category. AWS accounts subscribed to Business or higher support levels are entitled to access all categories' checks, making calls to the Trusted Advisor API, enable an organizational view (from the AWS Organizations management account), and integrate with AWS Compute Optimizer, AWS Config, and AWS Security Hub. For each validated check, Trusted Advisor will provide you with a result in the form of a recommended action (error status), a recommended investigation (warning status), or no further action (no problems detected; ok status).

AWS Trusted Advisor keeps a list of observations about how you can improve your environment. In addition to the Trusted Advisor checks, observations can come from AWS Config rules, from AWS Security Hub controls, and from Compute Optimizer recommendations. For accounts subscribed to Enterprise Support, recommendations can also come manually from AWS team experts and provided as part of the Trusted Advisor Priority feature. These observable records are available within the AWS Management Console (and via API calls for Business and higher support plan subscribers). From the AWS Console, you can also download a file containing all the observable records and configure your account contacts to receive a weekly email with a status report.

AWS Trusted Advisor checks your account resources throughout all regions. It is enabled or disabled at the account level (or at the organizational level if you enable the organizational view from your management account subscribed to Business support or higher).

Stage 4: Action

The action stage is the final step in this framework. Technically speaking, it represents the activities taken as a reaction to an observation as a way of improving a security posture, which is not explicitly part of the security logging and monitoring domain. This section focuses on Amazon EventBridge as a service that connects observations and analyzed insights that consumers can use to take action. In fact, Amazon EventBridge takes a key role in triggering automatic actions you learn about in Chapter 8, "Threat Detection and Incident Response."

Amazon EventBridge is a serverless AWS service that handles messages in a way that allows you to connect applications that produce and consume those messages. On one side, it receives messages (observable records in JSON format) that producers deliver, while on the other side, it routes events to consumers. EventBridge is a key component of implementing event-driven architectures. From the security point of view, EventBridge connects sources that deliver a stream of events representing changes to resources (usually within an AWS account, but it can also extend to external resources) with destinations that can act based on those events.

Amazon EventBridge is extremely useful because it provides services and applications with an easy way to connect with each other, without the need to build the response actions themselves. The flow shown in Figure 5.11 allows you to better understand the logic behind Amazon EventBridge. The process starts with the ingestion of events (generated by different sources, like AWS resources, partners' SaaS applications, custom applications, or message providers). Events are ingested into a message structure (event bus or pipe). Those structures provide message handling functionalities (like matching patterns, transformation, enrichment, or archiving). Applications then consume messages delivered from the message structure.

Amazon EventBridge provides different capabilities depending on the event structure that handles the messages: event buses or pipes. With event buses, you can connect multiple sources with multiple destinations. An event bus receives all messages on the ingestion side (without any filtering).

Amazon EventBridge provides a default bus and the option to set up additional managed event buses. Amazon EventBridge automatically provides a unique default event bus (that cannot be deleted) per region and per account.

AWS services deliver events to the default event bus. Those events are delivered either on a *best effort* or a *durable* basis. Best effort means the service sends all events to EventBridge, but in some cases the event could not be delivered. In a durable delivery, every event is delivered at least once in the default event bus. AWS public documentation provides the list of services that send events to EventBridge, and the type of delivery.

FIGURE 5.11 Amazon EventBridge flow representation.

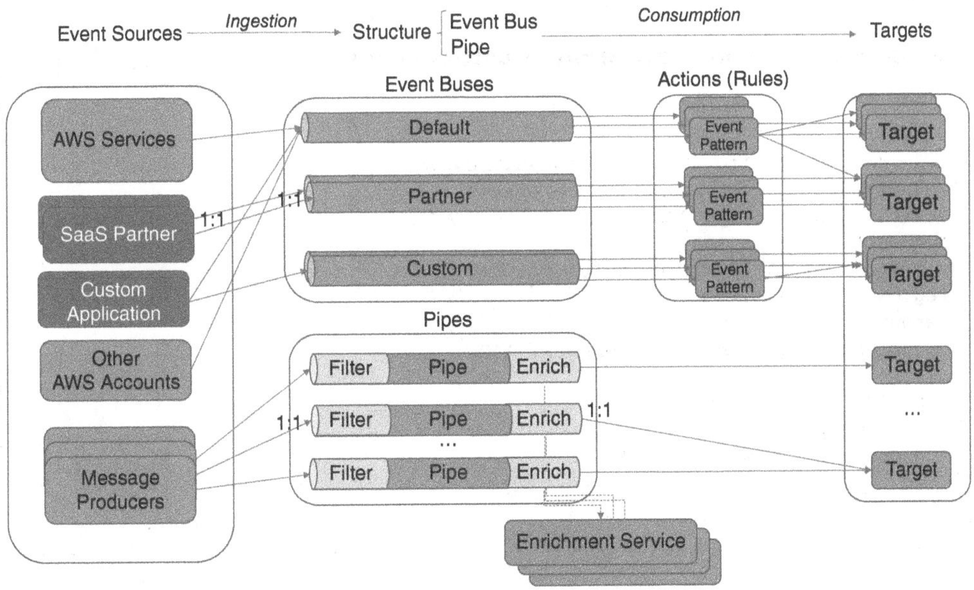

A special case of an AWS service delivering events to Amazon EventBridge is AWS CloudTrail. CloudTrail provides extensibility to capture events originated by other AWS services. Amazon EventBridge receives management, insights, and data events according to the configuration of the CloudTrail trails.

Managed event buses can be either partner event buses (receiving events from supported SaaS partners) or custom event buses (receiving events from custom applications).

To set up a partner event bus, complete the configuration on the partner SaaS application (AWS documentation provides the list of supported SaaS partner integrations). Once you complete that setup, you link the partner event source to a managed event bus in your AWS account. Each partner event source is attached to one, and only one, partner event bus. Conversely, a partner event bus can only receive events from one partner event source.

Amazon EventBridge also gives you the flexibility to create your own custom event buses. An application can ingest custom events into Amazon EventBridge through the PutEvents API. These custom events can be sent to the default event bus or to a custom event bus.

> The PutEvents API is a data-plane call. If the call results in an error, the call returns an error code and message. In the API documentation, AWS provides a list of retryable and non-retryable error codes.

In the Example 5.7, you can see the representation of a custom event on Amazon EventBridge.

Real World Scenario

Example 5.7: Amazon EventBridge Custom Event

```
{
  "version": "0",
  "id": "d1d7dcde-71fc-dbbd-1480-c5c85c7bb987",
  "detail-type": "Custom App Sample Event",
  "source": "custom.app.001",
  "account": "123456789012",
  "time": "2025-02-27T17:10:00Z",
  "region": "sa-east-1",
  "resources": [
    "colombia:bogota:bunidos:sensor/12345"
  ],
  "detail": {
    "custom-app-id": "id-2131580",
    "department": "accounting"
  }
}
```

On the consumption side, Amazon EventBridge applies pattern-matching rules to decide which messages route to which target applications. A target can be an AWS service, an API destination, or another EventBridge event bus.

An API destination is an HTTP endpoint that Amazon EventBridge can use as a target to deliver an event. To use an API destination, you define a connection, which is a construct that establishes the authorization parameters for the API call.

Within the rule, you establish an event pattern (attributes to select the events) and the targets to send the event to. Example 5.8 illustrates an event pattern that matches the previously discussed custom event.

 Real World Scenario

Example 5.8: Event Pattern for the Sample Custom Event

```
{
  "account": [
    "123456789012"
  ],
  "source": [
    "custom.app.001"
  ],
  "detail-type": [
    "Custom App Sample Event"
  ],
  "detail": {
    "custom-app-id": [
      "id-2131580"
    ]
  }
}
```

Amazon EventBridge keeps a repository of the event schemas called the Amazon EventBridge Schema Registry. This repository is already populated with event schemas for existing AWS services events. You can update the Schema Registry by uploading your own schemas or by starting the process of discovering schemas on an event bus. For every registered schema, you can download code bindings, embed them in your applications, and send custom events directly from them.

Another option is to use the rule to configure a transformation on the message to send only a section of the matched event, send a predefined static JSON message, or define an input transformer (create your own JSON message structure based on attributes and values from the matched event). A single rule can send messages to multiple targets, and an event bus can have multiple rules associated with it. However, a rule can only be associated with one event bus.

When configuring a target for an event bus rule, you can define retry configurations like the maximum age of an event and maximum retry attempts. Amazon EventBridge implements retries with exponential backoff and jitter within those limits.

An event bus also provides storing capabilities, such as archiving messages, replaying archived messages, and dead letter queues (DLQs). DLQs are customer-created Amazon SQS queues that hold messages not successfully delivered. Amazon EventBridge delivers the message to DLQ when a non-retryable error message is received from the target, or after exhausting the retrying attempts. Messages sent to DLQ will include information about the error code. Amazon EventBridge will also publish an Amazon CloudWatch metric.

In summary, by creating and attaching rules to an event bus, you have the capability to select and communicate an event to other applications, so they can trigger actions as a response.

AWS services like Amazon GuardDuty and AWS Security Hub rely on Amazon EventBridge to provide access to their findings in a stream-like structure.

In Exercise 5.6, you will create and attach a rule to an Amazon EventBridge default bus. The rule will capture AWS CloudTrail events logging the creation or deletion of Amazon S3 buckets. You will apply an input transformer and deliver the message to an Amazon SNS topic.

EXERCISE 5.6

AWS CloudTrail Integration with Amazon EventBridge

1. Open the Amazon EventBridge AWS Management Console.
2. Create a new rule, applied over the default bus.
3. Use the Custom Pattern option to configure the rule so that it captures every occurrence of an S3 bucket being created or deleted, as shown here:

```
{
  "source": [
    "aws.s3"
  ],
```

```
"detail-type": [
  "AWS API Call via CloudTrail"
],
"detail": {
  "eventSource": [
    "s3.amazonaws.com"
  ],
  "eventName": [
    "DeleteBucket",
    "CreateBucket"
  ]
}
}
```

4. Configure the Amazon SNS topic `security-chapter5` as the target for the rule.

5. Configure a transformation using an input transformer. For the input transformer, use the following:

```
{
  "bucket": "$.detail.requestParameters.bucketName",
  "action": "$.detail.eventName"
}
```

Use a template that uses the variables you defined in the input transformer. It should look something like this:

```
"The action <action> was executed on bucket <bucket>.This is an SNS
    notification from a CloudTrail event via EventBridge"
```

6. Delete the test S3 bucket you created in Exercise 5.4 (or execute any create or delete bucket action). Confirm that the notification of the action has arrived on the `security-chapter5` topic, with the message as you defined in the template.

Pipes are the second type of structure that Amazon EventBridge provides to handle messages. In contrast to event buses, pipes define a sequential workflow that connects exactly one source with one target: listen for source messages, filter, enrich, and deliver to the target. Sources for Amazon EventBridge pipes are message providers (stream sources like Amazon DynamoDB, Amazon Kinesis, or Apache Kafka implementations; message queues like Amazon SQS; and message brokers like Amazon MQ). Amazon EventBridge pipes listen for new messages from those sources and use filters to select events at ingestion time.

When configuring AWS stream sources (Amazon DynamoDB or Amazon Kinesis streams), you can define a DLQ (Amazon SNS topic or Amazon SQS queue), a maximum age, maximum retry attempts, and retry behavior for partial batch failures. Amazon EventBridge will automatically retry failed retrieves on retryable failures.

TABLE 5.5 Amazon EventBridge: Event Buses and Pipes

	Event Bus	**Pipe**
Pattern matching	Rules	Filters
Producer-to-target ratio	Many:many	One:one
Transformation capabilities	Part of matched event Constant JSON Input transformer	Enrichment capabilities (external calls) Input transformer
Sources	AWS services SaaS partners Custom app	Messages providers: streams, message queue, and message brokers
Long-term storage capabilities	Archive and replay	No

After a message is selected by the filter, Amazon EventBridge pipes can call an enrichment service, like an Amazon Lambda function, Amazon StepFunctions, Amazon API gateway, or an API destination. The transformed message received from the enrichment service is then sent to one target that can be an AWS service or an API destination. AWS documentation provides a list of supported Amazon EventBridge targets. When selecting a target, you can also configure an input transformer, similar to how you do with event buses.

> An event bus can be configured as the target of a pipe. In that case, you can use the advanced transformation capabilities of a pipe and fan out to multiple targets.

You can configure pipes to send log records of each execution to Amazon CloudWatch Logs, Amazon Firehose, or Amazon S3. When configuring the log recording, you can also define the level of logging you want to deliver (off, error, info, or trace) and if you want to include execution data (payloads, request, and response from enrichment services and targets).

Table 5.5 compares event buses and pipe structures.

Summary

Logging and monitoring services are a fundamental part of AWS Cloud security principles. Because of the high level of visibility that you reach when implementing your workloads in the cloud, these detection services are able to accomplish their goals in a comprehensive manner. In general, the job of the detection services starts by monitoring resources and keeping an up-to-date picture of their status. AWS services in the detection category provide visibility for AWS resources (such as API calls reported by AWS CloudTrail) and allows to collect user-related information (for example, by installing an AWS SSM agent inside monitored instances). Taking advantage of the automation provided by the cloud, these services are able to capture (as observable records) the events and changes affecting the resources. Using the cloud analytics capabilities, they can process those records and produce insights related to security events. Because of the integration capabilities of the cloud, the services can also automatically respond to different situations in a way that can remediate those findings.

Exam Essentials

Understand how AWS Config establishes a continuous compliance control. AWS Config expands its capabilities through the whole detective spectrum. Configuration items are the JSON-object representation of the monitored resources. They are stored in an AWS Config repository and can be accessed using different methods like API calls, queries, or processing of the files exported into S3 buckets. Configuration stream delivers a constant update of changes occurring to monitored resources, giving the opportunity to be notified or act upon a change in the environment. AWS Config extends its functionality with AWS Config Rules, which apply a sort of comparison with a desired state of configuration, establishing a continuous monitoring control on every monitored resource.

Understand how AWS CloudTrail monitors usage. AWS CloudTrail captures information about API calls occurring inside the AWS environment. For quick access to events reported in the last 90 days, AWS CloudTrail offers the event history feature. For longer retention and analysis of the information, a trail provides the mechanism of delivering the information into a S3 bucket. A trail constantly receives event information (usually reporting within 15 minutes of its occurrence). Integration with Amazon EventBridge allows you to create responses for specific API calls. AWS CloudTrail provides the mechanisms for you to protect the trails by applying the least privileged access control and using integrity validation methods.

Distinguish the differences and relationships between Amazon CloudWatch and Amazon CloudWatch Logs. Amazon CloudWatch is a metric repository that keeps track of important telemetry produced by monitored resources over time. It also alerts when they are outside predefined thresholds. Amazon CloudWatch Logs is a managed centralized repository that receives and stores logs generated by different sources. Amazon CloudWatch Logs offers management capabilities to query the stored log information. Using the EMF format, it converts logs into Amazon CloudWatch metrics.

Be familiar with Amazon Inspector capabilities.   Amazon Inspector analyzes the current state of computing instances (EC2 instances, containers, and Lambda functions) and reports detected vulnerabilities. Amazon Inspector allows you to run package vulnerability, code vulnerability, and network reachability scans. Amazon Inspector offers agent-based and agentless scans. The result of the scans are findings that can be accessed programmatically through the Amazon Inspector dashboard and shared with services like Amazon EventBridge and AWS Security Hub.

Understand how Amazon Security Lake simplifies security data management.   Amazon Security Lake is a managed data lake for security records. Using OCSF, Amazon Security Lake simplifies the standardization and subsequent analysis of security-related information. Record producers ingest data into Amazon Security Lake, which provides extraction, transformation, access control, analytics, and publishing capabilities. Subscribers can then consume security-related data using querying mechanisms.

Understand how Amazon EventBridge connects producers and consumers of events.   Amazon EventBridge allows sources of events to connect with consumers who act upon the received event. Events are ingested into Amazon EventBridge event buses or pipes, filtered, transformed, and delivered to targets (consumers). Using Amazon EventBridge, a source service can export relevant findings to a destination that will be in charge of taking actions.

Understand how to use AWS Health.   AWS Health notifies about performance or availability issues and planned maintenance activities that affect the underlying infrastructure supporting the workloads in the AWS account.

Internalize how AWS Trusted Advisor increases an account's security posture.   AWS Trusted Advisor provides actionable items to increase the security posture of the account. By periodically checking and acting based on AWS Trusted Advisor results, an account administrator can increase the security posture of the environment.

Recognize AWS Systems Manager capabilities.   AWS Systems Manager provides a comprehensive collection of capabilities to better operate instances and applications at scale. Some of these capabilities integrate with logging and monitoring processes. Inventory, application management, and operations management functionalities organize and provide information about the current status of monitored resources. Compliance, Patch Manager, and State Manager compare and update the status of the resources with the desired up-to-date standards.

Review Questions

You can find the answers to the review questions in Appendix A.

1. Read the following statements and choose the correct option:

I. By default, a trail delivers management events.

II. By default, a trail delivers insights events.

III. By default, a trail delivers data events.

    A. I, II, and III are correct.

    B. Only I is correct.

    C. Only II is correct.

    D. Only III is correct.

2. What is the representation of a point-in-time view of the attributes of a monitored resource in AWS Config called?

    A. Configuration snapshot

    B. Configuration item

    C. Configuration stream

    D. Configuration record

3. Read the following statements about AWS Config rules and choose the correct option:

I. A rule can be a custom rule.

II. A rule can be a managed rule.

III. A rule can be a service-linked rule.

    A. I, II, and III are correct.

    B. I and II are correct.

    C. Only I is correct.

    D. Only II is correct.

4. Which option do you use to validate the integrity of the log files delivered by AWS CloudTrail?

    A. The Amazon S3 `validate-files` action

    B. The AWS Config `cloud-trail-log-file-validation` managed rule

    C. The AWS CloudTrail `validate-logs` action

    D. There is no way to validate the integrity of those log files

188   Chapter 5 ▪ Security Logging and Monitoring

5. How could you centralize AWS CloudTrail log files from different accounts?

I. Configure the trail as an organization trail.

II. Configure the trail from different accounts to deliver to the same S3 bucket.

III. Configure the Consolidate Trails feature in AWS Organizations.
- **A.** I, II, and III are correct.
- **B.** I and II are correct.
- **C.** Only I is correct.
- **D.** Only II is correct.

6. How can you encrypt data within an Amazon CloudWatch Logs log group?

I. Use an Amazon CloudWatch Logs service encryption key

II. Use an AWS KMS symmetric key

III. Use an AWS KMS asymmetric key
- **A.** I, II, and III are correct.
- **B.** I and II are correct.
- **C.** Only I is correct.
- **D.** Only II is correct.

7. How could you receive "high resolution" metrics in Amazon CloudWatch?

I. Publish a custom metric of type "high resolution."

II. Selected AWS services produce "high resolution" metrics by default.

III. Use the `modify-resolution` request to modify the attribute resolution of a standard metric to `high resolution`.
- **A.** I, II, and III are correct.
- **B.** I and II are correct.
- **C.** Only I is correct.
- **D.** Only II is correct.

8. Which of the following is *not* part of the definition of an Amazon EventBridge rule?
- **A.** Bus
- **B.** Event pattern
- **C.** Remediation action
- **D.** Target

9. How can you manage Amazon Security Lake for accounts in an AWS Organizations?

A. Amazon Security Lake is not aware of AWS Organizations structure. Each AWS account manages the Amazon Security Lake implementation independently.

B. Amazon Security Lake is managed from the AWS Organizations management account.

C. Amazon Security Lake central configuration is managed from the AWS Organizations management account. Each member account can customize configuration at the account level.

D. Amazon Security Lake is managed from a delegated account for the AWS Organizations.

10. Which of the following statements is true about using different patch baselines for patch compliance reporting in AWS Systems Manager?

A. Compliance uses information from the more recent patch baseline to generate reports.

B. When running compliance scans, AWS Systems Manager does not allow using different patch baselines for the same instance to generate a report.

C. If two compliance scans use different patch baselines, AWS Systems Manager will overwrite the results with the more recent compliance scan.

D. If two compliance scans use different patch baselines, AWS Systems Manager will compare the results and patch baselines to provide a merged report.

Chapter 6

Infrastructure Protection

THE AWS CERTIFIED SECURITY SPECIALTY EXAM OBJECTIVES THAT LEVERAGE CONCEPTS EXPLAINED IN THIS CHAPTER INCLUDE THE FOLLOWING:

✔ **Domain 3: Infrastructure Security**

- 3.1. Design and implement security controls for edge services.
- 3.2. Design and implement network security controls.
- 3.3. Design and implement security controls for compute workloads.
- 3.4. Troubleshoot network security.

Introduction

Amazon Web Services relies on traditional and new infrastructure concepts to support applications on the AWS Cloud. And as new networking constructs are introduced (and old ones slightly changed), security policies and your cloud infrastructure must adapt to them accordingly.

This chapter introduces AWS networking concepts such as Amazon VPC, subnets, and route tables, as well as other features that are related to network address translation (NAT) gateways and traffic filtering (such as security groups, network access control lists, and network firewall). You learn how AWS adds features that will help you to do troubleshooting in networking services as well. You also learn how AWS Elastic Load Balancing works and how security services such as AWS Web Application Firewall can provide secure access to your web-based applications deployed in the cloud. This chapter also discusses how to integrate security services that enable AWS customers to protect compute workloads (e.g., managing, hardening, and scanning vulnerabilities) at both the instance and container levels.

Finally, you explore AWS's unique approach to mitigate distributed denial-of-service (DDoS) attacks while being introduced to AWS Shield services and its advanced features.

AWS Networking Constructs

Computer networking in the AWS Cloud is a critical discipline that focuses on a secure and efficient data communication among distributed computing resources. To fully grasp AWS infrastructure security, it's essential to understand the foundational networking concepts that underpin the AWS ecosystem. This section explores key AWS networking components such as Amazon Virtual Private Cloud (VPC), subnets, route tables, and network access control lists (NACLs). You explore how these elements work in conjunction with AWS security services like AWS Network Firewall, AWS Web Application Firewall (WAF), and AWS Shield to create a robust, scalable, and secure network architecture. Additionally, the chapter discusses the implementation of security groups, VPC endpoints, and AWS Transit Gateway to enhance network isolation and control. By mastering these concepts, you'll be better equipped to design and maintain secure, compliant, and highly available network infrastructures in the AWS Cloud, leveraging the latest advancements in cloud networking technology.

AWS has a series of constructs—or objects—that can compose a cloud networking topology. The first one you should know is Amazon Virtual Private Cloud, which is an abstraction that represents a virtual network within the AWS Cloud. Within a VPC, you can deploy cloud resources in a logically isolated part of the AWS Cloud, securely apart from other accounts and networks.

Of course, very few computing resources are created to be totally isolated from other systems. Therefore, within a VPC you need to employ other network constructs to allow (and, most importantly, control) the communication between cloud resources.

One of the advantages of cloud computing is its agility, which enables you to quickly spin up resources to deploy full applications in minutes. Such a characteristic facilitates experimentation and learning since you can always deprovision these resources without risks or a high investment. Therefore, if you are a beginner to AWS Cloud networking concepts, try to repeat the configurations shown in this whole chapter. Even if you are already familiar with these objects, you can follow the steps, but watch for notes or tips (like this one) to learn the details that fully characterize them.

In the AWS Management Console, the VPC configuration is currently available in the Networking and Content Delivery part of the list of AWS Cloud Services. After selecting it, you will be automatically taken to your Amazon VPC dashboard, which is shown in Figure 6.1.

As Figure 6.1 shows, the VPC dashboard presents a considerable variety of VPC-related objects. To fully understand their function, you will not follow the wizard (VPC setting --> VPC and more) in the Create VPC button (as Figure 6.2 shows). Instead, you will create your network objects one by one by using the VPC Only option.

It is important that you notice that the VPC dashboard in Figure 6.1 is associated with an AWS region (US East, N. Virginia) and therefore shows all VPCs (and their corresponding objects) that are configured within a single region. It is important to note that *VPCs do not extend beyond a region.*

Click Your VPCs in the menu at the left to open a screen that shows a list of VPCs you have already created and a button called Create VPC. Figure 6.3 shows the VPC settings you have access to. Click in one VPC and explore the different tabs available. The first one will give the general details of that specific VPC. One interesting view is the Resource Map tab, which will present the VPC and its different components like subnets, route tables, and connections. This view helps show some of the components and relationships in the VPC.

Chapter 6 ▪ Infrastructure Protection

FIGURE 6.1 Amazon VPC dashboard.

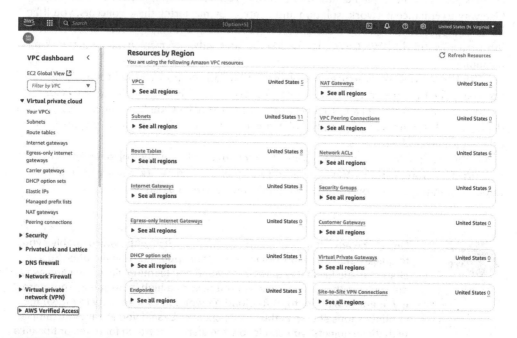

FIGURE 6.2 Create VPC dashboard (wizard view).

 Notice that by default you will see the Default VPC that is created by AWS to enable basic networking in the account. It's recommended that you create your own VPC according to the networking requirements of your applications.

FIGURE 6.3 VPC settings.

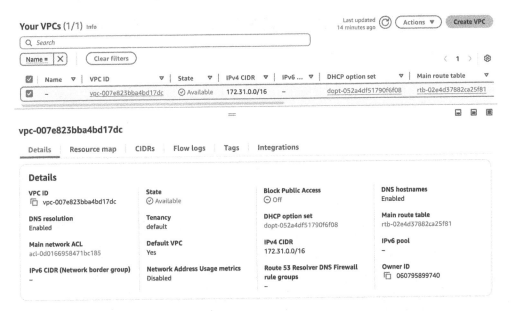

Now let's create a VPC. Click the orange Create VPC button (either in the Dashboard view or in the Your VPCs menu on the left panel). In the configuration screen shown in Figure 6.4, you can assign a name tag to a VPC (VPC1 in the figure), which will make the VPC more easily recognizable in future circumstances.

You can also define an IPv4 Classless Inter-Domain Routing (CIDR) block, which is an object that leverages public or private Internet Protocol (IP) addresses. You can also select an Amazon VPC IP Address Manager (IPAM) pool, if your organization already created one, to plan, track, and monitor IP addresses for your AWS workloads. In this example, you will assign the 10.0.0.0/16 CIDR using the manual input option. The Internet Corporation for Assigned Names and Numbers manages the assignment of public IP address blocks to service providers, which in turn can assign a subset of these addresses to another provider or organization. Such iterations may be repeated until a single public IP address is assigned to a host. Private IP addresses were defined in the Internet Engineering Task Force Request for Comments 1918, published in February 1996. In summary, these three special IP address blocks (which encompass addresses that are not valid on the Internet) are

- 10.0.0.0 to 10.255.255.255 (10/8 prefix)
- 172.16.0.0 to 172.31.255.255 (172.16/12 prefix)
- 192.168.0.0 to 192.168.255.255 (192.168/16 prefix)

In Figure 6.4, you can see that all IP addresses of VPC1 will belong to CIDR block 10.0.0.0/16. Also note that you can define the sixth version of the Internet Protocol (IPv6) to be used in VPC1 in the IPv6 CIDR block section. However, because this chapter focuses on

FIGURE 6.4 Create VPC: VPC settings.

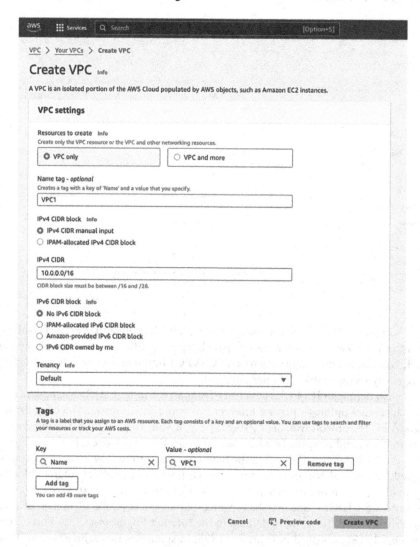

the AWS Cloud's most fundamental networking concepts, this option is not enabled in the examples throughout the chapter (the No IPv6 CIRD Block radio button is selected).

 You can have up to five IPv4 CIDR blocks per VPC (one primary and four secondaries). This quota can be increased up to a maximum of 50, if you request it. Check the AWS official documentation for complete and current information.

FIGURE 6.5 VPC1 network topology.

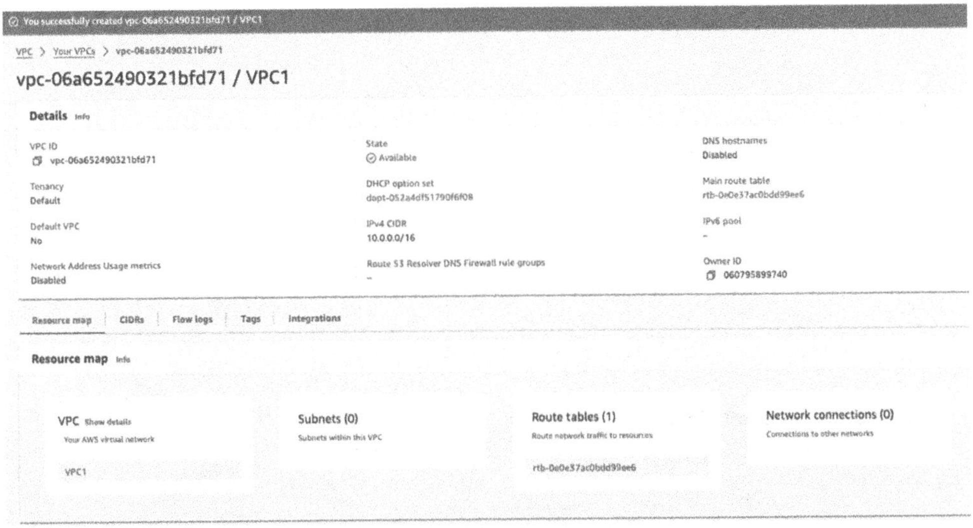

The last VPC configuration setting shown in Figure 6.4 refers to the concept of *tenancy*, which defines how VPC1 will share hardware with other accounts within the AWS Cloud. The options are as follows:

- **Default:** Amazon EC2 instances you deploy in this VPC will share hardware with other AWS accounts.
- **Dedicated:** Amazon EC2 instances deployed in a dedicated VPC will run on hardware dedicated to a single tenant (which can be understood as an AWS account).

The choice between either option depends on various factors, such as compliance regulations or existing software license specifics. For this example, you should assign VPC1 to the default option. Finish the VPC configuration by clicking Create VPC. Using the Resource map view, Figure 6.5 shows the topology that you have so far.

You can create a maximum of five VPCs per region. You can expand it, if you request it. Check the AWS official documentation for complete and current information.

Many seasoned networking engineers have surely heard the sentence "Nothing good comes out of a networking discussion that doesn't have a topology." Consequently, Figure 6.6 summarizes what you have created so far using the AWS Reference Architecture Icons.

The next concept you explore is the one called *subnet*. In the AWS Cloud context, this construct represents a range of IP addresses in your VPC. More importantly, deploying

FIGURE 6.6 Architecture VPC1 topology.

FIGURE 6.7 Subnet view.

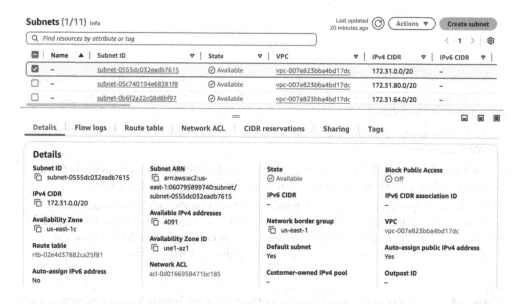

resources in a single subnet will make them inherit traffic policies that are applied to the subnet. Click on Subnets in the left panel to see a list of available subnets, and select one to see details, as shown in Figure 6.7.

You can use the Find Resources box, for example, to create a list of subnets in a specific VPC that you want to view. There are different filter criteria to use, such as VPC, route table, and tags.

Figure 6.7 shows what happens when you access the VPC dashboard again and click Subnets in the menu in the left. Now, to create a subnet, click the Create Subnet orange button.

Figure 6.8 shows the creation of a subnet called Subnet10-AZ1a. (The reason for this name will become clear over the next couple of paragraphs.) The subnet belongs to VPC1 (which is referred to by its VPC unique name identifier, vpc-06a652490321bfd71) and the availability zone (AZ) in which you are deploying this subnet. A subnet is, by definition, located within a single AZ. This fact will certainly influence your network designs and how you plan high availability for your applications.

FIGURE 6.8 Subnet creation.

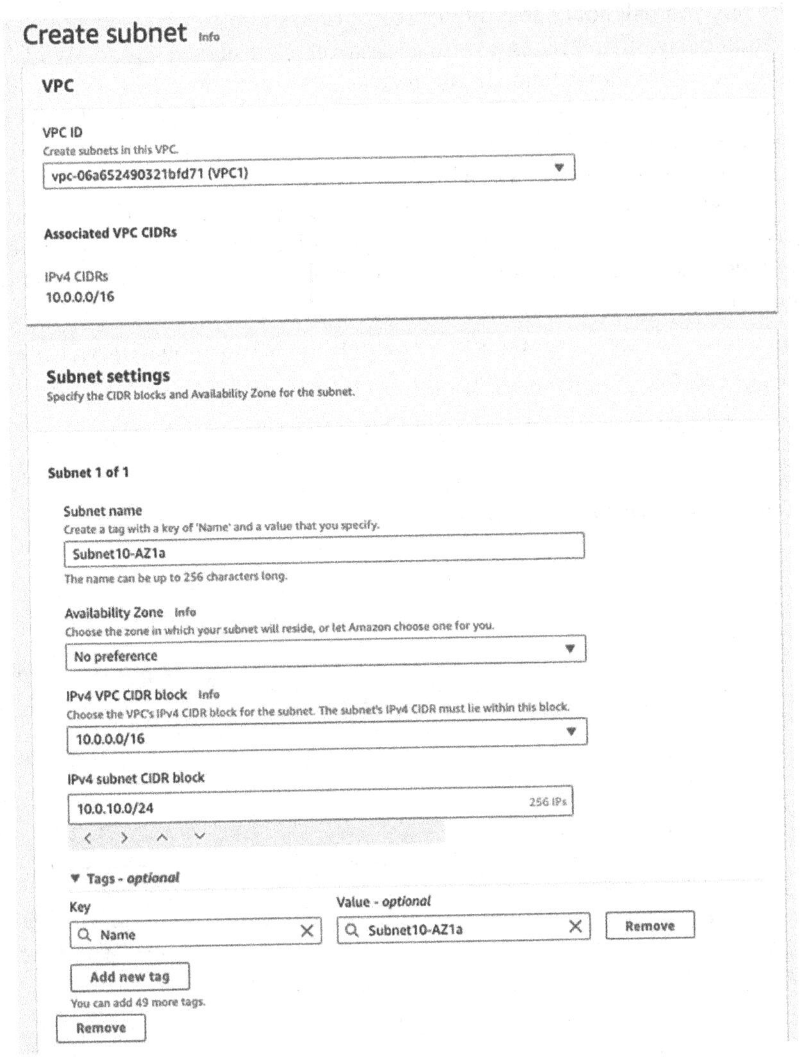

Figure 6.8 shows that you can define the subnet's IPv4 CIDR block, which in this case is 10.0.10.0/24. This network topology will use the CIDR block's third octet to differentiate subnets that belong to the defined VPC CIDR range. Hence, the naming convention chosen for Subnet10-AZ1a hopefully will facilitate your reading and quickly highlight which network and associated AZ each subnet is using.

You can have up to 200 subnets per VPC. Check the AWS official documentation for complete and current information.

Figure 6.9 shows some of Subnet10-AZ1a's parameters immediately after it is created.

In Figure 6.9, you will notice that Subnet10-AZ1a has a subnet ID (subnet-01e58c6cf92 09e8f8) that uniquely differentiates it from all other created subnets in the AWS Cloud. Furthermore, the figure shows familiar parameters such as to which VPC (VPC1) the subnet belongs and its configured IPv4 CIDR (10.0.10.0/24). Interestingly, it also shows the number of available IP addresses in this subnet.

Attentive readers will probably ask why a subnet with a 255.255.255.0 (/24) subnet mask is not showing all 254 addresses that are normally available in such configurations (256 minus 2, where the first is the subnet's network address and the last represents the subnet's broadcast address). The missing three addresses are predefined identifiers that AWS reserves in each subnet:

- **Second address:** Reserved for the VPC router (10.0.10.1 in Subnet10-AZ1a)
- **Third address:** Reserved for the DNS server (10.0.10.2 in Subnet10-AZ1a)
- **Fourth address:** Reserved for future use (10.0.1.3 in Subnet10-AZ1a)

FIGURE 6.9 Subnet10-AZ1a parameters.

AWS Networking Constructs   201

The AWS Cloud automation ensures that these IP addresses defined for the VPC router and DNS server will be automatically inserted in the Amazon EC2 instances as they are deployed on Subnet10-AZ1a.

> Unlike traditional networks, AWS does not support IP broadcast communication within a subnet.

Continuing the exploration of Figure 6.9, notice that Subnet10-AZ1a has two parameters that represent its availability zone. The first is simply called Availability Zone, which represents the choice you made during the subnet creation (in this case: us-east-1c). The zone names (such as us-east-1a and us-east-1b) are randomized per each account so that not everyone chooses the same zones. However, some users want to share resources centrally in a single account to leverage the high bandwidth and low latency from putting consumer and provider accounts in the same actual availability zones. For these scenarios, AWS created Availability Zone ID (in the image as use1-az1), which is a static reference that provides a cross-account identification of an AZ.

Finally, you will notice a Route Table parameter that points to a route table ID of rtb-0e0e37ac0bdd99ee6 listed with the subnet. In fact, this object represents the main route table associated with VPC1, which is shown in Figure 6.10 (click Route Tables in the menu at the left to see it).

FIGURE 6.10 VPC1 default route table.

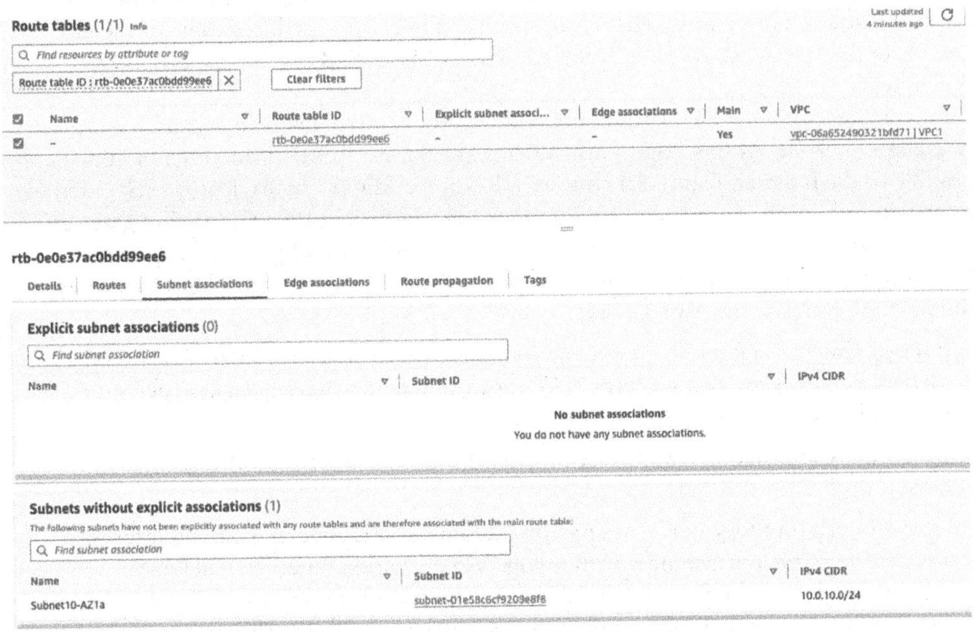

FIGURE 6.11 VPC1 subnet associations.

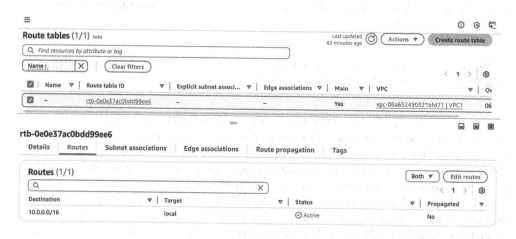

In Figure 6.11, the route table has a single route (10.0.0.0/16) declared to be a local target, which means that the VPC router can reach it within the VPC and that this route should not be propagated (or distributed) to external routers.

In Figure 6.11, once you click in the Subnet associations tab, you will see a subnet association of a route table to a specific subnet, which may surprise some network and security engineers who are more used to traditional on-premises network designs. However, through this noteworthy association, you can implement interesting routing schemes to redirect traffic from its default behavior in specific subnets. You will see some of these scenarios in the "Network Address Translation" and "VPC Endpoints" sections later in this chapter.

Now, create another subnet called Subnet20-AZ1b, whose name will suggest its address and availability zone. At this stage, both subnets are captive to VPC1 and are not at all accessible to the Internet. Figure 6.12 shows a Resource Map view. To deploy such external connectivity, you need to create yet another network construct called an Internet gateway.

An Internet gateway is a scalable, redundant, and highly available VPC component that allows communication between instances in your VPC and the Internet. There are two types of Internet gateways in the AWS Cloud:

- **Internet Gateways:** Provide a target in your VPC route tables for Internet-routable traffic (default route). They also perform NAT for instances that have been assigned public IPv4 addresses, and they support IPv6 traffic.

- **Egress Only Internet Gateways:** Are only used to enable outbound IPv6 traffic from the VPC.

In the network topology you are currently building in this chapter, you will insert an Internet gateway to make instances within your VPC reach the Internet. Click Internet Gateways in the menu at left in your VPC management console, and then click Create Internet Gateway. Figure 6.13 shows the only parameter required in this step.

FIGURE 6.12 VPC view: Resource Map.

FIGURE 6.13 Internet gateway IGW1 creation.

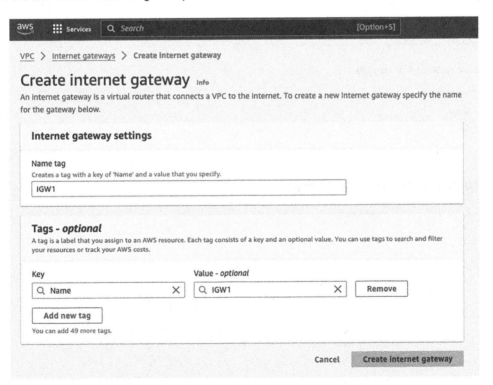

After you click Create, the state of IGW1 is red and is considered to be "detached." Such behavior occurs because you have to explicitly attach (or associate) an Internet gateway to a VPC so that it can route traffic to and from the Internet.

 There is a bidirectional relationship between these network constructs; therefore, you can have only one Internet gateway attached per VPC and each Internet gateway can only be attached to a single VPC. You can have up to five Internet gateways per region by default. Check the AWS official documentation for complete and current information.

To attach IGW1-VPC1, select IGW1 on the Internet Gateways screen, click the Actions drop-down menu, and select Attach To VPC. After you select VPC1 click the orange button labeled Attach Internet Gateway. You will reach the status shown in Figure 6.14.

Figure 6.15 represents the network topology you have built at this point.

FIGURE 6.14 IGW1 is attached to VPC1.

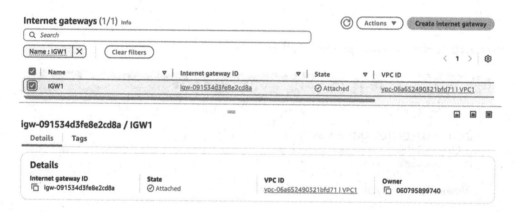

FIGURE 6.15 Updated topology.

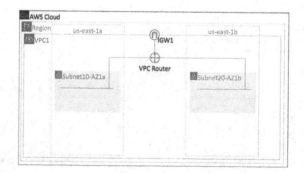

AWS Networking Constructs 205

In Figure 6.15, notice that IGW1 is serving both subnets in the VPC via the VPC router. To dive a little deeper into the inner workings of the VPC, let's look at the current status of the main route table by clicking Route Tables in the menu at left, as Figure 6.16 shows.

As you can see in Figure 6.16, this route table does not have a route to the Internet yet. Therefore, to leverage the recently created IGW1, you will add a default route (0.0.0.0/0) pointing to the Internet gateway. The VPC router will then direct any traffic that is not local (10.0.0.0/16) in VPC1 to the Internet gateway.

To make this happen, select the main route table, click Edit Routes, and add the default route (0.0.0.0/0 as Destination and IGW1 as Target), as shown in Figure 6.17.

Click Save Routes, and you now have ensured that traffic from both subnets in VPC1 will reach IGW1. However, since instances that are deployed on the created subnets will receive addresses within the range of 10.0.0.4 to 10.0.255.254, they cannot be reached on the Internet (recall that these are private addresses). Therefore, to offer a valid IP address as a target for Internet-sourced traffic, IGW1 will also have to perform network address translation (NAT).

FIGURE 6.16 Main route table after IGW1 creation.

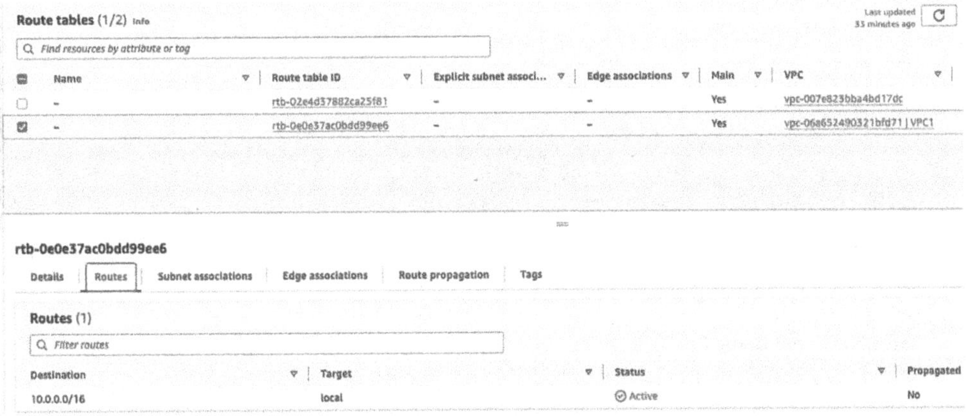

FIGURE 6.17 Adding the default route to the main route table.

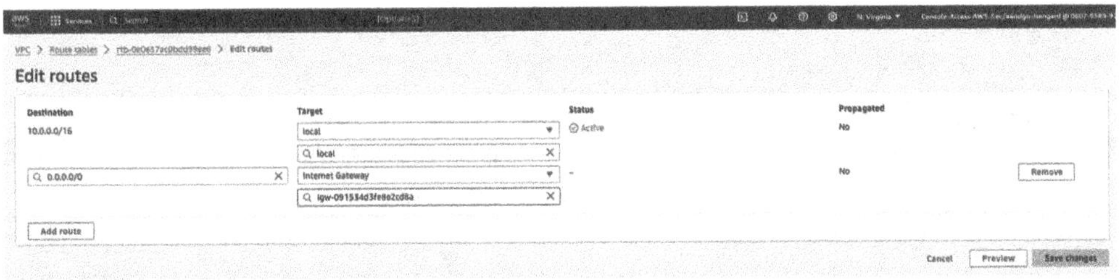

206   Chapter 6 • Infrastructure Protection

Through NAT, an Internet gateway can receive traffic directed to a public IP address and change it to a private IP address that is assigned to a resource located within a VPC. Such an endeavor can be achieved in different ways in the AWS Cloud, but for the sake of simplicity, you will rely on the simplest approach, where a public IP address is automatically assigned to instances deployed in a subnet.

Figure 6.18 shows what happens when, on the Subnets screen, you select Subnet10-AZ1a, and from the Actions drop-down menu, you select Edit Subnet Settings then the Modify Auto-Assign IP Settings option.

FIGURE 6.18   Modifying IP auto-assignment on Subnet10-AZ1a.

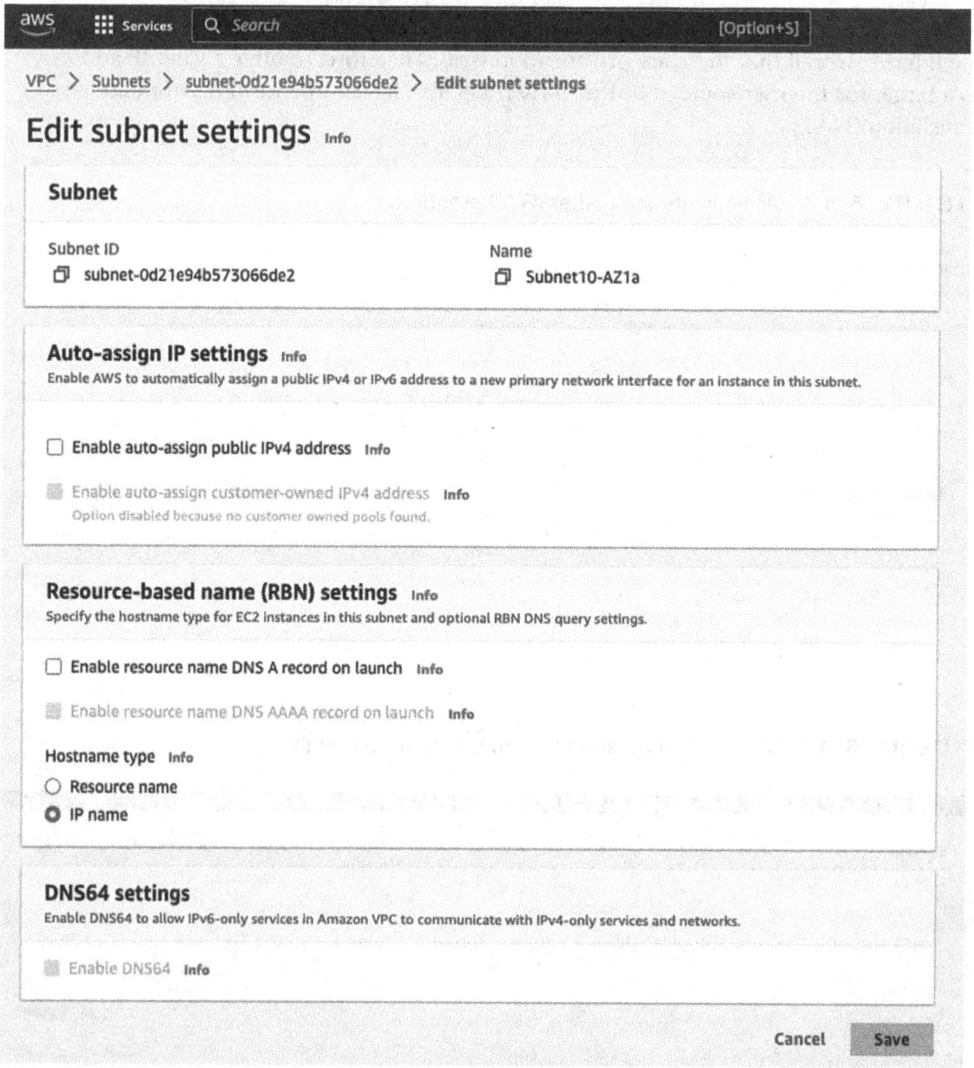

AWS Networking Constructs

FIGURE 6.19 Two instances deployed on Subnet10-AZ1a.

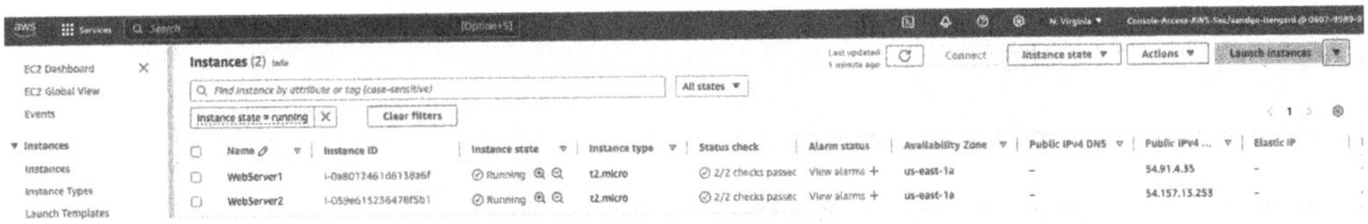

The configuration you executed in Figure 6.18 determines that an instance deployed in Subnet10-AZ1a will be automatically assigned a public IP address by default that will be registered in IGW1 (you can override this setting while launching an instance). As an experiment, you can add two Amazon EC2 instances to Subnet10-AZ1. Figure 6.19 shows a similar scenario of what you will find after deploying your instances.

As you can see in Figure 6.19, the *WebServer1* and *WebServer2* instances have IPV4 public IP addresses (54.91.4.35 and 54.157.13.253, respectively) that are routable on the Internet. That happened because the process of creating both instances took into consideration the default public IP address assignment you have performed, as shown in Figure 6.18. And because Subnet10-AZ1a can host resources that are reachable from the Internet, it can be classified as a public subnet.

The IP addresses assigned to both instances are called *elastic IP addresses*. These Internet-reachable IPv4 addresses are designed for dynamic cloud computing. You can also consider these addresses as a pool of public addresses AWS owns. They can be associated with and disassociated from resources deployed within the AWS Cloud to serve different objectives, such as temporary Internet access or application high availability.

A fair question you may have at this moment would be, "What happens when an instance is actually deployed on Subnet20-AZ1b, which does not have auto-assignment of public addresses?" If you create an Amazon EC2 instance named DBServer1 on Subnet20-AZ1b, it will not have a public IP address and therefore will not be directly accessible from the Internet via IGW1. Subnets such as Subnet20-AZ1b are commonly known as *private subnets*, and they are generally used when you are running a web application that relies on backend servers that are not accessible from the Internet but that can communicate with resources located in the same VPC.

Nonetheless, some resources deployed in private subnets (such as application or database servers) may need limited outgoing access to the Internet for various reasons, such as software updates. The next section shows you how such a need may be addressed in an Amazon VPC.

But first, you explore working with VPCs in a more hands-on way. In Exercise 6.1, you create a VPC and four subnets, and in Exercise 6.2, you create an Internet gateway for your VPC.

208   Chapter 6 ▪ Infrastructure Protection

EXERCISE 6.1

Create a VPC and Subnets

In this exercise, you create a VPC with four subnets.

1. Log in to your AWS account and choose a region of your preference.

2. Create a VPC called **SecureVPC** with a CIDR block of **192.168.0.0/16**.

3. Create a subnet called **PublicSubnet-A** in an availability zone that ends with the letter *a*, with the following CIDR block: **192.168.1.0/24**. Use the Auto-Assign Public IP Address configuration in this subnet.

4. Create a subnet called **PublicSubnet-B** in an availability zone that ends with the letter *b*, with the following CIDR block: **192.168.2.0/24**. Use the Auto-Assign Public IP Address configuration in this subnet.

5. Create a subnet called **PrivateSubnet-A** in an availability zone that ends with the letter *a*, with the following CIDR block: **192.168.3.0/24**.

6. Create a subnet called **PrivateSubnet-B** in an availability zone that ends with the letter *b*, with the following CIDR block: **192.168.4.0/24**.

EXERCISE 6.2

Create an Internet Gateway

After finishing Exercise 6.1, you create and attach an Internet gateway to your VPC.

1. Create an Internet gateway called **Internet-Gateway**.

2. Attach it to SecureVPC.

3. Create a route table called **PublicRouteTable**, associate it with Internet-Gateway, and assign it to PublicSubnet-A and PublicSubnet-B.

4. Create two free-tier Amazon EC2 instances (**Web-A** and **Web-B**) located at PublicSubnet-A and PublicSubnet-B, respectively. Allow SSH and web server in these instances and access them via the Internet. Use the following script to enable the web server on instance Web-A (and change it accordingly to Web-B):

```
#!/bin/bash
sudo -s
yum update -y
yum install httpd -y
```

```
echo "Web-A">/var/www/html/index.html
service httpd start
chkconfig httpd on
```

Network Address Translation

You can provide egress-only access to the Internet to a resource located on private subnets through a NAT gateway deployed on a public subnet. Select NAT Gateways in the menu at left in the VPC management console and click Create NAT Gateway to open the screen shown in Figure 6.20.

A NAT gateway is for use with IPv4 traffic only. To enable outbound-only Internet communication over IPv6, use an egress-only Internet gateway instead.

FIGURE 6.20 The Create NAT Gateway screen.

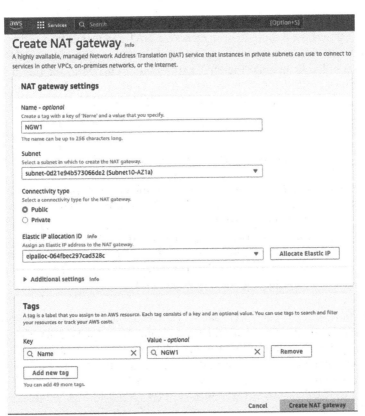

FIGURE 6.21 NAT gateway creation.

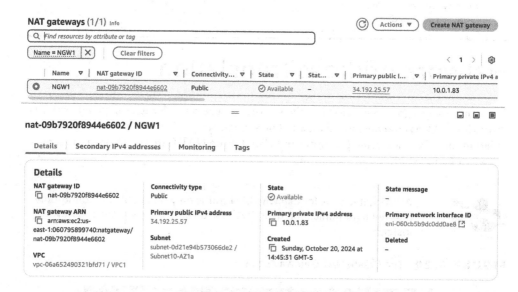

Figure 6.20 shows the required parameters of a NAT gateway: a name, that in this example will be NGW1; a subnet location in a public subnet such as Subnet10-AZ1a; connectivity set to Public because the NAT gateway needs access to the Internet; and allocation of an elastic IP address. By clicking Allocate Elastic IP Address, you will be able to assign one IP address to your NAT gateway. Figure 6.21 shows the resource after creation; once the state is set to Available, it's ready to be used in the environment.

NAT gateways support the following connectivity types:

- **Public (Default):** Instances in private subnets can connect to the Internet through a public NAT gateway but cannot receive inbound connections from the Internet.

- **Private:** Instances in private subnets can connect to other VPCs or your on-premises network through a private NAT gateway. You can route traffic from the NAT gateway through a transit gateway (TGW) or through a virtual private gateway.

The suggestion on the Create NAT Gateway screen (you can only imagine how many support cases AWS might receive with this issue) comes from the fact that the main route table currently points to IGW1, whenever an address out of the range 10.0.0.0/16 reaches the VPC router. Therefore, to steer the traffic from Subnet20-AZ1b to NAT-GW1, you need to create a separate route table and associate it with such a subnet.

Figure 6.22 shows the necessary parameters to create the new route table.

FIGURE 6.22 Route table creation.

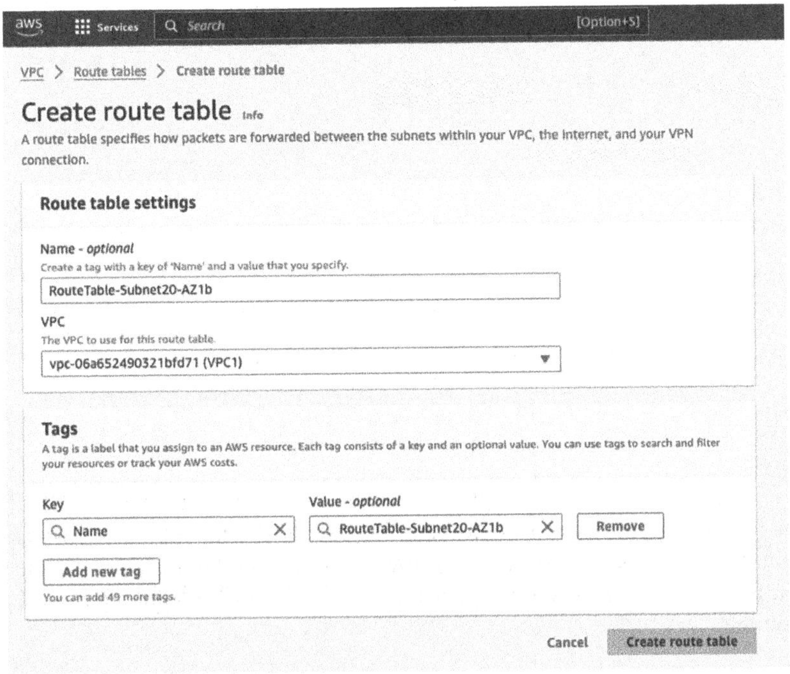

FIGURE 6.23 Adding a default route to RouteTable-Subnet20-AZ1b.

Because RouteTable-Subnet20-AZ1b comes with only one local route (10.0.0.0/16), you should also edit it and include a default route (0.0.0.0/0) pointing to NAT-GW1 as a target for Internet-bound traffic. If you are on the Route Tables screen of the VPC management console, you can do this by selecting RouteTable-Subnet20-AZ1b, selecting the Routes tab, and clicking Edit Routes.

Figure 6.23 shows the addition of a default route (0.0.0.0/0), but the default route points to NAT-GW1 (nat-09b7920f8944e6602 in the figure) right after you click the Add Route button.

FIGURE 6.24 Subnet associations.

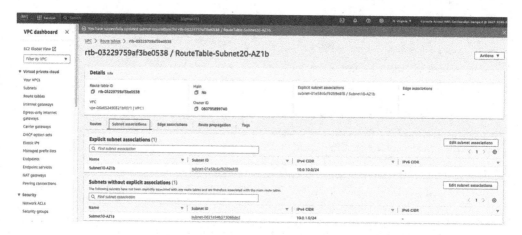

After saving the route, you must explicitly associate the route table with Subnet20-AZ1b in order for its routing policies to be enforced. You can do so on the Subnet Associations tab by clicking in the Edit subnet association button in the Explicit Subnet Associations section, as shown in Figure 6.24, which shows the association of RouteTable-Subnet20-AZ1b to its namesake subnet.

 Each subnet can have only one route table associated with it. However, within a VPC, each route table can be associated with multiple subnets. (As you have seen, the main route table is associated with all subnets by default.) You can have up to 200 route tables per VPC and 50 routes per route table. You may increase this number to a maximum of 1,000, but some network performance might be impacted.

After all these steps, you can validate your current configuration using the Resource Map tab. You just need to select Your VPCs in the left panel, then select the VPC1 and click on the Resource Map tab. Figure 6.25 shows the different components created so far.

Let's say you've deployed an Amazon EC2 instance called DBServer1 in Subnet20-AZ1b (as suggested earlier, in "AWS Networking Constructs"). Figure 6.26 shows your current VPC network topology status.

In Figure 6.26, DBServer1 does not have a public address because it is located on a private subnet (Subnet20-AZ1b). Therefore, traffic from DBServer1 has to first reach NAT-GW1, and from there be sent to the Internet using the NAT gateway's public IP address, through IGW1 to the destination host on the Internet.

Figure 6.27 shows how Amazon CloudWatch automatically monitors traffic from DBServer1 flowing through NAT-GW1. You can access these statistics on the Monitoring tab of the NAT Gateways screen.

FIGURE 6.25 Resource map.

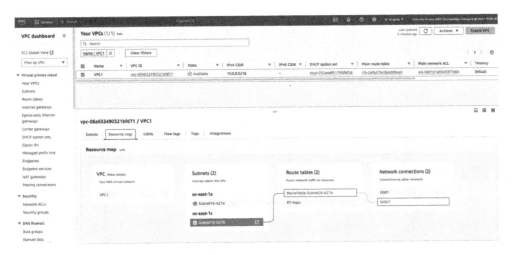

FIGURE 6.26 Topology with NAT gateway.

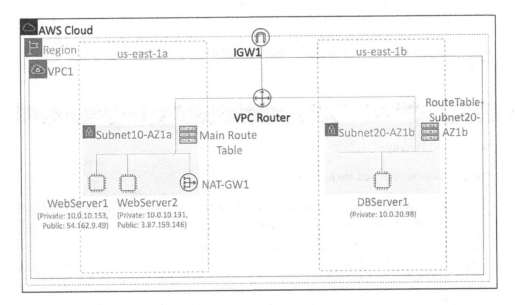

Before NAT gateways were presented on a screen in your VPC management console, you probably would have had to leverage NAT instances to allow resources in private subnets to reach the Internet. NAT instances are Amazon EC2 instances deployed from

FIGURE 6.27 NAT-GW1 CloudWatch statistics.

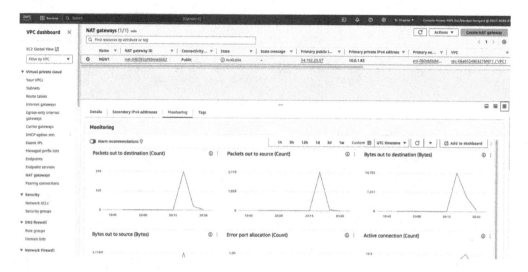

Amazon Machine Images (AMI) that were available from community or AWS Marketplace vendors. This service is no longer supported. Visit https://docs.aws.amazon.com/vpc/latest/userguide/vpc-nat-comparison.html#nat-instance-migrate to learn how to migrate from a NAT instance to a NAT Gateway. In Exercise 6.3, you see how to create NAT gateways.

EXERCISE 6.3

Create NAT Gateways

Building on Exercise 6.2, you create two NAT gateways.

1. Create two NAT gateways called **NAT-GW-A** and **NAT-GW-B** located at PublicSubnet-A and PublicSubnet-B, respectively. Do not forget to allocate elastic IP addresses for them.

2. Create two route tables: **PrivateRouteTable-A** (whose default route has NAT-GW-A as target) and **PrivateRouteTable-B** (whose default route has NAT-GW-B as target). Associate these route tables to PrivateSubnet-A and PrivateSubnet-B, respectively.

3. Create two free-tier Amazon EC2 instances (**DB-A** and **DB-B**) located at PrivateSubnet-A and PrivateSubnet-B, respectively. Check that they are reaching the Internet via their corresponding NAT gateways.

Security Groups

You can think of a security group as a virtual firewall that controls inbound and outbound traffic on an elastic network interface (ENI) that belongs to an Amazon EC2 instance or another resource deployed on a VPC. An ENI is basically a virtual network adapter card. Therefore, you can define rules in terms of IP addresses, transport protocols (TCP or UDP), and ports that define which type of communication your instance can receive or transmit.

During the creation of the instances in the AWS Networking Constructs screen, you need to select (or even create) security groups. To provide communication with the exterior world (in the case of WebServer1 and WebServer2), this chapter uses a group called SG1, as shown in the Security Groups screen in the VPC management console in Figure 6.28.

As you can see in Figure 6.28, SG1 has three inbound rules that allow HTTP, HTTPS, and SSH to instances that are associated with it. Consequently, these rules allow TCP connections that use destination ports 80, and 443, and 22, respectively. So, when you are adding inbound rules to a security group, you are actually allowing specific connections to reach the instances associated with it. Moreover, each security group by default denies all connections not specified on the ruleset.

If you have a traditional security background, you are probably trying to draw analogies between this cloud networking concept and other security on-premises solutions. However, if you are comparing security groups to agent-based software firewalls, you must be aware that security groups are part of the AWS Cloud infrastructure (more specifically, AWS hypervisor) and are not dependent on the operating system installed on the instance.

FIGURE 6.28 Security group SG1.

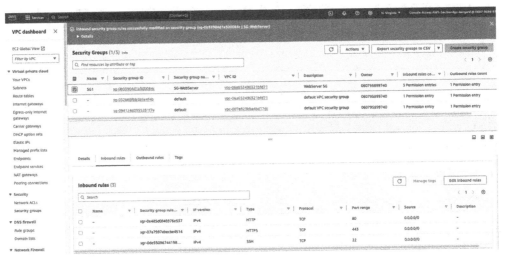

216 Chapter 6 ▪ Infrastructure Protection

Security groups are stateful, which means that the return traffic from an allowed inbound connection is automatically permitted to reach the instance without having to define a corresponding outbound rule to allow it. To illustrate this behavior, Figure 6.29 represents an HTTP connection as it reaches the WebServer1 instance.

In Figure 6.29, SG1 allows the inbound connection to the destination TCP port (80). The return traffic, whose destination TCP port is 9006, is automatically allowed due to the stateful nature of the security group.

In this chapter's examples, SG1's outbound rules are left unchanged. They allow all connections leaving the instances associated with this security group, as Figure 6.30 shows.

Of course, because security groups are stateful, the return traffic for the outbound connections is automatically permitted. However, you can change the outbound configuration to limit outbound connections to specific destinations, protocols, and ports, depending on the trust boundary on the deployed instance.

    Through security groups, you can deploy the principle of least privilege,
    allowing only expected inbound and outbound connections and nothing
    else, thus avoiding attacks and exploits that may generate unexpected
    traffic.

FIGURE 6.29 Security groups and an inbound connection.

FIGURE 6.30 SG1 outbound rules.

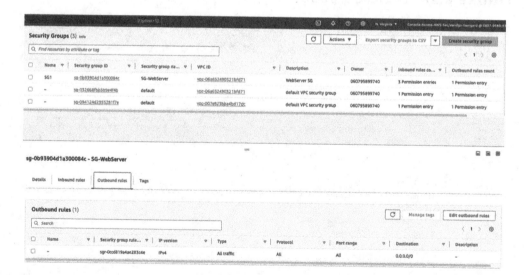

When you create an instance via the AWS Software Development Kit or command-line interface, and you do not specify a security group. It will be automatically associated with a default security group (the AWS Console will ask you to choose the default security group or create one). This special group is shown in Figure 6.31.

As shown in Figure 6.31, the default security group (sg-032668fbb3b9e4f4b) has only one inbound rule allowing all connections, but with an unusual source: only from other instances that are associated with the same security group. Therefore, this rule allows free communication between instances *within* the same security group.

The outbound rule in the default security group is exactly the same as SG1 (all traffic allowed to any destination).

Of course, you can edit these security groups by creating new rules that will allow traffic to flow through them. Table 6.1 gives you a full picture of what parameters you can use to build a rule in a security group.

You can deploy up to 2,500 security groups per region. You can also have 60 inbound and 60 outbound rules per security group (making a total of 120 rules). A rule that references a security group or prefix list ID counts as one rule. Check the AWS official documentation for complete and current information.

FIGURE 6.31 VPC1 default security group.

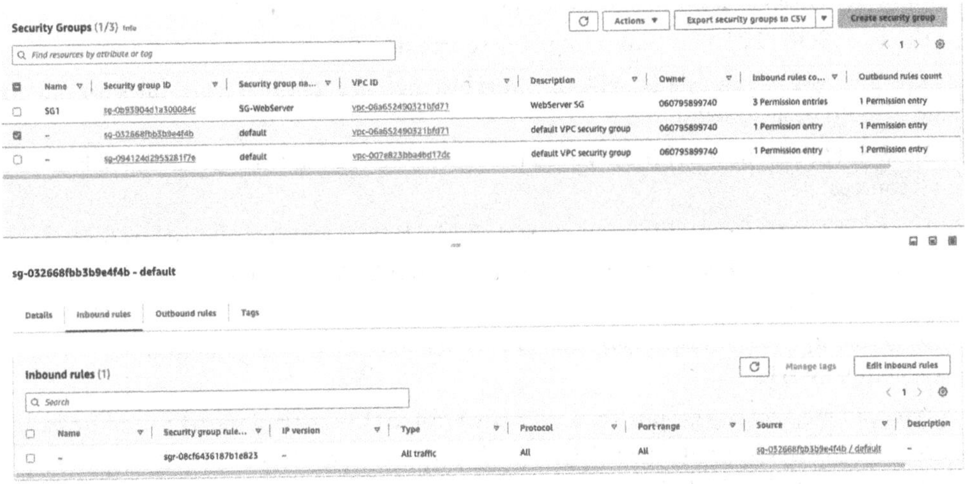

Chapter 6 ▪ Infrastructure Protection

TABLE 6.1   Security Group Rules Parameters

Parameter	Description
Type	Description of the protocol that will be allowed. You can choose well-known protocols, such as SSH, RDP, HTTP, or HTTPS. You can also choose to insert a custom TCP or UDP port, or even port ranges.
Protocol	Type of transport protocol (TCP or UDP) or ICMP.
Port Range	Manually entered port number or port number range.
Source (for inbound rules) or Destination (for outbound rules)	IP address range in CIDR format (for example, 192.168.0.0/16 or 10.1.1.1/32) or your own IP address. You can also specify the name or ID of another security group in the same region, as well as prefix lists.
Description	A string to provide insights for a security group rule.

When you are deploying Amazon EC2 instances to subnets in your VPC, you can associate them to previously created security groups or to a new one that you create. You can add up to five security groups per network interface. When you add two or more security groups to the same instance, the rules from each security group are effectively aggregated to create a unique set of rules, as if they belonged to a single security group. The resulting ruleset will be equal, or more permissive, when compared to each of the original security groups. As an example, imagine that you create a security group SG2 with the following inbound rules:

- Allow SSH from a single IP address 1.2.3.4
- Allow MySQL (TCP port 3306) from any source (0.0.0.0/0)

If SG1 and SG2 are associated with the same instance, the resulting set of rules for the instance would be as follows:

- Allow SSH (TCP port 22) from any source (0.0.0.0/0) due to SG1 permitting SSH from all sources
- Allow HTTP (TCP port 80) from any source (0.0.0.0/0), which is allowed by SG1
- Allow HTTPS (TCP port 443) from any source (0.0.0.0/0), which is also allowed by SG1
- Allow MySQL (TCP port 3306) from any source (0.0.0.0/0), which in turn is permitted by SG2

As you can see, security groups are a very powerful tool to control traffic to and from instances. But as you learn in the next section, they are not the only resource you can use to provide traffic filtering within your VPC.

Network Access Control Lists

Because security group rules only *allow* traffic, the order in which they are inserted is not relevant.

As you may have noticed in Table 6.1, security group inbound rules specify source addresses, whereas outbound rules specify destination addresses. Therefore, when you select Source/Destination Check, the destination for inbound rules and the source for outbound rules must be tied to the ENI.

In Exercise 6.4, you create two security groups and associate their instances.

EXERCISE 6.4

Create Security Groups

Building on Exercise 6.3, you create two security groups and associate their instances.

1. Build a security group named **WebSG** that allows HTTP from any host on the Internet and only allows SSH from your own personal computer's public IP address.
2. Associate WebSG to instances Web-A and Web-B.
3. Build a security group called **DBSG** that permits inbound ICMP Echo requests and replies (also known as "pings").
4. Associate DBSG to instances DB-A and DB-B.
5. Test all communications defined in this exercise.

Network Access Control Lists

Network access control lists are network traffic control objects that act as firewalls when traffic enters or leaves a subnet in your VPC. You can add this extra layer of traffic filtering to prevent unexpected traffic between subnets, regardless of what you have actually deployed on them.

In fact, the VPC you have created in "AWS Networking Constructs" had an associated NACL, as you can see on the Network ACLs screen in the VPC management console (see Figures 6.32 and 6.33).

These figures show the inbound and outbound rules from VPC1 default network ACL (acl-07c3d2d4085da0c6d). Because you already know how security group rules are built, it will be easier for you to notice some of the differences between these security group

FIGURE 6.32 Default NACL inbound rules.

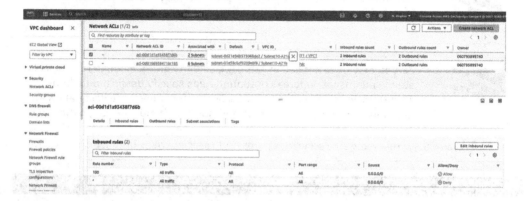

FIGURE 6.33 Default NACL outbound rules.

rules and NACL rules. In both inbound and outbound rules of the default NACL, there are two rules:

- **Rule 100:** Allowing all traffic from all protocols, all port ranges, from any source
- **Rule*:** Denying all traffic from all protocols, all port ranges, from any source

The rule number (such as 100) defines how traffic will be filtered. In NACLs, each traversing packet is compared to each rule and, if there is a match, the action (allow or deny) is performed against that packet and the rule evaluation stops. In the case of the default NACL shown in Figures 6.32 and 6.33, all traffic is allowed in Rule 100, which means that Rule* (which is always the last rule) does not have a match.

 Also notice that you can change the rules of the default NACL at any time.

As its name implies, the default NACL is associated with all subnets. So, considering VPC1, Subnet10-AZ1a, and Subnet20-AZ1b, Figure 6.34 explains how the default NACL is positioned in the VPC1 network topology.

As you can see in Figure 6.34, NACLs are positioned at the border of VPC subnets. Such a mental model will be important when you are troubleshooting connectivity issues.

Contrary to security groups, NACLs are stateless, which means that return traffic must be explicitly allowed (or denied) via additional rules to define a proper bidirectional communication filter. Therefore, when building NACLs, you must be mindful of both inbound and outbound rules.

Using Figure 6.34 as a visual aid, you can see how a functional connection from WebServer1 in Subnet10-AZ1a toward DBServer1 in Subnet20-AZ2 goes through the following traffic filters:

1. Outbound rules in SG1 (which is associated with WebServer1)
2. Outbound rules in the default NACL (which is associated with Subnet10-AZ1a)
3. Inbound rules in the default NACL (which is associated with Subnet20-AZ1b)
4. Inbound rules in SG2 (associated with DBServer1)

Conversely, when DBServer1 responds to such a connection, the return traffic follows these steps before reaching WebServer1:

5. Automatic stateful permission in SG2 (which is associated with DBServer1)
6. Outbound rules in the default NACL (which is associated with Subnet20-AZ1b)

FIGURE 6.34 Network topology showing the default NACL.

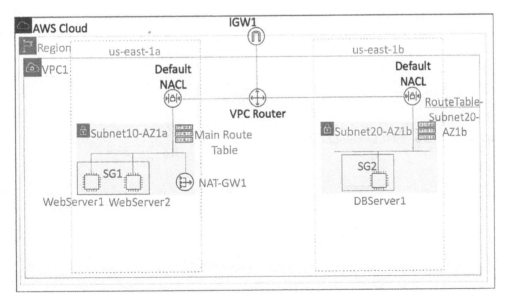

222   Chapter 6 ▪ Infrastructure Protection

7. Inbound rules in the default NACL (which is associated with Subnet10-AZ1a)

8. Automatic stateful permission in SG1 (which is associated with WebServer1)

You will create an NACL that will be associated with Subnet20-AZ1b, allowing specific MySQL communication from Subnet10-AZ1a, ICMP traffic for connectivity testing purposes, and software updates from a specific IP address (1.2.3.4) on the Internet via HTTPS.

Figure 6.35 shows a new NACL called NACL1 immediately after its creation on the NACL screen (under the Create Network ACL button).

As you can see in Figure 6.35, the only inbound rule in NACL1 is the (explicit) final rule that essentially denies everything. Because NACL1's only outbound rule is the same, if you associate this NACL as it is to Subnet20-AZ1b, it will block any traffic from and to this subnet (which can be an extremely secure approach, but not practical for real-world applications).

Consequently, to implement the aforementioned MySQL, ICMP, and software update traffic filtering, Figures 6.36 and 6.37 show the inbound and outbound rules you should add to NACL1.

FIGURE 6.35   Recently created NACL1.

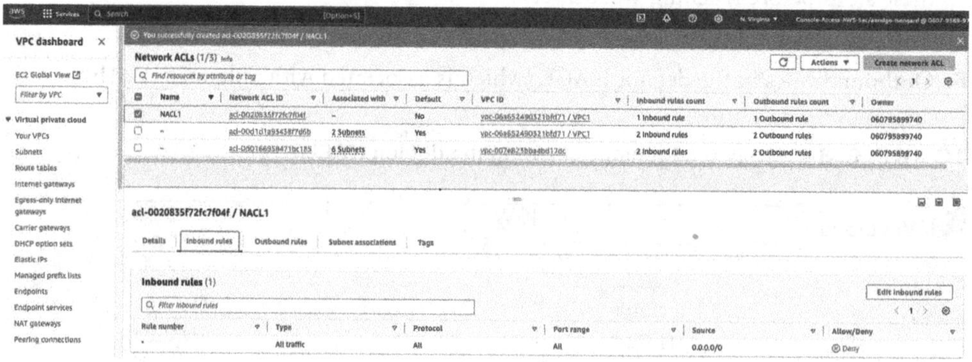

FIGURE 6.36   NACL1 inbound rules.

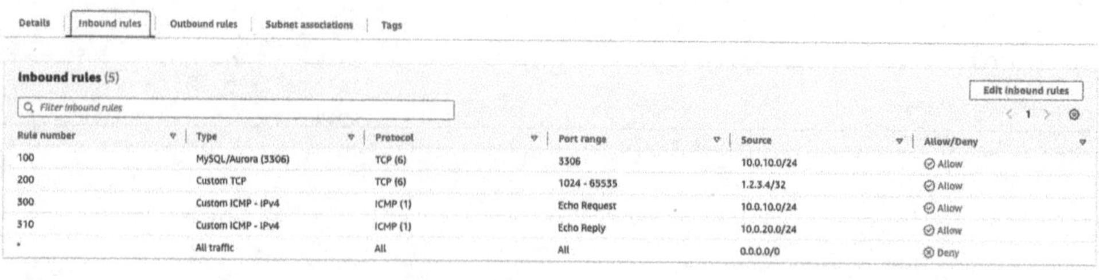

FIGURE 6.37 NACL1 outbound rules.

Rule number	Type	Protocol	Port range	Destination	Allow/Deny
100	Custom TCP	TCP (6)	1024 - 65535	10.0.10.0/24	Allow
200	HTTPS (443)	TCP (6)	443	1.2.3.4/32	Allow
300	Custom ICMP - IPv4	ICMP (1)	Echo Reply	10.0.20.0/24	Allow
310	Custom ICMP - IPv4	ICMP (1)	Echo Request	10.0.10.0/24	Allow
*	All traffic	All	All	0.0.0.0/0	Deny

It is important that you examine both figures to understand how the NACL's statelessness influences how the rules are built. Because NACL1 will be associated with Subnet20-AZ1b (via the Subnet Associations tab), try to focus on how the NACL allows MySQL/Aurora traffic between Subnet10-AZ1a and Subnet20-AZ1b: Inbound rule number 100 allows all TCP port 3306 traffic (which characterizes the aforementioned database traffic) from IP addresses on the prefix 10.0.10.0/24 (CIDR block from Subnet10-AZ1a). At the same time, outbound rule number 100 permits the return traffic, which is characterized by the use of ephemeral ports as destination TCP ports destined for subnet 10.0.10.0/24.

Ephemeral ports are random source port numbers that are generated in TCP connections or UDP communications. When a client establishes these communications with a server, an ephemeral port is chosen from the range of 1,024 to 65,535 to be the client's source port. The designated ephemeral port then becomes the destination port for return traffic from the service, so outbound traffic from the ephemeral port must be allowed in the NACLs.

Outbound rule number 200 in NACL1 allows HTTPS (TCP port 443) to leave Subnet20-AZ1b and reach IP address 1.2.3.4, which represents the server that will provide software updates to the connection source. Consequently, inbound rule number 200 allows its corresponding return traffic by allowing ephemeral ports as the destination.

Remember that this traffic is being steered to NAT-GW1 via RouteTable-Subnet20-AZ1b. Therefore, you should follow every traffic hop to guarantee that your NACLs are correctly allowing the bidirectional communications to work. Luckily, in this scenario, the default NACL permits all traffic that leaves and enters Subnet10-AZ1a.

Finally, rules numbers 300 and 310 were provisioned to allow ICMP Echo (Request and Reply) traffic from Subnet10-AZ1a to Subnet20-AZ1b, and vice versa.

You do not need to choose the same rule numbers to identify corresponding inbound and outbound rules that allow or deny specific bidirectional communications. However, this best practice can facilitate rule writing and connectivity troubleshooting.

To give you a more complete view of the potential of NACLs, Table 6.2 further describes the parameters that can be added to inbound and outbound rules.

Network ACLs can't block DNS requests to or from the Route 53 Resolver (also known as the VPC+2 IP address or AmazonProvidedDNS). To filter DNS requests through the Route 53 Resolver, you can enable Route 53 DNS Resolver Firewall.

TABLE 6.2 Network ACL Rule Parameters

Parameter	Description
Rule #	Can range from 1 to 32,766 but should be created in increments (such as by every 10 or 100) to allow the later insertion of new rules where necessary; because the rule with the lowest number is evaluated first, when a rule matches the traffic, it is immediately applied independently of any higher-numbered rule that may contradict it.
Type	Options are Custom TCP rule, Custom UDP rule, Custom ICMP rule, Custom Protocol Rule, ALL TCP, ALL UDP, ALL ICMP—IPv4, ALL ICMP—IPv6, ALL Traffic, or specific protocols such as SSH, Telnet, nameserver, DNS (TCP or UDP), HTTP, HTTPS, POP3, IMAP, LDAP, SMB, SMTPS, IMAPS, POP3S, MS SQLS, Oracle, MySQL/Aurora, NFS, RDP, PostgreSQL, Redshift, WinRM-HTTP, WinRM-HTTPS, HTTP*, or HTTPS*.
Protocol	Characterizes the IP protocol number for the packets referred to in the rule. It is automatically defined when you choose the rule type, except for a Custom Protocol Rule, which allows the selection of different protocols such as ICMP, IGMP, or GGP.
Port Range	Used on custom rules and protocols, in which you can enter a port number or a port range, such as 443 or 1024-65535.
Source (inbound rules only) or Destination (outbound rules only)	Determines the IP address or range that is allowed or denied by the rule via CIDR notation (for example, 10.0.10.183/32 for hosts or 10.0.10.0/24 for network address ranges).
Allow/Deny	Identifies the rule action according to its characterized traffic.

> VPC subnets are always associated with an NACL. If you do not associate a specific NACL with a certain subnet, that subnet will be automatically associated with the default NACL. You can associate an NACL with multiple subnets. However, a subnet can be associated with only one NACL at a time.

In Exercise 6.5, you create an NACL.

EXERCISE 6.5

Create an NACL

Building on Exercise 6.4, you create an NACL.

1. Create an NACL named **PrivateNACL** that allows Oracle connections (TCP destination port 1521 with ephemeral ports as TCP source) and blocks ICMP Echo communication from PublicSubnet-A and PublicSubnet-B.
2. Associate PrivateNACL to PrivateSubnet-A and PrivateSubnet-B.
3. Test whether the ICMP communications between subnets are working.

Amazon VPC Transit Gateways

Amazon VPC Transit Gateway is a network transit hub service designed to interconnect VPCs and on-premises networks within the AWS ecosystem. This powerful networking solution acts as a central point of connectivity, simplifying network architecture and enabling seamless communication between multiple VPCs and on-premises networks.

One of the key features of transit gateways is their ability to scale horizontally, allowing organizations to connect thousands of VPCs and on-premises networks through a single gateway. This centralized VPC approach significantly reduces the complexity of managing multiple peering connections and simplifies network topology.

> By carefully planning and implementing Amazon VPC Transit Gateways, organizations can create a more efficient, scalable, and manageable network infrastructure in the AWS Cloud. Currently Amazon VPC Transit Gateway supports five transit gateways per account, 20 transit gateway route tables per transit gateway, 5000 attachments per transit gateway, and up to 100 Gbps bandwidth per VPC attachment per availability zone. Check https://docs.aws.amazon.com/vpc/latest/tgw/transit-gateway-quotas.html for updated information.

To create a transit gateway, you have to click in the left panel on the VPC Dashboard view and then click on Transit Gateways. You will see the configurations options for the TGW. This example sets the name as TGW1 and a description as shown in Figure 6.38 and leaves the fields as described in the figure (leave the ASN field in black to get the default configuration). Click Create Transit Gateway.

For the Autonomous System Number (ASN) in the Amazon side Autonomous System Number (ASN) field, you can use the default ASN, or you can specify a private ASN in the ranges of 64512–65534 or 4200000000–4294967294. Here you set the configuration for the AWS side of a Border Gateway Protocol (BGP) session.

FIGURE 6.38 Transit gateway creation.

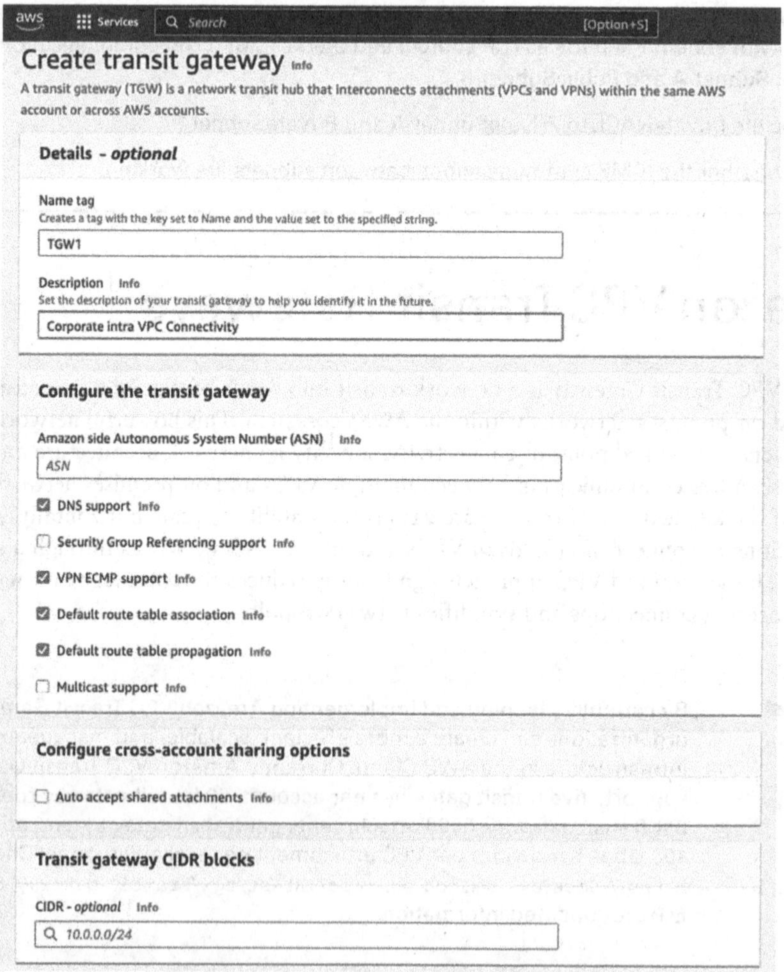

FIGURE 6.39 Transit gateway information.

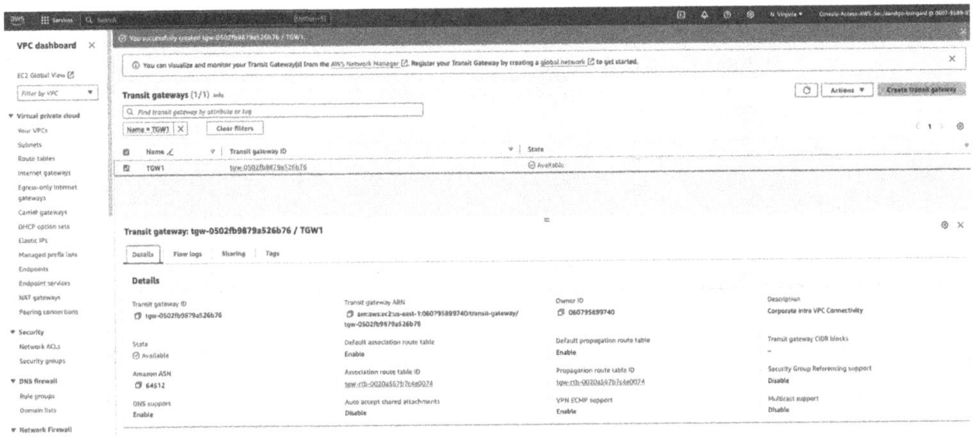

Once the creation is completed, you should see the transit gateway state as Available (see Figure 6.39). As you can see in the Details tab, you get an Amazon ASN number (64512) and AWS created a route table (tgw-rtb-0020a567b7c4e0074) that will help you control the communication flow (Routing) in the inter-VPC connectivity.

The next step is to create an association—in other words, connect the VPCs and the subnets. Amazon VPC Transit gateway supports various types of attachments, including VPCs (known as VPC Attachments), AWS Direct Connect gateways, and VPN connections. This versatility enables businesses to create a hub-and-spoke network architecture, where the transit gateway serves as the hub connecting multiple network spokes. This design pattern is particularly useful for large enterprises with complex network requirements. To create an attachment, click the left panel in the Transit Gateway section and select Transit Gateway Attachments. Click the orange button at the top-right, labeled Create Transit Gateway Attachment. To create the attachment, provide the name (VPC1-TGW-Attach), select the TGW1 from the TGW ID, and then select the attachment type as VPC. In the VPC Attachment configuration, select the VPC ID and the subnet Subnet10-AZ1b (which is the private subnet). Click Create. See Figure 6.40.

> **NOTE** In this example, you are selecting just one private subnet for intra-VPC communication. In real-world scenarios, you should have multiple private subnets in different AZs to have high availability.

Once it has been created, you will notice that the attachment is Associated and it has an Association route table ID (tgw-rtb-0020a567b7c4e0074) and Resource ID that correspond to the VPC1 (vpc-06a652490321bfd71), as shown in Figure 6.41.

FIGURE 6.40 Transit gateway attachment creation.

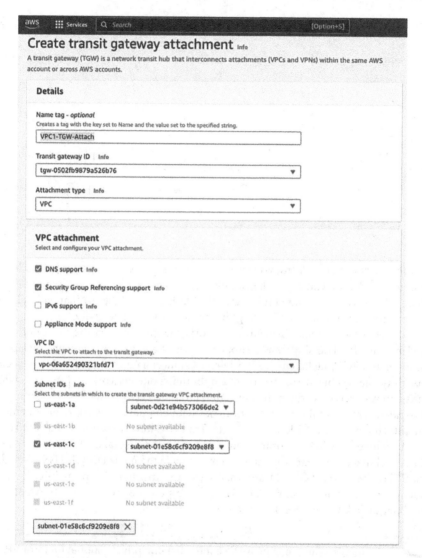

The next step is to update the route table (RouteTable-Subnet20-AZ1b) in VPC1. This route table was associated with the Transit Gateway attachment you created in the previous step. The update will configure the route table to send traffic to TGW1 through this attachment. Click the left panel, select Route Tables in the Virtual Private Cloud section, and select the RouteTable-Subnet20-AZ1b. Click the Routes tab and update the table to add 192.168.0.0/24 (CIDR for SecureVPC created in the VPC exercise), as shown in Figure 6.42.

FIGURE 6.41 Transit gateway attachment configuration.

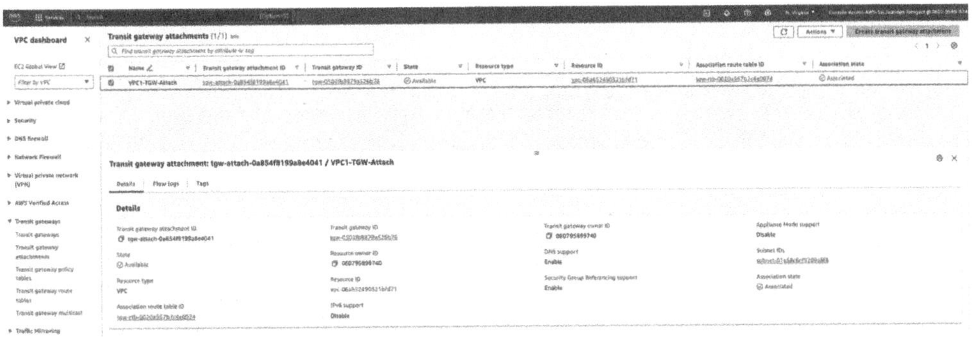

FIGURE 6.42 Route table with Transit gateway as a target.

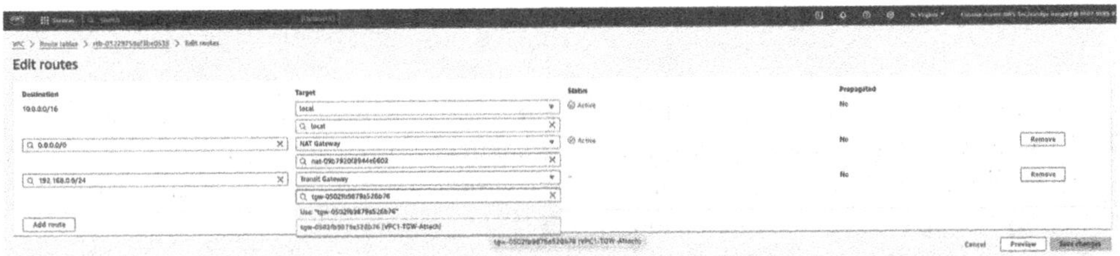

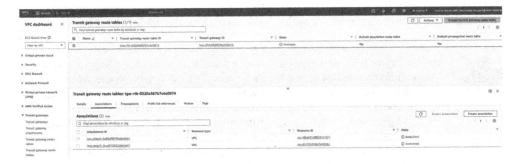

FIGURE 6.43 Associations for a Transit gateway route table.

It is important to note that, in this example, every attachment that you create gets the default transit gateway route table (you can assign a different route table to each attachment to define traffic flow and how the transit gateway will handle it). In Figure 6.43, you can see the associations that are currently created. Notice that the figure has two associations. The first one was the one created previously and the second one will be created in the Exercise 6.6, where you connect the TGW to communicate with SecureVPC from the previous exercise.

Chapter 6 • Infrastructure Protection

FIGURE 6.44 Transit gateway route table.

You can also explore in Figure 6.44 the current routes that are created in the associated TGW route table. Those routes were created automatically when you created the attachment and selected the propagation option (this could be disabled). You can also create static routes, depending on your communication needs.

A notable feature of transit gateways is *inter-region peering*, which allows organizations to connect transit gateways across different AWS regions. You can also peer transit gateways with third-party SD-WAN routers using connect attachments. This capability is crucial for businesses operating globally, as it facilitates efficient data transfer and communication between geographically dispersed networks, while leveraging the AWS Global Infrastructure.

 In Figure 6.40, you may have noticed the Appliance Mode Support. You should enable Appliance Mode on your TGW VPC attachment when using stateful network appliances in a shared services VPC. This ensures that bidirectional traffic flows through the same AZ, maintaining flow stickiness and preventing traffic drops. Appliance Mode is particularly useful for centralized inspection architectures, as it guarantees that both the request and response traffic are processed by the same appliance, improving the effectiveness of stateful inspection.

Security is an important concern in cloud networking, and transit gateways address this by providing built-in encryption for all traffic traversing the AWS backbone network. This ensures that data remains protected as it moves between different parts of your cloud infrastructure. Transit gateways also offer granular routing control through the use of route tables. Administrators can define specific routing rules for each attachment, enabling fine-grained control over network traffic flows. This level of control is essential for implementing complex networking policies and ensuring optimal traffic management.

Another significant advantage of using TGWs are their simplified billing and cost management. Instead of managing multiple connection charges for individual VPC Peering or VPN connections, organizations can consolidate their networking costs under a single transit gateway, making it easier to track and optimize expenses related to network connectivity.

In Exercise 6.6, you create a TGW.

EXERCISE 6.6

Create a Transit Gateway Attachment for VPC

Building on Exercise 6.4, you create a TGW attachment. The idea is to use the TGW1 and interconnect VPC1 and SecureVPC.

1. Create a TGW attachment named **SecureVPC-TGW-Attach** using the TGW1 that you created in this chapter.
2. Associate **SecureVPC-TGW-Attach** with PrivateSubnet-A and PrivateSubnet-B.
3. Test whether the ICMP communications between subnets in the private subnet in VPC1 and PrivateSubnet-A are working. (Be aware of the security group permissions to allow ICMP and the NACL rules created in the VPC1 associated with Subnet10-AZ1b.)

Elastic Load Balancing

Server load balancers (SLBs) are network devices that have been present in data centers since the 1990s. These devices were created to provide the following capabilities to the applications:

- **Scalability:** Whenever an application server saturates one of its hardware resources (e.g., CPU, memory, storage, or connectivity), connected users may suffer performance impacts, such as a higher response time or service unavailability. In these scenarios, SLBs allow a group of application servers to share user requests in order to avoid this situation.
- **High Availability:** Even if an application server is not properly functioning, the SLB can direct user traffic to other servers without them noticing any changes.
- **Content Switching:** In certain occasions, users that access the same application should be treated differently. For example, a user accessing an application through a mobile device should have a different experience from one doing the same on a desktop. An SLB can analyze data above the transport layer (such as browser type or complete URL) to determine the best server for each user.

AWS offers four types of server load balancing services under the name *elastic load balancing* (ELB). These network services are used to distribute client traffic across multiple targets (such as Amazon EC2 instances or application containers) in distinct availability zones, in order to increase application availability and scale.

Elastic load balancing implementations follow the same basic architecture, which is represented in Figure 6.45.

In this figure, the following configuration elements are identified:

- **Target:** Parameter that represents instances or IP addresses, as well as the transport protocol and port (HTTP, HTTPS, TCP, TLS, UDP) from AWS resources that will receive the connections ELB is dispatching.
- **Health Checks:** Synthetic requests that verify whether an application is available on a server. These requests can leverage communication on HTTP, HTTPS, TCP, TLS, UDP, or even a combination of TCP and UDP.

FIGURE 6.45 Elastic load balancing architecture.

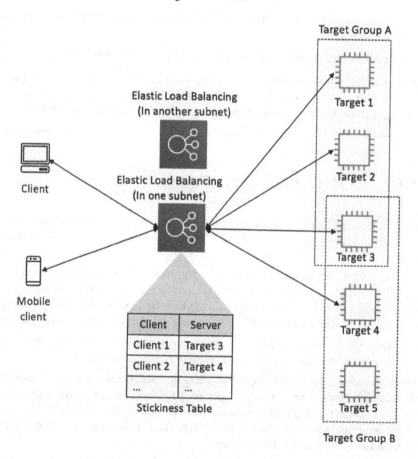

- **Target Group:** A group of instances, IP addresses, or AWS Lambda functions that deploy the same application, use the same health check, and are balanced via a load-balancing algorithm such as round robin (each time a different target receives the connection) or least outstanding requests (the target with fewer associated connections receives the next connection). You can register a target with multiple target groups.

- **Listener:** Entity that checks for connection requests from clients, using the protocol and port that you configure. This configuration element is also informally called virtual IP (VIP).

- **Stickiness:** An optional feature that enables ELB to bind a user's session to a specific target. This ensures that all requests from a specific user during the session are subsequently sent to the same target. The stickiness can last between one second and seven days.

AWS ELB receives a user connection from one of its listeners and verifies whether the user is already registered in the stickiness table. If the user is not in the table, the elastic load balancer analyzes the target group associated with the listener and determines through health check results which targets have the application healthily working at that specific moment. Using the listener-configured load-balancing algorithm, the ELB selects the target that will receive the client request. Then, it records a client characteristic (such as source IP) and the selected target in the stickiness table and splices both connections (client to ELB and ELB to target), until the client receives its intended response from the load-balanced application. If the user is already registered in the stickiness table, the ELB repeats the splicing process with the preregistered target (meaning that it waives the target selection).

AWS ELB supports the following load balancers: application load balancer, network load balancer, gateway load balancer, and classic load balancer. They can support the following features: health checks, Amazon CloudWatch metrics, logging, availability zone failover, cross-zone load balancing, stickiness, SSL offloading, and backend server encryption.

An application load balancer (ALB) operates at layers 5 to 7 of the OSI model, routing traffic to targets based on content associated with these layers. It is designed to load-balance web traffic (HTTP and HTTPS) and improve the security of applications by ensuring that the latest ciphers and protocols are used. Some of the exclusive ALB features are slow start (to avoid target overload when they are included in a target group), source IP address CIDR-based routing, and routing based on parameters such as path, host, HTTP header and method, query string, redirects, or fixed response. It also supports AWS Lambda functions as targets, as well as user authentication.

A network load balancer (NLB) operates at layer 4 of the OSI model, routing connections based on IP, TCP, or UDP protocol data. It is capable of handling millions of requests per second while maintaining ultra-low latencies. Exclusive NLB features include the use of static IP address, elastic IP address, and preservation of the client source IP address (for logging purposes).

A *gateway load balancer* (GWLB) operates at the network layer (layer 3) of the OSI model. It is designed to handle traffic for virtual appliances, such as firewalls, intrusion detection and prevention systems (IDPS), and deep packet inspection (DPI) systems. The primary use case for a GWLB is to simplify the deployment, scaling, and management of third-party virtual appliances in an AWS environment. Traditional virtual appliance deployments often required complex networking configurations and manual management of appliance instances. With GWLB, you can easily integrate virtual appliances into your network architecture without modifying your existing applications or infrastructure. GWLB integrates well with other AWS services, such as Amazon VPC, AWS Transit Gateway, and AWS Network Firewall. The GWLB and its registered virtual appliance instances exchange application traffic using the GENEVE protocol on port 6081.

Finally, a classic load balancer (CLB) enables basic load balancing across Amazon EC2 instances. This type of load balancer corresponds to the previous generation of AWS Load Balancer solutions. A CLB is intended for applications that were built within the EC2 Classic network. Exclusive CLB features include the support of the EC2 Classic platform, as well as custom security policies.

Unlike all the networking services explained in previous sections, ELB configurations are available on the Amazon EC2 management console, and not on the VPC management console. Figure 6.46 illustrates what happens when you select Load Balancing in the EC2 management console and click Create Load Balancer.

FIGURE 6.46 Select Load Balancer Type screen.

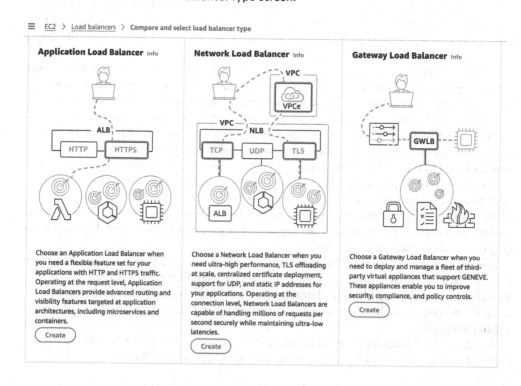

It is important to understand the security considerations when you have a load balancer in your application:

- **Encryption:** Elastic load balancing supports SSL/TLS termination, allowing you to offload the decryption process from your application servers to the load balancer. NLB supports both TCP and TLS listeners. With TLS listeners, NLB can perform TLS termination, offloading the encryption/decryption overhead from the backend instances. ALB supports SSL/TLS termination, which means it can decrypt incoming HTTPS traffic and encrypt outgoing traffic. This also offloads the encryption overhead from the backend servers.

- **Access Control:** Use security groups and network ACLs to control traffic to and from your load balancers.

- **AWS WAF Integration:** Application load balancers can be integrated with AWS WAF to protect applications against common web exploits. ALBs natively integrate with AWS WAF, a web application firewall that helps protect web applications against common vulnerabilities, such as SQL injection, cross-site scripting, and other application-level security threats. You can associate an AWS WAF access control list (ACL) with an ALB to define security rules and filter out malicious traffic before it reaches your applications.

- **Logging and Monitoring:** Enable access logs and CloudWatch metrics to monitor and audit your load balancer traffic. ALB generates access logs that contain detailed information about the processed requests, including client IP addresses, response times, HTTP status codes, and more. These logs can be sent to Amazon S3, Amazon CloudWatch Logs, or third-party services for analysis and monitoring. CloudWatch metrics can be enabled for LB, allowing you to monitor metrics such as request count, latency, and errors. This helps identify security and performance issues.

- **AWS Services Integration:** ALB integrates with AWS Shield, a DDoS protection service that automatically safeguards applications hosted behind ALB from layers 3 and 4 DDoS attacks. ALB can be used in conjunction with AWS Firewall Manager to simplify security policy management across multiple accounts and applications. NLB integrates with services like AWS Certificate Manager for certificate management. It also integrates with security groups for network-level security and supports AWS PrivateLink for secure communication between VPCs and services. NLB can be used as an endpoint for AWS Global Accelerator, a service that improves the availability and performance of applications by routing traffic through the AWS global network infrastructure. By using NLB with Global Accelerator, you can enhance the security and performance of your applications by leveraging AWS's globally distributed edge locations and advanced routing techniques.

As an experiment, you will configure an ALB to further understand how ELB works in a VPC. When configuring ELB, you must start with the definition of at least one target group. Figure 6.47 shows some elements of the basic configuration of a simple target group called TG1.

236 Chapter 6 ▪ Infrastructure Protection

FIGURE 6.47 TG1 basic configuration.

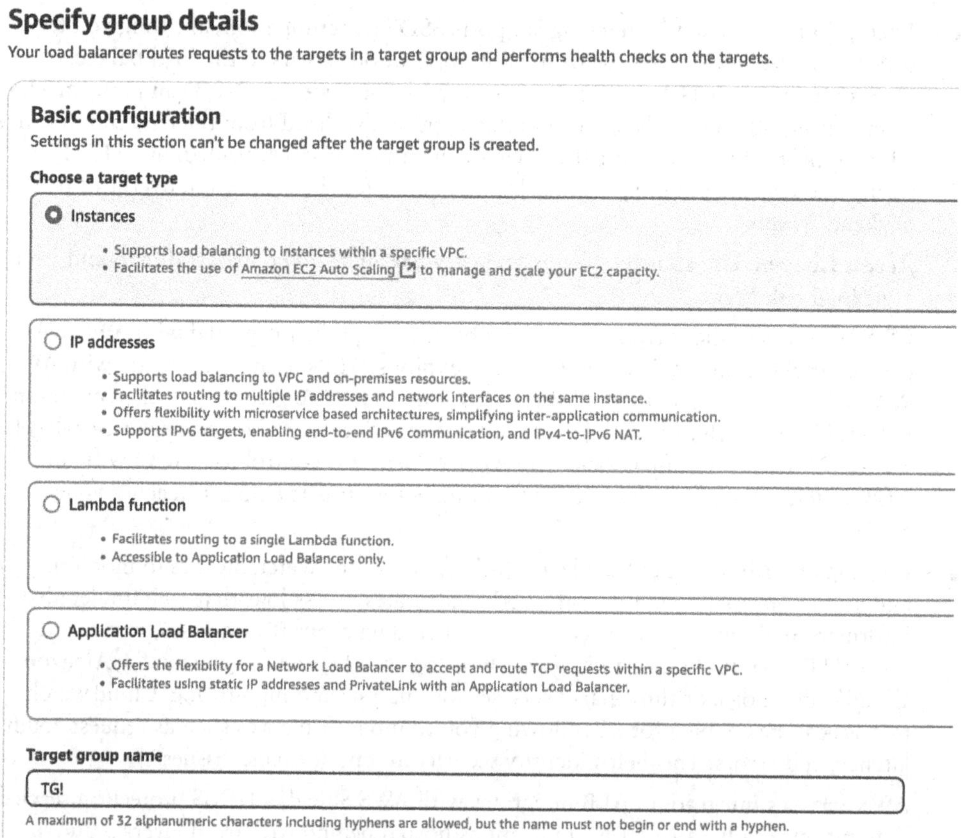

Specify group details
Your load balancer routes requests to the targets in a target group and performs health checks on the targets.

Basic configuration
Settings in this section can't be changed after the target group is created.

Choose a target type

○ **Instances**
- Supports load balancing to instances within a specific VPC.
- Facilitates the use of Amazon EC2 Auto Scaling [↗] to manage and scale your EC2 capacity.

○ **IP addresses**
- Supports load balancing to VPC and on-premises resources.
- Facilitates routing to multiple IP addresses and network interfaces on the same instance.
- Offers flexibility with microservice based architectures, simplifying inter-application communication.
- Supports IPv6 targets, enabling end-to-end IPv6 communication, and IPv4-to-IPv6 NAT.

○ **Lambda function**
- Facilitates routing to a single Lambda function.
- Accessible to Application Load Balancers only.

○ **Application Load Balancer**
- Offers the flexibility for a Network Load Balancer to accept and route TCP requests within a specific VPC.
- Facilitates using static IP addresses and PrivateLink with an Application Load Balancer.

Target group name

> TG!

A maximum of 32 alphanumeric characters including hyphens are allowed, but the name must not begin or end with a hyphen.

Figure 6.47 shows the group's name (TG1), protocol (HTTP), and TCP port (80), as well as a couple of attributes, such as Deregistration Delay (the amount of time the ALB continues to send traffic to a target after it has been removed from this group), Slow Start Duration (whose value is 0 seconds, which means disabled), Load Balancing Algorithm (round robin), and Stickiness (which is enabled), which are listed once you create the Target Group. Then, you would select the targets that you want to have, in this case, the EC2 instances that you created in previous sections.

Figure 6.48 shows the registered targets that belong to TG1.

As you can see in Figure 6.48, there are three targets: WebServer1, WebServer2, and WebServer3, where the first two are located in AZ us-east-1a and the last one is deployed in us-east-1b.

Now, you can finally configure the ALB. The configuration is shown in Figure 6.49.

Elastic Load Balancing   237

FIGURE 6.48 TG1 registered targets.

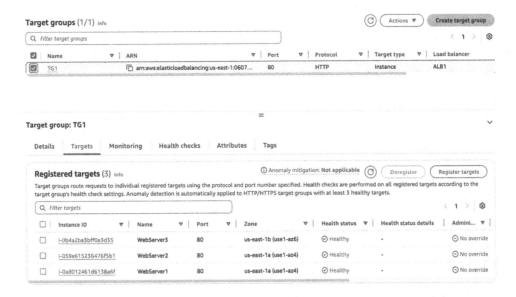

FIGURE 6.49 ALB1 description settings.

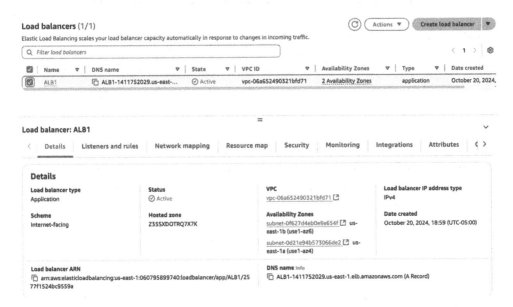

Figure 6.49 shows the following ALB1 settings: Amazon Resource Name (ARN), DNS Name (ALB1-1411752029.us-east-1.elb.amazonaws.com), State (Active), Type (Application), Schema (Internet-facing, rather than internal), IP Address Type (IPv4), and VPC. More importantly, it shows that the ALB is deployed in two different AZs. If one of them goes through a catastrophic failure, the ALB1 DNS name will direct user connections to the corresponding ALB1 listener IP address in the remaining AZ (without exposing such failure to users). In Figure 6.50, you can see a tab called Resource Map, which shows the configuration map for the created environment.

As you start to send HTTP traffic to the ALB1 DNS name, the ALB Monitor tab will show Amazon CloudWatch metrics such as Target Response Time, Requests, Rule Evaluations, HTTP 5XXs, HTTP 4XXs, ELB 5XXs, ELB 4XXs, and HTTP 500. The same tab on the Target Groups screen will show you the following Amazon CloudWatch metrics: Unhealthy Hosts, Healthy Hosts, Target Response Time, Requests, HTTP 5XX, HTTP 4XXs, Backend Connection Errors, and Target TLS Negotiation Errors. See Figure 6.51 for an example.

Finally, Figure 6.52 showcases how ALB1 is inserted in the topology that you have built during this chapter.

From a security perspective, ALB1 can provide the following benefits to the environment illustrated in Figure 6.52:

- Encryption offload from the web servers
- Operating system and web server isolation from nonconformant traffic (with AWS responsible for maintenance and vulnerability patching of the elastic load balancer)

FIGURE 6.50 ALB1 Resource Map view.

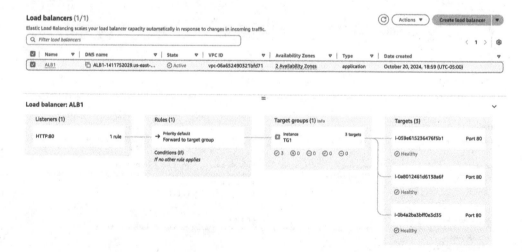

FIGURE 6.51 ALB1 Requests Amazon CloudWatch Metric.

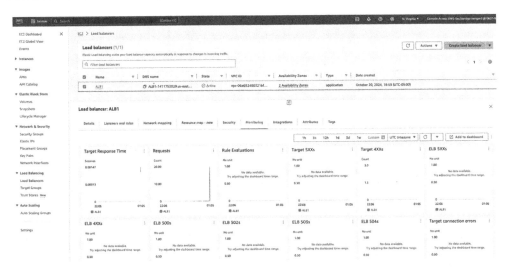

FIGURE 6.52 Network topology with ALB1.

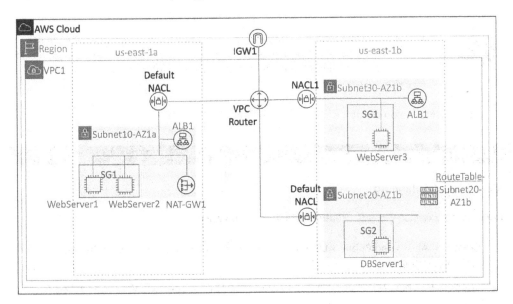

Also, you can have different integrations, such as in the security perspective, where you can integrate an AWS WAF. Figure 6.53 shows a list of available integrations. For web application firewall protection, you can select the AWS WAF integration and associate a WAF web ACL to secure your application.

Chapter 6 ▪ Infrastructure Protection

FIGURE 6.53 ALB integrations: AWS WAF.

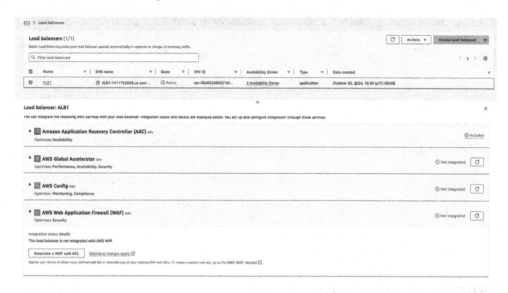

To optimize application security, associate either a predefined AWS WAF web ACL or an existing web ACL to your ALB. This association can be made during or after load balancer creation, from its Integrations tab or from the AWS WAF console.

In Exercise 6.7, you set up an elastic load balancer.

EXERCISE 6.7

Elastic Load Balancing

Building on Exercise 6.6, you create an elastic load balancer.

1. Create an ALB called **Public-ALB** to distribute web access (HTTP) between instances Web-A and Web-B.
2. Check that Public-ALB is actually load-balancing HTTP requests to Web-A and Web-B.
3. Create an NLB called **Private-NLB** to distribute internal Oracle traffic to instances DB-A and DB-B. You do not need to test this network load balancer.

VPC Endpoints

One of the main advantages of developing applications on the AWS Cloud is the inherent proximity to other computing, storage, and networking resources deployed in it. Nonetheless, there are different ways you can design internal connectivity for your different services deployed on AWS.

One approach you could adopt is to treat anything external to your VPC as the Internet and only provide connectivity via Internet (and NAT) gateways, as you did earlier in "AWS Networking Constructs" and "Network Address Translation." As you have learned, such a method would require public IP addresses to allow communication and traffic to leave the Amazon network, even though both communicating resources are located within the AWS Cloud.

Through VPC endpoints, you can privately connect resources in your VPC to multiple AWS services without imposing additional traffic on your Internet gateways or relying on the Internet for such communications. There are two types of VPC endpoints:

- **Interface endpoint:** An elastic network interface with a private IP address on a subnet that serves as an entry point for traffic between this subnet and AWS services such as Amazon API Gateway, Amazon Elastic Container Service (ECR), Amazon EMR, AWS Key Management Service (KMS), and Amazon SageMaker. Interface endpoints enable connectivity to services over AWS PrivateLink.
- **Gateway endpoint:** A gateway (or virtual device) that you specify as a target for a route in your route table for traffic destined to AWS services such as Amazon S3 and Amazon DynamoDB. Gateway endpoints do not use AWS PrivateLink.

Figure 6.54 illustrates a network diagram where you can see the connectivity architecture and understand how VPC endpoints provide private access to AWS resources without traversing the public Internet.

You will put such concepts in action to enable a direct connectivity to an Amazon S3 bucket from an Amazon EC2 instance in the topology you built. In such a scenario, Figure 6.55 illustrates the creation of a gateway endpoint. In VPC service, inside the Virtual Private Cloud section, click on Endpoints and then Create Endpoint.

VPC Endpoint Policies: When you create an interface or gateway endpoint, you can control access to the service to which you are connecting by attaching an endpoint policy to it. Endpoint policies must be written in JSON format. Not all services support endpoint policies. By default, they are set to *Full Access* at the moment of creation; however, this setting may be updated after creation to define a more restrictive access to the endpoint.

242 Chapter 6 ▪ Infrastructure Protection

FIGURE 6.54 Connectivity to AWS services using VPC endpoints.

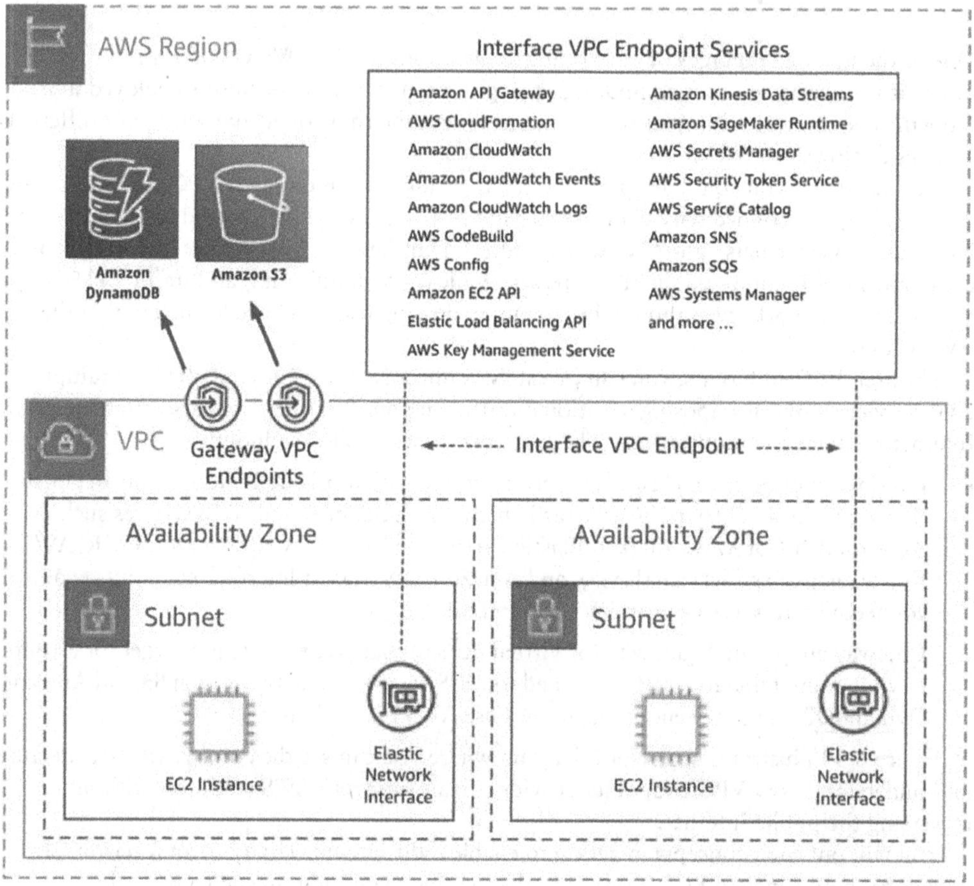

In Figure 6.55, you will notice that the following parameters are required for the gateway endpoint deployment:

- **Service Category:** This allows you to look for different methods to search for services to be connected to your VPCs. Its options include:
  - AWS Services
  - PrivateLink Ready Partner Services
  - AWS Marketplace Services
  - EC2 instance Connect Endpoint
  - Other Endpoint Services

FIGURE 6.55 VPC gateway endpoint creation.

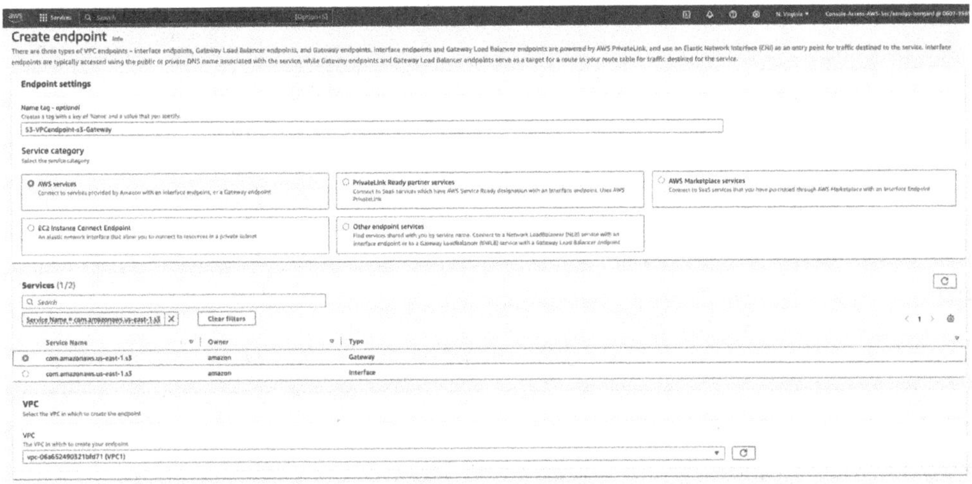

For configuration, select AWS Services. Once it has been selected, you will see the Services section that provides a search bar. Select Find Service By Name, and then select S3. This will display the existing endpoints. In the example, leave the default option set to AWS Services.

- **Services:** The console helps you with the reverse DNS name of the service you will connect to using this VPC gateway. Figure 6.55 shows the Amazon S3 service in the N. Virginia region (com.amazonaws.us-east-1.s3). You should use the search bar, type S3, and select the service. Then, you can select the VPC.

- **VPC:** This drop-down list allows you to select the VPC where the VPC endpoint will be created (vpc-06a652490321bfd71 represents VPC1 in this scenario, which will be different in your implementation).

The Create Endpoint screen allows you to define which route tables will be adjusted to redirect traffic to this service. Figure 6.56 shows how VPC1's main route table was adapted to send Amazon S3 traffic through the VPC gateway you just created.

In Figure 6.57, you can see that there is a more specific route that sends IP traffic to Amazon S3 in the region. The destination is a prefix list pl-63a5400a (com.amazonaws.us-east-1. s3, 52.216.0.0/15, 54.231.0.0/16, 3.5.0.0/19, 18.34.232.0/21, as shown in Figure 6.58). Consequently, the main route table redirects any IP packets with a destination among these networks toward this VPC endpoint (whose identifier is vpce-0f94d4e3d511904db, in this scenario).

You can also create a VPC interface endpoint using a configuration similar to the one shown in Figure 6.59.

FIGURE 6.56 VPC endpoint in VPC1.

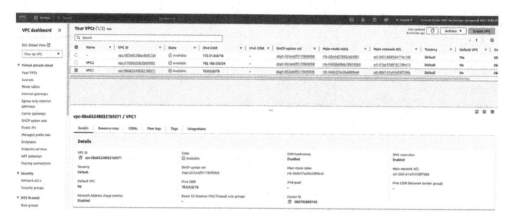

FIGURE 6.57 Updated main route table in VPC1.

In Figure 6.59, you can see that similar parameters from the gateway endpoint are required for the interface endpoint creation: Service Category, Service Name, and VPC. The configuration includes the following:

- **Subnets:** Indicates where the elastic network interfaces will be provisioned.
- **Enable DNS Name:** Enables the use of a private DNS name for this endpoint.
- **Security Group:** Associates a security group with the endpoint's elastic network interfaces.

FIGURE 6.58 Prefix list for S3.

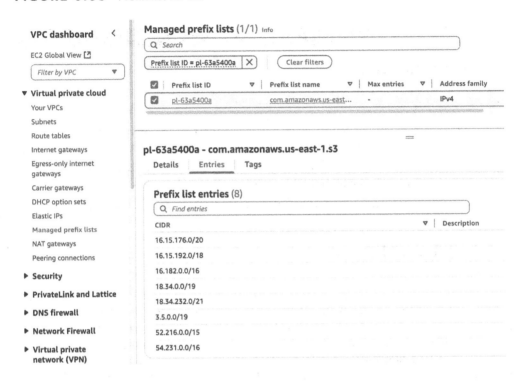

FIGURE 6.59 VPC interface endpoint creation.

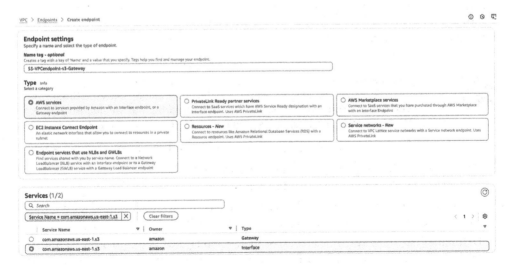

In Exercise 6.8, you work with VPC endpoints.

EXERCISE 6.8

Work with VPC Endpoints

Building on Exercise 6.7, you work with VPC endpoints.

1. Create a VPC gateway endpoint called **GW-EP** to connect PrivateSubnet-A and PrivateSubnet-B to Amazon S3 in the region you have chosen.

2. Verify that Private-RouteTable-A and Private-RouteTable-B were changed to provide communication between the subnets and the VPC gateway endpoint.

VPC Flow Logs

Connectivity without visibility can be as troublesome as driving a car without a dashboard. To provide traffic transparency in your VPCs, AWS has created *VPC Flow Logs*. This feature enables you to capture flow information (which includes IP addresses, transport protocol, and ports) about the traffic going to and from network interfaces in your VPC.

You can create a flow log for a VPC, a subnet, or a specific network interface. If you define a flow log for a subnet (or VPC), each network interface in that subnet (or VPC) is then monitored.

There are two places where you can send VPC Flow Log information: Amazon CloudWatch Logs or Amazon S3. Figure 6.60 shows the creation of the flow logs for a subnet (Subnet10-AZ1a).

 To access the screen shown in Figure 6.60 from the VPC management console, click Subnets in the menu at the left and then click the Create Flow Log button. You cannot enable flow logs for VPCs that are peered with your VPC (and their subnets) unless the peer VPC belongs to your AWS account.

Figure 6.60 shows the parameters required for AWS to log the IP traffic in this subnet:

- **Filter:** Choose All to log accepted and rejected traffic by the network interface, Reject to record only blocked traffic, or Accept to record only forwarded traffic.

- **Maximum Aggregation Interval:** This specifies the time interval during which a flow of packets is captured and aggregated into a flow log record.

- **Destination:** Options available are: (a) Send To CloudWatch Logs, (b) Send To An S3 Bucket, (c) Send to Amazon Data Firehose in the same account, and (d) Send to Amazon Data Firehose in a different account.

FIGURE 6.60 Flow Log creation.

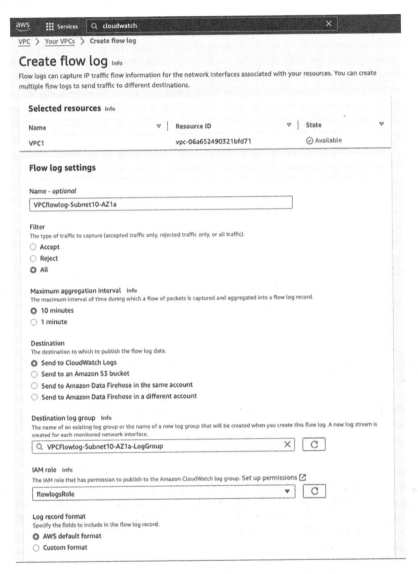

- **Destination Log Group:** This specifies the name of the Amazon CloudWatch Log group to which the flow log is published. A new log stream is created for each monitored network interface. (Figure 6.60 shows VPCFlowlog-Subnet10-AZa-LogGroup as the chosen name for the log group.)
- **IAM Role:** This specifies the AWS Identity and Access Management (IAM) role that has permission to publish to the Amazon CloudWatch Log group (flowlogsRole, in this scenario). You can create this role at this point by clicking the Set Up Permissions link.

FIGURE 6.61 VPC Flow Log example.

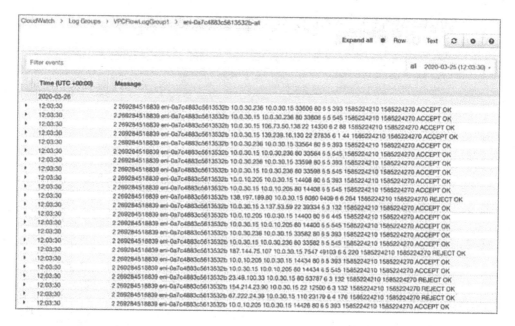

 You cannot change the configuration of a flow log after you have created it.

Figure 6.61 shows some flow logs generated via the previously specified configuration as they are visible on Amazon CloudWatch.

 VPC Flow Logs can monitor all IP traffic except Amazon DNS server traffic (although all other DNS server traffic can be monitored), Amazon Windows license activation traffic, instance metadata (169.254.169.254) traffic, DHCP traffic, and IP communication directed to the default VPC router's reserved IP address.

You can also create flow logs for network interfaces that belong to other AWS services, such as elastic load balancing, Amazon RDS, Amazon ElastiCache, Amazon Redshift, Amazon WorkSpaces, NAT gateways, and TGWs.

In Exercise 6.9, you check how the VPC Flow Logs present traffic information in your system.

AWS Web Application Firewall **249**

EXERCISE 6.9

Check VPC Flow Logs

Building on Exercise 6.8, you view the VPC Flow Logs.

1. Enable VPC Flow Logs in your Secure-VPC.

2. Observe the flows in Amazon CloudWatch. Test the Echo Reply (ping) communication allowed via the NACL you've built in Exercise 6.5 and locate at least one example of this traffic in the VPC Flow Logs.

AWS Web Application Firewall

Not all attacks can be detected using traditional layer 3 and layer 4 traffic filtering techniques. In time, hackers have continued to develop more sophisticated attacks in order to exploit vulnerabilities in many different ways of computer communications, including the higher layers of the OSI model, to compromise popular protocols such as HTTP.

To defend applications against such attacks, web application firewalls are used to detect and block HTTP malicious activity. In on-premises environments, such a security feature can be implemented in software or appliances (both physical or virtual), but in the AWS Cloud, you can easily deploy it as a service.

AWS Web Application Firewall (WAF) protects your applications and APIs from known web attacks. Through this service, you can create rules that block well-known attacks, such as SQL injection and cross-site scripting, or specific traffic patterns that you can define. Within AWS WAF, you can filter any part of the web request, including IP addresses, HTTP headers, HTTP body, and requested uniform resource identifiers (URIs).

The most fundamental object in an AWS WAF implementation is the creation of a Web Access Control List (Web ACL). These objects are available on the WAF & Shield console in the AWS Management Console.

Figure 6.62 shows the first step in the creation of a Web ACL named WebACL1.

In Figure 6.62, you can see some important aspects of the WebACL1 creation. First, its scope is regional, and it applies to region us-east-1. WebACL1 is regional because it is associated with application load balancer ALB1, which is firmly established in the Eastern US (N. Virginia) region. If WebACL1 was applied to an Amazon CloudFront distribution, it would have a global scope due to the nature of this service.

FIGURE 6.62 WebACL1 creation.

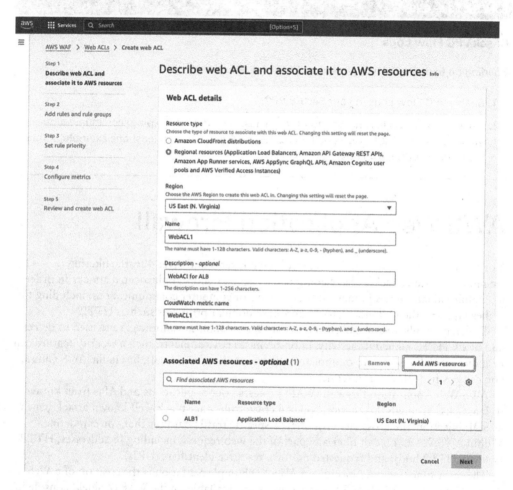

 AWS WAF can also be associated with Amazon API Gateways and to Amazon CloudFront distributions that are serving websites that can be hosted outside of the AWS Cloud.

You can do more with WebACL1's configuration. You can add your own rules or managed rule groups, which are preconfigured sets of rules defined by AWS or AWS Marketplace sellers. These managed rule groups support protection against vulnerabilities defined on the OWASP Top 10 Security Risks, threats specific to content management systems (CMSs), or emerging common vulnerabilities and exposures (CVE).

Figure 6.63 illustrates a configuration step that allows the addition of two managed rule groups.

FIGURE 6.63 Adding rules to WebACL1.

The managed rule groups shown in Figure 6.63 are as follows:

- **Amazon IP Reputation List (AWS-AWSManagedRulesAmazonIpReputationList):** Contains rules that are based on Amazon threat intelligence to block sources associated with bots or other threats.
- **Linux Operating System (AWS-AWSManagedRulesLinuxRuleSet):** Specifies rules that block request patterns associated with exploitation of vulnerabilities specific to Linux systems. It can help prevent attacks that expose file contents or execute code for which the attacker should not have had access.

252 Chapter 6 ▪ Infrastructure Protection

In Figure 6.63, you can also see that each of these groups has a defined capacity unit (25 and 200, respectively). Be aware that each web ACL has a limit of 5000 capacity units. The total WCUs for a web ACL can't exceed 5000. Using over 1500 WCUs affects your costs.

 You can deploy 100 Web ACLs per region. There are also other quotas that you should be aware of, such as rule groups (100 per region), IP sets (100 per region), and requests per second per web ACL deployed on an ALB (25,000 per region). Check the AWS official documentation for complete and current information.

Figure 6.63 shows Allow as the default action WebACL1 should take if a web request does not match any of the managed rule groups previously discussed.

In order to make this web ACL even more interesting, you can also create your own rules and rule groups. Figure 6.64 illustrates the creation of a new custom rule called BlockAdminPages. Select WebACL1 and click on the Rules tab. Then in the Rules section, click the Add Rules button and select the Add My Own Rules and Rule Groups.

This will open a new window to create your custom rule (see Figure 6.65). Select Rule Builder Option and add Name to the Rule.

In Figure 6.65, you can see the following parameters for the creation of this rule:

- **Name:** BlockAdminPages string.
- **Type:** Regular Rule, which will use string recognition.
- **If a request:** Matches the statement (where the characteristic that should be matched is described in statements that will follow).
- **Statement:** URI path, which specifies that it should look into the URIs of the HTTP request.
- **Match Type:** Contains string.
- **String To Match:** Admin, in this case.

FIGURE 6.64 Custom rule creation.

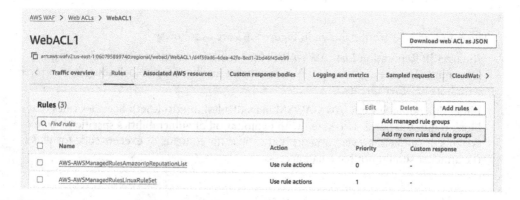

FIGURE 6.65 BlockAdminPages custom rule creation.

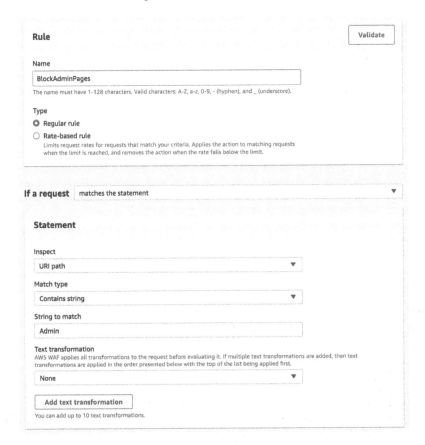

- **Text Transformation:** URL Decode, which eliminates a formatting known as URL encoding that some hackers use to bypass web application firewalls. Other text transformation options can be added if you want AWS WAF to compress whitespace, replace encoded HTML entities, such as (&)lt with decoded characters such as <, or convert uppercase letters (A–Z) to lowercase (a–z).
- **Action:** Block. Other choices are Allow, Count (where only matches would be counted), CAPTCHA, and Challenge (Token) (see Figure 6.66).

With the configuration shown in Figure 6.66, the BlockAdminPages rule actually obstructs all requests whose URI contained the word *admin* (which, for example, could refer to administrative pages on targets balanced by ALB1). In such a scenario, blocked web accesses are sent an HTTP 403 Forbidden reply.

FIGURE 6.66 BlockAdminPages custom rule creation: Action.

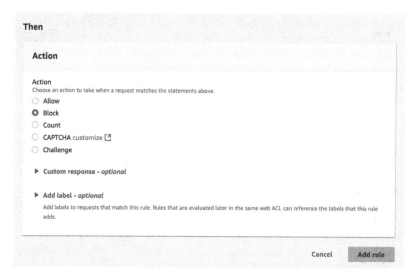

The conditions presented in Figure 6.65 are just a few of the many available for rule creation on AWS WAF. These include source IP addresses (in CIDR blocks), countries, request length, and specific HTTP request headers.

AWS WAF also provides logging data from each inspected web request for use in security automation, analytics, or auditing purposes. AWS WAF offers near real-time visibility into your web traffic, allowing you to create alerts in Amazon CloudWatch. In the case of WebACL1, you can follow how each of its rules is actually matched in CloudWatch or in the Overview tab of WebACL1, as shown in Figure 6.67.

By default, WebACL1 has logging disabled. To enable this option, select WebACL1 and click the Logging and Metrics tab. In the Logging section, click Enable. Here, you can select the different logging options supported. Use logging to capture information about the requests that this web ACL evaluates. Before you can enable this option on your web ACL, you must configure your logging destination in its AWS service. The name of any logging destination must start with "aws-waf-logs-." For additional information and requirements for each destination type, see the AWS WAF documentation for logging web ACL traffic.

FIGURE 6.67 Enable AWS WAF logging.

Figure 6.68 shows that after testing the custom rule, the WAF blocked four attempts during the five-minute period that ended at 12:25 P.M. on October 20, 2024.

 Depending on the web traffic that reaches your AWS environment, AWS WAF may generate an enormous number of log records. You can use the S3 configuration or the Amazon Kinesis Data Firehose to load a stream of AWS WAF logging, filter unneeded records, and store them in a different place or a log analysis tool. You can find more details about this implementation here: https://aws.amazon.com/blogs/security/trimming-aws-waf-logs-with-amazon-kinesis-firehose-transformations.

FIGURE 6.68 WebACL1 overview graph.

AWS WAF also includes a full-featured API that you can use to automate the creation, deployment, and maintenance of security rules.

In Exercise 6.10, you create and test a firewall.

EXERCISE 6.10

Create and Test an AWS Web Application Firewall

Building on Exercise 6.9, you work with an AWS WAF.

1. Create an AWS WAF Web ACL called **Web-ACL** with one managed group rule of your choice and a blocking default action. Then associate it to Public-ALB, which you created in Exercise 6.7.
2. Test the access to Public-ALB several times in your browser.
3. Create a custom rule allowing HTTP web access to Public-ALB.
4. Again, test the access to Public-ALB several times in your browser.
5. Check both test results via a graphical diagram.

AWS Shield

Distributed denial-of-service attacks can be defined as cyberattacks in which many different compromised sources generate traffic intended to make a computer or network resource unavailable to its originally intended users. Classic firewalling techniques are challenged by DDoS attacks for two main reasons: blocking traffic requires the characterization of all sources, and firewall capacity may also be at risk when dealing with a high number of connections.

To protect applications deployed in the AWS Cloud from such attacks, Amazon offers AWS Shield. This service provides constant detections and automatic inline mitigations that minimize application downtime or performance degradation against DDoS attacks at two different levels: AWS Shield Standard and AWS Shield Advanced.

AWS Shield Standard is a no-cost version that defends your environment against the most common network (layer 3) and transport (layer 4) known infrastructure attacks. It relies on detection techniques such as network flow monitoring, a combination of traffic signatures, and anomaly algorithms. Additionally, it mitigates attacks through inline mechanisms, which include deterministic packet filtering, priority-based traffic shaping, and rules in AWS WAF. And more importantly, AWS Shield Standard is activated by default in all AWS accounts, without any configuration required. On the other hand, AWS Shield Advanced requires a subscription and configuration. Figure 6.69 displays the AWS Shield Advanced Overview page, where you can find guidance for service setup and additional configuration options that facilitate more effective collaboration with the AWS Shield Response Team (SRT).

 AWS Shield Advanced is not activated by default. As of this writing, AWS charges $3,000 per month, including all accounts on AWS Organizations (with a 12-month commitment), plus additional data transfer fees for AWS Shield Advanced.

AWS Shield Advanced enables additional detection and mitigation against larger and more sophisticated DDoS attacks on Amazon EC2, ELB, Amazon CloudFront, AWS Global Accelerator, and Amazon Route 53. AWS Shield Advanced provides the following distinct features:

- **Near Real-Time Visibility and Reporting:** With layers 3 and 4 attack notifications and attack forensic reports as well as layers 3, 4, and 7 attack historical reports.
- **Integration with AWS WAF:** You can respond to incidents as they occur via customizable rules that you can deploy instantly in AWS WAF (which is also included in AWS Shield Advanced at no extra cost) to quickly mitigate attacks.
- **24/7 Access to the AWS Shield Response Team (SRT):** For manual mitigation of edge cases affecting your availability, such as custom rules intended to mitigate application layer DDoS attacks in your environments.

FIGURE 6.69 Shield Advanced General view.

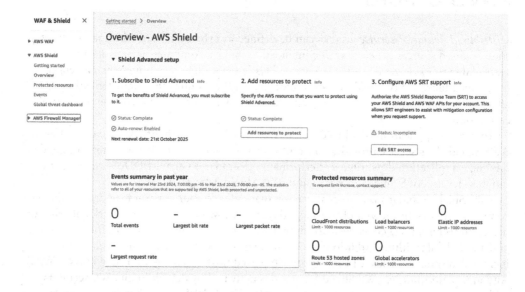

FIGURE 6.70 Shield Advanced protected resources.

- **Cost Protection:** Against DDoS-related cost spikes in AWS Shield Advanced protected resources, with service credits related to increased utilization of Amazon EC2, ELB, Amazon Route 53, Amazon CloudFront, and AWS Global Accelerator.

 To protect your organization from a DDoS attack, it is important to add those resources to the Protected Resources section. This can be done manually or by using a Firewall Manager rule to automate the process. Resources not included in that list are not protected. In Figure 6.70, you can see the ALB1 that was created in previous sections.

AWS Shield Advanced provides enhanced detection through network flow inspection, resource specific monitoring, resource and region-specific granular detection of DDoS attacks, application layer DDoS attacks like HTTP floods or DNS query floods by baselining traffic, and identification of anomalies. It offers advanced attack mitigation via routing techniques, SRT manual mitigations, and attack notifications via Amazon CloudWatch, as well as post-attack analysis.

AWS Network Firewall

AWS Network Firewall is a managed network security service that provides protection for your Amazon VPC networks. It allows you to deploy network security across your VPCs with just a few clicks, without the need to provision or manage any infrastructure.

Network Firewall provides fine-grained control over network traffic, allowing you to create firewall rules that provide protections like blocking outbound Server Message Block (SMB) requests to prevent the spread of malware, or disallowing domains and IP addresses that pose threats. AWS Network Firewall includes stateful inspection, intrusion prevention, and web filtering. The service uses rule groups to define network traffic inspection and filtering behaviors. These rule groups can be shared and reused across multiple firewalls, simplifying management for large or complex networks. Network Firewall integrates with other AWS services like CloudWatch for logging and monitoring, and AWS Firewall Manager for centralized management of the firewalls across your accounts and VPCs.

When implementing AWS Network Firewall, it is crucial to consider your network architecture and traffic flow patterns. The service is designed to protect traffic at the perimeter of your VPC, so proper placement within your network topology is essential. You'll need to update your VPC route tables to direct traffic through the firewall endpoints (based in AWS gateway load balancer endpoints).

AWS Network Firewall can be integrated into various network designs. In a simple single-AZ Internet gateway setup, you can place the firewall between your VPC and the Internet gateway, inspecting all inbound and outbound traffic. See Figure 6.71.

For multi-zone architectures, you can deploy firewall endpoints in multiple AZs for high availability and fault tolerance. In more complex setups involving NAT gateways, you can position the firewall to inspect traffic both before and after NAT translation, providing a comprehensive protection. Another common architecture involves using AWS Network Firewall with a TGW. In this design, the firewall can be placed between the transit gateway and the Internet gateway, allowing it to inspect traffic from multiple VPCs that are connected via the TGW. This centralized approach can simplify management and provide consistent security policies across your entire network infrastructure.

FIGURE 6.71 AWS Network Firewall deployed in a single AZ and traffic flow for a workload in a public subnet.

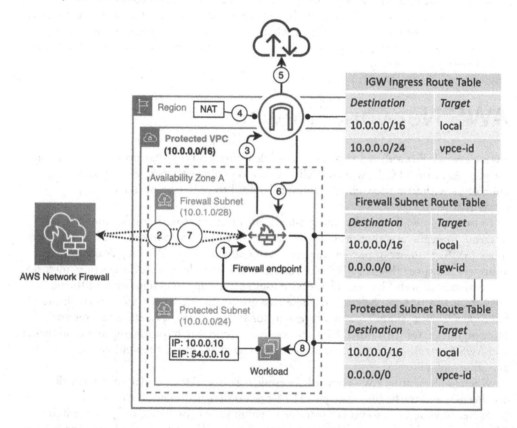

You can review different topologies on the AWS blog "Deployment models for AWS Network Firewall" at https://aws.amazon.com/blogs/networking-and-content-delivery/deployment-models-for-aws-network-firewall/.

Here are examples of the most common models:

- **Distributed AWS Network Firewall Deployment Model:** AWS Network Firewall is deployed into each individual VPC.
- **Centralized AWS Network Firewall Deployment Model:** AWS Network Firewall is deployed into centralized VPC for East-West (VPC-to-VPC) and/or North-South (Internet egress and ingress or on-premises) traffic. They refer to this VPC as *inspection VPC* throughout the blog post.

- **Combined AWS Network Firewall Deployment Model:** AWS Network Firewall is deployed into centralized inspection VPC for East-West (VPC-to-VPC) and a subset of North-South (on premises/egress) traffic. Internet ingress is distributed to VPCs, which require dedicated inbound access from the Internet, and AWS Network Firewall is deployed accordingly.

In Figure 6.72, you can see a partial view of the configuration parameters for creating this element; the complete set of parameters is described here:

- **Name:** NFW1 string.
- **VPC and Subnets:** Associated VPC and subnets to create the firewall endpoints.
- **Advanced settings:** Enable protection against changes and configure a customer-managed key (using AWS KMS) to encrypt and decrypt your resources.

FIGURE 6.72 AWS Network Firewall creation.

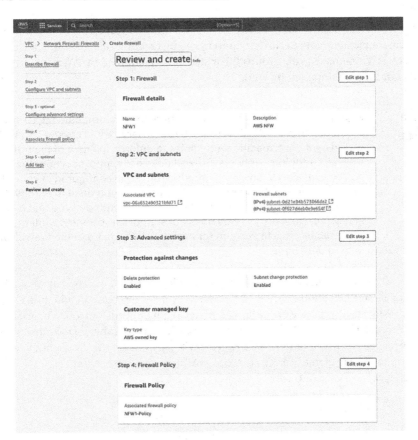

- **Associated Firewall policy:** The firewall policy contains a list of rule groups that define how the firewall inspects and manages web traffic. You can configure the associated firewall policy after you create the firewall.
  - **Firewall Policy:** Create and associate an empty firewall policy or associate an existing firewall policy.
  - **New Firewall Policy Name:** NFW1-Policy.
  - **Rule Evaluation Order:** Strict order recommended. Rules are processed in the order that you define, starting with the first rule.
  - **Drop Action:** Set to Drop established, which means that you are only allowing the traffic that you explicitly allow via your firewall rules, and everything else is denied/dropped.
  - **Alert Action:** Selected All and Established, which generates alert messages for each matching rule. To send the alert messages to the firewall logs, add a logging configuration to the firewall after creation.
- **Tags**

Figure 6.73 displays the overview after AWS Network Firewall creation is complete. From here, you can implement your security requirements by creating rule groups, which come in two types: AWS-managed rule groups (provided and maintained by AWS) or custom rule groups (created and maintained by you).

Best practice: Allocate a separate subnet to accommodate the Firewall Endpoints that the AWS Network Firewall service will create. This will allow you to configure specific route tables to enforce the flow of the traffic to the firewall endpoints. Network Firewall does not support asymmetric routing, so you will need to ensure symmetric routing is configured in your VPC. When you deploy Network Firewall into a VPC, you need to modify the route tables to ensure traffic is sent through firewall endpoints so that it can be inspected. Network Firewall does not support asymmetric routing, so the route tables have to account for network flows going to the firewall endpoint in both directions.

In Figure 6.74, you could create different rules inside the NFW1-Policy that were added in the Network Firewall creation process. In the Stateful rule group you can add unmanaged rules (Custom) or Managed stateful Rule groups (BotNetCommandAndControlDomainsStrictOrder, AbusedLegitBotNetCommandAndControlDomainsStrictOrder, MalwareDomainsStrictOrder). Click in the managed rules to add new rules. This will open the screen shown in Figure 6.75. More information is available at https://docs.aws.amazon.com/waf/latest/developerguide/aws-managed-rule-groups-list.html.

FIGURE 6.73 AWS Network Firewall overview.

FIGURE 6.74 Managed Rules overview.

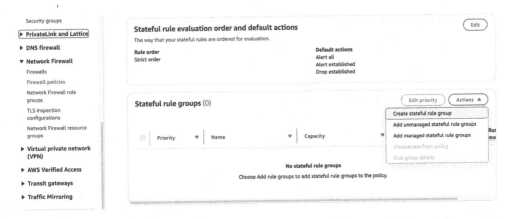

Amazon Inspector

An important component within the security management of organizations is the Technical Vulnerability Management part that involves carrying out a continuous process of reviewing the exposure and vulnerability status of your applications and all their associated components. Aligned with the Well-Architected Framework, precisely in the workload protection component, you have item SEC06-BP01: Perform Vulnerability Management, which recommends that you should "Frequently scan and patch for vulnerabilities in your

264 Chapter 6 ▪ Infrastructure Protection

FIGURE 6.75 Managed Rules to add at NFW1-Policy.

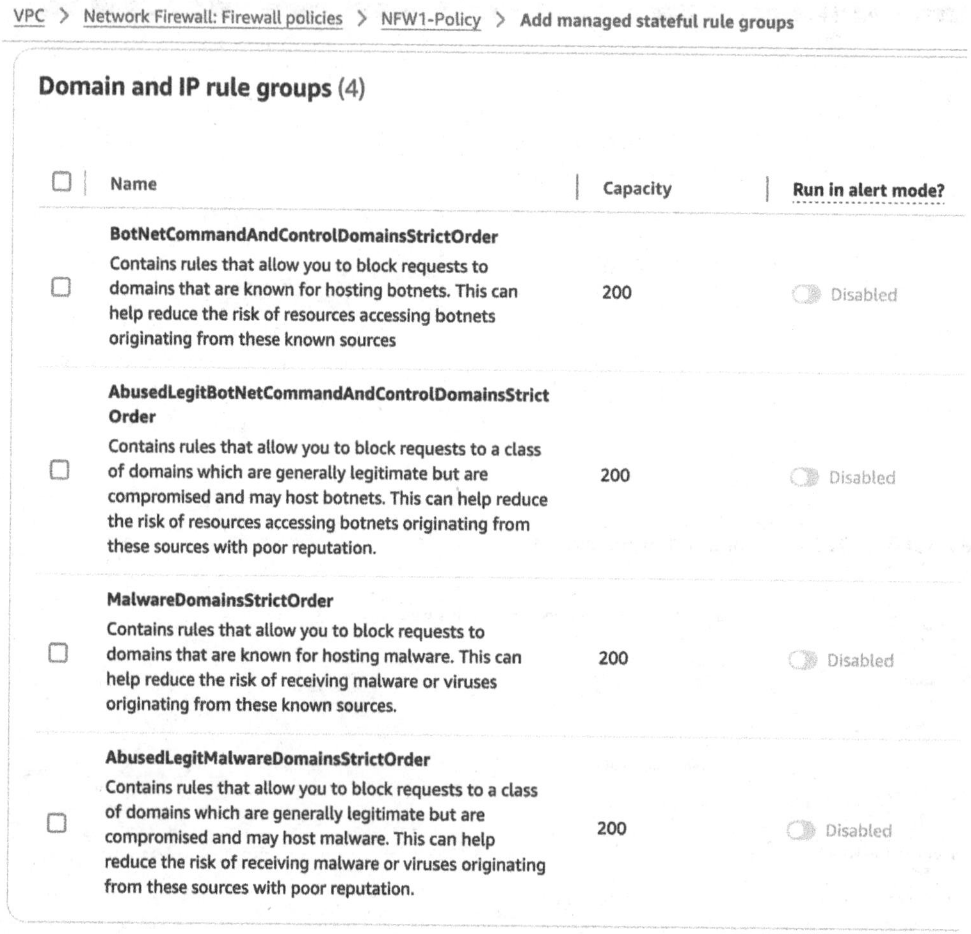

VPC > Network Firewall: Firewall policies > NFW1-Policy > **Add managed stateful rule groups**

Domain and IP rule groups (4)

	Name	Capacity	Run in alert mode?
☐	**BotNetCommandAndControlDomainsStrictOrder** Contains rules that allow you to block requests to domains that are known for hosting botnets. This can help reduce the risk of resources accessing botnets originating from these known sources	200	◯ Disabled
☐	**AbusedLegitBotNetCommandAndControlDomainsStrict Order** Contains rules that allow you to block requests to a class of domains which are generally legitimate but are compromised and may host botnets. This can help reduce the risk of resources accessing botnets originating from these sources with poor reputation.	200	◯ Disabled
☐	**MalwareDomainsStrictOrder** Contains rules that allow you to block requests to domains that are known for hosting malware. This can help reduce the risk of receiving malware or viruses originating from these known sources.	200	◯ Disabled
☐	**AbusedLegitMalwareDomainsStrictOrder** Contains rules that allow you to block requests to a class of domains which are generally legitimate but are compromised and may host malware. This can help reduce the risk of receiving malware or viruses originating from these sources with poor reputation.	200	◯ Disabled

code, dependencies, and in your infrastructure to help protect against new threats." In this sense, AWS offers the ability to address this important issue through Amazon Inspector. In Figure 6.76, you can see the general view. You just need to enable the service and it will automatically start the discovery process for EC2 instances, Container repositories, Container images, and Lambda functions.

Amazon Inspector is an automated vulnerability management service provided by AWS. It is designed to continuously discover workloads and scan them for software vulnerabilities and unintended network exposure. This regional service is crucial for maintaining the security posture of your AWS environment by automatically identifying potential security issues in your EC2 instances, container images in Amazon ECR, and Lambda functions.

As a fully managed (regional) service, Amazon Inspector reduces the operational overhead associated with vulnerability management. It eliminates the need for maintaining separate vulnerability scanning infrastructure, making it a cost-effective solution for organizations of all sizes. Figure 6.77 shows the discovered instances that were created along the chapter.

FIGURE 6.76 Amazon Inspector dashboard.

FIGURE 6.77 Amazon Inspector Resources coverage.

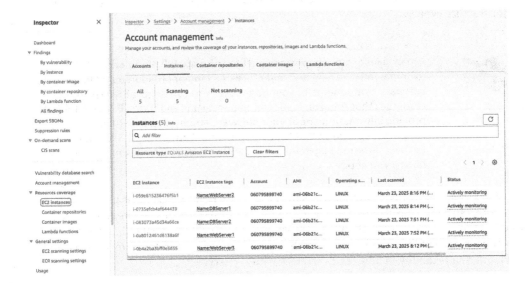

Amazon Inspector supports hybrid scanning, which includes agent-based scanning and agentless scanning. Agent-based scans are performed continuously using the SSM agent (on all eligible instances). It uses SSM associations, and plugins installed through these associations, to collect software inventory from your instances. For agentless scans, Amazon Inspector uses EBS snapshots to collect a software inventory from your instances. Agentless scanning checks instances for operating system and application programming language package vulnerabilities.

One of the standout features of Amazon Inspector is its ability to centrally manage multiple accounts. For organizations with complex AWS environments spanning multiple accounts, Amazon Inspector can be managed through a single delegated administrator account using AWS Organizations. This centralized approach allows for efficient management of findings data and settings across the entire organization.

Amazon Inspector eliminates the need for manual scheduling or configuration of assessment scans. It automatically discovers eligible resources and begins scanning them immediately. This continuous scanning approach ensures that your environment is constantly monitored for new vulnerabilities and network exposures, providing up-to-date security insights.

The service covers a wide range of resources within your AWS environment. It scans Amazon EC2 instances, container images stored in Amazon ECR, Lambda functions, and Lambda code scanning (scans for code vulnerabilities in your application package dependencies). These scan types can be activated based on your specific needs. The service automatically discovers new resources as they are added to your AWS environment. This ensures that new instances, containers, or functions are immediately brought under the security umbrella of Amazon Inspector, maintaining consistent security coverage as your infrastructure evolves.

Amazon Inspector supports export to software bill of materials (SBOMs) to create/retrieve a nested inventory of all the open-source and third-party software components in your codebase. You can export SBOMs for all resources that Amazon Inspector supports and monitors. Exported SBOMs provide information about your software supply. Amazon Inspector supports exporting SBOMs in CycloneDX 1.4 and SPDX 2.3 compatible formats. Amazon Inspector exports SBOMs as JSON files to the Amazon S3 bucket you choose.

When Amazon Inspector detects a software vulnerability using CVEs or unintended network exposure, it generates a detailed finding. These findings provide in-depth information about the issue, allowing security teams to quickly understand and address potential risks. Findings can be managed through both the Amazon Inspector console and API, offering flexibility in how teams interact with the service.

Amazon Inspector supports integration with CI/CD pipelines. You can integrate Amazon Inspector container image scans with your CI/CD pipeline to scan for software vulnerabilities and produce vulnerability reports, which allow you to investigate and remediate risks before deployment. For this integration, the service utilizes the Amazon Inspector SBOM Generator and Amazon Inspector Scan API to produce vulnerability reports.

Amazon Inspector integrates seamlessly with AWS Security Hub, providing a centralized view of security alerts and compliance status. This integration allows for a more holistic approach to security management within your AWS environment.

AWS Systems Manager Patch Manager

Once you have identified the vulnerabilities in your applications, it is important to start taking corrective and preventive actions to reduce the level of exposure of your applications. This is when establishing remediation capabilities comes into play by managing the updates and patches that address the identified vulnerabilities.

AWS Systems Manager Patch Manager automates the process of patching managed instances with both security-related and other types of updates. Patch Manager can be used to apply patches on Amazon EC2 instances for both operating systems and applications, including Microsoft applications, Windows service packs, and minor version upgrades for Linux-based instances. In addition to Amazon EC2, Patch Manager can also be used to patch on-premises servers. This comprehensive approach ensures that all critical components of your infrastructure remain up-to-date and secure. To create a Patch Manager policy, type Systems Manager in the search box, and in the left panel, click on Node Management, then click Patch Manager (see Figure 6.78). Next, click the Start with Overview link that is behind the Create Policy button to show the dashboard view.

FIGURE 6.78 Systems Manager Patch Manager: Dashboard view.

268 Chapter 6 ▪ Infrastructure Protection

As mentioned in the documentation, Systems Manager provides support for patch policies in Quick Setup, a capability of AWS Systems Manager. Using patch policies is the recommended method for configuring your patching operations. Using a single patch policy configuration, you can define patching for all accounts in all regions in your organization, for only the accounts and regions you choose, or for a single account and region pair. This requires using the Quick Setup to patch managed instances.

Now click the Create Patch Policy button to start the configuration process, as shown in Figure 6.79. Here are some important configurations to keep in mind:

- **Patch Policy Name:** Name of the policy that you will create.

FIGURE 6.79 Systems Manager Patch Manager: Create Policy.

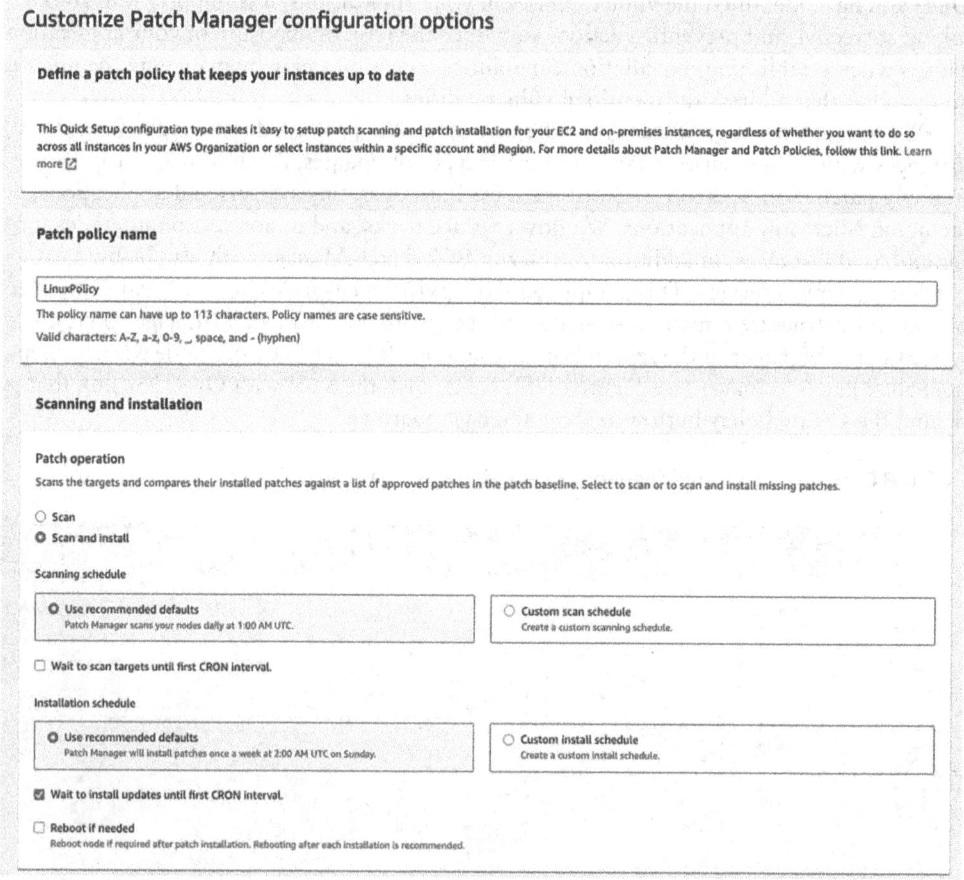

AWS Systems Manager Patch Manager   **269**

- **Scanning and Installation: Patch Operation:** Scans the targets and compares their installed patches against a list of approved patches in the patch baseline. Select to scan or to scan and install missing patches. You can start with scan and install (this will add the Installation Schedule to define the install window).

- **Patch Baselines (see Figure 6.80):** Define the way the patch will be installed. AWS provides you with managed (recommended defaults) and custom baselines. With Managed, you can use these baselines as they are currently configured (you cannot customize them), or you can create your own custom patch baselines, as shown in Figure 6.81. Custom patch baselines allow you greater control over which patches are approved or rejected for your environment.

- **Patching Log Storage:** Select or create an S3 bucket to store patching operation logs.

- **Targets:** Set to Current region.

- **Target Nodes:** Define the scope of the nodes in the policy. This could be All Managed nodes, or specify resources by tag, resource group, or defining specific instances (manual).

FIGURE 6.80   Patch Manager: Create Policy: Patch baseline custom.

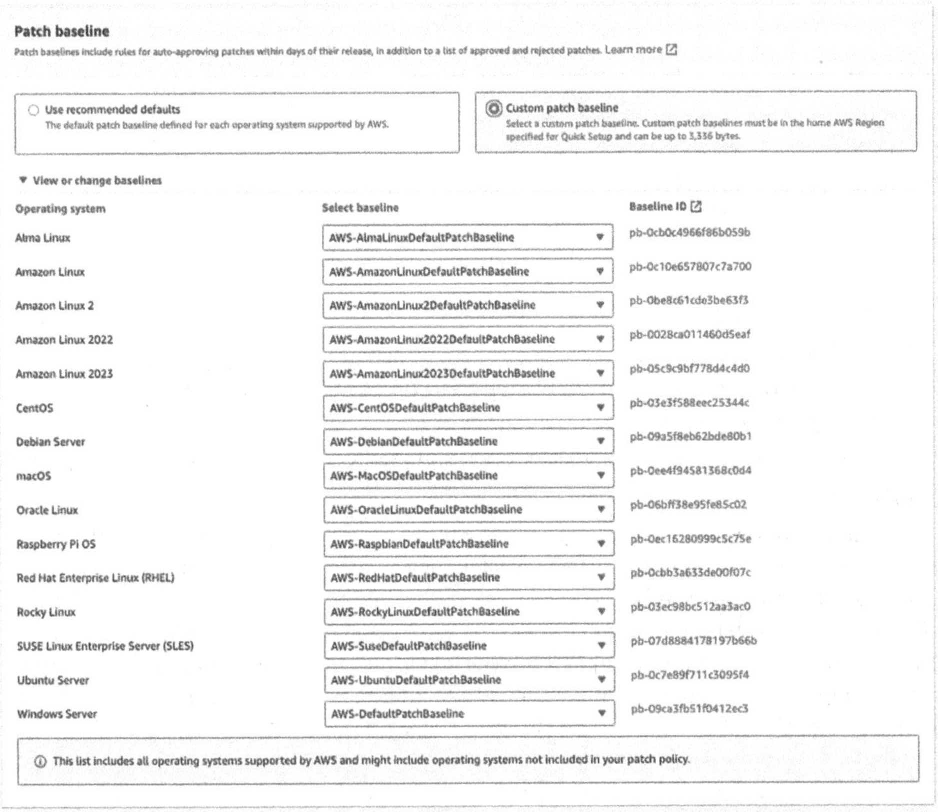

Chapter 6 · Infrastructure Protection

FIGURE 6.81 Patch Manager: Create Policy: Targets.

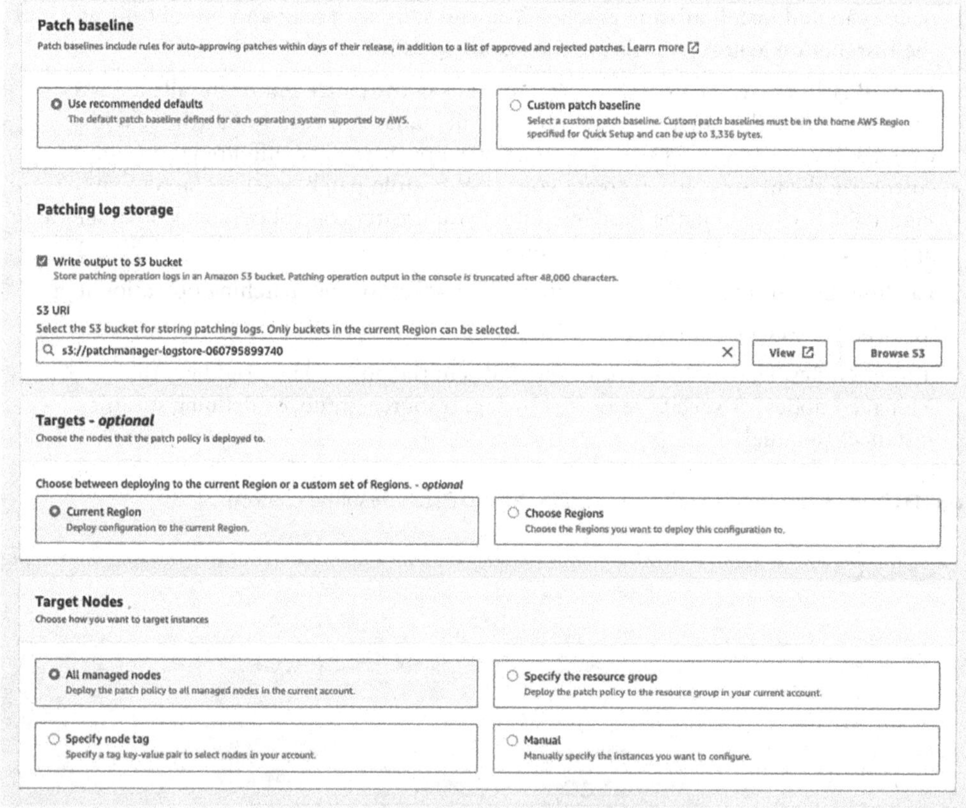

- **Rate Control:** Specify concurrency and rate to execute the process (see Figure 6.82).

- **Instance Profile Options:** Select Add Required Policies to Existing Instance Profiles Attached to Your Instances to enable the creation of policies and permissions needed for the configuration you choose (see Figure 6.82).

- **Local Deployment Roles:** Select the Create and Use New IAM Local Deployment Roles option (see Figure 6.82).

Once this is configured, you can use the Compliance Reporting tab to review the policy associated with the resources (EC2 instances), which you created in the chapter in Figure 6.83. To view fast results, you can click the Patch Now button to run the policy.

Patch Manager offers flexibility in how you apply patches. It uses patch baselines to define which patches should be applied to your managed nodes and where you can choose to scan instances, to generate a report of missing patches, or you can scan and automatically install all missing patches. Figure 6.84 shows an Amazon Linux 2 Default Patch Baseline.

FIGURE 6.82 Patch Manager: Create Policy: Rate control and profile options.

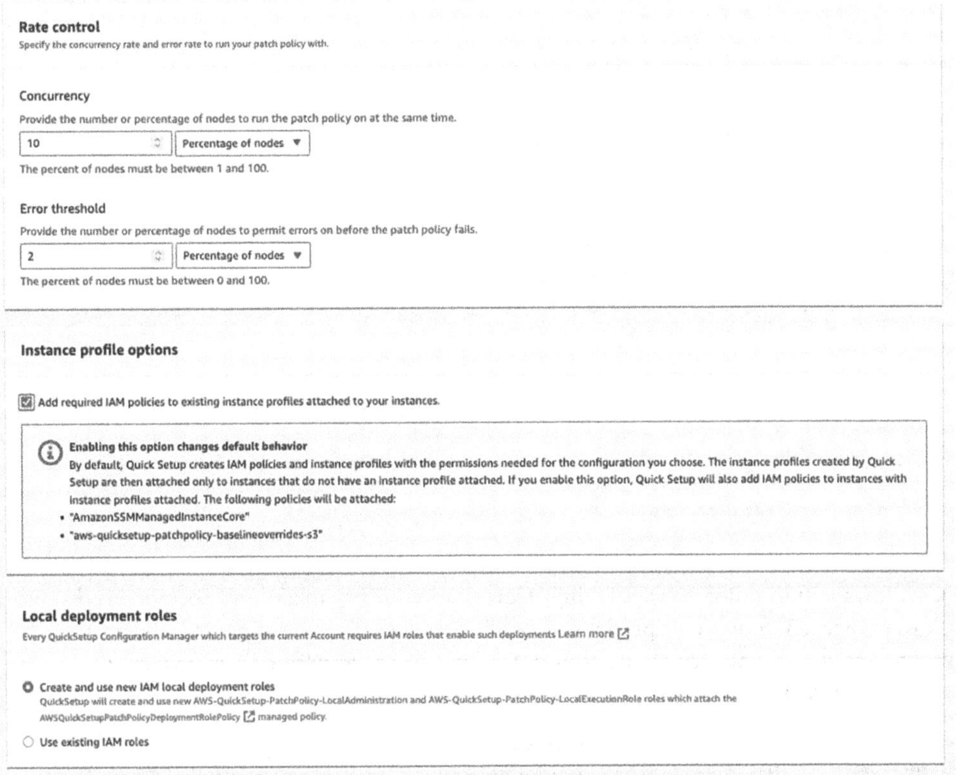

FIGURE 6.83 Patch Manager: Compliance Reporting.

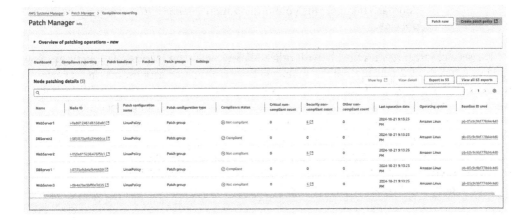

FIGURE 6.84 Patch Manager: Patch Baseline example.

This allows you to tailor your patching strategy to your organization's specific needs and risk tolerance. AWS provides predefined patch baselines for each supported operating system, but you can also create custom patch baselines that define your own set of approved patches.

 It's important to consider your patching strategy carefully. While Patch Manager can automatically apply all missing patches, in some environments, it may be more appropriate to review and approve patches before rollout. Patch Manager's flexibility allows you to implement the approach that best fits your organization's needs and risk management policies.

The service integrates seamlessly with other AWS services and features. For example, you can use Amazon EC2 tags to organize managed nodes into patch groups, making it easier to manage patching across large and complex environments. Additionally, Patch Manager works with AWS IAM to provide fine-grained access control to patching operations.

An important feature of Patch Manager is its support for compliance reporting. After a patching operation, Patch Manager generates detailed compliance reports that show which patches were applied, which ones failed, and which instances are compliant with your patch baseline. This information is crucial for maintaining security standards and meeting regulatory requirements (see Figure 6.85).

FIGURE 6.85 Patch Manager: Summary.

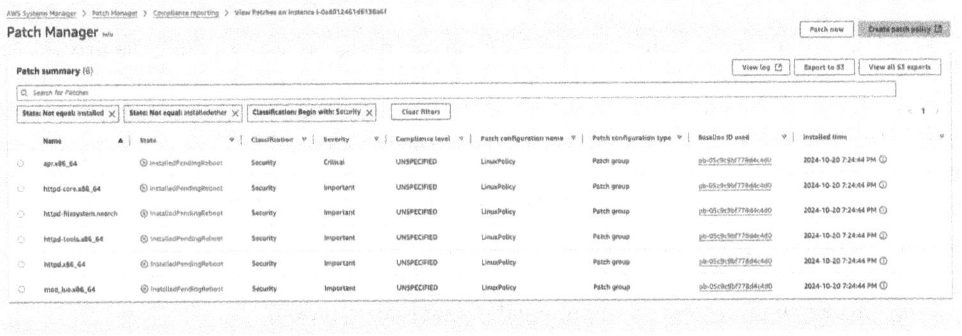

Patch Manager also offers scheduling capabilities through integration with AWS Systems Manager Maintenance Windows. This allows you to define specific time windows for patching operations, ensuring that updates are applied during off-peak hours to minimize disruption to your business operations.

For organizations managing patching across multiple AWS accounts and regions, Patch Manager supports the use of patch policies through AWS Systems Manager Quick Setup. This feature allows you to define patching configurations that can be applied across your entire organization, specific organizational units, or individual accounts and regions.

EC2 Image Builder

Another key component in protecting your workloads in any environment involves properly managing the images used for EC2 instances or containers. These images must be appropriate to fulfill application requirements while also incorporating necessary security hardening practices. By effectively controlling and maintaining standardized images deployed in your environment, you can significantly reduce potential attack vectors.

The AWS Well-architected framework, in the security pillar for the Infrastructure Protection component, recommends in item SEC06-BP02 to provision your computing with hardened images (images with your baseline). Hardened images help reduce the number of paths available in a runtime environment that can allow unintended access to unauthorized users or services. It also can reduce the scope of impact should any

274 Chapter 6 ▪ Infrastructure Protection

unintended access occur. With this in mind, AWS provides a capability to effectively manage the process of creating and managing images, both for EC2 Instances and containers, through EC2 Image Builder.

EC2 Image Builder is a fully managed AWS service designed to streamline the process of creating, managing, and deploying customized, secure, and up-to-date server or container images. This powerful tool allows users to automate the creation of custom images within their AWS accounts, using the AWS Management Console, AWS Command Line Interface, or APIs.

Key features and benefits of the EC2 Image Builder include the following:

- **Automated Image Creation:** Image Builder enables users to configure pipelines that automate updates and system patching for owned images. This ensures that images remain current and secure with minimal manual intervention.

- **Customization Capabilities:** Users can choose a base image, and then add or remove software, customize settings, and incorporate scripts using build components. This flexibility allows for tailored images that meet specific organizational requirements.

- **Testing and Validation:** The service includes the ability to run selected tests or create custom test components, ensuring that images meet quality and functionality standards before deployment. For hardening image purposes, you can select in the build image process components for hardening images that are managed components, such as Security Technical Implementation Guides, created by the Defense Information Systems Agency, or you can create your own components for that specific purpose, such as those created by the Center for Internet Security.

- **Multi-Region Distribution:** Image Builder facilitates the distribution of AMIs to multiple AWS regions and accounts, simplifying the process of maintaining consistent images across a global infrastructure.

- **Sharing and Authorization:** For custom AMIs created through Image Builder pipelines, users can authorize other AWS accounts, organizations, and organizational units (OUs) to launch the image from their account, promoting collaboration while maintaining control.

- **Ownership and Control:** All customized images created by Image Builder remain owned by the user's account, providing full control over the assets and their usage.

In Figure 6.86, you can see a pipeline that included the image creation for an Amazon Linux 2 image, and with components defined that should be included, like the latest version of Python 3 and a test to run Amazon Inspector.

In Figure 6.87, you can review the recipe that will be used to create the image. To create the final product (AMI), you should select the recipe and, in Actions, select Run Pipeline to create the image, using the information in the recipe.

EC2 Image Builder 275

 EC2 Image Builder integrates with Amazon Inspector to scan your test instances for vulnerabilities in operating system and programming language packages that are included in your Image Builder resources. After it's activated, Amazon Inspector is switched on for all services for the AWS account, including Image Builder. This also enables automatic security scanning, and Image Builder saves a snapshot of the findings for your test instances when you create a new image.

FIGURE 6.86 EC2 Image Builder summary.

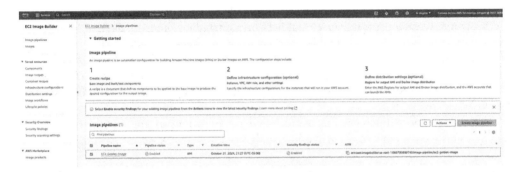

FIGURE 6.87 EC2 Image Builder recipe.

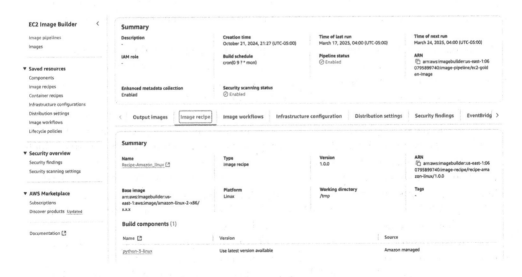

Network and Connectivity Troubleshooting Scenarios

One of the biggest challenges for professionals who operate distributed systems is the identification of network-related problems. In a cloud environment, it is no different. As you have read in this chapter, it is critical that you understand the operation of the main network and security components available on AWS to troubleshoot common connectivity scenarios in your environments.

Amazon VPC allows the provisioning of a logically isolated network portion on AWS. In a VPC, you have total control over virtual networks, including choosing the IP address to use and creating subnets, routing tables, and network gateways.

Currently, VPC supports up to five IP address ranges, one primary and four secondaries for IPv4. Each of these ranges can have a size between /28 (in CIDR notation) and /16. In IPv6, VPC has a fixed size of /56 (in CIDR notation). A VPC can have IPv4 and IPv6 CIDR blocks associated with it.

AWS also provides different tools that can help organizations troubleshoot network security. This section explores Reachability Analyzer and Network Access Analyzer.

VPC Network Reachability

Reachability Analyzer is a powerful network diagnostics tool for analyzing and debugging network reachability between resources within a VPC. This static configuration analysis tool is designed to help AWS users understand and troubleshoot connectivity issues in their cloud infrastructure.

Reachability Analyzer's primary function is to analyze the potential network paths between two specified resources in a VPC. It provides detailed, hop-by-hop information about the virtual path between these resources, when they are reachable. In cases where connectivity is not possible, Reachability Analyzer identifies the blocking component, allowing for quick and efficient problem resolution. One of the tool's strengths lies in its ability to detect and highlight configuration issues that may be impacting network reachability. For example, it can identify missing or misconfigured route table entries, which are often the root cause of connectivity problems in complex network setups.

Reachability Analyzer supports analysis between a wide range of AWS resources. These include EC2 instances, Internet gateways, network interfaces, transit gateways and their attachments, VPC endpoint services, VPC endpoints, VPC Peering connections, and VPN gateways. This comprehensive coverage ensures that users can troubleshoot connectivity issues across their entire VPC infrastructure. In Figure 6.88, you can see a test to validate connectivity between two EC2 instances: the DBServer1 located in the VPC1 and the DBServer2 located in the SecureVPC through the TG1 (as proposed in the exercise). You can see in the figure that the destination was reachable.

FIGURE 6.88 Reachability Analyzer.

In Figure 6.89, you can even view a detailed path to reach the DBServer2 instance.

The tool significantly reduces the time and effort required to diagnose and resolve network issues. Instead of manually tracing network paths or running multiple tests, administrators can quickly get a clear picture of their network's behavior, leading to faster problem resolution and improved operational efficiency. While Reachability Analyzer is primarily used for on-demand analysis, it can also be incorporated into continuous monitoring strategies. By regularly running reachability analyses, teams can proactively identify and address potential issues before they impact operations.

Network Access Analyzer

AWS Network Access Analyzer is a tool that enables users to analyze and monitor network accessibility within their AWS environment. This solution provides valuable insights into potential network misconfigurations and helps identify unintended network access to resources. By leveraging Network Access Analyzer, organizations can enhance their security posture, ensure compliance with security best practices, and streamline network troubleshooting processes.

One of the primary features of Network Access Analyzer is its ability to perform comprehensive network reachability analyses. Figure 6.90 shows the Network Access Scopes included with the service. It examines resource configurations, security groups, and network ACLs to determine the accessibility of resources from different network entities. This enables users to identify potential security gaps and unauthorized access points. Additionally, Network Access Analyzer provides detailed findings and recommendations, empowering users to take proactive measures to secure their network infrastructure. You simply need to select the scope that you want to test and click the Analyze button.

278 Chapter 6 ▪ Infrastructure Protection

FIGURE 6.89 Path details.

Network and Connectivity Troubleshooting Scenarios

FIGURE 6.90 Network Access Scopes (Amazon created).

FIGURE 6.91 Network Access Scopes custom.

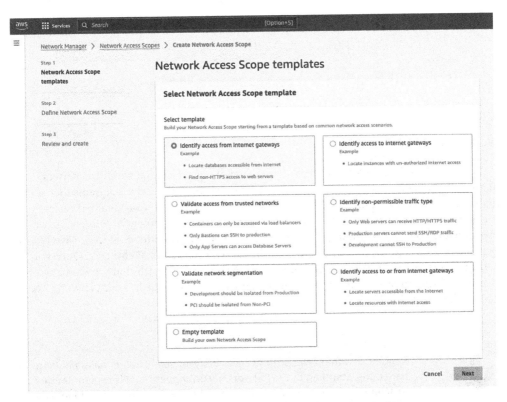

Another significant benefit of Network Access Analyzer is its integration with AWS IAM. It allows users to evaluate the effectiveness of IAM policies in controlling network access. By simulating network traffic based on IAM permissions, Network Access Analyzer helps identify any gaps between intended and actual network access. This feature is particularly valuable for organizations with complex IAM configurations, as it ensures that access controls are properly implemented and maintained. Figure 6.91 shows the templates you can use to create your own test based on your own specific requirements.

FIGURE 6.92 Findings example.

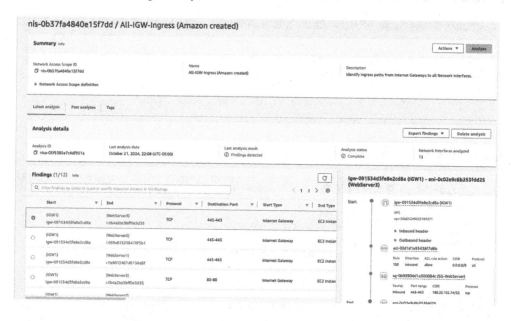

Network Access Analyzer also offers a user-friendly interface that simplifies network analysis and troubleshooting. It provides visualizations and interactive diagrams that show network paths and accessibility between resources. These visualizations make it easier for users to understand the flow of network traffic and identify potential bottlenecks or misconfigurations. Furthermore, Network Access Analyzer generates comprehensive reports that can be exported for further analysis or shared with relevant stakeholders. Once you run a test, you get the findings (a *finding* is a potential network path that matches any of the MatchPath statements and none of the ExcludePath statements in your Network Access Scope). See Figure 6.92.

 Regularly running Network Access Analyzer scans helps maintain an up-to-date understanding of the network security posture. It is recommended to schedule periodic scans and review the results to promptly identify any changes or potential vulnerabilities.

 When planning the IP addressing of a VPC, you should always check whether the network assigned to a subnet is overlapping with IP networks from another VPC or on-premises data center networks. Doing so will help avoid connectivity problems when these environments are later interconnected.

VPC Security and Filtering

Keep in mind that two components can be used to filter traffic within the VPC: the security group and the NACLs.

Security groups can be used to help protect instances within the VPC. Security groups in a VPC are used to specify the allowed inbound and outbound network traffic to and from each Amazon EC2 instance. Traffic that is not explicitly permitted for an instance is automatically dropped. As you read earlier, security groups are stateful, so they track traffic being allowed in one direction and automatically permit response traffic.

Security Group Example

A stateful filter that allows incoming traffic on TCP port 80 on a web server will allow return traffic to pass through the stateful filter between the client and the web server, usually on a high-numbered port (for example, port 63912). The filtering device maintains a status table that monitors the source and destination port numbers and IP addresses.

Security groups block all traffic by default, with the possibility of creating allow policies only; if you want to combine allows and denies, you must use a network ACL.

In addition to security groups, network traffic entering and leaving each subnet can be allowed or denied through network access control lists. NACLs operate at the subnet level and evaluate traffic coming in and out of a subnet. They can be used to define the Allow and Deny rules. NACLs do not filter traffic between instances on the same subnet.

If you need to filter traffic between instances on the same subnet, you can use security groups.

NACLs perform stateless filtering, so stateless filtering analyzes only the source and destination IP address and destination port, ignoring whether the traffic is a new request or a response to a request.

In the "Security Group Example" sidebar, it would be necessary to implement two rules on the filtering device: one rule to allow incoming traffic to the web server on TCP port 80 and another rule to allow outgoing traffic from the web server (for example, TCP port range of 49152 to 65535).

Route Tables

A route table contains a set of rules that are used to determine where network traffic is directed. Every subnet in the VPC must be associated with a route table. This table controls the routing for a subnet, and each subnet can be associated with only one route table at a time. Still, it is possible to associate several subnets with the same route table.

When you are troubleshooting routing tables, you must remember the following:

- Your VPC already has implicit routing and comes with a default route table that can be modified.

- It is possible to create more route tables for your VPC.

- It is not possible to delete the main route table. However, you can customize the routes in it. The VPC main route table will be automatically associated with newly created subnets.

- When traffic matches more than one entry on the route table, the most specific route will be used.

To determine how traffic should be routed, a route table prioritizes the most specific route in it. The routes for IPv4 and IPv6 addresses or CIDR blocks are independent of each other, so a route table uses the most specific route corresponding to IPv4 or IPv6 traffic.

Table 6.3 contains a route for IPv4 Internet traffic (0.0.0.0/0) directed to an Internet gateway (IGW) and a route for IPv4 traffic 172.31.0.0/16 directed to a peering connection (pcx-1a2b3c4d). Any traffic on the subnet directed to the 172.31.0.0/16 range uses the peering connection because this route is more specific than the route to the IGW. Any traffic to a VPC destination (10.0.0.0/16) is covered by the local route and is therefore routed within the VPC. All other traffic on the subnet uses the IGW.

Network Gateways

NAT gateways (see Figure 6.93) are used in network address translation to allow instances on a private subnet to connect to the Internet or other AWS services, and to prevent the Internet from initiating a connection to those instances. Each NAT gateway is created in

TABLE 6.3 Routing Table

CIDR	Destination
10.0.0.0/16	Local
172.31.0.0/16	pcx-1a2b3c4d
0.0.0.0/0	igw-11aa22bb

FIGURE 6.93 Architecture of a NAT gateway.

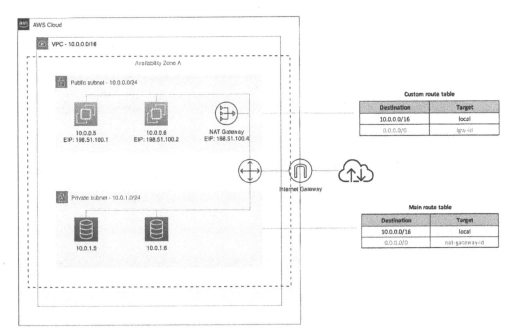

a specific availability zone and implemented with redundancy, and it supports 5 Gbps of bandwidth, and automatically scales up to 100 Gbps (at the time of this writing). If you require more bandwidth, you can distribute the workload into different subnets and create a NAT gateway.

An Internet gateway (see Figure 6.94) is a redundant and highly available component of the VPC that allows communication between the instances in the VPC and the Internet. In this case, starting the connection from the Internet is allowed. To enable Internet communication for IPv4, your instance must have a public IPv4 address or an elastic IP (EIP) associated with a private IPv4 address.

Since your instance only knows the private address defined in the VPC, IGW provides a one-to-one NAT for your instance. When traffic leaves your subnet and goes to the Internet, the reply address field is defined as the public IPv4 address or the EIP of your instance, not your private IP.

The AWS TGW connects VPCs and their local area networks through a central hub, such as a cloud router. Traffic between an Amazon VPC and AWS Transit Gateway remains on the AWS global private network.

Your TGW routes IPv4 and IPv6 packets between attachments using route tables. You can configure these tables to propagate routes from the route tables to the attached VPCs and VPN connections. Also, you can use static routes in your routing tables.

FIGURE 6.94 Architecture of an Internet gateway.

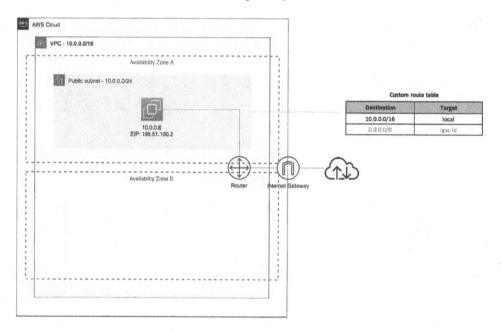

 If you are using NAT instances, make sure you disable the Source/Destination Check and validate whether the security group assigned to it correctly allows all desired traffic.

VPC Peering

It is a common scenario to need to connect two VPCs. In AWS, this functionality is delivered using a feature called VPC Peering. VPC Peering is a network connection between two VPCs that allows you to direct traffic between them using private IPv4 or IPv6 addresses. Instances in different VPCs can communicate with each other as if they were on the same network. You can create a peering connection between your VPCs or with a VPC from another AWS account. VPCs can also be in different regions.

Figure 6.95 shows the architecture of the peering between two VPCs.

A VPC can have more than one peering configured, so there is no transitivity using an intermediate VPC. Figure 6.96 shows an example of peering between three VPCs. VPC B and VPC C can each communicate with VPC A. However, transitive routing between VPC B and VPC C through VPC A is not possible.

Network and Connectivity Troubleshooting Scenarios 285

FIGURE 6.95 Peering example.

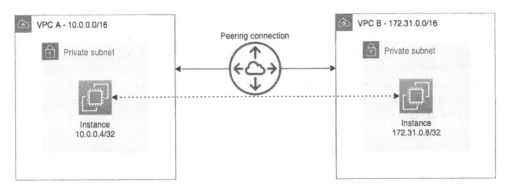

FIGURE 6.96 No transitivity example.

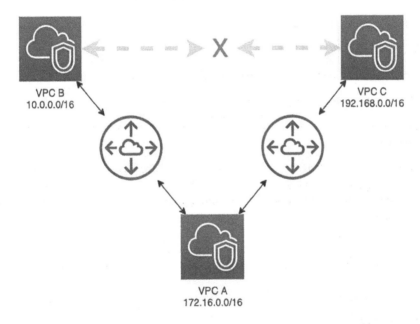

 It is not possible to create a VPC Peering connection between VPCs that have matching or overlapping IPv4 or IPv6 CIDR blocks.

VPC Flow Logs

VPC Flow Logs is a feature that makes it possible to capture information about IP traffic on VPC network interfaces. Flow log data can be published to Amazon CloudWatch Logs and Amazon S3. When creating a flow log, you can use the standard flow log record format or specify a custom format. The custom format is only available for publication on Amazon S3.

The standard format for a flow log record is a space-separated string that has the following set of fields, in this order (depending on the version selected and customizations made for the specific flow recording):

```
<version> <account-id> <interface-id> <srcaddr> <dstaddr> <srcport> <dstport>
<protocol> <packets> <bytes> <start> <end> <action> <log-status>
```

To learn more about the fields available in VPC Flow Logs, see `https://docs.aws.amazon.com/vpc/latest/userguide/flow-logs.html`.

Troubleshooting Peering

Keep these factors in mind when troubleshooting peering connectivity:

- Check that the route is configured correctly on both VPCs.

- Check that the security group of the source and destination instances allow the necessary traffic.

- Check if there are any NACLs blocking requests. It is important to remember that network ACLs are stateless, so it is necessary to configure the rules for allowing IPs and ports in a bidirectional way (inbound and outbound), as explained at the beginning of this chapter.

Use VPC Flow Logs to view accepted and rejected traffic in the communication.

Summary

As infrastructure evolves from manual configurations in on-premises data centers to automated functions in cloud computing, infrastructure security is developing accordingly. In the AWS Cloud, objects such as Amazon VPC, subnets, route tables, Internet gateways, and NAT gateways help millions of customers deploy their network topologies with simplicity and agility. Furthermore, traffic filter techniques such as security groups and NACLs allow fine-grained traffic control within these topologies in order to protect resources from unexpected connections.

Infrastructure protection in the AWS Cloud is further reinforced by the following services:

- **AWS Elastic Load Balancing:** Provides scalability, high availability, and content switching to your applications deployed in Amazon EC2 instances, containers, or AWS Lambda functions.
- **VPC Endpoints:** Provide direct connectivity between your VPCs and the AWS Cloud services you have deployed in the same region.
- **VPC Flow Logs:** Enable historical traffic visibility in your VPCs, subnets, or network interfaces.
- **AWS Web Application Firewall:** Protects your applications against well-known web attacks through the identification of patterns in the layer 7 HTTP protocol.
- **AWS Shield:** Defends your applications against DDoS attacks with two levels of protection (AWS Shield Standard and AWS Shield Advanced).
- **Amazon VPC Transit Gateway:** A network transit hub service designed to interconnect VPCs and on-premises networks within the AWS ecosystem.
- **AWS Network Firewall:** A managed network security service that provides protection for your Amazon VPC networks. It allows you to deploy network security across your VPCs with just a few clicks, without the need to provision or manage any infrastructure.
- **Amazon Inspector:** An automated vulnerability management service provided by AWS. It is designed to continuously discover workloads and scan them for software vulnerabilities and unintended network exposure.
- **AWS Systems Manager Patch Manager:** Automates the process of patching managed instances with both security and non-security updates.
- **EC2 Image Builder:** A fully managed AWS service designed to streamline the process of creating, managing, and deploying customized, secure, and up-to-date server or container images.
- **Reachability Analyzer:** A powerful network diagnostics tool for analyzing and debugging network reachability between resources within a VPC.
- **AWS Network Access Analyzer:** A tool that enables users to analyze and monitor network accessibility within their AWS environment.

Exam Essentials

Know the AWS main network constructs. The Amazon Virtual Private Cloud represents a virtual network within the AWS Cloud. VPCs were created to isolate cloud resources from other systems, networks, or accounts. Within these abstractions, one or more CIDR blocks are distributed among subnets, which characterize a range of IP addresses in a VPC. Each subnet has assigned traffic policies, such as a route table, which defines how IP traffic will be handled by the VPC router. A subnet belongs to a single availability zone, and their design must take application high availability into account. An Internet gateway provides a target in route tables for Internet-routable traffic.

Understand the various methods of network address translation.   Although Internet gateways can provide NAT services and Internet access to resources located in public subnets, other methods of IP address translation are used for instances and other cloud resources located in private subnets. NAT gateways are enterprise-class specialized virtual devices that AWS manages to enable NAT services in such scenarios. NAT instances are Amazon EC2 instances developed by communities and AWS Marketplace vendors that can provide NAT services. When compared to NAT gateways, NAT instances require additional care from an infrastructure and operations standpoint.

Understand the differences between security groups and NACLs.   There are two main ways of implementing traffic filtering within an Amazon VPC. Security groups are a set of inbound and outbound stateful rules that control traffic on elastic network interfaces that belong to Amazon EC2 instances or other cloud resources (such as VPC interface endpoints) in terms of IP addresses as well as transport protocols and ports. NACLs are traffic filters that control traffic that travels from one subnet to another through inbound and outbound stateless rules.

Understand Amazon VPC Transit Gateways.   Transit gateways act as a central hub to interconnect multiple VPCs and on-premises networks. They simplify network architecture, reduce operational complexity, and enable scalable connectivity across AWS accounts and regions. The key features of TGWs include centralized route tables, bandwidth aggregation, and comprehensive network monitoring capabilities. They facilitate implementing network segmentation through route table associations and enable centralized network management in complex AWS environments.

Understand how elastic load balancing works.   AWS provides ELB as a network service to ensure application scalability, high availability, and forwarding decisions based on higher-layer information from user requests. AWS Cloud currently offers ELB in three different formats: application load balancer, network load balancer, and classic load balancer.

Know about VPC endpoints.   VPC endpoints enable direct connectivity, within the Amazon network, between resources in your VPC and other AWS Cloud services. They are available in two types: interface endpoint and gateway endpoint. An interface endpoint is an elastic network interface that extends a private IP address from a subnet to services such as Amazon API Gateway and AWS Key Management Service (KMS). A gateway endpoint is a virtual routing table that targets AWS services, such as Amazon S3 and Amazon DynamoDB.

Understand VPC Flow Logs.   VPC Flow Logs provide traffic capture on network interfaces from specific AWS services (such as Amazon EC2, ELB, Amazon RDS, Amazon ElastiCache, Amazon Redshift, Amazon WorkSpaces, NAT gateways, and TGWs), subnets, or VPCs. You can send and review VPC Flow Logs in two different places: Amazon CloudWatch Logs or Amazon S3.

Be familiar with the AWS Web Application Firewall. AWS WAF protects web applications and APIs from known HTTP layer 7 attacks that exploit systems via malicious activity. The service leverages web ACLs (with managed and custom rules) that are applied to application load balancers, Amazon API gateways, or Amazon CloudFront distributions.

Understand AWS Shield and its offerings. AWS Shield protects applications deployed in the AWS Cloud from DDoS attacks with two levels of services: AWS Shield Standard and AWS Shield Advanced.

Comprehend AWS Network Firewall solution. AWS Network Firewall provides network protection for VPCs. It deploys granular network security rules across AWS accounts and VPCs. It integrates with other AWS services like AWS Firewall Manager for centralized management. Its features include stateful inspection, intrusion prevention, and web filtering. It is important in implementing defense-in-depth strategies and meeting compliance requirements.

Amazon Inspector. Amazon Inspector provides capabilities for automated security assessments across AWS environments. It can identify vulnerabilities, deviations from best practices, and potential security issues without requiring manual configuration. Amazon Inspector assesses EC2 instances, container images in ECR, and Lambda functions, generating detailed findings with remediation guidance. The service integrates with AWS Security Hub, EventBridge, and Systems Manager, enabling continuous monitoring and comprehensive compliance reporting through its agentless scanning approach.

AWS Systems Manager Patch Manager. Patch Manager automates the process of patching managed instances. It can scan for missing patches, deploy patches across large fleets of EC2 instances and on-premises servers, and report on patch compliance status. It integrates with other Systems Manager capabilities and supports both Linux and Windows systems, and it is important in maintaining system security and compliance.

EC2 Image Builder. EC2 Image Builder automates the creation, maintenance, validation, and testing of EC2 AMIs and container images. Its key components include pipelines, recipes, and test suites. It can enhance security by ensuring consistent, up-to-date, and compliant images across the organization, and it can integrate with other AWS services for comprehensive image management and distribution.

Reachability Analyzer. Reachability Analyzer can perform network connectivity testing between resources in a VPC. It helps identify and troubleshoot network configuration issues that might impact resource reachability. It can analyze connectivity for EC2 instances, load balancers, and VPN gateways and is important in ensuring proper network segmentation and security group configurations.

AWS Network Access Analyzer. Network Access Analyzer identifies unintended network access to resources. It helps implement least-privilege network access by analyzing network configurations and identifying potential security risks. It can provide findings on overly permissive security group rules, network ACLs, and Internet gateways and is important in maintaining a secure network posture and meeting compliance requirements.

290   Chapter 6 · Infrastructure Protection

Review Questions

1. Read the following statements and choose the correct option:

I. A VPC can extend beyond AWS regions.

II. A VPC can extend beyond AWS availability zones.

III. A subnet can extend beyond AWS availability zones.
   - **A.** I, II, and III are correct.
   - **B.** Only I is correct.
   - **C.** Only II is correct.
   - **D.** Only III is correct.

2. Considering that you gave the CIDR block 172.16.100.128/25 to a subnet, which option is correct?
   - **A.** The IP address of the VPC router is 172.16.100.128.
   - **B.** The IP address of the DNS server is 172.16.100.130.
   - **C.** The IP address 172.16.100.131 is the first one available for use in the subnet.
   - **D.** You cannot assign this CIDR block to a subnet.

3. Read the following statements about security group rules and choose the correct option:

I. You can allow HTTP from 10.0.40.0/24.

II. You can block HTTP from your own public IP address.

III. You can allow HTTP from any source.
   - **A.** I, II, and III are correct.
   - **B.** I and III are correct.
   - **C.** II and III are correct.
   - **D.** Only III is correct.

4. Read the following statements about AWS Elastic Load Balancing and choose the correct option:

I. ALBs, NLBs, and CLBs support health checks, CloudWatch metrics, and AZ failover.

II. NLBs can support AWS Lambda functions as targets.

III. CLBs can only be used with EC2-classic implementations.
   - **A.** Only I is correct.
   - **B.** I and II are correct.
   - **C.** II and III are correct.
   - **D.** I, II, and III are correct.

Review Questions   291

5. A company needs to connect multiple VPCs and on-premises networks in different AWS Regions. Which AWS service should they use to simplify network architecture and reduce operational complexity?

   A. VPC Peering

   B. AWS Direct Connect

   C. Amazon VPC Transit Gateway

   D. AWS Site-to-Site VPN

6. Which AWS service provides network protection for your VPCs by allowing you to deploy granular network security rules across your AWS accounts and VPCs?

   A. AWS WAF

   B. AWS Shield

   C. Amazon GuardDuty

   D. AWS Network Firewall

7. A security team wants to automatically assess applications for exposure, vulnerabilities, and deviations from best practices. Which AWS service should they use?

   A. AWS Config

   B. Amazon Inspector

   C. AWS Trusted Advisor

   D. Amazon GuardDuty

8. Which AWS service should you use to automate the process of patching managed instances with both security-related and other types of updates?

   A. AWS Config

   B. AWS Systems Manager Patch Manager

   C. Amazon Inspector

   D. AWS CloudFormation

9. A DevOps team needs to automate the creation, maintenance, validation, and testing of EC2 AMIs. Which AWS service should they use?

   A. AWS CodeBuild

   B. Amazon EC2 Auto Scaling

   C. EC2 Image Builder

   D. AWS CloudFormation

10. Which AWS service allows you to perform network connectivity testing between resources in your VPC?

   A. Amazon VPC Flow Logs

   B. AWS Network Access Analyzer

   C. Amazon VPC Reachability Analyzer

   D. AWS Config

Chapter 7

Data Protection

THE AWS CERTIFIED SECURITY SPECIALTY EXAM OBJECTIVES THAT LEVERAGE CONCEPTS EXPLAINED IN THIS CHAPTER INCLUDE THE FOLLOWING:

✔ **Domain 5: Data Protection**

- 5.1. Design and implement controls that provide confidentiality and integrity for data in transit.
- 5.2. Design and implement controls that provide confidentiality and integrity for data at rest.
- 5.3. Design and implement control to manage the lifecycle of data at rest.
- 5.4. Design and implement controls to protect credentials, secrets, and cryptographic key materials.

Chapter 7: Data Protection

Introduction

In this chapter, you learn how to leverage the AWS-native security services and best practices available in the AWS Cloud to protect your data. AWS offers you the ability to add a layer of security to your data at rest and in transit in the cloud, providing scalable and efficient encryption features. These include:

- Data at rest encryption capabilities available in AWS services, such as Amazon EBS, Amazon S3, Amazon RDS, Amazon Redshift, Amazon ElastiCache, AWS Lambda, and Amazon SageMaker
- Data encryption in transit, where AWS services use security standard algorithms (HTTPS endpoints using TLS for communication) to enable secure communication to AWS Services providing encryption in transit when communicating with the AWS APIs
- Flexible key management options, including AWS Key Management Service (KMS), that allow you to choose whether to have AWS manage the encryption keys or enable you to keep complete control over your own keys
- Dedicated, hardware-based cryptographic key storage using AWS CloudHSM, allowing you to help satisfy your compliance requirements
- Encrypted message queues for the transmission of sensitive data, using server-side encryption (SSE) for Amazon SQS

In addition, AWS provides APIs for you to integrate encryption and data protection with any of the services you develop or deploy in an AWS environment. For that reason, the chapter addresses the following AWS services and capabilities so you understand the different mechanisms that AWS solutions and services offer to protect your data in the cloud:

- Working with the AWS KMS
- Creating a customer-managed key (CMK) in AWS KMS
- Understanding the cloud hardware security module (CloudHSM)
- Using AWS Certificate Manager

- Handling secrets in AWS
- Protecting Amazon S3 buckets
- Understanding how Amazon Macie deploys machine learning to identify personal identifiable information

Using a variety of AWS Cloud security controls, services, and practices, a security team goal is to create mechanisms and implement the necessary controls to protect sensitive data stored in the AWS Cloud, thus meeting regulatory, security, and data privacy needs. With such measures, this team can properly protect the most valuable asset of companies in the digital age: data and information.

With the emergence of data privacy and protection regulations around the world, such as the European Union's General Data Protection Regulation (GDPR), which came into action in May 2018, data protection and privacy are becoming even more strategic topics for all kinds of businesses and governmental organizations.

Different regulations all over the world enforce severe financial penalties to address information leaks and even negligence in implementing security controls, best practices, and reporting security incidents. In such scenarios, the use of data protection mechanisms—especially cryptographic mechanisms—is crucial in increasing the resilience of information technology systems. *Cryptography* is defined as the ability to transform standard text information into ciphertext, using cryptographic algorithms and keys, as in the symmetric encryption operation shown in Figure 7.1.

In Figure 7.1, on the left is plain text (unprotected data) that is passing through an encryption algorithm using a symmetric key (Key A), generating a ciphertext (protected data) in the middle of Figure 7.1. The same algorithm and symmetric key (Key A) are applied again (on the right) to open the ciphertext, generating the same plain text (unprotected data) again.

When deploying encryption, you have two types of cryptographic algorithms you can implement, symmetric and asymmetric, which are explored next.

FIGURE 7.1 Plain text and ciphertext.

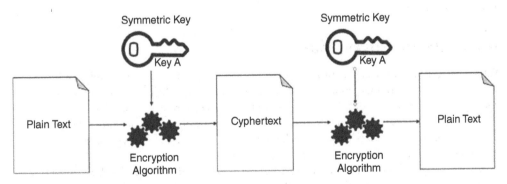

296 Chapter 7 ▪ Data Protection

TABLE 7.1 Symmetric Cryptographic Encryption Algorithms

Name	Key Size
Advanced Encryption Standard (AES)	128, 192, and 256 bits
Twofish	128, 192, and 256 bits
Serpent	128, 192, and 256 bits
Blowfish	32 to 448 bits
Carlisle Adams and Stafford Tavares (CAST5)	40 to 128 bits
Data Encryption Standard (DES)	64 bits
Triple Data Encryption Standard (3DES)	128 and 192 bits, effectively 56, 112, and 168 bits
IDEA	128 bits

Symmetric Encryption

Keys are a sequence of bytes used to encrypt and decrypt data. In symmetric encryption algorithms, the same key is used in both operations, as shown in Figure 7.1. The size of such keys also determines how hard it is for an attacker to try all possible key combinations (brute-force attack) when attempting to decrypt a protected message. Table 7.1 presents some examples of symmetric cryptographic encryption algorithms.

AWS cryptographic tools and services extensively support symmetric encryption through the Advanced Encryption Standard (AES). This algorithm is implemented with 128-, 192-, or 256-bit keys and is frequently used in combination with Galois/Counter Mode (GCM), known as AES-GCM.

Asymmetric Encryption

When using asymmetric encryption, two distinct keys are required—one public and one private—and both are mathematically derived. There are two different uses of asymmetric encryption to guarantee confidentiality and authenticity/nonrepudiation. Consider a scenario where you have two users, defined as Alice and Bob. In this scenario, Alice wants to send information to Bob, protecting the data using asymmetric encryption mechanisms to guarantee that only Bob will be able to access the protected data.

To achieve the desired confidentiality protection, Alice will encrypt the data using Bob's public key, as shown in Figure 7.2, and Bob will decrypt the data information using his private key.

FIGURE 7.2 Asymmetric encryption.

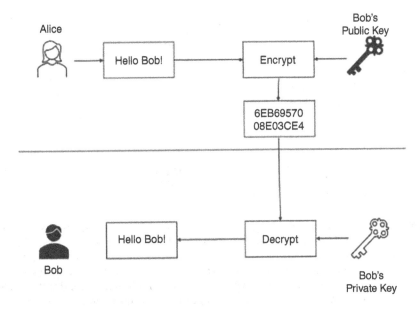

In this scenario, only the owner of the respective private key can decrypt the information encrypted by the public key. Consequently, the private key must be adequately protected against any improper access, which could expose the visibility of encrypted information.

In the same scenario, if Bob then wants to send data back to Alice, using encryption to protect the data confidentiality, Bob must encrypt the data using Alice's public key, and Alice will decrypt the data using her private key.

AWS services typically support Rivest–Shamir–Adleman (RSA) and elliptic-curve cryptography (ECC) for asymmetric cryptographic key algorithms. RSA uses key sizes of 2048, 3072, and 4096 bits. ECC supports ECC_NIST_P256, ECC_NIST_P384, and ECC_NIST_P521.

Additionally, the public and private key mechanism can be used to ensure the authenticity of the data source. Therefore, when private keys are used to digitally sign a message, it assures the receiver that only the owner of the private key can sign it correctly. This way, the destination that receives the message can validate whether the message came from the expected source, which is done through the use of the public key, as shown in Figure 7.3.

You can use a CMK with a key spec that represents an RSA key pair or an ECC key pair to encrypt, decrypt, sign messages, and verify signatures. The key spec you choose is determined by the signing algorithm that you want to use. In some cases, the users who will verify signatures are outside AWS and can't call the verify signature operation. In that case, choose a key spec associated with a signing algorithm that these users can support in their local applications.

FIGURE 7.3 Signature using an asymmetric algorithm.

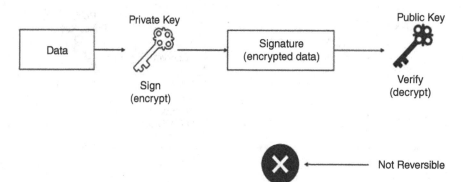

 AWS KMS supports post-quantum hybrid key exchange for the Transport Layer Security (TLS) network encryption protocol that is used when connecting to KMS API endpoints. To support post-quantum resistance in the current public key cryptography that is used for key exchange in every TLS connection, AWS KMS also supports finite-field–based Diffie-Hellman ephemeral (FFDHE) keys and elliptic curve Diffie-Hellman ephemeral (ECDHE) keys. For more information, see https://aws.amazon.com/blogs/security/post-quantum-tls-now-supported-in-aws-kms.

Hash Algorithms

Another essential concept is the use of hash algorithms. Hashing is a feature that applies an algorithm to a piece of information, generating a message digest, which is a string of digits created by a one-way hashing to generate summary information (you can't recover information starting from a hash result), as shown in Figure 7.4.

As you can see in Figure 7.4, different input sizes generate different digest outputs, but with the same size. Even if you change a single bit in the input (in third phrase, "Red" starts with capital letter), it will have a different digest output (right box in Figure 7.4), but always with the same size. In reverse, different inputs, with the same hash function applied, result in different hashes (digests), but still with the same size. In this case, looking at the digest alone, you cannot infer the input data, size, or even the input data type.

In a perfect scenario, based on the message digest, you cannot obtain the original information, so in theory, a good hash algorithm is irreversible. But since hashed values are generally smaller than the originals, a hash function can generate duplicate hashed values. These are known as *collisions*, and they occur when identical values are produced when using different data sources.

Collisions can be avoided by using larger hash values, or they can be resolved with multiple hash functions, overflow tables, or salts. Salts are often used to store passwords to

FIGURE 7.4 Hash algorithm usage.

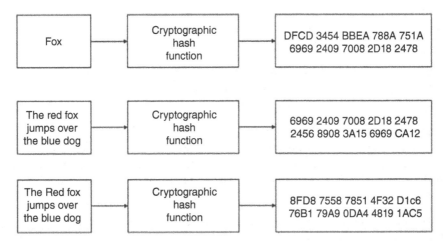

TABLE 7.2 Hash Algorithms Examples

Name	Hash Code Size (Bits)
Message-Digest 5 (MD5)	128
SHA-1	160
SHA-256	256
SHA-384	384
SHA-512	512

prevent the use of precalculated password hash tables, known as *rainbow tables*, which can significantly accelerate brute-forcing.

A *salt* is random data used as an additional input to safeguard a one-way function, like a hash algorithm. A new salt is randomly generated for each hash operation. You can find more examples of hash algorithms in Table 7.2.

Table 7.2 shows the algorithm name, as well as the fixed output size in bits for each hash function.

The use of encryption is essential to increasing the level of data protection. However, encryption should be seen as a layer of defense and not the only defense. As one of the components of a data protection strategy, encryption should be used throughout the information lifecycle, including its creation, transport, and even when data is stored at rest, adopting an end-to-end encryption model.

However, in traditional environments, there are several challenges to the implementation of an end-to-end cryptographic model, such as

- Integration of distinct technology platforms
- Proper encryption key protection
- Implementation of encryption key use and audit trails
- Minimization of performance impact due to encryption deployed on various components of a solution and architecture
- Periodic rotation of cryptographic keys

The AWS Cloud enables the deployment of data protection mechanisms using large-scale cryptography, protecting data throughout its lifecycle and natively addressing the challenges outlined earlier, enabling the implementation of an end-to-end encryption model that allows

- Protection of cryptographic keys based on the highest industry standards
- Accountability of who is using the cryptographic keys through native logs in the AWS Cloud, using the AWS CloudTrail service
- Large-scale encryption without impacting component performance, working natively and seamlessly with a range of AWS Cloud services
- Continuous rotation of cryptographic keys
- High availability

The next sections demonstrate and explain how these capabilities are deployed in the AWS Cloud to provide data protection for your applications.

AWS Key Management Service

The AWS Cloud has a security service called AWS Key Management Service, which allows you to natively encrypt data in a seamless and integrated manner, with more than 117 available services.

Here are some examples of services that can integrate with AWS KMS:

- Amazon Simple Storage Service (Amazon S3)
- Amazon Relational Database Services (Amazon RDS)
- Amazon Elastic Block Store (Amazon EBS)
- Amazon Elastic File System (Amazon EFS)
- Amazon Aurora
- AWS CloudTrail
- Amazon DynamoDB
- Amazon Redshift
- Amazon EMR

AWS Key Management Service 301

 The KMS service cannot be used to generate SSH access keys for your Amazon Elastic Compute Cloud (EC2) instances. Key pairs (public and private keys) are generated directly from the EC2 service.

A complete list of services that natively integrate with AWS KMS can be obtained directly from the service's public page in the AWS Service Integration section at https://aws.amazon.com/kms/features/#AWS_Service_Integration (see Figure 7.5).

Using the KMS service, you can implement an end-to-end encryption strategy, thus enabling you to encrypt data stored on Amazon services, such as Elastic Block Storage (EBS) attached to your servers, objects stored on Amazon S3 storage, and relational database service (RDS) in your AWS Cloud environment.

Figure 7.6 shows how AWS KMS can provide encryption for various AWS Cloud services.

FIGURE 7.5 AWS KMS service integration.

AWS Key Management Service   Overview Features Pricing Getting Started Resources FAQs

AWS service integration

AWS KMS integrates with AWS services to encrypt data at rest, or to facilitate signing and verification using an AWS KMS key. To protect data at rest, integrated AWS services use envelope encryption, where a data key is used to encrypt data and is itself encrypted under a KMS key stored in AWS KMS. For signing and verification, integrated AWS services use asymmetric RSA or ECC KMS keys in AWS KMS. For more details about how an integrated service uses AWS KMS, see the documentation for your AWS service.

Alexa for Business[1]	Amazon FSx	Amazon Rekognition	AWS CodePipeline
Amazon AppFlow	Amazon GuardDuty	Amazon Relational Database Service (RDS)	AWS Control Tower
Amazon Athena	Amazon HealthLake	Amazon Route 53	AWS Data Exchange
Amazon Aurora	Amazon Inspector	Amazon Simple Storage Service (Amazon S3)[3]	AWS Database Migration Service
Amazon Chime SDK	Amazon Kendra	Amazon SageMaker	AWS DeepRacer
Amazon CloudWatch Logs	Amazon Keyspaces (for Apache Cassandra)	Amazon Simple Email Service (SES)	AWS Elastic Disaster Recovery
Amazon CloudWatch Synthetics	Amazon Kinesis Data Streams	Amazon Simple Notification Service (SNS)	AWS Elemental MediaTailor
Amazon CodeGuru	Amazon Kinesis Firehose	Amazon Simple Queue Service (SQS)	AWS Entity Resolution
Amazon CodeWhisperer	Amazon Kinesis Video Streams	Amazon Textract	AWS GameLift
Amazon Comprehend	Amazon Lex	Amazon Timestream	AWS Glue
Amazon Connect	Amazon Lightsail[1]	Amazon Transcribe	AWS Glue DataBrew
Amazon Connect Customer Profiles	Amazon Location Service	Amazon Translate	AWS Ground Station
Amazon Connect Voice ID	Amazon Lookout for Equipment	Amazon WorkMail	AWS IoT SiteWise
Amazon Connect Wisdom	Amazon Lookout for Metrics	Amazon WorkSpaces	AWS Lambda
Amazon DocumentDB	Amazon Lookout for Vision	Amazon WorkSpaces Thin Client	AWS License Manager
Amazon DynamoDB	Amazon Macie	Amazon WorkSpaces Web	AWS Mainframe Modernization
Amazon DynamoDB Accelerator (DAX)[1]	Amazon Managed Blockchain	AWS AppConfig	AWS Network Firewall
Amazon EBS	Amazon Managed Service for Prometheus	AWS AppFabric	AWS Proton

FIGURE 7.6 Implementing an end-to-end encryption strategy using AWS KMS.

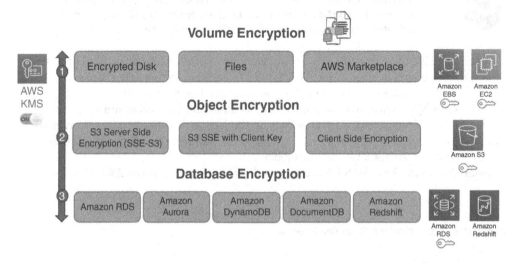

Figure 7.6 shows an example where AWS KMS service can be used to encrypt your data in three layers:

1. Data at rest in your EBS disks
2. Data at rest in your S3 buckets (object storage)
3. Data at rest in your database, like RDS, Aurora, DynamoDB, and Redshift

 The AWS KMS service backs up cryptographic keys to maintain 11 nines of durability: 99.999999999%.

Although AWS KMS has its protection methods for cryptographic keys, AWS also allows the use of dedicated hardware security modules (HSMs) to provide more sophisticated protection of your keys. An HSM is dedicated hardware that has a variety of logical and physical controls designed to protect cryptographic keys, preventing their exposure and mitigating the risk of compromising the entire cryptographic model. AWS KMS natively uses HSMs to protect their keys, but these HSMs are not dedicated to a single user; in other words, they are multitenant. Nonetheless, with proper isolation and security controls implemented, the native HSMs behind the AWS KMS service can be securely shared among different customers.

When you are using AWS KMS, you do not have access to manage the HSMs behind the service. Generally speaking, a dedicated HSM is usually required by regulatory, security, or compliance policies, and this requirement can be addressed through an AWS CloudHSM deployment.

Before creating a cryptographic key and seeing how simple it is to manage large-scale encryption in the AWS Cloud, you must understand how the AWS KMS service works in detail. This section examines how encryption and decryption occur, and especially how these keys are securely generated and stored. Let's start with a couple of foundational concepts.

Managed and Data Keys

One of the biggest challenges when you are implementing symmetric key encryption models is the protection of the keys. In extreme scenarios, you could still protect the key with another key, but chances are that a clear and unprotected key could be stored somewhere at the end of the process.

Because repeatedly encrypting one key with another would not solve the problem completely (since you will always have the challenge of protecting the key), the last unencrypted key requires the highest level of protection and is commonly known as the *managed key*. Figure 7.7 shows how multiple data keys can be used in conjunction with a managed key.

It is imperative to protect the managed keys in your environments because these are the keys that ensure data key protection and guarantee data encryption. Consequently, AWS KMS creates the environment to manage and protect your managed keys, as Figure 7.8 shows.

Using AWS KMS, your managed key is protected and is never exposed in cleartext, so in this scenario, the key is never handled in cleartext to protect the boundary established by the

FIGURE 7.7 Managed and data keys.

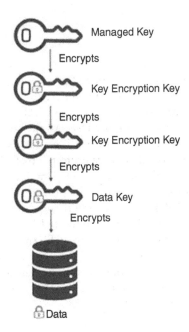

FIGURE 7.8 KMS managed key protection.

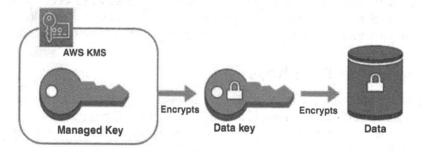

FIGURE 7.9 User access methods to the managed key.

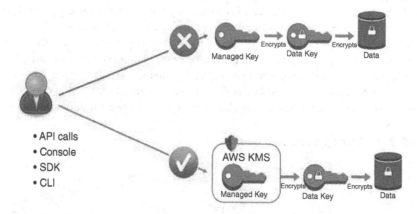

KMS HSMs. The master key is used to encrypt and protect your data key, and the data key is used to encrypt and decrypt your data in many different services, as shown in Figure 7.8.

When you are using AWS KMS, you must interact with the service to use and manage your managed keys using the console, CLI, or SDKs. All the interactions with the service are through API calls, because the managed keys never leave the AWS KMS unencrypted; thus, there is no exposure, and the managed keys are protected by Federal Information Processing Standard (FIPS) 140-2 Level 3 validated cryptographic modules (https://csrc.nist.gov/projects/cryptographic-module-validation-program/Certificate/3139).

When you're using the AWS SDKs to make programmatic API calls to AWS KMS, it is recommended that you always use the latest supported TLS version. Clients must also support cipher suites with Perfect Forward Secrecy (PFS), such as Diffie-Hellman ephemeral (DHE) or ECDHE. Most modern systems, such as Java 7 and later, support these modules.

As you can see in Figure 7.9, you cannot access the managed key directly. To access AWS KMS, you must use API calls using the console, SDK, or CLI, with authenticated and authorized level of access to interact with the service.

FIGURE 7.10 Customer-managed key examples.

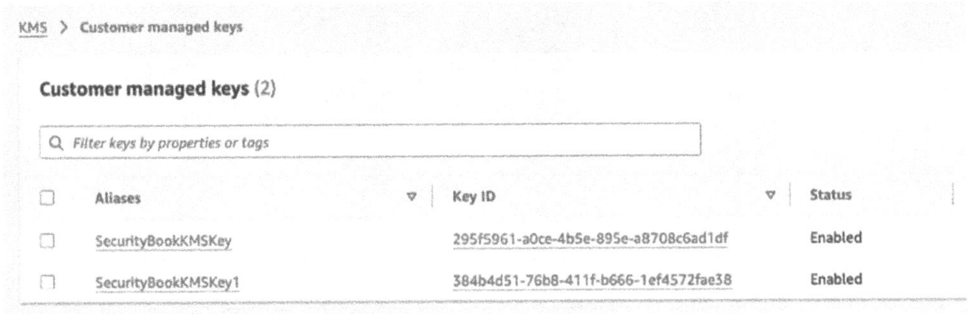

KMS > Customer managed keys

Customer managed keys (2)

Aliases	Key ID	Status
SecurityBookKMSKey	295f5961-a0ce-4b5e-895e-a8708c6ad1df	Enabled
SecurityBookKMSKey1	384b4d51-76b8-411f-b666-1ef4572fae38	Enabled

Customer-Managed Key and Key Hierarchy

A CMK is a 256-bit AES symmetric key that has a unique key ID, alias, and ARN, and it is created based on a user-initiated request through AWS KMS. It resides at the top of your key hierarchy and is not exportable, spending its entire lifecycle within AWS KMS.

Figure 7.10 shows two customer-managed keys that were created in AWS KMS.

Once you use the AWS KMS service, it is possible for a CMK to use multiple data keys to protect the data in an integrated manner with other services in an AWS environment, as shown in Figure 7.11.

KeyID, Alias, and ARN

Customer-managed keys have four additional attributes that can be used for identification:

- **KeyID:** A unique key identifier for a CMK.
- **Alias:** A user-friendly name that can be associated with a CMK. The alias can be used interchangeably with the KeyID in many of the AWS KMS API operations. The alias is important when you are rotating keys with imported material.
- **ARN:** A file-naming convention used to identify a particular resource in the AWS Cloud, helping administrators and users track and use AWS KMS keys across AWS services and API calls.
- **Regionality:** AWS KMS supports multiregion keys, which are AWS KMS keys in different AWS regions that can be used interchangeably, as though you had the same key in multiple regions. Each set of related multiregion keys has the same key material and key ID, so you can encrypt data in one AWS region and decrypt it in a different one without re-encrypting or making cross-region calls to AWS KMS. Like all KMS keys, multiregion keys never leave AWS KMS unencrypted.

Figure 7.12 shows these attributes in the AWS Console.

FIGURE 7.11 AWS KMS service integration.

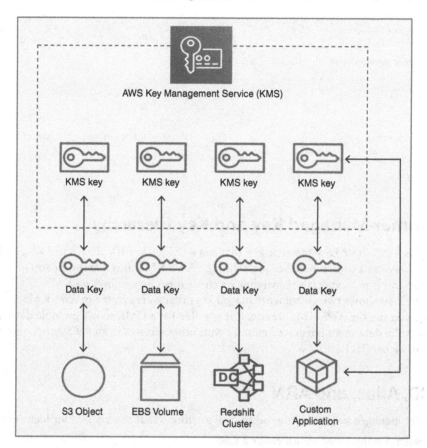

FIGURE 7.12 Customer-managed key details: ARN, alias, KeyID.

Permissions

The permissions represent the level of access granted in a JSON policy that is attached to a CMK. Permission defines the principals (as defined in Chapter 4, "Identity and Access Management") that are allowed to use the keys for encryption and decryption, and also who can administer and add Identity and Access Management (IAM) policies to the key.

When you are creating CMKs, all the keys must have at least two policy roles (see Figure 7.13):

- **Key Administrators:** IAM users or IAM roles that can manage the key
- **Key Users:** IAM users or IAM roles that can use the key to encrypt or decrypt data

Figure 7.13 shows two different IAM users (or roles) with distinct privileges. In this example, the Key Administrator role can create a key but cannot encrypt, decrypt, or generate a data key. On the right, the Key Users role can access and use the CMK to generate, decrypt, and encrypt a data key.

It is only possible to use IAM roles and IAM users, so IAM groups cannot be used as principals in KMS policies.

Figure 7.14 shows two different users, one with administrator access and one with user access.

Figure 7.14 shows the AWS KMS Key policy option in the AWS Console. Two IAM users are created for the specific key. SEC_AWS_BOOK_KMS_ADMIN is a key administrator and SEC_AWS_BOOK_KMS_USER is a key user.

FIGURE 7.13 Two roles used to control access to the CMK.

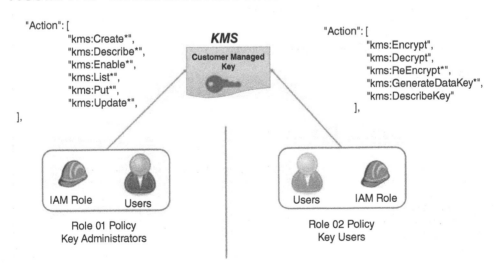

308 Chapter 7 ▪ Data Protection

FIGURE 7.14 Role configuration in KMS to control access to the CMK.

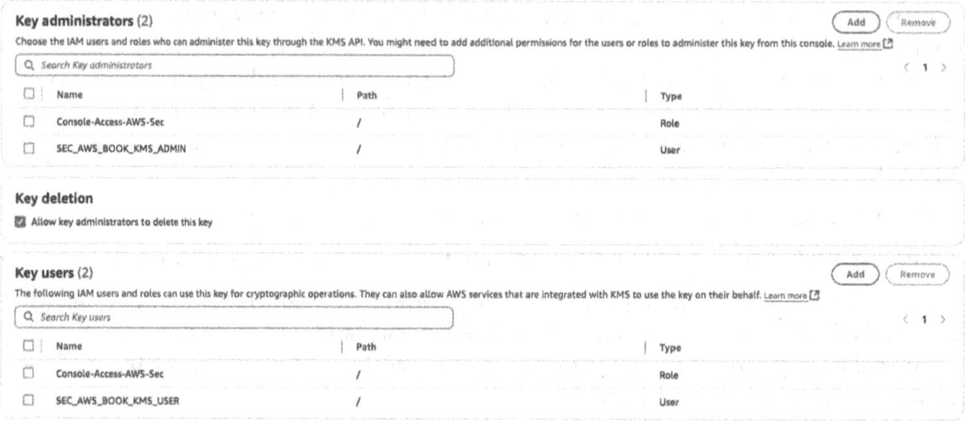

Key administrators (2)   `Add` `Remove`

Choose the IAM users and roles who can administer this key through the KMS API. You might need to add additional permissions for the users or roles to administer this key from this console. Learn more ☐

🔍 *Search Key administrators*   ‹ 1 ›

☐	Name	Path	Type
☐	Console-Access-AWS-Sec	/	Role
☐	SEC_AWS_BOOK_KMS_ADMIN	/	User

Key deletion

☑ Allow key administrators to delete this key

Key users (2)   `Add` `Remove`

The following IAM users and roles can use this key for cryptographic operations. They can also allow AWS services that are integrated with KMS to use the key on their behalf. Learn more ☐

🔍 *Search Key users*   ‹ 1 ›

☐	Name	Path	Type
☐	Console-Access-AWS-Sec	/	Role
☐	SEC_AWS_BOOK_KMS_USER	/	User

Example 7.1 shows a KMS JSON policy created based on the access permissions defined in Figure 7.14.

> 🌐 **Real World Scenario**
>
> **Example 7.1: KMS JSON Policy**
>
> ```
> {
> "Id": "key-consolepolicy-3",
>  "Version": "2012-10-17",
>  "Statement": [
>     {
>       "Sid": "Enable IAM User Permissions",
>       "Effect": "Allow",
>       "Principal": {
>         "AWS": "arn:aws:iam::112233445566:root"
>       },
>       "Action": "kms:*",
>       "Resource": "*"
>     },
>     {
>       "Sid": "Allow access for Key Administrators",
>       "Effect": "Allow",
>       "Principal": {
>         "AWS": "arn:aws:iam::112233445566:user/SEC_AWS_BOOK_KMS_ADMIN"
>       },
>       "Action": [
>         "kms:Create*",
>         "kms:Describe*",
>         "kms:Enable*",
> ```

```
            "kms:List*",
            "kms:Put*",
            "kms:Update*",
            "kms:Revoke*",
            "kms:Disable*",
            "kms:Get*",
            "kms:Delete*",
            "kms:ImportKeyMaterial",
            "kms:TagResource",
            "kms:UntagResource",
            "kms:ScheduleKeyDeletion",
            "kms:CancelKeyDeletion"
          ],
          "Resource": "*"
        },
        {
          "Sid": "Allow use of the key",
          "Effect": "Allow",
          "Principal": {
            "AWS": "arn:aws:iam::112233445566:user/SEC_AWS_BOOK_KMS_USER"
          },
          "Action": [
            "kms:Encrypt",
            "kms:Decrypt",
            "kms:ReEncrypt*",
            "kms:GenerateDataKey*",
            "kms:DescribeKey"
          ],
          "Resource": "*"
        },
        {
          "Sid": "Allow attachment of persistent resources",
          "Effect": "Allow",
          "Principal": {
            "AWS": "arn:aws:iam::112233445566:user/SEC_AWS_BOOK_KMS_USER"
          },
          "Action": [
            "kms:CreateGrant",
            "kms:ListGrants",
            "kms:RevokeGrant"
          ],
          "Resource": "*",
          "Condition": {
            "Bool": {
              "kms:GrantIsForAWSResource": "true"
            }
          }
        }
      ]
    }
```

FIGURE 7.15 JSON permission policy example diagram.

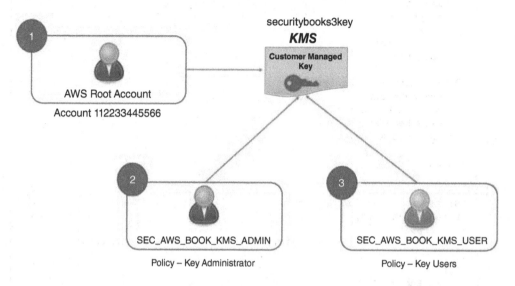

From now on, whenever you see a JSON policy example, take the time to read it more carefully. You should be able to interpret a KMS JSON policy to pass the AWS Certified Security Specialty exam. The remainder of this section explains how to identify a JSON policy's block (see Figure 7.15):

- **AWS Account:** All principals of the account with access to KMS CMKs are added by default in the policy, to protect from key lockout. The default key policy gives the AWS account (roles and users) full access to the CMK, which reduces the risk of the CMK becoming unmanageable, and enables IAM permissions to allow access to the CMK.
- **Key Administrator:** The SEC_AWS_BOOK_KMS_ADMIN user.
- **Key User:** The SEC_AWS_BOOK_KMS_USER user.

Each user has a set of permissions defined in JSON policy, allowing them to perform different activities with the keys (see Figure 7.16). Note that this is a default configuration that can be changed by the key administrator.

As Figure 7.17 shows, the SEC_AWS_BOOK_KMS_ADMIN IAM user can call all the admin APIs but cannot use the encrypt or decrypt operations. The permissions for IAM principal (and users in this example) can create, revoke, delete, and update the keys, among other API calls, and so can execute many different administrative actions within the respective key(s).

And finally, Figure 7.18 shows the permitted API calls that a typical principal (an IAM user in this case) can execute based on the JSON policy. The SEC_AWS_BOOK_KMS_USER IAM user can call all the APIs to encrypt, decrypt, generate, reencrypt, and describe a key and also to create, list, and revoke a grant, but cannot use administration API calls.

FIGURE 7.16 JSON permission policy, all AWS principals in the account.

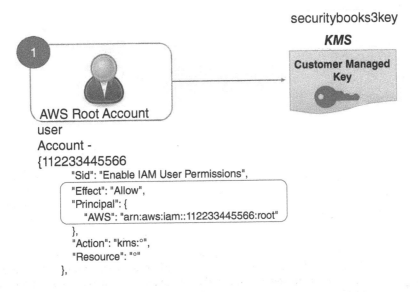

FIGURE 7.17 JSON permission policy, IAM user `SEC_AWS_BOOK_KMS_ADMIN`.

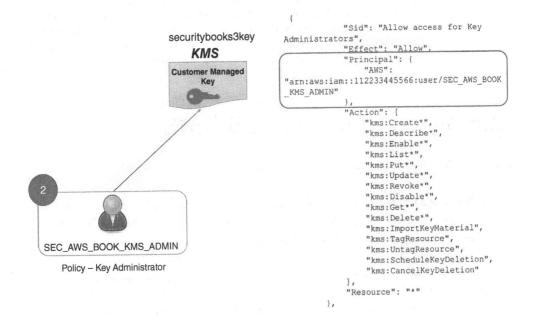

FIGURE 7.18 JSON permission policy, IAM user `SEC_AWS_BOOK_KMS_USER`.

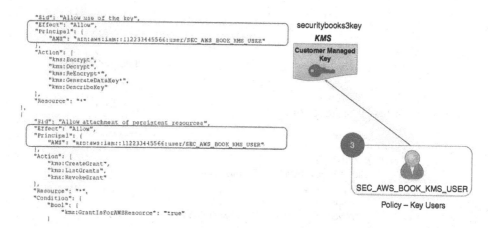

 AWS KMS provides an additional set of predefined condition keys that you can use in key policies and IAM policies. You can use conditions with KMS, for instance, to control what accounts can use the key, using the `kms:CallerAccount` condition, or to control what specific AWS services can call the key using the `kms:ViaService` condition. You do not need to know in detail all the conditions for the exam, but you must know how to read and interpret a JSON KMS policy. If you need more details about KMS conditions, you can find them in the following KMS documentation: https://docs.aws.amazon.com/kms/latest/developerguide/policy-conditions.html#conditions-kms.

Managing Keys in AWS KMS

In the AWS KMS service console shown in Figure 7.19, you can see that there are three categories of keys:

- **AWS-managed keys** are the default keys that protect S3 objects, Lambda functions, and Workspaces, when no other keys (customer-managed keys) are defined for these services.
- **Customer-managed keys** are keys that the users can create and administer using JSON policies.
- **Custom key stores** are used when you want to manage your CMKs using a dedicated AWS CloudHSM cluster, giving you direct control to the HSMs that generate and manage the key material for your CMKs and perform cryptographic operations

FIGURE 7.19 Key categories in AWS KMS.

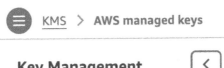

with them. "Understanding the Cloud Hardware Security Module," later in this chapter, addresses the AWS CloudHSMs and how you can use them to protect your environment.

Creating a Key Using the Console

You can create a key directly from the AWS Console. Exercise 7.1 shows you how to do so.

EXERCISE 7.1

Create a KMS Key

Follow these steps to create a KMS key:

1. Log in with an account with permissions that allow you to access the KMS service and create keys.
2. Access the AWS Key Management Services using the AWS Management Console.
3. Click the Create Key button.
4. Select Symmetric.
5. Click Advanced Options and define the KMS key material origin.
6. Click Next and create a CMK with an alias such as `awssecuritycertificationkeytest`.

EXERCISE 7.1 *(continued)*

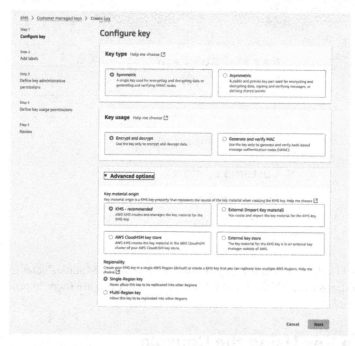

7. Define the key description, such as "**This is the key I'm using to study and pass the exam.**"
8. Click Add Tag and specify the tag key and value.
9. Click Next.

10. Select the key administrators (if you do not have any, you can create a user or a role by using the IAM Management Console).
11. Click Next.

Key deletion
☑ Allow key administrators to delete this key

12. Select the IAM principals that will be able to use the CMK to encrypt and decrypt data with the AWS KMS API and click Next.
13. Review the KMS policy and click Finish.

14. Use the KMS Console to verify that your `awssecuritycertificationkeytest` key was created.

Aliases	Key ID	Status
awssecuritycertificationkeytest	ecf6a0e2-2a97-43cc-8522-e3e988868848	Enabled

It is recommended to tag resources with AWS KMS. The tag can be used to help you evaluate costs by assets and resources, aggregating the costs by tags. So, when you use the Tag resource with AWS KMS, you can map costs for a project, application, or cost center. You can also use tags to define and categorize the keys by information type and projects.

Deleting Keys in AWS KMS

When you delete a CMK, you are also deleting all the metadata associated with it, and after that, you cannot decrypt data that was encrypted under that CMK anymore, which means that data encrypted with the deleted CMK becomes unrecoverable (the only exceptions are multiregion replica keys, asymmetric keys, and hash-based message authentication code [HMAC] KMS keys with imported key material).

You should only delete a CMK when you are sure that you don't need it anymore. If you are in doubt, it is possible to disable the CMK and enable it again later if necessary (and cancel the scheduled deletion of a KMS key), but you cannot recover a deleted CMK.

To help avoid a disastrous scenario where you might inadvertently delete a CMK, AWS KMS enforces a minimum of 7 days and a maximum of 30 days (default configuration) as a waiting period for deleting a CMK. Moreover, it is also important to remember that a CMK pending deletion cannot be used, and KMS does not rotate or generate other derived keys from pending CMKs. For asymmetric keys, the procedure to schedule the deletion is the same; however, scheduling deletion has no effect on public keys (remember that asymmetric keys use public and private keys) outside of AWS KMS. Users who have the public key can continue to use it to encrypt messages. They do not receive any notification that the key state is changed. Unless the deletion is canceled, ciphertext created with the public key cannot be decrypted.

You can only schedule the deletion of a customer-managed key. You cannot delete AWS-managed keys or AWS-owned keys.

When you create the key, you still have the option to prevent the administrator from deleting it, thus adding another layer of protection for accidental deletion, as shown in Figure 7.20.

FIGURE 7.20 Allow key administrators to delete this key option.

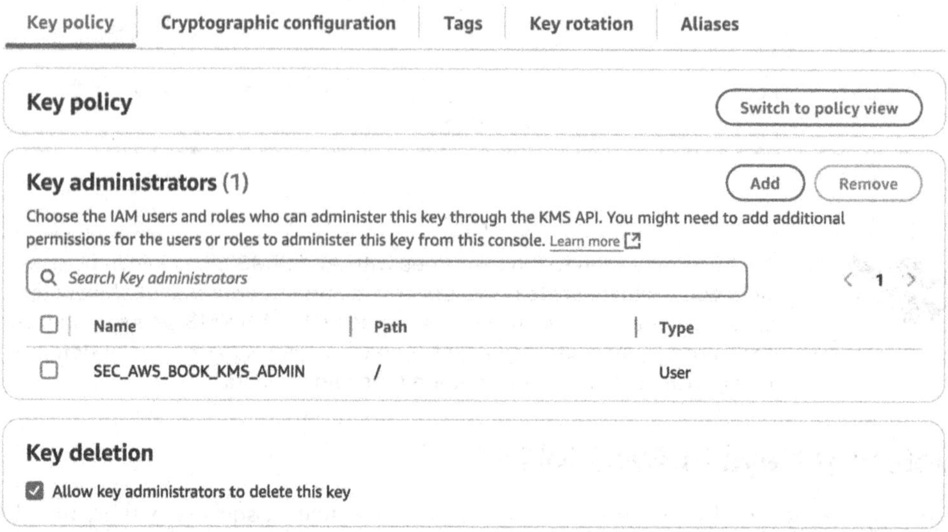

| Key policy | Cryptographic configuration | Tags | Key rotation | Aliases |

Key policy — Switch to policy view

Key administrators (1) — Add Remove

Choose the IAM users and roles who can administer this key through the KMS API. You might need to add additional permissions for the users or roles to administer this key from this console. Learn more

Search Key administrators   < 1 >

	Name	Path	Type
☐	SEC_AWS_BOOK_KMS_ADMIN	/	User

Key deletion

☑ Allow key administrators to delete this key

To delete a key in the AWS KMS Console, perform the following steps:

1. Select AWS Key Management Services in the AWS Management Console.
2. Select the Customer Managed Keys option in the left panel.
3. Search for and select the key that you want to delete or disable.
4. Click the Key Actions button.
5. From the drop-down menu, select either Disable or Schedule Key Deletion. See Figure 7.21. If you choose the second option, define the waiting period.
6. Confirm your disable or deletion action from the previous step. Figure 7.22 shows the confirmation screen for disabling a key.

When considering deleting a key, even if there is a waiting period imposed by the AWS KMS service, you should disable the key for a period of time before performing the final deletion.

Rotating Keys in KMS

You can use the AWS KMS Console, CLI, or the KMS API to enable and disable automatic key rotation, as well as view the rotation status of any CMK. When you enable automatic key rotation, AWS KMS automatically rotates the CMK every 365 days after the enable date. This process is transparent to the user and the environment.

FIGURE 7.21 Key disable and schedule key deletion options.

FIGURE 7.22 Confirm that you want to disable the key.

When an S3 bucket is using KMS keys to protect data, KMS manages the entire rotation process, keeping the previous cryptographic material available to decrypt the data encryption keys. Encryption of objects after the key rotation generates data keys transparently, using the new cryptographic material.

When you have to decrypt data that was encrypted using the old cryptographic material, AWS KMS transparently identifies the right key material to use. That is one of the many advantages of using the AWS KMS service, because if you are not using the KMS to rotate the key, you must manage the entire key lifecycle and keep all the historical keys somewhere so that you can decrypt old data.

318   Chapter 7 ▪ Data Protection

Figure 7.23 shows the key rotation policy.

Select Edit to change the rotation that you want to define, which can be set from 90 to 2560 days, as shown in Figure 7.24.

Manual key rotation may be needed because of a "Bring your own key" (BYOK) situation. More information on manual key rotation can be found at `https://docs.aws.amazon.com/kms/latest/developerguide/rotate-keys.html#rotate-keys-manually`.

FIGURE 7.23 Configuring and checking key rotation.

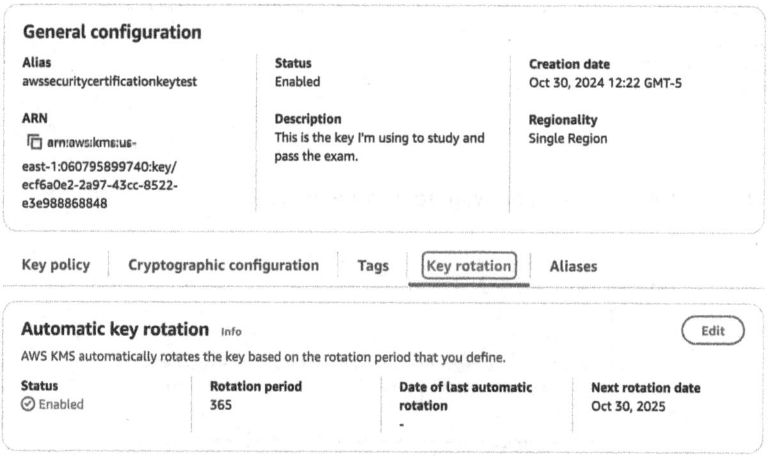

General configuration

Alias	**Status**	**Creation date**
awssecuritycertificationkeytest	Enabled	Oct 30, 2024 12:22 GMT-5
ARN	**Description**	**Regionality**
arn:aws:kms:us-east-1:060795899740:key/ecf6a0e2-2a97-43cc-8522-e3e988868848	This is the key I'm using to study and pass the exam.	Single Region

Key policy | Cryptographic configuration | Tags | Key rotation | Aliases

Automatic key rotation Info   Edit

AWS KMS automatically rotates the key based on the rotation period that you define.

Status	**Rotation period**	**Date of last automatic rotation**	**Next rotation date**
✓ Enabled	365	-	Oct 30, 2025

FIGURE 7.24 Enabling key rotation.

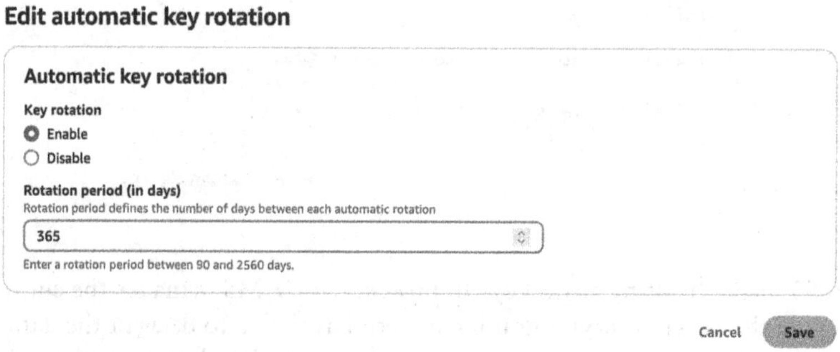

Edit automatic key rotation

Automatic key rotation

Key rotation
- Enable
- Disable

Rotation period (in days)
Rotation period defines the number of days between each automatic rotation

| 365 |

Enter a rotation period between 90 and 2560 days.

Cancel   Save

In Exercise 7.2, you create an S3 bucket using a KMS key to protect your data.

EXERCISE 7.2

Create an S3 Bucket and Use a KMS Key to Protect It

In this exercise, you create an S3 bucket and use the key created in Exercise 7.1 to protect the bucket content. Then you upload a picture to the bucket, turn the object public, and try to access it as a standard/external unauthenticated Internet user.

1. Open the S3 service in the AWS Console.
2. Click the Create Bucket button.
3. Assign a unique name.
4. Click Create.
5. Create an S3 bucket with a unique name.
6. Select the bucket and select the Properties tab.
7. Click the Edit button for Default Encryption.

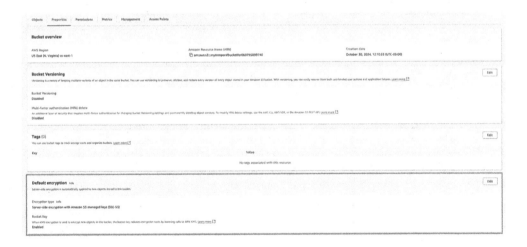

8. Select server-side encryption as Enabled, encryption key type as AWS Key Management Service Key, and AWS KMS Key as Choose From Your AWS KMS keys. Then search for the key that you created in Exercise 7.1.

320 Chapter 7 ▪ Data Protection

EXERCISE 7.2 (continued)

Amazon S3 > Buckets > mytemporalbucketfor060795899740 > Edit default encryption

Edit default encryption Info

Default encryption
Server-side encryption is automatically applied to new objects stored in this bucket.

Encryption type Info

○ Server-side encryption with Amazon S3 managed keys (SSE-S3)

◉ Server-side encryption with AWS Key Management Service keys (SSE-KMS)

○ Dual-layer server-side encryption with AWS Key Management Service keys (DSSE-KMS)
 Secure your objects with two separate layers of encryption. For details on pricing, see **DSSE-KMS pricing** on the **Storage** tab of the
 Amazon S3 pricing page. [↗]

AWS KMS key Info

◉ Choose from your AWS KMS keys

○ Enter AWS KMS key ARN

Available AWS KMS keys

| arn:aws:kms:us-east-1:060795899740:key/ecf6a... ▼ | | C | | Create a KMS key [↗] |

Bucket Key
Using an S3 Bucket Key for SSE-KMS reduces encryption costs by lowering calls to AWS KMS. S3 Bucket Keys aren't supported for DSSE-KMS. Learn more [↗]

○ Disable

◉ Enable

> ⚠ Changing the default encryption settings might cause in-progress replication and Batch Replication jobs
> to fail. These jobs might fail because of missing AWS KMS permissions on the IAM role that's specified in
> the replication configuration. If you change the default encryption settings, make sure that this IAM role
> has the necessary AWS KMS permissions. Learn more [↗]

Cancel   **Save changes**

---

9. Click Save Changes.

10. Upload a picture to the bucket.

11. Change the object permissions from private to public and disallow Block Public Access
 (BPA) protection for that bucket, to test it.

12. Click Save.

Managing Keys in AWS KMS **321**

13. Now that the object is public, try to access the object using the public URL shown in the object's Overview tab. You will see an access denied error.

```
- <Error>
    <Code>InvalidArgument</Code>
  - <Message>
      Requests specifying Server Side Encryption with AWS KMS managed keys require AWS Signature Version 4.
    </Message>
    <ArgumentName>Authorization</ArgumentName>
    <ArgumentValue>null</ArgumentValue>
    <RequestId>A5A3425D7B286298</RequestId>
  - <HostId>
      IIsKDOuf4nyYeFF40F3HQQI/fEGFPKKgApB14paF6zm/I1r0Mq7fnb8xQzDZz/MMCeJ4yg/JxXo=
    </HostId>
  </Error>
```

14. Now try to access the object from the S3 Console by clicking Open.

Were you able to open the object? Do you know why? Why could you not open it in your browser even when you defined the object as a public object?

When you are opening the object using the link in the S3 Console, you are authorized as a user who has access to the bucket and the KMS CMK, so you can see the object. However, when you are trying to open it as an unauthenticated user from the Internet, even with a public S3 bucket, you cannot access the KMS service and decrypt the object. In that case, you have no access to decrypt and visualize the data, and the encryption works as another access control layer.

In Exercise 7.3, you create an RDS database using a KMS key to protect your data.

EXERCISE 7.3

Protecting RDS with KMS

In this exercise, you create an RDS database and create a KMS key (in the same way that you did in Exercise 7.1) and use it to protect the RDS database.

1. Log in with an account with permissions to access the KMS service and create keys.

2. Access the KMS service using the AWS Management Console.

3. Click the Create Key button.

4. Click Advanced Options and define the KMS key material origin.

EXERCISE 7.3 (continued)

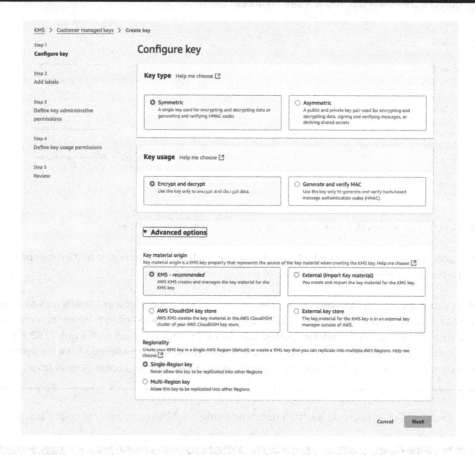

5. Click Add Tag and define the tag key and value.

6. Create a CMK with a unique name and define the alias for the key, such as **RDSencryptionkey**.

7. Define the key description, such as "**This is the key I'm using to study, encrypt RDS, and pass the exam.**"

8. Click Next.

9. Select the key administrators. (If you do not have any, you can create a user or a role by using the IAM Management Console.)

10. Click Next.

11. Select the IAM principal that will be able to use the CMK to encrypt and decrypt data with the AWS KMS API. Click Next.

12. Review the KMS policy and click Finish.
13. Verify that RDSencryptionkey was created by using the KMS Console.

14. Create an RDS MySQL database using the AWS Management Console.

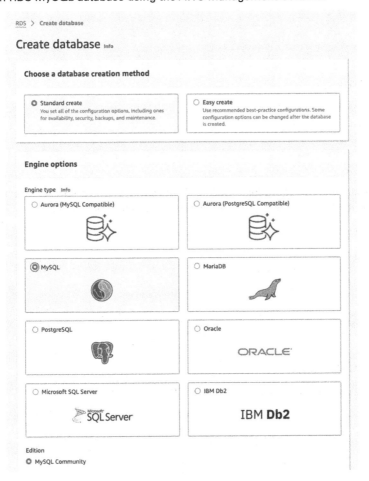

EXERCISE 7.3 (continued)

15. Find the Credential Settings session and define the admin password.

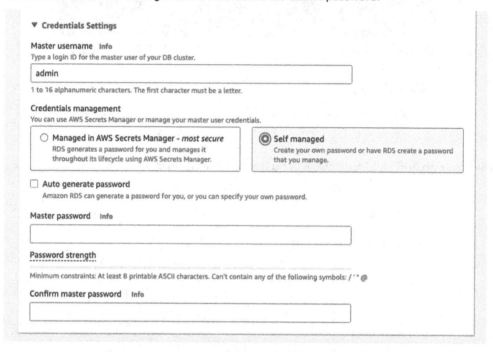

16. Under Additional Configuration, select RDSencryptionkey. If you do not select the predefined key, the RDS service will encrypt the RDS using a default service key.

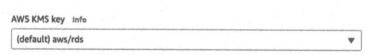

17. Click Create Database.

18. Check that your database was created using the right key.

Managing Keys in AWS KMS

Now that you have created your database using a KMS key, you have an encrypted RDS. As you can see, the process was very simple; however, pay attention to the tips in the "Tips for Protecting RDS with KMS" sidebar, because they may be on your exam.

Tips for Protecting RDS with KMS

- You can only enable encryption for an Amazon RDS database instance while you are creating it, not after it is created.

- You cannot have an encrypted read replica of an unencrypted database instance or an unencrypted read replica of an encrypted database instance.

- You cannot restore a backup of an unencrypted snapshot to an encrypted database instance.

- Encrypted read replicas must be encrypted with the same key as the source database instance.

- If you copy an encrypted snapshot within the same AWS region, you can encrypt the copy with the same KMS encryption key as the original snapshot, or you can specify a different KMS encryption key.

- If you copy an encrypted snapshot between regions, you cannot use the same KMS encryption key for the copy used for the source snapshot because the KMS keys are region specific. Instead, you must specify a valid KMS key in the target AWS region.

326 Chapter 7 ▪ Data Protection

In Exercise 7.4, you create an EBS disk using a KMS key to protect your data.

EXERCISE 7.4

Protecting EBS with KMS

In this exercise, you create an EBS volume and a KMS key (in the same way that you did in Exercise 7.1) to use with EBS volumes.

1. Log in with an account to access the KMS service and create keys.

2. Access the KMS service using the AWS Management Console.

3. Click Customer Managed Keys.

4. Click Create Key.

5. Select Symmetric.

6. Click Advanced options and select KMS.

7. Click Next.

8. Create a CMK with an alias for the key, such as `EBSencryptionkey`.

9. Define the key description, such as **"This is the key I'm using to study, encrypt EBS volumes, and pass the exam."**

10. Click Add Tag.

11. Define the tag key and value.

12. Click Next.

13. Select the key administrators. (If you do not have any, you can create a user or a role by using the IAM Management Console.)

14. Click Next.

15. Select the IAM principals that will be able to use the CMK to encrypt and decrypt data with the AWS KMS API. Click Next.

16. Review the KMS policy and click Finish.

17. Verify that `EBSencryptionkey` was created using the KMS Console.

18. Create an EBS using the AWS Console inside EC2. (If you need help, check the documentation at `https://docs.aws.amazon.com/AWSEC2/latest/UserGuide/ebs-creating-volume.html`.)

Managing Keys in AWS KMS 327

▼ Elastic Block Store

　Volumes

　Snapshots

　Lifecycle Manager

19. Select the Encryption option.

20. Specify the key.

21. Define the KMS key for encryption.

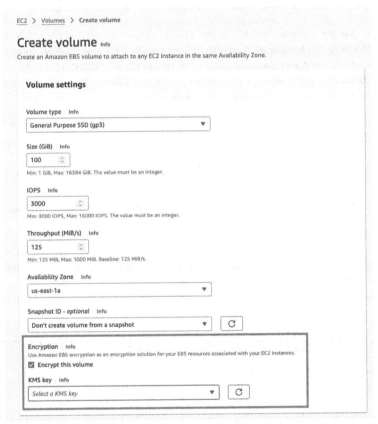

22. Click Create Volume.

Now that you have enabled the EBS encryption using a KMS key, you have an EBS volume that you can attach to an EC2 instance with an encrypted volume. As you can see, the process was very simple; however, pay attention to the "Tips for Protecting EBS with KMS" sidebar because they may be on your exam.

Tips for Protecting EBS with KMS

- Encryption by default is a region-specific setting. If you enable it for a region, you cannot disable it for individual snapshots or volumes in that region. To enable the EBS encryption by default, you can use this command in the AWS CLI (or use the AWS Management Console):

  ```
  aws ec2 enable-ebs-encryption-by-default
  ```

- EBS volumes are encrypted by your account's default AWS-managed key unless you specify a customer-managed CMK in EC2 settings or on deployment.

- Volumes that are created from encrypted snapshots are automatically encrypted using the same key as the snapshot, or using a different key that you specify. Volumes that are created from unencrypted snapshots are automatically unencrypted, but you can choose to encrypt them using a specific key. If no snapshot is selected, you can choose to encrypt the volume and specify your own key.

- By enabling encryption by default, you can run an Amazon EC2 instance with EBS encryption.

- Without encryption by default enabled, a restored volume of an unencrypted snapshot is unencrypted by default.

- When the CreateVolume action operates on an encrypted snapshot, you have the option of encrypting it again with a different CMK.

- The ability to encrypt a snapshot while copying lets you apply a new CMK to an already encrypted snapshot belonging to you. Restored volumes from the resulting copy are only accessible using the new CMK.

Understanding the Cloud Hardware Security Module

A hardware security module (HSM) is a hardware-based encryption device. An HSM implements robust physical and logical security mechanisms that enable the generation, storage, and protection of cryptographic keys, both symmetric and asymmetric. Acting as a secure cryptographic vault, it prevents keys from being exposed outside its protected boundaries, thereby safeguarding the confidentiality of data encrypted with those keys.

AWS CloudHSM is a managed service that automates administration tasks such as hardware provisioning, software patching, high availability configurations, and backups.

AWS CloudHSM lets you scale quickly by adding (or removing) on-demand HSM instances, in a pay-as-you-go model.

> AWS CloudHSM runs in your own Amazon VPC, so that you can easily use your HSMs with applications that run on your Amazon EC2 instances. With CloudHSM, you can use standard VPC security controls to manage access to your HSMs. Your applications connect securely and with better performance.

With AWS CloudHSM, you can still implement multiregional clustering and replication, further enhancing your level of protection, resiliency, and business continuity. You can also integrate the solution with your applications using Cryptography APIs: Microsoft CryptoNG (CNG) libraries, Public Key Cryptography Standards (PKCS) #11, and Java Cryptography Extensions (JCE).

Generally, the use of a Cloud HSM is directly related to meeting regulatory needs, such as FIPS 140-2 Level 3 standards. To create an HSM cluster in the AWS Management Console, you must configure the VPC, subnets, and their availability zones where cluster members will be provisioned.

Figures 7.25 and 7.26 show how Amazon CloudHSM is provisioned through the AWS Console.

Once you have created a cluster, you need to initialize it by validating the HSM certificate chains, verifying the identity of your cluster, and then importing the signed cluster certificate and your issuing certificate. Figure 7.27 shows the relationship between certificates.

> A cluster is a collection of individual HSMs. AWS CloudHSM synchronizes the HSMs in each cluster so that they function as a logical unit. AWS CloudHSM offers two types of HSMs: hsm1.medium and hsm2m.medium. When you create a cluster, you choose which of the two will be in your cluster.

Once you initialize the cluster, you will be prompted to download the certificate signing request (see Figure 7.28). In order to understand the relationship between certificates, you first need to understand each of these certificates:

- **AWS Root Certificate:** This is AWS CloudHSM's root certificate.
- **Manufacturer Root Certificate:** This is the hardware manufacturer's root certificate.
- **AWS Hardware Certificate:** AWS CloudHSM created this certificate when the HSM hardware was added to the fleet. This certificate asserts that AWS CloudHSM owns the hardware.
- **Manufacturer Hardware Certificate:** The HSM hardware manufacturer created this certificate when it manufactured the HSM hardware. This certificate asserts that the manufacturer created the hardware.

- **HSM Certificate:** The HSM certificate is generated by the FIPS-validated hardware when you create the first HSM in the cluster. This certificate asserts that the HSM hardware created the HSM.
- **Cluster Certificate Signing Request (CSR):** The first HSM creates the cluster CSR. When you sign the cluster CSR, you claim the cluster. Then, you can use the signed CSR to initialize the cluster.

FIGURE 7.25 CloudHSM configuration.

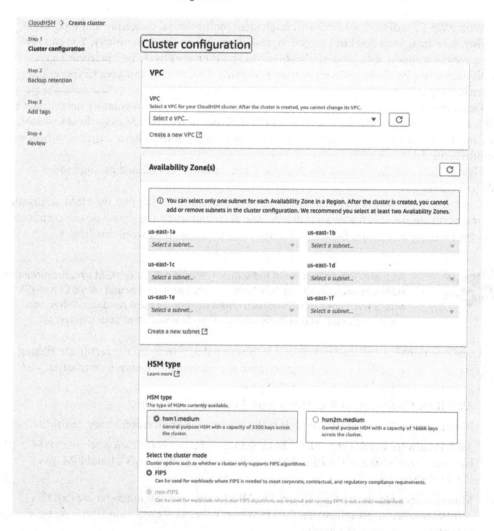

FIGURE 7.26 CloudHSM configuration validation.

FIGURE 7.27 CloudHSM certificates hierarchy.

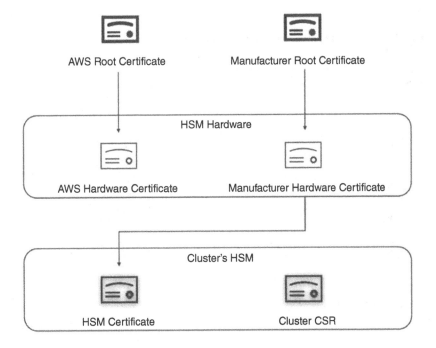

 AWS CloudHSM provides secure access to your HSMs so you can create users and set HSM policies. The encryption keys that you generate and use with CloudHSM are accessible only by the HSM users that you specify. AWS has no visibility or access to your encryption keys.

FIGURE 7.28 CloudHSM cluster initialization.

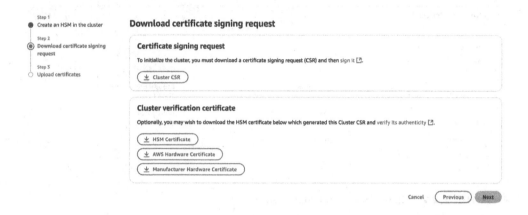

FIGURE 7.29 VPC architecture to access Cluster HSM.

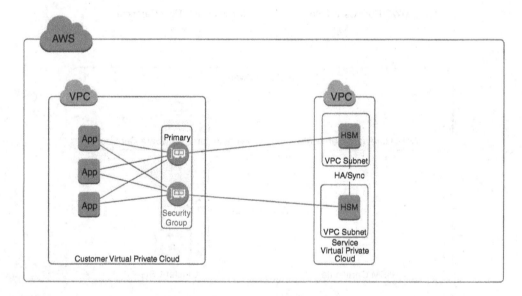

Once the Cluster HSM (a collection of individual HSMs) is configured, the client can access the service through network interfaces and security group configurations directly from their VPC, as shown in Figure 7.29.

In Figure 7.29, applications in the Customer VPC must use an ENI to access CloudHSM and keys provisioned in the service VPC.

Understanding the Cloud Hardware Security Module

You don't need to know how to provision, export, validate, and start a CloudHSM for the certification exam, but if you want to do a complete lab, you can find step-by-step instructions in the CloudHSM documentation at `https://docs.aws.amazon.com/cloudhsm/latest/userguide/getting-started.html`.

Using CloudHSM with AWS KMS

It is also possible to integrate AWS CloudHSM with the AWS KMS service (using the AWS KMS Custom Key Stores). This allows you to use an AWS CloudHSM cluster to protect the CMKs and thus the keys and data in the most diverse AWS Cloud services.

Figure 7.30 shows how to configure AWS KMS custom key stores to use with a Cloud HSM.

A custom key store is a key store within AWS KMS that is backed by a key manager outside of AWS KMS, which you own and manage. Custom key stores combine the convenient and comprehensive key management interface of AWS KMS with the ability to own and control the key material and cryptographic operations. When you use a KMS key in a custom key store, the cryptographic operations are performed by your key manager using your cryptographic keys. As a result, you assume more responsibility for the availability and durability of cryptographic keys, and for the operation of the HSMs.

When you are using your own key store using AWS CloudHSMs that you control (you can also use an external key store), KMS generates and stores the key material for the CMK inside the CloudHSM cluster that you own and manage. In this use case, the cryptographic operations under that key are performed by your CloudHSM cluster.

FIGURE 7.30 AWS KMS custom key stores configuration with HSM.

Here are three scenarios in which you'd want to use your own key store using CloudHSMs BYOK:

- You have keys that are required to be protected in a single-tenant HSM or in an HSM over which you have direct control.

- You must store keys using an HSM validated at FIPS 140-2 Level 3 overall.

- You have keys that are required to be auditable independently of KMS.

There are other scenarios that require the use of an external key store. An external key store is a custom key store backed by an external key manager that you own and manage outside of AWS. All encryption or decryption operations that use a KMS key in an external key store are performed by your external key manager using your cryptographic key material, a feature known as hold your own keys (HYOKs). This advanced feature is designed for regulated workloads that you must protect with encryption keys stored in an external key management system that you control.

External key stores are designed for use in server-side encryption so you can protect your AWS resources with your own cryptographic keys. Most AWS services that support customer-managed keys also support KMS keys in an external key store.

SSL Offload Using CloudHSM

You can use AWS CloudHSM to offload SSL encryption and decryption of traffic to your servers or instances, improving private key protection, reducing performance impact into your application, and raising your application security when using AWS Cloud.

The following steps describe the communication process followed by the client, the server, and CloudHSM once the configuration is created:

1. The client connects to the server.
2. The server responds and sends the server's certificate.
3. The client verifies that a trusted root certificate authority signs the SSL/TLS server certificate and extracts the public key from the server certificate.
4. The client generates a secret premaster key.
5. The client encrypts the premaster key with the server's public key and sends it to the server.
6. The server sends the client's premaster secret to the HSM.
7. The HSM uses the private key in the HSM to decrypt the premaster secret.
8. The HSM sends the premaster secret to the server.
9. The handshake process ends, and all subsequent messages sent between the client and the server are encrypted with derivatives of the premaster secret.

Figure 7.31 graphically represents these steps.

FIGURE 7.31 Custom key store KMS integration to CloudHSM.

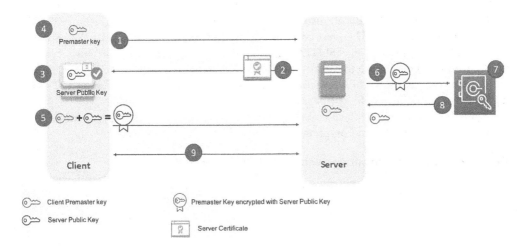

AWS Certificate Manager

With the increasing use of APIs, services exposed to the Internet, and integration with third parties, it is a requirement to implement secure protocols, especially for communications through Internet environments. The use of such protocols is fundamental to increase the security level of your applications and environments, as well as the confidentiality of your environment.

Consequently, with more elements exchanging information securely, the challenge to generate, manage, install, and control digital certificates for highly scalable environments also increases.

AWS Certificate Manager (ACM) is a managed service that allows you to quickly provision, manage, and deploy Secure Sockets Layer (SSL)/Transport Layer Security (TLS) certificates for use with both AWS Cloud–native services and your internal resources.

Through ACM, you can quickly request an SSL certificate; deploy it to ACM-integrated AWS services such as elastic load balancers (ELBs), Amazon CloudFront distributions, and APIs on the Amazon API Gateway; and let the AWS Certificate Manager manage the renewals of these certificates. The service can also be used for internal digital certificate generation, functioning as an internal certificate authority (CA).

A CA issues SSL digital certificates accepted by most browsers and is responsible for validating the ownership of a domain by a company or organization, ensuring that information is being exchanged with the correct entity.

ACM has no cost when used within the AWS-native environment and resources; however, when using it as an internal certificate authority or for on-premises environments, it has a monthly cost.

Figure 7.32 shows a scenario where ACM is integrated with native AWS services.

In Figure 7.32, ACM automates the creation and renewal of SSL/TLS certificates and deploys them to AWS CloudFront distributions and ELB in Step 1, considering your predefined configurations. The users communicate with CloudFront over HTTPS in Step 2, and CloudFront terminates the SSL/TLS connection at the edge location. You can configure CloudFront to communicate to the origin over HTTPS in Step 3, using an S3 bucket or even an ELB that can distribute the connections to different EC2 instances in the same AZ, or in multiple AZs, as defined in Step 4.

Figure 7.33 shows how you can integrate your ACM in the AWS Cloud, generating certificates to your traditional on-premises environments.

FIGURE 7.32 ACM integration with AWS-native services scenario.

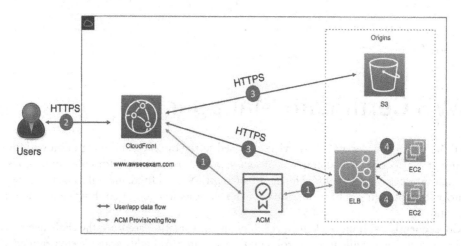

FIGURE 7.33 ACM private CA scenario.

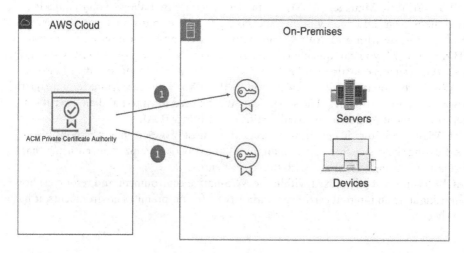

When using as a private CA, ACM can generate the certificates to your legacy, on-premises environment and protect IoT device communications. Figure 7.34 shows the AWS Certificate Manager Service dashboard.

ACM Private Certificate Authority (ACM PCA) is a managed private CA service that helps you easily and securely create private certificates to identify resources and protect communication in your organization. It allows you to create your own CA hierarchy, giving you full control over your private PKI. One key feature of ACM PCA is its integration with AWS services and your existing IT infrastructure. It enables you to issue private certificates for use with AWS services like ELB, API Gateway, and IoT, as well as with your on-premises resources. This seamless integration helps streamline certificate management across your entire environment. Figure 7.35 displays the main interface that appears when you access the service console.

FIGURE 7.34 ACM General dashboard.

FIGURE 7.35 Private CA general dashboard.

AWS Private CA

Private certificate authorities are regional resources. To use PCAs in more than one region, you must create a new CA in those regions. You cannot copy private CAs between regions.

AWS PCA enables creation of Private CA hierarchies, including root and subordinate CAs, without the investment and maintenance costs of operating an on-premises CA. Your private CAs can issue end-entity X.509 certificates, useful in scenarios including:

- Creating encrypted TLS communication channels
- Authenticating users, computers, API endpoints, and IoT devices
- Cryptographically signing code
- Implementing Online Certificate Status Protocol (OCSP) for obtaining certificate revocation status

AWS Secret Protection Mechanisms

In the world of cloud computing, protecting sensitive information is key. Amazon Web Services offers various mechanisms to safeguard secrets, such as passwords, API keys, and other confidential data. This section explores the different secret protection solutions provided by AWS, their key features, and important considerations for implementation.

The AWS Secrets Manager and AWS Systems Manager Parameter Store are two primary services that AWS provides for secret management. Each has its own strengths and use cases, catering to different organizational needs and security requirements. As you navigate through this document, you'll explore how these services can be integrated into your existing AWS infrastructure, enhancing your overall security strategy and ensuring compliance with various regulatory standards.

AWS Secrets Manager

AWS Secrets Manager is a dedicated service designed to protect secrets needed to access your applications, services, and IT resources. It helps you easily rotate, manage, and retrieve database credentials, API keys, and other secrets throughout their lifecycle.

One of the key features of Secrets Manager is its ability to automatically rotate secrets. This functionality significantly reduces the risk associated with long-lived credentials and helps maintain a strong security posture. The service can rotate secrets for Amazon RDS, Amazon Redshift, and Amazon DocumentDB without requiring downtime.

Choosing the Right AWS KMS Key

When creating a secret, you can choose to use the default AWS-managed key for Secrets Manager or specify a customer-managed key. Consider your compliance requirements and key management needs when making this decision.

AWS Secret Protection Mechanisms

Secrets Manager integrates seamlessly with other AWS services, allowing you to use secrets directly in your applications without hard-coding sensitive information. This integration extends to services like AWS Lambda, Amazon ECS, and Amazon EKS, enhancing the overall security of your AWS ecosystem.

The service also provides fine-grained access control through AWS IAM. This allows you to define who can access which secrets, ensuring that sensitive information is only available to authorized entities. You can use identity-based policies and resource-based policies to control who can access your secrets and what actions they can perform.

Cross-Account Access

Secrets Manager supports cross-account access to secrets. This allows you to centralize the secret management, while still maintaining proper access controls.

Secrets Manager offers encryption at rest and in transit. All secrets are encrypted using AWS KMS, providing an additional layer of security. This ensures that your sensitive information remains secure even when stored in AWS databases. You can use AWS-managed keys or create and manage your own for more control. All communication with AWS Secrets Manager occurs over HTTPS, providing encryption in transit. Secrets Manager supports TLS 1.2 and 1.3 in all regions, as well as a hybrid post-quantum key exchange option for TLS (PQTLS) network encryption protocol.

To start using AWS Secrets Manager, follow these steps:

1. Sign in to the AWS Management Console.
2. Navigate to the AWS Secrets Manager service.
3. Click on Store a New Secret to create your first secret.
4. Choose the type of secret you want to store (e.g., database credentials, API key) (see Figure 7.36).
5. Enter the secret details and configure additional settings like description and tags.
6. Set up rotation settings if desired:
    a. Choose a rotation schedule.
    b. Select or create a Lambda function for rotation.
    c. Configure the rotation strategy.
7. Define secret replication (another region).
8. Review and create the secret.

Once your secrets are created, you can manage them through the AWS Management Console, AWS CLI, or AWS SDKs. Figure 7.37 shows the way you can access the secret via AWS SDK using Boto3 in Python.

FIGURE 7.36 Secret creation.

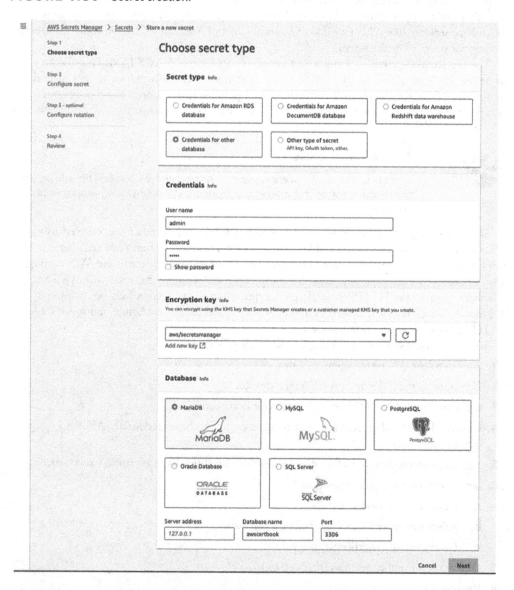

 Cross-Region Replication

You can replicate your secrets in multiple AWS regions to support applications spread across those regions to meet regional access and low latency requirements.

AWS Secret Protection Mechanisms 341

FIGURE 7.37 Python code to access a secret.

```
1   # Use this code snippet in your app.
2   # If you need more information about configurations
3   # or implementing the sample code, visit the AWS docs:
4   # https://aws.amazon.com/developer/language/python/
5
6   import boto3
7   from botocore.exceptions import ClientError
8
9
10  def get_secret():
11
12      secret_name = "DBawssecuritybook"
13      region_name = "us-east-1"
14
15      # Create a Secrets Manager client
16      session = boto3.session.Session()
17      client = session.client(
18          service_name='secretsmanager',
19          region_name=region_name
20      )
21
22      try:
23          get_secret_value_response = client.get_secret_value(
24              SecretId=secret_name
25          )
26      except ClientError as e:
27          # For a list of exceptions thrown, see
28          # https://docs.aws.amazon.com/secretsmanager/latest/apireference
                /API_GetSecretValue.html
29          raise e
30
31      secret = get_secret_value_response['SecretString']
32
33      # Your code goes here.
34
```

AWS Systems Manager Parameter Store

AWS Systems Manager Parameter Store provides secure hierarchical storage for configuration data management and secrets management. It offers a centralized store to manage your application configurations, feature flags, and secrets across multiple AWS accounts and regions. Parameter Store seamlessly integrates with other AWS services, including Amazon EC2, Amazon ECS, AWS Lambda, and AWS CloudFormation. This integration allows you to dynamically reference stored parameters in your applications and AWS CloudFormation templates.

One of the key features of Parameter Store is its support for different parameter types. It allows you to store data as String, StringList, or SecureString. SecureString parameters are encrypted using AWS KMS, ensuring that sensitive information remains protected at rest.

Cross-Account Parameter Sharing

You can now use AWS Resource Access Manager to share parameters with other accounts in your organization. Sharing advanced parameters simplifies configuration data management in a multi-account environment. You can centrally store and manage your parameters and share them with other AWS accounts that need to reference them.

Parameter Store offers version tracking for your parameters. This feature allows you to maintain a history of changes and roll back to previous versions, if needed, providing an additional layer of data management and security. The service provides hierarchical storage, allowing you to organize and manage your parameters efficiently. You can group related parameters and control access at different levels of the hierarchy using IAM policies.

To start using AWS Systems Manager Parameter Store, follow these steps:

1. Sign in to the AWS Management Console.
2. Navigate to the AWS Systems Manager service.
3. In the left panel, select Parameter Store from the Application Management section.
4. Click on the Create Parameter button to create your first parameter/secret. The configuration options are illustrated in Figure 7.38.
5. Select the tier. Parameter Store offers two tiers: standard parameters (supporting up to 4 KB of data) and advanced parameters (supporting up to 8 KB of data). Select Standard for this example.
6. Choose the type of parameter that you want to store (e.g., String, StringList, SecureString). Select SecureString to protect the information with a KMS Key (encrypt sensitive data using KMS keys from your account or another).
7. Enter the secret value.
8. Click Create Parameter. After creation, the console displays the My Parameters view (see Figure 7.39), which lists all your current parameters.

While both services can store secrets, they have different strengths and use cases that are important to understand:

- **Secret Rotation:** Secrets Manager offers built-in secret rotation, while Parameter Store does not.
- **Cost:** Parameter Store is generally more cost-effective for storing a large number of parameters or secrets.
- **Integration:** Secrets Manager has deeper integration with database services for automatic rotation.

AWS Secret Protection Mechanisms 343

- **Complexity:** Parameter Store is simpler and more suitable for storing configuration data and less sensitive information.
- **Cross-Region Replication:** Secrets Manager supports cross-region replication, while Parameter Store does not.

FIGURE 7.38 AWS Systems Manager Parameter Store creation.

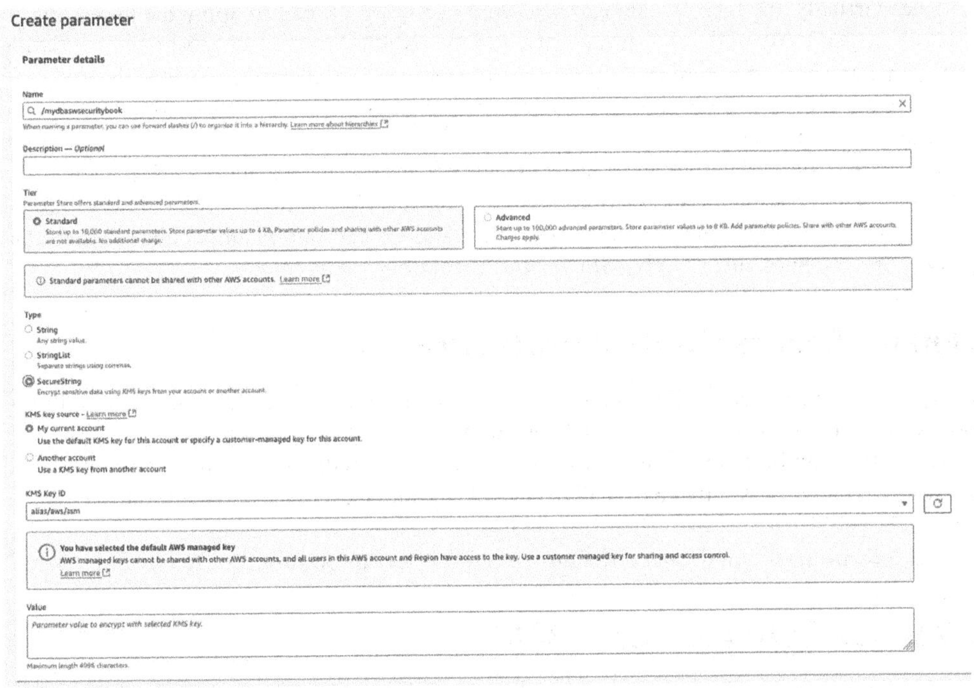

FIGURE 7.39 AWS Parameter Store: My Parameters view.

Protecting Your S3 Buckets

Amazon S3 is an object storage service that offers the ability to store large amounts of data for a variety of use cases, such as public site files that can be accessed by users, backing up and restoring files, images, business applications, and IoT devices. It is also a centerpiece for using big data and analytics in the AWS environment.

Since virtually any type of data can be stored in S3, it is crucial to apply the necessary security measures (confidentiality, integrity, and availability) to protect sensitive information that may have been stored in this type of object storage. The following sections discuss fundamental mechanisms in the AWS environment that you should use to protect your data when using S3 buckets.

S3 offers a comprehensive set of features that allow users to protect their data from unauthorized access, maintain data integrity, and ensure high availability. By understanding and implementing these security measures, organizations can significantly enhance their data protection strategies and comply with various regulatory requirements.

Default Access Control Protection

Every bucket in S3 is created by default as a private bucket, that is, the bucket is initially protected from public external access. Even so, when a bucket is created as private, its configuration can be changed by a customer if they have predefined permissions to do so, which could mistakenly make the bucket public, due to an operational or automation process error.

The following section details different ways to protect information stored in S3 buckets.

S3 Block Public Access (BPA)

S3 Block Public Access is a set of controls that can be applied at the account level or to individual buckets to prevent unintended public access to S3 resources. This feature provides an additional layer of protection against data exposure due to misconfigured bucket policies or ACLs. S3 BPA provides settings to help you avoid inadvertent public exposure of your resources.

When enabled (this is a default feature in S3), as shown in Figure 7.40, BPA overrides any existing policies or ACLs that might allow public access, ensuring that even if a bucket or object is accidentally configured to be public, it remains protected. This feature can be particularly useful in maintaining compliance with regulations that require strict control over data access and preventing data breaches due to misconfiguration. You can also configure Block Public Access (BPA) protection at the bucket level, allowing you to set specific protections for each individual bucket, as shown in Figure 7.41.

FIGURE 7.40 Block Public Access: Account Level.

FIGURE 7.41 Block Public Access: Bucket Level.

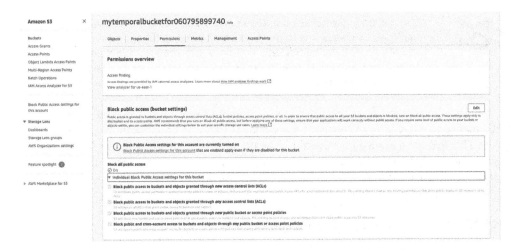

BPA settings can be managed through the S3 Console, AWS CLI, or AWS SDKs, allowing for easy integration into existing security workflows and automation processes. It's recommended that you enable these settings as a best practice for all S3 buckets that don't explicitly require public access.

If you require public access to your general-purpose buckets, it's recommended that you grant access through bucket policies, CloudFront, or access point policies instead of ACLs. Using these policy-based approaches rather than ACLs simplifies permission management.

S3 Access Points

S3 access points simplify managing data access for shared datasets in S3. They provide a way to create unique hostnames with dedicated access policies for any S3 bucket, making it easier to manage access for applications with different permission requirements. Amazon S3 access points are named network endpoints with dedicated access policies that describe how data can be accessed using that endpoint.

Access points simplify managing data access at scale for shared datasets in Amazon S3. Access points are named network endpoints that are attached to buckets that you can use to perform S3 object operations, such as GetObject and PutObject. Each access point has its own access point policy, similar to a bucket policy, which allows you to customize access controls for specific use cases. This granular control helps enhance data confidentiality by ensuring that each application or user group only has access to the specific data they need.

You can only use access points to perform operations on objects. You can't use access points to perform other Amazon S3 operations, such as modifying or deleting buckets. For more information, check access point restrictions and limitations at https://docs.aws.amazon.com/AmazonS3/latest/userguide/access-points-restrictions-limitations.html.

Similar to S3 buckets, access points can be configured to accept requests only from a VPC, adding an extra layer of security for workloads that don't require public network access. This feature is particularly useful for maintaining compliance with regulations that require strict control over data access. In Figure 7.42, you can see an access point for a bucket that is restricted to be used inside a VPC for the finance team.

FIGURE 7.42 An access point named finance.

Permissions granted in an access point policy are effective only if the underlying bucket also allows the same access. You can accomplish this in two ways:

- (Recommended) Delegate access control from the bucket to the access point.
- Add the same permissions contained in the access point policy to the underlying bucket's policy.

S3 Object Lock and S3 Glacier Vault Lock

S3 Object Lock and S3 Glacier Vault Lock are two powerful features provided by AWS to help users implement robust data protection, retention, and compliance controls. Both features offer write once read many (WORM) capabilities, ensuring that data remains immutable for a specified period (or indefinitely).

Object Lock works only on versioned buckets. You must enable versioning on the bucket before you can enable Object Lock.

S3 Object Lock enables users to store objects using a WORM model directly within Amazon S3. To configure this option, select the bucket where you want to implement this, select the Properties tab, then go to the Object Lock section and click on Edit to see the options (see Figure 7.43).

Be aware that once Amazon S3 Object Lock is enabled, you can't disable Object Lock or suspend versioning for the bucket.

You can configure the S3 Object Lock at the bucket creation (new buckets), in the advanced settings section, or with existing buckets, as shown in Figure 7.43.

Object Lock can be configured in two modes (by enabling the default retention):

- **Governance mode:** Users with specific IAM permissions can override or delete protected object versions.
- **Compliance mode:** Protected object versions cannot be overwritten or deleted by any users, including the root account.

S3 Glacier Vault Lock, on the other hand, is designed specifically for Amazon S3 Glacier, which is AWS's low-cost storage service for data archiving and long-term backup. Vault Lock allows users to easily deploy and enforce compliance controls for individual S3 Glacier

FIGURE 7.43 Object Lock setup.

vaults using a Vault Lock policy. A Vault Lock policy can prevent future changes, providing strong enforcement for your compliance controls. This policy can specify various controls, including WORM protection, to meet specific compliance objectives. In Figure 7.44, you can see the options for securitybook-vault.

To create a Vault Lock policy, click in the Initiate Vault Lock policy button and check the options in Figure 7.45. In this example, you can see a policy that denies the glacier:DeleteArchive action on securitybook-vault, if the archive being deleted is less than one year old. You can view more policies in the following link: https://docs.aws.amazon.com/amazonglacier/latest/dev/vault-lock-policy.html.

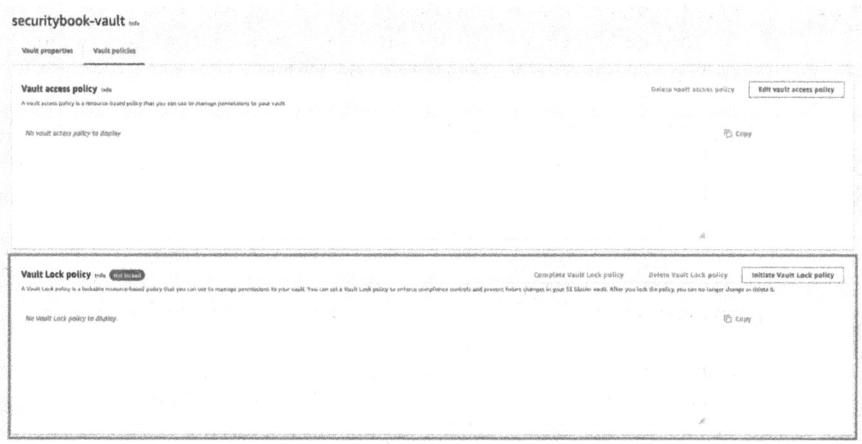

Protecting Your S3 Buckets 349

FIGURE 7.44 Glacier S3 vault policies.

FIGURE 7.45 Glacier S3 Vault Lock policy example.

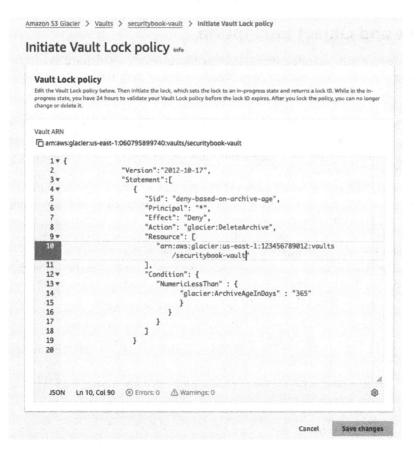

For S3 Glacier Vault Lock, the process involves creating a lock policy, initiating the lock, and then completing the lock within 24 hours. It's crucial to thoroughly review and test your Vault Lock policy before initiating the lock, as it cannot be changed once completed.

A crucial aspect of S3 Glacier Vault Lock is its immutability once locked. After a Vault Lock policy is locked, it can no longer be changed or deleted. This ensures that the specified compliance controls remain in place for the entire duration of data storage, providing a high level of assurance for regulatory requirements and internal governance policies.

To maximize the benefits of S3 Object Lock and S3 Glacier Vault Lock, it's recommended that you integrate them into your overall data lifecycle management strategy. For instance, you can use S3 Object Lock in conjunction with S3 Lifecycle policies to automatically transition objects to Glacier storage classes while maintaining WORM protection throughout the object's lifecycle.

Bucket and Object Encryption

When created with the default settings, buckets are automatically defined as private. You should also define the encryption mechanisms (mandatory for new buckets), so the administrator or the bucket owner must determine which of the available encryption mechanisms to use.

Figure 7.46 shows the default encryption configuration when you create an S3 bucket.

Amazon S3 supports both encryption in transit and encryption at rest. In encryption in transit, you want to protect data during transmission. S3 supports encryption in transit using HTTPS (TLS). This ensures that data remains confidential as it travels between the client and S3 servers. AWS recommends using HTTPS for all S3 API requests to maintain data confidentiality. Additionally, S3 bucket policies can be configured to deny any requests that do not use SSL, further enhancing security.

For encryption at rest, S3 provides different options, ensuring that stored information remains confidential, even if unauthorized access to the storage infrastructure occurs. The Amazon S3 service allows four different mechanisms to be used to encrypt stored data, so that information is automatically encrypted when sent to buckets:

- **SSE-S3:** Server-side encryption with Amazon S3–managed keys
- **SSE-KMS:** Server-side encryption with KMS customer-managed keys
- **DSSE-KMS:** Dual-layer server-side encryption with AWS KMS keys that apply two layers of encryption to objects
- **SSE-C:** Server-side encryption with customer-provided encryption keys

FIGURE 7.46 Default S3 creation with encryption.

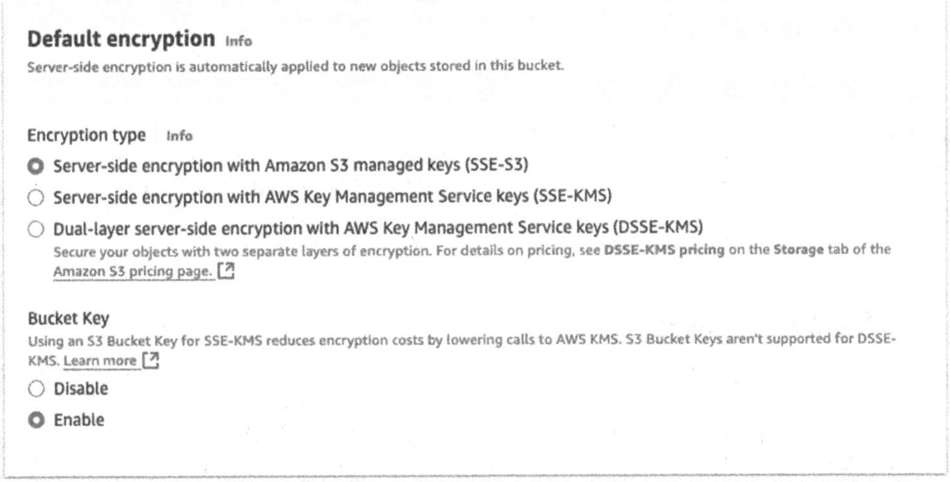

Default encryption Info
Server-side encryption is automatically applied to new objects stored in this bucket.

Encryption type   Info
● Server-side encryption with Amazon S3 managed keys (SSE-S3)
○ Server-side encryption with AWS Key Management Service keys (SSE-KMS)
○ Dual-layer server-side encryption with AWS Key Management Service keys (DSSE-KMS)
    Secure your objects with two separate layers of encryption. For details on pricing, see **DSSE-KMS pricing** on the **Storage** tab of the Amazon S3 pricing page.

Bucket Key
Using an S3 Bucket Key for SSE-KMS reduces encryption costs by lowering calls to AWS KMS. S3 Bucket Keys aren't supported for DSSE-KMS. Learn more
○ Disable
● Enable

 Amazon S3 evaluates and applies bucket policies before applying bucket encryption settings. If you enable bucket encryption settings, your PUT requests without encryption information will be rejected because your bucket policy rejects such PUT requests. So, it is very important to implement the encryption mechanism and review your bucket policies.

SSE-S3 Encryption

SSE-S3 is the native encryption functionality of the AWS S3 service. This functionality allows you to natively encrypt objects inserted into a bucket using an AES-256 symmetric key, which is automatically generated and managed directly by the S3 service, at no additional cost. Buckets and new objects are encrypted with server-side encryption with an Amazon S3 managed key as the base level of encryption configuration.

In such a scenario, Amazon S3 encrypts each object with a unique key and additionally protects the data encryption key with a key that is rotated regularly. This feature can be enabled directly in the bucket's setting properties by following these steps through the AWS Console:

1. Select the Amazon S3 service inside the AWS Management Console.
2. Select the bucket that you want to encrypt (for existing unencrypted buckets) or update the encryption mechanism by clicking its name in the list or by searching for it with the search tool at the top of the screen.
3. Click the Properties Configuration tab of the bucket.

4. Search for the Default Encryption and click Edit.
5. Select the SSE-S3 Encryption method.
6. Save the configuration.

> Changing the default encryption settings might cause in-progress replication and batch replication jobs to fail. These jobs might fail because of missing AWS KMS permissions on the IAM role specified in the replication configuration. If you change the default encryption settings, make sure that this IAM role has the necessary AWS KMS permissions.

SSE-KMS Encryption

SSE-KMS is the encryption functionality of the S3 service that uses encryption keys managed with KMS. This functionality sets the behavior of S3 to encrypt by default every object uploaded into the specified bucket using keys managed through KMS, regardless of whether they are AWS-managed keys or customer-managed keys. Objects uploaded in the bucket after this configuration is performed will be encrypted even if no encryption option is specified in the request.

You have the option to choose from a list of available KMS keys. Both the AWS-managed key (AWS/S3) and your customer-managed keys appear in this list. The first time you add an SSE-KMS encrypted object to a bucket in a region, a default CMK is created and used for SSE-KMS encryption, when you are using AWS-managed keys (AWS/S3).

It is also important to know that there may be an extra cost in this configuration. Figure 7.47 highlights how to configure the bucket encryption using the Properties tab and choosing to edit the default encryption, and then how to select and use the AWS-managed keys for S3 within KMS.

You can also select CMKs previously created within KMS, which allows flexibility, including the ability to set access controls, a managed key rotation, and audit key usage to protect your data. In this scenario, the S3 service benefits from the full AWS KMS features such as auto-rotation, key management model, and usage auditability.

Figure 7.48 shows how to select a preexisting KMS CMK to use with an S3 bucket.

To enable the encryption service using AWS KMS, follow these steps:

1. Select the Amazon S3 service in the AWS Management Console.
2. Select the bucket that you want to encrypt by clicking its name in the list or by searching for it with the search tool at the top of the screen.
3. Select the Properties Configuration tab of the bucket.
4. Select the section Default Encryption and click the Edit button.
5. Select the Server-Side Encryption with AWS Key Management Service keys (SSE-KMS) option.
6. Select the key in the drop-down menu (AWS/S3 or preexisting keys).
7. Save the configuration.

Protecting Your S3 Buckets   **353**

FIGURE 7.47   S3 SSE-KMS configuration.

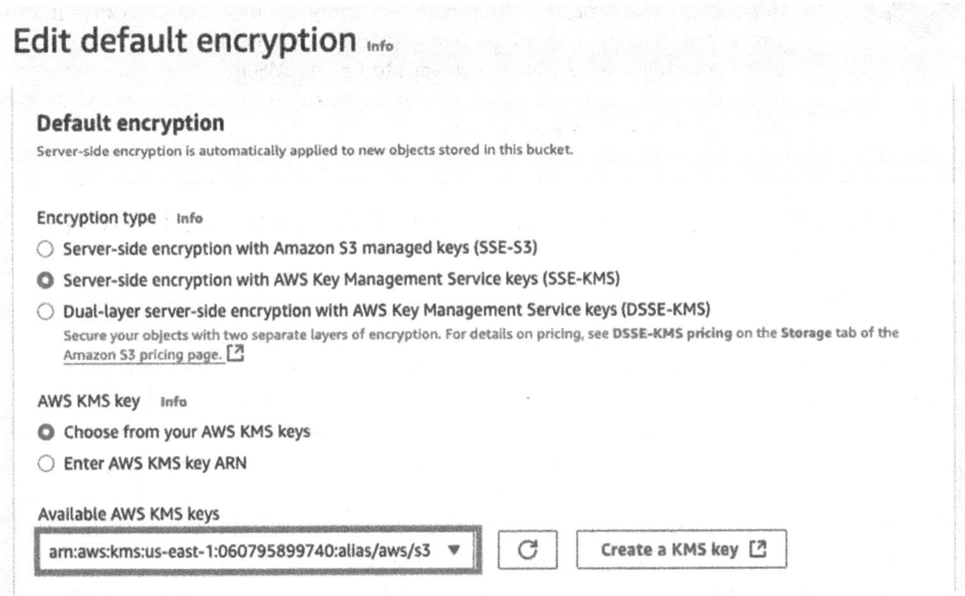

FIGURE 7.48   S3 SSE-KMS with preexisting CMK.

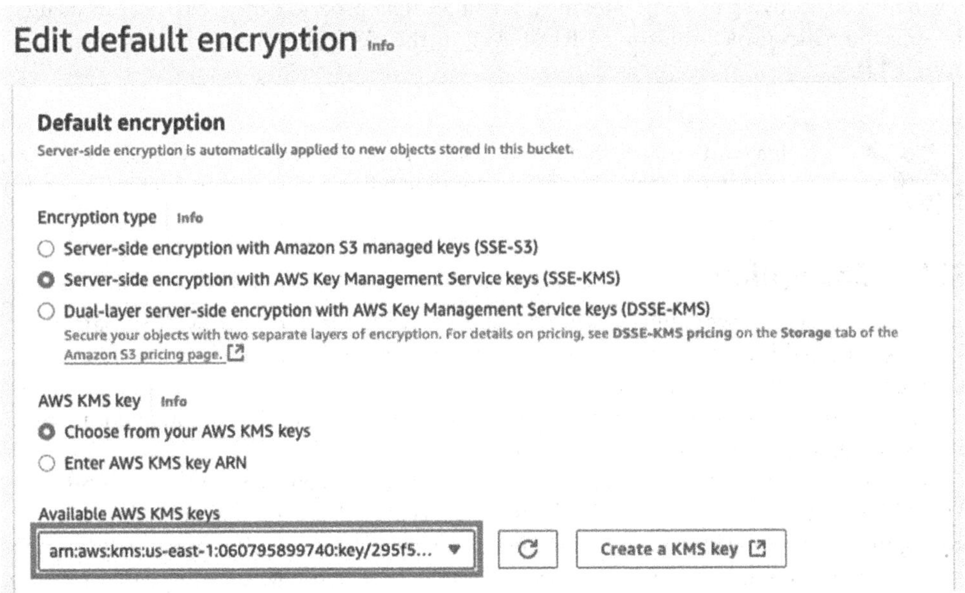

You can only use KMS keys that are available in the same AWS region as the bucket. The Amazon S3 Console lists only the first 100 KMS keys in the same region as the bucket. To use a KMS key that is not listed, you must enter your KMS key ARN. If you want to use a KMS key that is owned by a different account, you must first have permission to use the key, and then you must enter the KMS key ARN.

Dual-Layer Server-Side Encryption with AWS Key Management Service Keys

Dual-layer server-side encryption with AWS Key Management Service (DSSE-KMS) is an advanced encryption method offered by Amazon S3. This approach applies two separate layers of object-level encryption to the object when it is uploaded to S3, providing an additional level of security compared to the single-layer encryption methods.

DSSE-KMS is similar to SSE-KMS. This dual-layer encryption is performed on the server side, which means you can still use various AWS services and tools to analyze your data stored in S3, while meeting stringent compliance requirements.

One of the key advantages of using DSSE-KMS is the increased control over your encryption keys. With AWS KMS, you can view the keys, edit control policies, and track key usage in AWS CloudTrail. You also have the flexibility to create and manage your own customer-managed keys or use AWS-managed keys that are unique to your account, service, or region.

When implementing DSSE-KMS, you can specify this encryption method when uploading new objects or copying existing ones in Amazon S3. The process can be carried out using the Amazon S3 Console, Amazon S3 REST API, or the AWS Command Line Interface (AWS CLI).

It's worth noting that DSSE-KMS supports the use of multiregion AWS KMS keys in Amazon S3, offering additional flexibility for your encryption needs.

SSE-C Encryption

Using SSE-C, you can set your own encryption keys, which you must provide as part of a request. So, in this case, the S3 manages encryption and decryption when storing and accessing objects using the customer key provided.

The customer is in charge of managing the keys provided in each request, and only the data is encrypted, not the object's metadata.

When you upload an object, Amazon S3 uses the provided encryption key to apply AES-256 encryption to the data and deletes the encryption key from memory, thus not storing the encryption key you provided. Instead, it stores a randomly salted HMAC value from the encryption key to validate future requests. The salted HMAC value cannot be used to derive the value of the encryption key or to decrypt the contents of the encrypted object. So, if the customer loses the encryption key, the stored object data is also lost.

An HMAC is a specific type of message authentication code involving a cryptographic hash function and a secret cryptographic key. The cryptographic strength of the HMAC depends on the cryptographic strength of the underlying hash function, the size of its hash output, and the size and quality of the key.

When using the SSE-C feature, you must use HTTPS because requests made over general HTTP are rejected for security reasons, as using HTTP may compromise the confidentiality of the keys sent. Also, since S3 does not store the keys used, the client is responsible for managing and controlling which key was used to encrypt each object. If the customer loses the encryption key, any GET request for an object without its right encryption key fails, and the S3 object is lost.

SSE-KMS Encrypted Objects Replication

By default, Amazon S3 doesn't replicate objects that are encrypted with SSE-KMS or DSSE-KMS. You must modify the bucket replication configuration to tell Amazon S3 to replicate these objects using the right KMS keys.

To configure the replication, you must change the replication definitions in the Management tab, adding a replication rule for the specific bucket, as shown in Figure 7.49.

FIGURE 7.49 S3 Replication configuration.

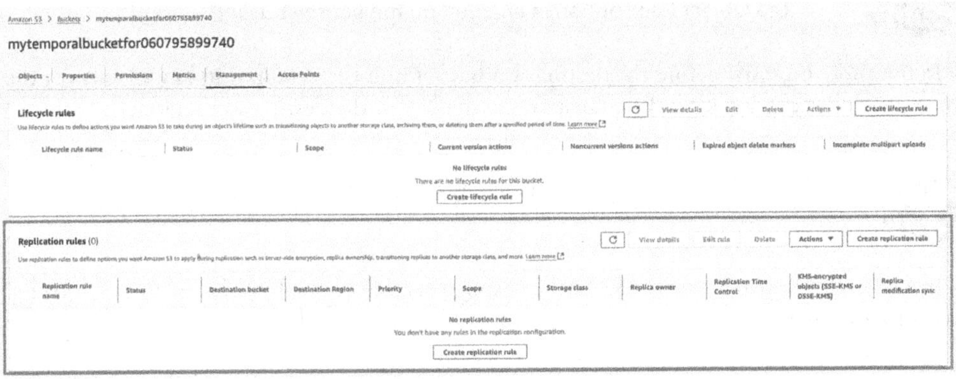

FIGURE 7.50 Key that must be used to replicate encrypted objects.

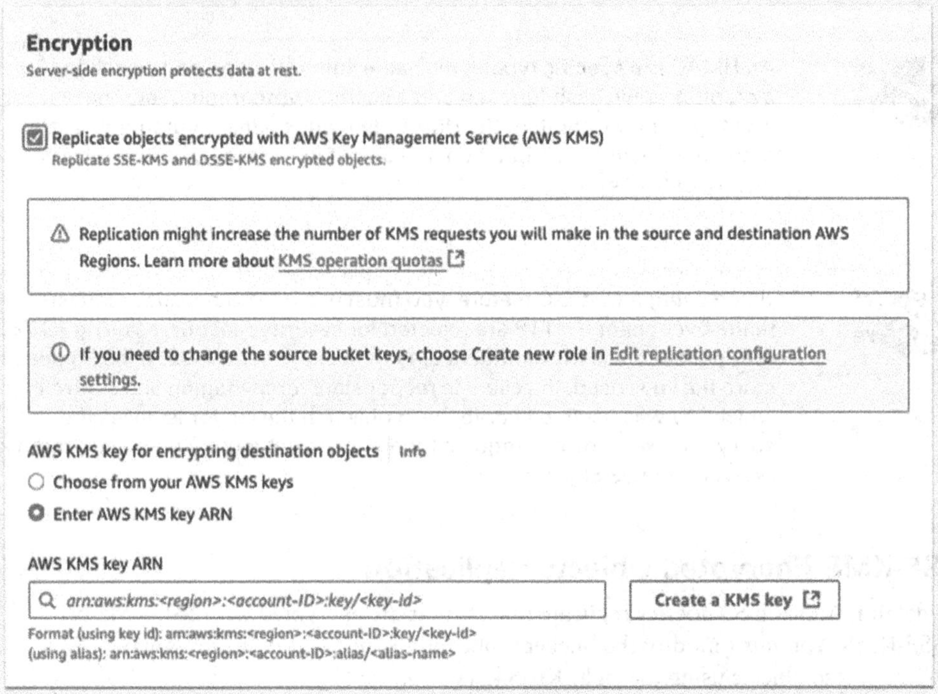
Encryption
Server-side encryption protects data at rest.
Replicate objects encrypted with AWS Key Management Service (AWS KMS)
Replicate SSE-KMS and DSSE-KMS encrypted objects.
Replication might increase the number of KMS requests you will make in the source and destination AWS Regions. Learn more about KMS operation quotas
If you need to change the source bucket keys, choose Create new role in Edit replication configuration settings.
AWS KMS key for encrypting destination objects Info
Choose from your AWS KMS keys
Enter AWS KMS key ARN
AWS KMS key ARN
arn:aws:kms:<region>:<account-ID>:key/<key-id>
Create a KMS key
Format (using key id): arn:aws:kms:<region>:<account-ID>:key/<key-id>
(using alias): arn:aws:kms:<region>:<account-ID>:alias/<alias-name>

Once you start the creation of a replication rule, you will find the Encryption section. Here, you must select the right CMK to replicate objects encrypted, as you can see in Figure 7.50.

> **NOTE** Replication requires Object Lock to be enabled on the destination bucket if the Object Lock option is enabled on the source bucket.

In the end, you must define the destination bucket and the destination key to encrypt the objects with destination keys. You must create the key in the destination region.

> **TIP** The S3 versioning must be enabled to replicate the bucket.

In Exercise 7.5, you create an S3 bucket using a service control policy (SCP) to protect access to your data.

EXERCISE 7.5

Protect Your S3 Buckets with Block Public Access Settings and Service Control Policy

In this exercise, you create an S3 bucket and use the BPA functionality to protect and prevent an S3 bucket from becoming public. You also configure an SCP to enforce a protection policy in your accounts. To complete the exercise, the account must be part of an AWS Organization, and the user must have permissions to the organization management account to change the SCPs.

1. Open the S3 Console.
2. Select the account settings for Block Public Access.

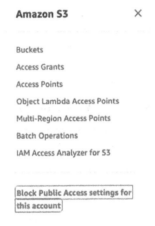

3. Click Edit.
4. Select Block All Public Access and click Save Changes (this is set to Block by default).

EXERCISE 7.5 *(continued)*

5. Click Confirm.

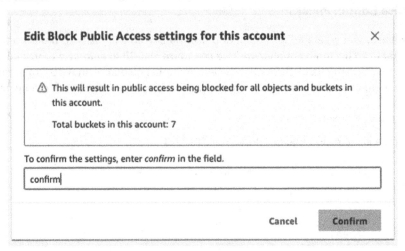

6. Make sure that you applied the configuration correctly.
7. Now you can create an S3 bucket and try to change the configuration to make the bucket public. You will see an access error message.

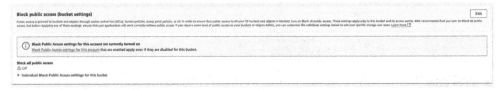

You received this message because the Block Public Access setting was enabled, and you cannot change the bucket configuration to make it public.

8. Now try to change an existing bucket to public access. You will see a message that says you are blocked from changing the bucket to public access.

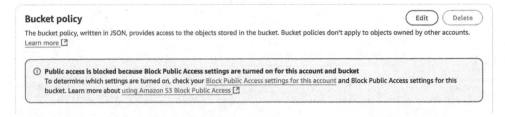

You can also create an SCP at the management account level of the AWS Organizations that will apply to all member accounts to prevent someone from changing the BAP configuration.

9. Open the AWS Organization Console and create an SCP.

Protecting Your S3 Buckets   359

10. Apply the policy to your account at the organization level using this code:

```
{
  "Version": "2012-10-17",
  "Statement": [
    {
      "Sid": "Stmt1548173791000",
      "Effect": "Deny",
      "Action": [
        "s3:PutAccountPublicAccessBlock",
        "s3:PutBucketPublicAccessBlock"
      ],
      "Resource": [
        "*"
      ]
    }
  ]
}
```

11. Try to change the Block Public Access settings. You will receive an access error message.

12. Use an SCP to block access to the following APIs:

- s3:PutAccountPublicAccessBlock
- s3:PutBucketPublicAccessBlock

You can block access to change the Block Public Access settings at the account level or the whole organization, so even if you log in as the root user, you will not be able to change this configuration.

It is also essential to note that the SCP does not restrict the management account.

In Exercise 7.6, you replicate S3 bucket objects using KMS keys to protect your data across regions.

EXERCISE 7.6

Replicate Encrypted S3 Objects Across Regions

In this exercise, you create an S3 bucket and then configure it to replicate objects in different regions, using different encryption keys.

1. Create two different S3 buckets in two different regions.

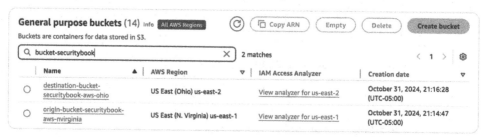

2. Create two different CMKs, one in each region in which you created the buckets (N. Virginia and Ohio, for example).
3. Select the origin bucket.
4. Click Properties.
5. Select Default Encryption.
6. Select the origin KMS key and click Save.

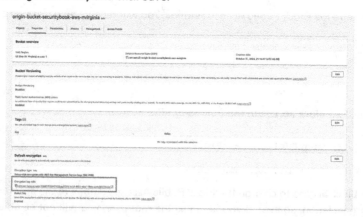

7. In the selected S3 bucket, click Management and then select Replication.

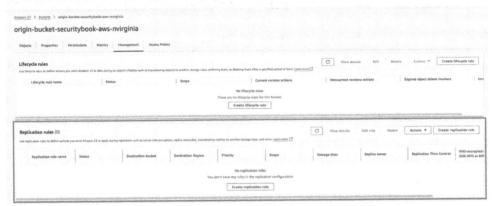

8. Add a rule (remember that you need to enable S3 bucket versioning first).
9. Select the Replicate Objects Encrypted with AWS KMS option.

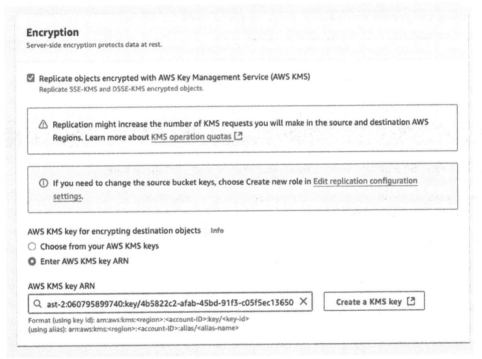

10. Select the bucket to replicate into the destination region and the respective key and click Next.
11. Define a new IAM role for replication (select Create a New Role).

EXERCISE 7.6 *(continued)*

12. Give the rule a name and save the replication rule.

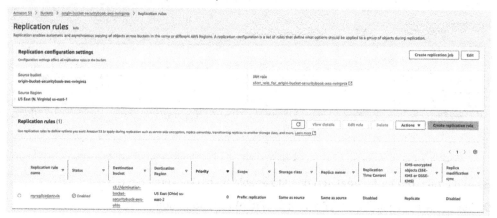

13. Insert a test object into the original bucket and validate the replication.

In Exercise 7.7, you protect data inside an S3 bucket object using a resource policy and VPC endpoints.

EXERCISE 7.7

Protect Your S3 Buckets with a Resource Policy and VPC Endpoints

In this exercise, you create an S3 bucket, and then you use the S3 bucket resource policy to limit access to a specific predefined VPC.

1. Create a new bucket.

2. Create two different VPCs. (If you need more information on how to create a VPC, you can refer to `https://docs.aws.amazon.com/vpc/latest/userguide/vpc-getting-started.html`.)

Protecting Your S3 Buckets   **363**

	Name	▽	VPC ID	▽	State	▽
☐	S3-Denied-VPC		vpc-01530c6d5b8082861		⊘ Available	
☐	S3-Allowed-VPC		vpc-09d15378d7d77081f		⊘ Available	

3. Start two EC2 instances—one in the S3-allowed and other on the S3-denied VPC—so that you can use the AWS CLI to test access to the S3 bucket.

	Name 🖉		Instance ID		Instance state	▽	Instance type	▽
☐	S3 Allowed		i-0735efcb4af644439		⊘ Running ⊕ ⊖		t2.micro	
☐	S3 Denied		i-083073a45d34a66ca		⊘ Running ⊕ ⊖		t2.micro	

4. Create the following policy in your bucket. Change **vpc-id** to your corrected ID and change the S3 ARN to your ARN.

```
{
 "Id": "Policy1569592276562",
 "Version": "2012-10-17",
 "Statement": [
  {
   "Sid": "Stmt1569592272181",
   "Action": "s3:*",
   "Effect": "Deny",
   "Resource": ["arn:aws:s3:::s3-vpc-limited-securitybook-aws",
         "arn:aws:s3:::s3-vpc-limited-securitybook/*"],
   "Condition": {
    "StringNotEquals": {
     "aws:SourceVpc": "vpc-73ad900b"
    }
   },
   "Principal": "*"
  }
 ]
}
```

You can also use the AWS Policy Generator to generate the S3 resource policy.

5. Insert an object inside the bucket and apply the policy.

6. Create a VPC endpoint to the S3 service that is connected to your allowed VPC.

EXERCISE 7.7 (continued)

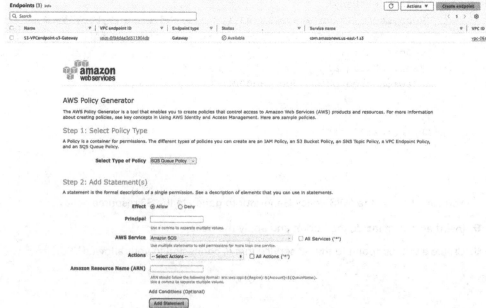

7. You will need to configure an EC2 AWS LINUX instance to run the CLI and execute the proposed tests. You will also need to configure a credential with valid permissions and use the command AWS configure. If you need help with this, see `https://docs.aws.amazon.com/cli/latest/userguide/cli-chap-configure.html#cli-quick-configuration`.

8. Try to access the bucket from the allowed VPCs using the EC2 instance.

```
[cloudshell-user@ip-10-134-55-106 ~]$ aws s3 ls s3://s3-vpc-limited-securitybook-aws
2025-03-22 00:24:17      49243 My image.png
[cloudshell-user@ip-10-134-55-106 ~]$ █
```

As you can see, it was possible to access the bucket using the VPC endpoint and predefined resource policy.

9. Now try to access the bucket using another VPC that is not allowed to access the S3 bucket, using another EC2 in this VPC. The access will be blocked because you can only access the bucket from the allowed VPC. Even if you define the bucket as public, you cannot access the bucket from the Internet, because only the predefined VPC, using the S3 endpoint, can access your bucket. Even if you try from the console now, you cannot access the bucket.

Amazon Macie

In today's data-driven world, protecting sensitive information is not just a regulatory requirement but a business imperative. Amazon Macie plays a crucial role in this context by automating the process of data discovery and classification, which is often labor-intensive and error-prone when done manually. By providing continuous monitoring and alerts, Macie helps organizations stay ahead of potential data security threats and compliance issues.

Amazon Macie is a fully managed data security and privacy service that uses machine learning and pattern matching to discover, monitor, and protect sensitive data in AWS environments. As organizations increasingly store vast amounts of data in the cloud, protecting this information from unauthorized access and potential breaches becomes paramount. Amazon Macie addresses this critical need by providing automated, intelligent data discovery and classification capabilities.

Its key features are as follows:

- **Automated Data Discovery:** Macie continuously scans your Amazon S3 buckets to identify and catalog sensitive data such as personally identifiable information (PII), financial data, and intellectual property.

- **Machine Learning–Powered Classification:** Leveraging advanced machine learning algorithms, Macie can accurately classify data types and sensitivity levels, even for custom data formats specific to your organization.

- **Comprehensive Data Visibility:** Macie provides detailed insights into your data landscape, helping you understand where sensitive information resides and how it's being accessed and used.
- **Continuous Monitoring and Alerts:** The service continuously monitors your data for security risks and policy violations, sending alerts when potential issues are detected.
- **Integration with AWS Services:** Macie seamlessly integrates with other AWS services like CloudTrail, GuardDuty, and Security Hub for a holistic security approach.

Once you enable the service, you see a summary view of three components (see Figure 7.51):

- The **Automated Discovery panel** displays a snapshot of aggregated sensitivity statistics for your Amazon S3 data in the current AWS region (if automated sensitive data discovery is enabled).
- The **Data Security panel** shows the security posture of your buckets, showing buckets with public access, encryption settings, and if buckets are shared.
- The **Coverage Issues panel** displays a snapshot of aggregated coverage statistics for automated sensitive data discovery. The statistics indicate whether certain types of issues prevented Macie from analyzing objects in your Amazon S3 general purpose buckets. The data can help you identify gaps in coverage of your buckets in the current AWS Region.

The Macie service administrator for an organization can view the dashboard that aggregates data for all your member accounts. To filter the dashboard and display data for only a particular account, enter the account ID in the Account box.

FIGURE 7.51 Amazon Macie summary.

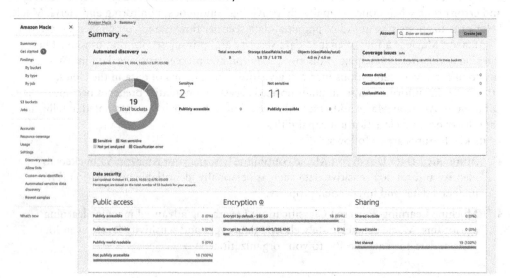

Macie supports two categories of sensitive data types:

- Fully managed sensitive data types that include common PII and other sensitive data types as defined by data privacy regulations, such as GDPR, PCI DSS, and HIPAA
- Custom-defined data types using regular expressions to discover proprietary or unique sensitive data

Because it is a managed service, Amazon Macie continually monitors the activities of users and resources accessing data in S3 buckets, identifying possible data copying or data movement, and generating alerts of possible anomalies on a centralized dashboard. The Amazon Macie service can be enabled with few clicks:

1. In the AWS Console, select the Amazon Macie service.
2. Click the Get Started button.
3. Click the Enable Macie button.
4. When the service is enabled, click S3 Buckets, where you can have a view of current bucket (you can change the view to see each bucket or consolidated by account).

At this point, the service is enabled, and you can have a view of the general status of the account. Figure 7.52 shows the Bucket view, and in Figure 7.53, you can see the legend to understand the findings.

Now, you can create sensitive data discovery jobs to analyze objects in S3 buckets and report occurrences of sensitive data in those objects. When you create a discovery job, you specify which S3 buckets stored objects that you want the job to analyze, and you can choose additional settings to refine the scope of the analysis. You also specify how often to run the job (once or periodically).

FIGURE 7.52 Amazon Macie bucket view.

FIGURE 7.53 Amazon Macie findings legend.

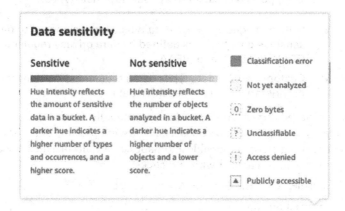

FIGURE 7.54 Amazon Macie job creation.

5. Click Create a Job.
6. Review the S3 buckets (select one bucket to review) and click Next, as shown in Figure 7.54.
7. For this test, schedule a one-time job and click Next.
8. Leave the recommended option and click Next.
9. There are no custom identifiers, so click Next.
10. The is no Allow list, so click Next.
11. Define a name and description and click Next.

12. The final (optional) step is to click Submit, but doing so may incur costs. The goal here is only to validate the console options, which you can do without clicking Submit. See Figure 7.55.

After these steps, Macie starts to monitor the data movements in the S3 bucket and uses bucket events to identify bad behaviors to generate alerts.

You can enable Automated Discovery in the Settings section (see Figure 7.56). If you enable automated sensitive data discovery, Macie continually evaluates the S3 bucket inventory in the current AWS region, using sampling techniques to identify and select representative objects from your buckets. Macie retrieves and analyzes the selected objects, inspecting them for sensitive data.

You can view a snapshot of aggregated sensitivity statistics for your Amazon S3 data in the current AWS region (in the Summary section). The statistics capture the status and results of the automated sensitive data discovery activities that Macie has performed so far. In these statistics, you will see the following levels:

- **Sensitive (red):** The number of buckets with a score ranges of 51 through 100.
- **Not sensitive (blue):** The number of buckets with a score of 1 through 49.
- **Not yet analyzed (light gray):** The number of buckets with a score of 50.
- **Classification error (dark gray):** The number of buckets with a score of −1.

Publicly accessible statistics report the number of buckets that the general public is allowed to access. To calculate these values, Macie analyzes account- and bucket-level settings for each S3 bucket.

FIGURE 7.55 Amazon Macie job creation: Final.

FIGURE 7.56 Automated sensitive data discovery.

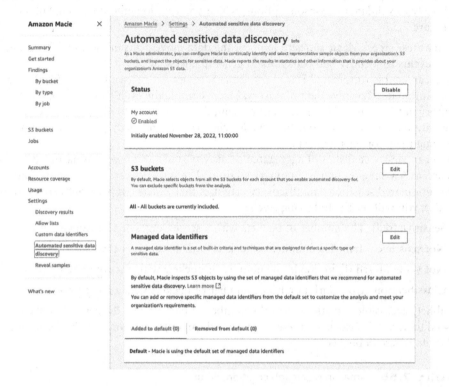

 Once the service for inventory and data movement monitoring in S3 buckets is enabled, Amazon Macie executes a scan to identify and classify the data types within the selected buckets. It is essential to evaluate the data volume present inside the buckets, and the cost of using the service, before triggering an extensive data analysis, especially when the evaluation is related to the use of a large volume in data lakes and S3 buckets.

Protecting Data on the Move in AWS

Data in transit refers to information that is being transferred over a network, whether it's within an organization's internal network or across the public Internet. As part of data protection, it's important to understand the solutions that AWS offers and also be able to design and implement controls that provide protection to data in transit, as a crucial way to maintain the confidentiality and integrity of sensitive information as it moves between different systems or services.

Before we start, let's review a couple of topics that are important regarding data protection:

- **Encryption:** Converting data into a coded form that can only be decrypted by authorized parties. This prevents unauthorized access to the data if it's intercepted during transmission.

- **Authentication:** Verifying the identity of communicating parties to ensure that data is being sent to and received from legitimate sources. This is typically achieved through digital certificates and cryptographic protocols.

- **Integrity checking:** Ensuring that data hasn't been tampered with during transmission, typically through the use of cryptographic hash functions or digital signatures. This protects against man-in-the-middle attacks and data corruption.

- **Non-repudiation:** Providing proof of the integrity and origin of data, making it difficult for the sender to deny having sent the message. This is often accomplished through digital signatures and secure logging mechanisms.

- **Perfect forward secrecy:** Ensuring that past communications cannot be decrypted if long-term secrets are compromised in the future. This is achieved through ephemeral key exchange methods.

- **Traffic analysis protection:** Preventing attackers from inferring information based on traffic patterns, even if they can't decrypt the data itself. This may involve techniques like padding or mixing real traffic with decoy data.

AWS offers a comprehensive suite of solutions to help customers protect their data in transit, shown in in Table 7.3.

TABLE 7.3 AWS Services That Support Protection of Data in Transit

AWS Service	Key Features
AWS VPN creates encrypted tunnels between your network and your Amazon VPCs or AWS Transit Gateway, providing secure remote access and site-to-site connectivity.	• Site-to-site VPN for connecting on-premises networks to AWS • Client VPN for secure remote access to AWS and on-premises resources • Accelerated site-to-site VPN using AWS Global Accelerator for improved performance • Support for multiple VPN connection types, including policy-based and route-based • Integration with AWS Direct Connect for backup connectivity • Automatic failover capabilities for high availability • Support for custom encryption algorithms and key lengths

(Continued)

372 Chapter 7 ▪ Data Protection

TABLE 7.3 (Continued)

AWS Service	Key Features
AWS Transit Gateway acts as a central hub to route traffic between VPCs, AWS accounts, and on-premises networks, simplifying network architecture and enhancing security.	• Simplified network architecture with fewer peering connections required • Enhanced security with centralized control and policy enforcement • Support for multicast routing across connected networks • Integration with AWS Direct Connect and VPN for hybrid cloud connectivity • Cross-region peering for global network architectures • Centralized network address translation (NAT) capabilities • Support for equal-cost multipath (ECMP) routing for improved performance and redundancy
Amazon Virtual Private Cloud (VPC) lets you provision a logically isolated section of the AWS Cloud, providing a secure foundation for your network architecture.	• Network access control lists (NACLs) for stateless packet filtering at the subnet level • Security groups for stateful traffic filtering at the instance level • VPC Flow Logs for detailed network traffic monitoring and analysis • VPC endpoints for private access to AWS services without traversing the public Internet • VPC peering for connecting VPCs within and across AWS accounts • IPv6 support for enhanced addressing and security capabilities • Traffic mirroring for in-depth packet inspection and threat detection
AWS Direct Connect establishes a dedicated network connection from your premises to AWS, offering enhanced security and performance for hybrid cloud architectures.	• Increased bandwidth throughput, with options up to 100 Gbps • Consistent network performance with reduced latency and jitter • Reduced network costs for large volume data transfers • Support for AWS Direct Connect SiteLink for direct communication between Direct Connect locations • Ability to establish private connectivity to multiple VPCs across different regions • Support for Link Aggregation Groups (LAG) to combine multiple connections for increased bandwidth and redundancy • Integration with AWS Transit Gateway for simplified network architectures

AWS Service	Key Features
AWS PrivateLink provides private connectivity between VPCs, AWS services, and on-premises applications, reducing exposure to the public Internet.	• Enhanced security by keeping network traffic within the AWS network • Simplified network architecture by eliminating the need for Internet gateways, NAT devices, or public IP addresses • Improved performance with reduced latency and increased bandwidth • Support for inter-region connectivity, allowing secure communication between resources in different AWS regions • Integration with AWS Direct Connect for secure hybrid cloud architectures • Ability to share services across multiple AWS accounts and VPCs

 You can enforce HTTPS communication to access S3 information using a bucket policy condition "aws:SecureTransport": "false."

```
{
    "Version": "2012-10-17",
    "Statement": [{
        "Sid": "RestrictToTLSRequestsOnly",
        "Action": "s3:*",
        "Effect": "Deny",
        "Resource": [
            "arn:aws:s3:::amzn-s3-demo-bucket",
            "arn:aws:s3:::amzn-s3-demo-bucket/*"
        ],
        "Condition": {
            "Bool": {
                "aws:SecureTransport": "false"
            }
        },
        "Principal": "*"
    }]
}
```

Check the following link to review examples of policies in S3: https://docs.aws.amazon.com/es_es/AmazonS3/latest/userguide/example-bucket-policies.html.

Data Protection Troubleshooting Scenarios

AWS KMS is a managed service that facilitates the creation and control of the keys used to encrypt your data. The customer-managed keys that you create in AWS KMS are protected by HSMs. This section focuses on troubleshooting common issues in AWS KMS and provides guidance on correctly handling policy permissions. Understanding these concepts is essential for maintaining a secure and efficient key management system in your AWS environment.

AWS KMS is integrated with AWS services that enable the encryption of your data. AWS KMS is also integrated with AWS CloudTrail to provide logging of encryption key usage and to help meet your audit, regulatory, and compliance requirements.

You can use the encryption keys created in different AWS accounts. For that, you need to perform cross-account access configuration for the KMS.

When configuring access to KMS through other accounts, you have to configure two types of policies: the key policy and the IAM policy. The key policy is a resource-based policy attached to the CMK, and it defines controls for the management and use of the key. The IAM policy is responsible for defining which users, groups, and roles can perform operations, such as kms:Encrypt or kms:Decrypt.

It is essential to know the most common problems when using AWS KMS and CMK keys. Table 7.4 provides a general view of some common issues that could happen using AWS KMS.

Monitoring and logging are critical components in the troubleshooting process for any AWS service, including KMS. These practices provide invaluable insights into system behavior, performance, and security events. By implementing comprehensive monitoring through services like Amazon CloudWatch and enabling detailed logging with AWS CloudTrail, administrators gain visibility into their KMS operations.

This visibility allows for quick detection of anomalies, performance issues, or security breaches. Proper monitoring and logging facilitate proactive management by allowing the setup of alerts for specific events or thresholds. This proactive approach can significantly reduce downtime and improve overall system reliability.

In the context of KMS, monitoring key usage patterns and logging access attempts are particularly crucial for maintaining the security and integrity of cryptographic operations. Ultimately, robust monitoring and logging practices are not just tools for troubleshooting; they are essential for maintaining a secure, efficient, and compliant AWS environment. Table 7.5 compares two AWS solutions to monitor KMS keys.

Data Protection Troubleshooting Scenarios   375

TABLE 7.4   Common Issues in AWS KMS

Common Issue	Problem	Solution
Key State Issues: One of the most frequent issues with KMS is related to key states. AWS KMS keys can be in various states, including enabled, disabled, pending deletion, and deleted.	Unable to use a KMS key for encryption or decryption operations	• Check the key state using the AWS Management Console or AWS CLI: `> aws kms describe-key --key-id <key-id>` • If the key is disabled, enable it: `> aws kms enable-key --key-id <key-id>` • If the key is pending deletion, cancel the deletion process: `> aws kms cancel-key-deletion --key-id <key-id>`
Permissions and Access Issues: Incorrect permissions can prevent users or services from using KMS keys.	Access Denied errors when attempting to use a KMS key	• Review the key policy and ensure the necessary permissions are granted. • Check IAM policies for the user or role attempting to access the key. • Verify that the key policy allows the AWS account to use the key, and IAM policies to control access to the key.
Encryption Context: Mismatch: Encryption context is an additional way to authenticate data, used to add an extra layer of security to encryption operations.	Decryption fails due to encryption context mismatch	• Ensure that the same encryption context used for encryption is provided during decryption. • Review your application code to verify that encryption context is being correctly handled.

TABLE 7.5   Monitoring and Logging for KMS

AWS Solution	Description	Recommendation for Troubleshooting
CloudTrail Logs	AWS CloudTrail logs all KMS API calls, which can be invaluable for troubleshooting.	• Enable CloudTrail logging for your account, if not already done. • Configure CloudTrail to log KMS events to a dedicated S3 bucket. • Use Amazon Athena or other log analysis tools to query and analyze CloudTrail logs.
CloudWatch Metrics	AWS KMS publishes metrics to Amazon CloudWatch, which can help identify issues proactively.	• Monitor KMS-specific metrics such as `SecondsUntilKeyDeletion` and `PendingDeletionWindowInDays`. • Set up CloudWatch Alarms for critical KMS metrics to receive notifications of potential issues.

Summary

The implementation of encryption is a critical factor in the success of any data protection strategy. Although it does not solve every challenge related to secure data access, data encryption is an important layer for increasing the level of data protection, resilience, and privacy.

Using native AWS Cloud data protection solutions enables you to solve many end-to-end security implementation difficulties that are usually observed in traditional environments, such as the ability to deploy cryptographic mechanisms without impacting environment performance, securely protecting and rotating keys automatically, transparently auditing key usage, and scaling the environment without compromising security.

Using the AWS KMS service also allows you to implement encryption natively within various AWS services, such as RDS databases, EBS volumes, and S3 storage. In such integrations, the customer can use their own keys or keys automatically generated by AWS KMS service.

Key access can be granularly controlled, allowing you to define who can create and delete keys or who can access and use the keys to encrypt or decrypt data. Use the Principle of Least Privilege to grant only the permissions necessary for users or services to perform their tasks, and also use condition keys in policies to restrict key usage based on specific criteria (e.g., encryption context, VPC endpoint).

It is also possible to leverage AWS CloudHSM, thus implementing dedicated cryptographic hardware to protect your keys, meeting the highest security standards, such as FIPS140-2 Level 3.

A multi-AZ or even multiregional architecture can be used to create a highly scalable, on-demand, pay-as-you-go model.

You can use ACM for SSL/TLS digital certificate generation to secure communication of your applications by protecting data in transit in your AWS environment. You can also use it to generate and manage internal digital certificates for your traditional on-premises environments.

By leveraging AWS Secrets Manager and AWS Systems Manager Parameter Store effectively, organizations can implement a comprehensive strategy for managing secrets and configuration data. Secrets Manager's automatic rotation and deep integration with database services make it ideal for high-value secrets, while Parameter Store's simplicity and cost-effectiveness make it suitable for application configuration and less sensitive data. Understanding the strengths of each service allows you to create a robust and secure environment for your AWS resources.

Amazon Macie allows you to inventory data in S3 buckets, classifying and identifying critical and sensitive data, and using AI/ML capabilities to identify potential suspicious actions in your environment.

Finally, effective troubleshooting of AWS KMS and proper handling of policy permissions are essential skills for AWS security professionals. By understanding common issues, implementing best practices, and avoiding typical pitfalls, you can ensure a secure and efficient KMS in your AWS environment. Remember to regularly review and update your policies, monitor KMS activities, and stay informed about new AWS KMS features and best practices. It's important to implement proper error handling in your applications to catch and log KMS-related errors. Also, regularly review and audit KMS key usage and permissions and implement monitoring and logging capabilities using AWS Services like AWS CloudTrail and CloudWatch metrics to effectively troubleshoot KMS issues.

Exam Essentials

Understand encryption fundamentals. Symmetric encryption uses a single key for both encryption and decryption. AWS supports AES (128, 192, and 256-bit keys), which is used extensively across services like S3, EBS, and RDS. Asymmetric encryption uses public and private key pairs where data encrypted with one key can only be decrypted with the other. AWS supports RSA and ECC algorithms for services like CloudFront, Certificate Manager, and KMS. Hashing involves one-way functions that generate fixed-length outputs from arbitrary inputs. AWS supports SHA-256 and SHA-512 for integrity verification. Protecting data while it moves across networks is encryption in transit, and protection while stored on disks or in databases is encryption at rest.

Know AWS Key Management Service (KMS) operations. KMS stores customer-managed keys (CMKs) in highly available, durable hardware security modules (HSMs) that never leave AWS unencrypted. Three types of data keys are CMKs, AWS-managed keys, and AWS-owned keys. Data keys are generated by KMS but used outside KMS for envelope encryption of large data volumes. Key lifecycle management involves creating, enabling, disabling, rotating, and scheduling deletion of keys with appropriate waiting periods (7–30 days). Key material options include AWS-generated key material, imported key material, and custom key stores.

Comprehend the structure and components of KMS access control profiles. AWS Key Management Service (KMS) employs a comprehensive access control system centered on key policies. When creating a new Customer Master Key (CMK), KMS automatically generates a default key policy that grants full administrative access to the AWS account root user, ensuring the key remains manageable. KMS key policies follow the standard AWS policy structure with elements including principal (who can access), action (what operations they can perform), resource (which keys are affected), and condition (constraints on permissions). Access control for KMS separates permissions into two primary categories: administrative actions that govern key lifecycle operations such as `kms:CreateKey`, `kms:ScheduleKeyDeletion`, and `kms:EnableKey`; and usage actions that control cryptographic operations including `kms:Encrypt`, `kms:Decrypt`, and `kms:GenerateDataKey`. Organizations can enhance security and reduce data exposure by implementing VPC endpoints for KMS, ensuring that all API calls to KMS remain within the AWS network rather than traversing the public Internet, while still maintaining granular access control

Chapter 7 ▪ Data Protection

through endpoint policies that can restrict specific operations or keys accessible through the endpoint.

Know how to create and use a KMS security policy. The structure of KMS key policies is hierarchical. The outer JSON container includes version and statement elements. Individual statement objects have unique IDs for clarity and management. Principal elements specify AWS accounts, IAM users, roles, or services. Effect declarations (allow or deny) determine access behavior. The policy statement components for access control include principal specification, which defines exactly who can access keys—from specific IAM roles to AWS service principals; action elements, which control which specific KMS API operations can be performed; resource identifiers, which target specific keys using their ARNs; and condition blocks, which implement context-based access rules.

Know how to use KMS with other AWS-native services. AWS KMS integrates seamlessly with numerous AWS services to provide robust encryption capabilities. When working with Amazon S3, KMS enables server-side encryption for both buckets and individual objects using CMKs, allowing granular encryption control over your stored data. For Amazon EBS, KMS provides encryption for volumes and snapshots, ensuring that data remains protected even when volumes are backed up or replicated. Amazon RDS leverages KMS to encrypt database instances and their underlying storage, including automated backups and read replicas, with minimal performance impact. DynamoDB tables can be encrypted with KMS keys, protecting table data, local secondary indexes, and global secondary indexes while maintaining millisecond performance. AWS Lambda functions benefit from KMS through environment variable encryption, securing sensitive configuration information. For managing sensitive credentials, both Secrets Manager and Systems Manager Parameter Store use KMS to encrypt information (secrets and parameters) with KMS keys. CloudTrail integrates with KMS to encrypt log files, ensuring that audit records remain tamper-evident. These integrations demonstrate how KMS provides consistent encryption capabilities across the AWS ecosystem while allowing centralized key management.

Understand the four S3 encryption models. Amazon S3 provides multiple encryption models to protect data at rest. Server-side encryption with Amazon S3–managed keys (SSE-S3) is the most straightforward option, where AWS handles both the encryption process and key management using AES-256 encryption with automatically rotated keys. Server-side encryption with KMS-managed keys (SSE-KMS) leverages AWS KMS, offering enhanced security through separate permissions for key usage, detailed audit trails, and customer-controlled key rotation policies. Dual-layer server-side encryption with KMS keys (DSSE-KMS) provides additional protection by performing two separate encryption operations, creating two layers of encryption for each object to mitigate against vulnerabilities in a single encryption algorithm. Server-side encryption with customer-provided keys (SSE-C) allows S3 to perform the encryption using keys that customers provide with each request, giving organizations complete control over their encryption keys while still offloading the computational complexity to AWS. For the highest level of control, client-side encryption enables customers to encrypt data before uploading it to S3, ensuring the data is never exposed in unencrypted form during transit or while stored in the cloud, using either KMS-managed keys or client-side master keys managed within the customer's infrastructure.

Understand CloudHSM's role in secure key management. AWS CloudHSM provides FIPS 140-2 Level 3 validated hardware security modules that offer the highest level of key protection within the AWS ecosystem. CloudHSM operates as a single-tenant service where each HSM instance is physically isolated hardware dedicated to a single customer, unlike shared services like KMS. Customers maintain exclusive control and ownership of their encryption keys—AWS has no ability to access or recover these keys. CloudHSM is designed for high availability and resilience through cluster architecture that allows deployment across multiple AZs with automatic synchronization of keys and policies. For disaster recovery scenarios, CloudHSM supports cross-region architectures, though clusters themselves are region-specific and require proper planning for global deployments. CloudHSM integrates with AWS KMS through custom key stores, enabling organizations to combine KMS's ease of use with CloudHSM's enhanced security and compliance controls. Common use cases include satisfying strict regulatory compliance standards, meeting contractual obligations requiring hardware-based key management, and serving organizations with stringent key ownership requirements that necessitate exclusive control over cryptographic operations.

Master AWS Certificate Manager (ACM) capabilities and integrations. AWS Certificate Manager simplifies SSL/TLS certificate management by providing automated provisioning, renewal, and deployment capabilities for both public and private certificates. ACM seamlessly integrates with numerous AWS services, including Elastic Load Balancing, CloudFront, API Gateway, AWS Nitro Enclaves, Amazon Cognito, and AWS Amplify for automatic certificate deployment, eliminating manual certificate installation. For public certificates, ACM supports two validation methods: DNS validation (recommended for automation and auto-renewal) and email validation (requiring manual action for renewals). ACM Private Certificate Authority enables organizations to establish and manage private certificate hierarchies for internal applications, microservices, and IoT devices with full control over the certificate authority. When organizations have existing certificates from external providers, ACM supports importing third-party certificates for use with integrated AWS services, though these imported certificates require manual renewal. For hybrid architectures, organizations can deploy private certificates to on-premises resources through ACM Private CA while managing cloud resources through standard ACM integrations. ACM public certificates are automatically logged to Certificate Transparency logs (CT logs) as required by browsers, but customers can opt out of transparency logging when issuing private certificates through ACM Private CA to maintain confidentiality of internal domains and infrastructure.

Understand how Macie can protect your data. Amazon Macie is a fully managed data security service that uses machine learning and pattern matching to discover, monitor, and protect sensitive data stored in Amazon S3. Macie automatically identifies and categorizes sensitive information, including personally identifiable information (PII), protected health information (PHI), financial data, and credentials through managed data identifiers covering over 100 unique data types. Organizations can also create custom data identifiers using regex patterns, keywords, and proximity rules to detect company-specific sensitive data like employee IDs or internal project codes. Macie integrates with AWS CloudTrail to monitor access patterns and API calls, helping detect suspicious activities such as unusual data access or exfiltration attempts. When Macie discovers sensitive data or detects a potential security issue, it generates detailed findings that can be automatically routed to AWS Security Hub for centralized visibility and to Amazon EventBridge for triggering automated workflows. Organizations can implement automated remediation processes using EventBridge rules to invoke Lambda functions or Step Functions workflows that quarantine exposed data, modify bucket policies, or notify security teams. For cost efficiency when deploying Macie across large S3 estates, organizations can implement sampling techniques, focus on high-risk buckets, use account-level suppression rules to exclude certain data patterns, and leverage multi-account management through AWS Organizations to optimize monitoring coverage while controlling costs.

Review Questions

1. Which of the following methods can be used to encrypt data in S3 buckets? (Choose three.)
    - **A.** ACM using symmetric keys
    - **B.** SSE-S3
    - **C.** SSE-KMS
    - **D.** SSE-C

2. A company is designing a multiregion application that uses Amazon RDS for PostgreSQL. Their security team requires that all database content be encrypted with keys that are automatically rotated every year without manual intervention. They also want detailed audit logs of all encryption and decryption operations for compliance purposes. Which approach should they implement?
    - **A.** Use Amazon RDS encryption with AWS KMS CMKs and enable automatic key rotation.
    - **B.** Use Amazon RDS encryption with AWS-owned keys and manually rotate them annually.
    - **C.** Create a custom encryption solution using AWS CloudHSM with application-level encryption.
    - **D.** Use Amazon RDS encryption with default AWS-managed keys and enable CloudTrail.

3. You are configuring a CMK using the KMS service console. Which permissions should you define and configure in the JSON security policy? (Choose three.)
    - **A.** The IAM groups that can read the key
    - **B.** IAM users that can be the CMK administrators
    - **C.** IAM roles that can be the CMK administrators
    - **D.** The application pool that will access the CMK
    - **E.** IAM roles that can use the CMK
    - **F.** The asymmetric algorithms that can be used
    - **G.** The Cognito pool that will be used to authenticate the user to read the keys

4. What happens when you delete a CMK using KMS?
    - **A.** The key is deleted immediately.
    - **B.** AWS KMS enforces a 60-day waiting period before you can delete a CMK.
    - **C.** AWS KMS enforces a waiting period minimum of 7 days up to a maximum of 30 days before you can delete a CMK.
    - **D.** It is impossible to delete a CMK.

382 Chapter 7 • Data Protection

5. Which AWS service should you use to implement a ubiquitous encryption strategy in your AWS environment?

   A. Amazon Macie

   B. Amazon Inspector

   C. ACM

   D. AWS KMS

   E. CloudHSM

6. When should you consider using CloudHSM? (Choose two.)

   A. To meet regulatory needs, such as FIPS 140-2 Level 3 standards

   B. To protect EC2 instances

   C. For SSL offloading

   D. All the times that you need to use KMS

7. How does key rotation work when you are using a CMK?

   A. AWS KMS rotates automatically every 30 days.

   B. AWS KMS cannot rotate the key, so the user must rotate it manually.

   C. AWS KMS rotates the CMK every 365 days after the user enables automatic key rotation.

   D. There is no key rotation functionality, and only ACM can rotate keys automatically.

8. A company hosts a web application on Amazon EC2 instances behind an Application Load Balancer (ALB). They need to implement TLS encryption for their customer-facing website with the following requirements:

   1. Automatic certificate renewal without service interruption

   2. Support for wildcard certificates

   3. Certificate usage across multiple AWS regions

   4. Minimum operational overhead

   Which solution best meets these requirements?

   A. Request certificates from a third-party CA and manually install them on each EC2 instance.

   B. Use AWS Certificate Manager (ACM) to provision public certificates and associate them with the ALB.

   C. Create a private CA using ACM Private CA and issue certificates for the ALB.

   D. Generate self-signed certificates on EC2 instances and configure the ALB to use them.

9. A company maintains sensitive customer information in Amazon S3 buckets across multiple AWS accounts within their organization. They need a scalable solution that will automatically discover and protect personally identifiable information (PII) in these buckets. The solution should generate alerts if sensitive data is found in buckets with public access settings enabled. Which AWS service should they implement?

   A. AWS Key Management Service

   B. Amazon Inspector

   C. Amazon Macie

   D. AWS Shield Advanced

10. A financial services company needs to comply with strict regulatory requirements for their encryption key management. They require exclusive control of their encryption keys with no possibility of AWS having access to the key material. They also need FIPS 140-2 Level 3 compliance and the ability to perform operations like key generation and cryptographic operations. Which solution should they implement?

   A. AWS KMS with imported key material

   B. AWS CloudHSM

   C. AWS KMS with AWS-managed keys

   D. Server-Side Encryption with S3-managed encryption keys (SSE-S3)

Chapter 8

Threat Detection and Incident Response

THE AWS CERTIFIED SECURITY SPECIALTY
EXAM OBJECTIVES THAT LEVERAGE
CONCEPTS EXPLAINED IN THIS CHAPTER
INCLUDE THE FOLLOWING:

✔ **Domain 1: Threat Detection and Incident Response**
- 1.1. Design and implement an incident response plan.
- 1.2. Detect security threats and anomalies by using AWS services.
- 1.3. Respond to compromised resources and workloads.

Introduction

In this chapter, you learn about how to detect different types of threats in AWS and how to respond. You learn about incident response best practices and how to identify the resources you will need in your incident response plan.

As you learned in Chapter 1, "Security Fundamentals," *incidents* are defined as a violation (or a threat of violation) of security policies, acceptable usage policies, or standard security practices. They can be as harmful as the compromise of an access key that is subsequently used to create resources for cryptomining or as mundane as an incorrect configuration in a firewall rule that leaves a resource exposed. In either case, they need to be detected as soon as possible and demand action from responsible personnel—in the first example, to eradicate the adversary's footprint and return to normal operations, and in the latter, to reconfigure the rule to decrease the risk to an acceptable level by preventing unauthorized access to a specific resource.

There are multiple threat detection services from AWS and from third parties that can assist you in detecting vulnerabilities, misconfigurations, anomalies, or malicious activity.

Incident response can be *manual* or *automated*. Using the firewall misconfiguration example, you may receive a notification when a firewall rule is changed to an undesired setting (such as allowing SSH or RDP from anywhere) and manually decide if the rule change needs to be reverted. Or in the context of the AWS Cloud, you can establish an AWS Config rule that receives the change notification, automatically compares it with the desired state, and takes immediate action to correct the misstep. The set of actions created to address incidents composes an incident handling program, which is also known as an *incident response plan*.

In this chapter, you learn best practices that will help you define and implement security controls to detect threats, and to develop your own incident response plan for workloads in the AWS Cloud.

Threat Detection

Threat detection is a general security concept that goes beyond the technology used to implement it. Before going deeper into the available AWS services, it is important for the security practitioner to understand different categories of detection and response.

Identifying Risks vs. Detecting Active Threats

There are multiple services in AWS that support detection of threats. Some controls analyze resources and policies to identify risks to prevent future active security incidents. For example, Amazon Inspector can identify security vulnerabilities in instances, containers, and AWS Lambda functions, and AWS IAM Access Analyzer can identify external accesses or unused permissions before an adversary actually tries to use those resources.

Other services, like Amazon GuardDuty, analyze activity to detect potentially malicious actions taken by an adversary, such as an EC2 Instance opening a connection to a known command and control IP server. Security Information and Event Management (SIEM) solutions also analyze events and flows, correlating them into each order using rules to detect malicious activity (i.e., offenses or alerts) and investigating them.

The Security Standards in AWS Security Hub can identify a lack of alignment to security best practices in cloud workload configurations (what Gartner calls *Cloud Security Posture Manager*) and can also centralize security findings from multiple security services, including Amazon GuardDuty, Amazon Inspector, and many more. This provides a single pane of glass or dashboard view of your risks and malicious activity happening in real time.

As discussed in Chapter 5, "Security Logging and Monitoring," a *security event* is a record of an activity that may not be of interest by itself to the security team, such as a login success or a single firewall deny. A *security finding* is a set of events or discoveries that, by themselves, are relevant for a security analyst to review, such as a port scanning or a brute-force attack. Sometimes, a security finding may be triggered by a single event, such as a connection to a command and control server or the discovery of a vulnerability.

A key aspect of threat detection is to remember that using any detective controls without taking action to remediate the issue will not contain the threat and will not mitigate risks. Someone (manual) or something (automatic) needs to take action.

On the exam, pay attention to which type of control the question is asking you about. If the question is asking you to *detect*, you can use a detective control, but if they ask you to *protect*, pure detective controls will not achieve the desired outcome, and you can discard that option.

Automated vs. Custom Threat Detection

You can leverage native services such as Amazon GuardDuty to detect common threats, and you can implement your own threat detection capabilities, creating rules and alerts on solutions such as SIEM. You can also build your own AWS Lambda functions to inspect certain events and alert if a specific combination of events occurs. For example, Amazon EventBridge rules can trigger a notification upon root login, or billing alarms on your compute resources can detect potential misuse.

All organizations require threat detection, but not all organizations have the resources to implement SIEM solutions. They can be costly to purchase, maintain, and scale, and they require a team of security specialists to curate the rules to detect the threats defined by the use cases in an organization (i.e., which set of actions you want to know about if they happen in your environment).

People trained with SIEM solutions tend to think that the SIEM is the place to resolve every requirement with a custom rule. People with a development background tend to think that everything can be resolved with an AWS Lambda function. Beware that on the exam (and as well in your workplace), you will often need to choose the option that is simpler and more efficient. If you can comply with your requirement in minutes by using a managed service such as Amazon GuardDuty, which provides multiple additional benefits, a custom approach is likely not the best answer. Always remember to consider the total cost of ownership (TCO), particularly the maintenance cost of custom rules and code, which has the greatest impact on the most constrained resource in most organizations: the humans on the security team.

If your organization needs to quickly implement a SIEM solution with limited budget, evaluate using the AWS Sample solution called "SIEM on Amazon OpenSearch Service" at `https://github.com/aws-samples/siem-on-amazon-opensearch-service`. The capabilities of the next-gen SIEM solutions on the market are more advanced, but this solution achieves great cost efficiency and speed for the deployment and integration with AWS services.

Threat Detection Services

AWS offers a series of services to help you with threat detection, using complementary approaches like a set of security rules, machine learning for anomaly detection, and consolidation of different sources to produce a more complete assessment of the environment. In this section, you learn about Amazon GuardDuty, AWS Security Hub, AWS Trusted Advisor, and Amazon Detective.

Amazon GuardDuty

Amazon GuardDuty analyzes logs to produce observable records of suspicious activities, which are known as security findings. Its basic service analyzes logs from Amazon VPC Flow Logs, AWS CloudTrail, and DNS queries (specifically, the queries solved by AWS VPC DNS resolvers in the account). Nonetheless, Amazon GuardDuty does not require you to enable VPC Flow Logs, create a trail in AWS CloudTrail, or even configure an Amazon Route

53 zone. Instead, Amazon GuardDuty automatically gathers information from these services, without affecting the performance of your applications or your costs for these services.

Amazon GuardDuty's analysis is based on rules maintained by the service team, leveraging threat intelligence information (such as IP addresses and domain-based lists) as well as machine learning models. You can create your own lists of trusted IPs to avoid false positives from your penetration testing activities and your own list of known malicious IPs (i.e., threat lists). These lists can consist of publicly routable network IPs. Activity from IP addresses on a trusted IP list will not generate any findings. On the other hand, Amazon GuardDuty generates findings from every activity involving IP addresses on threat lists. Figure 8.1 shows a high-level representation of how Amazon GuardDuty works.

The basic entity in Amazon GuardDuty is called a *detector*. The detector consumes information and generates findings within a specific AWS account and region. An Amazon GuardDuty finding contains several attributes, such as ID, time of the finding, severity, finding type, affected resources, and action details. The naming convention adopted for finding types is important, since it contains valuable information for security teams. The example in Figure 8.2 illustrates the naming convention.

As you can see in the name of this finding, the threat purpose (i.e., the objective of the attack; in this example, it signals a Trojan) appears first. Then, the EC2 string represents the resource type affected by the suspicious activity. Next is the threat family name (DGADomainRequest; it informs that the instance is querying algorithmically generated DNS domains) and variant (not always present; in this case, the known variant "C"). Finally, the artifact indicates the type of resource owned by the attacker (a DNS server in this example).

Events corresponding to the same finding type and affecting the same resource are considered recurrent occurrences. Each finding will keep a count of its number of recurrent occurrences.

FIGURE 8.1 How Amazon GuardDuty works.

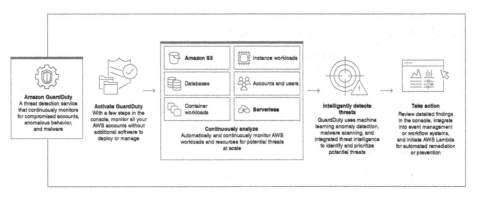

FIGURE 8.2 Sample finding details in Amazon GuardDuty.

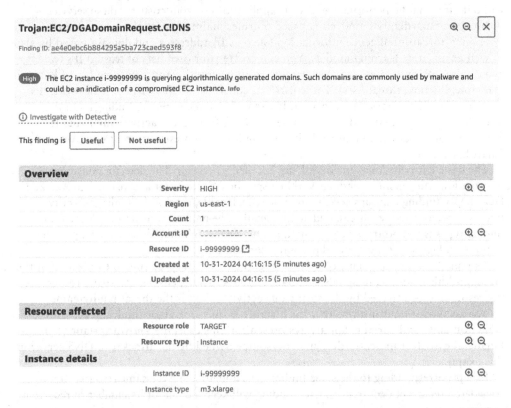

Once a detector is enabled, Amazon GuardDuty starts reporting findings. You can access the list of findings at any time through the management console or via the GetFindings API. You can also see findings-related statistics by calling the GetFindingsStatistics API.

Integration with AWS Organizations

Amazon GuardDuty has native integration with AWS Organizations. This supports delegated administration, a feature that allows you to access the organization's management account once and delegate the administration of Amazon GuardDuty to the Security Account, and then centrally enable the service in multiple accounts and centrally control which of the additional security features are enabled (protection plans).

Amazon GuardDuty's Protection Plans

Amazon GuardDuty offers a series of additional features called *protection plans* that you can enable individually to provide additional visibility of threats in your environment. You can monitor the cost for each feature in the navigation pane by selecting Usage.

The available protection plans are as follows:

- **GuardDuty S3 Protection:** This feature monitors and generates findings on S3 data events, such as anonymous connections to an S3 bucket, connections from potential hacking tools such as Kali Linux. It can also detect potential data exfiltration or abnormal data deletion based on machine learning models.

- **EKS Protection:** This feature continuously monitors Kubernetes audit logs that capture API activities within your EKS cluster. It detects suspicious activities such as malicious IPs or unauthenticated users calling API commonly used to access credentials or secrets in the EKS cluster, or a default service account being granted admin privileges on cluster or executions on a Kubernetes system pod.

- **Runtime Monitoring:** This feature monitors runtime activities using an agent to detect threats to your compute workloads on Amazon ECS, Amazon EKS, AWS Fargate, and Amazon EC2. The agent is managed by the Amazon GuardDuty service (or you can manage it yourself). It identifies the process within a specific container with abnormal activity, enhancing the visibility and reducing the impact of the containment tasks, as well as providing detection capabilities that can only be detected from the host, such as the execution of a recently modified binary file. When runtime monitoring is enabled, the detail of the finding is much more complete, as it can identify the container that performed the suspicious action and even the specific process ID. The containment tasks, then, may be more precise and have less impact to the business.

- **Malware Protection for EC2:** When enabled, this feature automatically initiates a malware scan on the EBS volumes when findings suggest that there may be malware in an EC2 instance, such as a port scan, an outbound SSHBruteForce, or a connection to a command-and-control URL. You can also execute on-demand malware scans on instances. The malware scan is performed by taking a snapshot of the EBS volume and scanning it on a service account; therefore, it has no performance impact on the instance, nor additional costs on your EC2 resources. Although it is called malware *protection*, be aware that it only detects malware; it does not replace antimalware or endpoint detection and response (EDR) solutions, as it does not have blocking capabilities. This feature complements these solutions, thereby increasing coverage, especially for short-lived or legacy instances that do not have the EDR or antimalware agent installed. You can trigger remediation actions through EventBridge rules such as an AWS Lambda function to contain the instance.

- **Malware Protection for S3:** When a file is uploaded to an S3 bucket monitored by this feature, a malware scan is performed and the service tags your S3 object with a scan status such as NO_THREATS_FOUND or THREATS_FOUND. You can block access to the infected files using bucket policies or service control policies, or you can trigger an EventBridge rule to execute an AWS Lambda function, sending the file to a sandbox or deleting the object.

- **RDS Protection:** This feature monitors and analyzes login events from your RDS databases, generating findings for anomalous login attempts (whether it is successful or it failed), brute-force attempts, or probes from malicious or anonymous IPs

(TOR nodes). Check the documentation to identify which database types are supported by this feature.
- **Lambda Protection:** This feature adds visibility of the network activity logs from Lambda functions to detect potential threats such as anonymous or known malicious IPs connecting to your functions.

During the 30-day free trial period, the cost estimation feature projects what your estimated costs will be after the trial period. Protection plans have individual free trial periods allowing you to enable them only when you are going to test that feature.

Enabling Amazon GuardDuty

In Exercise 8.1, you will enable GuardDuty in your account and check the information provided as part of the findings.

EXERCISE 8.1

Enable Amazon GuardDuty in Your Account

1. Open the Amazon GuardDuty Management Console.
2. If this is your first time configuring Amazon GuardDuty, click Enable GuardDuty. If it's already configured, open the settings and confirm that Amazon GuardDuty is enabled. That's all you need to do to enable the service.
3. Go to the Settings section and generate sample findings.
4. (Optional) Use the AWS CloudFormation template and procedure to generate an environment and produce simulated findings, as described here: https://docs.aws.amazon.com/guardduty/latest/ug/sample_findings.html#guardduty_findings-scripts.
5. Navigate through the Findings menu and explore the detailed information reported for the different findings.

Amazon GuardDuty offers a workflow to deal with findings so that you can document the manual actions taken as a response. You can archive or unarchive findings (so you can only focus on interesting findings). Also, you can automatically send findings to an archive by creating suppression rules. Each suppression rule is represented by a filter. When a finding matches the filter, the finding is automatically marked as archived. When visualizing GuardDuty findings, you can choose to visualize current, archived, or all findings.

Amazon GuardDuty also allows you to export findings. Each exported file is a JSON-formatted file containing findings as elements of an array. Each finding is represented by all its attributes in a JSON structure.

You can also configure the automatic export of findings to an S3 bucket you own. Amazon GuardDuty will export active findings (findings matching suppressed rules will not be exported) within 5 minutes of its first occurrence. If an active finding receives recurrent events, you can configure how frequently those events are reported (e.g., every 15 minutes, every hour, or every 6 hours). Exported files of findings are encrypted with an AWS KMS key you choose.

Amazon GuardDuty adheres to the concept of an administrator account. The administrator account receives findings from other (member) accounts. It also has the capability to manage the detectors, the findings workflow (archive and create suppression rules), protection plans, and threat lists for those member accounts. You can select the member accounts on a per-account basis (by invitation) or include the accounts in your AWS Organization.

Amazon GuardDuty allows you to disable or suspend the service in one or multiple accounts, on a per-region basis. Suspending the service stops the detection of new findings but keeps information about previously detected findings. Disabling the service stops the detection and deletes all related findings.

AWS Security Hub

AWS Security Hub is a service that consolidates security findings about your AWS resources and presents it in a single pane. AWS Security Hub receives information from other AWS security services (such as Amazon GuardDuty, Amazon Inspector, Amazon Macie, AWS Firewall Manager, and IAM Access Analyzer) as well as from integrated third-party security products and from your own custom security applications.

AWS Security Hub gathers data about the current control implementation status of your AWS account (via services such as AWS Config) to complement its information and to deliver a series of findings and compliance verdicts. In that sense, AWS Security Hub acts as a concentrator of security information, correlator, and processor of data to provide filtered information about the security status of your environment. Figure 8.3 shows at a high level how AWS Security Hub works.

Input and output data in AWS Security Hub conforms to a standardized format called AWS Security Finding Format (ASFF).

FIGURE 8.3 How AWS Security Hub works.

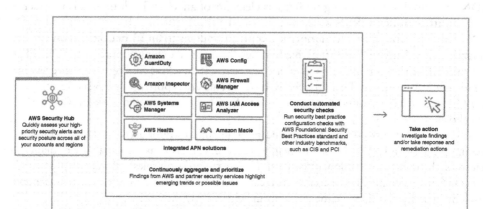

AWS Security Hub relies on the concept of *security standards* when gathering information from the accounts. Each security standard is composed of a list of security controls and the definition of how those should be configured (best practices). Then, the service compares the current environment status with the expected controls the security standard establishes. As a result of the comparison (or check), AWS Security Hub produces a verdict of compliance for each of the controls. The service executes two types of checks in order to keep the information up to date: change-triggered and scheduled. Change-triggered checks are run when a change in the monitored resource is detected. This method requires the resource to be supported by AWS Config. When there is no AWS Config support to monitor changes for a check, AWS Security Hub executes a periodic check no later than 12 hours after the last execution.

One of the main benefits of Security Hub is to provide a centralized view of the security findings. Such findings are presented in the Security Hub console (or through the GetFindings API). Figure 8.4 shows a centralized view of findings in AWS Security Hub, showing an aggregation by different sources of events.

AWS Security Hub also provides a process called a *workflow* to manage the findings. A workflow is a series of stages in which a finding can be positioned at any point in time. Each finding contains an attribute called WorkflowStatus, which has one of the following values: New, Notified, Suppressed, or Resolved. You can modify the workflow status of a finding, giving you the flexibility to implement your own process to deal with the security findings.

Findings also contain an attribute named RecordState. This attribute can take the value Active or Archived. By default, findings with an archived value in the RecordState attribute are filtered out from the lists shown in the Management Console (nonetheless, you can modify the visualization filter).

Along with findings, AWS Security Hub presents an additional view to consume the information via *insights*. Insights are filters and groupings that allow you to see affected

FIGURE 8.4 Centralized view in AWS Security Hub grouped by product name.

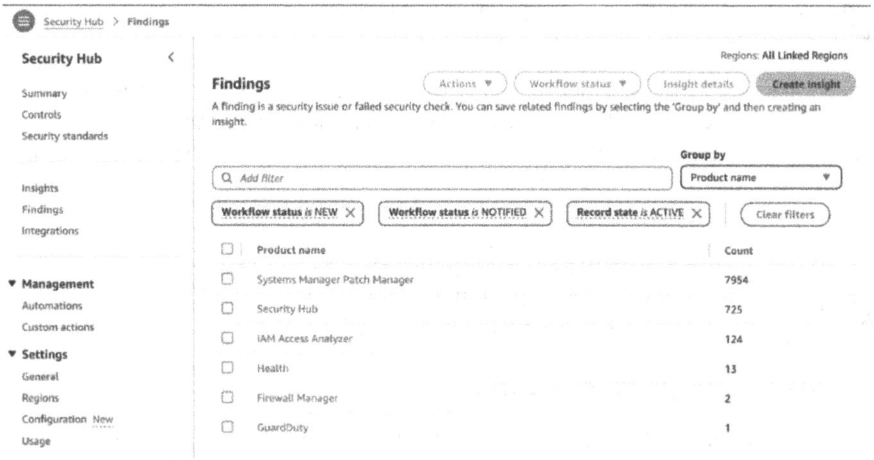

FIGURE 8.5 AWS Security Hub—insights example.

resources in groups to facilitate the human analysis. AWS Security Hub provides a predefined list of insights, but you can also create your own. For example, Figure 8.5 shows an example of an insight showing the AWS resources with the greatest number of findings. Each insight is defined by a query on the findings view that uses a `group by` clause, so the result of an insight is a grouped view of findings.

AWS Security Hub provides automation rules that can elevate the severity of findings that relate to important resources or suppress informational findings in non-prod accounts without any coding required. AWS Security Hub relies on Amazon EventBridge for the integration required when defining rules for all other automations involving external services.

> **NOTE** You learn about Amazon EventBridge and its integration with AWS Security Hub in the "Automating Incident Response" section.

AWS Security Hub receives findings from other AWS services or from third-party integrations. AWS Security Hub can also send findings to other AWS services and external systems. Sending findings to third parties allows you to track your observable records in external systems, such as your own SIEMs, instant messaging notifications, or ticketing systems.

> **NOTE** Disabling AWS Security Hub will stop the generation of new findings but keep existing findings for the retention period of 90 days. AWS Security Hub will also stop the verification of security standards.

Integration with AWS Organizations

AWS Security Hub has native integration with AWS Organizations supporting delegated administration, a feature that allows you to access the organization's management account once and delegate the administration of AWS Security Hub to the Security Account, and then centrally enable the service in multiple accounts.

With this service, you can create a central configuration that simplifies management across accounts and regions, allowing you to specify which security standards to enable in your organization, on each business unit, or on each account. You can even enable all controls or only a subset.

The AWS Security Hub services support multi-region aggregation of findings as well, as shown in Figure 8.6.

FIGURE 8.6 AWS Security Hub multi-region aggregated view.

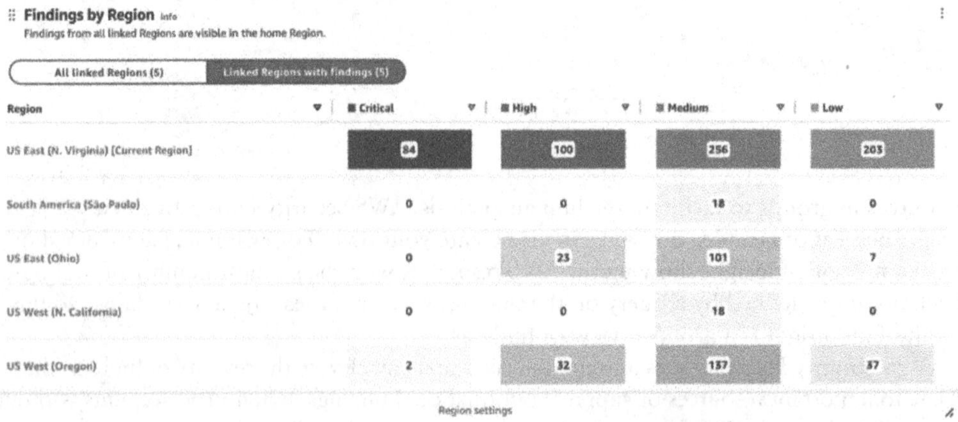

Region	Critical	High	Medium	Low
US East (N. Virginia) [Current Region]	84	100	256	203
South America (São Paulo)	0	0	18	0
US East (Ohio)	0	23	101	7
US West (N. California)	0	0	18	0
US West (Oregon)	2	32	157	57

Threat Detection Services 397

Enabling AWS Security Hub

Exercise 8.2 explores the AWS Security Hub concepts, including enabling the service and reviewing findings and insights.

EXERCISE 8.2

Enable AWS Security Hub in Your Account

1. Open the AWS Security Hub Management Console.

2. If this is your first time configuring AWS Security Hub, click Enable Security Hub (confirm that at least the CIS Benchmark and AWS Foundational security standards are selected). If it's already configured, click Settings, select the General tab, and confirm that AWS Security Hub is enabled. That's all you need to do to enable the service.

3. Navigate to the Security Standards menu and check your account compliance.

4. Go to Findings and confirm that the sample findings from Amazon GuardDuty were also reported in AWS Security Hub. Explore the details provided for these findings.

5. Navigate through the Insights page. In the AWS Resources with the Most Findings insight, look for the instance with ID i-99999999 (generated by the sample findings in Amazon GuardDuty during the previous exercise).

AWS Trusted Advisor

Any discussion about gathering security insights on your AWS account would be incomplete without mentioning AWS Trusted Advisor. Available to every AWS account, this service provides a list of checks that compare your current account status against a set of good practices grouped into four categories: security, cost optimization, reliability, and performance. You can control access to specific checks through IAM access control policies. AWS Trusted Advisor also has the capability to monitor how close you are to reaching service limits. Moreover, if your account has a Business or Enterprise support plan, your AWS Trusted Advisor service will cover additional checks, such as confirming unrestricted access rules in security groups or whether AWS IAM is enforcing a password policy.

AWS Trusted Advisor keeps a list of observations about how you can improve your environment. These observable records are available within the AWS Console (Business and Enterprise support users can also access them via API calls). From the AWS Console, you can also download a file containing all the observable records and configure your account contacts to receive a weekly email with a status report.

Finally, AWS Trusted Advisor checks your account resources throughout all regions. It is enabled or disabled at the account level.

398 Chapter 8 ▪ Threat Detection and Incident Response

> **NOTE** The focus of AWS Security Hub's security standards is to provide detailed findings, and the focus of AWS Trusted Advisor security checks is to report mostly on serious red flags. If AWS Security Hub is not enabled, it's strongly recommended to leverage this free service.

Amazon Detective

Amazon Detective is a service that simplifies the analysis and visualization of security data to investigate potential security issues. Amazon Detective allows the security analyst (or incident responder) to investigate incidents, analyzing all the resources involved in the issue, performing triage, and saving time and effort on root-cause analysis.

The service receives security findings from Amazon GuardDuty and AWS Security Hub and generates graph models that show the relation between the security finding, external IP addresses or domains, IAM Principals, and resources. This enables you to quickly determine the extent of an incident and how to contain the threat, to find the source actor for the issue, and to prevent the issue from happening again. Figure 8.7 shows at a high level how Amazon Detective works.

> **NOTE** The name of the service is Amazon Detective because it allows the security analyst to play the role of a detective investigating an issue. Do not confuse this security *investigation* service with a detective control; it's only meant for investigation of issues detected by Amazon GuardDuty and other sources.

FIGURE 8.7 How Amazon Detective works.

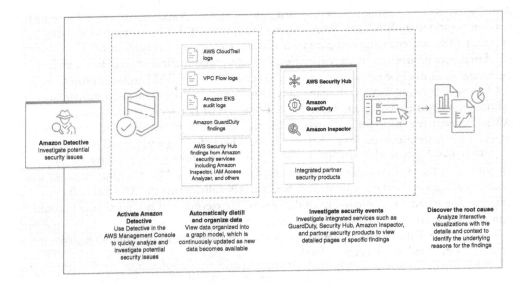

In Amazon Detective, the analyst is the one who leads the investigation, pivoting through the data, starting with a security finding such as a connection to a command and control, and analyzing EC2 resources, IAM principals, VPC flow logs, and successful/failed API calls, driving the investigation toward the root cause.

In the service, you can search on a malicious remote IP address or other indicator of compromise and see if the current issue is the only one from that source in the past 12 months or if perhaps the same actors were responsible for a previous compromise.

One of the most interesting features of Amazon Detective is its capability to create groups of findings and generate a visualization that allows the analyst to explore a security incident (see Figure 8.8). A summary of the issue is created with generative artificial intelligence (GenAI) to provide a natural language explanation of what happened, which may not be trivial when there are numerous indicators of compromise or resources involved. Using the visualization of finding groups, you can do a deep dive into the resources or security findings.

The scope time of a finding group will be automatically set from the moment that the service saw the first appearance of the initial finding until the last event related to the issue, but you can also adjust the scope time if required by your analysis.

FIGURE 8.8 Finding group visualization: Node graph.

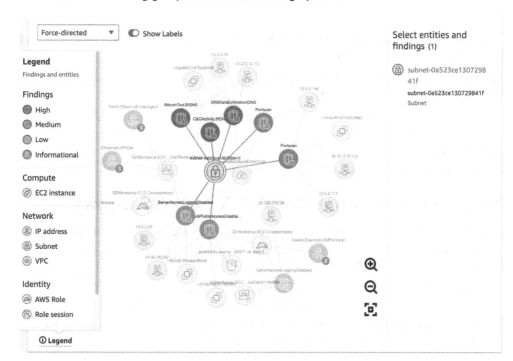

400 Chapter 8 ▪ Threat Detection and Incident Response

Integration with AWS Organizations

Amazon Detective has native integration with AWS Organizations supporting delegated administration. This feature allows you to access the organization's management account once to delegate the administration of Amazon Detective to the Security Account, and then centrally enable or disable the service in multiple accounts.

Enabling Amazon Detective

Exercise 8.3 explores how to enable Amazon Detective and analyze its findings.

EXERCISE 8.3

Enable Amazon Detective in Your Account

1. Open Amazon Detective in the AWS Management Console.

2. If this is your first time configuring Amazon Detective, click Get Started and then Enable Amazon Detective. That's all you need to do to enable the service.

3. Use the AWS CloudFormation template and procedure to generate an environment and produce findings (if you didn't do this in Exercise 8.1), as described here: https://docs. aws.amazon.com/guardduty/latest/ug/sample_findings.html#guardduty_findings-scripts.

4. Go to the Summary page. Review the Roles and Users with the Most API Call Volume and Newly Observed Geolocations sections.

5. Choose Investigations → Run Investigation, then select one of the recommended resources to investigate.

6. Navigate to the Investigations page. Choose View Details on the report with the highest severity, and then explore the View Details page with the Summary, Indicators, and Tactics Techniques and Procedures (TTPs).

Other Threat Detection Capabilities in AWS Services

Many other services can be used to detect issues or threats. Here are some examples:

- **AWS CloudTrail:** You can configure through Amazon EventBridge for a notification about sensitive events like a successful root login.

- **Amazon CloudWatch:** You can configure billing alarms, which are great for identifying potential adversarial launches of EC2 instances for cryptomining or botnets.

- **AWS Systems Manager:** You can identify a missing patch and auto-remediate. State Manager can detect a service that went down and start it again.

AWS Systems Manager OpsCenter helps aggregate operational issues and is not intended for security teams.

Incident Response

Incident response is a comprehensive and wide-scoped topic. It directly deals with the main goal of any security organization: to reduce risks to acceptable levels in order to achieve business objectives. It also often involves communication with external parties in addition to the internal organization, such as law enforcement agencies, customers, media, and regulators.

A successful incident response plan deals with actions along the full life cycle of a security event, from having the right tools for detection and protection, to going through the automation of security protections, and applying lessons learned from every incident. In other words, you cannot do a good job responding to incidents if you do not deploy security controls. You must also consciously acknowledge that the security issues will happen and the maturity of your incident response process along with the training of your people and the technology you have implemented will determine the impact to your organization. You need to be prepared to handle potential security issues.

To simplify the approach, think about three clearly visible components of an incident response plan: the incident's *management* (or how it can improve over time), its *constituent factors* (people, technology, and processes), and its *life cycle* (preparation, detection and analysis, containment eradication and recovery, and post-incident activities such as forensics and lessons learned). There are multiple frameworks and guides for incident response. Most of the AWS documentation is aligned with NIST Special Publication 800-61 Computer Security Incident Handling Guide.[1]

Incident Response Life Cycle

This section explains each phase in the incident response life cycle shown in Figure 8.9. These steps are defined by NIST Computer Security Incident Handling Guide SP 800-61 r2.

Because an incident response plan is inherently a process, it is subject to a continuous improvement cycle, where post-incident activities provide input to better prepare and protect against similar attacks in the future. Within the operations, after detecting and analyzing threats, containment, eradication, and recovery activities are executed. Then, after initial efforts, there is additional analysis to make sure that the threat is no longer present; if it is found that additional tasks are needed, new actions are then executed.

---

[1] NIST SP 800-61 Computer Security Incident Handling Guide: https://csrc.nist.gov/publications/detail/sp/800-61/rev-2/final.

FIGURE 8.9 The incident response life cycle.

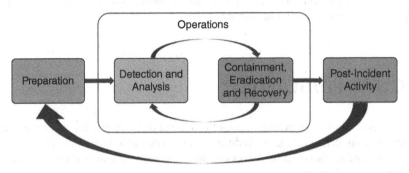

The *preparation* phase presented in Figure 8.9 involves gathering as much information about your protected resources as you can and defining your goals and important outcomes. During this phase, you also define the adequate training level you require for the people involved as well as any required improvements to the processes already in place. Another task is to assess any gaps between the current and the desired levels, including technical controls required to achieve your security goals. Then, you implement security controls to close the gaps you discover. An important portion of this phase focuses on increasing incident visibility (along with incident notifications) in a comprehensive way for the responsible personnel.

During the *detection and analysis* phase, you effectively put your security incident response plan into action. You can do that proactively by simulating security incident conditions (with table-top or live exercises), or you can evaluate the performance of the process when facing a real security event situation. In either case, during the events, you document and measure your capabilities to respond, and gather and preserve as much forensics information related to the incident for analysis.

During the *containment, eradication*, and *recovery* phase, you do the following:

1. Isolate the compromised resources: Change firewall rules and IAM permissions, rotate access keys, or isolate the compromised resources.

2. Remove the presence of adversaries in your workloads: Eliminate resources created by the adversary and unrecognized IAM users or roles, and in general reverse all the activity performed by the adversary that you see on the logs.

3. Recover operations: Get the business back to normal operations. As mentioned previously, you cycle between the previous phase and this one, until you have verified that the threat is completely eradicated and operations are restored.

During the *post-incident activity* phase, you perform forensic analysis to learn from the incident, identify potential opportunities for improvement, and identify what went wrong, which security controls were not in place to prevent or detect the issue earlier, which procedures during containment failed or took too much time, and which additional training is needed for your team. Metrics of the incident are reviewed during this phase, such as attacker dwell time, mean time to detect, mean time to acknowledge and prioritize the

Incident Response   **403**

potential security incident, and mean time to respond, contain, and recover. Measuring and making sure your program improves over time in these metrics for similar issues is strongly recommended. An additional task is to perform root-cause analysis not only to identify the actors that caused the issue (if possible), but also to prevent similar threats from reappearing in the future, which brings you back to the first phase of a new cycle. In this phase, if you realize that this may be a recurring issue, you can also design security automations to reduce the operational workload next time. You need to make sure that you are learning from incidents so that your team's skills improve based on those experiences.

People, Technology, and Processes

As explained previously, there are three constituent factors of an incident response plan: *people*, *technology*, and *processes*.

People refer to the humans, both internal and external to your organization, who are involved in an incident response. Internally, in addition to IT and information security departments, you should consider other stakeholders such as legal, compliance, physical security, business owners, human resources, public relations, and organizational leadership. Externally, you should also acknowledge entities such as your own customers, the general public, authorities (including law enforcement), industry associations, security research organizations, and forensics specialists. Due to the potential number of parties involved, a comprehensive training and communications plan is critical to the success of an incident response plan.

In addition to the security awareness training in your company, you should have a special learning path for the security personnel, specifically for incident responders, that covers what they should learn the first day, the first week, the first month, and the first quarter in their role.

Technology refers to the technical tools to use in an incident response. Throughout the previous sections of this book, you have learned about the available AWS Cloud tools that handle identity and access management, threat detection controls, and infrastructure and data protection.

In the context of an incident response plan, a *process* is a human-triggered or automated predefined sequence of actions to respond to a security incident. The flexibility of AWS Cloud makes the automation of the processes a critical part (as well as an advantage) of executing an incident response process in the cloud. It allows you to dramatically reduce the response times for suspicious activities and to correct misconfigurations long before a malicious actor can attempt to exploit them.

In the next sections, you learn about best practices and how they help you improve your incident response plan. If you are interested in going beyond the scope of the AWS Certified Security Specialty certification, you can find additional information here:

- **AWS Well-Architected Framework.** Incident response is one of the five best practices areas defined in the security pillar. For more information, see `https://docs.aws.amazon.com/pdfs/wellarchitected/latest/framework/wellarchitected-framework.pdf`.

- **AWS Cloud Adoption Framework.** Incident response is one of the capabilities of the security perspective. For more information, see https://docs.aws.amazon.com/pdfs/whitepapers/latest/aws-caf-security-perspective/aws-caf-security-perspective.pdf.

- **AWS Security Incident Response Guide.** This documentation discusses general incident response concepts and how they match with AWS Cloud capabilities. For more information, see https://docs.aws.amazon.com/whitepapers/latest/aws-security-incident-response-guide/introduction.html.

AWS Customer Incident Response Team

In Chapter 2, "Cloud Security Principles and Frameworks," you learned about the shared responsibility model. In a nutshell, AWS is responsible for the security *of* the cloud and the customer is responsible for security *in* the cloud. AWS deploys a security incident response plan as part of its accountability in the shared responsibility model (with evidence available to you through the security and compliance reports AWS Artifact creates). For the workloads you implement, you, as the customer, are responsible for developing the incident response plan, covering your part of the shared responsibility model.

When a customer has an active security incident in their workloads, such as when an adversary has taken control of some of the customer's resources or credentials, the customer is responsible for the response, but they are not alone in this task. AWS has a team of security incident responders that assists the customer's security team during these situations, to investigate and contain the threat: the AWS Customer Incident Response Team (AWS CIRT).

This team guides the customer to identify what happened and how to isolate the affected resources and mitigate the impact. The team provides assistance to all customers at no cost, regardless of the support level.

If you have an active security incident, to engage with the AWS CIRT, open a support ticket indicating that you have an active security incident and you need assistance from the AWS CIRT.

Creating Your Incident Response Plan

In this section, you find general steps and best practices to consider when creating an incident response plan for workloads on AWS Cloud. Any plan will contain some general activities and some detailed activities aligned to specific types of incidents. The plan should also include playbooks for each of those specific incidents based on types of situations that are commonly seen, that are trending, or that would generate major impact to the workload if not handled properly.

To accelerate the creation of your own incident response playbooks, you can leverage these sample playbooks created by the AWS CIRT: https://github.com/aws-samples/aws-incident-response-playbooks.

Step 1: Prepare

In this step, you should consider deploying the following best practices in your incident response plan:

- Identify the personnel required to deal with security incidents along the whole life cycle.
- Establish the gap between the current and desired state in incident response training.
- Conduct a risk assessment that clearly identifies information classification and the factors that define the severity of an incident.
- Establish an inventory of your monitored resources using AWS Config and AWS Systems Manager capabilities.
- Implement a tagging strategy for your monitored resources to help with the incident response. For example, tagging resources according to their classification level, owners, and workload name allows for faster identification of risk level at the time of the incident.
- Conduct training. Have a clear understanding of the different controls and countermeasures available in AWS Cloud.
- Establish a mechanism to stay up to date with the latest AWS services and features.

Step 2: Implement

Most of the preparation tasks for the incident response are executed in this step. You should consider the following best practices:

- Implement detailed logging and monitoring across the whole infrastructure, explained in Chapter 5, "Security Logging and Monitoring."
- Make sure to include logging at the different levels of the workload, including services, resources, and applications. Centralize logs and prepare the data structure for the analysis:
  - Using Amazon Security Lake, which will normalize and structure many AWS and third-party logs using Open Cybersecurity Schema Framework (OCSF).
  - If you're delivering AWS CloudTrail logs to an Amazon S3 bucket, configure the data catalog in AWS Glue so that you will be able to query data using analytics tools like Amazon Athena or Amazon EMR. Create and update the data catalog for every centralized log delivered to the Amazon S3 repository, including logs from components like Elastic Load Balancing, AWS WAF, and Amazon API Gateway.

406   Chapter 8 ▪ Threat Detection and Incident Response

- Establish relevant metrics from the reported logs and plot them using Amazon CloudWatch metrics. For every metric, define thresholds and alarms.

- Configure notifications to be delivered through the right channels, providing relevant information and reaching the appropriate subscribers.

- Create AWS CloudFormation templates (infrastructure as code) for your AWS Cloud environment that define and implement the guardrails and technical specifications for detection of security events. Include technical specifications for the various detective controls defined earlier in this chapter.

- Consider pre-provision tools for incident response, including tools available from AWS, AWS Partner Network (APN) members, and other external parties (such as open-source tools or adequately licensed external solutions).

- Consider automation to take snapshots of the involved systems (including storage systems and volatile information like memory content). Establish and test backup and restore procedures. You can also use Automated Forensics Orchestrator for Amazon EC2 (`https://aws.amazon.com/solutions/implementations/automated-forensics-orchestrator-for-amazon-ec2`) to capture and examine data from EC2 instances and attached volumes for forensic analysis.

- For forensics analysis, consider preparing a *clean room*, an isolated environment where you can deploy the infrastructure with the tools required for investigation. As a requirement for the clean room, keep an up-to-date Amazon EC2 AMI Image vetted by the security team with the required set of tools.

- Use an AWS CloudFormation template to automate the creation of the clean room environment when needed.

- Put your incident response plan in writing. Document the processes to analyze findings, query logs, and metrics and respond to incidents following the life cycle of the security incidents (from detection to forensics). Classify these documents and make sure they are accessible in case of an incident. Consider options to store these documents offline (or printing them).

- Automate the responses to security events as much as possible.

- Implement a training and awareness program for personnel to know and successfully execute the documented incident response processes. Include topics such as how to query and analyze logs and findings, how to react when an alarm is triggered, how to classify the severity of an incident, and how to respond, following the actions depending on the life cycle of the incident. Make sure you provision access to the personnel dealing with incident response in accordance with the least privilege principle.

- Define the process and mechanisms for summoning a *war room,* a virtual or physical meeting of the team in charge of dealing with the incident.

- Develop a clear communications guideline, establishing official communication mechanisms and points of contact. Make sure your contact information is up to date (both for internal and external contacts). In the case of external stakeholders, understand their operating model and, when applicable, whether you have a valid contract and SLA to use their services. Also, take the appropriate measures to guarantee that all stakeholders have a clear understanding of the chain of communication, communication tools, war rooms, and PR guidelines during the incident response.

Step 3: Monitor and Test

This step corresponds to a thorough execution of the incident response plan in a testing scenario. During the whole execution, you should document your responses with the goal of monitoring how your response plan performs and to gather metrics from your process. Therefore, you should do the following:

- Arrange to carry out the plan in a controlled environment (after all, it is better to find gaps in a simulation and not when dealing with a real incident in a production environment).

- Prepare and execute security incident response simulations (SIRS) as a tabletop exercise using role play. Another option is to have an incident response game day, which uses a simulation on an isolated or temporary learning environment such as AWS Jams. This provides challenges that emulate real use cases. Design your simulations to be as realistic as possible, while not affecting production environments. In more mature organizations, consider blind exercises where the response team does not know in advance about the simulation.

- Although it's not desirable, executing your incident response plan in a real situation is also useful for monitoring and testing your plan.

- Regardless of whether it is a simulated or a real scenario, make sure you are documenting every action along the life cycle of the incident. This includes having an activity log for both the manual and automated processes. Also, gather metrics during the process that will allow you to compare and establish improvement goals for future executions.

Step 4: Update

After an incident response plan has been effectively executed with thoughtful monitoring of the process, you will probably uncover some gaps. You'll then have an opportunity to improve the plan's real value for your organization. Consequently, as part of the update phase, you should do the following:

- Document a root cause analysis (RCA) after every execution of the incident response plan. The RCA is a document in which you identify the reason behind the incident and describe the actions to avoid in the future, as well as any improvements to the plan.

- In addition to technical improvements, consider the people and processes dimensions. Human-related actions that deviated from the documented processes can be improved by creating training and awareness activities.

- Review and update procedures that failed to solve the incidents at every stage of the life cycle in a timely manner.

At this point, you will take the lessons learned from the execution of the incident response and enter them in the prepare and implement phases, considering all three incident response factors: people, technology, and processes. This is an iterative cycle you will keep improving over time.

Reacting to Specific Security Incidents

In this section, you learn how to react to well-known security incidents that may happen in your AWS Cloud. You should always remember that incidents happen, so it is better to be prepared to address them than have to find out later what to do.

Abuse Notifications

The AWS Customer agreement, in Section 6, "Temporary Suspension," specifies the following:

6.1 Generally. We may suspend your or any End User's right to access or use any portion or all of the Service Offerings immediately upon notice to you if we determine: (a) your or an End User's use of the Service Offerings (i) poses a security risk to the Service Offerings or any third party, (ii) could adversely impact our systems, the Service Offerings or the systems or Content of any other AWS customer, (iii) could subject us, our affiliates, or any third party to liability, or (iv) could be fraudulent.

As you can see, if your account gets compromised and a bad actor uses it to attack other accounts or third parties, AWS may suspend your account to prevent attacks from spreading through the Internet if you do not take proper countermeasures to contain the threat.

For this reason, it is particularly important that you protect your workloads in the AWS Cloud. Additionally, you should detect and contain compromised instances while also keeping your security contacts updated in the account information. With such information, AWS Security teams can contact your security engineers to warn them about suspicious activities in the account. Figure 8.10 shows where you should add the contacts related to your organization's security personnel.

To reach that page, access your AWS Management Console. In the upper bar, click the AWS Account ID (or the AWS account alias if you defined one), select the Account option, and look for the Alternate Contacts section.

It is also a best practice to define a dedicated alias (such as aws-notifications@example.com) that will deliver notifications to a team of security analysts. Make sure your team will receive instant messaging alerts when an email reaches this alias so that any member can act quickly.

AWS may use that contact information to inform you about suspicious activity that could affect the operation of your account, such as detected leaked access keys from your account or if one of your Amazon EC2 instances is attacking someone else.

FIGURE 8.10 AWS account security contacts.

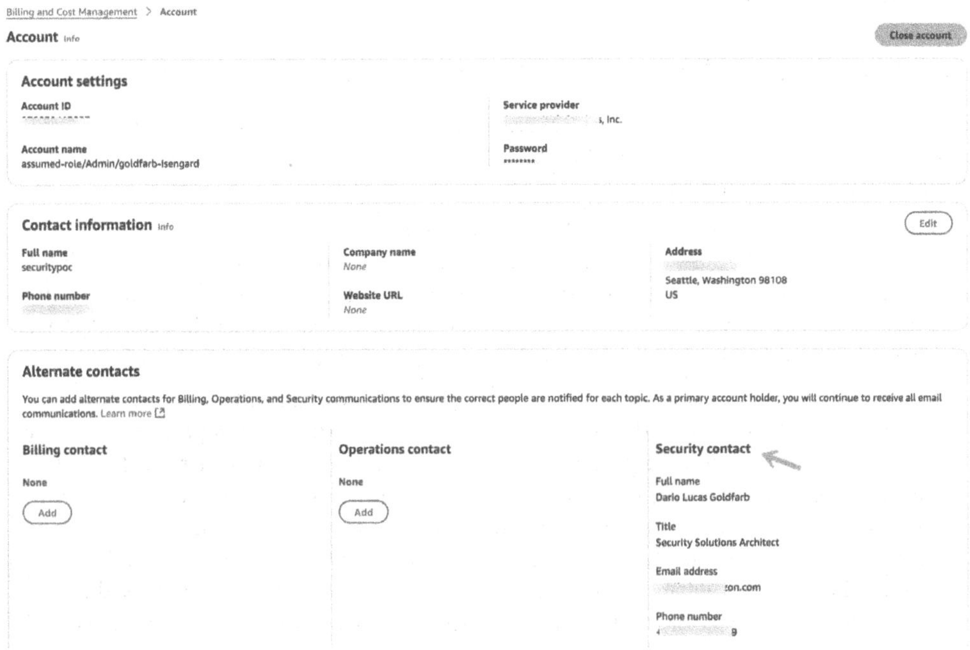

> Later in this chapter, you learn about security automations that can be configured to isolate compromised instances, reducing the risk of account suspension.

Insider Threat and Former Employee Access

When a user with privileged access leaves the company, you, as a security engineer, need to remove all of the former user's access according to your security policies. If the former employee was an IAM user, you should delete the AWS IAM user or revoke AWS IAM access keys while disabling their AWS Console password to remove all privileges for the AWS environment.

Alternatively, if you are using external authentication repositories such as Okta, OneLogin, or Microsoft Active Directory Federation Services, you need to disable or delete the user on that external identity provider solution. If you're using AWS IAM Identity Center with its own user repository, you should remove the user from that service.

If any security group with IP validation allowed access from the user's home IP address, you should remove that access as well.

You should also rotate other access keys that the employee had access to, such as access keys for services that they configured, or keys that allowed access to the secret access key.

Chapter 8 ▪ Threat Detection and Incident Response

Since this may be a complex task, strive to avoid using long-term credentials such as access keys in favor of temporary permissions, such as roles.

Amazon EC2 Instance Compromised by Malware

Different organizations may apply distinct reactions in case an Amazon EC2 instance is compromised by installed malware. Nonetheless, you should consider performing the following best practices in your response plan:

- Take a snapshot of the EBS Volume at the time of the incident to allow the forensics team to work on the root cause of the compromise, capture the malware for analysis, and capture any other forensic information prior to shutting down the instance. If the impact is high, you may want to shut down the instance immediately, but doing so may mean that evidence needed for forensic reconstructions is lost.

- To isolate the instance, change its security group by removing the allowed entries and detach any IAM role attached to the instance, also by revoking the temporary credentials. Remove it from Auto Scaling groups so that the service creates a new instance from the template and service interruption is reduced. Beware that tracked connections (which are established from a rule with a specific IP address or segment) in security groups may persist for some moments after the change in the security group to remove all inbound/outbound rules because the security group considers it to be response traffic for the original traffic that was allowed. Therefore, terminating the connection blocking the malicious IP with a Network Access Control List (NACL) or moving the instance to an isolated VPC is a more comprehensive solution for the isolation.

- Tag the instance as compromised, together with an AWS IAM policy or service control policy that explicitly restricts all operations related to the instance to anyone outside the incident response and forensics teams. Following such a procedure is a great way to reduce the risk of unintentionally destroying the evidence due to human mistakes. These tags can be applied programmatically using Amazon EventBridge upon the detection of specific Amazon GuardDuty finding types.

- When the incident forensics team wants to analyze the compromised instance based on an EBS snapshot, they should deploy it into an isolated environment—ideally a private subnet (without Internet access) on an isolated Amazon Virtual Private Cloud that is exclusively accessed only by a forensics workstation (i.e., a clean room). This special instance can be a hardened Amazon Workspaces virtual desktop preinstalled with the appropriate forensic tools (such as Wireshark or Volatility) to speed up analysis.

- Analyze the logs and findings, such as Amazon GuardDuty findings related to that instance, operating system logs, application logs, AWS CloudTrail logs, and Amazon VPC flow logs, if available. Consider using Amazon Detective to assist in the root cause analysis.

There are several options to automate incident responses. AWS Lambda functions can be an option if you prefer coding, but you can also use AWS Step Functions to define

Reacting to Specific Security Incidents   **411**

workflows that can have an execution time of up to one year. You can also leverage the Security Orchestration, Automation, and Response (SOAR) solution of your choice, such as Palo Alto Cortex SOAR (formerly Demisto) or Splunk SOAR (formerly Phantom).

Leaked Credentials

Developers sometimes enjoy sharing their code with open-source communities or another community of their preference. If they used access keys hardcoded into the codebase instead of following the best practices related to using temporary credentials (such as AWS IAM roles attached to Amazon EC2 instances), they may be inadvertently making their AWS credentials public. In addition, there are various reports that malicious actors are constantly looking for credentials of all sorts on shared repositories like GitHub.

If the AWS Security team finds those credentials, they will notify you by sending an email to your configured security contact and apply an inline policy to the user to restrict highly destructive actions like eliminating an Amazon RDS database, but AWS cannot block all access as it could disrupt your operations. If a malicious actor finds your credentials first, and your policies did not have IAM conditions restricting their usage, they can use those credentials to cause damage.

If any access key is leaked to a shared repository (like GitHub), even if only for a couple of seconds, you should assume that the access key was compromised and revoke it immediately.

In Exercise 8.4, you practice rotating credentials for an AWS IAM user. Note that you do not assign access policies to this user.

EXERCISE 8.4

Rotate AWS IAM Credentials

1. Create a new AWS IAM user named `security-chapter8` and assign the following credentials: Console Password, Access Key, HTTPS Git Credentials, and Amazon Keyspaces.

2. Access the AWS IAM Management Console. Click Users under the Access Management category.

3. Click the `security-chapter8` user.

4. Select the Security Credentials tab.

5. Under Access Keys, make the current access keys inactive.

6. Under HTTP Git Credentials for AWS Code Commit, make the current key inactive.

7. Under Credentials for Amazon Keyspaces, make the current key inactive.

8. Delete the `security-chapter8` user.

412   Chapter 8 ▪ Threat Detection and Incident Response

EXERCISE 8.4 *(continued)*

Remember that rotating existing credentials will require you to update any system or application currently using the previous credentials. IAM users allow the creation of two access keys so that you can create the new access key, assign it to the application that had the old or compromised key, and then disable and later eliminate the old access key.

The principle of least privilege is a critical factor in reducing risk in cases like this. If credentials are leaked, the impact depends on how restrictive your security policies are.

Also, if you have Business or Enterprise support plan, you can use the AWS Trusted Advisor Exposed Access Keys check to monitor popular code repositories and learn whether your access keys have been exposed to the public.

Application Attacks

Some of the more frequent attacks are the ones that leverage a vulnerability on your web applications. Regardless of how you analyze the AWS WAF logs, as developers usually prioritize the development of functional aspects of the applications, there may be a delay in correcting vulnerabilities that could create an exposure window on your application.

As you learned in Chapter 6, "Infrastructure Protection," AWS WAF can effectively address such vulnerabilities. Keep in mind that, in addition to using AWS Managed Rules, AWS WAF allows the creation of custom rules that can act as a virtual patch to the vulnerability until the development team can fix the issue in their code.

If you're experiencing EC2 compromise on a web server for multiple instances, there may be a vulnerability in the application allowing the adversary to run operating systems commands. Enabling the operating system rules in block mode (such as `AWSManagedRulesLinuxRuleSet` and `AWSManagedRulesWindowsRuleSet`) will likely prevent other instances from being compromised.

If your AWS WAF rules are in "count" mode and you detect attacks analyzing the logs, the simple response would be to change from count mode to block on the rules triggering, while monitoring the availability of your applications.

DDoS attacks on the network level (OSI Layers 3 and 4) will be automatically mitigated by AWS with no action required by customers (AWS Shield Standard), but if the type of attack you are receiving is a DDoS attack on the application level (OSI Layer 7), you have two options. If you have AWS Shield Advanced with automatic application layer DDoS mitigation, it will protect you from Layer 7 attacks and you don't have to take any action. If you did not configure automatic mitigation, you can open a ticket to involve the AWS Shield Response Team (SRT), and they will help you analyze and block the malicious traffic. You can also configure AWS Route 53 health check to involve the SRT if your website or application goes down, to investigate whether it was related to a DDoS attack. AWS Shield Advanced will also protect your AWS bill; you will be able to request a refund of the charges related to your infrastructure growth due to the DDoS attack (a cost protection feature).

remediating, and are valid for security invariants, which you don't expect to change over time. Keep in mind, however, that unlike the security automations, SCPs prevent future undesirable configurations, not the resources that are currently misconfigured, so users get an "access denied" error. With automations, you can send notifications to the person making the change, with explanations as to why the change was reverted to the secure configuration. Automations are significantly more flexible.

Structure of a Security Automation

When analyzing incident response playbooks to find opportunities for improving automation, you will often get to a logical sequence such as the one shown in Figure 8.11.

1. A detective control receives data from one or more data sources.
2. Using rules or machine intelligence, the detective control recognizes an undesired condition and then triggers an Amazon EventBridge rule, creates a finding in AWS Security Hub, or creates a ticket in the Incident Response Platform or ticketing tool.
3. A response task is triggered that contains the threat, alerts the security team, and/or resolves the configuration drift.

The following elements are some examples of common data sources:

- **Logs:** AWS CloudTrail logs, DNS records, VPC Flow Logs, web application firewall logs, operating systems logs, application logs, or AWS CloudWatch Logs
- **Infrastructure:** Configurations or inventory
- **Data:** Amazon S3 buckets data analytics

The following services are examples of detective capabilities that can identify a risk or detect an active security incident:

- Amazon GuardDuty
- AWS Security Hub Security Standards
- AWS Config
- Amazon Inspector
- Amazon Macie
- AWS IAM Access Analyzer

FIGURE 8.11 Security automation logical sequence.

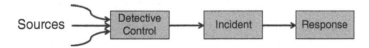

The following findings and events are frequently used to trigger an automation:

- Unsafe configurations (from AWS Config or Amazon Inspector), such as open buckets, RDP/SSH open to all IPs, and others
- AWS Security Hub findings from AWS services and solutions from the AWS Partner Network, such as antimalware and endpoint detection and response (EDR)
- Potential security incidents, such as connections to anonymization networks (TOR), connections to botnets, or other malicious actors
- Other events from Amazon EventBridge that can trigger a response task

The Onion Router (TOR) Network routes traffic through a series of relays using cryptography for anonymization. The origin node cannot know where the destination is located, and vice versa.

The following AWS service features are some examples of common response tasks:

- An AWS Lambda function can use AWS APIs to change security groups or network ACLs. In scenarios using attribute-based access control (ABAC), an AWS Lambda function can change tags to isolate access to the object or limit access to the blue team.
- Systems Manager Automation documents are frequently used to correct configuration drifts detected by AWS Config.
- If an action needs to be performed at the OS level, AWS Systems Manager Run Command can be used to execute commands to multiple hosts at scale.
- Coordinated responses, especially when confirmation is required from a human, can be accomplished by using AWS Step Functions to follow a workflow of actions with conditionals, or by using AWS Systems Manager Automation documents, which support multiple steps, such as the following:
  1. Preserve evidence using a snapshot.
  2. Collect additional information on the incident from different sources to enrich the data available for the analysis.
  3. Contain the incident by isolating the compromised instances.

Depending on your objective for security automation, each of the boxes in Figure 8.11 will be mapped to a different component, with a different service or code. Throughout this chapter, you explore a variety of automated processes that can be accomplished using AWS Services.

Automating Incident Response **417**

Know the Art of the Possible

Regarding security automations, for the exam it is important that you identify the security objective that is requested in the question, and how it could be achieved by a combination of components. One option could provide an answer with a single service solving a similar issue but not exactly what is requested, while a second option provides the right answer by integrating different services.

Know Which Service Can Detect Which Needs to Trigger the Automation

If you are trying to detect configuration drifts in the configuration of Amazon S3 Buckets, you could use Amazon Macie or AWS Config, both of which are capable of detecting weak configurations on Buckets, but AWS Config provides an auto-remediate feature to correct that configuration drift through an AWS Systems Manager Automation. If you are trying to build an automation to react to a potential compromised instance or malicious actors' connections (based on their IP Reputation), then Amazon GuardDuty will be used to detect the instance, and an AWS Lambda function will be used to isolate the instance.

How to Automate

AWS offers different services to automate the incident response in your environment. In this section you learn about some of the services and patterns you can use to implement such automation.

AWS Security Hub and Amazon EventBridge

These two services play a key role in security automations. Because many different types of issues generate findings on AWS Security Hub, this service is the perfect place to centralize the remediation of potential vulnerabilities in semi-automatic or automatic mode. Figure 8.12 shows the interaction of AWS Security Hub with other AWS services and third-party solutions.

As you can see in Figure 8.12, AWS Security Hub can receive findings from many AWS services (such as Amazon GuardDuty and Amazon Inspector) that provide detective controls, as well as solutions from AWS partners. Additionally, AWS Security

FIGURE 8.12 AWS Security Hub as the centerpiece of security automation.

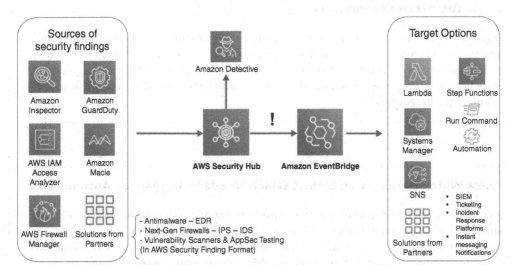

Hub can trigger automated remediation actions through the events triggered in Amazon EventBridge that can target AWS Lambda or Amazon Simple Notification Service (SNS).

Within the AWS Security Hub, you can take one of the following three approaches to resolve a security finding:

- **Manual:** You can correct a finding manually (or archive it if you recognize it as a false positive).

- **Semi-Automatic:** With one or many preconfigured custom actions in AWS Security Hub, once you analyze a finding, you can decide that a remediation action should be launched by selecting the finding and selecting the desired action from the drop-down menu. For example, Close S3 Bucket enables Block Public Access at that bucket, or the Resolve action could trigger a response action that has a different action to be triggered depending on the finding type.

- **Automatic:** All findings from AWS Security Hub generate Amazon EventBridge events, so a completely automated response can be triggered immediately. From the Amazon EventBridge console, you can create a rule using Security Hub as the service name and setting Security Hub Findings - Imported as Event Type. You can also create a rule in JSON, as Example 8.1 shows.

Real World Scenario

Example 8.1: JSON Rule

```
{
 "source": [
  "aws.securityhub"
 ],
 "detail-type": [
  "Security Hub Findings - Imported"
 ]
}
```

Automated Security Response on AWS

Configurations that are not aligned to CIS AWS Foundational Benchmark will be detected by AWS Security Hub provided that the security standard with that name is enabled. A quick win for security analysts to improve the speed of resolution of these misalignments to the best practice is to implement the solution called Automated Security Response on AWS (see Figure 8.13). This solution will simplify the remediation task by creating several custom actions in AWS Security Hub that can be used to resolve many of these issues automatically.

The solution can be found here: https://aws.amazon.com/solutions/implementations/automated-security-response-on-aws.

Using AWS Lambda

Many security automations use Amazon EventBridge with AWS Lambda functions, and there are a couple of reasons why this makes sense. AWS Lambda is a service that allows executing

FIGURE 8.13 Automated Security Response on AWS.

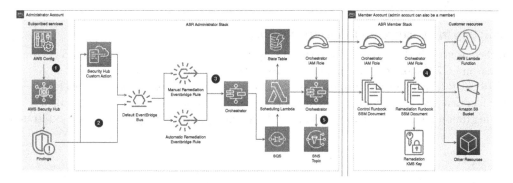

custom code, including calls to AWS APIs. Being serverless, AWS Lambda is very appropriate for event-driven security for the following reasons:

- It does not generate costs while it is not invoked.
- It does not have the need for infrastructure management, which is also very valuable for security teams, where human operators are frequently the most constrained resource.

The following sections explore some common ways of using AWS Lambda for automating security responses.

Using AWS Step Functions

The AWS Lambda functions' 15-minute limit may be an issue for actions that require waiting one step to complete in order to start the next one. AWS Step Functions allow you to define a workflow with many steps, human confirmations, and loops, and they can live for up to a year—much longer than what's needed for incident response, for more complex remediations.

Using AWS SSM Automation Documents

AWS Systems Manager automation documents are linear, therefore less flexible than the Step Functions, but they are great for most playbooks and are easy to create. They can also be used directly from AWS Config for auto remediation.

Using AWS Config

AWS Config can auto-remediate noncompliant resources by launching AWS Systems Manager automation documents.

Examples

This section examines some examples that integrate AWS Services to provide an automated incident response.

Isolating Instances with Malicious Activity

If there is no valid business reason for allowing anonymous access to remote resources from Amazon EC2 Instances (as is the case for most organizations), you can assume that any TOR client activity on such instances is probably malicious. This conclusion comes from the fact that many types of malware use this network to anonymously reach out to their owner (botnet master) for many reasons, such as remote command-and-control, to exfiltrate information (credentials, personally identifiable information), or in some cases just to report progress (as with destructive malware).

A TOR client (such as the TOR browser) routes web traffic through the TOR network, anonymizing it. The client connects randomly to any entry point that bounces that traffic to a middle relay and then sends the traffic through a third and final exit node using cryptography to ensure that the origin node doesn't know the destination node (and therefore can't reach it directly or even know where it's located).

Let's examine a simple scenario of a security automation that isolates an instance that is communicating using TOR. Figure 8.14 shows an example of a security automation that uses an Amazon CloudWatch rule to act upon the Amazon GuardDuty event executing an AWS Lambda function that quarantines the Amazon EC2 Instance.

As Figure 8.14 shows, Amazon GuardDuty detects connections to TOR network nodes and the presence of a TOR client.

As you can see in Figure 8.15, GuardDuty produces a finding that an EC2 Instance is communicating with an IP address that is an entry node for the TOR anonymization network. With a simple Amazon EventBridge rule that looks for the UnauthorizedAccess:EC2/TorClient event and triggers an AWS Lambda function that isolates the compromised instance, you can automatically contain the threat. (See Examples 8.2 and 8.3.)

FIGURE 8.14 Simple security automation example.

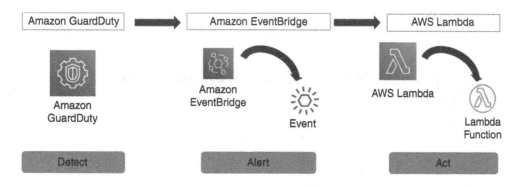

FIGURE 8.15 GuardDuty's TOR Client detection message.

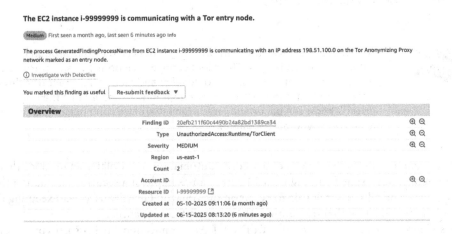

Real World Scenario

Example 8.2: Amazon EventBridge Rule

```
{
 "source": [ "aws.guardduty" ],
 "detail": { "type": [ "UnauthorizedAccess:EC2/TorClient" ] }
}
```

Real World Scenario

Example 8.3: AWS Lambda Function (Using Python Runtime and Boto3 AWS SDK)

```
import boto3
from botocore.exceptions import ClientError
import os

def lambda_handler(event, context):
  response = 'Error isolating the instance.'
  try:
    # Set Variables
    instanceID = event['detail']['resource']['instanceDetails']['instanceId']
    security_group_id = os.environ['QUARANTINE_SG']
```

```
    # Get instance details
    ec2 = boto3.resource('ec2')
    instance = ec2.Instance(instanceID)

    # Change instance Security Group attribute
    instance.modify_attribute(Groups=[security_group_id])
    response = 'Incident auto-remediated'

except ClientError as e:
    print(e)
return response
```

As you can see in Example 8.3, the Python code sets the `security_group_id` variable to a value received as a parameter from the AWS Lambda Function, an environment variable called QUARANTINE_SG, which contains the identifier of the security group that does not have outgoing access to other instances (or to the Internet) and allows incoming traffic only from the Incident Forensics IP address. Therefore, the code is changing the security groups for that Amazon EC2 instance.

A best practice is to use a virtual desktop on Amazon Workspaces with all the forensic tools like Wireshark, Volatility, and Nmap preinstalled. Doing so speeds up investigation and reduces the probability of infection of the security analyst's desktop.

As you can see in Figure 8.16, the security group is passed as a parameter to the AWS Lambda function. This security group allows the instance to be reached through the network only by the Forensics workstation's IP address and explicitly denies access for outgoing communications.

For the AWS Lambda function to be able to change security groups and write its logs to Amazon CloudWatch logs, it needs an execution role granting the proper permissions. Therefore, you need to create a role including the AWS managed policy AWSLambdaBasicExecutionRole for granting access to write Amazon CloudWatch logs

FIGURE 8.16 AWS Lambda environment variable pointing to the forensics security group.

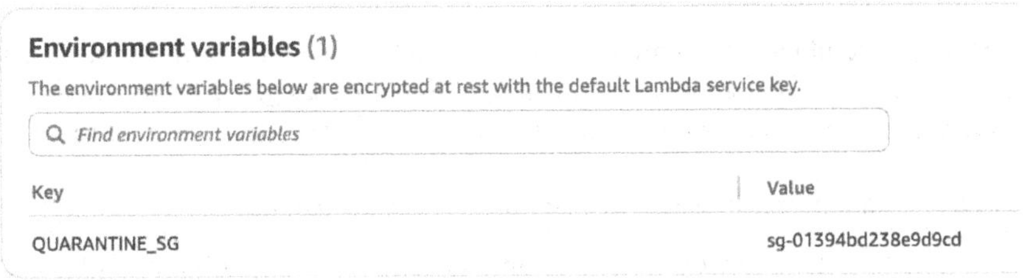

Key	Value
QUARANTINE_SG	sg-01394bd238e9d9cd

Environment variables (1)
The environment variables below are encrypted at rest with the default Lambda service key.

(or one more specific for production), as well as a custom policy that allows changing the security group of Amazon EC2 instances.

An example of such a policy is shown in Example 8.4.

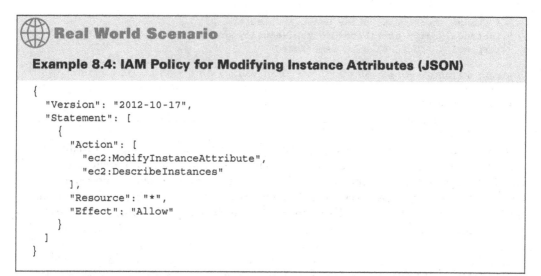

Real World Scenario

Example 8.4: IAM Policy for Modifying Instance Attributes (JSON)

```
{
  "Version": "2012-10-17",
  "Statement": [
    {
      "Action": [
        "ec2:ModifyInstanceAttribute",
        "ec2:DescribeInstances"
      ],
      "Resource": "*",
      "Effect": "Allow"
    }
  ]
}
```

You can see in the JSON policy in Example 8.4 that the ability to describe instances and modify instance attributes is given to the role that uses the AWS Lambda function while running.

With such security automation in place, the initial security group will be replaced with the forensics security group once a TOR client is detected in near real time, just minutes after it is discovered.

In Exercise 8.5, you configure an automation to react to a TOR client detection. This will allow you to gain hands-on experience with event-driven security and see a quick way to isolate potential connections to malicious actors using command-and-control tools leveraging the TOR network to protect their identity.

EXERCISE 8.5

Isolate Instances Using a TOR Anonymization Network

In this exercise, you configure an automation to react to a TOR client detection by Amazon GuardDuty. The automation will isolate the instance by changing the security group to an Incident-Forensics security group that allows access only from a specified IP address (used by that group).

1. Log in as an admin user in a sandbox or nonproduction account.

2. Create a security group called Incident-Forensics that allows inbound SSH only from the IP of the forensics team (it could be the IP address of a virtual desktop preinstalled

with forensics tools in Amazon WorkSpaces), without allowing any outbound access.

3. Create an instance and configure a security group that allows RDP (or SSH if you chose to use a Linux instance).

4. Connect to the instance using RDP/SSH.

5. Download and install TOR browser within the instance (`www.torproject.org/download`).

6. Configure an Amazon EventBridge rule to trigger an AWS Lambda function upon finding `UnauthorizedAccess:EC2/TorClient`.

7. Write the code to change the security group to the Incident-Forensics security group.

8. Create a role that can be assumed by AWS Lambda with the permissions to change security groups and add it as an execution role.

9. Open the TOR client on the instance.

10. Review the finding on Amazon GuardDuty (wait 10–20 minutes).

11. Verify that the security group was changed and that all the connections were terminated.

Beware of More Complex Options When There Are More Straightforward Alternatives

In some exam questions, there is a native functionality that addresses what was requested, and another option that is technically feasible but would be more costly and harder to set up and maintain. These kinds of questions usually include a hint requesting the easiest or most effective way to accomplish the goal.

Automated Termination for Self-Healing (Using Auto Scaling Groups)

When working within AWS to auto scale groups of instances that do not have any state (when all data is stored externally in databases, or using services such as Amazon Elastic File Systems or Amazon S3), you can terminate an instance as part of an automated action, since a new one will be created. This behavior certainly accomplishes self-healing, but always check with your forensics team to determine which information they need for root cause analysis. They will probably require you to take a snapshot of the Amazon EBS volume before an instance can be terminated.

Summary

Dealing with incident response plans means understanding a wide spectrum of security services. Taking the three-axis model as a reference will help you navigate through the spectrum, considering best practices for the different activities related to the process.

First, it is important to understand that incident response is a continuous process requiring constant improvement. Enhancement comes from practice. So it is critical to periodically test your incident response plan and consolidate the lessons learned.

Each iteration of your incident response plan follows the whole life cycle of an incident, from preparation to detection to forensics to post-incident. To be able to perform the actions in a timely and efficient way, you need to know which tools are available. Be prepared to contain the spread of a security issue by isolating resources, rotating credentials, responding to notifications of suspicious activity, and using tools to analyze and understand root causes of the incidents.

As a dynamic business practice, the incident response cycle is subject to agents of change: people, processes, and technology. Those are the pillars to consider when implementing new actions as part of the plan. Regarding technology, AWS Cloud provides tools to improve the effectiveness of an incident response plan. Arguably, one of the main factors that implies a more secure environment in the cloud is related to automation. By automating security response, you can reduce the time required to react to a security incident, reducing your window of exposure and thereby reducing the overall risk.

Exam Essentials

Know that abuse notifications require attention.   Keep in mind that when AWS Security teams send abuse notifications, they require attention from your security team and usually require your action as well. Ignoring them could potentially lead to account suspension. Respond to the notifications that you received from AWS Support through the AWS Support Center.

Know how to react to compromised credentials.   When credentials are compromised, you need to ensure that no resource created by malicious actors remains in the account, including resources on your account that you didn't create, such as EC2 instances, AMIs, EBS volumes and snapshots, and IAM users. You need to rotate all potentially compromised credentials. Changing the password for other users is a safety measure as well.

Know how to react to compromised instances.   Investigate compromised instances for malware, isolate them in the network, and stop or terminate them (ideally taking an Amazon EBS snapshot for the forensics team to do their root cause analysis). In AWS Marketplace, you'll find available partner products that can help detect and remove malware.

Know how to use AWS WAF and AWS Shield Advanced to mitigate attacks on applications. Remember to consider AWS Shield Advanced as a potential answer whenever you see DDoS attacks and to prepare your architecture to withstand the load until AWS Shield Advanced acts. Using AWS CloudFront, AWS Elastic Load Balancing, and Route 53 helps as well. Remember that you can use AWS WAF to mitigate many different application attacks by adding custom rules, such as a rate limit to prevent scraping and other malicious bot activity.

Understand how to use Amazon EventBridge for security integrations. Amazon EventBridge is frequently used to trigger response actions when a specific event is detected. This can include remediation using an AWS Lambda function.

Understand common remediation actions. Some of the most common remediation actions include executing AWS Lambda functions to isolate threats and running AWS Systems Manager Automations to fix configuration drifts.

Know what each service detects in order to trigger an automation. You can use Amazon Macie or AWS Config to detect weak configurations of Amazon S3 buckets. AWS Config also provides the Auto Remediation feature to correct configuration drift through AWS Systems Manager Automation or AWS Lambda. If you are trying to build an automation to react to a potential compromised instance or malicious actor's connections (based on their IP Reputation), then Amazon GuardDuty will be used to detect the instance, and an AWS Lambda function can be used to isolate the instance.

Understand AWS Systems Manager's capabilities. The AWS Systems Manager OpsCenter helps aggregate operational issues. AWS Systems Manager State Manager helps ensure that services restart automatically when they go down and when it detects configuration drifts. AWS Systems Manager can help you manage the security of resources at scale by creating groups of resources, improving visibility of patch compliance and operational issues, and automating remediation actions on groups of resources.

Review Questions

1. What is the first action to take when a probable compromise of AWS IAM credentials is detected?

    A. Update the security contact of the AWS account.

    B. Deactivate the AWS IAM credentials.

    C. Delete the AWS IAM credentials.

    D. Modify the apps that use the AWS IAM credentials.

2. Which of the following AWS services (alone or combined) would better suit the remediate phase of an incident life cycle?

    I. AWS Config

    II. AWS CloudTrail

    III. AWS Systems Manager

    A. Only I

    B. Only III

    C. Combination of II and III

    D. Combination of I and III

3. Which of the following is NOT contact information you should always keep updated in your AWS account?

    A. Billing contact

    B. Administrative contact

    C. Security contact

    D. Operations contact

4. What should you do when the AWS team sends you an abuse report from your resources?

    A. Review only when you receive more than one abuse notice for the same incident.

    B. Review and reply to the abuse report team as soon as possible.

    C. Review and reply to the abuse report team, only after you are totally sure what caused the issue.

    D. Review and solve the issue. No need to reply to the abuse report team, unless you have questions about the notification.

Review Questions   **429**

5. Which of the following options minimizes the risk to your environment when testing your incident response plan?

   A. Automate containment capability to reduce response times and organizational impact.

   B. Develop an incident management plan that contains incidents and procedures to return to a known good state.

   C. Execute security incident response simulations to validate controls and processes.

   D. Use your existing forensics tools on your AWS environment.

6. The security team detected a user's abnormal behavior and needs to know if there were any changes to the AWS IAM permissions. What steps should the team take?

   A. Use AWS CloudTrail to review the user's IAM permissions prior to the abnormal behavior and compare them to their current IAM permissions.

   B. Use Amazon Macie to review the user's IAM permissions prior to the abnormal behavior and compare them to their current IAM permissions.

   C. Use AWS Config to review the user's IAM permissions prior to the abnormal behavior and compare them to their current IAM permissions.

   D. Use AWS Trusted Advisor to review the user's IAM permissions prior to the abnormal behavior and compare them to their current IAM permissions.

7. Amazon GuardDuty reported finding an instance of `Backdoor:EC2/C&CActivity.B!DNS` in the production environment, outside business hours, and the security team is wondering how to react. What would be the most appropriate action to take?

   A. Instruct the forensics team to review the instance early tomorrow, since it does not reflect any immediate threat.

   B. Investigate the image for malware, and isolate, stop, or terminate the instance as soon as possible.

   C. Explicitly deny access to security groups to isolate the instance.

   D. Use Amazon Inspector to analyze the vulnerabilities on the instance and shut down vulnerable services.

8. You, the IAM access administrator, receive an abuse notification indicating that your account may be compromised. You do not find any unrecognized resource, but you see one of your IAM users with the following policy attached, which you did not attach: `AWSExposedCredentialPolicy_DO_NOT_REMOVE`. What would be the most appropriate action to immediately start remediation?

   A. Remove the policy since you did not create it, as it may be the source of the issue.

   B. Change the access keys for the user and detach the policy as the issue was remediated.

   C. No action is needed since the policy restricts the usage of the user. The user should not be deleted. Open a support ticket for instructions on how to proceed.

   D. Delete the user and be sure to check all regions for unrecognized resources or other users with the policy attached.

430   Chapter 8 ▪ Threat Detection and Incident Response

9. Amazon GuardDuty reported the finding `UnauthorizedAccess:EC2/TorClient` related to an Amazon EC2 instance. You, as part of the security team, are determining how to react. What would be the most appropriate action to take?

   A. Unless you know that the Amazon EC2 instance uses an anonymization network for valid business needs, you should isolate or stop the instance since it can indicate that your instance is compromised.

   B. You should immediately terminate the instance.

   C. You can safely ignore this finding since it's only informational, and it's probably an end user using TOR browser to access your site for privacy reasons.

   D. Use traffic mirroring to analyze the traffic to verify whether it is legitimate.

10. You are a security analyst at a company. You recently discovered that developers embed access keys on the code of many business applications. You are concerned about potential credentials being exposed by mistake. Which are the simplest and most effective actions to mitigate the risk? (Choose three.)

   A. Instruct the developers to use AWS Secrets Manager or AWS Systems Manager Parameter Store to avoid storing credentials in code.

   B. Enable Amazon Macie to detect access keys exposed to the public.

   C. Upgrade the support plan to Business or Enterprise Support and use AWS Trusted Advisor to detect exposed credentials.

   D. Build an AWS Lambda function to check repositories and notify using Amazon Simple Notification Service.

   E. Use Amazon CodeGuru to detect exposed credentials.

Appendix A

Answers to Review Questions

Chapter 1: Security Fundamentals

1. **B.** The concept of vulnerability is related to a fragility in a computer system, whereas a threat is defined by an entity exploiting a vulnerability. A security risk also considers the impact resulting from a threat being materialized. Therefore, the definitions for the terms in options b and c are swapped.

2. **A.** Confidentiality is concerned with preventing unauthorized disclosure of sensitive information and ensuring that the suitable level of privacy is maintained at all stages of data processing. Integrity deals with the prevention of unauthorized modification of data and with ensuring information accuracy. Availability focuses on ensuring reliability and an acceptable level of performance for legitimate users of computing resources. All statements present valid methods of addressing such concepts.

3. **B.** The sentence refers to the undeniable confirmation that a user or system had in fact performed an action, which is also known as nonrepudiation.

4. **D.** The classic AAA architecture refers to authentication, authorization, and accounting.

5. **A.** The seven layers of the Open Systems Interconnection (OSI) model, which are numbered 1–7, are physical, data link, network, transport, session, presentation, and application.

6. **C.** The Internet Control Message Protocol (ICMP) is not a dynamic routing protocol. It is used for reporting errors and performing network diagnostics, being a very important troubleshooting resource within the TCP/IP stack. All the other options are correct.

7. **E.** The intention of denial of service (DoS) is to exhaust processing resources (either on connectivity devices or computing hosts), thus keeping legitimate users from accessing the intended applications.

8. **C.** Some VPN technologies, such as multiprotocol label switching (MPLS), do not natively provide data confidentiality features such as encryption. All the other options are correct.

9. **C.** The Payment Card Industry Data Security Standard (PCI DSS) requires that credit card merchants meet minimum levels of security when they handle card holder data. The Health Insurance Portability and Accountability Act (HIPAA) is a set of security standards for protecting health information that is transferred or held in electronic form. The National Institute for Standards and Technology Cybersecurity Framework (NIST CSF) is a framework that assembles security standards, guidelines, and practices that have proved effective and may be used by entities belonging to any market segment. The General Data Protection Regulation (GDPR) is a set of rules created by the European Union (EU), requiring businesses to protect the personal data and privacy of EU citizens.

10. **C.** The zero-trust security model is based on the principle of least privilege, which states that organizations should grant the minimal amount of permissions that are strictly necessary for each user or application to work. Option A cites the phases of the security wheel model. Option B refers to the attack continuum model phases. Option D defines methods of data encryption. Option E is not directly related to the zero-trust model.

Chapter 2: Cloud Security Principles and Frameworks

1. A. AWS is always in charge of the facilities' security, including their data center, regardless of the type of service used. Options B and C are wrong because the customer is not accountable for AWS data center facilities security in the Shared Responsibility Model. Option D is wrong because the Shared Responsibility Model applies to all AWS regions.

2. C. When you are using an Amazon RDS database, AWS is in charge of most of the security layers, such as physical security, operating system security, database patching, backup, and high availability. However, you still need to define the maintenance windows to patch the operating system and applications. Options A and B are wrong because the customer does not manage the operating system in the Shared Responsibility Model for the container services category (which includes Amazon RDS). Option D is wrong because the Shared Responsibility Model applies to all AWS regions.

3. B. The AWS Artifact portal is your go-to resource for compliance-related information. It provides on-demand access to AWS's security and compliance reports and a selection of online agreements. Option A is wrong because there is no such portal. Option C is wrong because AWS GuardDuty is a service that provides monitoring on AWS Cloud environments. Option D is wrong because the AWS public website does not offer such certifications.

4. A. The AWS SOC 1 Type 2 report evaluates the effectiveness of AWS controls that might affect internal controls over financial reporting (ICFR), and the auditing process is aligned to the SSAE 18 and ISAE 3402 standards. Options B and C refer to definitions that do not apply to the mentioned report.

5. C. The AWS SOC 2 Security, Availability, and Confidentiality Report evaluates the AWS controls that meet the AICPA criteria for security, availability, and confidentiality. Options A and B refer to definitions that do not apply to the mentioned report.

6. C. The Well-Architected Framework was created to help cloud architects build secure, high-performing, resilient, and efficient infrastructure for their applications. The framework is freely available to all customers. Option A is wrong because the AWS Well-Architected Framework is not only related to security best practices. Option B is wrong because the framework is not a paid service. Option D is wrong because the framework is more than a tool.

7. D. The AWS Well-Architected security pillar dives deep into seven design principles for security in the cloud, and the seven principles are: Implement a strong identity foundation, enable traceability, apply security at all layers, automate security best practices, protect data in transit and at rest, keep people away from data, and prepare for security events. Options A, B, and C are wrong because they contain items that do not include all of the previous principles.

8. A. AWS is always in charge of the hypervisor security. When you start the operating system in your Amazon EC2 instance, you are in charge of updating the patches, implementing system configuration best practices, and defining security policies aligned with your own security

434 Appendix A ▪ Answers to Review Questions

rules. Still, AWS is in charge of implementing the security patches, hardening and guidelines, and best practices in the hypervisor layer. Options B and D are wrong because the customer is not accountable to the hypervisor security in the AWS Shared Responsibility Model. Option C is wrong because the model applies to all Amazon EC2 instances that use AWS hypervisors.

9. D. The AWS Marketplace is where you can find many security solutions that you can use to improve your security posture. You can use strategic AWS security partners. You can also use your own licenses in a bring-your-own-license model. The pay-as-you-go model is also available to you. Option A is wrong because it is too general. Option B is wrong because the AWS website does not provide such a service. Option C refers to a web page that does not provide such services.

10. D. The security pillar of the Well-Architected Framework provides a general overview of design principles and best practices to help you take advantage of cloud technologies to improve your security. Options A and C refer to pillars that focus on different topics. Option B refers to an extension of the guidance provided by the framework focusing on the financial industry.

Chapter 3: Management and Security Governance

1. D. AWS Organization allows you to set up IAM Identity Center to centrally manage access to AWS account and resources. Options A, B, and C are not offered by AWS Organization.

2. B. Service control policies do not restrict actions in the management account of an AWS Organization. SCPs only affect member accounts in the organization, which includes accounts that are designated as delegated administrators.

3. A. Using Amazon Macie, you can configure the service to automatically detect resources in new accounts and get alerts for policy misconfiguration across S3 buckets in your organization. Options B, C, and D do not support becoming delegated administrators.

4. C. AWS Control Tower implements three types of controls—preventive, detective, and proactive. They help you govern your resources and monitor compliance across your organization. Corrective control is not a type included by the service.

5. C. Using AWS CloudFormation StackSets extends the capability of stacks by allowing you to create, update, and delete stacks across multiple accounts and regions in one single operation. A template is just a file with a specific format used as a blueprint for building AWS resources, while a stack is a collection of resources defined within a template. A CloudFront distribution allows you to distribute static and dynamic web content for your users.

6. A. Option A is correct since you can share Private Certificate Authorities (CAs) with other accounts in your organization using AWS Resource Access Manager (AWS RAM). This configuration allows users of AWS Certificate Manager to issue certificates signed by your

shared CA. Option B, AWS Tag Editor, is a service that allows you to manage tags for your AWS resources; it's not for sharing resources. Amazon Share Services does not exist. Option D is not correct because it is a service that takes advantage of shared resources as your CA, but it does not share the resources by itself.

7. A. You can configure Amazon Macie to analyze S3 objects by using managed data identifiers provided by the same service, or custom data identifiers that you define. Option A, PII, is one of the types of managed data that you can select, along with financial information and credential data. PCI DSS and HIPAA are security standards that help you protect your data.

8. B. There are two valid channels that you can use to deliver configuration item updates: S3 buckets and SNS topic. Event Bridge notifications and Amazon SES are not supported as a delivery channel. Amazon ACLs are rules that define access to S3 buckets and objects.

9. C. If you have Basic and Developer Support plan, you can use the Trusted Advisor console to access all checks in the Service Limits category and five checks in the Security category.

10. D. PCI DSS version 4 is a valid pre-built framework available in the AWS Audit Manager library. Options A, B, and C are not correct versions of frameworks available to final users.

Chapter 4: Identity and Access Management

1. D. Enabling multifactor authentication is a good practice to provide secure access to your AWS account. All the other options are not recommended when you first create your account.

2. B. It is not possible to identify a user group as principal in a resource-based policy because groups are related to permissions, not authentication, and principals are authenticated IAM entities.

3. C. Answer C is the correct list of mandatory elements in a resource-based policy. SID is an optional statement to differentiate among others. Condition is optional to specify circumstances under which the policy grants permissions. The principal must be specified using an account, user, role, or federated user to which you want to grant or deny access.

4. C. That policy defines the maximum permissions that the identity-based policies can grant to an entity, but does not grant permissions. SCPs limit permissions that identity-based policies or resource-based policies grant to IAM users or IAM roles within the account. SCPs do not grant permissions. Session policies limit the permissions that the role or user's identity-based policies grant to the session, but do not grant permissions.

5. C. By default Amazon S3 enforces SSL encryption for cross-region replication. Options A and B are not available during configuration of cross-region replication. Option B is a condition to enforce encrypted connection using TLS to access bucket's objects but not include cross-region replication.

436 Appendix A ▪ Answers to Review Questions

6. C. ACLs are suitable for specific scenarios. For example, if a bucket owner allows other AWS accounts to upload objects, permissions to these objects can only be managed using ACLs by the AWS account that owns the object.

7. B. You can configure the amount of time that the temporary credentials are valid from 15 minutes to 12 hours.

8. A, C. With Amazon Cognito identity pools, you can authenticate users with identity providers (IdPs) through SAML 2.0. You can use an IdP that supports SAML with Amazon Cognito to provide a simple onboarding flow for your users. Your SAML-supporting IdP specifies the IAM roles that your users can assume. This way, different users can receive different sets of permissions.

9. A, D. Using a pre-signed URL will allow an upload without requiring additional credentials or permissions. A pre-signed URL is limited by the permissions of the user who creates it. That is, if you receive a pre-signed URL to upload an object, you can upload an object only if the creator of the URL has the necessary permissions to upload that object. When pre-signed URLs are created, you must specify an expiration, so it is possible that this URL has expired.

10. A, B. Using the principle of least-privilege will help you reduce the risk of unauthorized access of sensitive information. Using MFA is a good practice to provide secure access to your AWS account. It is not recommended to review and remove unused users on a daily basis but it a best practice to use custom password policies to enforce complex passwords for users accessing AWS resources.

Chapter 5: Security Logging and Monitoring

1. B. By default, an AWS CloudTrail trail only delivers the events of type management. You intentionally need to enable data and insights type events for them to appear in a trail.

2. B. In AWS Config terms, a configuration item is the representation of a single resource's attributes. A configuration snapshot is a JSON file containing the configuration of all the monitored resources. A configuration stream is the notification of a change in a monitored resource as soon as it happened, delivered in an Amazon SNS topic.

3. A. There are three types of AWS Config rules: custom rules (trigger a custom AWS Lambda function), managed rules (predefined by AWS Config), and service-linked rules (created by other AWS services).

4. C. AWS CloudTrail provides the CLI-based validate-logs command to validate the integrity of log files of the trail. In addition to this, you can use a custom method by validating the PKI-generated signature strings. No other AWS services (like Amazon S3 or AWS Config) provide a mechanism to validate the integrity of the AWS CloudTrail files.

Chapter 6: Infrastructure Protection   **437**

5. B. An AWS CloudTrail trail can be set up as an organizational trail if configured in a manager AWS Organizations account. Another possible centralization mechanism is to store log files produced by different accounts into the same Amazon S3 bucket. There is no Consolidate Trails feature in AWS Organizations.

6. B. Amazon CloudWatch Logs log group data is always encrypted and supports only symmetric encryption. By default, CloudWatch Logs uses server-side encryption with AES. You can also encrypt log group data using a symmetric KMS key.

7. C. High-resolution metrics (sub-minute reporting period) are only available for metrics reported by external sources (custom metrics). AWS Services publish metrics in Standard resolution. The metric's resolution is defined at the metric's creation time; there is no modify attribute action in Amazon CloudWatch.

8. C. An Amazon EventBridge rule contains information about the event bus the rule is attached to, the event pattern (expression that matches the events of interest), and the target service. There is no remediation action in an Amazon EventBridge rule.

9. D. When integrating Amazon Security Lake with AWS Organizations, the Organizations management account must designate a Security Lake delegated administrator account. This delegated administrator account will have the capability of collecting logs and events for all member accounts in all regions (where Security Lake is enabled). The Organizations management account cannot be assigned as the Security Lake delegated administrator account.

10. C. The SSM Compliance module works with patch data from Patch Manager. To provide the information, Patch Manager runs a patch scan task. When this task runs, it overwrites the compliance details of any previously executed scan.

Chapter 6: Infrastructure Protection

1. C. Statement I is wrong because a VPC is contained within an AWS Region. Statement II is correct because a VPC can contain multiple AWS availability zones in a single region. Statement III is wrong because a subnet is contained within an AWS availability zone.

2. B. Option A is wrong because the VPC router address in this subnet is 172.16.100.129 (the first available address in the CIDR). Option B is correct because the DNS server in this subnet is 172.16.100.130 (the second available address in the CIDR). Option C is wrong because the first available address in the subnet is 172.16.100.132 (the fifth available address in the CIDR). Option D is wrong because you can assign 172.16.100.128/25 as a CIDR block in a VPC.

3. B. Statements I and III are correct configurations in security groups. Statement II is not possible because security groups only have allow rules.

4. A. Statement I is correct because these load balancers indeed support such features. Statement II is incorrect because NLBs do not support AWS Lambda functions as targets. Statement III is incorrect because CLBs are not restricted to EC2-classic implementations.

438 Appendix A ▪ Answers to Review Questions

5. C. Amazon VPC Transit Gateway is the correct solution for this scenario because it is specifically designed to act as a central hub that can interconnect multiple VPCs, simplifying the network topology from a potential full mesh architecture to a hub-and-spoke model. It also easily scales as more VPCs are added, without requiring additional configuration between each pair of VPCs.

6. D. AWS Network Firewall is the correct solution for this scenario because it is specifically designed to protect VPCs by filtering network traffic at the perimeter. It allows you to create highly customized network security rules for traffic inspection and filtering based on protocols, ports, IP addresses, domains, and patterns in traffic content.

7. B. Amazon Inspector is the correct solution for this scenario because it is specifically designed to automatically assess applications for vulnerabilities, security exposures, and deviations from best practices. Inspector provides continuous scanning of resources, giving security teams real-time visibility into their security posture.

8. B. AWS Systems Manager Patch Manager is the correct solution for this scenario because it is specifically designed to automate the process of applying patches to managed instances across your AWS environment. It handles both security-related patches and other types of updates (such as feature updates and bug fixes) for operating systems and applications.

9. C. EC2 Image Builder is the correct solution for this scenario because it is specifically designed to automate the creation, maintenance, validation, and testing of EC2 Amazon Machine Images (AMIs). It provides a complete workflow for building, testing, and distributing AMIs, addressing the entire process the DevOps team needs to manage. EC2 Image Builder includes built-in testing and validation capabilities to ensure AMIs meet security and compliance requirements before deployment.

10. C. Amazon VPC Reachability Analyzer is the correct solution for this scenario because it is specifically designed to analyze and test network paths between source and destination resources within your VPC. It performs a detailed analysis of the potential network path between two endpoints, identifying any network configurations that might block traffic.

Chapter 7: Data Protection

1. B, C, D. There are three possible options for encrypting data using S3 buckets: SS3-S3, SSE-KMS, and SSE-C. ACM is not a valid option in this case and can work only with asymmetric certificates and not symmetric encryption.

2. A. Using Amazon RDS encryption with AWS KMS CMKs with automatic key rotation enabled is the correct solution for this scenario.

3. B, C, E. When you are defining a CMK, you must define three levels of access: The AWS root account level of access to the CMK, the IAM roles or users that have admin rights, and the IAM roles or users that have access to use the keys to encrypt and decrypt data. It is also important to remember that you cannot use IAM groups inside the CMK JSON security policy.

Chapter 8: Threat Detection and Incident Response

4. C. AWS KMS enforces a waiting period minimum of seven days up to a maximum of 30 days (default configuration) before you can delete a CMK.

5. D. AWS Key Management Service allows you to encrypt data natively, in addition to the ability to integrate with more than 50 available services in the AWS Cloud.

6. A, C. Typically, the use of CloudHSM is directly related to meeting regulatory needs, such as FIPS 140-2 Level 3 standards. Another widespread use case is to protect web applications' private keys and offloading SSL encryption.

7. C. When you enable automatic key rotation, AWS KMS rotates the CMK every 365 days from the enabled date, so once a year automatically. This process is transparent to the user and the environment. The AWS-managed keys are the default master keys that protect the S3 objects, Lambda functions, and WorkSpaces when no other keys (CMKs) are defined for these services.

8. B. Using AWS Certificate Manager (ACM) to provision public certificates and associate them with the ALB is the correct solution for this scenario. ACM automatically handles the renewal of public certificates before they expire, with no manual intervention required and no application downtime during renewal. ACM can issue and manage wildcard certificates (e.g., *.example.com) that cover multiple subdomains.

9. C. Amazon Macie is the correct solution for this scenario. Macie is specifically designed to automatically discover, classify, and protect sensitive data stored in Amazon S3. It uses machine learning and pattern matching to identify sensitive data types like PII, financial data, and credentials.

10. B. AWS CloudHSM is the correct solution for this scenario. CloudHSM provides dedicated HSMs in the AWS Cloud that enable organizations to maintain complete and exclusive control over their encryption keys.

Chapter 8: Threat Detection and Incident Response

1. B. If an AWS IAM credential is leaked, the best practice is to revoke it as soon as you detect the compromise. Only then should you modify the apps, and once the functionality is restored, you can proceed with the deletion of the credentials. It is important to keep the security contact on your AWS account updated, but it is not the more critical action to execute immediately after detecting a possible compromise.

2. D. Using AWS Config rules and the remediation feature with an AWS Systems Manager automation document is an effective way to remediate a deviation from a compliant configuration affecting a monitored resource. AWS CloudTrail helps with the detection phase of the suspicious activity.

440 Appendix A • Answers to Review Questions

3. B. You should keep all of the contacts for your AWS account updated because, as they receive important notifications, some of them will require action to keep your account and services in good standing. Administrative is not a contact definition inside the AWS account; billing, operations, and security are the alternate contact options within an AWS account.

4. B. You should constantly check and immediately review every abuse report you receive from AWS. To avoid any disruption, reply to the report as soon as possible explaining the actions you plan to take so that the AWS team is aware you are executing your incident response. Keep them informed until the incident is resolved.

5. C. Although all answers are valid mechanisms for developing a sound incident response plan, the security incident response simulations are specifically oriented to minimize the risk when testing your plan.

6. C. AWS Config is the most appropriate service to check if there were changes to an AWS resource. AWS CloudTrail gives you information of executed actions, Amazon Macie helps in the classification of information in Amazon S3 buckets (and detecting failures in protecting that information), and AWS Trusted Advisor informs you about your implementation of best practices.

7. B. First, the security team should be able to assess the criticality of the incident. A backdoor report in the production environment requires immediate attention. Isolation is part of the reaction, but it should be complemented with the root cause analysis of the incident to detect the blast radius.

8. The user had an IAM policy attached without the administrator's knowledge, which is suspicious. So, the first action is to delete the suspicious user and check other possible actions taken by that user. Removing the policy or changing access keys does not remediate the issue.

9. If you detect suspicious activity (in this case an Amazon EC2 instance using a TOR client without a valid business need to do so), your next step is to try to isolate the incident; then you will contain, remediate, recover, and do a forensic analysis. Terminating the instance will not allow a comprehensive forensic analysis. Traffic mirroring is not effective since TOR clients use encryption to connect to the anonymization network. It is not a best practice to ignore a finding without further investigation (in addition, the finding reports an outbound traffic using a TOR client, not the other way around).

10. A, B, C. The constituent factors of an incident response plan are people, technology, and processes. Instructing the developers deals with *people*. Enabling Amazon Macie to detect access keys on Amazon S3 buckets deals with *technology* (use relevant AWS services). Using the right support plan helps with the *processes* that deal with incident. Although you can create an AWS Lambda function to check repositories, it is not the simplest way to do that. Amazon CodeGuru helps in checking code quality (such as discovering inappropriate handling of credentials) but not in mitigating the risk.

Appendix B

Creating Your Security Journey in AWS

Introduction

In this appendix, you learn how to put together all the skills you learned in previous chapters into a cloud security strategy.

A security strategy should have a set of initiatives that your teams will implement to mitigate risks in your workloads.

Some risks may be particular to the application you're running, but many of the risks your workload will face are common to other workloads that may include all public web applications, all virtual machines, or most AWS customers.

While many security specialists would like to know in detail all potential risks and to have security controls in place to mitigate them before launching any applications to production, reality often doesn't allow this. Resources are scarce, even for organizations with significant monetary investments, and it's hard to find and hire senior security specialists experienced in the cloud.

In the AWS Cloud, there are dozens of security services and dozens of security configurations on other services. Many security services or configurations are free or have a free tier (such as AWS Shield, with a Standard tier for free network-level DDoS mitigation and an Advanced tier that is paid) or a free trial that allows you to see the actual cost that you would have in your billing if there was no free trial. A free trial is intended for you to see that AWS Security services are cost efficient.

There are recommendations available on AWS Cloud Adoption Framework (CAF) Security Perspective and on the Security pillar of the Well-Architected Framework (WAF). There are also plenty of other recommendations that come from the Center for Internet Security (CIS) in their AWS Foundations benchmark.

With so many recommendations, so many services, and so many configurations, you may wonder where to start or how to prioritize these tasks.

While this topic may be one of the most important aspects in real life, it is not included on the exam, as prioritization strategy varies for different organizations (startup vs. enterprise; some are more risk averse than others). Because of the relevance of the topic, we chose to include this content as an appendix in this book.

How to Prioritize Your Security Initiatives

Most security teams define security initiatives with different recommendations based on risk. They focus on implementing security controls that mitigate the most significant risks first, considering their potential impact and likelihood of occurrence.

Obviously, this perspective is valid, but another factor that you should consider is how much effort the implementation of that security control requires, considering not only how quick it is to

FIGURE B.1 Identifying quick wins.

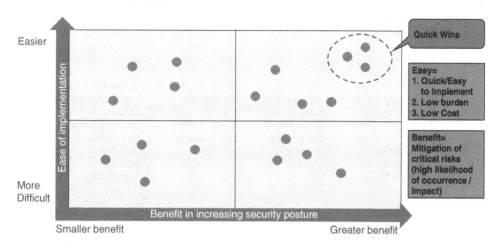

implement, but also what the cost is and what the operational or administrative impact is once it is implemented.

Why is it important to consider the effort? Without this consideration, you could have your whole team working for three months on IAM, as it's probably the most critical capability, and completely neglect threat detection, which could be resolved in minutes by enabling Amazon GuardDuty to show potential active security threats in your environment.

Security recommendations that mitigate significant threats *and* are quick to implement are your quick wins. These should go first, as shown in Figure B.1.

In Figure B.1, each dot represents a security initiative; some of them are quick wins. During the first phase of your security journey, it is recommended that you define and then implement these quick wins.

Consistency is another critical aspect. You should balance recommendations from multiple pillars (IAM, threat detection, incident response application protection, etc.) to prevent adversaries from breaking the chain at the weakest link.

In AWS Cloud, there are many quick wins, such as enabling MFA, assigning security contacts, establishing a billing alarm, enabling Amazon GuardDuty, and protecting the root account. These are all actions that will take minutes to implement and will help significantly improve the security posture.

It's a Journey

After the quick wins (Phase 1), it becomes a journey, where you evolve your security capabilities over time, in phases.

In Phase 2, you should focus on the foundational aspects that may not be as quick to implement but are mandatory for launching production applications, such as temporary credentials, the cloud

FIGURE B.2 Phases.

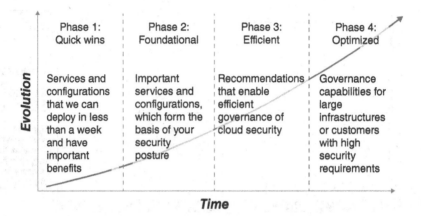

foundations with multi-account management, Amazon VPCs to isolate workloads, and encryption configuration.

In Phase 3, you should address all the recommendations required to be efficient in the security program that are not present at launch of the first production application. All organizations should strive to implement these recommendations, for example, using infrastructure as code or establishing DevSecOps pipelines with application security scans as part of the pipeline.

In Phase 4, you should have the security recommendations that will optimize your security program, but it only makes sense to implement these capabilities if you are mature on the recommendations in previous phases, if you have a large organization, or you have a particular compliance requirement or security stringent policies. For example, if you have not defined a disaster recovery plan, it doesn't make sense to perform chaos engineering (injecting faults to simulate incidents such as an AZ becoming unavailable). In Figure B.2, you can see a sample set of generally advisable phases.

Security Maturity Model

Each journey is going to be particular, and there is no one recipe for all organizations, but to help you design your journey, you can use the AWS Security Maturity Model (available at https://maturitymodel.security.aws.dev) as a sample to create your own journey. This community reference model provides prescriptive guidance (advice based on experience from the field) regarding how to prioritize recommendations. They help you build your journey toward improving your cloud security in a coherent and efficient order and to minimize risks as soon as possible.

Security Maturity Model   **445**

FIGURE B.3   Security Maturity Model Phase 1: Quick Wins.

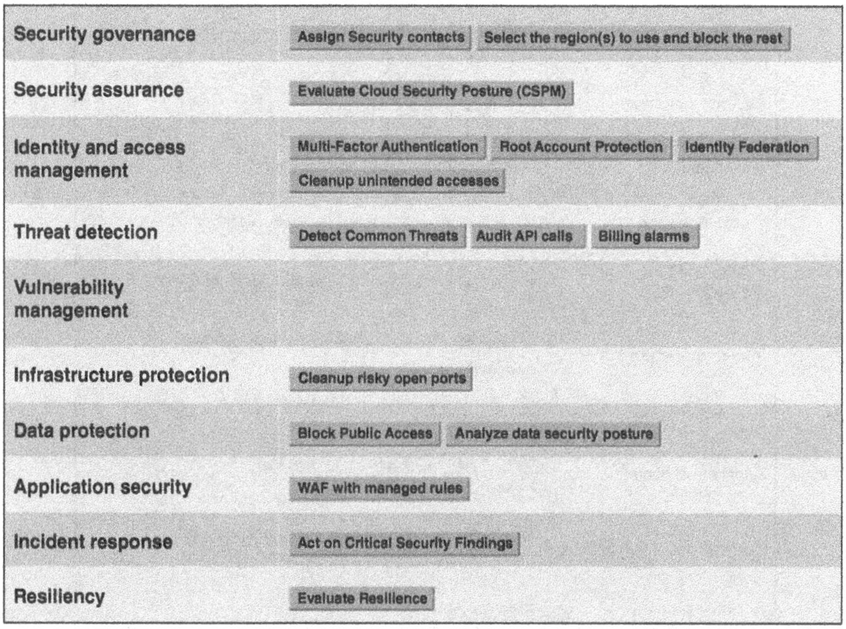

Security governance	Assign Security contacts	Select the region(s) to use and block the rest
Security assurance	Evaluate Cloud Security Posture (CSPM)
Identity and access management	Multi-Factor Authentication / Root Account Protection / Identity Federation / Cleanup unintended accesses
Threat detection	Detect Common Threats / Audit API calls / Billing alarms
Vulnerability management	
Infrastructure protection	Cleanup risky open ports
Data protection	Block Public Access / Analyze data security posture
Application security	WAF with managed rules
Incident response	Act on Critical Security Findings
Resiliency	Evaluate Resilience

FIGURE B.4   Security Maturity Model Phase 2: Foundational.

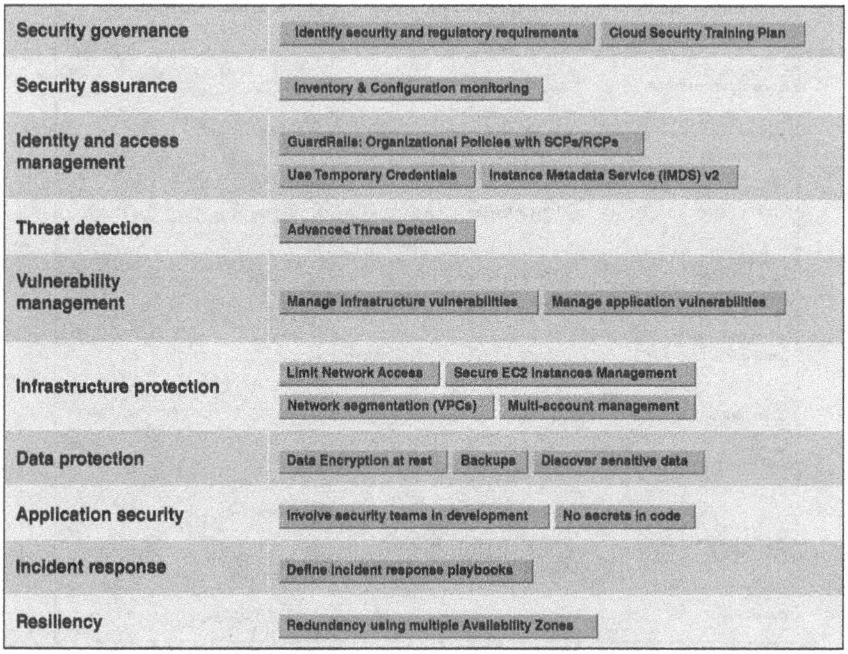

Security governance	Identify security and regulatory requirements / Cloud Security Training Plan
Security assurance	Inventory & Configuration monitoring
Identity and access management	GuardRails: Organizational Policies with SCPs/RCPs / Use Temporary Credentials / Instance Metadata Service (IMDS) v2
Threat detection	Advanced Threat Detection
Vulnerability management	Manage infrastructure vulnerabilities / Manage application vulnerabilities
Infrastructure protection	Limit Network Access / Secure EC2 Instances Management / Network segmentation (VPCs) / Multi-account management
Data protection	Data Encryption at rest / Backups / Discover sensitive data
Application security	Involve security teams in development / No secrets in code
Incident response	Define incident response playbooks
Resiliency	Redundancy using multiple Availability Zones

446   Appendix B ▪ Creating Your Security Journey in AWS

FIGURE B.5   Security Maturity Model Phase 3: Efficient.

Security governance	Design your secure architecture Use infrastructure as code Tagging strategy
Security assurance	Create your compliance reports
Identity and access management	Least Privilege Review Customer IAM: security of your customers
Threat detection	Custom Threat Detection capabilities (SecLake / SIEM)
Vulnerability management	Security Champions Program DevSecOps: Security in the Pipeline
Infrastructure protection	Image Generation Pipeline Anti-Malware / EDR / Runtime Protection Outbound Traffic Control
Data protection	Encryption in transit
Application security	Perform threat modeling WAF with custom rules Advanced DDoS Mitigation (L7)
Incident response	Run TableTop Exercises - Simulations Automate Critical Playbooks Security Investigations - Root cause analysis
Resiliency	Disaster Recovery Plan

FIGURE B.6   Security Maturity Model Phase 4: Optimized.

Security governance	Sharing security work and responsibility
Security assurance	Automate Evidence Gathering
Identity and access management	IAM Data Perimeters IAM Policy Generation Pipeline Temporary Elevated Access
Threat detection	Threat Intelligence Network Flows analysis (VPC Flow Logs)
Vulnerability management	Vulnerability Management Team
Infrastructure protection	Zero Trust Access Use abstract services
Data protection	GenAI Data protection
Application security	Forming a Red Team (Attacker's Point of View)
Incident response	Forming a Blue Team (Incident Response) Advanced security automations Security Orchestration & Ticketing Automate deviation correction in configurations
Resiliency	Multi-region Disaster Recovery Automation Chaos Engineering

In Figures B.3 through B.6, you can see a set of sample recommendations in each phase and capability, as you will find on the security maturity model, that can be your starting point for your strategy.

For more details on each recommendation, access the model that is available at `https://maturitymodel.security.aws.dev`.

The model also provides assessment tools to self-evaluate how aligned you are with the recommendations and to track your progress over time.

Appendix C

AWS Security Services Portfolio

AWS currently offers more than 200 cloud services across more than 30 regions and more than 100 availability zones. The company classifies some of these services under the security, identity, and compliance category.

Because remembering what each service does is a challenge for the novice cloud security practitioner, this appendix provides a brief description of these dedicated services in alphabetical order, a summary of their relationship with other AWS services, and the icon that represents each of the services.

Much like a family photo, the AWS Security Service Portfolio will continue to change in the future, with the addition of new members to the list each year (and most probably announced during the company's conferences AWS re:Invent and re:Inforce). Therefore, we highly recommend that you check the following website to meet new "family members": `https://aws.amazon.com/products/security`.

Many of these AWS services are offered with a free trial for a certain period of time, such as a month, or for a certain amount of usage (such as storage, events, users, or other parameters). Charges, parameters, and offerings can change. Always refer to the AWS official documentation for the most current charges, updates, and other information.

Amazon Cognito

Amazon Cognito (see Figure C.1) allows you to add user sign-up, user sign-in, and user access control to web and mobile applications, sparing you the effort of designing or developing such components. Amazon Cognito has federation resources that support the use of identity providers such as Facebook, Google, and Amazon. Additionally, the service follows open identity standards such as Open Authorization (OAuth) 2.0, OpenID Connect (OIDC), and Security Assertion Markup Language (SAML) 2.0. Such integrations facilitate the management of user access control from these applications, both to AWS resources and to user-defined resources in their applications.

The feature set of Amazon Cognito includes multifactor authentication (MFA), data-at-rest and data-in-transit encryption, and a built-in customizable user interface. The service also offers threat protections. One example is adaptive authentication, which provides detection for unusual sign-in requests from new locations or devices, risk score, additional verification, user blocking, SMS, and a time-based one-time password generator, such as Google Authenticator. It also offers compromised credentials protection when it detects that a password configured in Cognito has been compromised in other places.

FIGURE C.1 Amazon Cognito icon.

Amazon Cognito brings value to organizations by providing support for compliance regulations such as the Health Insurance Portability and Accountability Act (HIPAA), Payment Card Industry Data Security Standard (PCI DSS), System and Organization Control (SOC), International Standards Organization/International Electrotechnical Commission (ISO/IEC) 27001, ISO/IEC 27017, ISO/IEC 27018, and ISO 9001.

AWS currently offers Amazon Cognito in three pricing categories: Lite, Essentials, and Plus. Both Lite and Essentials are free for 10,000 monthly active users (MAUs) directly managed by Cognito and 50 MAUs for federated users. Always refer to the AWS official documentation for updated information.

You can find the Amazon Cognito documentation here: `https://docs.aws.amazon.com/cognito`.

Amazon Detective

Amazon Detective (see Figure C.2) enables you to investigate, analyze, and identify root causes of security issues or suspicious activities in your AWS environments. Amazon Detective does this through the collection of log data from AWS resources, such as VPC flow logs, AWS CloudTrail, Amazon EKS, AWS Security Hub, and Amazon GuardDuty. Within its engine, Amazon Detective leverages machine learning models, statistical analysis, and graph theory to build a data set that facilitates faster security investigations.

From an administrative perspective, Amazon Detective creates a consolidated and interactive view of resources, users, and the relationships among them over time (a Detective behavior graph) in order to allow historical analysis and triage of findings.

Amazon Detective pricing is based on the amount of data ingested. It offers a 30-day free trial for new users, providing access to the full set of features of the service.

You can find the Amazon Detective documentation here: `https://docs.aws.amazon.com/detective`.

FIGURE C.2 Amazon Detective icon.

Amazon GuardDuty

Amazon GuardDuty (see Figure C.3) is AWS's threat detection service that continuously searches for malicious activities and unauthorized operations in AWS resources deployed on your environment. Leveraging machine learning, anomaly detections, and threat intelligence from AWS

Security and third-party companies such as CrowdStrike and Proofpoint, Amazon GuardDuty identifies potential threats across AWS CloudTrail, VPC flow logs, and DNS logs. It can also rely on AWS EventBridge and AWS Lambda to provide threat response automation.

Being able to act on multiple accounts simultaneously, Amazon GuardDuty detects cryptocurrency mining, credential compromise behavior, communication with known command-and-control servers (C&C), API calls from well-known malicious IP addresses, unusual API activity, intra-VPC port scanning, unusual patterns of failed login requests, outbound denial-of-service activity, unusual high volumes of network traffic, uncommon network protocols, data exfiltration using DNS, API calls from an unfamiliar geolocation, attempts to disable AWS CloudTrail logging, changes that weaken the account password policy, and unexpected infrastructure launches. It also can detect anomalies and threats in Amazon S3 buckets, EKS, Lambda, runtime protection (EC2, ECS, and EKS), RDS, and malware protection (EC2 and S3).

Amazon GuardDuty currently offers a 30-day free trial period. You can find the Amazon GuardDuty documentation here: https://docs.aws.amazon.com/guardduty.

FIGURE C.3 Amazon GuardDuty icon.

Amazon Inspector

Amazon Inspector (see Figure C.4) offers an automated assessment of the security posture for compute resources in your AWS account. The service searches for exposures, vulnerabilities, and deviations from best practices and produces a detailed list of security findings across Amazon EC2 instances, containers, and Lambda functions. These findings are then divided into different levels of severity. Amazon Inspector provides a contextualized severity score for each finding, based on its knowledge of your environment and the base score of the vulnerabilities. Amazon Inspector can continuously inspect your compute resources and automatically update the resulting findings.

FIGURE C.4 Amazon Inspector icon.

Amazon Inspector also helps you discover unplanned network access in your Amazon EC2 instances. Additionally, Amazon Inspector can provide a software bill of materials (SBOM) that is an inventory of the software components in your applications.

Amazon Inspector pricing is based on the number of covered resources (EC2 instances, containers in ECR, and Lambda functions) and the type of scan. Users get a 15-day free trial for accounts that have never activated Amazon Inspector before. The free trial covers continuous scans of EC2 instances, containers pushed to ECR, Lambda functions, and 25 on-demand container image assessments.

You can find the Amazon Inspector documentation here: https://docs.aws.amazon.com/inspector.

Amazon Macie

Amazon Macie (see Figure C.5) automatically discovers, classifies, and protects sensitive data, such as personally identifiable information (PII) or intellectual property, via machine learning techniques. When Amazon Macie detects information such as credit card numbers, Social Security numbers, or a match with a (customizable) pattern, it provides detailed alerts in a dashboard that shows which accounts, S3 buckets, and objects are at risk. Amazon Macie also provides automation capabilities to respond to such risks.

Amazon Macie pricing is based on the number of Amazon S3 buckets evaluated, the number of Amazon S3 objects monitored, and the amount of data inspected. Amazon Macie offers a 30-day free trial period for new accounts, which includes up to 150 GB of inspected data.

You can find the Amazon Macie documentation here: https://docs.aws.amazon.com/macie.

FIGURE C.5 Amazon Macie icon.

Amazon Security Lake

Amazon Security Lake (see Figure C.6), as its name implies, is a data lake for security data. AWS resources, third-party providers, and custom sources ingest information in Amazon Security Lake following the Open Cybersecurity Schema Framework (OCSF) standard. Amazon Security Lake then normalizes, consolidates, and presents the security information.

FIGURE C.6 Amazon Security Lake icon.

Amazon Security Lake gives you the capability of centralizing your security data for storage, analysis, and lifecycle management. You can visualize and analyze data using other tools like Amazon QuickSight, Amazon Detective, Amazon SageMaker, or Amazon Bedrock.

Amazon Security Lake pricing is based on the amount of ingested and normalized data. While all data normalization is charged, data sourced outside of AWS services is not charged for ingestion. Amazon Security Lake offers a 15-day free trial for new users, covering all the service features.

You can find the Amazon Security Lake documentation here: `https://docs.aws.amazon.com/security-lake`.

Amazon Verified Permissions

Amazon Verified Permissions (see Figure C.7) is an authorization service that allows you to specify the access you want to provide to your custom application. Amazon Verified Permissions relies on the Cedar policy language to express the permissions to enforce. This policy language provides automated reasoning capabilities, having the means to mathematically prove the correctness of the expressed permissions. The policy language uses familiar constructs like roles, attributes, principals, actions, and resources to document the permissions.

Amazon Verified Permissions allows for decoupling the authorization decisions from the business logic of the applications. In addition to providing a better focus for developers, it gives organizations the capability of independently reviewing the access control definitions and centralizing authorization decisions.

You can find the Amazon Verified Permissions documentation here: `https://docs.aws.amazon.com/verifiedpermissions`.

FIGURE C.7 Amazon Verified Permissions icon.

AWS Artifact

AWS Artifact (see Figure C.8) is a service portal that empowers you to obtain compliance reports and online agreements related to your environments deployed on the AWS Cloud. Consequently, you can use AWS Artifact if you require formal information associated with regulations such as service organization control (SOC), payment card industry (PCI), and agreements such as the business associate agreement (BAA) and nondisclosure agreement (NDA).

This service intends to provide a comprehensive resource to auditors looking for reports, certifications, accreditations, and third-party attestations from regulation bodies across geographic areas and compliance industry organizations. It also provides governance for your agreements with AWS and insights from the AWS security control environment.

AWS Artifact is currently offered at no cost. You can find the AWS Artifact documentation here: https://docs.aws.amazon.com/artifact.

FIGURE C.8 AWS Artifact icon.

AWS Audit Manager

AWS Audit Manager (see Figure C.9) allows you to collect evidence from your AWS infrastructure to identify and report adherence with a set of compliance frameworks.

AWS Audit Manager provides continuous auditing functionalities for a set of prebuilt frameworks. The service also gives you the option to build your own compliance framework (for example, to adhere to internal audit requirements).

AWS Audit Manager active assessments run continuously, collecting data based on the defined scope and framework and providing evidence for each control within the framework.

AWS Audit Manager billing is based on the number of executed resource assessments. The service offers a two-month free tier of 35,000 resource assessment per month for new users.

You can find the AWS Audit Manager documentation here: https://docs.aws.amazon.com/audit-manager.

FIGURE C.9 AWS Audit Manager icon.

AWS Certificate Manager

Certificates provide secure data communication and ensure the identity of entities exchanging such data. AWS Certificate Manager (see Figure C.10) provisions, imports, manages, and deploys Secure Socket Layer (SSL) or Transport Layer Security (TLS) X.509 digital certificates.

Those certificates can then be deployed on integrated AWS services. AWS Certificate Manager centralizes the management of certificates and streamlines the traditional manual process of acquiring, uploading, and renewing digital certificates.

Within AWS Cloud, AWS Certificate Manager can directly assign certificates to elastic load balancers, Amazon CloudFront distributions, APIs deployed on Amazon API Gateway, AWS Elastic Beanstalk, Amazon Cognito, AWS App Runner, AWS Nitro Enclaves, AWS Amplify, Amazon OpenSearch service, and AWS Network Firewall. In addition, you can audit the use of each certificate on AWS Certificate Manager via Amazon CloudTrail logs and import certificates issued by third-party certificate authorities.

Digital certificates provided by AWS Certificate Manager for use with an AWS integrated service are currently free (you only pay for the AWS resources that consume these certificates).

You can find the AWS Certificate Manager documentation here: `https://docs.aws.amazon.com/acm`.

FIGURE C.10 AWS Certificate Manager icon.

AWS CloudHSM

A hardware security module (HSM) is a computing device that safeguards and manages encryption keys for authentication and provides cryptoprocessing. AWS CloudHSM (see Figure C.11) is a cloud-based, single-tenant, Federal Information Processing Standard

FIGURE C.11 AWS CloudHSM icon.

(FIPS)-validated hardware security module that allows you to generate, manage, and use your own encryption keys. Because it is a cloud service, AWS CloudHSM releases the customer from the time-consuming administrative tasks of hardware provisioning, software patching, high-availability deployment, and backup coordination. It also provides low latency to applications running in AWS Cloud.

AWS CloudHSM provides general-purpose HSMs in FIPS and non-FIPS mode. CloudHSM in FIPS mode offers HSM clusters that are FIPS 140-2 Level 3 or FIPS 140-3 Level–validated. AWS CloudHSM follows industry standards such as Public Key Cryptography Standards (PKCS) #11, Java Cryptography Extensions (JCE), Cryptography API: Next Generation (CNG), and Key Storage Provider (KSP). It is also compliant with regulations, such as HIPAA, Federal Risk and Authorization Management Program (FedRAMP), and PCI.

As a dedicated hardware security module, AWS CloudHSM instances are deployed with single-tenant access inside your own Amazon Virtual Private Cloud (VPC). AWS CloudHSM has no visibility or access to your encryption keys, while providing a clear separation of management duties, such as AWS administrator (a role that manages the appliance) and crypto users (who perform key management and cryptographic operations).

AWS CloudHSM is billed per hour of running HSM.

You can access the AWS CloudHSM documentation here: `https://docs.aws.amazon.com/cloudhsm`.

AWS Directory Service

AWS Directory Service (see Figure C.12) is a managed Microsoft Active Directory deployed on the AWS cloud and built on Microsoft software. This service is also known as AWS Managed Microsoft AD and can be used by your directory-aware workloads and AWS resources, such as Amazon EC2 instances, Amazon RDS for SQL Server, and Amazon WorkSpaces.

With AWS Directory Service, you can use the same management tools that Microsoft AD administrators use to centrally manage application access and devices, as well as to take full advantage of Microsoft AD features such as Group Policies and Single Sign-On. Although this service does not require you to synchronize or replicate data from your existing AD to the AWS Cloud, you can easily deploy Microsoft AD trust relationships from existing domains to AWS Directory Service.

FIGURE C.12 AWS Directory Service icon.

Similar to other AWS managed services, AWS Directory Service simplifies administration by providing native high availability through multi-AZ deployment, automatic monitoring to detect failures, data replication, and automated daily snapshots, with no need for software installation, patching, or updates. You can also scale your implementation using a multiregion replication feature that automatically replicates a single directory across multiple AWS regions.

AWS Directory Service is available in two editions: Standard (for small and midsize businesses with up to 5,000 employees and 30,000 directory objects, including users, groups, and devices) and Enterprise (for organizations with up to 500,000 directory objects).

AWS Directory Service currently provides a 30-day free trial, limited to 1,500 hours of use across all your eligible Directory Service–managed directories. You can find the AWS Directory Service documentation here: `https://docs.aws.amazon.com/directory-service`.

AWS Firewall Manager

AWS Firewall Manager (see Figure C.13) enables you to define and control firewall rules across accounts deployed in AWS Organizations from a central location. This service allows the creation and enforcement of firewall rules and security policies in a centralized way from services like AWS WAF, AWS Shield Advanced, Amazon VPC Security Groups, AWS Network Firewall, and Amazon Route 53 Resolver DNS Firewall. It can also centrally manage firewall rules for supported third-party firewalls like Palo Alto Networks NGFW and Fortigate CNF.

Through the AWS Firewall Manager, you can roll out AWS WAF rules for your application load balancers, Elastic IP addresses, and Amazon CloudFront distributions. In addition, you can control AWS Shield Advanced configurations, security groups for your Amazon EC2 instances, and Elastic Network Interfaces (ENIs) in Amazon VPCs. To achieve automatic protection on the aforementioned services deployed on your AWS environments, you can leverage grouped rules and policies that are centrally managed in AWS Firewall Manager. These constructs ensure compliance both for existing resources and for new resources as they are created across accounts.

AWS Firewall Manager also brings vulnerability protection through subscription to managed rules for WAF from the AWS Marketplace (for example, for Common Vulnerabilities and Exposures [CVE] patch updates). Furthermore, AWS Firewall Manager provides a dashboard with compliance notifications to further help regulatory demands.

AWS Firewall Manager charges by the type of protection policy you implement, by AWS region.

FIGURE C.13 AWS Firewall Manager icon.

You can find the AWS Firewall Manager documentation here: `https://docs.aws.amazon.com/firewall-manager`.

AWS Identity and Access Management

AWS Identity and Access Management (AWS IAM; see Figure C.14) is a security service that controls access to AWS services and resources. It creates and manages users, groups, and permissions, which allow and deny access to AWS resources in a granular way. AWS IAM enables customizable access control through conditions, such as MFA, and encryption implementations, such as TLS, source IP addresses, or time of day.

AWS IAM adheres to the concept of zero-trust because, by default, users have no authorization to access any AWS resources until permissions are explicitly declared. Natively integrated in AWS services, AWS IAM differentiates the validation of public or cross-account access using policies from Amazon S3 buckets, AWS KMS keys, Amazon SQS queues, AWS IAM roles, and AWS Lambda functions. Moreover, the service can also be integrated with your corporate directory, such as Microsoft Active Directory, and is extensible via SAML 2.0.

There is currently no charge for using AWS IAM. You can find the AWS IAM documentation here: `https://docs.aws.amazon.com/iam`.

FIGURE C.14 AWS Identity and Access Management (IAM) icon.

AWS IAM Identity Center

AWS IAM Identity Center (formerly known as SSO; see Figure C.15) centrally controls access of your workforce to AWS accounts and AWS managed applications. This service manages access and user permissions to your AWS accounts in a single place. It also centralizes access to other AWS applications like Amazon Redshift or your custom application (using SAML 2.0). AWS IAM Identity Center allows you to federate your workforce, connecting to your identity provider (like MS Active Directory, CyberArk, Google, Ping Identity, and Okta, among others), or you can create local users directly in IAM Identity Center.

AWS IAM Identity Center is a managed service that provides native high availability. This service is available at no charge. You can find the AWS IAM Identity Center documentation here: `https://docs.aws.amazon.com/singlesignon`.

FIGURE C.15 AWS IAM Identity Center icon.

AWS Key Management Service

AWS Key Management Service (KMS; see Figure C.16) provides you with the means to create, import, control, and manage encryption keys (both symmetric and asymmetric). You can integrate those keys with your applications or across AWS services. With AWS KMS, you can encrypt data, digitally sign, and generate and verify message authentication codes (MACs). AWS KMS also helps you support your regulatory and compliance needs via AWS CloudTrail logging of all key-related operations in your environment. Additionally, this service is validated under FIPS 140-2, SOC 1–3, PCI DSS Level 1, FedRAMP, and HIPAA.

AWS KMS is charged based on the number of KMS keys created, the number of rotations, and the number of requests. AWS KMS currently provides a free tier of 20,000 requests per month.

You can find the AWS KMS documentation here: https://docs.aws.amazon.com/kms.

FIGURE C.16 AWS Key Management Service (AWS KMS) icon.

AWS Network Firewall

AWS Network Firewall (see Figure C.17) allows you deploy network rules to control and authorize traffic across your Amazon VPCs. It is a managed service, so you do not need to manage infrastructure, and it scales according to the traffic requirements. AWS Network Firewall enforces security rules that can be created directly on the service, imported from common open-source formats (Suricata), or automatically integrated from threat intelligence feeds managed by AWS partners. The AWS Network Firewall supports both stateful and stateless inspection.

FIGURE C.17 AWS Network Firewall icon.

AWS Network Firewall organizes rules in rule groups, which then are grouped in firewall policies. AWS Network Firewall can filter on attributes like protocol, domain, or IP address. It can also inspect for threat signatures, filter web traffic (FQDN), and inspect encrypted traffic.

AWS Network Firewall charges both per firewall (on a per-hour, per-region, and availability zone basis) and for the amount of traffic inspected. The TLS inspection feature has an additional charge.

You can find the AWS Network Firewall documentation here: https://docs.aws.amazon.com/network-firewall.

AWS Organizations

AWS Organizations (see Figure C.18) is a service to manage your AWS accounts under a common set of policies. Using AWS Organizations, you consolidate all your AWS accounts under a single structure (called an organization). Within your organization, you can create organizational units (OU), which are subsets of AWS accounts. You can even create OUs under other OUs. AWS Organizations then allows you to apply security policies that provide boundaries to the access privileges on the accounts. You can apply policies at different levels (organizations or OUs). AWS Organizations also simplifies billing requirements, consolidating billing for your AWS accounts under a single payment method.

While AWS Organizations is not considered a security service, it offers key features for security services to organize, manage, and share resources across AWS accounts.

There is no additional charge for using AWS Organizations.

You can find the AWS Organizations documentation here: https://docs.aws.amazon.com/organizations.

FIGURE C.18 AWS Organizations icon.

AWS Payment Cryptography

AWS Payment Cryptography (see Figure C.19) is a managed service that allows you to process card payments following PCI standards by managing the lifecycle of cryptographic keys and providing AWS native APIs for payment cryptographic functions.

AWS Payment Cryptography offers compliance with industry standards like PCI PIN, PCI P2PE, and PCI DSS. AWS Payment Cryptography relies on PCI PTS HSM v3 and FIPS 140-2 Level 3 certified hardware. The service provides regional endpoints to support low latency calls from your applications hosted in AWS Cloud.

AWS Payment Cryptography billing is based on the amount of API calls to the service endpoints and the number of active cryptographic keys.

You can find the AWS Payment Cryptography documentation here: `https://docs.aws.amazon.com/payment-cryptography`.

FIGURE C.19 AWS Payment Cryptography icon.

AWS Private Certificate Authority

AWS Private Certificate Authority (CA; see Figure C.20) establishes a private key infrastructure with a hierarchy of CAs. You can then have the CAs issue private X.509 digital certificates for consumption within your organization.

Implementing a Private Key Infrastructure allows you to customize your internal digital certificates. AWS Private CA can issue digital certificates directly or certificates can be requested via AWS Certificate Manager. When you use AWS Certificate Manager to request private certificates from AWS Private CA, you can integrate those certificates with the AWS services

FIGURE C.20 AWS Private Certificate Authority icon.

supported by AWS Certificate Manager. Digital certificates issued directly by AWS Private CA can be exported for usage inside or outside AWS. You can also integrate AWS Private CA to issue certificates inside an Amazon EKS cluster. AWS Private CA offers connectors for Kubernetes, for Active Directory, and for Simple Certificate Enrollment Protocol (SCEP; for issuing certificates for mobile device management [MDM] systems).

AWS Private CA provides revocation functionality via Online Certificate Status Protocol (OCSP) or via Certificate Revocation Lists (CRL). You can also implement a short-lived certificate operating mode, where certificates issued by AWS Private CA expire in up to seven days.

AWS Private CA billing involves a monthly fee per AWS Private CA implemented (with different fees for short-lived and general-purpose modes), the number of digital certificates issued, the number of digital certificates with OCSP enabled, and the number of OCSP requests. AWS Private CA offers a 30-day free operations charge trial.

You can find the AWS Private CA documentation here: https://docs.aws.amazon.com/privateca.

AWS Resource Access Manager

AWS Resource Access Manager (AWS RAM; see Figure C.21) gives you the power to securely share AWS resources with any other AWS account. If the account is part of AWS Organizations, you can easily share the resources with the whole organization or with accounts in specific OUs. For some resource types, you can also share the resource with a specific IAM user or role. The service's main benefit is that, through the sharing of a resource among multiple accounts, it avoids duplication of cloud resources and management efforts.

Through three configuration steps (create a resource share, specify resources, and select accounts), AWS RAM allows you to securely share AWS Transit Gateways, AWS License Manager configurations, and Amazon Route 53 resolver rules, for example. In addition, to improve accountability, all API calls to this service are logged in AWS CloudTrail.

AWS RAM currently charges no additional fee. You can find the AWS RAM documentation here: https://docs.aws.amazon.com/ARG.

FIGURE C.21 AWS Resource Access Manager icon.

AWS Secrets Manager

AWS Secrets Manager (see Figure C.22) enables you to rotate, manage, and retrieve secrets, such as database credentials and API keys. Because this service releases you from storing sensitive information in clear text, AWS Secrets Manager protects secrets that are essential for your applications and resources.

This service provides secret rotation with built-in integration for Amazon RDS, Amazon Aurora, Amazon Redshift, and Amazon ECS. AWS Secrets Manager is also extensible to other types of secrets (such as OAuth tokens and API keys).

To better protect your secrets, AWS Secrets Manager transmits them securely over TLS, provides fine-grained permissions, and does not save or cache them on any persistent storage. It also helps you adhere to compliance regulations such as HIPAA, PCI DSS, ISO/IEC 27001, ISO/IEC 27017, ISO/IEC 27018, and ISO 9001.

AWS Secrets Manager is currently available without additional charge for a 30-day trial period. After the trial period, AWS Secrets Manager charges a fee per secret, and by volume of API calls.

You can find the AWS Secrets Manager documentation here: https://docs.aws.amazon.com/secretsmanager.

FIGURE C.22 AWS Secrets Manager icon.

AWS Security Hub

AWS Security Hub (see Figure C.23) provides a centralized view of security alerts and automated compliance verifications across your AWS accounts. Moreover, it collects information from multiple AWS services, such as Amazon GuardDuty, Amazon Inspector, Amazon Macie, AWS

FIGURE C.23 AWS Security Hub icon.

IAM Access Analyzer, AWS Firewall Manager, and third-party solutions such as Check Point, CrowdStrike, Palo Alto Networks, Qualys, and Symantec.

All security findings in AWS Security Hub are collected via standardized AWS Security Findings Format (ASFF). In addition, AWS Security Hub automates the verification of security standards like Center for Internet Security (CIS), AWS Foundational Security Best Practices (FSBP, a set of well-defined, unbiased, consensus-based industry best practices), NIST SP 800-53, PCI DSS, and AWS Resource Tagging Standard. AWS Security Hub also provides access to service-managed standards (standards managed by other AWS services, like AWS Control Tower).

AWS Security Hub pricing is based on the number of enabled security checks, the number of findings ingested, and the number of rules evaluated. AWS Security Hub offers a 30-day free trial period for new users that covers all the functionalities of the service. You can find the AWS Security Hub documentation here: https://docs.aws.amazon.com/securityhub.

AWS Shield

AWS Shield (see Figure C.24) offers managed DDoS protection for applications running on AWS. It provides constant detections and automatic inline mitigations that minimize application downtime or performance degradation.

AWS Shield is available in two tiers: Standard and Advanced. AWS Shield Standard is a no-cost version that protects your environments against the most common Network and Transport Layer DDoS attacks that target your website or applications, available by default when you host your applications on AWS Cloud. This edition relies on detection techniques such as network flow monitoring, a combination of traffic signatures, and anomaly algorithms. Additionally, it mitigates attacks through inline mechanisms, which include deterministic packet filtering and priority-based traffic shaping.

AWS Shield Advanced enables additional detection, mitigation, and response capabilities against sophisticated DDoS attacks targeting Amazon EC2 Elastic IP addresses, ELBs, Amazon CloudFront distributions, AWS Global Accelerator standard accelerators, and Amazon Route 53 hosted zones. The service provides near real-time visibility, integration with AWS WAF, 24×7 access to the AWS Shield Response Team (SRT), and protection against DDoS-related spikes in charges related to the covered services (cost protection). This enhanced detection is provided through network flow inspection, resource-specific monitoring, resource- and region-specific granular detection of DDoS attacks, and application layer DDoS attacks (like HTTP floods or

FIGURE C.24 AWS Shield icon.

DNS query floods) through baselining traffic and identifying anomalies. It also offers advanced attack mitigation via routing techniques, SRT manual mitigations, AWS WAF rules free of charge for Shield-protected resources, visibility and attack notification (Amazon CloudWatch), DDoS cost protection, and global availability.

AWS Shield Advanced is charged as a monthly fee, plus a fee based on the data transfer out from selected protected resources.

You can find the AWS Shield documentation here: `https://docs.aws.amazon.com/shield`.

AWS Web Application Firewall

AWS Web Application Firewall (AWS WAF; see Figure C.25) protects your web applications and APIs from known web attacks that could affect application availability, compromise data security, or invoke a denial-of-service condition. With AWS WAF, you can create rules that block common attacks, such as SQL injection and cross-site scripting, or specific traffic patterns you can define. You can filter any part of the web request, including IP addresses, HTTP headers, HTTP body, or URI strings. You create and organize rules under a web access control list (web ACL).

When applied to Amazon CloudFront, ALB, Amazon API Gateway, AWS AppSync GraphQL API, Amazon Cognito user pool, AWS App Runner, or an AWS Verified Access instance, AWS WAF offers automated protection via managed rules, a preconfigured set of rules from AWS and partners on the marketplace that protects against vulnerabilities defined on OWASP's Top 10 Security Risks, threats specific to CMSs, or emerging CVEs. AWS WAF also includes a full-featured API, which you can use to automate the creation, deployment, and maintenance of security rules.

In terms of monitoring and automated protection, AWS WAF offers near real-time visibility into your web traffic, allowing you to create new rules or alerts in Amazon CloudWatch. It also provides logging from each inspected web request for use in security automation, analytics, or for auditing purposes.

AWS WAF pricing is based on the number of web ACLs, the number of rules, and the number of requests inspected by the service.

You can find the AWS Web Application Firewall documentation here: `https://docs.aws.amazon.com/waf`.

FIGURE C.25 AWS Web Application Firewall (WAF) icon.

Appendix D

DevSecOps in AWS

Appendix D ▪ DevSecOps in AWS

The DevSecOps practice is not yet covered by AWS Security Certification, but we believe it is essential to define the concept, introduce the AWS family of services that implement DevOps practices, and demonstrate in a practical way how security controls can be implemented in an automated pipeline.

Introduction

This appendix introduces you to the principles of DevSecOps and shows you how to implement a continuous integration and continuous deployment (CI/CD) process using security best practices. It presents a practical example of how to create an automated pipeline using AWS Developer Tools services (and some third-party tools) in order to illustrate such concepts.

A CI/CD pipeline helps you automate software delivery steps, such as building, testing, and deploying the application. The pipeline provides a standardized process of minimizing the chance of failures to improve the speed of feedback when errors occur during the process.

Before being properly introduced to DevSecOps, you need to understand what a DevOps process is and the main benefits of implementing it in software development.

DevOps

The term "DevOps" first came up at the Velocity event in 2009, where John Allspaw and Paul Hammond presented the talk "10+ Deploys per Day: Dev and Ops Cooperation at Flickr," which explored the results and challenges of closer engagement between development and operations teams on Flickr. Patrick Debois, who attended the lecture online and would later co-create the term, came up with the idea of creating the "DevOps Days" event.

DevOps is a set of software development practices that combines software development and information technology operations to reduce the systems development lifecycle while delivering features, fixes, and frequent updates in close alignment with business objectives.

With the need for faster software deliveries, various techniques and tools have been created to automate development and release steps. Perhaps due to the strong mindshare some development tools possess, it is fairly common for people to confuse DevOps with the purchase or implementation of a toolkit. Nonetheless, the DevOps adoption process involves three complementary pillars: cultural philosophies, practices, and tools.

Cultural Philosophies

Many of the problems that occur during deployment processes are related to the lack of information from the operations team about what needs to be done at deployment time. In addition, developers are not always aware of the infrastructure that will support the application.

To minimize these problems, information about what is being developed and how the application should behave after deploying it to environments must flow correctly among these teams.

To implement a DevOps process, development and operations teams must work together, without silos, with shared responsibility from development to application support. Therefore, a philosophy of open communication has to drive their work on a daily basis.

Practices

DevOps practices mainly address the process of continuous integration, continuous delivery, continuous deployment, infrastructure as code, and monitoring.

Continuous integration is the practice of merging all developers' local copies of the software to a shared branch several times a day. With such a practice, it is possible to anticipate the problems that may occur when integrating the code of the various developers working in the same project and consequently fix it more quickly.

Continuous delivery is a software development practice where code changes are automatically prepared for production release. A cornerstone of modern application development, continuous delivery expands on continuous integration by deploying all code changes to a testing environment and, optionally, to a production environment after the build stage. When properly implemented, developers will always have access to a deployment-ready build artifact that has passed through a standardized test process.

Continuous delivery lets developers automate testing beyond just unit tests so that they can verify application updates across multiple steps before deploying to customers. These evaluations may include user interface testing, load testing, integration testing, and API reliability testing. Such processes help developers thoroughly validate updates and preemptively discover issues. One of the benefits of cloud computing in such scenarios is the ease of automating the creation and replication of multiple environments for testing, which is a difficult task in on-premises data centers.

Continuous deployment is a strategy for software releases in which any code commit that passes the automated testing phase is automatically released to the production environment, implementing changes that are visible to users of the software being developed.

Other techniques should also be considered for a successful continuous deployment process. One of the main methods is the use of a development pattern called Feature Flag (also known as Feature Toggle). With this functionality, you can enable and disable parts of your code so that a specific feature can be enabled and disabled at runtime.

As an example, you can use Feature Flag when you need to enable a feature that has a specific date and time to go live to mobile users. In this situation, the code has already been delivered to the production environment, so now you will only be able to activate it when other areas are ready to consume the feature, or eventually when the application becomes available in its app store.

As shown in Figure D.1, with continuous delivery, every code change is built, tested, and then pushed to a nonproduction testing or staging environment. There can be multiple parallel test stages before production deployment. Where continuous delivery requires human intervention

FIGURE D.1 Continuous delivery vs. continuous deployment.

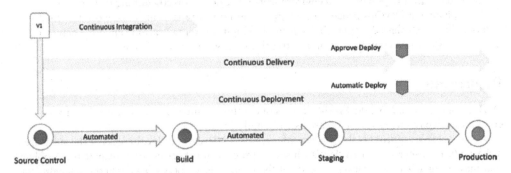

through a manual approval for code deployment to production, continuous deployment does it automatically.

Infrastructure as code is the process of provisioning and managing cloud resources via a template file that is both human-readable and machine-consumable. Within the AWS Cloud, the built-in choice for infrastructure as code is the AWS CloudFormation service.

 The code generated for the deployment of the infrastructure must be treated as the software of your application. It must be versioned and undergo tests, vulnerability checks, and compliance validation.

The monitoring practice is used to give teams visibility into application behavior, not only after production deployment but also during the build and deployment processes. Each organization may set different goals when implementing its DevOps process. Keep in mind that to achieve the highest levels of maturity, application changes may be required.

One of the most common changes observed in enterprise organizations today is the breaking down of monolithic applications into smaller parts, also known as *microservices*. With the adoption of microservices, you can speed up the software development process to achieve more frequent deliveries. Another significant benefit of adopting microservices is the ability to scale each component of your application independently, which could not be accomplished using monolithic applications.

 Software engineering defines a monolithic application as a single-layered software application where the user interface and data access code are part of a single program.

A monolithic application describes a software application that is designed without modularity, is stand-alone, and is generally independent of other applications. It consists of an application that is not only responsible for a particular task but can also perform all the necessary steps to solve a problem.

As you break the application into smaller parts, multiple teams can be formed, each working on different components of the system. Each team becomes responsible for all stages of their components, from development to support.

It is important to note that when adopting the microservices strategy, you must clearly define how components will communicate with one another in the application. This is usually done by setting API contracts, which makes each part less dependent on the others. As a result, the evolution of the whole application is simpler.

Tools

To better understand the role of tools in DevOps, consider the steps of the software release process and what should be covered in each of the steps, as shown in Figure D.2.

The *source* step is where source code versioning and revision of the committed codes are performed. The details behind the different strategies for branch management are beyond the scope of this appendix. Instead, we focus on what should be controlled and the possible variations of implementation.

In the *build* step, you must compile the application, perform unit tests, perform code style checks, collect code metrics, package the software, and possibly generate container images.

In the *test* phase, you must run load tests, usability tests, and vulnerability tests, and perform integrated tests with other systems. In this phase, you address the application and its related infrastructure.

During the *deployment* stage, you deliver the artifacts generated to the production environment. Then, you should monitor the application metrics to identify any issues. One important observation: the term "monitor" here does not refer to metrics like CPU, memory, and disk usage. The process should be mostly concerned with business metrics, such as the percentage of successful responses in the API layer.

The closer the user is to a monitored metric, the more critical it should be considered. With metrics that reflect user experience, it is easier to understand whether they are being impacted by an incident or a change in the software that you just delivered to the production environment. For example, if an application typically has a failure rate of 0.3 percent, and after the deployment of a new version it increases to 0.8 percent, the change is directly impacting users as long as a correlation between both events is correctly identified.

FIGURE D.2 Steps of software release process.

Dev + Sec + Ops

DevSecOps (derived from "development," "security," and "operations") is the combination of cultural philosophies, practices, and tools that leverage the advances made in IT automation to achieve a state of production immutability, frequent delivery of business value, and automated enforcement of security policies. It aims to reduce the risk of security breaches by automating security testing, vulnerability scanning, and compliance checks throughout the software development lifecycle (SDLC). By doing so, DevSecOps ensures that applications are secure, reliable, and compliant with industry standards from the outset.

To fully comprehend the need for DevSecOps, you should be aware of the competing demands that exist within organizations. The development team must deliver more quickly, the security team must ensure that deliveries are secure, and the operations team must keep systems stable.

DevSecOps is achieved through the integration and automation of the enforcement of preventive, detective, and responsive security controls into the pipeline. Its implementation has three main stages:

- **Security of the CI/CD Pipeline:** Encompasses tasks such as the creation of automated IAM roles, hardening of automation servers, and other configurations that protect the infrastructure that supports the software build and deployment process.

- **Security in the CI/CD Pipeline:** Includes security-related tasks such as automated security tests and codebase analysis as part of the software development process.

- **Enforcement of the Pipeline:** Includes procedures that provide monitoring and proactive protection, such as automated incident response remediation and forensics

---

Key Principles of DevSecOps

- **Automation:** Automate security tasks to reduce manual errors and increase efficiency.

- **Integration:** Integrate security into every stage of the development process.

- **Collaboration:** Foster a culture of collaboration between developers, security teams, and operations teams.

- **Feedback:** Continuously gather feedback from users and stakeholders to improve application security.

According to the Chalk Talk, "Building a DevSecOps Culture," presented during AWS re:Inforce 2019, DevSecOps has four tenets:

1. **Test security as early as possible to accelerate feedback.** It is essential to create mechanisms to test the application and to identify potential shortcomings as early as possible. It is common to see companies performing pipeline security checks only when they are going to make a

production release. Sometimes they identify serious security issues that will take a longer time to fix and can sometimes cause production software to be delayed.

2. **Prioritize preventive security controls to stop bad things from happening.** When dealing with security issues, it is critical to avoid problems in the production application. For this reason, preventive safety controls must be implemented.

3. **When deploying a detective security control, ensure that it has a complementary responsive security control.** Even with the implementation of preventive safety controls, you must be ready to act in case of production failures. It is essential to keep the application runbooks up to date and teams adequately trained to act in case of problems. It is usual for companies to adopt red team and blue team strategies to conduct application intrusion simulations. This ensures that everyone knows what to do in a real security incident.

Application Runbook

An *application runbook* is a compilation of routine procedures and operations that the system administrator or operator carries out. People in IT departments use runbooks as a reference. Runbooks can be in either electronic or physical book form.

---

4. **Automate, automate, and automate.** To facilitate the identification and remediation of security issues, strive to automate everything in the system deployment process. Create automated scripts to contain security issues in production, such as isolating a compromised server so that a forensic team can evaluate it.

AWS Developer Tools

The AWS Cloud provides a series of services that support DevOps software development pipelines. This section addresses which services can be used at each stage of the software release process and the main benefits of each service.

AWS CodeCommit

AWS CodeCommit is a fully managed source control service that hosts Git-based protected repositories. It enables teams to easily collaborate on code in a secure and highly scalable ecosystem. This service eliminates the need to operate your source control system or worry about infrastructure scalability. You can use CodeCommit to securely store anything from source code to binary files. In addition, it works perfectly with your existing Git tools.

> **AWS CodeCommit Deprecation**
>
> AWS has made the decision to close new customer access to AWS CodeCommit, effective July 25, 2024. AWS CodeCommit existing customers can continue to use the service as normal. AWS will continue to invest in security, availability, and performance improvements for AWS CodeCommit, but they do not plan to introduce new features.
>
> Here you can find a blog that explain how to migrate current AWS CodeCommit repositories to another Git provider: `https://aws.amazon.com/blogs/devops/how-to-migrate-your-aws-codecommit-repository-to-another-git-provider/`
>
> Other services, like AWS Cloud9 and AWS CodeStar, were also deprecated.

AWS CodeBuild

AWS CodeBuild is a fully managed continuous integration service that compiles source code, performs testing, and produces ready-to-deploy software packages. With AWS CodeBuild, you don't have to provision, manage, and scale your build servers. AWS CodeBuild scales continuously and processes multiple builds at the same time, preventing them from waiting in a queue. You can quickly start using predefined build environments or create custom build environments with your build tools. When you are using AWS CodeBuild, the used computational resources are charged per minute.

AWS CodeBuild runs your builds in preconfigured build environments that contain the operating system, programming language runtime, and building tools like Apache Maven, Gradle, and npm, which are required to complete the task. Just specify your source code's location and select the settings for your build. AWS CodeBuild builds your code and stores the artifacts in an Amazon S3 bucket, or you can use a build command to upload them to an artifact repository.

> To speed up the process of building your build scripts, you can use AWS CodeBuild's local testing support, which is available here: `https://aws.amazon.com/blogs/devops/announcing-local-build-support-for-aws-codebuild`.

During the build process, you will need to perform different types of tests on your software. The most common are unit tests, load tests, integration or API tests, and vulnerability tests. In addition, to successfully implement a CI/CD process, you must automate an entire test suite.

With AWS CodeBuild, you can add your test calls directly to your build script. In some cases, you will need to install third-party tools for testing. You can also install these features in your build script; however, because AWS CodeBuild charges for the computation time spent during the process, you will be spending money to install the tools and make the build time longer. For these cases, we recommend that you create a custom Docker image containing all the tools you will use in the build process so that your build process becomes faster and cheaper.

AWS CodeDeploy

AWS CodeDeploy is a fully managed deployment service that automates software deployments on a variety of computing services, such as Amazon EC2, AWS Fargate, and AWS Lambda, as well as local servers. AWS CodeDeploy facilitates the rapid launch of new features, helps you avoid downtime while deploying applications, and deals with the complexity of updating them. You can use AWS CodeDeploy to automate software deployments and eliminate the need for error-prone manual operations. The service scales to meet your deployment needs.

AWS X-Ray

AWS X-Ray helps developers analyze and debug distributed production applications, such as those created by using a microservices architecture. With X-Ray, you can review the performance of applications and their underlying services in order to identify and troubleshoot the root cause of performance issues and errors. X-Ray provides a complete view of requests as they move through the application, and it shows a map of the underlying components of the application. You can use X-Ray to analyze both development and production applications, varying from simple three-tier applications to complex microservices applications consisting of thousands of services.

Figure D.3 shows a service map that helps you identify the components of your application. You can quickly identify the percentage of affected customers in case of problems.

FIGURE D.3 AWS X-Ray service map.

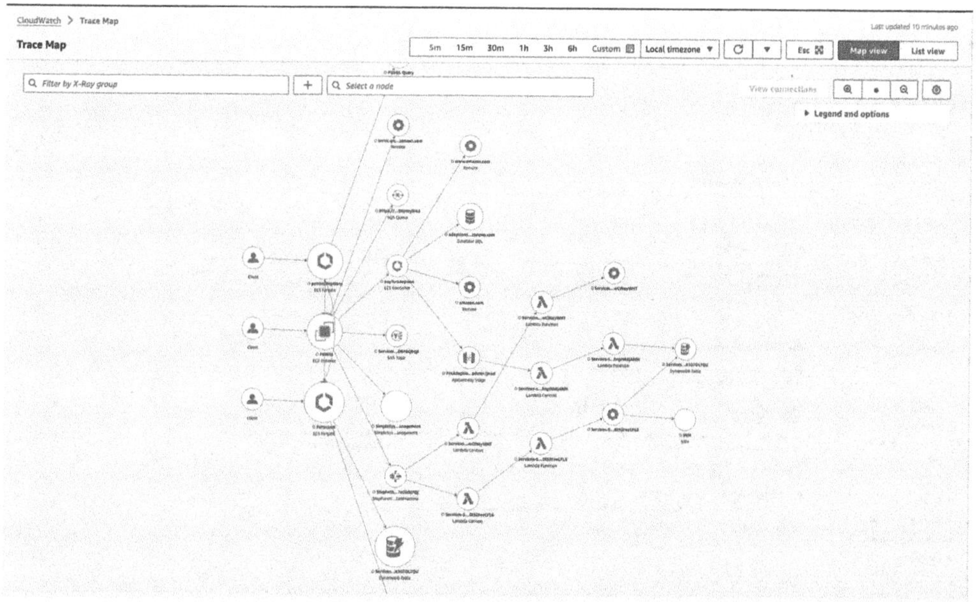

Amazon CloudWatch

Amazon CloudWatch is a monitoring and observation service designed for DevOps engineers, developers, site reliability engineers (SREs), and IT managers. CloudWatch provides useful data and insights so that you can monitor applications, respond to systemwide performance changes, optimize resource utilization, and gain a unified view of operational integrity. CloudWatch collects monitoring and operations data in the form of logs, metrics, and events, providing a unified view of AWS resources, applications, and services running on AWS and on-premises servers. You can use CloudWatch to detect anomalous behavior in your environments, set alarms, view logs and metrics side by side, perform automated actions, troubleshoot, and discover insights to keep your applications running smoothly.

Figure D.4 shows the main panel of the Amazon CloudWatch service, where you see alarms by service, recent alarms of the platform, and some metrics from other AWS services. CloudWatch also allows you to create your own dashboards.

AWS CodePipeline

AWS CodePipeline is a managed continuous delivery service that helps automate release pipelines to provide fast and reliable application and infrastructure updates. CodePipeline automates the build, test, and deployment phases of the release process whenever a code change occurs, according to the release model you have defined. This enables you to make features and updates available quickly and reliably. You can easily integrate AWS CodePipeline with third-party services like GitHub or with your custom plugin.

FIGURE D.4 Amazon CloudWatch panel.

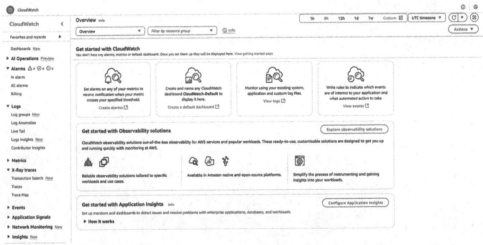

Creating a CI/CD Using AWS Tools

In this section, you create a software development pipeline. This exercise is very important since it provides a practical illustration of how to add security checks to a software delivery pipeline.

As a first step, you set up a code repository to save the source of a Lambda application. To create the repository, we recommend that you use an external Git repository service (the AWS CodeCommit service is currently available to accounts that already have a repository created).

Creating a Repository

To execute the commands in this section, you need to install the AWS CLI tool. The installation steps can be found here: `https://docs.aws.amazon.com/cli/latest/userguide/cli-chap-install.html`.

After installing AWS CLI, you need to configure it. The configuration steps can be found here: `https://docs.aws.amazon.com/cli/latest/userguide/cli-chap-configure.html`.

This example uses a private GitHub repository. First, go to GitHub and create an empty repository called **MyLambdaApp.**

The next step is to clone the created repository, using the following command for GitHub:

```
git clone https://github.com/cloud-nativo/MyLambdaApp.git
```

After this process, open the `MyLambdaApp` folder and create a new folder called **src:**

```
cd MyLambdaApp
mkdir src
```

Open the `src` folder, create a new file named **handler.js,** and insert the following code. This is the unique file inside the `src` folder.

```
export const handler = async (event, context) => {

  const length = event.length;
  const width = event.width;
  let area = calculateArea(length, width);
  console.log(`The area is ${area}`);
  console.log('CloudWatch log group: ', context.logGroupName);

  let data = {
    "area": area,
  };
    return JSON.stringify(data);

  function calculateArea(length, width) {
```

Appendix D ▪ DevSecOps in AWS

```
    return length * width;
  }
};
```

Return to the previous `src` folder using this command:

```
cd ..
```

Create a file named **buildspec.yml** and insert the following code in the file:

```
version: 0.2

phases:
  install:
    runtime-versions:
      nodejs: 18

  build:
    commands:
      # Create deployment directory
      - mkdir -p dist
      # Copy Lambda function files
      - cp src/handler.js dist/
      # Install dependencies
      - cd dist
      - npm init -y
      - npm install moment-timezone
      - cd ..
      # Debug - list files to verify template exists
      - pwd
      - ls -la
      # Package application
      - aws cloudformation package --template-file template.yaml --s3-bucket
<YOUR_BUCKET NAME> --output-template-file outputtemplate.yaml

artifacts:
  files:
    - outputtemplate.yaml
    - template.yaml
    - dist/*/*
  discard-paths: no
```

Replace *<YOUR BUCKET NAME>* with the name of an existing bucket in your AWS account. Create a file named **template.yaml** and insert the following code in the file:

```
AWSTemplateFormatVersion : '2010-09-09'
Transform: AWS::Serverless-2016-10-31
Description: A sample SAM template for deploying Lambda functions.
```

```
Resources:
# Details about the CalcArea Lambda function
  CalcAreaFunction:
    Type: AWS::Serverless::Function
    Properties:
      CodeUri: dist/
      Handler: handler.handler
      Runtime: nodejs18.x
      Timeout: 3
      MemorySize: 128
      # Grants this function permission to call lambda:InvokeFunction
      Policies:
        - Version: "2012-10-17"
          Statement:
          - Effect: "Allow"
            Action:
              - "lambda:InvokeFunction"
            Resource: '*'
```

Use the following `git` commands to send your source to GitHub. (you should configure your computer with the credentials required to push the files, and you can also use the GitHub Desktop app to do this easily):

```
git add .
git commit -m "My First Commit"
git push origin master
```

Figure D.5 shows your repository with the committed source code.

FIGURE D.5 Committed source code.

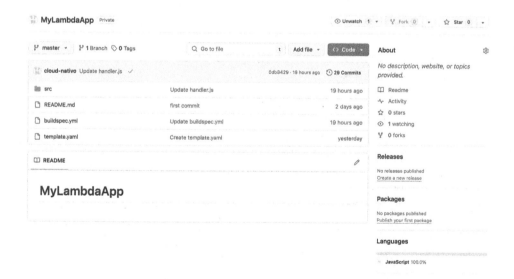

Creating an AWS CodePipeline Pipeline

Before creating a pipeline with AWS CodePipeline, you need to set up some other components, such as an IAM role to execute AWS CloudFormation. You must also create an AWS CodeBuild project. The next sections describe what you need to do.

Create a Role to AWS CloudFormation

Follow these steps to create a new IAM role:

1. While logged in with sufficient permissions, open IAM and create a CloudFormation service type role named `cfn-lambda-pipeline`.

2. Select the CloudFormation use service.

3. Type `cfn-lambda-pipeline` in the Role Name field.

4. Select the `AWSLambdaExecute` policy.

5. Review your role configurations (see Figure D.6) and click Create Role.

6. Edit the created role and add an inline policy.

FIGURE D.6 Role configuration.

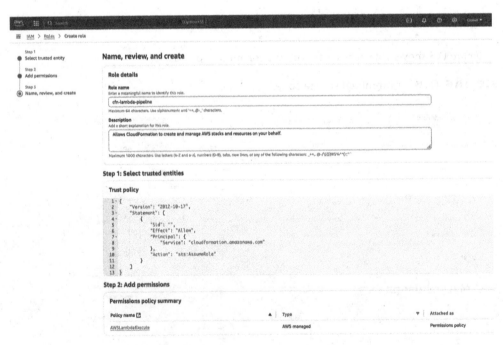

7. Select the JSON tab.

8. Enter the following code as a JSON policy:

```
{
    "Version": "2012-10-17",
    "Statement": [
        {
            "Action": [
                "codedeploy:*",
                "lambda:*",
                "cloudformation:CreateChangeSet",
                "iam:GetRole",
                "iam:CreateRole",
                "iam:DeleteRole",
                "iam:PutRolePolicy",
                "iam:AttachRolePolicy",
                "iam:DeleteRolePolicy",
                "iam:DetachRolePolicy",
                "iam:PassRole",
                "s3:GetObjectVersion",
                "s3:GetBucketVersioning",
                "iam:TagRole"
            ],
            "Resource": "*",
            "Effect": "Allow"
        }
    ]
}
```

9. Click Review Policy.

10. Type `deploy-lambdaapp-policy` as the policy name.

11. Click Create Policy.

Create an AWS CodeBuild Project

Follow these steps to create a new AWS CodeBuild project:

1. While logged in with sufficient permissions, open AWS CodeBuild.

2. Create a new project named `LambdaAppBuild` (see Figure D.7).

3. On the Source screen, select GitHub from the Source Provider menu. Currently you have several options, such as Amazon S3, AWS CodeCommit, GitHub, BitBucket, and GitLab.

4. For this case, use Default Source Credential and click on Manage Default Source Credential to set the access to the repository (see Figure D.8). Use the GitHub App to create a GitHub Connection, by using an AWS managed GitHub app.

5. On the Environment screen, select Ubuntu from the Operating System menu.

Appendix D ▪ DevSecOps in AWS

FIGURE D.7   Project configuration.

Developer Tools > CodeBuild > Build projects > **Create build project**

Create build project

Project configuration

Project name

LambdaAppBuild

A project name must be 2 to 255 characters. It can include the letters A-Z and a-z, the numbers 0-9, and the special characters - and _.

Public build access - *optional*
Public build access allows you to make the build results, including logs and artifacts, for this project available for the general public.

☐ Enable public build access

▶ **Additional configuration**
Description, Build badge, Concurrent build limit, tags

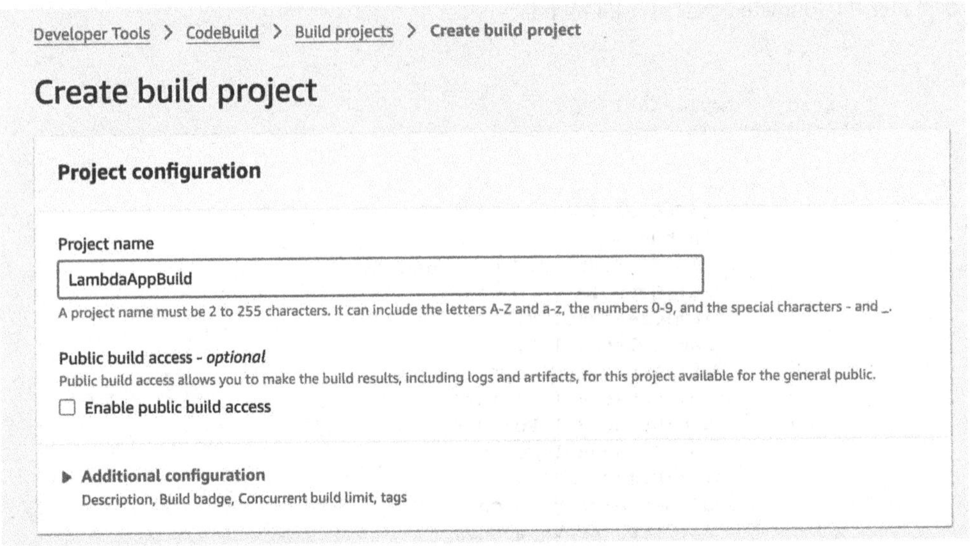

6. Select the Standard runtime.

7. For Image, select the latest image using the version as a reference.

8. From the Image Version menu, choose Always Use the Latest Image for this Runtime Version, as shown in Figure D.9.

9. On the next screen, enter `buildspec.yml` as the file location and select the Use a Buildspec File option (see Figure D.10).

10. In the Artifact section, select the S3 bucket where you want to put the build artifacts.

11. Under Artifacts Packaging, select the Zip option, as shown in Figure D.11.

12. On the Logs screen, type `LambdaAppBuild` as the group name for CloudWatch logs (see Figure D.12).

13. Click Create Build Project. Figure D.13 displays how the project appears after it has been created.

Create the Pipeline

Follow these steps to create a pipeline:

1. While logged in with sufficient permissions, open AWS CodePipeline.

2. Select the Build Custom Pipeline option and click on Next (see Figure D.14).

Creating a CI/CD Using AWS Tools   483

FIGURE D.8 Source screen.

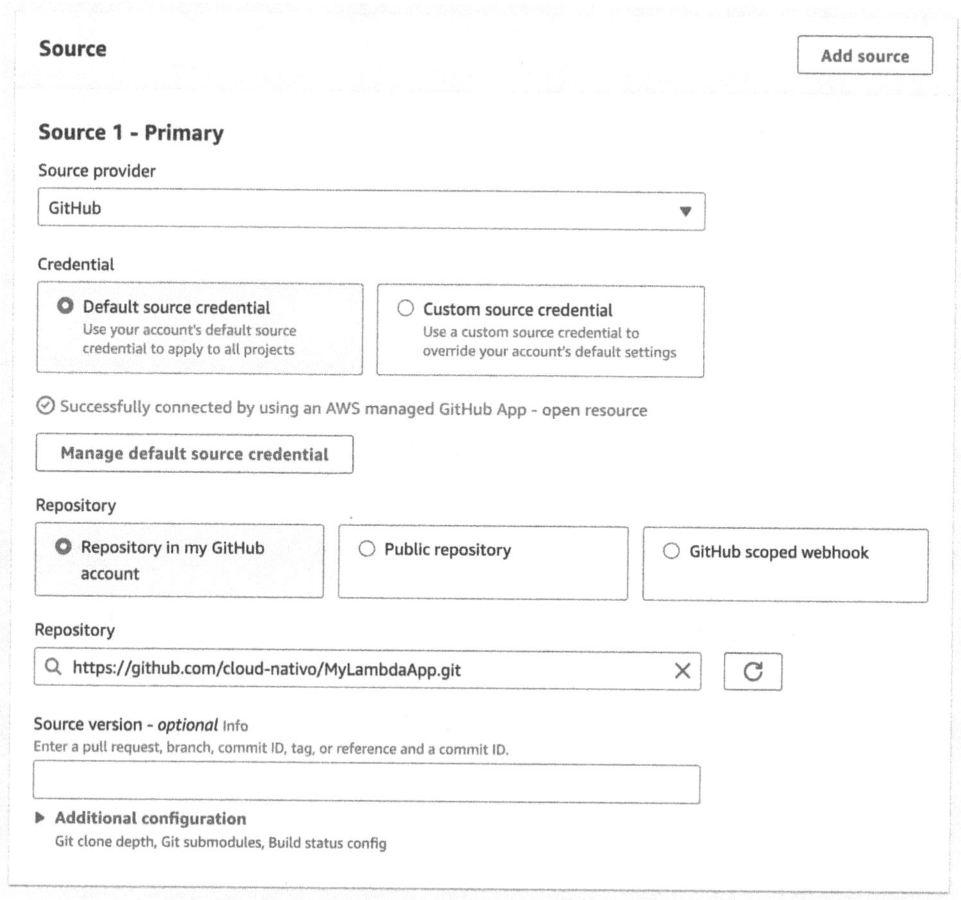

Source   [Add source]

Source 1 - Primary

Source provider

| GitHub   ▼ |

Credential

◉ **Default source credential**
Use your account's default source
credential to apply to all projects

○ **Custom source credential**
Use a custom source credential to
override your account's default settings

⊘ Successfully connected by using an AWS managed GitHub App - open resource

[**Manage default source credential**]

Repository

◉ **Repository in my GitHub
account**

○ Public repository

○ GitHub scoped webhook

Repository

| 🔍 https://github.com/cloud-nativo/MyLambdaApp.git   ✕ | [⟳]

Source version - *optional* Info
Enter a pull request, branch, commit ID, tag, or reference and a commit ID.

| |

▶ **Additional configuration**
   Git clone depth, Git submodules, Build status config

3. Create a new pipeline named `LambdaAppPipeline`. Leave the defaults and click Next.

4. In Source, select GitHub (via GitHub App) as the source provider. Select the connection (it is recommended that you use Connect to GitHub and the App).

5. Select the MyLambdaApp repository.

6. Select the Master branch name. Click Next (see Figure D.15).

7. In Step 4, in the Build stage, select the Other Build Providers option and select AWS CodeBuild as the build provider.

484 Appendix D • DevSecOps in AWS

FIGURE D.9 Environment screen.

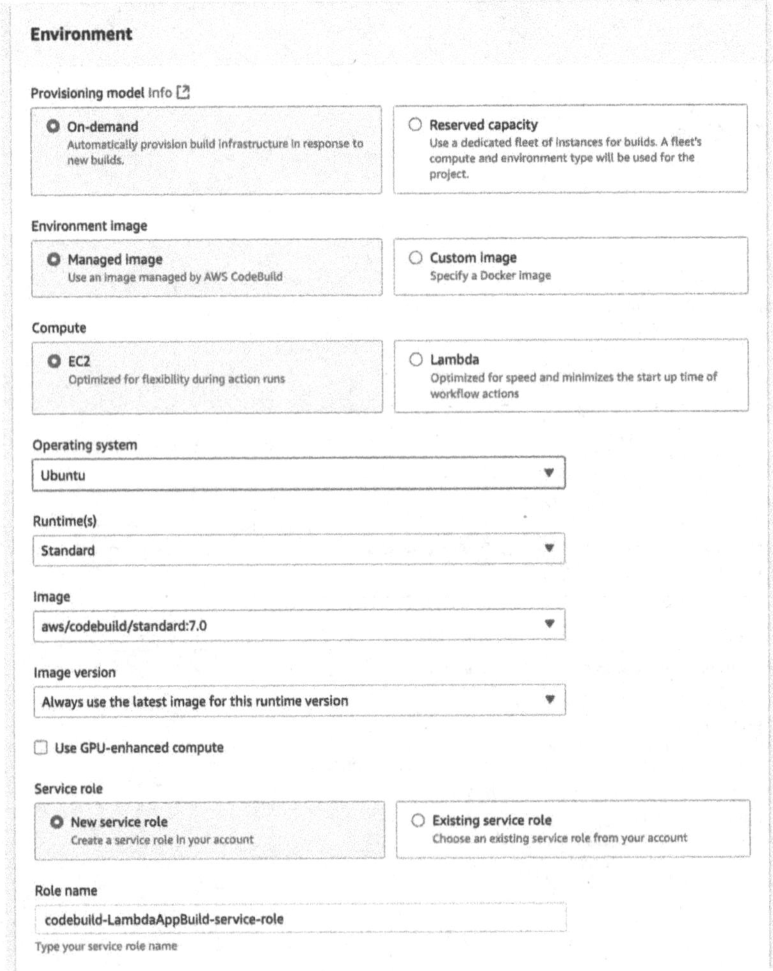

Environment

Provisioning model Info ☐

- ● On-demand
  Automatically provision build infrastructure in response to new builds.

- ○ Reserved capacity
  Use a dedicated fleet of instances for builds. A fleet's compute and environment type will be used for the project.

Environment image

- ● Managed image
  Use an image managed by AWS CodeBuild

- ○ Custom image
  Specify a Docker image

Compute

- ● EC2
  Optimized for flexibility during action runs

- ○ Lambda
  Optimized for speed and minimizes the start up time of workflow actions

Operating system

Ubuntu ▼

Runtime(s)

Standard ▼

Image

aws/codebuild/standard:7.0 ▼

Image version

Always use the latest image for this runtime version ▼

☐ Use GPU-enhanced compute

Service role

- ● New service role
  Create a service role in your account

- ○ Existing service role
  Choose an existing service role from your account

Role name

codebuild-LambdaAppBuild-service-role

Type your service role name

FIGURE D.10 Buildspec screen.

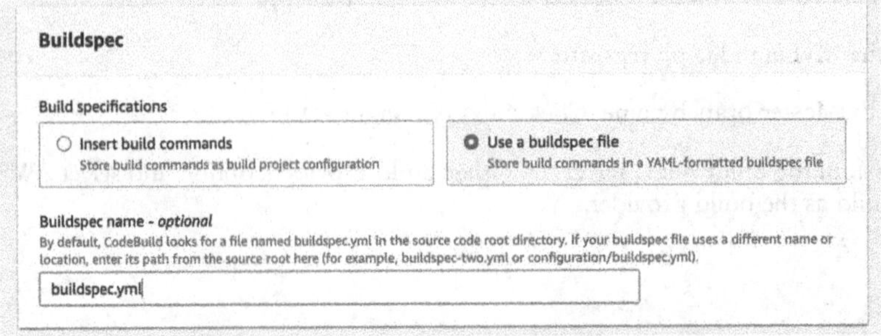

Buildspec

Build specifications

- ○ Insert build commands
  Store build commands as build project configuration

- ● Use a buildspec file
  Store build commands in a YAML-formatted buildspec file

Buildspec name - *optional*
By default, CodeBuild looks for a file named buildspec.yml in the source code root directory. If your buildspec file uses a different name or location, enter its path from the source root here (for example, buildspec-two.yml or configuration/buildspec.yml).

buildspec.yml

Creating a CI/CD Using AWS Tools 485

FIGURE D.11 Artifacts screen.

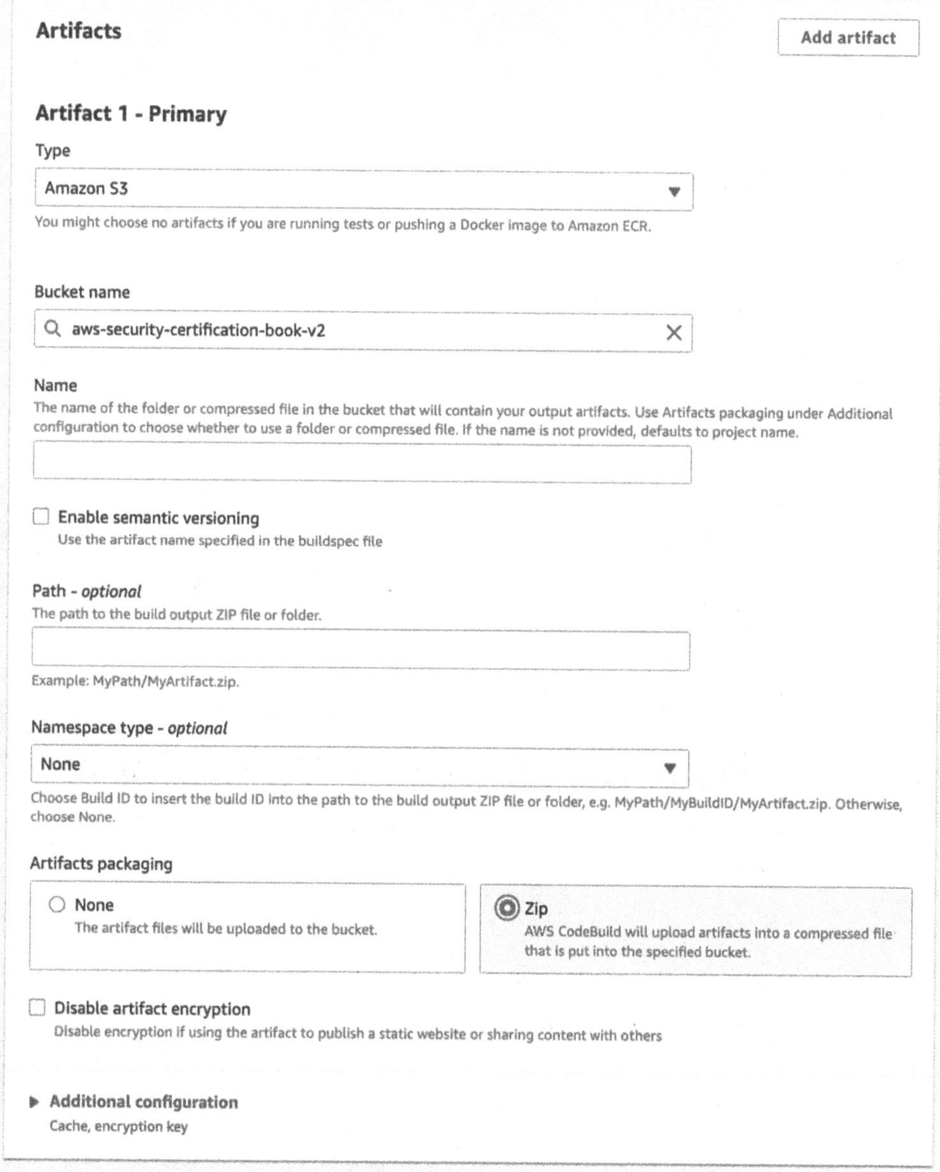

Artifacts

[Add artifact]

Artifact 1 - Primary

Type

| Amazon S3 ▼ |

You might choose no artifacts if you are running tests or pushing a Docker image to Amazon ECR.

Bucket name

| 🔍 aws-security-certification-book-v2 ✕ |

Name

The name of the folder or compressed file in the bucket that will contain your output artifacts. Use Artifacts packaging under Additional configuration to choose whether to use a folder or compressed file. If the name is not provided, defaults to project name.

☐ **Enable semantic versioning**
Use the artifact name specified in the buildspec file

Path - *optional*
The path to the build output ZIP file or folder.

Example: MyPath/MyArtifact.zip.

Namespace type - *optional*

| None ▼ |

Choose Build ID to insert the build ID into the path to the build output ZIP file or folder, e.g. MyPath/MyBuildID/MyArtifact.zip. Otherwise, choose None.

Artifacts packaging

| ○ **None**
The artifact files will be uploaded to the bucket. | ◉ **Zip**
AWS CodeBuild will upload artifacts into a compressed file that is put into the specified bucket. |

☐ **Disable artifact encryption**
Disable encryption if using the artifact to publish a static website or sharing content with others

▶ **Additional configuration**
Cache, encryption key

FIGURE D.12 Logs screen.

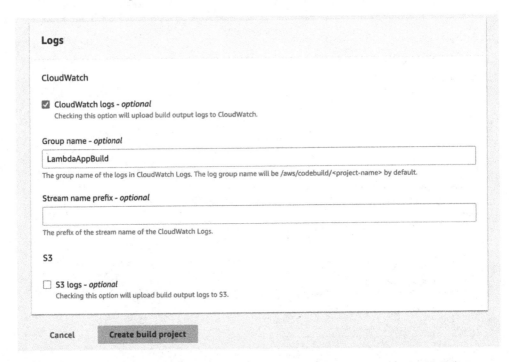

FIGURE D.13 Build screen.

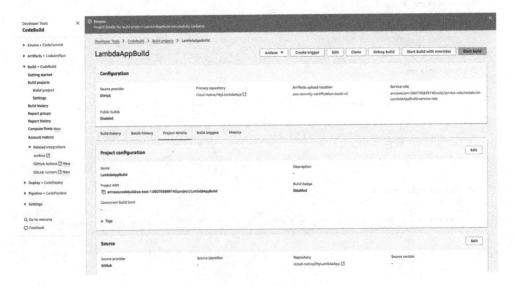

Creating a CI/CD Using AWS Tools 487

FIGURE D.14 Pipeline settings.

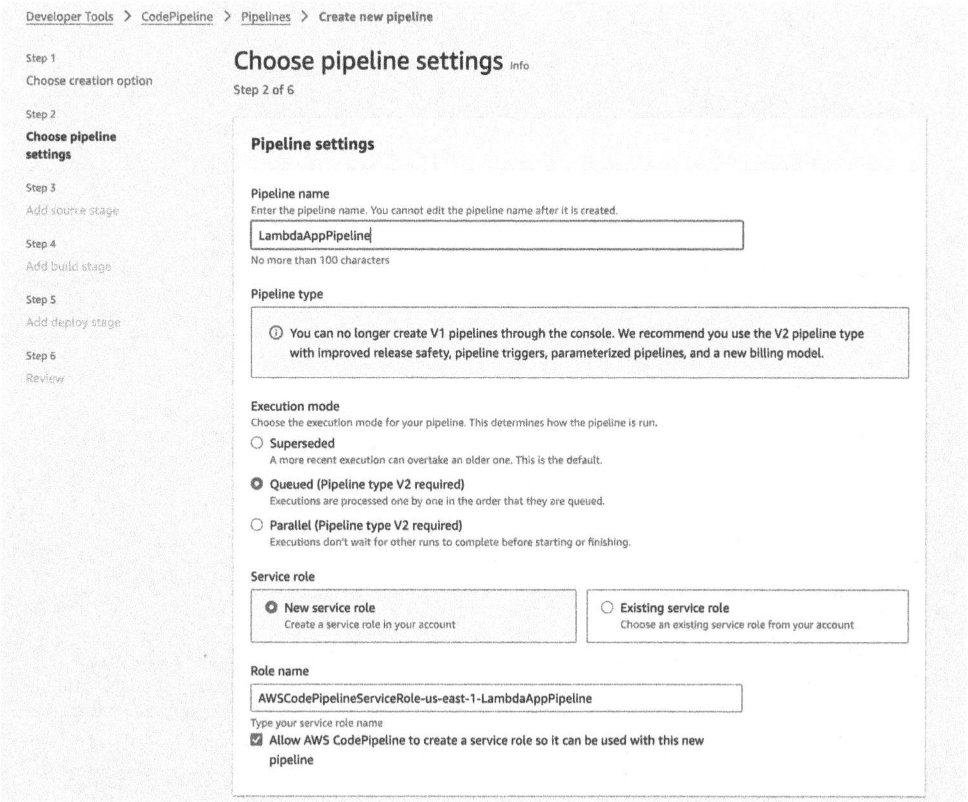

Developer Tools > CodePipeline > Pipelines > Create new pipeline

Step 1
Choose creation option

Step 2
Choose pipeline settings

Step 3
Add source stage

Step 4
Add build stage

Step 5
Add deploy stage

Step 6
Review

Choose pipeline settings Info
Step 2 of 6

Pipeline settings

Pipeline name
Enter the pipeline name. You cannot edit the pipeline name after it is created.

```
LambdaAppPipeline
```
No more than 100 characters

Pipeline type

ⓘ You can no longer create V1 pipelines through the console. We recommend you use the V2 pipeline type with improved release safety, pipeline triggers, parameterized pipelines, and a new billing model.

Execution mode
Choose the execution mode for your pipeline. This determines how the pipeline is run.

○ Superseded
A more recent execution can overtake an older one. This is the default.

◉ Queued (Pipeline type V2 required)
Executions are processed one by one in the order that they are queued.

○ Parallel (Pipeline type V2 required)
Executions don't wait for other runs to complete before starting or finishing.

Service role

◉ New service role	○ Existing service role
Create a service role in your account	Choose an existing service role from your account

Role name

```
AWSCodePipelineServiceRole-us-east-1-LambdaAppPipeline
```
Type your service role name

☑ Allow AWS CodePipeline to create a service role so it can be used with this new pipeline

488   Appendix D ▪ DevSecOps in AWS

FIGURE D.15   Add source stage screen.

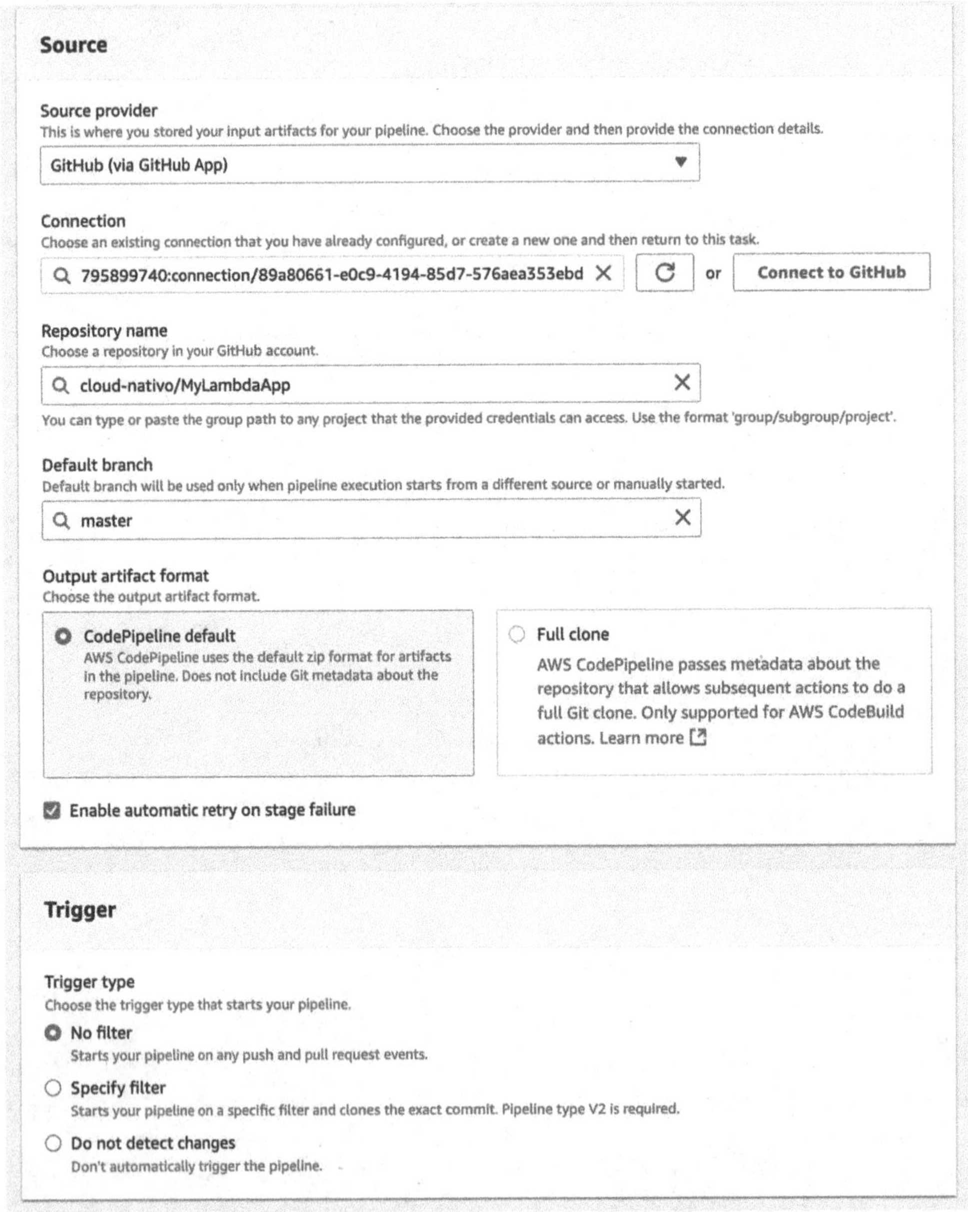

Source

Source provider
This is where you stored your input artifacts for your pipeline. Choose the provider and then provide the connection details.

GitHub (via GitHub App)   ▼

Connection
Choose an existing connection that you have already configured, or create a new one and then return to this task.

🔍 795899740:connection/89a80661-e0c9-4194-85d7-576aea353ebd   ✕   ⟳   or   **Connect to GitHub**

Repository name
Choose a repository in your GitHub account.

🔍 cloud-nativo/MyLambdaApp   ✕

You can type or paste the group path to any project that the provided credentials can access. Use the format 'group/subgroup/project'.

Default branch
Default branch will be used only when pipeline execution starts from a different source or manually started.

🔍 master   ✕

Output artifact format
Choose the output artifact format.

◉ **CodePipeline default**
AWS CodePipeline uses the default zip format for artifacts in the pipeline. Does not include Git metadata about the repository.

○ **Full clone**
AWS CodePipeline passes metadata about the repository that allows subsequent actions to do a full Git clone. Only supported for AWS CodeBuild actions. Learn more ↗

☑ **Enable automatic retry on stage failure**

Trigger

Trigger type
Choose the trigger type that starts your pipeline.

◉ **No filter**
Starts your pipeline on any push and pull request events.

○ **Specify filter**
Starts your pipeline on a specific filter and clones the exact commit. Pipeline type V2 is required.

○ **Do not detect changes**
Don't automatically trigger the pipeline.

Creating a CI/CD Using AWS Tools   **489**

8. Select/set the project name for that build (LambdaAppBuild), leaving the other options at their defaults. Click Next (see Figure D.16).

9. In Step 5 (add deploy stage), select CloudFormation as a deploy provider and click Build Custom Pipeline.

FIGURE D.16   Add build stage screen.

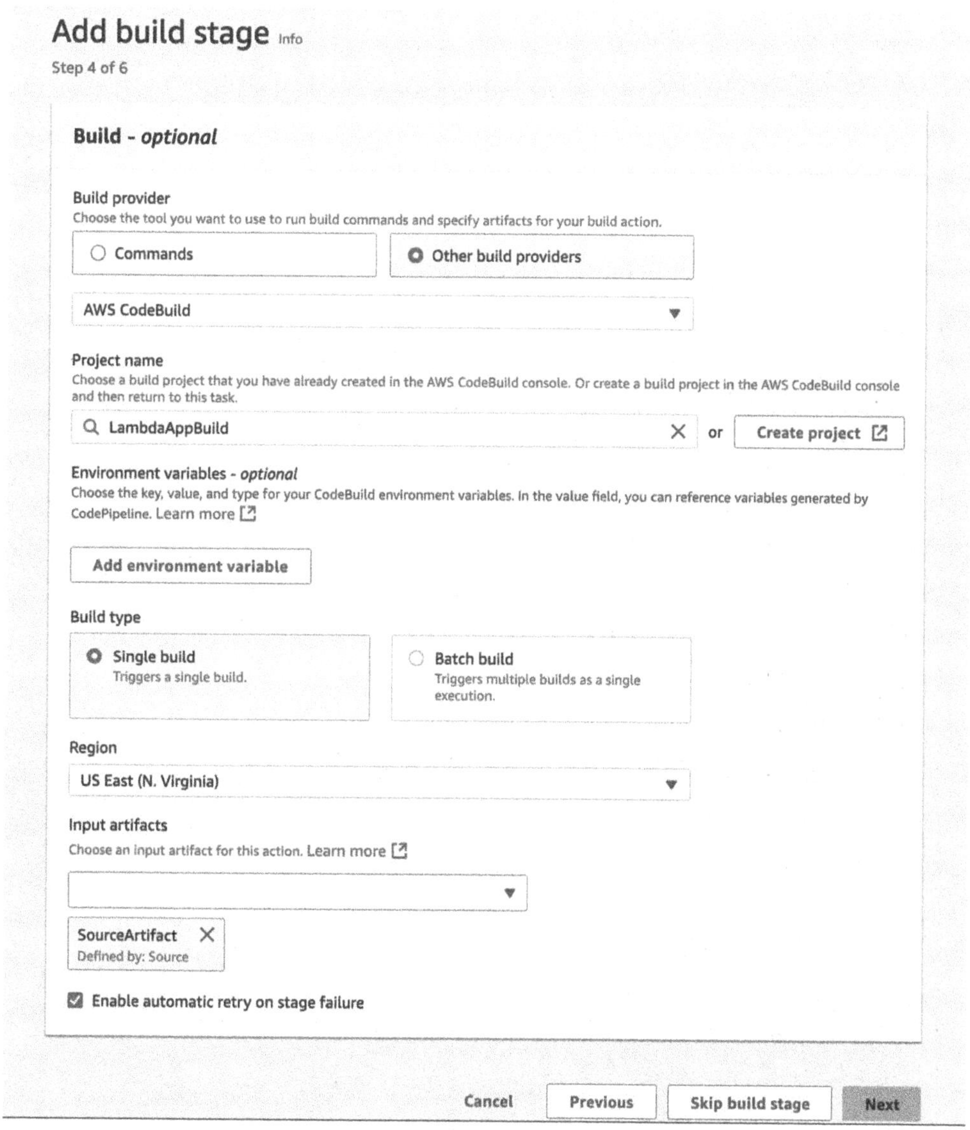

Add build stage Info
Step 4 of 6

Build - *optional*

Build provider
Choose the tool you want to use to run build commands and specify artifacts for your build action.

○ Commands   ● Other build providers

AWS CodeBuild   ▼

Project name
Choose a build project that you have already created in the AWS CodeBuild console. Or create a build project in the AWS CodeBuild console and then return to this task.

🔍 LambdaAppBuild   ✕   or   Create project ⬏

Environment variables - *optional*
Choose the key, value, and type for your CodeBuild environment variables. In the value field, you can reference variables generated by CodePipeline. Learn more ⬏

Add environment variable

Build type

● Single build
Triggers a single build.

○ Batch build
Triggers multiple builds as a single execution.

Region

US East (N. Virginia)   ▼

Input artifacts
Choose an input artifact for this action. Learn more ⬏

▼

SourceArtifact   ✕
Defined by: Source

☑ Enable automatic retry on stage failure

Cancel   Previous   Skip build stage   Next

490 Appendix D ▪ DevSecOps in AWS

FIGURE D.17 Add deploy stage screen.

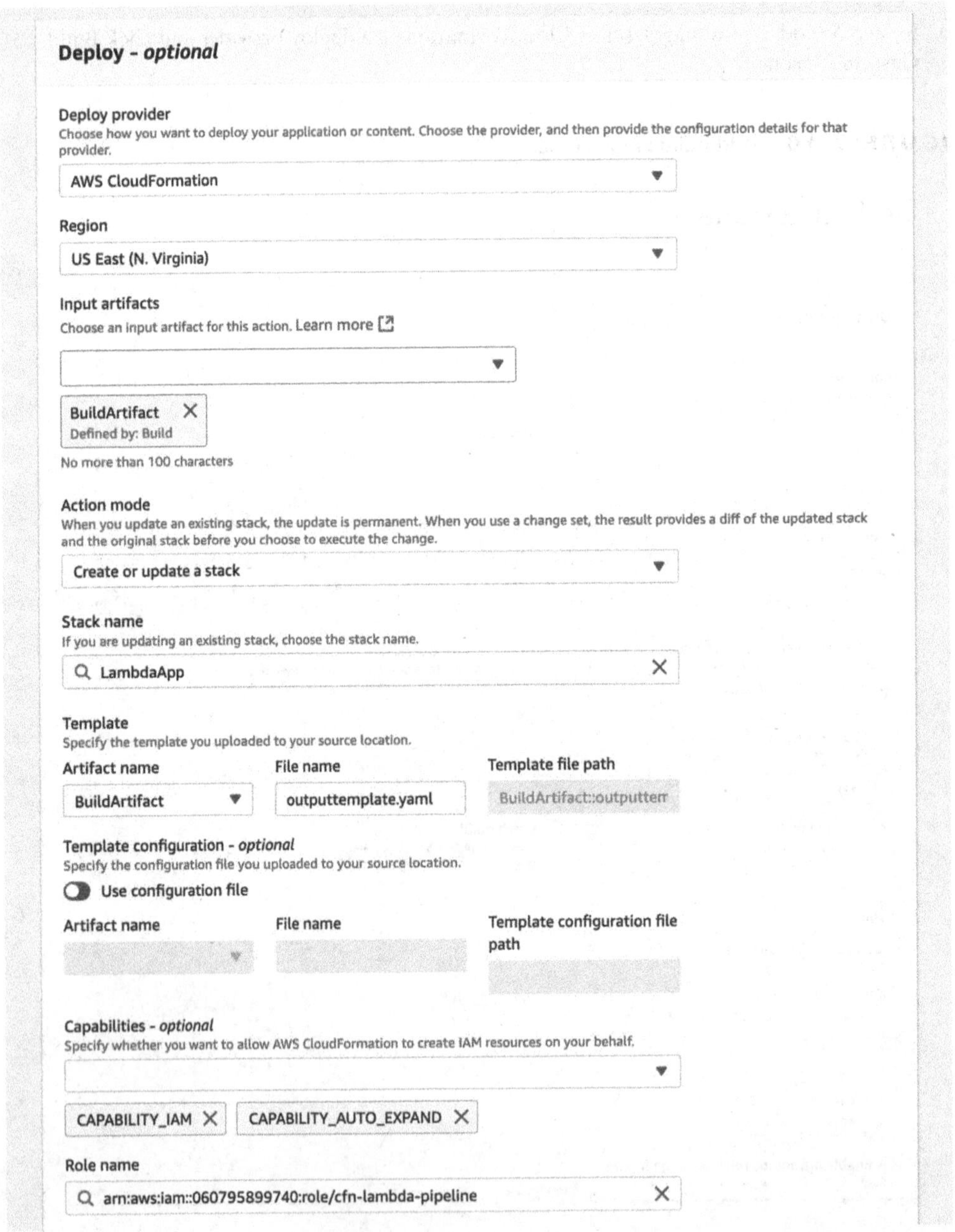

Deploy - *optional*

Deploy provider
Choose how you want to deploy your application or content. Choose the provider, and then provide the configuration details for that provider.

AWS CloudFormation ▼

Region

US East (N. Virginia) ▼

Input artifacts
Choose an input artifact for this action. Learn more ⤴

▼

BuildArtifact ✕
Defined by: Build

No more than 100 characters

Action mode
When you update an existing stack, the update is permanent. When you use a change set, the result provides a diff of the updated stack and the original stack before you choose to execute the change.

Create or update a stack ▼

Stack name
If you are updating an existing stack, choose the stack name.

🔍 LambdaApp ✕

Template
Specify the template you uploaded to your source location.

Artifact name	File name	Template file path
BuildArtifact ▼	outputtemplate.yaml	BuildArtifact::outputtem

Template configuration - *optional*
Specify the configuration file you uploaded to your source location.

⬤ Use configuration file

Artifact name	File name	Template configuration file path
▼		

Capabilities - *optional*
Specify whether you want to allow AWS CloudFormation to create IAM resources on your behalf.

▼

CAPABILITY_IAM ✕   CAPABILITY_AUTO_EXPAND ✕

Role name

🔍 arn:aws:iam::060795899740:role/cfn-lambda-pipeline ✕

Creating a CI/CD Using AWS Tools 491

10. Select Create or Update a Stack from the Action Mode drop-down menu.

11. Type in the StackName box **LambdaApp.**

12. Select BuildArtifact from the Artifact Name menu in the Template section.

13. Type `outputtemplate.yaml` in the File Name field.

14. In the Capabilities section, select CAPABILITY_AUTO_EXPAND and CAPABILITY_IAM.

15. Select the role name arn:aws:iam::123456789012:role/cfn-lambda-pipeline.

16. Click Next (see Figure D.17).

17. Review the configurations.

18. Click Create Pipeline.

After you finish the pipeline creation, click Release Change and wait for the complete pipeline execution. You can see the result in Figure D.18.

FIGURE D.18   Pipeline result.

Evaluating Security in Agile Development

Agile software development is a less complex, more efficient, and results-oriented way to collaborate between the project teams and other stakeholders. Agile development often entails evaluating things earlier and more regularly in the process and proactively making adjustments to your process as you go. With cybersecurity risks increasing and enterprises becoming more aware of their liabilities, software development teams need effective ways to build security into software. Threat modeling is a risk-based approach to designing secure systems. It is based on identifying threats in order to develop mitigations against them.

One way to check code security is by implementing a peer code review process at the beginning of your pipeline. The biggest challenge with this approach is the fact that it is not automated, meaning that it is not simple to scale. In addition, when other team members are executing code review, they are also subject to failure, making the whole process more time-consuming and sometimes even ineffective.

To make security checks scalable and more reliable when implementing a DevSecOps process, you need tools to evaluate the security of all artifacts that are used in your software development. Several third-party tools can be used in conjunction with AWS CodeBuild to perform this task. Here is a list of solutions that you can integrate into the pipeline to help you identify security breaches:

- **Haskell Dockerfile Linter:** A smart Dockerfile *linter*, which is a static code analysis tool used to flag programming errors, bugs, stylistic errors, and suspicious constructs, can help you build best practice Docker images (`https://github.com/hadolint/hadolint`).

- **Detect-Secrets:** As the name suggests, it detects secrets within a codebase (`https://github.com/Yelp/detect-secrets`).

- **Anchore:** The Anchore Engine allows developers to perform detailed analysis on their container images, run queries, produce reports, and define policies that can be used in CI/CD pipelines. Developers can extend the tool to include new plugins that add new queries, new image analysis, and new policies (`https://anchore.com/opensource`).

- **Cfn_nag:** The cfn-nag tool looks for patterns in CloudFormation templates that may indicate insecure infrastructure. It will look for IAM rules or security groups that are too permissive, access logs that are not enabled, and encryption features that are not activated (`https://github.com/stelligent/cfn_nag`).

Now is the time to put into practice some of these concepts and tools. You should start by changing the pipeline you created in previous sections to include additional security checks. As a first step, change your `buildspec.yml` file to the following code. (Replace *<YOUR BUCKET NAME>* with the name of an existing bucket in your AWS account.)

```
version: 0.2

phases:
  install:
    runtime-versions:
      nodejs: 18
```

Evaluating Security in Agile Development 493

```
    commands:
      - pip install detect-secrets

build:
    commands:
      # Detect Secrets in code
      - detect-secrets scan src/ --all-files> results.
json #scan the src directory
      - cat results.json
      - node -pe "if (Object.keys(JSON.parse(process.argv[1]).results).
length>=1) { process.exit(1) } else { process.exit() }" "$(cat results.
json)" #Break pipeline if found something

      # Create deployment directory
      - mkdir -p dist
      # Copy Lambda function files
      - cp src/handler.js dist/
      # Install dependencies
      - cd dist
      - npm init -y
      - npm install moment-timezone
      - cd ..
      # Debug - list files to verify template exists
      - pwd
      - ls -la
      # Package application
      - aws cloudformation package --template-file template.yaml --s3-bucket
aws-security-certification-book-v2 --output-template-file outputtemplate.yaml

artifacts:
  files:
    - outputtemplate.yaml
    - template.yaml
    - dist/**/*
  discard-paths: no
```

Now, change your `src/handler.js` file to the following code:

```
export const handler = async (event, context) => {

  const length = event.length;
  const width = event.width;
  let area = calculateArea(length, width);
  console.log(`The area is ${area}`);

  console.log('CloudWatch log group: ', context.logGroupName);

  var key = "AKIAWE7XI6O6QGGPDZEZ";
  var secret = "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";

let data = {
    "area": area,
  };
```

```
    return JSON.stringify(data);

  function calculateArea(length, width) {
    return length * width;
  }
};
```

Commit your changes, and after the pipeline finishes, you will see the failed status (see Figure D.19).

 If you have problems using credentials, you can go to the following site to see how to solve that problem: https://docs.aws.amazon.com/codecommit/latest/userguide/setting-up-https-unixes.html#setting-up-https-unixes-credential-helper.

This build failed because you added a secret key to the Lambda function. By removing lines 10 and 11 from the `src/handler.js` file and committing your changes, the pipeline will finish with the Success status again (see Figure D.20).

FIGURE D.19 Pipeline with failed status.

FIGURE D.20 Pipeline with Success status.

Creating the Correct Guardrails Using SAST and DAST

SAST and DAST are different styles of application security testing (AST), which are tests performed automatically by specialized tools. Static Application Security Testing (SAST) is the source code scan for signs of vulnerable code. Dynamic Application Security Testing (DAST) corresponds to the analysis for conditions indicative of vulnerability performed with the application running, so the specialized tool will "navigate" through the application, simulating known attack approaches.

SAST and DAST are often used together because SAST will not find runtime errors and DAST is not going to flag coding errors (at least not down to the code line number). SAST performs well when it finds an error in a line of code, such as weak random number generation, but it is usually not very efficient in finding data-flow flaws. Furthermore, SAST solutions are notorious for their large number of false positives and false negatives.

Security as Code: Creating Guardrails and Implementing Security by Design

The Open Web Application Security Project (OWASP) is a nonprofit community of software developers, engineers, and freelancers that provides resources and tools for web application security.

OWASP has several studies that you can use as the basis for your software development. These studies produce two main reports: The Top Ten Proactive Controls and The Ten Most Critical Web Application Security Risks. This section summarizes these reports and explains how they can be leveraged in modern software development.

The Top 10 Proactive Controls

The OWASP Top Ten Proactive Controls 2024 is a list of security techniques that should be considered for every software development project. The report is written for developers to assist those new to secure development. One of the main goals of this project is to provide concrete, practical guidance that helps developers build secure software. These techniques should be applied proactively at the early stages of software development to ensure maximum effectiveness.

The full OWASP Top 10 Proactive Controls 2024 report can be accessed at `https://top10 proactive.owasp.org/archive/2024/`.

1. **Implement Access Control:** Access control, or authorization, is crucial for managing user privileges and protecting sensitive resources. It should be implemented across all levels of an application, including business logic and database access. Remember that authentication (verifying identity) is distinct from authorization.

2. **Use Cryptography to Protect Data:** Sensitive data like passwords, credit card numbers, and personal information must be protected using strong cryptography. This is especially important for compliance with regulations like GDPR and PCI DSS. Implement proper encryption for data in transit and at rest.

3. **Validate All Input and Handle Exceptions:** Input validation is critical to prevent injection attacks. Implement thorough validation for all user inputs to protect against SQL injection, remote command injection, and cross-site scripting (XSS) attacks. Proper exception handling is also crucial to avoid exposing sensitive information.

4. **Address Security from the Start:** Incorporate security into the design phase of your application. Follow the Keep It Simple, Stupid (KISS) principle, make secure behavior the default, and design for defense-in-depth. Minimize the attack surface by identifying and reducing exposed components.

5. **Secure by Default Configurations:** Ensure that your application starts in a secure state without requiring extensive user configuration. This approach reduces the burden on developers and users, increasing the likelihood of maintaining a secure environment over time.

Security as Code: Creating Guardrails and Implementing Security by Design 497

6. **Keep Your Components Secure:** Leverage secure libraries and frameworks to prevent security-related design and implementation flaws. Regularly update and monitor third-party components for vulnerabilities. When possible, use existing secure features of frameworks rather than importing additional libraries.

7. **Secure Digital Identities:** Implement robust authentication and session management. Follow guidelines like NIST Special Publication 800-63B for digital identity management. Ensure that your most skilled engineers are responsible for maintaining identity solutions due to their complexity.

8. **Leverage Browser Security Features:** Utilize browser security features and HTTP headers to enhance client-side security. This includes implementing Content Security Policy (CSP), using secure cookies, and enabling HSTS (HTTP Strict Transport Security).

9. **Implement Security Logging and Monitoring:** Incorporate security logging to detect and respond to potential security incidents. Implement monitoring systems to review application and security logs in real-time, using automation where possible. This helps in identifying and responding to threats quickly.

10. **Stop Server-Side Request Forgery (SSRF):** Protect against SSRF attacks by implementing strict input validation and access controls on server-side request functionality. Be aware that SSRF attacks can bypass security controls by leveraging the server's identity to make unintended requests to internal or external services.
    Additional considerations include the following:

- Regularly perform security assessments and penetration testing to identify vulnerabilities.

- Stay informed about the latest security threats and best practices in web application security.

- Train developers in secure coding practices and maintain a security-aware development culture.

- Implement a robust incident response plan to handle security breaches effectively.

- Use HTTPS for all communications to ensure data integrity and confidentiality.

- Implement strong password policies and consider multifactor authentication for sensitive operations.

- Regularly update and patch all software components, including the operating system, web server, and application frameworks.

By following these best practices, you can significantly improve the security posture of your web applications and protect against common threats and vulnerabilities.

The 10 Most Critical Web Application Security Risks

The primary goal of the Top 10 Most Critical Web Application Security Risks report (https://owasp.org/Top10/) is to educate developers, designers, architects, managers, and organizations about the consequences of the most common and most critical web application security weaknesses. The report provides basic techniques to protect against these high-risk problem areas and guides on where to go from there.

Broken Access Control

Restrictions on what authenticated users are allowed to do are often not properly enforced. Attackers can exploit these flaws to access unauthorized functionality and/or data, such as accessing other users' accounts, viewing sensitive files, modifying other users' data, or changing access rights.

Cryptographic Failures

The first thing is to determine the protection needs of data in transit and at rest. For example, passwords, credit card numbers, health records, personal information, and business secrets require extra protection, mainly if that data falls under privacy laws (e.g., the EU's GDPR) or regulations (financial data protection, such as PCI DSS).

Injection

Injection flaws, such as SQL, NoSQL, OS, and LDAP injection, occur when untrusted data is sent to an interpreter as part of a command or query. The attacker's hostile data can trick the interpreter into executing unintended commands or accessing data without proper authorization.

Insecure Design

Insecure design is a broad category representing different weaknesses, expressed as "missing or ineffective control design." Insecure design is not the source for all other Top 10 risk categories. There is a difference between insecure design and insecure implementation. OWASP differentiates between design flaws and implementation defects for a reason, as they have different root causes and methods of remediation. A secure design can still have implementation defects, leading to vulnerabilities that may be exploited. An insecure design cannot be fixed by a perfect implementation, as by definition, needed security controls were never created to defend against specific attacks. One of the factors that contributes to insecure design is the lack of business risk profiling inherent in the software or system being developed, and thus the failure to determine what level of security design is required.

Security Misconfiguration

Security misconfiguration is the most commonly seen issue. This is usually a result of insecure default configurations, incomplete or ad hoc configurations, open cloud storage, misconfigured HTTP headers, and verbose error messages containing sensitive information. Not only must all operating systems, frameworks, libraries, and applications be securely configured, but they must be patched and upgraded in a timely fashion.

Vulnerable and Outdated Components

You are likely vulnerable:

- If you do not know the versions of all components you use (both client-side and server-side). This includes components you directly use, as well as nested dependencies.
- If the software is vulnerable, unsupported, or out of date. This includes the OS, web/application server, database management system (DBMS), applications, APIs and all components, runtime environments, and libraries.
- If you do not scan for vulnerabilities regularly and subscribe to security bulletins related to the components you use.
- If you do not fix or upgrade the underlying platform, frameworks, and dependencies in a risk-based, timely fashion. This commonly happens in environments when patching is a monthly or quarterly task under change control, leaving organizations open to days or months of unnecessary exposure to fix vulnerabilities.
- If software developers do not test the compatibility of updated, upgraded, or patched libraries.
- If you do not secure the components' configurations (see A05:2021-Security Misconfiguration at `https://owasp.org/Top10/A05_2021-Security_Misconfiguration/` for more detail).

Identification and Authentication Failures

Confirmation of the user's identity, authentication, and session management is critical to protect against authentication-related attacks. There may be authentication weaknesses if the application:

- Allows automated attacks such as credential stuffing, where the attacker has a list of valid usernames and passwords.
- Allows brute-force or other automated attacks.
- Allows default, weak, or well-known passwords, such as `Password1` or `admin/admin`.
- Uses weak or ineffective credential recovery and forgot-password processes, such as "knowledge-based answers," which cannot be made safe.
- Uses plain text, unencrypted, or weakly hashed password data stores (see A02:2021-Cryptographic Failures at `https://owasp.org/Top10/A02_2021-Cryptographic_Failures/` for more details).
- Has missing or ineffective multifactor authentication.
- Exposes a session identifier in the URL.
- Reuses a session identifier after a successful login.
- Does not correctly invalidate session IDs. User sessions or authentication tokens (mainly single sign-on [SSO] tokens) are not properly invalidated during logout or after a period of inactivity.

...thentication

...nctions related to authentication and session management are often implemented ...owing attackers to compromise passwords, keys, or session tokens, or to exploit ...entation flaws to assume other users' identities temporarily or permanently.

...ware and Data Integrity Failures

Software and data integrity failures relate to code and infrastructure that does not protect against integrity violations. An example of this is where an application relies upon plugins, libraries, or modules from untrusted sources, repositories, and content delivery networks (CDNs). An insecure CI/CD pipeline can introduce the potential for unauthorized access, malicious code, or system compromise. Lastly, many applications now include auto-update functionality, where updates are downloaded without sufficient integrity verification and are applied as the previously trusted application. Attackers could potentially upload their own updates to be distributed and run on all installations. Another example is where objects or data are encoded or serialized into a structure that an attacker can see and modify, to exploit insecure deserialization.

Security Logging and Monitoring Failures

This category is to help detect, escalate, and respond to active breaches. Without logging and monitoring, breaches cannot be detected. Insufficient logging, detection, monitoring, and active response occur any time:

- Auditable events, such as logins, failed logins, and high-value transactions, are not logged.
- Warnings and errors generate inadequate or unclear log messages.
- Logs of applications and APIs are not monitored for suspicious activity.
- Logs are only stored locally.
- Appropriate alerting thresholds and response escalation processes are not in place or effective.
- Penetration testing and scans by dynamic application security testing (DAST) tools (such as OWASP ZAP) do not trigger alerts.
- The application cannot detect, escalate, or alert for active attacks in real-time or near real-time.

Server-Side Request Forgery

SSRF flaws occur whenever a web application is fetching a remote resource without validating the user-supplied URL. It allows an attacker to coerce the application to send a crafted request to an unexpected destination, even when protected by a firewall, VPN, or another type of network ACL.

As modern web applications provide end users with convenient features, fetching a URL becomes a common scenario. As a result, the incidence of SSRF is increasing. Also, the severity of SSRF is becoming higher due to cloud services and the complexity of the architectures.

The full Top 10 Most Critical Web Application Security Risks report can be accessed at https://owasp.org/Top10/.

Index

A

Abuse notifications, 408–409, 426
Access control, 124–125
Access control lists (ACLs), 105, 219–225, 240, 249–256, 281, 288, 345
Access control profiles, KMS, 377–378
Access keys, root user, 123
Access management, 100–113, 122. *See also* Identity and access management (IAM)
Access points, S3, 346–347
Accountability, 7
Account Factory feature, 75
Accounting process, 8
ACM Private Certificate Authority (ACM PCA), 337–338
Action stage of detective framework, 178–184
Administrator permissions, 92–94
Administrator user policy, 104
Agile development, 492–495
Agility, of cloud computing, 193
Alarms, 165–166
Alias, customer-managed key, 305
Amazon API Gateways, 250
Amazon CloudFront, 250
Amazon CloudWatch, 158, 162–166, 185, 375, 476
Amazon CloudWatch Logs, 150, 157–162, 185
Amazon Cognito, 115–118, 450–451
Amazon Detective, 72, 398–400, 451
Amazon DynamoDB, 70
Amazon EC2, 99, 273–275, 289, 410–411
Amazon EventBridge, 150, 178–184, 186, 395, 417–418, 422, 426
Amazon GuardDuty, 72, 174, 388–393, 451–452
Amazon Inspector, 72, 170–172, 186, 263–267, 275, 289, 452–453

Amazon Kinesis Data Firehose, 255
Amazon Macie, 73, 78–79, 365–370, 379–380, 453
Amazon S3, 126–127
  access management in, 106–113
  access points in, 346–347
  BPA controls in, 344–345, 357–359
  creating buckets in, 108
  cross-region replication in, 112
  default access control protection, 344
  encryption models, 350–365, 378–379
  Glacier Vault Lock feature, 347–350
  lock features, 347–350
  Macie's activity monitoring of, 367–370
  Object Lock feature, 347, 348, 350, 356
  policy conflicts in, 109
  policy that allows CloudTrail to write events, 156–157
  pre-signed URLs in, 113
  protecting buckets, 319–321, 344–365
  secure data transport in, 109–111
  VPC endpoint to route traffic to, 243, 245
  WAF logging with, 255
Amazon Security Lake, 172–174, 186, 453–454
Amazon Verified Permissions, 454
Amazon Virtual Private Cloud (VPC), 192–214, 225–231, 288, 329, 372
Amazon Web Services (AWS). *See also entries beginning* AWS
  abstracted services from, 51
  container services from, 50–51
  infrastructure services from, 50
  responsibilities of customer vs., 47–51
  for security automation, 417–425
  for threat detection, 388–400
Anonymous access to S3 bucket, 106

502 Index

API destination, Amazon EventBridge, 181
Appliance Mode Support, 230
Application attacks, 412
Application load balancer (ALB), 236–240
Application Programming Interfaces (APIs), 23–25
Application runbook, 473
Architecture review, 80–81
ARN convention, 305
Art of the possible, 417
AssumeRole permission policy, 97
Asymmetric encryption, 296–298
Attachments, transit gateway, 227–229
Attack continuum model, 35–38, 41
Authentication, 8
Authorization, 8, 70–71
Automated incident response, 409, 413–425
Automated sensitive data discovery, 369, 370
Automated threat detection, 388
Automation documents, 175
Autonomous System Number (ASN), 226
Auto scaling groups, 425
Availability, 7
AWS Account Management, 71
AWS Artifact, 56–58, 455
AWS Audit Manager, 71, 80, 455
AWS Certificate Manager (ACM), 335–338, 379, 456
AWS CLI tool, 113
AWS Cloud Adoption Framework, 404
AWS CloudFormation, 75–76, 480–481
AWS CloudHSM, 328–335
AWS CloudTrail, 72, 143–157, 160, 182–183, 185, 375, 400
AWS CloudWatch, 400
AWS CodeBuild, 474, 481–482
AWS CodeCommit, 473–474
AWS CodeDeploy, 475
AWS CodePipeline, 476, 482–491
AWS compliance programs site, 52–58
AWS Config, 72, 79–80, 135–142, 167–170, 420
AWS Console, 101, 313–315

AWS Control Tower, 73–75, 83
AWS Cost Explorer, 81–82, 84
AWS Customer Incident Response Team (AWS CIRT), 404, 405
AWS Developer Tools, 473–491
AWS Direct Connect, 372
AWS Directory Service, 457–458
AWS Firewall Manager, 72, 458–459
AWS Health, 166–167, 186
AWS IAM Identity Center, 73, 118, 459–460
AWS Identity and Access Management (AWS IAM), 89–96, 100–105, 121–123, 126, 411–412, 459
AWS Identity and Access Management Roles Anywhere service, 99
AWS Key Management Service (AWS KMS), 149, 160, 298, 300–328, 333–335, 338, 375, 377–378, 460
AWS Lambda, 419–420, 422–423
AWS Management Console, 140
AWS Marketplace, 61–62
AWS Network Access Analyzer, 277–280, 289
AWS Network Firewall, 259–263, 289, 460–461
AWS Organizations, 68–75, 390, 395–396, 400, 461
AWS Payment Cryptography, 462
AWS Private Certificate Authority (AWS Private CA), 462–463
AWS PrivateLink, 373
AWS Resource Access Manager (AWS RAM), 77–78, 342, 463
AWS Secrets Manager, 120–121, 338–343, 464
AWS Security Finding Format (ASFF), 174, 393
AWS Security Hub, 73, 174–175, 393–398, 417–418, 464–465
AWS Security Incident Response Guide, 404
AWS Security Maturity Model, 444–447
AWS Security Service Portfolio, 239–240, 449–466. *See also specific programs*
AWS Security Token Service (AWS STS), 96–99
AWS Service Catalog, 78
AWS Service Role, 99

AWS Shield, 257–259, 289, 426, 465–466
AWS Step Functions, 420
AWS Systems Manager, 142–143, 175–177, 186, 273, 400, 420, 426
AWS Systems Manager OpsCenter, 401
AWS Systems Manager Parameter Store, 121, 341–343
AWS Systems Manager Patch Manager, 267–273, 289
AWS Transit Gateway, 225–231, 288, 372
AWS Trusted Advisor, 73, 81, 177–178, 186, 397–398
AWS VPN, 371
AWS Web Application Firewall (AWS WAF), 249–256, 289, 426, 466
AWS Well-Architected Framework, 58–59, 403
AWS Well-Architected Lenses, 59–60
AWS Well-Architected Tool, 60–61
AWS X-Ray, 475

B

Block Public Access (BPA) controls, 344–345, 357–359
Blue teams, 414
Broadcast addresses, 16

C

Centralized AWS Network Firewall Deployment Model, 260
CIA triad, 7
CI/CD (software development pipeline), 267, 477–491
Classless Inter-Domain Routing (CIDR) block, 195–196
Cloud computing, agility of, 193
Cloud security:
    AWS compliance programs, 52–58
    Marketplace for, 61–62
    overview, 46–47

Shared Responsibility Model of, 47–52
Well-Architected Framework for, 58–61
Cluster, of modules, 329, 332
Combined AWS Network Firewall Deployment Model, 261
Command documents, 175
Compliance, evaluating, 78–80
Compliance reporting, 271, 272
Condition keys, 312
Confidentiality, 7
Configuration drift, 417
Configuration history files, 139
Configuration recorder, 135, 140
Configuration snapshot, 139
Configuration stream, 139
Connectivity problems, 276–286
Cost analysis, 80–82, 84
Cost Anomaly Detection feature, 82, 84
Cost Estimation feature, GuardDuty, 392
Cost management, transit gateway, 231
Credentials:
    leaked, 411–412, 426
    protecting, 120–121
    root user, 90–91, 123
    temporary, 96, 99, 122
    using, 494
Cross-account access, 96–98, 103, 339–340
Cross-account parameter sharing, 342
Cross-region replication (CRR), 112, 340–341, 360–362
Customer identity, 115
Customer-managed key (CMK), 305–312, 316–318, 350, 352–356
Custom events, EventBridge, 180, 181
Custom key store, 333–334
Cyberattacks, 18–21

D

Data classification, 78–79, 83
Data events, 153
Data identifiers, 79

504 Index

Data key, 303
Data movement, monitoring, 370
Data protection, 293–383
   with Amazon Macie, 365–370
   for Amazon S3 buckets, 344–365
   asymmetric encryption, 296–298
   AWS Certificate Manager, 335–338
   AWS KMS, 300–328
   AWS Secrets Manager, 338–341
   AWS Systems Manager Parameter
     Store, 341–343
   CloudHSM service, 328–335
   for data in transit, 370–373
   hash algorithms, 298–300
   symmetric encryption, 296
   troubleshooting scenarios, 374–375
Dead letter queues (DLQs), 182, 183
Default access control protection, 344
Delegated administration, 71–73, 83
Denial-of-service (DoS) attacks, 19–20
Detective controls, 387, 398
   action stage, 178–184
   events analysis stage, 167–178
   events collection stage, 143–167
   resources state stage, 134–143
DevOps, 467–500
   in agile development, 492–495
   creating CI/CDs, 477–491
   cultural philosophies for, 468–469
   Developer Tools that support, 473–476
   and DevSecOps, 472–473
   and OWASP reports, 496–500
   practices, 469–471
   SAST and DAST guardrails, 495
   tools in, 471
DevSecOps, 472–473
Digest files, CloudTrail, 149–150
Disabling AWS Security Hub, 395
Distributed AWS Network Firewall
   Deployment Model, 260
Domain Name System (DNS),
   27–28, 224

Dual-layer server-side encryption with
   AWS KMS keys (DSSE-KMS
   encryption), 350, 356
Dynamic Application Security Testing
   (DAST), 495

E

Eavesdropping attacks (sniffing), 19
EC2 Image Builder, 273–275, 289
Elastic block store (EBS) disks,
   protecting, 326–328
Elastic IP addresses, 207
Elastic load balancing, 231–240, 288
Email services, protecting, 26–27
Encryption, 296–298, 350–355,
   375, 378–379
Ephemeral ports, 223
Event buses, EventBridge, 182, 184
Events, CloudTrail, 156–157
Event data stores, CloudTrail, 154–155
Events analysis stage of detective
   framework, 167–178
Events collection stage of detective
   framework, 143–167

F

Feature Flag, 469
Find Resources box, 198
Firewalls, 22–23, 40, 262. *See also* Web
   application firewalls (WAFs)
Former employee access, 409–410

G

Gateway endpoints, 242–243
General Data Protection Regulation
   (GDPR), 34, 40
Glacier Vault Lock feature, S3, 347–350

H

Hardware security module (HSM), 328, 329, 332. *See also* AWS CloudHSM
Hash algorithms, 298–300
Hash-based message authentication code (HMAC), 354, 355
Health Insurance Portability and Accountability Act (HIPAA), 34, 40
Host Management configuration, Systems Manager, 176
HTTPS, 109–110, 355, 373
Hybrid scanning, with Inspector, 266

I

IAM Access Analyzer, 72
IAM groups, 94, 95, 107–109, 307
IAM policy, 374, 423–424
IAM roles, 94–99, 122, 480–481
IAM user permissions, 92–94
Identity and access management (IAM), 87–130
    access control troubleshooting, 124–125
    in Amazon S3, 106–113
    AWS IAM principals, 89–96
    AWS Security Token Service, 96–99
    IAM Roles Anywhere service, 99
    identity federation, 114–120
    overview, 88–89
    policies and permissions, 100–105, 122
    protecting credentials, 120–121
    security best practices, 121–123
Identity-based policies, 101–102
Identity federation, 114–120, 122–125, 127
Identity pools, Cognito, 116–118
Images, protecting, 273–275
Implementation, of incident response plan, 405–407
Inbound rules, 220–222, 224
Incident response, 32–33, 401–425
    automating, 413–425
    by AWS CIRT, 404
    for specific types of incidents, 408–412

Incident response lifecycle, 401–403
Incident response plans, 403–408
Infrastructure, deployment of, 75–78
Infrastructure security, 191–291
    Amazon Inspector, 263–267
    Amazon VPC Transit Gateway, 225–231
    AWS Network Firewall, 259–263
    AWS networking constructs, 192–209
    AWS Shield, 257–259
    AWS Systems Manager Patch Manager, 267–273
    AWS WAF, 249–256
    EC2 Image Builder, 273–275
    elastic load balancing, 231–240
    network access control lists, 219–225
    network address translation, 209–214
    network and connectivity troubleshooting, 276–286
    security groups, 215–219
    VPC endpoints, 241–246
    VPC flow logs, 246–249
Insider threat, 409–410
Insights, Security Hub, 396
Insight events, 146–148, 153
Integrity, 7
Interface identifiers, 17
Internet gateways, 208–209
Internet Protocol (IP) activities, 11–14, 40, 280
Internet Protocol version 4 (IPv4), 14–15, 209
Internet Protocol version 6 (IPv6), 14–17
Intrusion-detection systems (IDSs), 25
Intrusion-prevention systems (IPSs), 25–26
Inventory, 370
IP spoofing attacks, 19
ISO 27001 standard, 58
ISO 27017 standard, 58

J

JavaScript Object Notification (JSON):
    identity-based policies, 101–102
    incident response rules, 419
    KMS permission policy, 308–312

506 Index

JavaScript Object Notification (JSON): (*Cont.*)
    modifying instance attributes, 423–424
    policy documents in, 100–101
    resource-based policies, 102–103

K

KeyID, 305
Key policy, configuring, 374
Key state issues, 375

L

Landing zone, 74
Leaked credentials, 411–412, 426
Linux Operating System rule group, 251
Log collection, disabling, 153
Logging and monitoring, 131–189
    action stage, 178–184
    events analysis stage, 167–178
    events collection stage, 143–167
    for Key Management Service, 375
    resources state stage, 134–143

M

Malware, 20–21, 33, 36–38, 40, 410–411
Managed key, 303–305
Management and security governance, 67–86
    architecture review/cost analysis, 80–82
    evaluating compliance, 78–80
    infrastructure deployment, 75–78
    multi-account management, 68–75
Management events, 144–145, 153
Management policies, 70
Man-in-the middle (MitM) attacks, 19
Microsoft Active Directory (AD) credentials,
    118–120, 127
Monitoring. *See also* Logging and monitoring
    of incident response plan, 407
    root account access and usage, 123

Monolithic applications, 470
Multi-account environments, 68–75, 77–78, 83
Multifactor authentication, 91, 92, 121

N

National Institute for Standards and
    Technology Cybersecurity Framework
    (NIST CSF), 34, 40
Network access control lists (NACLs),
    219–225, 281, 288
Network access problems, 277–280
Network address translation (NAT) gateways,
    205–206, 209–214, 282–284, 288
Network Detection and Response (NDR)
    systems, 30–31, 40
Networking, 9–17
    for infrastructure security, 192–209
    IPv6, 14–17
    OSI model, 9–11
    TCP/IP protocol stack, 11–14
Network problems, 276–286
Node graph, 399
Nonrepudiation, 8

O

Object Lock feature, 347, 348, 350, 356
Onion Router (TOR) Network, 416
Open Web Application Security Project
    (OWASP), 496–500
Organizational security policy, 4–9
OSI model, 9–11, 40
Outbound rules, 216–224

P

Password attacks, 18–19
Passwords, root user, 90–91, 123
Patch management, 267–273
Patch Manager, 175–177

Patch policies, 268–271
Payment Card Industry Data Security Standard
 (PCI DSS), 33, 40, 55, 57–58
Permissions, 92–94, 97–98, 100–105, 122,
 307–312, 375, 454
Permissions boundaries, 103–104
Phishing attacks, 21
Pipes, Amazon EventBridge, 183, 184
Policy conflicts, 109
Policy documents, 100–101, 175
Portfolios of resources, deploying, 78
Post-quantum hybrid key exchange, 298
Preparation phase, incident response, 405
Pre-signed URLs, 113
Principals, IAM, 89–96
Principle of least privilege, 41, 93, 122, 216
Private certificate authority (CA), 336–338
Private connectivity, 210
`ProdAccess` permission policy, 97–98
Protection plans, GuardDuty, 390–392
Public connectivity, 210
`PutEvents` API, 180

R

Reachability Analyzer, 276–277, 289
Read-only policy, 101
Reconnaissance, for attacks, 18
Red teams, 414
Regionality, key, 354
Relational databases (RDS databases),
 protecting, 321–325
Remediation, after Config rule violation, 168
Replication, 352, 355–356, 360–362
Repository, creating, 477–479
Resource-based policies, 102–103, 362–365
Resource Map tab, 212, 213
Resources state stage of detective
 framework, 134–143
Retention period, configuration item, 136
Risk identification, 387
Risk management, 21–33

API discovery and protection, 23–25
firewalls, 22–23
handling security incidents, 32–33
intrusion-detection and prevention
 technologies, 25–26
malware protection, 33
network detection and response
 systems, 30–31
protecting DNS, 27–28
protecting email services, 26–27
SIEM solutions, 29–30
TLS/SSL offload and visibility, 31–32
virtual private networks, 27
vulnerability analysis tools, 28–29
web application firewall, 23
web proxies, 23
Root users, 89–92, 123, 126
Route 53 Resolver, 224
Route tables, 205, 211, 212, 228–230,
 243, 244, 282

S

Schema Registry, EventBridge, 181
Secret protection, 339–343
Secure data transport, 109–111
Secure design, 59
Secure Sockets Layer (SSL) protocol, 31, 334
Security:
 context for current practice, 8–9
 defining, 2–6
Security, orchestration, automation, and
 response (SOAR), 33, 40
Security automation, 409, 413–425
Security countermeasures or controls, 7, 34, 74
Security frameworks, 33–34
Security groups, 215–219, 281, 288
Security information and event management
 (SIEM) solutions, 29–30, 40
Security initiatives, prioritizing, 442–443
Security journey, 441–447
 designing, 444–447

Security journey (*Cont.*)
  phases in, 443–444
  prioritizing security initiatives, 442–443
Security models, 34–39
  attack continuum model, 35–38
  categories of security controls, 34
  security wheel, 34–35
  zero-trust model, 38–39
Security risk, 6
Security wheel, 34–35, 41
Sensitive data discovery jobs, Macie, 367–369
Server-side encryption with Amazon
  S3-managed keys (SSE-S3
  encryption), 350–352
Server-side encryption with customer-provided
  keys (SSE-C encryption), 350, 354–355
Server-side encryption with KMS
  customer-managed keys (SSE-KMS
  encryption), 350, 352–356
Service control policies (SCPs), 70–71,
  105, 357–359
Session policies, 105
Sever load balancers (SLBs), 231–232
Shared Responsibility Model, 47–52
Software bill of materials (SBOMs), 266
Stacks, CloudFormation, 76
StackSets feature, CloudFormation, 76
State Manager, 175–177
Static Application Security Testing (SAST), 495
Subnets, 211–212, 225, 227, 262
Suspending service, GuardDuty, 393
Symmetric encryption, 296

T

Tagging strategies, 76, 83
Target groups, load balancing, 235–237
Technical vulnerability management, 263–267
Testing, 407
Third-party trust policy, 98
Threats, 6, 8

Threat detection, 387–401
  automated vs. custom, 388
  AWS services for, 388–400
  risk identification vs., 387
TOR anonymization network, 424
TOR client, 421
Transit, protecting data in, 370–373
Transit gateways, 225–231
Translation layer, OSI model, 11
Transmission Control Protocol
  (TCP), 11–14, 40
Transport Layer Security (TLS), 31–32,
  110–111
Trust relationship policy, 97, 98

U

Update Account Settings page, 91
Update management, 267–273
Updating incident response plan, 407–408
User pools, Amazon Cognito, 116

V

Virtual multifactor authentication, 91, 92
Virtual private clouds (VPCs). *See also* Amazon
  Virtual Private Cloud (VPC)
  creating, 208
  endpoints, 241–246, 288, 362–365
  filtering traffic within, 281
  flow logs, 246–249, 286, 288
  IP addressing for, 280
  network access control lists for, 219–225
  Network Firewall to protect, 259–263
  network reachability problems, 276–277
  peering connections, 284–286
  transit gateway attachments for,
    225–231, 288
Virtual private networks (VPNs), 27,
  28, 40, 371

Visibility, of threats, 8
VPC endpoints, 241–246, 288, 362–365
VPC Flow Logs, 246–249, 286, 288
VPC Peering, 284–286
Vulnerabilities, 6, 28–29

W

Web access control list (WACL), 249–256

Web Application and API Protection (WAAP), 25
Web application firewalls (WAFs), 23, 40
Web proxies (web gateways), 23, 24
Workforce identity, 115, 122–123

Z

Zero-trust model, 38–39, 41